VIOLENCE AND SOCIETY

VIOLENCE AND SOCIETY

A Reader

Edited by
Matthew Silberman

Prentice
Hall

Upper Saddle River, New Jersey 07458

Library of Congress Cataloging-in-Publication Data

Violence and society: a reader / edited by Matthew Silberman.
   p. cm.
  Includes bibliographical references.
  ISBN 0-13-096773-4
    1. Violence—United States. 2. Violent crimes—United States. 3.
  Aggressiveness—United States. 4. Anger—United States. I. Silberman, Matthew.

  HN90.V5.V5343 2003
  303.6'0973—dc21
                                                  2002030375

Publisher: Nancy Roberts
Acquisitions Editor: Chris DeJohn
Production Liaison: Joanne Hakim
Project Manager: Rosie Jones
Prepress and Manufacturing Buyer: Mary Ann Gloriande
Copyeditor: Pamela B. Rockwell
Art Director: Jayne Conte
Cover Designer: John Boylan
Marketing Manager: Amy Speckman

This book was set in 10/11 Berkeley Book by The Clarinda Company and
was printed and bound by Hamilton Printing, Inc. The cover was printed by Phoenix Color Corp.

 © 2003 by Pearson Education, Inc.
Upper Saddle River, New Jersey 07458

Printed in the United States of America

10 9 8 7 6 5 4 3 2 1

ISBN 0-13-096773-4

Pearson Education Ltd., London
Pearson Education Australia, PTY. Limited, Sydney
Pearson Education Singapore, Pte. Ltd
Pearson Education North Asia Ltd, Hong Kong
Pearson Education Canada, Ltd., Toronto
Pearson Educacion de Mexico, S.A. de C.V.
Pearson Education—Japan, Tokyo
Pearson Education Malaysia, Pte. Ltd
Pearson Education, Upper Saddle River, New Jersey

Contents

Part VI: CRIMINAL VIOLENCE   279

Preface

Some years ago, I attended a conference at which Murray Straus, whose work on family violence brought to light one of America's hidden problems, spoke about his commitment to the principle that we should have zero tolerance for family violence of any kind. Even spanking, he argued, reflects an acceptance of violent solutions to societal problems that perpetuates itself from generation to generation. Around the same time (April 1991), I attended a conference on aggression and violence sponsored by the Department of Sociology at SUNY-Albany. Both of these events inspired the development of a course on social violence that I now teach at Bucknell University. The collection of readings in this book derives from the materials in the course. In this work, I include excerpts from *Behind Closed Doors,* the groundbreaking work on family violence by Murray Straus, Richard Gelles, and Suzanne Steinmetz. I also include the published version of one of the SUNY-Albany conference papers on sexual coercion by Richard Felson, one of the principal organizers of the conference.

Donald Black's work on the social structure of right and wrong, the moral and legal regulation of social conduct, has been an additional source of inspiration for the design of my course on violence (see Black 1998). The core of the materials in this course focuses on the normative aspect of social violence, including behavior usually understood to be predatory in nature. But no course on the sociology of violence would be complete without paying attention to the social construction of the emotions that underlie violent conduct. Carol Tavris' work on the social construction of anger, the "misunderstood emotion," forces us to think about anger in ways that are counterintuitive to those raised in the individualistic, psychologically-oriented popular culture of late twentieth century America. According to Tavris, anger serves a *judicial* function, regulating everyday conduct in a variety of social situations.

This book is intended for upper-level undergraduate courses in sociology, criminology, and legal studies. The course on violence that I teach at Bucknell is part of the legal studies curriculum in the sociology program. No examination of contemporary American society can be complete without understanding the central role of the legal system in both contributing to, and regulating, social violence at all levels. It is from anthropologist Henry Lundsgaarde's description of "Homicide as Custom and Crime" in Houston, Texas that we learn how important legal norms are to our understanding of the production of violence in society. Statutes that provide legal justifications for homicides committed in a variety of social situations both reflect and support cultural traditions that legitimate the use of deadly force.

The chapters in the book are organized into six parts, each emphasizing an important theme in the emerging literature on the sociology of violence. The first half of the book explores the social contexts that give rise to anger and violence in general. We begin in Part I with three articles on the social construction of anger. In Part II, we explore the role that social inequality, based on class, race, and gender, plays in contributing to increased levels of violence. Part III examines the role that cultural values play in justifying violence in a variety of situations and locations in American society. In this section, we also see how legal norms, by expressing some of the core values of the wider society, may contribute to, rather than deter, violence in America.

The second half of the book includes chapters on specific topics of substantive concern in the literature. Part IV focuses on family violence, first by exploring the extent and nature of the problem, including child abuse and domestic violence. We then explore the issues involved in the legal regulation of family violence, examining the history of the criminalization of family violence, the issue of self-defense when battered women kill their partners, and the impact of mandatory arrest policies in domestic violence cases. And, finally, we examine the role of vigilante justice in the Old South in response to a "wife-killing."

Part V explores the extent and nature of sexual coercion in American society. This part is divided into two sections, the first dealing with sexual assault and the second with sexual harassment. The first chapter asks: Why do men rape? The next three chapters explore the social situations in which most rapes occur, by men whom women know as acquaintances, dates, and spouses. The last chapter in the section on sexual assault summarizes the research on the impact of rape law reform on rape prosecutions in the United States. In the second section, we begin with an article on the social origins of sexual harassment, then continue with a description of the history of the legal regulation of sexual harassment in the United States. The final chapter presents a review of the current literature on sexual harassment research and the most recent legal developments concerning sexual harassment in the workplace.

The last part of the reader focuses on an array of different types of criminal violence that are usually considered to be predatory in nature, including serial murder, armed robbery, organized crime (the "hit man"), and domestic terrorism. These selections were chosen to include in this section because they demonstrate the underlying normative character of violence, even in the most overtly predatory cases. And, finally, we examine the role of the prison system as a major factor in the production of violence in the wider society.

The book includes a mixture of articles, some of which were originally written to be accessible to general audiences, and some published in peer-reviewed academic journals. All the selections were chosen for their accessibility to the advanced undergraduate reader. One or two articles may be less accessible to the average reader, not because they are difficult to read, but because they represent major paradigm shifts in the way we think about crime and violence. Nevertheless, they are included here because of the importance of their contribution to the emerging literature in the sociology of violence. Such is the case with Donald Black's article, "Crime as Social Control." Black clearly shows that much of what is called criminal violence in contemporary America is governed by cultural norms that legitimize violence as "moralistic" acts in defense of traditional values.

The goal of this book is to enhance our understanding of the social causes of violence and, in doing so, make it possible to reduce the level of violence in families, in gender relations, and in a wide variety of social contexts in which violence appears to be an all-too-frequent occurrence. This becomes conceivable with changes in social structural factors, such as economic, racial, and gender inequality, associated with greater levels of social violence. Inequality produces the sense of injustice that yields righteous anger and the cultural values that legitimize violence in resistance to, or defense of, the existing social order. In such a world, there would be less reliance on direct interpersonal violence. There would also be less need for law, as organized state violence, to regulate social conduct.

Acknowledgments

I would like to thank those students, especially in the early days, whose challenging questions and inquiring minds pushed me to develop the ideas and select the materials for the course that have become the core of this reader. Too many to mention, I hope that I will be forgiven if I fail to thank each one individually. I would also like to thank the reviewers, Kimberly Davies of Augusta State University and Lynda Dickson of the University of Colorado at Colorado Springs, for their helpful comments. And finally, it would have been difficult to have made the progress that I did in assembling this book without the assistance of Emily Novick, whose hard work and dedication has made the completion of this book possible.

Reference

Black, Donald (1998) *The Social Structure of Right and Wrong.* Second edition. San Diego, CA: Academic Press.

Matthew Silberman
Bucknell University

Introduction

The purpose of this reader is to introduce the student to a distinctly sociological perspective on the production of violence in contemporary society. Such a perspective differs from the typical criminology text because it treats as problematic the social contexts that give rise to violent conduct, whether or not these acts are defined as crimes. In fact, central to such an argument is that violence itself may be an expression of socially approved forms of social control. A separate question, one for a theory of law, concerns the conditions under which acts of violence are treated as crimes.

As we shall see from the readings, family violence has not always been treated as problematic in our society. For many, it is still "normal and necessary" to beat your wife. Texas law historically sanctioned wife-killing following the discovery of an adulterous affair. In this book we learn how violence can be seen as a moralistic expression of support for cultural values. Even crimes that are often thought of as predatory in nature can be interpreted within a normative framework. As Jack Katz clearly shows, the most impulsive acts of deadly violence can be viewed as "righteous" from the perspective of the perpetrator. As the reader will see, armed robbery, or "banditry," also has a strong normative component. From Jesse James to the contemporary terrorist, those who attack the institutions of the dominant social order (banks, railroads, federal buildings, or the twin towers of the World Trade Center) justify their acts in terms of the perceived injustice that those institutions represent to the perpetrator.

Additionally, the typical rapist views the rape victim as someone who "deserved" to be raped because she "asked for it."

This perspective differs from the psychological perspective on violence in a number of ways. One need not assume individual motives to commit acts of violence to understand how and why they occur. In the book's first chapter, Tavris clearly shows that anger is a socially constructed symbolic process, or "uncivil rite," in reaction to a perceived threat to traditional cultural values. Anger, she notes, is the *judicial emotion* and, as such, seeks to punish those who violate the norms that govern everyday life. Stearns and Stearns, in their history of anger construction in America describe how boys and girls have been socialized to express anger differently. From this perspective, anger expressed in the form of overt acts of violence is a reflection of existing social arrangements. Acts of violence in support of the status quo may express dominant cultural values, as in the lynching of an accused rapist in the Old South, or enforce legal norms, as in the execution of a mass murderer.

In order to understand the social production of violence, it is necessary to examine the social arrangements that contribute to the sense of injustice that appears to be a root cause of the sort of anger that gives rise to acts of violence. Structural inequality, on the basis of ethnic background, gender, or social class, plays a role in the production of violence by both the "haves" and "have-nots" in such arrangements. For those in positions of power, violence may be instrumental in keeping that power, as in acts of intimidation that occur through racial or sexual harassment. On the other hand, acts of rebellion against the existing order may occur. Thus, when a battered woman kills her partner in self-defense, her act of violence can be understood as an inevitable act of resistance against the patriarchal system that made her a victim in the first place. More generally, inequality has been linked to higher levels of "diffuse" violence, violence that is not particularly directed at maintaining or challenging the existing order, but rather represents the accumulated collective rage of a subordinated population. Thus, the relatively high incidence of situational violence (e.g., street fights, drive-bys, and muggings) and other forms of criminal violence by young African American males is the result of generations of exclusion from the opportunity structures that have been available to most other segments of the American population.

The culture of violence in America reflects both social and legal traditions that legitimate the use of violence in support of the existing normative order. As such, the contemporary American culture of violence is both moralistic and legalistic in nature. These moral and legal traditions exist in a complex relationship of both mutual support and opposition. The moral order is reproduced by customs that dictate how and when it is appropriate to use force to protect the sanctity of property, personal integrity, or life itself. Whether this is the "righteous" expression of the husband who kills his wife because she violated some perceived rule of the patriarchal order, or the shooting of muggers by the so-called "subway vigilante" in New York City, there are cultural rules for defining when it is appropriate to engage in acts of violence. Moreover, these rules vary regionally and over time. Similarly, legal order consists of a set of procedural rules that define how and when the state and its agents (police, prosecutors, judges) shall legitimately coerce compliance to a set of substantive norms that govern the conduct of citizens in everyday life. Thus, rules that govern when the use of violence is legally justified in self-defense vary over time and place. On the other hand, the use of violence in

a "preemptive strike" is rarely considered legally justified. Thus, for example, vigilante action is often praised by the community while condemned by the courts.

Studies of family violence in America provide a unique opportunity to understand how profound changes in the social and legal traditions surrounding one social institution can occur so dramatically over time. Late twentieth century America saw a profound change in official attitudes concerning family violence. Earlier traditions treated both children and women as "possessions" of their fathers and husbands, respectively. The Anglo-American common law not only legitimized family violence, it also prescribed it under certain conditions. The marriage license became a "hitting license" and the "rod" was often used to "beat the devil" out of unruly children. Family values have recently changed as a matter of both law and custom. No longer can a parent beat a child without risking accusations of child abuse. Husbands can no longer beat their wives in some jurisdictions without being subject to mandatory arrest. The complicated issues raised by the battered women's syndrome as a defense to homicide raises issues that are both moral and legal in nature. And the mixed results of the research on the impact of mandatory arrest laws on domestic violence alerts us to the complicated relationship between law and custom when they contradict one another.

The social arrangements that reproduce gender inequality contribute to the production of violence against women at school, at home, at work, and on the street. Sexual coercion in its various forms is a product of the structural subordination of women. As a result, women may become victims of sexual assault and sexual harassment. The basic framework of this book questions the traditional psychologically-oriented theory that sexual violence is motivated primarily by men seeking power over, or expressing anger at, women. In a culture that objectifies women's bodies and eroticizes acts of sexual violence, sexual aggression acquires instrumental value in the pursuit of sexual gratification. It is only when the broader context of the relationship between sexuality and violence is understood that an explanation of sexual aggression can include the full range of acts of violence against women. For these reasons, the book includes sociological studies of date rape, marital rape, and sexual harassment as forms of sexual aggression.

A culture that has such deeply ingrained traditions of sexual aggression is not likely to change without substantial transformation in the laws that both define and control sexual aggression. Rape law itself has reproduced the cultural dynamics that legitimate rape through social constructions that characterize women who violate the norms of the wider patriarchal culture as "asking" to be raped. Women who walk alone at night, meet men at bars, or dress "provocatively" may discover that police are reluctant to arrest, prosecutors are reluctant to prosecute, and juries are reluctant to convict their assailants. Comprehensive rape law reform that narrowly defines acts of sexual aggression as criminal sexual *assault* and clearly specifies the elements of the crime requiring proof, such as the use of force and the degree of injury, has been effective in encouraging rape prosecutions. The shift in perspective from viewing sexual harassment as a specific harm against an individual to a form of sexual discrimination directed at a status group has also dramatically changed the nature of gender relations in the American workplace over the past 10–15 years.

In the final section of the book, we turn to studies of a variety of conventional forms of criminal violence. In this context, conventional criminality is defined in terms of what most Americans view as "typical" of the kinds of predatory acts usually regulated by the criminal justice system. Nevertheless, each type of criminal violence has distinct normative elements and reflects the political and social realities of the society in which they occur. The "mind" of the serial killer, even someone like Jeffrey Dahmer who killed gay men and boys, must be understood to be a consequence of the social construction of gender in the wider culture. How does the shame and humiliation of his own early sexual experiences get transformed into the sort of rage that ends in the targeting of gay men and boys? Caputi's work on the sexual politics of murder helps us to understand how "monsters" like the Hillside Strangler are an inevitable product of the patriarchal society in which we live. To understand serial killers as "evil" implies that they are produced by a society that has a particular construction of the Good.

Armed robbery (banditry) must be understood in historical context as organized attacks on the dominant social institutions at that time. Organized crime can be understood as a specific form of banditry that emerges when particular resources are made scarce through legal prohibition, yet the demand for those services still exist. So much has been written about the violence associated with organized crime, especially the Mafia, that including such work in this reader seemed superfluous. Instead, I have included an article on the socialization of the professional "hit man" who must neutralize conventional values in order to conform his behavior to the norms of his profession.

Now that we have experienced extraordinary acts of both domestic and foreign terrorism in the United States in the past decade, we can begin to understand why the Russians refer to the Chechen rebels as terrorists and bandits. In fact, the social conditions that give rise to banditry are very similar to those that give rise to terrorism. When attacks on the dominant institutions become politicized and the goals shift from economic justice (as in Robin Hood's attacks on the persons and property of the English aristocracy) to political change, banditry may evolve into political rebellion and terrorism. Similarly, when the political objectives of the terrorist (rebel) become less viable, yet the organizational skills associated with the guerrilla tactics of the rebel army remain, so-called terrorists may devolve into banditry. Such has been the case of the narco-terrorists in Columbia, the Contras in Nicaragua, and many of the right-wing groups in the United States. As President Reagan said in defense of his support for the Contras, "One man's terrorist is another man's freedom fighter." When the terrorists lose essential political and economic support, they may resort to armed robbery, the drug trade, and other forms of organized crime to support their cause. And when their cause itself is lost, they may resort to simple banditry to support themselves.

Attempts to control those who commit ordinary crimes may have a number of unanticipated side effects. The final chapter of the book examines the social origins of violence in the American prison system and the impact the violent world of the American prison has on the wider society. Much of the violence that occurs in contemporary America can be understood as a by-product of the way we organize and run our prisons.

About the Editor

Matthew Silberman, Professor of Sociology and Coordinator of Legal Studies at Bucknell University, has taught numerous courses in the area of criminology and violence. He received a Ph.D. from the University of Michigan and his undergraduate degree from McGill University. He has also served as the chair of the Sociology Department at Bucknell University.

Dr. Silberman's current research is on the production of violence in prison, the effect of legal environments on the social organization of prison life, and the role of patriarchy in shaping policies and practices in prisons for women. His research has taken him into numerous correctional institutions, including maximum security prisons for men and women, to interview hundreds of convicted felons, giving him a unique perspective on the minds and social backgrounds of violent offenders.

Professor Silberman's previous books include *A World of Violence: Corrections in America* (Wadsworth, 1995) and *The Civil Justice Process: A Sequential Model of the Mobilization of Law* (Academic Press, 1985). In addition to authoring several articles on prison violence, he has written on the deterrence of crime, welfare regulation, and gun control. He regularly teaches courses in Law and Society, Criminology, Deviant Behavior, Social Control, and the Sociology of Violence.

A gifted violinist who once considered music as a career, Dr. Silberman even enjoyed a brief stint at the Julliard School of Music in the early 1960s. Of course, that was before he became fascinated with correctional systems and prison life. In his spare time, he plays first violin with the Bucknell University Orchestra.

VIOLENCE AND SOCIETY

Part I: THE SOCIAL CONSTRUCTION OF ANGER

The readings in this section explore the role that anger plays in defending social institutions against threats to their integrity. Anger is a socially constructed emotion to the extent that the feelings associated with this emotion derive from the relationships that give them meaning. In her chapter, "Uncivil Rites—the Cultural Rules of Anger," Tavris helps us to understand how everyday expressions of anger operate to defend the established moral order against attacks from within or without. Tavris shows us how anger can be understood as the "judicial emotion." As such, anger often occurs in response to violations of cultural rules or perceived injustice. Yet, the way we display our anger is itself subject to cultural traditions or standards that define appropriate forms of self-expression. Today, with Americans facing attacks on innocent civilians from both domestic and foreign terrorists, our anger is justified, yet measured, as we retaliate against those who commit such acts. Characteristic of the American response to attacks on the twin towers of the *World Trade Center* on September 11, 2001 has been our careful targeting of military sites in Afghanistan, while providing assistance to innocent civilians who may have come in harm's way.

In the second chapter, Stearns and Stearns describe how the cultural rules of anger changed during the nineteenth and early twentieth centuries in America. Girls were socialized in families to control their anger, while boys learned to "channel" their anger into constructive activities. As children, boys learned to channel their energy into athletic competition, skills that would prove useful in the competitive economic world they were to face as adults. This shift toward an emphasis on emotional control in middle-class America corresponds to parallel shifts in the delegitimation of violence in family life, as we shall see in Part IV. Nevertheless, just as family violence is a reality in contemporary America, so the expression of anger in families is commonplace. In this chapter, we learn that anger expression occurs within a normative framework. How and when we express ourselves is subject to cultural rules that are learned in childhood and perpetuated throughout our adult lives.

In the third and final chapter in this section, we see how some individuals may come to internalize anger as a part of their socially constructed identity. Unable to acknowledge the source of his shame, the angry person directs his rage at the perceived symbols of his humiliation. In his own world, the targets of his rage "deserve" to be punished for a perceived transgression. Thus, for example, in a world in which masculinity is defined in terms of heterosexist norms, homophobia is the consequence of anger directed at those who are perceived to violate the norms of the wider patriarchal culture. Those who carry out acts of violence in defense of the existing patriarchal order are likely to be individuals who are unable to acknowledge the source of their own inadequacies or failures and turn their rage against an available target. In this chapter, we learn how Hitler's experiences in childhood created the sort of enraged personality that led to his blaming the Jewish people for the humiliation Germany had experienced at the hands of the Allies in World War I. Invoking the anti-Semitic traditions of the German nation, Hitler could turn the humiliation of Germany at the hands of the Allies into a symbolic substitution for his own humiliation.

All of the readings mentioned share the common theme that anger is a moralistic expression against injustice, perceived or real. Whether it is the American response to the unjustified killing of civilians by terrorists, the anger that parents express toward children who have disobeyed their rules, or Hitler's attributing Germany's ills to the Jews, each occurs in defense of the cultural values expressed in particular social institutions. In the first case, it is the symbolic attack on the American way of life; in the second, it may be the decorum of the proper young lady; and in the last, it is the traditional anti-Semitic values that permeated European culture at that time.

Uncivil Rites—the Cultural Rules of Anger

Carol Tavris

The young wife leaves her house one afternoon to draw water from the local well. She saunters down the main street, chatting amiably with her neighbors, as her husband watches from their porch. On her return from the well, a stranger stops her and asks for a cup of water. She obliges, and in fact invites the man home for dinner. He accepts. The husband, wife, and guest spend a pleasant evening together, and eventually the husband puts the lamp out and retires to bed. The wife also retires to bed—with the guest. In the morning, the husband leaves early to bring back some breakfast for the household. Upon his return, he finds his wife again making love with the visitor.

At what point in this sequence of events will the husband become angry or jealous? Is his anger inevitable? The answer, observes psychologist Ralph Hupka, depends on the tribe and culture he belongs to:

• A Pawnee Indian husband, a century ago, would, in fury, bewitch any man who dared to request a cup of water from his wife.

• An Ammassalik Eskimo husband who wants to be a proper host invites his guest to have sex with his wife; he signals his invitation by putting out the lamp. (The guest might feel angry if this invitation were not extended.) An Ammassalik husband would be angry, however, if he found his wife having sex with a man in circumstances other than the lamp game, such as that morning encore, or without a mutual agreement to exchange mates.

• A middle-class husband belonging to most modern American tribes would tend to get angry with any guest who, however courteously, tried to seduce his wife, and with the wife who, however hospitably, slept with their guest.

• A husband who belonged to the polyandrous Toda tribe of southern India at the turn of the century would find the whole sequence of events perfectly normal; nothing to raise a fuss about. The Todas practiced *mokhthoditi,* a custom that allowed both spouses to take lovers. If a man wanted to make love to a married woman, he first got her permission and then the permission of her husband or husbands; a yearly fee was negotiated; and then the wife was free to visit her new lover and the lover free to visit the wife at her home. But a Toda husband and wife would undoubtedly be angry with any man who tried to establish an affair by sneaking around the husband's back (and not paying the proper fee).

People everywhere get angry, but they get angry in the service of their culture's rules. Sometimes those rules are explicit ("Thou shalt not covet thy neighbor's wife"); more often they are implicit, disguised in the countless daily actions performed because "That's the way we do things around here." These unstated rules are often not apparent until someone breaks them, and anger is the sign that someone has broken them. It announces that someone is not behaving as (you think) she or he *ought.* This "assertion of an ought" is, according to psychologist Joseph de Rivera, the one common and essential feature of anger in all its incarnations. "Whenever we are angry," he writes, "we somehow believe that we can influence the object of our anger. We assume that the other is responsible for his actions and ought to behave differently."

This "ought" quality suggests that a major role of anger is its policing function. Anger, with its power of forcefulness and its threat of

---

retaliation, helps to regulate our everyday social relations: in family disputes, neighborly quarrels, business disagreements, wherever the official law is too cumbersome, inappropriate, or unavailable (which is most of the time). Psychologist James Averill observes that for most of Western history, it has been up to individuals to see to it that their rights were respected and justice seen to; in the absence of a formal judiciary, anger operates as a personal one.

Perhaps the best way to understand the policing power of anger is to step outside of our own complex environment, and observe the way anger works in small societies. Small societies are highly revealing, whether they are families, tribes, high-school marching bands, or the U.S. Congress. Members of such groups understand very well the importance of the rules that govern anger, because everyone has to get along with each other in the morning. Anger is society's servant, and you can see this in the day-to-day life of small tribes. They may seem exotic, but they are, close up, a mirror on ourselves.

The Judicial Emotion

N!uhka, age seventeen, was furious. Her father had reminded her that she was getting on in years and that it was high time for her to marry. N!uhka, who was rebellious and vain, was uninterested in the eligible young men her father suggested, and at last, in the heat of argument, she cursed him aloud. He was shocked. *She* was shocked. So were all the neighbors and relations who had overheard her.

Now N!uhka was angry and also ashamed of her disrespectful outburst. She grabbed her blanket and stormed out of the camp to a lone tree some seventy yards away. There she sat, all day, covered in the blanket. This was not a trivial penance, since the temperature that day was 105 degrees Fahrenheit in the shade (without a blanket), but by the time she returned to camp her anger and embarrassment had subsided.

The !Kung hunter-gatherers of the Kalahari Desert are called "the harmless people" because of their renowned lack of aggression. This does not mean that they are free from the petty plagues of human life, such as jealousies, resentments, suspicions, and sulks. Teenagers dis-

agree with their parents' wishes, relatives squabble about who owes what to whom, and husbands and wives bicker about marital matters. The difference is that the !Kung know that they must manage these emotions and dampen them down to tolerable levels, and that if they don't their very survival is endangered.

The !Kung are nomadic, foraging constantly for food, and their only insurance against hard times is each other. No individual can lay in a supply of frozen pizzas and beer in the event of famine and drought, and no individual could long survive on his or her own. Sharing is therefore the dominant value and obsession of their society. As one of their principal ethnographers, Elizabeth Marshall Thomas, observed: "It has never happened that a Bushman [today they are called !Kung or !Kung-san] failed to share objects, food, or water with the other members of his band, for without very rigid co-operation Bushmen could not survive the famines and droughts that the Kalahari offers them." Under such conditions, any antisocial or angry outburst threatens the whole group; so it is to the !Kung interest to avoid direct physical confrontation or violence, and to be suspicious of individuals who cannot control their behavior or their tempers. "Their hold on life," says Thomas, "is too tenuous to permit quarreling among themselves."

The same structure of camp life that increases the chances of group solidarity and survival—lack of privacy, each hut close to the other huts, extended family nearby—also means that every flare-up and dispute is immediately available for public discussion and resolution. Such lack of privacy would be cause enough for anger in the West, where "It's none of your business" is an accepted refrain. Among the !Kung, everything is everyone's business. "Once a person attacks his victim he is like a fly that attacks an insect already caught in a spider's web," writes anthropologist Patricia Draper. "Immediately both are caught. If the combatants forget the sticky web in the heat of their anger, the onlookers do not. Real anger frightens and sickens the !Kung, for it is so destructive of their web of relationships." Anyone who becomes angry will have the assistance ("interference" to the West) of the entire tribe, if need be. Perhaps this is why, in nearly a year and a half of fieldwork, one anthropologist saw only four examples of overt discord and heard of only a few others. Another recorded only three serious disputes: one over possession of an animal that had been killed, another about a marital disagreement, and a third in which a mother raged at a curer who failed to attend her sick child.

Although the !Kung are not aggressive, they are expert at bickering and complaint. "The outsider wonders how the !Kung can stand to live with each other," says Patricia Draper. "In the early months of my own fieldwork I despaired of ever getting away from continual harassment." Some psychoanalytically inclined observers take this as evidence of the !Kung's "displaced" aggressive instinct, which, if not released physically (they say), takes this verbal outlet. But a closer look at the content of the bickering reveals two things about it: It has a distinct social purpose, and although it may seem to outsiders like a sign of anger it is really a ritual game, devoid of anger's heat.

After several months, Draper discovered that the key to !Kung bickering was its emphasis on dunning for food. What idle conversation about the weather and the economy is to Europeans, she noticed, reminders about food obligations were to the !Kung. In time she learned the "properly melodramatic disclaimers" that allowed her to join the game:

> You expect *me,* one lonely European, a stranger in this territory, living away from my own kin, without even one spear or arrow or even a digging stick, and with no knowledge of the bush . . . you expect *me* to give *you* something to eat? You are a person whose hut is crammed full of good things to eat. Berries, billtong, sweet roots, stand shoulder high in your hut and you come to me saying you are hungry!

The !Kung visitor would be delighted with such a spirited reply (as would the inevitable onlookers), and once this exchange was completed, Draper and the !Kung could go on to talk about other things. But food-dunning jokes and complaints are important because they remind everyone of the responsibility to recirculate food and property. The have-nots press for their share; the haves are reminded that their fortune is only temporary.

I have found Draper's observations useful in understanding my own particular tribe, Eastern European Jews whose forebears came from the shtetls of Russia and Poland, and for whom ritual dunning has been a long tradition. Indeed, the rich curse repertoire of Yiddish makes the four-letter-word grunts of English a pale and gutless thing. As Barbara Myerhoff recorded in *Number Our Days:*

JAKE: In those days, everybody gave curses. You couldn't live without it. A woman there was on our street who could curse like Heifetz plays the violin. The things she would fix up for her enemies! "May your teeth get mad and eat your head off." "May you inherit a hotel with one hundred rooms and be found dead in every one." "May you have ten sons and all your daughters-in-law hate you." "May all your teeth fall out but one, and that one has a cavity." "May your chickens lay eggs in your neighbor's house." "May the gypsies camp on your stomach and their bears do the *kazotskhi* in your liver."

BASHA: This last one you are getting from Sholom Aleichem.

JAKE: And where do you think Sholom Aleichem learned it?

Today these curses are a fading talent (I think they require the original Yiddish), just as the ritual dunning is a mere shadow of its former self: "You don't call me any more"; "Write your Aunt Hannah a thank-you letter *today*"; "Do your fingers have leprosy that you can't pick up your socks?" But the curses and the dunning have their origin in survival needs as great as those for food in the African bush. The repeated bickering reminded shtetl Jews of their social obligations to the family and the culture, emphasizing the importance of staying in line and paying attention to the traditions that kept the precarious group together. A visitor to such cultures is likely, as Patricia Draper was among the !Kung, to feel under attack, at least until he or she learns the rules and can play the game.

Catherine Lutz, who lived among the Ifaluk in the Southwest Pacific, offers a good example of the deeply rooted community perspective of these close-knit tribes. She had asked a group of women: "Do you (all) want to come with me to get drinking water?" Their faces fell, until Lutz realized "that my pronouns were at fault"—*you* being separate from *me* in her sentence. The correct form of the question, she realized in time, is: "We'll go get water now, OK?"

Whenever a tribe must cooperate and struggle to survive—on the frozen tundra of the Northwest Territories, in the steamy jungles of South America, in the arid bush of Africa, as a persecuted minority in the heart of "civilization"—it must find a way to settle disputes without causing the offended party to leave the tribe in a huff. In the absence of formal laws to govern distribution of goods—in fact, in the absence of predictable supplies of goods—the problem of sharing is never permanently resolved. It is always vulnerable to dispute, and anger is the policeman of that dispute. Did I get my fair share? Did he get too much? Should I get more because I was sick or less because I couldn't hunt? The Siriono of Bolivia, for example, are forever accusing each other angrily of hoarding food, not sharing what they have, eating at night, or stealing off into the forest to eat. (Most of their remaining disputes have to do with sex, which also has its intrinsically uncertain aspects.) But anger over food distribution is not widespread in places such as Tahiti, where the food supply and other staples of survival are abundant and predictable.

The analogy of anger as policeman can be carried a step further, since policemen must themselves follow certain rules and are constrained from excessive violence. The anger that may be expressed in small tribes likewise must follow certain rules and constraints to ensure that anger does not become disruptive. The Siriono, for example, may throw a drinking feast in which serious complaints are aired. This is not an American-style drinking feast, where drinking is often assumed to lead to violence. The most that two Siriono men may do is wrestle, but if either man uses his fists he is promptly accused of "fighting like a white man" and stops, embarrassed, at once. More likely, Siriono men who feel angry with each other go hunting; if successful, they are too elated to be angry, and if not, they are too tired.

Perhaps the most vivid and charming example of anger being used to influence recalcitrant members of a tribe, while itself being controlled by ritual limits, is the "mad dance" of the Kapauku Papuans of West New Guinea. The Kapauku Papuans may not be familiar to you, but every culture, including our own, has its version of the mad dance.

A Kapauku wedding is, more than most, an obvious economic exchange, since the bride and groom have invariably been living together for some time before the ceremony. On the big day, the two families gather together for official payment of the bride price, and clan members gather from far and wide. Throughout the day, the groom's family displays the gifts they are offering, while the bride's family inspects them carefully, exchanging derogatory comments about their quality and quantity, muttering audibly about the stinginess of the groom's clan.

The groom's closest relatives, having set forth what they can afford to pay, now call upon their visiting kin to raise the ante. A few more shells and necklaces are added, but the bride's father still looks displeased. The local headmen, hoping to settle the matter quickly and avoid disputes, now try to drum up some financial support from the groom's kin with appeals to their pride and family loyalty. If this effort fails, the headmen will start *wainai,* the "mad dance," which is just what it sounds like: the dancers yell and scream their requests for the relatives to cough up some booty, all the while stamping their feet furiously in a fast rhythm, their arms mimicking the shooting of arrows.

If the mad dance doesn't produce the desired results, some of the bride's male relatives may get into the act, hurling insults and reproaches—not at the poor groom, who is broke, but at the groom's distant relatives. If all of this pressure fails, the bride's kin may be forced to join the mad dance themselves. Then all hell will break loose, for it means the end of negotiations. But usually the dance is effective, the bride's father gives his OK, the deal is settled, the groom gives his new in-laws a pig or two, and everyone goes home happy.

Now, apart from the pigs and the arrows, this is not so different from some American weddings, in substance if not form. I've watched a few mad dances in my time, and they usually get the same result: The errant relative shapes up. One woman I interviewed told me that her daughter's marriage was nearly called off by the groom's *mother* because the bride's family wasn't prepared to buy the newlyweds a house. After an exchange of enraged calls, foot stamping, and accusations of stinginess and bullying, a compromise was reached. The wedding went off as planned.

These economic exchanges are not simply outbursts of greed, however, in the Kapauku or any other tribe. They play an important cohesive role for the family and for the tribe; a lot more is going on than getting a few beaded necklaces or a silver teapot. Among the Kapauku, successful settlement for the bride price includes these benefits: The mother of the bride, who gets to keep most of the wealth, now has raised her status, for she has money to lend. The bride's brother receives a large enough portion to be able to get married too. The father of the bride, who has refereed the transaction, confirms his importance and position as head of the family. On the groom's side, the relatives who contributed to the bride price gain enormous public prestige for their generosity and, more important, the groom's undying gratitude. The groom will now call his creditors *naitai,* "my father," and be expected to assist them in their future troubles or debates. In sum, a satisfactory bride price unifies both sets of kin, forming alliances within each clan as well as between them. No wonder a mad dance might be called for.

Bickering, drinking feasts, and mad dances represent a spectrum of solutions that cultures have evolved to regulate disputes. Are the participants actually *feeling* angry? As observers, we cannot know for sure; but I don't think it matters. I suspect that among the Kapauku, as among Americans, some mad dancers are feeling enraged and others are behaving as if they were. Some jealous husbands actually do feel angry with wives who flirt, and others simply think they should. Some ritual bickerers, such as Pat Draper's !Kung friends, are playing a game quite consciously; others aren't kidding. The point is that the rules of the tribe regulate both the feelings of anger and angry behavior, establishing when anger may be expressed, and how, and to whom, and for what reasons.

To make sure, however, that anger does not become excessive and threaten the delicate internal mechanism of the group, small tribes rely on informal (but highly effective) ways to keep *inappropriate* anger in check: gossip, ridicule, witchcraft, public discussion, and in extreme cases ostracism. One of the most popular methods invokes the individual's bond to the community: shame.

"The only authority here," said the astute Semai informant, is "*slniil.*" Among the Semai of West Malaysia, *slniil* (variously defined as "shame," "nervousness," or "reluctance") is the typical response to anger, whether one feels the anger personally or is the recipient of someone else's. A man who feels *slniil* will avert his eyes from the target of his wrath and refuse to talk or listen to him, thereby retreating from the conflict instead of confronting or escalating it. This is considerate behavior for a Semai, and no one will accuse him of repression, depression, or passive-aggressive manipulativeness.

Both parties to a Semai conflict feel shame; indeed, most close-knit tribes are as concerned about the person who provokes anger as about the individual who feels it. Arapesh adults (one of the tribes studied by Margaret Mead), who worry that strong bursts of rage will make their whole society vulnerable, will join in punishing the individual who *causes* another to engage in violence. Similarly, the Utku Eskimo worry about anyone with a volatile temper, even if that temper is, by Western standards, justified. Anthropologist Jean Briggs learned this the hard way. She lost her temper—"very mildly as we ourselves would view it"—with some Caucasian fishermen who, while visiting the area, broke one of the Eskimo canoes. Although she was angry on behalf of the Utku, although her annoyance was not remotely directed at them, the Eskimo saw only her anger, not its cause. She had revealed a sign of decidedly un-Eskimo volatility, and it was now uncertain whether she could be trusted. "As a result of my unseemly and frightening wrath at the fishermen," Briggs reported, "I was ostracized, very subtly, for about three months." (I think she felt a touch of *slniil.*)

Among the Temiar of Malaysia, according to Marina Roseman, anger in its late stages is expressed indirectly and formally in a "harangue." During the night, protected by darkness, the angry person speaks out from his or her sleeping compartment separate from the person being criticized. The target is referred to as "he" or "she" rather than "you" to further distance the confrontation. The target may respond in like fashion, or listen silently. In spite of these precautions of indirection, says Roseman, the Temiar still consider this expression of anger to be dangerous, capable of shocking the souls of participants or bystanders into taking flight. (The Temiar would be right at home among the haranguing inhabitants of a New York apartment building.)

Or consider the Toraja of South Sulawesi, Indonesia, who, like other groups in Malaysia and Indonesia, fear and dislike anger. The overt display of anger is "likened to that of amoral animals and is thought to be unworthy of human beings," says Douglas Hollan, an anthropologist who lived among them. In Hollan's year of fieldwork, he saw only three incidents of openly expressed anger, despite the occurrence of many events that "certainly tried people's patience." To "cool out," the Toraja call on their fatalistic philosophy, a belief that one's fate is determined at birth and can be changed only by the gods. They told Hollan they also avoid active rumination and brooding about their problems, and try to "talk themselves" out of it. In dealing with another person who is angry, the Toraja get out of the way and let the person calm down; challenging or confronting someone who is angry, the Toraja know, just enrages the person all the more.

I prefer the anger-calming approach of the Mbuti hunter-gatherers of northeast Zaire, who use humor to dissipate a quarrel. When rational discussion breaks down, Mbuti disputants (and their inevitable observers) begin to ridicule each other, acting out the argument, until everyone is rocking with laughter. Significantly, this stratagem is learned early in life. When a child teases another child into tears, guess whom the other children will rally around? The tearful victim. They will then begin a joyful game from which the teaser is excluded (a small but potent lesson in the hazards of antisocial behavior) until the teaser, the target, and the rest of the children are laughing and have forgotten the incident. Bullies don't succeed among the Mbuti.

Ridicule and humor are effective antidotes to anger in many small societies. Verbal dueling is high art where "fighting like a white man" is taboo or dangerous. In some Eskimo tribes, one man may challenge another to a drum match or song duel. He starts with a few brash insults and obscenities. His target replies in kind. The (inevitable) audience, which is enjoying the show, begins to take sides. Now the insults get juicier and the obscenities hilarious. The audience determines the winner by laughing louder and longer at his jokes, and the bloodless contest is over. "And that is precisely the point of the Eskimo song duel," writes Peter Farb. "Two disputants batter each other by the singing of insults rather than by blows, in that way preventing a quarrel from turning into a socially divisive feud." And a good time is had by all, besides.

A culture's values and needs determine not only our everyday angers but even when we may be allowed to "go crazy" with rage. "Anger," wrote Horace some two thousand years ago, "is a brief madness," succinctly noting the affinity between "mad" and "angry." The match is psychological as well as linguistic, because in many cultures (including our own) an enraged individual and an insane one are both regarded as being out of control, unable to take responsibility for their actions. Yet other cultures, such as the Eskimo, distinguish the two conditions: A person who is legitimately insane cannot be expected to control himself, but one who is merely angry can and must control himself. What distinguishes us from the Eskimo, aside from the weather? What role does the *belief* in the similarity between rage and madness play?

A Brief Madness

• One evening, apparently out of the blue, a young Malay man armed himself with traditional weapons, the parang and the kris, and embarked on a killing spree. By the time his rampage was over, several hours later, he had accosted customers in three local coffeehouses and murdered five innocent men. His friends were surprised that the young man had "run amok"; he seemed so polite and well mannered.

• In San Francisco in 1979, a civil servant named Dan White resigned his seat on the city's Board of Supervisors. Shortly thereafter he changed his mind, but he was too late: Mayor George Moscone had decided to give the job to someone else. White took his snub-nosed revolver, climbed in through the window of City Hall (so the metal detectors wouldn't reveal his gun), and pumped nine bullets into Moscone and supervisor Harvey Milk, who had been one of White's outspoken opponents (and who was a homosexual whom White disliked). In what the press played up as the "Twinkie defense," White's lawyers argued that his excessive consumption of junk food had caused his "diminished mental capacity," leaving him unable to premeditate anything, much less murder. The jury agreed. White was convicted of voluntary manslaughter and given a maximum sentence of seven years and eight months in jail. (Twenty months after his release, he committed suicide.)

• The Gururumba tribesman was behaving strangely. He had suddenly taken to looting his neighbors' huts, stealing food and objects, and one afternoon his kinsmen found him hiding behind a tree, shooting arrows at passersby. He was clearly suffering a mental aberration, the tribe agreed, which they diagnosed as "being a wild pig."

• In New York in 1980, Jean Harris shot and killed Herman Tarnower, her lover of fourteen years, in what the prosecution called a "jealous rage" and the defense a "tragic accident." Tarnower was found with four bullets in his body; Harris said she was trying to kill herself, not him. The jury did not believe her. She was convicted of intentional murder and given a minimum sentence of fifteen years in prison.

Running amok, being a wild pig, and temporary insanity are, within their respective tribes, legitimate signs of "a brief madness." These rages are, however, regarded as something other than psychosis, true mental illness, or other sorts of "long" madnesses, and they are often treated differently. Certainly some individuals who suffer organic abnormalities or psychoses that produce rage attacks can properly be diagnosed as insane; they do not, for one thing, revert to normalcy after a violent episode. And there are other individuals, such as the disturbed loners who have tried to assassinate or succeeded in assassinating our presidents and heroes, whose aggressive acts have little to do with anger and more to do with fantasies of power and fame. But most cases of "temporary insanity" caused apparently by rage, those heralded cases that capture

the public eye, can be explained better in terms of their social causes than their organic ones, junk food to the contrary notwithstanding.

Start with "running amok," a phenomenon that originally referred to violent, often homicidal attacks among the indigenous peoples of the Malay Archipelago. Most people assume that the acts committed while a person is in such a state are unconscious, random, and without purpose. The *pengamok* (those who run amok) themselves think so, and so do their neighbors and relatives. But a closer look suggests otherwise. The frequency of this supposedly impulsive, uncontrollable act declined precipitately when the cultural response to it shifted from supportive tolerance to vicious punishment (at one point in Malay history, the *pengamok* were drawn and quartered).

Further, the objects of amok attacks are not random victims: Almost all of them are known to the amok and have been continuing sources of provocation. In one study that compared true *pengamok* to a control group of psychotics, the victims of the *pengamok* proved to be "rational" choices: a wife suspected of infidelity, a quarrelsome neighbor, an oppressive religion teacher. The Malay who killed the five customers of coffeehouses had carefully assured that his victims were Chinese: As his record showed, he had harbored anger at the Chinese who had killed some Malays several years before. The so-called psychotic symptoms of the *pengamok* vanish within a month or two of the episode, which is hardly the case for true psychotics.

Traditionally, the Malay are expected to be courteous and self-effacing, never to reprimand each other, and never to strive for success at the expense of another. Other cultures that have invaded the Malay Archipelago, such as the Chinese, have had rather more aggressive values, and therefore interpreted Malay behavior as signs of weakness and inferiority—which they promptly exploited. "Running amok," whether on an individual level or at a group level of rebellion, is a brilliant solution for Malay conflict: It allows the Malay to remain true to his cultural values while attacking the sources of his oppression and rage.

"Being a wild pig" is to the Gururumba what "running amok" is to the Malay. The Malay think that amok results from witchcraft or possession by evil spirits; the Gururumba think it comes from being bitten by a ghost. But wild pigs, like the *pengamok,* are not randomly distributed throughout the society. The only people who seem to get bitten, for example, are men between the ages of twenty-five and thirty-five, which is an especially stressful decade for the Gururumba male. He must abandon his youthful irresponsibility, take a wife, and assume a sudden burden of social obligations to the group. Success or failure at meeting these obligations will reflect not only on him, but on his clan.

Anthropologist P. L. Newman thinks that "being a wild pig" is a way of calling attention to the difficulties of shouldering these obligations. The victim of ghost bite, by his wild behavior, thereby announces to the tightly knit group that he wants to do something that his kinsmen might otherwise prohibit: change wives, move somewhere else, give up a particular responsibility. In the same way that a vociferous display of anger in our own culture finally convinces the recipient that the angry person *means* it, wild-pigdom convinces the Gururumba that the victim really is having a hard time and that something must be done. (Some Gururumba, consciously or not, put themselves in places where they are likely to be bitten by a ghost—a remote part of the forest or a gravesite.)

The Gururumba react with tolerance to a man who is being a wild pig. They are sympathetic to him, because they believe he is not responsible for his actions; they expect the seizure to run its course in a few days, like the flu. While the man is in this state they gently direct his "craziness": They leave food and little things for him to steal, and they don't let him hurt anyone seriously. The victim retreats to the forest for a few days on his own—not unlike our paid vacations—and if he returns still in a "wild" state, the tribesmen set up a ritual to cure him. They "capture" him and treat him as if he *were* a pig that had gone wild: They hold him over a smoking fire and rub him all over with pig fat. (This, the anthropologists assure us, is not as bad as it sounds.) A prominent person kills a real pig in the victim's name, and the victim is given a feast of pig meat and roots. Most important, however, are the reassessment and usually reduction of his obligations that occur after this ritual. That

component of the procedure seems most likely to prevent remissions.

The Malay and Gururumba examples suggest that acceptable varieties of "temporary insanity" occur in cultures in which two equally powerful value systems conflict. In Western culture, a powerful taboo exists against intentional acts of violence, especially murder, yet the culture often counteracts that taboo with as great a passion for revenge, retribution, and defense of moral values. In America, when "an eye for an eye" meets "turn the other cheek," when "thou shalt not kill" meets "thou shalt not commit adultery," temporary insanity is a temporary solution. This is a legal loophole in a Gordian knot: the law allows individuals to become angry enough to kill, but only if they kill in the service of society's dominant values, and only if they kill without premeditation or self-control—"in the heat of passion."

This is one reason, I think, that Dan White got off with such a light sentence for murdering two men and Jean Harris got a severe sentence for killing one. White and Harris both had had time, before their actions, to think about what they were doing. Both packed up their little guns at home and sought their victims. Both believed that they had been cruelly and unfairly treated by their victims. But Dan White's lawyers played on his "diminished mental capacity" to the hilt, bringing in plenty of psychiatrists to testify to his unstable mental condition. "The killing was done out of a passion," the foreman of the jury later said, "given the stress he was under." Jean Harris's defense emphasized the "tragic accident" explanation, and called on no psychiatrists to exonerate her behavior or describe the stress she was under. The only person to describe her mental state was Harris herself, and that was her undoing; for the anger she expressed, even there on the witness stand, was cold and deliberate. She gave no evidence of having been enraged at Tarnower; angry with the "other woman," yes, but with the lover who left her, no. Had she done so, had she used the enormous sympathy usually extended to scorned lovers, had she argued that she had committed a crime of passion, I believe the outcome would have been different. But she did not. She took responsibility for her emotions. And so the jury had to find her guilty of her actions.

Although people frequently deplore the association between anger and violence in the United States, our customs and our laws (to say nothing of the easy availability of handguns) encourage the link. Why do we resist the idea that we can control our emotions, that feeling angry need not inevitably cause us to behave violently? Seneca the Stoic had a good idea of the answer. We refuse to follow his philosophy of self-restraint, he suggested, "Because we are in love with our vices; we uphold them and prefer to make excuses for them rather than shake them off." And why do we make excuses for them? *Because they excuse us.*

In a timely update of Seneca's observation, James Averill notices that we do not abdicate responsibility for all of our emotions, just the negative ones. No one apologizes for being swept away by a tidal wave of kindness and donating five thousand dollars to a worthy cause. A bystander who intervenes to prevent an assault or mugging is unlikely to apologize for acting courageously. We want credit for our noble emotions and tolerance for our negative ones; and losing one's temper, "misplacing" it in a fleeting hour of insanity, is the apology that begs such tolerance. While anger serves our private uses, it also makes our social excuses.

Manners, Emotions, and the American Way

The class was basic English for foreign students, and an Arab student, during a spoken exercise, was describing a tradition of his home country. Something he said embarrassed a Japanese student in the front row, who reacted the proper Japanese way: He smiled. The Arab saw the smile and demanded to know what was so funny about Arab customs. The Japanese, who was now publicly humiliated as well as embarrassed, could reply only with a smile and, to his misfortune, he giggled to mask his shame. The Arab, who now likewise felt shamed, furiously hit the Japanese student before the teacher could intervene. Shame and anger had erupted in a flash, as each student dutifully obeyed the rules of his culture. Neither could imagine, of course, that his rules might not be universal.

Because a major function of anger is to maintain the social order, through its moralizing implications of how people "should" behave, it is predictable that when two social orders collide they would generate angry sparks. It is easiest to see this when the colliding cultures are foreign to each other, but we have plenty of such collisions within our society as well. For some groups in America, anger is an effective way to get your way; for others it is the last resort. (Some groups have to learn assertiveness training to deal with others.) You may find your attitudes about anger, and the rules you learned to govern it, in conflict with those of different groups. Often it is this conflict about anger rules, not the rules per se, that can stir up trouble.

Each of us is tied to a group—a minitribe, if you will—by virtue of our sex, status, race, and ethnicity, and with countless unconscious reactions we reveal those ties as surely as Eliza Doolittle did when she opened her mouth. Anthropologist Edward T. Hall speaks of the "deep biases and built-in blinders" that every culture confers on its members. You can observe them at work every time you hear someone grumble, "I'll never understand women," or, "Why can't he just say what he feels?" or, "The (Japanese) (Mexicans) (Irish) (etc.) are utterly inscrutable."

Hall, who lives in New Mexico, has long observed the clash that occurs between groups when deeply felt rules about the "correct" management of anger are broken. The Spanish are sensitive to the slightest suggestion of criticism, Hall explains. "Confrontations are therefore to be avoided at all costs." The resulting misunderstandings between Spanish- and Anglo-Americans, he says, would be amusing if they weren't so often tragic.

When Anglo-Americans are angry, they tend to proceed in stages from small steps to larger ones: First, they hint around ("Mort, are you sure that fence is on *your* side of the property line?"). Then they talk to neighbors and friends of Mort. If they get no results, they may talk directly, and calmly, to Mort ("Mort, can we discuss our fence problem?"). Next they will express anger directly to Mort ("Dammit, that fence is on my property"). Eventually, if they are angry enough, they will take the matter to the courts.

And as a last resort, they may resort to violence—and burn the fence down.

These steps, from smallest to largest, seem natural, logical, and inevitable. Actually, they are not only not natural, they are not even very common, worldwide. In many societies, such as in Latin cultures and in the Middle East, the first step is . . . to do nothing. Think about it. Brood. This brooding may go on for weeks, months, or even years (some cultures have long memories). The second step is . . . to burn the fence down. Now that matters are back to square one, participants are ready for direct discussions, negotiations, lawyers, and intermediaries. But notice, says Hall, that the act of force, which is the last step to Anglos, signaling the failure of negotiation, is the start of the conversation to Hispanics.

A culture's rules of anger are not arbitrary; they evolve along with its history and structure. The Japanese practice of emotional restraint, for example, dates back many centuries, when all aspects of demeanor were carefully regulated: facial expressions, breathing, manner of sitting and standing, style of walking. Not only were all emotions—anger, grief, pain, even great happiness—to be suppressed in the presence of one's superiors, but also regulations specified that a person submit to any order with a pleasant smile and a properly happy tone of voice. At the time of the Samurai knights, these rules had considerable survival value, because a Samurai could legally execute anyone who he thought was not respectful enough. (You may notice the similarity to American blacks and to women, who likewise had to be careful to control anger in the presence of the white man.)

Even today in Japan, an individual who feels very angry is likely to show it by excessive politeness and a neutral expression instead of by furious words and signs. A Japanese who shows anger the Western way is admitting that he has lost control, and therefore lost face; he is thus at the extreme end of a negotiation or debate. In other cultures, though, showing anger may simply mark the *beginning* of an exchange, perhaps to show that the negotiator is serious; a man may lose face if he does *not* show anger when it is appropriate and "manly" for him to do so.

Psychotherapy, of course, takes place within a culture and is deeply embedded in cultural rules. Arthur Kleinman, himself both an anthropologist and psychiatrist, tells of a psychiatrist in south-central China who was treating a patient who had become depressed and anxious ever since her demanding mother-in-law had moved in. "She is your family member. It is your responsibility to care for an old mother-in-law," the Chinese psychiatrist said. "You must contain your anger. You know the old adage: 'Be deaf and dumb! Swallow the seeds of the bitter melon! Don't speak out!'"

I am not recommending that Americans learn to "swallow the seeds of the bitter melon"; in our society, most of us would choke on them. Cultural practices cannot be imported from society to society like so many bits of cheese, because they are part of a larger pattern of rules and relationships. Indeed, that is the reason we cannot avoid the anger we feel when someone breaks the rules that we have learned are the only civilized rules to follow. But we might emulate the Arapesh, who criticize the provocateur; or the Eskimo, who settle in for a good round of verbal dueling; or the Mbuti, who have a good laugh, understanding as they do the healing power of humor. We might also retrieve the old-fashioned standard of manners, which is, as small tribes teach us, an organized system of anger management. The conventions of the U.S. Senate, for example—the ornate language, the rules of debate—regulate anger over disagreements into acceptable channels. A senator does not call his or her opposition a stupid blithering moron, for instance. He says, "My distinguished colleague from the great state of Blitzhorn, an otherwise fine and noble individual, is, in this rare moment, erring in judgment." The elaborate language that seems so comically deceptive to the rest of us is what keeps political conversation going without bloodshed and mayhem.

Good manners melt resentment because they maintain respect between the two disagreeing parties. Indeed, one of the basic principles of parliamentary law is courtesy, "respect for the rights of individuals and for the assembly itself." You don't have to join Congress to feel the effect of this principle at work. Someone steps on your toe, you feel angry, the person apologizes, your anger vanishes. Your toe may still hurt, but your dignity is intact. (A friend tells me he loudly shushed a talkative man sitting behind him at the movies, and immediately felt bad that he had expressed himself so angrily. After the show, the man touched him on the shoulder. "You were quite right to tell me to keep quiet," he said, "I was rude." "I could have kissed him," said my friend.)

Without rules for controlling anger, it can slip into emotional anarchy, lasting far longer than its original purposes require. Observe how friends and family react to someone undergoing a bitter divorce: They extend sympathy and a willing ear to the enraged spouse for a while, but eventually they expect the person to "shape up" and "get on with it." What these friends and relatives are doing is imposing unofficial rules of anger management. The victim may grouse and mutter about the loss of sympathy, but actually the friends and relatives are doing what any decent tribe would do: keeping anger in bounds after it has done its job and making sure the victim stays in the social circle. Well-meaning friends and therapists who encourage a vengeful spouse to ventilate rage for years are doing neither the spouse nor the tribe a service.

People in all cultures, even the pacifistic !Kung and the Utku, do occasionally feel irritable and angry. But they do not *value* anger. They strive for a state of mind that philosopher Robert Solomon calls "equanimity under trying circumstances," the worldview of small societies that live in dangerous environments. "The Utku," says Solomon, "much more than any of us, are used to extreme hardship and discomfort. Their philosophy, therefore, is that such things must be tolerated, not flailed against. Captain Ahab and Sisyphus would have no role in their literature."

In this country, the philosophy of emotional expression regards self-restraint as hypocrisy. The cultures of the Far East do not have this conflict; a person is expected to control and subdue the emotions because it is the relationship, not the individual, that comes first. Here, where the reverse is true, some people express their emotions even at the expense of the relationship, and manners seem to be as rare as egrets. This analogy is not arbitrary, for the same ideology that gave us emotional ventilation is responsible for the scarcity of egrets: the imperial "I."

Consider the gentle, forgiving environment of Tahiti, where people learn that they have limited control over nature and over other people. They learn that if they try to change nature, she will swiftly destroy them, but if they relax and accept the bounty of nature— and the nature of people—they will be taken care of. Anthropologist Robert Levy calls this resulting world view among the Tahitians "passive optimism."

Such a philosophy would not have lasted long among the ancient Hebrews, whose God gave them "dominion over the fish of the sea, and over the fowl of the air, and over the cattle, and over all the earth, and over every creeping thing that creepeth upon the earth" (Genesis 1:26). And a good thing He did, too, because in the harsh deserts of the Middle East, adherents of a laissez-faire Tahitian religion would have met a swift demise. The Judeo-Christian philosophy, however, produces "active pessimists": people who assume that nature and other people are to be conquered, indeed must be conquered, and that individual striving is essential to survival. But a universe defined as the Tahitians see it is intrinsically less infuriating than a universe in which almost everything is possible if the individual tries hard enough. The individualism of American life, to our glory and despair, creates anger and encourages its release; for when everything is possible, limitations are irksome. When the desires of the self come first, the needs of others are annoying. When we think we deserve it all, reaping only a portion can enrage.

Bibliography

Averill, James R. "Anger." In H. Howe and R. Dienstbier, eds. *Nebraska Symposium on Motivation, 1978,* vol. 26. Lincoln: University of Nebraska Press, 1979.

Averill, James R. "Emotion and Anxiety: Sociocultural, Biological, and Psychological Determinants." In M. Zukerman and C. D. Spielberger, eds. *Emotions and Anxiety.* New York: LEA-John Wiley, 1976.

Averill, James R. *Anger and Aggression.* New York: Springer-Verlag, 1982.

Briggs, Jean. *Never in Anger: Portrait of an Eskimo Family.* Cambridge, Mass.: Harvard University Press, 1970.

Carr, John E., and Eng Kong Tan. "In Search of the True Amok: Amok as Viewed Within Malay Culture." *American Journal of Psychiatry* 133, 1976, 1295–1299.

Dentan, Robert Knox. "Notes on Childhood in a Nonviolent Context: The Semai Case." In A. Montagu, ed. *Learning Non-Aggression.* New York: Oxford University Press paperback, 1978.

Dentan, Robert Knox. *The Semai.* New York: Holt, Rinehart & Winston, 1968.

De Rivera, Joseph. "A Structural Theory of the Emotions." *Psychological Issues* X(4), monograph 40. New York: International University Press, 1977.

Draper, Patricia. "The Learning Environment for Aggression and Anti-Social Behavior among the !Kung." In A. Montagu, ed. *Learning Non-Aggression.* New York: Oxford University Press paperback, 1978.

Draper, Patricia. "Social and Economic Constraints on Child Life among the !Kung." In R. B. Lee and I. DeVore, eds. *Kalahari Hunter-Gatherers: Studies of the !Kung San and Their Neighbors.* Cambridge, Mass.: Harvard University Press, 1976.

Farb, Peter. *Word Play: What Happens When People Talk.* New York: Bantam, 1975.

Hall, Edward T. *Beyond Culture.* Garden City, N.Y.: Doubleday, Anchor Press, 1976.

Hollan, Douglas. "Staying 'Cool' in Toraja: Informal Strategies for the Management of Anger and Hostility in a Nonviolent Society." *Ethos* 16, 1988, 52–72.

Holmberg, Allan R. *Nomads of the Long Bow: The Siriono of Eastern Bolivia.* Garden City, N.Y.: The Natural History Press, 1969.

Hupka, Ralph. "Cultural Determinants of Jealousy." *Alternative Life Styles* 4, August 1981, 310–356.

Kleinman, Arthur. *Rethinking Psychiatry: From Cultural Category to Personal Experience.* New York: The Free Press, 1988.

Levy, Robert I. "Tahitian Gentleness and Redundant Controls." In A. Montagu, ed. *Learning Non-Aggression.* New York: Oxford University Press, 1978.

Levy, Robert I. *Tahitians.* Chicago: University of Chicago Press, 1973.

Lutz, Catherine A. *Unnatural Emotions.* Chicago: University of Chicago Press, 1988.

Marshall, Lorna. "Sharing, Talking, and Giving: Relief of Social Tensions among the !Kung." In R. B. Lee and I. DeVore, eds. *Kalahari Hunter-Gatherers.* Cambridge, Mass.: Harvard University Press, 1976.

Mead, Margaret. *Male and Female.* New York: Dell, 1949; Laurel edition, 1968.

Myerhoff, Barbara. *Number Our Days.* New York: Dutton, 1978.

Newman, P. L. "'Wild Man' Behavior in a New Guinea Highlands Community." *American Anthropologist* 66, 1960, 1–19.

Pospisil, Leopold. *The Kapauku Papuans of West New Guinea.* New York: Holt, Rinehart & Winston, 1963.

Roseman, Marina. *Healing Sounds: Music and Medicine in Temiar Life.* Berkeley, Calif.: University of California Press, 1990.

Sebeok, Thomas A. *Play of Musement.* Bloomington: University of Indiana Press, 1982.

Seneca, Lucius Annaeus. "On Anger." In J. W. Basore, trans. *Moral Essays.* Cambridge, Mass.: Harvard University Press, 1963. (See also "On Self-Control," letter CXVI in *The Letters of Seneca.*)

Solomon, Robert. "Emotions and Anthropology: The Logic of Emotional World Views." *Inquiry* 21, 1978, 181–199.

Thomas, Elizabeth Marshall. *The Harmless People.* New York: Random House, 1959.

Turnbull, Colin M. *The Forest People.* New York: Simon and Schuster, 1961.

Turnbull, Colin M. "The Politics of Non-Aggression." In A. Montagu, ed. *Learning Non-Aggression.* New York: Oxford University Press paperback, 1978.

2

A New Approach to Anger Control

1860–1940, THE AMERICAN AMBIVALENCE

Carol Zisowitz Stearns
Peter N. Stearns

The early Victorian synthesis on anger depended on a more general synthesis of beliefs about the relationship between home and work and on a style that handled unpleasant subjects by pressing for more effort, more self-discipline, and more control. That home/work dichotomy began to undergo some modification in the second half of the century, and at the same time a new style emerged that encouraged dealing with unpleasantness through understanding rather than conquest. Not surprisingly, then, ideas about anger also began to change. These changes became evident, at first, in the child-rearing literature and only later began to be accommodated in thought on marriage. We will describe these changes and then attempt to explore in some detail the reasons for change. After this discussion of emotionology, we will then consider what form the actual expression of anger took during this period and offer some speculations about the relationship between the emotionology and the reality of anger in the American home.

Family emotionology at the turn of the century became more complex, which may ironically have made it more realistic. Two new ingredients entered the picture, altering the earlier Victorian stance: a recognition that anger existed as a natural personality trait and a belief that anger could be put to some good uses. These novelties were combined with continued insistence on avoiding anger in the home, which made for some careful statements about child-rearing strategies and new discussions of marital tactics as well.

During the decades between about 1860 and 1940, as Victorian idealism confronted new realities about the human personality and marriage, basic anger-control goals persisted. No one emerged directly to praise anger or to urge that restraint was less important than the Victorians had believed. Indeed, on the subjects of both child rearing and marriage statements of almost literal Victorianism continued to be made or could be revived when external reality seemed to turn particularly sour. But strategies did change, as it was realized, for various reasons, that literal avoidance of anger was more difficult than had previously been thought. Furthermore, particularly in child rearing, the definition of desirable personality shifted somewhat, so that a person devoid of anger's zest was now seen as unduly flaccid. The shift in tactics and the partial alteration of goals combined to create a new period in the American approach to anger, one still modern in its attack on anger itself but far more complicated than the Victorian decades had been.

Perhaps no character exemplifies this complexity so well as Melville's Billy Budd, whose demise may fairly be viewed as the result of his unsuccessful attempt to handle conflicts about anger. Melville, introducing his hero, tells us that his slowness to anger was viewed as unmanly by some peers. One man thought "such a 'sweet and pleasant fellow' as he mockingly designated

"A New Approach to Anger Control: 1860–1940, The American Ambivalence," pp. 69–109 in *Anger: The Struggle for Emotional Control in America's History,* by Carol Zisowitz Stearns and Peter N. Stearns (University of Chicago Press 1986). © 1986 by The University of Chicago. Abridged and reprinted with permission.

him . . . could hardly have the spirit of a game-cock." He tried unsuccessfully to provoke the hero, but finally, when he struck Billy, the hero "quick as lightening . . . let fly his arm." Melville commented on this through another character: "'Well, blessed are the peacemakers, especially the fighting peacemakers!'"[1] Anger, when justifiable, was manly and admirable. Billy's and Melville's confusion about how to express the anger, however, was the central problem of the tragedy.

This newly complex approach to anger that was epitomized by Billy Budd must be explored in detail for two reasons. First, several aspects of it seem quintessentially American, constituting a clearer national variant on a general modern-Western approach to emotionality than Victorian idealism had done. In child rearing, the characteristic ambivalence about goals generated during this period corresponded to some measurable and unusual features of American parenting. The approach in marriage advice was less clearly distinctive, on a comparative basis, but here too ambivalence corresponded to some unusual empirical aspects of the American scene, notably the rising national divorce rate. The American approach to anger during the turn-of-the-century decades sought still to discipline the emotion, but a confusing sense that the discipline could not or should not be complete was also present.

The second reason to attend to this period is that it provides a crucial baseline for evaluating subsequent developments. For Americans did not stick to an ambivalent approach to familial anger, despite its linkage to some important facets of national character. Recent alterations in approach must inevitably be measured against the turn-of-the-century style. And the existence of this style, coming after the more straightforward Victorian attempt to attack anger without qualification, might lend some encouragement to those who find contemporary Americans again too thoroughly repressive. For while it is clear that an effort to identify and discipline anger forms an important part of modern social norms from the late eighteenth century, the new twists that emerged after about 1860 demonstrated that this effort was compatible with some subtle usage of the emotion as well: it may be

tempting to appeal in future to the turn-of-the-century willingness to draw benefit from anger.

Child Rearing: A New Emotionology

The emergence of a new ambivalence toward anger in child-rearing advice was particularly striking in the decades after 1860, for it represented an attempt to preserve an anger-free home while developing a new kind of vigor in economic and public life. American child-rearing emotionology had already gone through two phases, and in each the approach to anger was quite clear-cut. In the first period, child-rearing advice ignored anger in favor of selective concern over its behavioral consequences. In the second, ultimately Victorian stage, anger had been thoroughly reproved, though the reproval was surrounded by idealistic assumptions of childish innocence that might mute its effects in practice. Now, while reproval continued, particularly within the family circle, properly controlled anger was seen as a useful goad to constructive behavior in the wider world. This was the pattern of advice that corresponded to measurable behavior on the part of many parents, producing the distinctive American approach to the handling of anger in children, indeed, a distinctive American approach to the definition of an emotionally appropriate personality.

Some portion of the new ambivalence may have resulted from a partial merger of expert advice with parental reality. We will see a similar realism enter, more hesitantly, into marital advice as well. Victorian advice had, after all, paid little attention to the actual personality traits of children, assuming that proper parental example was everything. It is very unlikely that many parents attempted to alter traditional disciplinary behavior to meet this ideal fully. Thus while there is some evidence that the strictest will-breaking behavior declined and evidence also of new anxiety on the part of parents about their own anger, it is clear that many parents did indeed encounter anger in children and that they often attempted to punish expressions of angry emotion. Certain child-rearing experts toward the end of the nineteenth century explicitly recognized childish anger; they also recognized, with the larger goal of anger control in mind, the need to do something about it, and were therefore sending more realistic signals and also picking up on actual parental experience. This is one reason, in turn, that the new pattern of advice had a wider demonstrable effect than Victorian idealism had won, even though this idealism had served an important stage in the development of anger-control goals.

The new approach toward anger in child-rearing unquestionably related to another trend in actual parenting, particularly for males, that took shape toward the end of the nineteenth century. Moral discipline, as part of character building, declined in favor. Fathers who advised and wrote to their sons increasingly pulled away from this Protestant-Victorian approach, replacing it in part with growing concern about physical health and athletic development.[2] This shift did not eliminate anger control as a purpose, but it required a new sense of tactics; moral restraint and parental example would no longer suffice.

Two new themes predominated in child-rearing emotionology concerning anger from the late nineteenth century through the interwar years. First, there was greater recognition that children did naturally get angry, as against Victorian assumptions of innocence, and that childish anger required some firm disciplinary approach. Anger remained unacceptable, but the mechanisms through which to achieve anger control inevitably became more complex and explicit. This was the area in which the new tone in advice corresponded most obviously with parental realities. The second change related in part to the new strategies sought, but it also reflected an alteration in personality goals. Anger, while unacceptable, was now seen as a desirable emotional spur that could be channeled into useful endeavor. The concept of channeling, into competitive drive or moral indignation, was the most significant innovation of turn-of-the-century emotionology.

Fairly literal Victorian statements did continue, particularly, of course, in the 1870s and 1880s but even into the 1920s. At first an ideal of the Christian gentleman maintained the Victorian approach toward anger in children, with an emphasis on complete anger avoidance through proper moral guidance and parental restraint. Evangelical pamphlets espoused this approach into the twentieth century. Thus, for example, the Christian gentleman school maintained that parents have a "sacred duty" to instill anger control by forming habits early through their own examples; and the Evangelical approach held, with an interesting increase in concern about violence, that "the same temper that smashes a toy in anger may, when the child is grown, kill a man."[3] Such continuity of idealistic concern means of course that diversity continued in the American approach to anger. This is no great surprise, but it is important because it underlines the fact that key Victorian goals persisted in this area, not only in the genteel Christian literature, but also in the more innovative materials. The changes that must be discussed were not reversals. Older goals were to a great extent retained, and this is why literal Victorianism could still be maintained without seeming hopelessly anachronistic. We will see a similar pattern in marital advice, in which real changes did not obscure an intense desire to keep the family largely free from anger.

But the most popular child-rearing advice manuals, soon joined by magazines for up-to-date parents, shifted away from literal Victorianism. Darwinian findings about the animal bases of human behavior, including elaborate inquiries into the evolutionary role of anger, helped alter the view of childish innocence in the mainstream literature from the 1860s on. The fact had to be recognized: many children, even when well treated, did grow angry and have tantrums. Indeed, it was during these decades, and initially through Darwinian usage, that the word *tantrum* finally settled into its contemporary form, designating an objectionable pattern of emotional outburst among young children and therefore a genuine problem for parents.[4]

The new empirical view of childish anger produced a growing concern about the issue of parental emotional control from the 1880s until about 1910. G. Stanley Hall inquired into anger in an elaborate research project, and he incorporated some of this concern in his discussion of adolescence. Partly under Hall's influence, several child-rearing manuals took up the problem of anger between 1900 and 1910, and the National Institute of Child Life issued a special pamphlet on the subject. After about 1910 attention grew less detailed because an acceptable range of approaches had been agreed on, at least among the advice givers; but any manual that went beyond physical health advice now regularly included a section on tantrums, a pattern that continues to the present day.[5]

For childish anger was a problem precisely because the new empirical view of children was combined with a basic desire to maintain older goals of anger control. The flurry of attention to the subject produced a general consensus that childish anger was an appropriate subject for discipline and that it required as well more elaborate strategies than the Victorians had suggested in order to avoid angry confrontations in the first place. Hall and his followers criticized parents who were too indulgent of anger in young children and urged physical punishment for its expression. They also saw anger control as part of a childhood-long process of parental guidance, one that would extend to advice on proper behavior for adolescents. During the 1920s and 1930s, concern about very young children increased, in advance of real acceptance of Freudianism.[6] John B. Watson and other behaviorists found childish anger easy enough to control, through elimination of unnecessary restraint and also of undue coddling; calm, nonangry discipline remained a key. Other experts handled growing parental concern about tantrums differently. Some urged neglect pure and simple; others favored careful inquiry into the causes of anger; others, including several authors in *Parents' Magazine,* urged outright punishment lest tantrums reveal a child unduly spoiled.[7] The increasing concern with childish anger, while it did not produce a single enduring recommended parental response, did show a new, or newly articulate, belief. Childish anger control was not only important, as earlier in the nineteenth century, but also somewhat difficult. Parents needed more than their own self-restraint if the child was to grow into a "self-controlled and useful adult."[8]

As part of this new concern, the need for patience and control of anger in relationships among brothers and sisters received growing emphasis, for, along with positive affection, the absence of sibling conflict was vital to family harmony. Authorities called to mind evil fraternal conflicts in the Bible. Louisa May Alcott, in *Little Women,* painted the problems of quick tempers among sisters: Jo lamented her "dreadful temper," and her mother assured her that this was a temptation that would require lifelong control. "You think your temper is the worst in the world, but mine used to be just like it. I've been trying to cure it for forty years, and have only succeeded in controlling it. I am angry nearly everyday of my life, but I have learned not to show it; and I still hope to learn not to feel it, though it may take me another forty years to do so."[9] Clearly, the later nineteenth century did not abandon the arduous goal of emotional control.

Growing recognition of childish anger as a problem did not produce a single strategy for coping. Child-rearing authorities got a good bit of mileage from arguments about whether ignoring anger was better than outright punishment of it, with advocates of the former approach (combined of course with greatest possible avoidance of childish fatigue and other irritants) gradually winning majority support in the advice manuals. This tactical disagreement was significant, for, as we will see, it corresponded to considerable diversity in parental approach. But the authorities did agree on key goals: childish anger should never be rewarded; childish anger, including sibling rivalry, should be excised as fully and as early as possible to preserve the proper emotional tone of the home and to start the process of building a civilized personality; and parents must see this aspect of the emotional life of their charges as a problem area.

Concern about childish anger spilled over, more clearly than in early Victorianism, into perceptions of social class. Experts, using the dominant emotionology, widely criticized the way working-class parents handled anger, from the late nineteenth to the mid-twentieth century. Worker or immigrant parents were judged likely to respond to childish tantrums with anger and physical punishments of their own. Some even encouraged and enjoyed their children's aggression against others as an outlet for their own feelings. The net result was inconsistency (so the experts held)—the generation of anger in reaction to parental anger, without firm and uniform rules against its expression. Here, the experts argued, was a major source of disproportionate delinquency, another theme that reveals growing recognition that childish anger could turn into a problem unless handled with care.[10]

In some ways the second new theme of child-rearing emotionology complicated the first, for it recognized that anger could mutate into useful drives. But the complication was not intentional, for the goal of anger control, particularly within the family, was not explicitly altered. And channeling anger—the strategy that resulted from the new theme—formed a widely agreed on technique for handling part of the problem now so widely perceived.

This second new theme, addressed particularly toward men, did, however, pull away from Victorian idealism quite decisively. For there was a growing belief that anger could be good as well as bad. Not in raw form: no one pulled back from disapproval of literal displays of personal temper. But, properly channeled, anger was a useful spur; indeed, its absence was to be lamented. Here indeed was another new parental worry by the late nineteenth century: children incapable of anger lacked individuality and independence and were truly "pathetic."[11] The notion that anger reflected a kind of admirable spunk, at least in males, had not been totally foreign to the earlier period, but now it became a central strain of the emotionology rather than an insignificant aside. Child-rearing experts, in the eighty years after 1860, produced the emotionological base for the American ambivalence about anger—the ambivalence that Lloyd Warner still discerned in middle-class families in the 1950s.

Some of the new tensions about anger emerged in outright disagreement, particularly during the 1860s and 1870s, when the transition to new beliefs was in progress. Thus handbooks on the Christian gentleman stressed control of anger at the same time as literature in the Horatio Alger school urged the importance of aggressive, competitive behavior, in which values such as anger were instrumental in personal advancement. Anger, in this literature, was by itself of no concern, for it could easily shift to spur achievement. Children's literature similarly provided examples of pacificity cheek by jowl with the more sensational stories of the post–Civil War era, which praised brawling and manly strength.[12]

By the end of the nineteenth century, and recurrently thereafter, the new tensions emerged in individual discussions, producing many near contradictions. G. Stanley Hall blasts anger as destructive and damaging to health, the sign of a weak will and of decaying intellectual power. But he also held that "a certain choleric vein gives zest and force to all acts" and, in an effort to reconcile, that "the best work of the world is done" in the tension between anger and control. According to the American Institute of Child Life: "Anger is not lovely"; children's rages, though inevitable to a point because of the fighting instinct, create such ugly physical symptoms that the person seems "a child no longer, but a creature under demoniacal possession." But while childish anger warrants some "counsel and punishment, an atmosphere of grief and disapproval," and efforts to prevent or distract, and while the aggression that leads to "wars, rapine and misery" is unquestionably bad, anger cannot and should not be entirely eliminated; it has many good qualities and should be "a great and diffused power in life, making it strenuous, giving zest to the struggle for power and rising to righteous indignation."[13]

The key to this new perception, the ultimate reconciler, was channeling, as part of character building. Thus a turn-of-the-century manual urged a balance between encouraging and discouraging anger as the fighting instinct. Too much combativeness is obviously bad, but a boy with no tendency to fight would be an unnatural nonentity. So fighting should never be promoted, but no parent should ever say never fight. Similarly for adults, competition "is a form of fighting that is very prominent all through life." In a similar vein, according to the founder of the National Congress of Mothers, while girls should be trained to prepare a tranquil home and face problems "cheerfully," boys should simply be trained in righteous indignation. The process was to be highly rational. Children could be taught to look at the results of ungoverned temper and then urged on to proper targets. Here, for example, is an uplifting conversation between mother and son on a dirty street: "'I'm sure, my little son, when you are a man, and serve in the City Council, you will see that the laws are enforced and that we have a clean town.' See the flash of righteous indignation in the boyish eyes. . . . the active brain has received an indelible impression, the emotional nature has found a legitimate vent." Even a violent temper, with such training, can be a "splendid force," providing "royal service."[14]

Thus the tension about the uses of anger, though it did produce some contradictory or confusing statements, was not fundamentally illogical. It did pull away from the simpler disapproval of anger that had developed by the mid-nineteenth century without returning to the lack of explicit concern characteristic of will breaking. To this extent the tension was more complex. Even when not illogical in theory, it could add new worries to the process of parenting. The decline of belief in the innocence of young children justified new admissions that some children had ungovernable tempers while other children might frighten by their passivity, their lack of anger.[15] Furthermore, the new, limited value found in anger did not remove the parental obligation of self-control. Children must be allowed some anger, but adults should have learned that anger was inappropriate in the home. Both competition and righteous indignation were for external use only. Thus the translation of the new tension into practice may have been constructive, but it raised several potential difficulties as well. It is also obvious that authorities who saw channeling as the solution to parental problems disagreed somewhat about direction. Advice produced by men, and also many stories for boys, tended to emphasize the competitive joys of channeled anger and suggested various specific devices, such as boxing, to begin the channeling process during boyhood. Other literature, particularly that produced by

women and directed toward the mothers of boys, focused more explicitly, Progressive fashion, on the moral utility of indignation. Their strategies rested more on sage maternal advice than on competitive sports, like the ideal mother who strolled down the streets with her son pointing out targets for reformist zeal.

Contradictions and complexities in the new approach to anger should not be overdrawn. Experts did disagree over precise methods of disciplining anger, just as they more implicitly argued about whether anger should be channeled into business or into reformist activities. But a sense that anger in children, though a problem, was a manageable problem developed widely. Children's stories could toss off glib, moralistic pronouncements about anger with a firm belief that the values of control were undoubted—they often focused on anger in boys since girls were not angry anyway. Thus Uncle Wiggily (the rabbit gentleman popular between the wars) disdained an angry boy: "And I think he stamped his foot on the floor, the least little bit. It may have been that he saw a tack sticking up, and wanted to hammer it down with his shoe. But I am afraid it was a stamp of the foot; and afterward that boy was sorry." Note that the angry gesture itself was wrong, even in private; this involved more than the traditional insistence on obedience and readily continued the Victorian emphasis on avoiding a nasty emotion.[16] Other stories, of course, showed teenagers, who had presumably mastered personal anger, displaying commendable emotional drive in pursuit of business success or in attacking social evils. No shadow of a psychological or philosophical dilemma entered these lessons.

Child-rearing literature also usually handled the complexity of the emotionology of anger with admirable brevity. Particularly after about 1910, when the Darwinian findings about children had been assimilated and the channeling approach widely accepted, the space devoted to anger problems was typically limited. This helps account for the confusing signals that resulted in some treatments, but it also expresses the real confidence that a satisfactory synthesis had been achieved. If anything, after the initial discussion, the new sense that anger could be channeled reduced the need to talk about it, in contrast to the more thorough uprooting projected in the mid-nineteenth-century approach, though, as we have seen, a subject such as sibling relations, involving family harmony, roused great interest still. Character building, of which Victorian anger control was a part, required repeated lessons and examples, for parents and children alike. The new approach, for all the disagreements over specifics, tended to assume that childish anger could be handled early, with channeling developed through a series of physically as well as mentally uplifting exercises until adulthood was achieved. Hence, again particularly after 1910, other issues easily predominated: sheer physical care (for infants), the treatment of sexuality, and even the handling of fear. Some manuals focused only on physical health; this was the official stance of the early editions of *Infant Care,* which viewed the emotional area as beyond really scientific judgment to date. Even manuals that did take up emotions tended to favor inculcation of temperance, chastity, honesty, and courage, though anger received its due formulas.[17] Most typical was the brief, confident comment. Children could usually learn to handle anger naturally, through interaction with peers under parental guidance. Wild anger had to be discouraged, though remedies varied somewhat. But parents should not exaggerate even a modest tantrum problem since anger was valuable when channeled and even tantrums might be channeled through vigorous exercise or competitive games.[18]

This general approach, including the central ambivalence about anger's value depending on private or public expression, survived several generational swings in other aspects of child-rearing advice. Historians have identified the cycles 1840–60, 1860–80, 1880–1910, and 1910–30 as marking shifts and sometimes outright reversals in such basic practices as toilet training and feeding schedules and in parental emotional tone.[19] These shifts, if carried through by actual parents, might have had a major effect on actual childish anger, the effect varying, of course, according to the school of experts listened to. Thus Watsonian benign neglect, intended among other things to limit anger, would be seen by later experts to be productive of anger in adults because of its strictness and coldness

toward young children. The shifts in child-rearing fads unquestionably revealed the ingenuity of experts in seeking an audience, for each succeeding generation had the awesome task of undoing its predecessor's work. And each of the shorter cycles undoubtedly had some real effect on the actual behavior of some real parents and, even more, on their professed goals and anxieties. However, with respect to anger, at least, the somewhat longer periodization 1860–1940 must also be emphasized, for a fairly consistent stance, calling for control but not repression, underlay the shorter cycles. The fact that such consistency can be discerned may possibly point to a more realistic connection between child-rearing advice and actual parental behavior. The assumptions of 1860–1940 did represent change from the previously dominant approach, and they were to change again. But as they were not quite as volatile as the cycles expertise in other areas went through, actual parents and children were exposed to them longer.[20]

The theme of controlling private anger while channeling it to good purpose continues from the Darwinians through the muscular Christians to the various child-rearing schools of the first third of our own century, creating vigorous appeals for less or for more anger, depending on the context. G. Stanley Hall cites the attitude of one of his teachers in the mid-1890s: "I plead for more anger in schools. There is a point where patience ceases to be a moral of pedagogical virtue, but is mere flabbiness."[21] Dorothy Canfield Fischer, a tireless writer of manuals for parents, felt that a child should never be permitted to gain anything by showing anger, for children must learn to solve problems by other means. *But* anger can spur useful energy. A recent manual for black parents regards anger as typically destructive; it should certainly never dominate action, for too often it leads to crime and violence. Mothers should prevent anger in children by large doses of affection. *But* anger energizes the fight for legitimate rights. According to a Watsonian of the 1930s, parents can easily teach children not to throw tantrums by ignoring them, and while some anger is indeed unavoidable since children must be restrained, it is a learned emotion and can largely be omitted from a child's emotional lexicon. *But* anger is valuable to individuals and to society: "If he is stirred, if he reacts powerfully, out of that very stirring may come achievements and performance of a high level." A more permissive approach, from the 1940s, stresses that civilization depends on rational control of anger and that a well-adjusted person is not angry. *But,* some pages later, anger is a great thing, from childhood on, in calling attention to individual rights.[22] Even specific aspects of anger elicit contradictions. After noting how tantrums can best be avoided and how they can signal problems with parent or child, a manual subsequently lauds the normalcy of tantrums as the root of a baby's individuality, self-respect, and strength of character.[23] *But* tantrums after two years of age show physiological and serious behavioral disturbance (though later in the same book the age is confusingly pushed back to three and a half). And, elsewhere, children's anger "serves an excellent purpose."[24]

The durability of the tensions in the new child-rearing emotionology suggests again that they served an important cultural function and represented a satisfactory amalgam to several generations of writers. We will turn later to the equally important and durable correspondence to actual parental styles. Clearly, many people found the turn-of-the-century complications in the anger-control effort a valid addendum, one that addressed real-world needs without sacrificing a proper definition of personality or the ongoing desire for an anger-free family environment. The channeling concept was of course the key reconciler of diverse purposes. Supplementing this was the implied division between the socialization of boys and that of girls. Early Victorian child-rearing ideals had merged the treatment of gender largely on a feminized base. The new approach to anger, which in part reacted to growing fears of feminization as women took on novel roles and gained predominance in the teaching corps, stipulated the importance of aggressive behavior for males.[25] A few child-rearing experts, such as representatives of the National Congress of Mothers who stood against the feminism of the day in the name of domestic authority, explicitly differentiated between the channeling needs of boys and the continued anger-free qualities of girls. Without question, as we will see, many parents adopted this dual approach, continuing to stress Victorian restraint on girlish anger. Such a division did help reconcile the channeling impulse with domestic idealism. Both boys and girls should shed literal anger, but girls, as future promoters of domestic bliss, should do their shedding without qualifications. Only boys, with business and public roles in mind, should work toward anger control through channeling.

It is important to note, however, as a final complication in this new emotionology, that most child-rearing authorities only implied this clear gender division; they did not state it outright. Examples of channeled anger used boys as subjects. Worries about angerless children were, mainly, worries about boys. Sports used as channeling mechanisms were boys' sports. Save for the few exceptions noted, few authorities actually stated that girls should not undergo a channeling experience or that they might not find the vigor of sublimated anger useful, as men would, in later life. In a period when many women, as feminists or temperance advocates, were in fact demonstrating high levels of moral indignation, this common omission is significant—as if child-rearing experts, like many women themselves, had not decided on an appropriate emotional definition for womanhood. This implicit hesitancy about gender divisions (or their absence) in emotionology carried over into some of the obliqueness of the treatment of anger in marriage, as we shall see. It may also have suggested that, in practice, some girls as well as boys were exposed to the new esteem for channeled anger, if with some confusion because of the lack of overt comment on this emotional outlet for women. This exposure, too, could bear on marriage.

Emotion and Emotional Expression

There is strong evidence that many parents stepped up their attempts to control their own anger from the later nineteenth century on, continuing the trend from the earlier period. Worries about angry children became more articulate, but channeling was also attempted and produced results that many parents found satisfactory. A striking correspondence between actual parental tactics and the new channeling idea was a fundamental aspect of emotional experience in this period. Results for children were less clear, as anger became a tantalizing emotion not always easy to express when it was felt. Anger in marriage may have been slightly less guilt ridden in practice than in emotionological theory, and some of the new control tactics were utilized. But marital anger remained a difficult and confused topic, as experience mirrored emotionological ambiguities. . . .

We know more about changes in expression of anger in child rearing than we do about trends in marriage, though the social scientific evidence about child rearing accumulates particularly from the 1920s on. The bows to greater realism in the turn-of-the-century emotionology by definition increased the correspondence between anger standards and the actual experience of anger. Insofar as experts were coming a bit closer to actual children, they inevitably picked up substantial echoes of real life. In child rearing, the link between emotionology and child-rearing behavior went beyond heightened realism. Parents, particularly in the middle class, adopted many of the precise cues of the channeling approach. Whether their stance was new, whether it partly resulted from the emotionology, or whether it merely corresponded to it cannot be ascertained. But there is no question that emotionology at this point suggested a distinctive American parenting style, despite some clashes on specific tactics.

Concern about unusually angry children prompted many parents to consult outside experts in this period, as we will see; and while this trend reflects the new secular expertise available, it may also have translated parents' growing anxiety about how to handle intense childish anger without using anger themselves. Even middle-class parents without problem children tried to translate the pervasive emotionology into their own styles. They did try to restrain their own anger. They did seek to channel childish aggression into socially or individually useful achievement. In contrast to what experts saw as the working-class model, middle-class parents by the twentieth century were more concerned about the intent behind a child's loss of temper than about manifestations in behavior; in this sense, workers more traditionally tended to stress obedience in deed. Even when middle-class parents diverged on tactics, they often shared emotionological goals with the advice literature. Thus parents who punished tantrums were expressing the kind of concern about anger that the experts urged in the decades around 1900, and they may have helped provoke responding anger in children that would permit subsequent channeling.[26] Certainly, many parents agreed that they themselves should set a good example by not punishing in anger, though intent may often have differed from fact. Sixty percent of all parents urged this strategy in one survey, 12 percent admitting that they fell short. Overall, behavior did change in the direction of less overt anger being expressed against children. This was consistent with a gradual, measurable decline in physical abuse.[27]

Thus parental behavior in the late nineteenth and early twentieth centuries revealed divisions that could be evaluated, and were evaluated by researchers and therapists, in terms of anger-control values, creating groups of "good" and "bad" parents, in part according to class. In the middle class, but also among some workers and Americanizing immigrants, a fairly high concern about anger control was manifest—a sign that the campaign launched in the eighteenth century was bearing ever greater fruit.

At some point, indeed, between the late eighteenth and the early twentieth century a generation or more of parents had broken with the disciplinary styles of their own parents, with distinctive mechanisms for handling anger a central element in this shift. The break was sometimes fragile. In the economic hard times of the 1930s (and, again, of the 1970s), job loss and other pressures would produce rising rates of physical anger, mainly by fathers, taken out against children. But these oscillations were not total reversals, and they occurred in the working class almost exclusively; middle-class fathers would not react to job loss with the same kind of overt anger. The impression of a distinct, if incomplete and sometimes inconsistent, transformation in parental style is inescapable,[28] a shift compatible with both the early nineteenth-century and the turn-of-the-century emotionological emphases, but one that for most families probably occurred after 1870, though it built on some modification of literal will breaking introduced earlier. Here the rather detailed attention to handling anger in advice literature written between 1890 and 1910 may well reflect not only intellectual currents but also real parental demand for information about a problem translated from behavioral into emotional terms. The transformation completed, it was small wonder that studies of actual middle-class parents from the 1920s to the 1950s would find substantial acceptance of the emotionology of anger control embodied in common child-rearing strategies.

Along with this general evolution, the particular twists of turn-of-the-century emotionology also showed up in actual parental attitude and behavior. The ambivalent emotionology produced or reflected ambivalence in real emotional guidance. This is where American parenting seemed uniquely complex, in comparative perspective. American parents translated the emotionological precepts quite precisely, in the following manner. A number of comparative studies conducted between the world wars or shortly after World War II rated Americans severe in punishments of anger directed against parents but unusually tolerant of angry behavior, particularly of retaliation directed against peers, a situation in which a child's ability to stand up for himself—the talisman of later competitiveness—could safely be tested. The absence of overall rules on anger was unusual: researchers found societies just as strict as Americans were as far as anger directed against parents was concerned or as permissive as Americans were as far as anger directed against a child's peers was concerned, but in no case, other than that of America, did they find both at once. American parents, then, really did seek to channel anger toward approved outlets, from quite an early age, instead of trying to excise it completely. Their approach contrasts not only with those of several non-Western cultures (some more permissive overall, some less) but also with that of Western Europe. Thus the American prompting to do battle with peers, at least when provoked, finds no counterpart in French or German child-

rearing culture. There children were encouraged to turn to adults to right the wrongs done to them. It was an adult supervisor who would step in when a child's toy was taken away, and the child himself was punished if he took direct action.[29]

Typically American was the fascination with contact sports, picked up and encouraged by channeling enthusiasts such as G. Stanley Hall around 1900. Boxing was a particular favorite. The physical energy it required made mastery of temper in daily life easier, while the sport also taught how channeled anger could generate competitive excellence. This interest in turn helped produce unusually high levels of American middle-class interest in boxing, not only as spectator sport, but also as a participant activity; it produced an almost obligatory gift of boxing gloves to middle-class boys, from early in the century through the 1940s (an obligation that revealingly has since died off, the victim of a newer emotional code).[30] Emotionology, in other words, nourished some distinctive American male sports interests, perhaps even helping to explain why some national sports gained in popularity over less violent West-European analogues, as both societies experienced the cresting modern interest in sports of some sort. For not only boxing but also football provided the expression of intense but channeled anger that sports like soccer or even the earlier American staple of baseball could not; and so what has become a rather parochial American sports interest might feed and be fed by a distinctive set of emotional values in child rearing.

Thus the late nineteenth-century/early twentieth-century American child-rearing culture moved partially away from otherwise general Western patterns, despite the common evolution toward anger control in Western society in the eighteenth and early nineteenth centuries. Elements of the American duality may go back to the colonial period, in the separation that Demos has noted between anger against neighbors and harmony within the all-important nuclear family. Protecting the family against childish anger may simply have been more important in a land of comparative strangers and protection of neighbors less so. But the duality was unquestionably deepened and legitimized by the child-rearing approach that took shape in the later nineteenth century. The particular appeal of social Darwinism in the United States was an element in the unique American approach to childish anger. More basically, the American middle class, free from concern about irrational effects of aristocratic temper (a concern evident in Western Europe in the ongoing debates over dueling), may also have been freer to shape a child-rearing style that seemed molded to the emotional context of business competitiveness. American indulgence of children, noted by travelers much earlier, may also have encouraged an approach that allowed legitimate outlets for childish emotion, rather than a stricter discipline, when it turned out that children were not angelic. Whatever the combination of causes, American experts, while sharing in interests such as competitive sports that developed more widely in Western middle-class culture, helped forge an ambivalence about anger whose effects would be visible for many decades.

The American child-rearing style was not the only one compatible with turn-of-the-century capitalism or high rates of indignant social protest. Though Europeans raised their children differently, with regard to anger, they produced their share of aggressive capitalists and certainly their share of protesters. Obviously, factors other than child rearing enter into adult emotional styles. The tendency of European parents to intercede, sometimes angrily, on behalf of their children—rather than encouraging angry response to slights by children themselves—suggests a high valuation of anger differently expressed. But the American style could relate, if not to protest or competitive levels, at least to specific forms. That social Darwinism spread more widely in the United States than in Europe, as a gloss for capitalist competition, owes something to the emotionology of child rearing. The tendency to righteous indignation in middle-class reform movements in the Progressive era also picked up elements of what children were being taught.

Emotionology and actual emotional standards applied in child rearing thus flowed together in the decades around 1900, particularly in the middle class. Expert advice was not taken literally, to be sure, even by parents who ap-

proved of it in principle. Thus twentieth-century studies showed that parents were not as willing to ignore childish tantrums as the advice literature urged they should be (though the literature was not unanimous on the point): in one study, 27 percent of all parents responded to tantrums with excited talk and 25 percent with spankings. On other occasions parents were surely less careful of restraining their own anger than the advice literature continued to urge.[31] However, on the whole there was a correspondence between the emotionology and the practice of child rearing. The correspondence was not perfect, and there is of course no way to demonstrate which came first; probably the interaction was mutual, as parents and children picked up cues from the literature and affected this literature in turn. The combination produced an important ingredient in the American character.

Before considering what effect this new child-rearing style may have had on the children, however, it must be noted that the new emotionology posed some hardships for the schools, which embraced the new emotionology less readily than did parents. Prior to the late eighteenth century, teachers had no difficulty supplementing the standard style of child rearing with stringent discipline and an often angry insistence on obedience to authority. Dutch schoolmasters in New York, though less severe than their Puritan counterparts in New England, were warned against discipline that was "too easy." Teachers, like parents, easily permitted themselves the right to grow angry at inferiors.[32]

Changing views of children and of education began to affect the emotional climate of some schools by the 1790s. Parents as well as educational theorists increasingly insisted on teachers of good character, and this in turn was to include mastery of temper.[33] Even earlier, Cotton Mather urged the translation of the new emotional style of the home into the schools: "I try to form in the children a temper of benignity. I caution them exquisitely against all revenges of injuries. . . . I would never come to give a child a blow, except in case of obstinacy or some gross enormity. . . . The slavish way of education, carried on with raving, kicking and scouring (in schools as well as families), 'tis abominable."[34]

But while the new concern about anger gained ground in pedagogical theory, practice lagged somewhat. Corporal punishment, for example, became more moderate in the early nineteenth century; it did not disappear.[35] Given the complexity of making a transition from will breaking to anger control in parenting, some parents were not loath to see others—such as teachers—administer discipline they could no longer countenance on their own part. And teachers, faced with large numbers of children and a setting unalleviated by the affection now encouraged in the family, understandably found it hard to make as complete a shift as some middle-class parents contemplated.[36] They continued to value obedience and had less compunction than parents did about using anger to elicit it. Thus the emotional atmosphere of schools differed from that of many families, just as actual classroom discipline often differed from official administrative recommendations.[37]

Ideas of anger control did spread gradually, however. Well into the twentieth century they worked in tandem with the obvious temptation to insist on a tranquil student body. Girls therefore so often seemed more desirable students because the docility urged at home blended nicely with teachers' expectations.[38] Teachers, for their part, were increasingly urged to keep an even temper. Educational theory that stressed greater equality between student and teacher and greater freedom from rigid constraint found some translation in teacher training manuals.[39] By the twentieth century, the idea of teacher responsibility for emotional guidance spread more explicitly: "Schools must be watchful that they do not contain the exciting causes of such emotion in their own inflexible or unreasonable program or treatment of children. . . . If the educator fails to deal with . . . the control of passion, he may properly be charged with . . . negligence."[40]

School programs certainly picked up the idea of channeling anger. Many a school athletic program was justified largely in these terms, as part of character building. George Creel, in 1916, urged that schools help immigrant children channel their "ferocity" to their own benefit and that of society.[41] It was in this context that some teachers could write authorities like G. Stanley Hall, bemoaning too-passive students and urging more, rather than less, anger in their

charges. This current particularly attracted those educators concerned about the effects of women teachers on the character of boys.

But there were limitations to the correspondence between teachers' attitudes and those of parents and child-rearing experts. Many women teachers found aggressive male students hard to channel and certainly hard to ignore. Here was a practical problem in classroom order but also a clash between gender styles that could be quite vivid in the decades after 1900. More than one such teacher unwittingly stimulated angry behavior by the attention they paid to it; more than one, in fact, responded by righteous anger of their own.[42] Certainly teachers found less value in childish anger than parents did, during the period in which the dominant emotionology stressed channeling. Regularly, from the early twentieth century through the 1950s, teachers reported far lower tolerance for acts of temper than did parents (particularly fathers) and child experts. Teachers correspondingly failed to share parental concern about the insufficiently aggressive child. Thus problems of temper produced three of the top fifteen behavior problems in teachers' ratings in the 1920s, whereas none made the parental top twenty; predictably, the disparity was particularly marked for boys and helped explain boys' ten to one lead in teacher-rated behavior problems. A lack of fit between home and school reactions may explain an important aspect of the experience of childhood, especially boyhood, just when school became a common requirement.[43]

Clearly, then, schools and teachers followed the dominant emotionology selectively, though they were touched by it. They preferred portions that stressed student anger control and therefore girls' ideal standards over boys'. They were wary of the complexity of translating channeling ideas into classroom practice, and while they increasingly adhered to temper-control standards—"freedom from over-aggressiveness," as one teacher personnel form put it[44]—as part of their emotional responsibility, they did not in fact abandon angry tones and punishments in response to what they saw as angry or disorderly acts in their charges. The problems of coping with large groups of children, some from families in which anger control seemed problematic in a period of working-class and immigrant exposure to mass education, easily explain the disparity.

If children received different messages from teachers and from parents, there is also some evidence of a disparity between mother and father. A number of studies, from the 1920s on, showed greater tolerance by fathers than by mothers of aggressive children. Mothers adhered to expert opinion more closely than fathers did in disciplining childish anger, but also they reported themselves as stricter than fathers and therefore may well have appeared angrier to their children. Fathers were more interested in channeling, more concerned about children (particularly sons) who lacked spunk.[45]

In sum, the new emotionology did have an effect on child-rearing behaviors, but not a simple one. Schools were slower to change than were families; fathers and mothers did not always behave consistently. This complexity served to translate much of the ambivalence of the dominant emotionology into the behaviors to which children were exposed.

Notes

1. Herman Melville, *Billy Budd, Foretopman* (1891), in *Four Short Novels,* ed. William Plomer (New York, 1959), pp. 201–2. David Brion Davis has noted occasional sympathy for justifiably aroused anger and an equation of such anger with morality in other novels (see *Homicide in American Fiction, 1798–1860: A Study in Social Values* [Ithaca, N.Y., 1968], pp. 289–90).

2. E. Anthony Rotundo, "Body and Soul: Changing Ideals of American Middle-Class Manhood, 1770–1920," *Journal of Social History* 16 (1983): 23–38; Peter G. Filene, *Him/Herself: Sex Roles in Modern America* (New York, 1975), pp. 68–77.

3. Flora H. Williams, *You and Your Children* (Nashville, Tenn., 1946), pp. 40, 43; R. Gordon Kelly, *Mother Was a Lady: Self and Society in Selected American Children's Periodicals, 1865–1890* (Westport, Conn., 1974).

4. Gabriel Compayré, *Development of the Child in Later Infancy,* trans. M. Wilson (New York, 1902), and *The Intellectual and Moral Development of the Child,* trans. M. Wilson (New York, 1901).

5. G. Stanley Hall, "A Study of Anger," *American Journal of Psychology* 10 (1899): 615–91; American Institute of Child Life, *The Problem of Temper* (Philadelphia, 1914).

6. Ernest Groves and Gladys Groves, *Wholesome Childhood* (Boston, 1931).

7. A. H. Arlitt, *Psychology of Infancy and Early Childhood* (New York, 1930); Leslie B. Hohman, *As the Twig Is Bent* (New York, 1941); *Parents' Magazine* from 1927 to 1938; John B. Watson, *Psychological Care of Infant and Child* (New York, 1928), pp. 41–43. Child guidance workers, as noted above, reported great parental concern about tantrums in the 1920s and 1930s, exceeding what the experts recommended.

8. D. A. Thom, *Guiding the Adolescent,* U.S. Department of Labor, Children's Bureau Publication (Washington, D.C., 1935), and *Child Management,* U.S. Department of Labor, Children's Bureau Publication (Washington, D.C., 1925).

9. Reverend Andrew Morton, *The Family Circle* (Edinburgh, 1865); Louisa May Alcott, *Little Women* (1868–69) (New York, 1946), p. 98; see also p. 93.

10. D. G. Harris, H. G. Gough, and W. E. Martin, "Children's Ethnic Attitudes: Relationship to Parental Beliefs Concerning Child Training," *Child Development* 21 (1950): 169–81; Albert Bandura and Richard Walters, *Adolescent Aggression* (New York, 1959), pp. 88–141; W. Lloyd Warner, *American Life: Dream and Reality* (Chicago, 1962), pp. 108, 210.

11. Garry Cleveland Myers, *Building Personality in Children* (New York, 1931), p. 190; M. H. Appel, "Aggressive Behavior in Nursery School Children and Adult Procedures in Dealing with Such Behavior," *Journal of Experimental Education* 11 (1942): 185–99.

12. Kelly, *Mother Was a Lady;* Abigail J. Stewart, David G. Winter, and H. David Jones ("Coding Categories for the Study of Child-Rearing from Historical Sources," *Journal of Interdisciplinary History* [1975]: 687–701) find some parallels in Britain, with reduction of references to obedience and mildness as virtues.

13. American Institute of Child Life, *Problem of Temper,* pp. 1–5; Hall, "Anger," p. 683.

14. Edwin Kirkpatrick, *Fundamentals of Child Study* (New York, 1919), p. 136; Alice M. Birney (Mrs. Theodore W.), *Childhood* (New York, 1904), pp. 66–67, 96.

15. Marion L. Faegre and John E. Anderson, *Child Care and Training* (Minneapolis, 1947); Percival M. Symonds, *The Psychology of Parent-Child Relationships* (New York, 1939), p. 151.

16. Howard R. Garis, *Uncle Wiggily's Story Book* (New York, 1921), p. 4. We are grateful to Clio Stearns, who called this passage to our attention.

17. Charlotte Gilman, *The Home, Its Work and Influence* (New York, 1903), p. 169; White House Conference on Child Health and Protection, *Growth and Development of the Child,* pt. 4, *Appraisement of the Child* (New York, 1932); U.S. Department of Labor, Children's Bureau, *Infant Care* (Washington, 1914).

18. Parent's Magazine, *The Mother's Encyclopedia* (New York, 1933), 1: 66, 2: 353.

19. Celia B. Stendler, "Sixty Years of Child Training Practices," *Journal of Pediatrics* 36 (1950): 122–34; A. Michael Sulman, "The Freudianization of the American Child: The Impact of Psychoanalysis in Popular Periodicals in the United States, 1919–1939" (Ph.D. diss., University of Pittsburgh, 1972); Clark Vincent, "Trends in Infant Care Ideas," *Child Development* 22 (1951): 199–210; Bernard Wishy, *The Child and the Republic* (Philadelphia, 1968).

20. Jay Mechling, "Advice to Historians on Advice to Mothers," *Journal of Social History* 9 (1975): 44–63; Martha Wolfenstein, "Trends in Infant Care," *American Journal of Orthopsychiatry* 23 (1953): 120–30; Leone Kell and Jean Aldous, "Trends in Child Care over Three Generations," *Marriage and Family Living* 22 (1960): 176–77.

21. Hall, "Anger," p. 638.

22. Ibid., pp. 670, 689; American Institute of Child Life, *Problem of Temper,* pp. 1, 10, 11; Dorothy Canfield Fisher, *Mothers and Children* (New York, 1914); John Anderson, *Happy Childhood: The Development and Guidance of Children and Youth* (New York, 1933), p. 101; Phyllis Harrison-Ross and Barbara Wyden, *The Black Child—a Parents' Guide* (New York, 1973), p. 180; Ruth W. Washburn, *Children Have Their Reasons* (New York, 1942), pp. 8, 53. See also Smiley Blanton and Margaret Blanton, *Child Guidance* (New York, 1927); G. Stanley Hall, *Adolescence* (New York, 1931), 1: 221; William Healy, *Personality in Formation and Action* (New York, 1938).

23. C. Anderson and Marty Aldrich, *Babies Are Human Beings* (New York, 1938), pp. 115–16; see also M. S. Smart and R. C. Smart, *Living and Learning with Children* (Boston, 1949); Marion L. Faegre et al., *Child Care and Training* (Minneapolis, 1928), p. 146; Emily Post, *Children Are People* (New York, 1940), p. 259; George Lawton, *How to Be Happy though Young* (New York, 1949), p. 110; Esther Lloyd-Jones and Ruth Fedder, *Coming of Age* (New York, 1941), pp. 35, 40.

24. Ada Hart Arlitt, *The Child from One to Twelve* (New York, 1931), pp. 93–97; see also Robert B. Sears, Eleanor Maccoby, and Harry Levin, *Patterns of Child Rearing* (New York, 1957), pp. 268–69.

25. Julius Sachs, "Co-education in the United States," *Educational Review* 33 (1900): 300 and passim; Edward H. Cooper, *The Twentieth Century Child* (London, 1906).

26. Melvin L. Kohn, "Social Class and the Exercise of Parental Authority," in *Personality and Social Systems,* ed. Neil Smelser and William Smelser (New York, 1963), p. 208.

27. Martha S. White, "Social Class, Child Rearing Practices, and Child Behavior," in Smelser and Smelser, eds., *Personality and Social Systems,* pp. 286–96; Sears et al., *Patterns of Child Rearing;* Appel, "Aggressive Behavior of Nursery School Children"; Kell and Aldous, "Trends in Child Care"; Myra Musto and Doris Sharpe, "Some Influential Factors in the Determination of Aggressive Behavior in Preschool Children," *Child Development* 18 (1947): 11–28; G. S. Gates, "An Observational Study of Anger," *Journal of Experimental Psychology* 9 (1926): 325–36; D. R. Peterson et al., "Child Behavior Problems and Parental Attitudes," *Child Development* 32 (1961): 151–62; Harold Orlansky, "Infant Care and Personality," *Psychological Bulletin* 49 (1949): 1–48.

28. Phyllis Moen, E. L. Kain, and Glen Elder, Jr., "Economic Conditions and Family Life: Contemporary and Historical Perspective," in *American Families and the Economy,* ed. R. Nelson and F. Skidmore (Washington, D.C., 1983), pp. 335–37.

29. Leigh Minturn and W. W. Lambert, *Mothers of Six Cultures* (New York, 1964), pp. 143 ff.; Margaret Mead and Martha Wolfenstein, eds., *Childhood in Contemporary Cultures* (Chicago, 1955), pp. 104, 223, 414; Sears et al., *Patterns of Child Rearing,* pp. 231ff.; Richard L. Rapson, "The American Child as Seen by British Travelers, 1845–1935," *American Quarterly* 17 (1965): 524; Lawrence Wylie, *Village in the Vaucluse* (New York, 1964), pp. 49–51, 196–200. These studies use data from the 1930s through the 1950s. See also Jerome Kagan, "The Child in the Family," in *The Family,* ed. A. S. Rossi, J. Kagan, and T. Hareven (New York, 1978), p. 39.

30. Hall, "Anger"; Benjamin Rader, *American Sports* (Englewood Cliffs, N.J., 1983).

31. Sophie Ritholz, *Children's Behavior* (New York, 1959), pp. 60–61 and passim.

32. Lawrence A. Cremin, *American Education—the Colonial Experience, 1607–1783* (New York, 1970), p. 51; William Kilpatrick, *The Dutch Schools of New Netherland and Colonial New York* (Washington, D.C., 1912), p. 31. See also Helen Sobehart, "Toward a History of Anger in the Schools" (Carnegie-Mellon University, Department of History, December 1983, typescript). We are grateful to Sobehart and also to Joan Francis for many of the data that follow.

33. Cremin, pp. 368, 483.

34. Ibid., *American Education,* pp. 487–89 (taken from *The Diary of Cotton Mather* [New York, 1957], 1: 534–37).

35. J. Manning, "Discipline in the Good Old Days," *Phi Delta Kappan* 41, no. 3 (1969): 96.

36. Rena L. Vassar, ed., *A Social History of American Education* (Chicago, 1965), 1:26 (taken from *The Autobiography of Reverend John Barnard* [Boston, 1766], pp. 178–87). See also Manning, "Discipline—Old Days," p. 96; Philip J. Greven, Jr., *The Protestant Temperament: Patterns of Childrearing, Religious Experience and the Self in Early America* (New York, 1977), p. 278; Cremin, *American Education,* p. 500.

37. Thus a Boston committee in 1845 found an average of sixty-five floggings daily in a population of four hundred students, despite administration advice against any such punishments (Manning, "Discipline—Old Days," pp. 94, 99; Otis Caldwell and Stuart Courtis, *Then and Now in Education* [New York, 1971], p. 20; Michael E. Katz, *The Irony of Early School Reform* [Cambridge, Mass., 1968], p. 129).

38. Charles E. Silberman, *Crisis in the Classroom* (New York, 1970), pp. 152–53.

39. Manning, "Discipline—Old Days," p. 96; Pennsylvania Retired School Employees Association, *So Your Children Can Tell Their Children* (Pittsburgh, 1961), pp. 101, 176, 210; Gerald L. Gutek, *A History of the Western Educational Experience* (New York, 1972), p. 383; Pittsburgh Public Schools, *Handbook for Counselors* (Pittsburgh, 1933), p. 34.

40. Daniel A. Prescott, *Emotion and the Educative Process* (Washington, D.C., 1938), pp. vi, vii, 29.

41. Vassar, ed., *American Education,* 2:219 (citing George Creel, "Hopes of the Hyphenated," *Century Magazine* 62 [January 1916]: 354–63).

42. Edwin I. Megargee and Jack E. Hokanson, eds., *The Dynamics of Aggression: Individual. Group and International Analyses* (New York, 1970), p. 106.

43. Ritholz, *Children's Behavior,* pp. 60–61; E. K. Wickman, *Children's Behavior and Teachers' Attitudes* (New York, 1928), pp. 17, 127, 161; Caroline B. Zachry, *Personality Adjustments in School Children* (New York, 1929).

44. Pittsburgh Public Schools, *Handbook of Personnel Procedures* (Pittsburgh, 1948), p. 37.

45. On mother-father differences, see Jerome Kagan, "Socialization of Aggression and the Perception of Parents in Fantasy," *Child Development* 29 (1958): 318; Jerome Seidman, ed., *The Child: A Book of Readings* (New York, 1958), p. 130; Arthur T. Jersild et al., *Joys and Problems of Child Rearing* (New York, 1949), pp. 212ff.

3

Hitler's Appeal: Alienation, Shame-Rage, and Revenge

Thomas J. Scheff
Suzanne M. Retzinger

> *Accurate scholarship can*
> *Unearth the whole offense*
> *From Luther until now*
> *That has driven a culture mad,*
> *Find what occurred at Linz,*[1]
> *What huge imago made*
> *A psychopathic god.*
>
> —W. H. Auden "September 1, 1939"

This chapter proposes a solution to the riddle of Hitler's appeal to the German masses. Following Lasswell (1960), we show how Hitler's psychopathology, his paranoia, and his continuous humiliated fury produced a program responsive to the craving of his public for a sense of community and pride rather than alienation and shame. Since neither their alienation nor their pride was acknowledged, both Hitler and his public were trapped in a never-ending cycle of humiliation, rage, and vengeful aggression. We describe the evidence for unacknowledged shame in Hitler's life and in his written statements (mainly *Mein Kampf*).

We propose that the alienation and shame-rage cycle in Germany was (and is) only part of a larger system of alienation and emotional repression within and between nations in the world social system. Hitler's rise to power was produced by the labeling, segregation, and stigmatization of Germany as a consequence of its defeat in World War I. Unless the social and emotional features of the world system change toward more solidarity and less repression, increasingly destructive wars are predicted.

Hitler's appeal to the German people has yet to be explained. In his person, he was singularly unprepossessing, to say the least. From a logical point of view, his speeches were disasters; he rambled incoherently, with little order and less substance. His political program was no better; it was disorganized, vague, and silent on key issues.

Beneath the surface, matters were still worse. From the testimony of his intimates, Hitler's personality was bizarre to the point of madness. His delusions, phobias, sadism, sexual aberrations, and utter isolation are well documented. All the biographies clearly show manifold symptoms of severe mental illness.

The puzzle is that this extraordinarily unattractive madman had charismatic appeal not

---

"Hitler's Appeal: Alienation, Shame-Rage, and Revenge," pp. 141–164 in *Emotions and Violence: Shame and Rage in Destructive Conflicts*, by Thomas J. Scheff and Suzanne M. Retzinger (Lexington Books 1991). Reprinted by permission.

only to the masses but also to a large coterie of devoted followers. These latter individuals knew most or all of the unsavory details, yet they were fanatically loyal. In this chapter we first review earlier attempts to resolve this problem. Then, building on these explanations, we outline a new approach, focusing on the emotional bases of charisma. We propose a new theory of the dynamics of shame, which suggests that unconscious vengefulness motivated Hitler and connected him to his followers.

Earlier Explanations of Hitler's Appeal

A conjecture by Lasswell (1960) provides the foundation for most discussions of Hitler's appeal. Lasswell proposed that successful leaders make assets out of their psychological difficulties by rationalization; they externalize their internal conflicts in political programs. Those whose personal needs exactly correspond to those of their countrymen have charismatic—that is, emotional—appeal.

Lasswell's proposal implies that if we are to understand Hitler's appeal during the years he came to power, we need to understand during that period (1) the personal needs of Germans in the mass; (2) Hitler's personality; and (3) the linkage between (1) and (2). This is a problem of culture and personality, the link between the one and the many. Such problems were much discussed several decades ago but are now neglected. The central difficulty was the lack of a theory and method for conceptualizing the link between individual and collective behavior. We use recent developments in theory and method for the study of emotions to outline a model that might provide such a link.

There are many studies of the first two issues listed above, but the third—the link between Hitler and his public—is treated only briefly and casually. As a framework for our discussion, we first summarize several approaches to this problem.

Of the many discussions of the social bases of Hitler's rise to power, we review three representative ones: Mitchell (1983), Dahrendorf

(1967), and Waite (1977). Like most of the other studies, Mitchell's (1983) explanation of Hitler's appeal is quite brief (259–66) and very late in the text—the last eight pages. He proposed that a sequence of disasters lead to a state of anomie, the breakdown of an entire society (Germany's defeat in World War I, the humiliation of the Treaty of Versailles, the Great Inflation, and finally, the Great Depression in 1929). These events created an economic, intellectual, political, and emotional crisis in Germany.

In this crisis, Hitler offered what seemed to many Germans attractive solutions. Of the several concepts which Mitchell and others propose, we emphasize two, anomie and shame. Instead of anomie, Hitler offered community (*Volksgemeinschaft,* "a community of the folk"), and instead of humiliation, he offered pride and self-confidence. The idea of the folk-community intimated a restoration of what had been lost, the traditional rural community from which many Germans had recently been deprived. The community Hitler offered, "race and blood," seemed easily attainable by the mass; it was heedless of most of the usual distinctions (such as region, class, income, and education). It excluded only a small proportion of the population—mainly the Communists and the Jews.

Most commentators have linked anomie, the breakdown of community and societal bonds, to the rise of Hitler. Dahrendorf (1967) treated this issue in greatest detail. He suggested that anomie was prevalent in German society even before World War I, because industrialization had come late, rapidly, and more completely than in England, the United States, and France. These countries had several hundred years to develop new forms of community during industrialization. But rapid and thorough industrialization led to a more extensive state of anomie in Germany than in the older industrial countries. Dahrendorf proposed that this condition provided the basis for the appeal of a totalitarian leader.

The other concept proposed by Mitchell and others was that Hitler offered pride instead of shame, the restoration of what Mitchell called self-confidence, and "an escape route from the deep pits of humiliation to nearly unlimited adventure" (262). This same solution is implied in Mitchell's discussion of Hitler's ability to "direct popular emotions" (262), although pride and shame are not named explicitly.

These two dimensions of Hitler's appeal—restoring a lost sense of community and pride—are also mentioned in virtually all the other discussions, with about the same amount of detail as Mitchell, or less. Waite's (1977) discussion, however, treated the issue of restoring lost pride at greater length. He noted several times that Germans referred to the Treaty of Versailles as the "Treaty of Shame," and the particular ways in which it triggered the crisis in the Weimar Republic. After coming to power, Hitler usually referred to the Weimar Republic only as "fourteen years of shame and opprobrium."

The Germans felt betrayed; because of Wilson's fourteen points, they had expected a treaty of reconciliation. Instead, the treaty transferred large parts of German territory to other nations, seized all German colonies, and excluded Germany from membership in the League of Nations as unworthy. The treaty spoke in general terms about disarmament, but in actuality, only Germany was forced to disarm. Apparently the most disturbing part of the treaty was one that involved a symbolic rather than a material issue.

In Article 231, Germany was required to confess sole responsibility for causing World War I—a patent absurdity. (We will return to the issue of blame in our discussion of conflict in family and social systems.) Furthermore, the Germans were compelled to sign the treaty since they were threatened with continued blockade until it was signed. The blockade was in fact extended ten months beyond the end of the war, causing starvation and a further sense of injustice and betrayal.

As it turned out, the Allied treatment of Germany in the Treaty of Versailles was neither fish nor fowl: it visited suffering and humiliation on Germans without destroying their capacity to make war. An earlier victor over the German tribes, Julius Caesar, had a different policy: after defeating them he either killed every member of a tribe or treated them generously, fearing revenge. Although the French feared revenge, the Allies neither scorched the German earth nor restored Germany to the community of nations.

After recounting the realistic bases for the German sense of betrayal and humiliation, Waite went on to describe the irrational ones: the legend of the *Dolschstoss* ("stab-in-the-back") and the anti-Semitism to which it was closely tied. The stab-in-the-back legend was that the "November criminals"—traitorous Jews and revolutionaries at home—surrendered, rather than the victorious armed forces. This legend was pure fiction (307). The military command compelled surrender well before the revolution; General Ludendorff forced an unwilling civilian government to sue for peace. Although both legends were false, Hitler always took them to be factual: they played an important role in his appeal. (We return to the emotional appeal of these legends later.)

Hitler's Personality

The need of Germans for solidarity and for pride are prominent in a reverse way in the many studies of Hitler's psychopathology. They all stress Hitler's complete isolation from other people and the prominence of shame (and anger) in his makeup. The descriptions of Hitler's isolation will be summarized first.

The biographies and psychological studies emphasize Hitler's isolation as a child and adult (Bromberg and Small 1983; Bullock 1964; Davidson 1977; Miller 1983; Stierlin 1976; Toland 1976). As an infant and youth, he was pampered by his mother. But even as young as three, his relationship with his father was charged with violence, ridicule, and contempt. By the age of six, he apparently was walled off from everyone, including his mother (Bromberg and Small 1983; Miller 1983; Stierlin 1976).

The three most likely candidates with whom he had a close relationship are August Kubizek, Eva Braun, and Albert Speer. Hitler and Kubizek were companions for three years, beginning when they were both sixteen. Kubizek's memoir of Hitler (1955) shows that his relationship to Hitler was not that of friend but that of an adoring admirer. Kubizek described Hitler as a compulsive talker, brooking no interruptions, let alone any disagreement. Lacking any other listeners at this age, Hitler used Kubizek as an audience.

Speer, an architect-engineer, was closest to Hitler among his officials during the last years of World War II. In an interview after the war, Speer revealed that although he spent countless hours with Hitler, there was no personal relationship between them (Bromberg and Small 1983: 112): "If Hitler had friends, I would have been his friend."

Eva Braun's diary (Bromberg and Small 1983: 107–108) shows that she, as Hitler's mistress, came no closer to him than Kubizek and Speer. For most of their fifteen-year relationship, he attempted to keep it hidden, confining her to her rooms during meetings with others. A few entries suggest the tone of the whole diary. In 1935, when she was twenty-three and Hitler forty-six, she complained that she felt imprisoned, that she got nothing from their sexual relationship, and that she felt desperately insecure: "He is only using me for definite purposes" (March 11). Most of the women with whom Hitler had sexual relations either attempted or committed suicide. (Small and Bromberg count seven such relationships, with three of them attempting, and three completing suicide [1983: 125].) Eva Braun herself made two such attempts.

In 1942, Hitler inadvertently suggested the extent of his isolation from Eva. Hearing of the death of one of his officials, Fritz Todt, chief of armaments, he said that he was now deprived of "the only two human beings among all those around me to whom I have been truly and inwardly attached: Dr. Todt is dead and Hess has flown away from me!" (Toland 1976: 666). As Bromberg and Small (1983) note, this statement leaves out Eva entirely, mentioning instead "a remote man who could rarely be induced to sit at Hitler's table and a man he could not bear to converse with, denounced as crazy, and wished dead" (150).

Neither as a soldier nor as a politician did Hitler have close attachments. His experience as an enlisted man in the army during and after World War I is illustrative. Although he was a dedicated soldier who demonstrated courage in battle, he was a "loner"; he had no intimates. This may be one of the reasons that although he was decorated for bravery, he was little promoted; after four years, he left the army at the rank of lance corporal—the equivalent of private first

class. In his evaluations, he was described as lacking in leadership.

After becoming the leader of the Nazi party, he moved no closer to human relationships. A description of his campaign the year before he gained power is representative:

> Hitler used superhuman energy to storm every German state by train, car, and still-novel airplane. Yet he had almost no real contact with people, not even with his associates, who felt they were touring with a performer. He did not permit them to be colleagues on a team and kept them away from any important people, storing information only in his own memory. He remained a lone wolf, now even harsher, often jealous, more distant from his senior associates, and contemptuous of them. (Small and Bromberg 1983: 108)

Although he was the adored leader of millions of people, Hitler apparently had no secure bond with anyone.

The other characteristic of Hitler's personality noted by most of the studies is the prevalence of shame and anger. Diagnostic studies (Bromberg and Small 1983; Miller 1983; Stierlin 1976) point to shame and humiliation as prominent features in Hitler's makeup, both as a child and as an adult. Hitler's father, Alois, was a brutal and tyrannical ruler of his family, but his most intense wrath was turned on Adolf, whom he repeatedly beat and humiliated. Hitler's mother, Klara, pampered him, but she did nothing to protect him from his father since she too was brutalized by Alois. The studies mentioned above interpret Hitler's early childhood experiences as the source of his later aberrations, his temper tantrums, his sadomasochism, and his fanatical anti-Semitism. (We will return to this issue after discussing the shame dynamics.)

Although the earlier studies are useful, they do not solve the puzzle. The discussions of the first issue, Hitler's psychopathology, are compelling enough. The argument about the needs of the German masses is merely plausible, however, since it is quite abstract in the main and is supported only in part by actual evidence. With respect to the third question—the basis of the overwhelming response to Hitler—the arguments are thin; they might be described as barely plausible.

The existing literature on this question is unconvincing because it lacks not only evidence but even the most rudimentary form of theory and method. The arguments lack a conceptual framework. For this reason, and because they are post hoc, it is unclear how one might choose between the different versions. None of the explanations propose directions for future research.

Our purpose here is to outline a theory linking the charismatic leader's personality and the response of his followers, and a method for the analysis of his discourse. As background, two steps are necessary. [Elsewhere] we have shown the connection between social structure and the emotions of pride and shame. In this chapter, we go on to develop a model of the dynamics of these two emotions within and between leader and followers.

Pride and Shame

The psychoanalytic idea of repression may be helpful in understanding defenses against inadequate bonding. If the ideology of the self-sufficient individual is a defense against the pain of threatened bonds, what is being repressed is the *idea* of the social bond. Freud, however, argued that repression concerns not only ideas but also the *feelings* that accompany them. He thought that repression could be lifted only if both the idea and the emotions were expressed. If modern societies repress the idea of the social bond, what are the associated feelings that are also repressed?

As we have seen, Cooley (1922) implied that pride and shame are the primary social emotions. These two emotions have a signal function with respect to the social bond. In this framework, pride and shame serve as intense and automatic bodily signs of the state of a system that is otherwise difficult to observe. Pride is the sign of an intact bond; shame is the sign of a threatened bond. The clearest outer marker of pride is holding up one's head in public, looking others in the eye, and indicating respect by taking turns looking and looking away. In *overt* shame, one shrinks, averts or lowers one's gaze, and casts

only furtive glances at the other. In *bypassed* shame, one stares, outfacing the other.

The two forms of shame are polar opposites in terms of thought and feeling. Overt shame involves painful feeling with little ideation, bypassed shame, the opposite pattern: rapid thought, speech, or behavior, but little feeling. Overt shame is marked by furtiveness, confusion, and bodily reactions such as blushing, sweating and/or rapid heartbeat. One may be at a loss for words, with flustered or disorganized thoughts or behavior, as in states of embarrassment. Many of the common terms for painful feelings appear to refer to this type of shame, or to its combinations with anger: feeling peculiar, shy, bashful, awkward, funny, bothered, or miserable; in adolescent vernacular, it is being freaked, bummed, or weirded out. The phrases "I feel like a fool" or "a perfect idiot" may be prototypical of overt shame.

Bypassed shame is manifested as a brief painful feeling, usually lasting less than a second, followed by obsessive and rapid thought or speech. A common example is feeling insulted or criticized. At that moment (or later, in recalling it), one may experience a jab of painful feeling (producing a groan or wince), followed immediately by imaginary but compulsive and repetitive *replays* of the offending scene. The replays are variations on a theme: how one might have behaved differently and thereby avoided the incident, or responded with better effect. One becomes *obsessed*.

In our theory, unacknowledged shame is the cause of revenge-based cycles of conflict. (This formulation was anticipated in the work of Geen [1968] and Feshbach [1971].) We argue that shame-rage may escalate continually to the point that a person or a group can be in a permanent fit of shame-rage, a kind of madness.

Studies of Shame and Aggression

The theory we outline is supported by several exploratory studies. Katz (1988) analyzed descriptions of several hundred criminal acts: vandalism, theft, robbery, and murder. In many of these cases, Katz found that the perpetrator felt humiliated, and had committed the crime as an act of revenge. In some of the cases the perpetrator's sense of humiliation was based on actual insults:

> [A] . . . typical technique [leading to a spouse being murdered] is for the victim to attack the spouse's deviations from the culturally approved sex role. . . . For example, a wife may accuse her husband of being a poor breadwinner or an incompetent lover . . . or the husband may accuse his wife of being "bitchy," "frigid," or promiscuous. (1988: chap. 2, page 8)

In other cases it was difficult to assess the degree to which the humiliations were real and/or imagined. Whatever the realities, Katz's findings support the model of the shame-rage feeling trap. In his analysis of the murder of intimates, he says, "The would-be-killer must undergo a particular emotional process. He must transform what he initially senses as an eternally humiliating situation into a blinding rage" (11). Rather than acknowledge his or her shame, the killer masks it with anger, which is the first step into the abyss of the shame-rage feeling trap, which ends in murder. Katz reported similar though less dramatic findings with respect to the other kinds of crimes he investigated.

One issue that Katz's study did not address is the conditions under which humiliation is transformed into blind rage. Since not all humiliations lead to blind rage, there must be some ingredient that is not indicated in Katz's cases. The studies of family violence by Lansky strongly suggest what this extra ingredient is. In order to lead to blind rage, the shame component in the emotions that are aroused must be *unacknowledged.*

Lansky has published three papers on family violence. The first paper (1984) describes six cases; the second (1987) describes four; and the third (1989), one. The third paper analyzes a session with a single couple. In most of the cases, Lansky reports similar emotional dynamics: in the cases he studied, violence resulted from the insulting manner that both husbands and wives took toward each other. Although some of their insults were overt, in the form of cursing, open contempt, and disgust, most of them were covert, taking the form of innuendo or double messages.

Underhanded disrespect gives rise to unacknowledged shame, which leads in turn to anger and violence, in the way predicted by Lewis. It is difficult for the participants to respond to innuendo and to double messages; these forms of communication confuse them. But instead of admitting their upset and puzzlement, they answer in kind. The cycle involves disrespect, humiliation, revenge, counter-revenge, and so on, ending in violence.

That both spouses seem to be unaware of the intense shame that their behavior generates can be seen in Lansky's description of one of the cases:

> A 32-year-old man and his 46-year-old wife were seen in emergency conjoint consultation after he struck her. Both spouses were horrified, and the husband agreed that hospitalization might be the best way to start the lengthy treatment that he wanted. As he attempted to explain his view of his difficult marriage, his wife disorganized him with repeated humiliating comments about his inability to hold a job. These comments came at a time when he was talking about matters other than the job. When he did talk about work, she interrupted to say how immature he was compared to her previous husbands, then how strong and manly he was. The combination of building up and undercutting his sense of manliness was brought into focus. As the *therapist* commented on the process, the husband became more and more calm. . . . After the fourth session, he left his marriage and the hospital for another state, and phoned the therapist for an appropriate referral for individual therapy. On followup some months later, he had followed through with treatment. (1984: 34–35, emphasis added)

The wife humiliates the husband in this case not through innuendo, since her disparagement is overt. Her shaming tactics seem to be disguised by her technique of alternately praising her husband, by stating how "strong and manly" he is, then cutting him down. (Perhaps she confused *herself* with this tactic as much as she did her husband.)

A lack of awareness of shaming and shame can be seen in Lansky's 1989 article, which reports a conjoint session with a violent man and his wife. In this session, Lansky reports, the wife was dressed in a sexually provocative way, and her bearing and manner were overtly seductive toward the interviewer. Yet neither spouse acknowledged her activity, even when the interviewer asked them whether the wife was ever seductive toward other men. Both answered affirmatively, but their answers concerned only past events. The lack of comment on what was occurring at that very moment in the interview is astounding. It would seem that blind rage requires not only shaming and shame, but blindness toward these two elements.

The relationship between collective violence and unacknowledged shame has been suggested in a recent analysis of the Attica riots (Scheff, Retzinger, and Ryan 1989). Violence of the guards toward the inmates began with a series of events that the guards perceived as humiliating: without consulting the guards, a new warden intent on reform increased the rights of the prisoners, which resulted in a series of incidents with prisoners that the guards experienced as humiliating. Since the guards did not acknowledge their humiliation, their assault on the prisoners followed the sequence predicted by the Lewis theory: insult, unacknowledged shame, rage, and aggression.

The conjecture that unacknowledged humiliation is the source of lethal aggression would seem to solve the problem both of Hitler's motivation and of his appeal to his public. Hitler himself continuously expressed the dominant affect among the Germans—bypassed shame-rage, humiliated fury—and he encouraged them to express it. Denying his own overwhelming shame and rage, he projected it onto the outside world, particularly upon the Jews. Unacknowledged shame was prevalent in Hitler's life and in his discourse.

Humiliated Fury as the Key Affect in Hitler's Life

The Swiss psychoanalyst Alice Miller (1983) has called attention to what may be the origin of Hitler's psychopathology—the conjunction of his father's physical and emotional violence and his mother's complicity in it. Miller argues that the rage and shame caused by his father's treatment may have been completely repressed because of his mother's complicity. Although she pampered Hitler and professed to love him, she didn't protect him from his father's wrath or allow Adolf *to express his feelings about it.* Klara, as much as Adolf, was tyrannized by her husband, but she offered obedience and respect in return. Because of his mother's "love" for him, as a young child Adolf was required not only to suffer humiliation by his father in silence but to respect him for it—a basic context for repression.

In *Mein Kampf,* Hitler glossed over his treatment by his parents, behavior that is congruent with repression. He described his father as stern but respected and his childhood as that of a "mother's darling living in a soft downy bed" (Bromberg and Small 1983: 40). But Alois's other son, Alois, Jr., left home at fourteen because of his father's harshness. His own son, William Patrick, reported that Alois, Sr., beat Alois, Jr., with a hippopotamus whip. Alois, Jr.'s, first wife, Brigid, reported that Alois, Sr., frequently beat the children, and on occasion, his wife Klara, Hitler's mother (Bromberg and Small 1983: 32–33).

It would appear that Hitler's early childhood constituted an external feeling trap from which he had no escape. This external trap is the exact analogue to the internal trap proposed by Lewis (1971): when shame is evoked but goes unacknowledged, it generates intense symptoms of mental illness and/or violence toward self or others. Under the conditions of complete repression that seem to have obtained, Hitler's personality might have been severely damaged. His biographies suggest that he was constantly in a state of anger bound by shame.

One indication of Hitler's continual shame-rage was his temper tantrums. Although in later life some of them may have been staged, there is no question that in most of his tantrums he was actually out of control. His older stepbrother reported that even before he was seven,

> He was imperious and quick to anger from childhood onward and would not listen to anyone. My stepmother always took his part. He would get the craziest notions and get away with it. If he didn't have his way he got

very angry. . . . [H]e had no friends, took to no one and could be very heartless. He could fly into a rage over any triviality. (Gilbert 1950: 18).

In his teens, Hitler's rages were frequent and intense, evoking such expressions as "red with rage," "exceedingly violent and high-strung," and "like a volcano erupting" (Kubizek 1955).

Hitler's early shame-proneness is suggested by the slightness of the provocations that triggered his rage. Kubizek's memoir provides two examples: an occasion when Hitler learned that he had failed to win a lottery, and another when he saw Stephanie, a girl whom Hitler longed to meet but never did, with other men. He was infatuated with her but never introduced himself (Bromberg and Small 1983: 55–56).

The most obvious manifestations of Hitler's shame-proneness occurred after he became chancellor. Although he was easily the most powerful and admired man in Germany, he was constantly fearful that he would appear ridiculous.

> Before he ventured on a political appearance in a new suit or headgear, he had himself photographed to study its effect. In addition to asking his valet whether he looked the part of the Fuehrer, he would check with Hess the manner of speech he should use on different occasions. His anxieties lest he appear ridiculous, weak, vulnerable, incompetent, or in any way inferior are indications of this endless battle with shame. (Bromberg and Small 1983: 183)

Further manifestations of chronic shame states occurred in his relationships with women and in his sexual relationships. In attempting to interest a woman in himself,

> even the presence of other persons would not prevent him from repulsive groveling. [He would] tell a lady that he was unworthy to sit near her or kiss her hand but hoped she would look on him with favor. . . . One woman reported that after all kinds of self-accusations he said that he was unworthy of being in the same room with her. (Bromberg and Small 1983: 183)

Bromberg and Small (1983: 243–47) establish that Hitler was never able to have a normal sexual relationship with a woman. Instead, he practiced a type of perversion in which both he and his partner were humiliated. Although the humiliation of the partner is not explicitly described, Hitler's part is: he first required that the partner squat over his face. After a lengthy inspection of her genitals, he demanded that his partner urinate on his face. Apparently this was the only way he could achieve satisfaction.

To this point, the descriptions of Hitler's shame states suggest overt, undifferentiated shame, emotionally painful states involving feelings of inadequacy and inferiority. How, then, is one to understand the other side of Hitler's personality—his arrogance, boldness, and extreme self-confidence? How could a man so shame-prone also be so shameless?

Lewis's concept of the bimodal nature of shame states—overt and bypassed—may provide the answer to this puzzle. In addition to the overt shame states already discussed, Hitler also had a long history of bypassed shame. Many aspects of his behavior suggest bypassed shame, but here we will review only three: his temper tantrums, his "piercing stare" (Bromberg and Small 1983: 309), and his obsessiveness.

Shame theory suggests that protracted and destructive anger is always generated by unacknowledged shame. Normal anger, when it is not intermixed with shame, is usually brief, moderate, and constructive, serving to call notice to adjustments that are needed in a relationship (Retzinger 1988). Long chains of alternating shame and anger, however, are experienced as blind rage, hatred, or resentment if the shame component is completely repressed. In this case, the expression of anger serves as a disguise for the hidden shame, projecting onto the outside world the feelings of shame that are unacknowledged within. According to Lewis, many "would rather turn the world upside down than turn themselves inside out." This idea exactly captures the psychology of Hitler's lifelong history of intense rage states and his projection of his inner conflict onto scapegoats.

The second indicator of bypassed shame is Hitler's demeanor, especially his gaze. As early as sixteen, it was described as "blank" or "cruel" (Bromberg and Small 1983: 51). On the other hand, at a later time (21) he was described as having "an evasive manner," as being "shy" and "never looking a person in the eye," except when he was talking politics (70). These descriptions suggest that Hitler may have been in a virtually permanent state of shame, manifested as either bypassed shame (the stare) or overt shame (avoiding eye contact). As his power increased, the bypassed shame was more and more in evidence, in the form of arrogance, extreme self-confidence, isolation, and obsession.

According to Lewis, the rapidity of speech and behavior that is the prime outer indicator of bypassed shame is usually accompanied by a primary inner manifestation—obsessiveness. Persons who are in a state of chronic shame may avoid and deny their emotional pain by obsessive preoccupation. Hitler's principal obsession, "the Jewish problem," is particularly indicative of unacknowledged shame. At the center of Hitler's belief system was the concept of racial superiority—that the "Aryan race" was the superior race and that the Jewish "race" was inferior. His many obsessions with superiority-inferiority, racial purity, pollution, and contamination can be interpreted as operations for bypassing shame. Textual evidence supports the conjecture that Hitler was motivated by unconscious shame.

Shame-Anger Sequences in *Mein Kampf*

Hitler's book, "My Struggle," was written during his imprisonment after a failed attempt to overthrow the government of Bavaria in 1923. The first half of the book is part autobiography, part a history of the Nazi party. The second half describes the program of the party. Although indications of shame and anger are scattered throughout the book, they are the most prevalent in the latter half.

The most frequent sequence is the progression from shame to pride. One example is his discussion of "scientific education":

> There is ground for *pride* in our people only if we no longer need to be *ashamed* of any class. But a people, half of which is wretched and careworn, or even depraved, offers so sorry a picture that no one should feel any *pride* in it. Only when a nation is healthy in all its members, in body and soul, can every man's joy in belonging to it rightfully be magnified to that high sentiment which we designate as national *pride*. And this highest *pride* will only be felt by the man who knows the greatness of his nation. (427, emphasis added)

There is a reference to pride in each of the four sentences in this passage, but only one reference to shame (the word *ashamed* in the first sentence). This pattern is characteristic: an initial reference to shame is followed by repeated references to pride. One intimation seems to be that although now ashamed, the future will be proud, but only if the Nazi program is carried out. This pattern also suggests the denial of shame, which is mentioned only once, compared with the repeated references to pride—a more "respectable"—that is, less shameful—emotion.

The meaning of the passage is also of interest because it may imply proneness to shame. The phrase *any pride* at the end of the second sentence suggests that if a group has *any* reason for shame, then *all* pride is lost. A more normal response would be that we always have reason for both pride and shame; that is the human condition.

In the passage just quoted, the references to pride and shame are explicit. In the following passage, which has the same structure, the references are indirect:

> Particularly our German people which today lies broken and defenseless, *exposed to the kicks of all the world*, needs that suggestive force that lies in *self-confidence*. This *self-confidence* must be inculcated in the young national comrade from childhood on. His whole education and training must be so ordered as to give him the conviction that he is absolutely *superior* to others. Through his physical strength and dexterity, he must recover his faith in the *invincibility* of his whole people. For what formerly led the German army to victory was the sum of the *confidence* which each individual had in himself and all together in their leadership. What will raise the German people up again is *confidence*. (411, emphasis added)

Once again there is a progression from shame to pride, and once again a single reference to shame is followed by repeated references to pride. But this time both feelings are evoked obliquely. In the middle of the first sentence is an image of the German people "exposed to the kicks of all the world." Although the word *shame* is not used, the image is clearly one of gross humiliation, of being subjected to a humiliating assault by anyone and everyone.

This passage too, moves very quickly from shame to many references to pride. But like the reference to shame, the references to pride are indirect, using the cognates *self-confidence* and *confidence* rather than the word *pride* itself. This passage contains three more references to confidence as well as two additional *pride* cognates—a conviction of "superiority to others" and a "faith in invincibility." This pattern, like that in the first passage, suggests the denial of shame, since references to it are quickly negated by many references to pride. The entire passage, like many others, is suggestive of the denial of emotions since shame and pride are referred to only indirectly.

Although direct references to pride are found throughout *Mein Kampf,* there are many more indirect references. In addition to *self-confidence, honor, superiority,* and *faith* in one's invincibility, Hitler frequently invokes "dignity" (and being "worthy") as valued characteristics. The task of the "folk-state" "is not to preserve the decisive influence of an existing social class, but to pick the most capable kinds from the sum of all the national comrades and bring them to office and *dignity*" (431; emphasis added). This passage contains both key elements in Hitler's appeal, community and pride; it negates social class in the interest of community, and it promises prideful office to the most capable, regardless of background.

Most of the manifestations of pride and shame are disguised, requiring reading between the lines. The emotional content of the following passage is invisible unless one realizes that the basic shame context is seeing oneself negatively in the eyes of the other (see Sartre 1956; Lewis 1971):

How terrible is the damage indirectly done to our Germanism today by the fact that, due to the ignorance of many Americans, the German-jabbering Jews, when they set foot on American soil, are booked to our German account. Surely no one will call the purely external fact that most of this lice-ridden migration from the East speaks German a proof of their German origin and nationality. (390)

In this passage, Hitler seems to be seeing himself (and the German people) negatively in the eyes of the other, the American people. Because the shameful ("lice-ridden") Jewish migrants speak German, the Americans denigrate Germans and Germany. In the second sentence, he goes on to protest the injustice of this situation produced by his imagination. There is a gratuitous element to this passage that is difficult to define explicitly, but it captures the kind of emotional aura characteristic of Hitler's prose; it is shame-haunted.

In *Mein Kampf,* the many manifestations of shame are virtually always hidden in encoded terms. Hitler repeatedly refers to disgrace, lack of self-confidence, inferiority, and "bowing and scraping" (625) in describing the German people or their representatives. Frequently shame manifestations are even more indirect, as in the passage quoted above about the "German-jabbering Jews." One of Hitler's frequent themes is other nation's lack of respect for Germany:

Will any [nation ally itself with] a state . . . whose characteristic way of life consists only in *cringing* submissiveness without and *disgraceful* oppression of national virtues within; . . . with governments which can boast of *no respect* whatsoever on the part of their citizens, so that foreign countries cannot possibly harbor any greater admiration for them? No, a power which itself wants to be *respected* . . . will not ally itself to present-day Germany. (621; emphasis added)

Like Hitler's statements, his actions were also haunted by the specter of shame. Bromberg and Small (1983: 119) note in passing Hitler's obsession with giantism, of building bigger than anyone. He explained to the workers on one of his building projects, "Why always the biggest? I do this to restore to each individual German his *self-respect*. . . . I want to say to the individual: We are not *inferior;* on the contrary, we are the complete equals of every other nation" (Speer 1970: 69, 107; emphasis added). Because the references to pride and shame are in code language, Bromberg and Small miss their significance. A huge part of Germany's resources, even during wartime, were devoted to the attempt to make Hitler and his followers feel large (proud) rather than small (ashamed).

The primary manifestation of shame in Hitler's behavior was not in construction, however, but in destruction. As Lewis's theory predicts, an individual in a state of chronic shame is very likely to perceive the source of this feeling as an attack by another, generating rage toward that other. Lewis's theory suggests that *protracted* rage *always* has its source in unacknowledged shame, without exception. In her theory, unacknowledged shame is *the* cause of destructive aggression because it generates blind rage.

The sequence "unacknowledged shame, followed by rage, followed by aggression" can be traced in particular passages in *Mein Kampf,* as well as in the book as a whole. The following passage is representative. In one of his many attacks on the Treaty of Versailles, after describing it as an instrument of "abject humiliation," Hitler states:

> How could every single one of these points have been burned into the brain and emotion of this people, until finally in sixty million heads, in men and women, a common sense of *shame* and a common hatred would have become a single fiery sea of flame, from whose heat a will as hard as steel would have risen and a cry burst forth:
> *Give us arms again!* (632, emphasis added)

In this excerpt, the text moves from humiliation to fury to aggression, the last in the form of rearmament for the battle that Hitler prescribes as the destiny of Germany.

What is the battle for which Hitler wants Germany to prepare? It is a battle against both external and internal enemies. At first glance it appears that France is the external enemy, since Hitler refers many times to the "eternal conflict"

between the two countries (674, for example). He also repeatedly refers to the French motive for destroying Germany, its "thirst for vengeance" (624, for example), with great indignation, quite oblivious to his own vengefulness. Hitler does not aver that revenge is his own motive, but he is quick to detect it in others; for example, he ascribes to another "hereditary enemy," Negroes, "the perverted sadistic thirst for vengeance" (624).

It becomes apparent quite quickly, however, that the ultimate enemy that Hitler sees everywhere is the Jewish people—or as he puts it, the "International Jew." Hitler had a classical idée fixe, a fanatical and unswerving belief, that behind every enemy nation, race, occupation, or class, the source of every disaster was the Jewish conspiracy, whose aim was world conquest. Hitler's rage is directed against Jews, whom he confabulates with all other enemies. In Hitler's discourse, all capitalists, traitors, revolutionaries, and Marxists are either Jews or are in the pay of Jews.

In *Mein Kampf,* Hitler's solution to what he calls the Jewish problem is only slightly disguised. Hitler repeatedly alludes to "the settling of accounts" and a "day of reckoning." In the middle of the last chapter, which has the ominous title "The Right of Emergency Defense," Hitler gives a foretaste of what he has in mind:

> If at the beginning of the War and during the War twelve or fifteen thousand of these Hebrew corrupters of the people had been held under poison gas, as happened to hundreds of thousands of our very best German workers in the field, the sacrifice of millions at the front would not have been in vain. On the contrary: twelve thousand scoundrels eliminated in time might have saved the lives of a million real Germans, valuable for the future. (679)

The cycle of shame and rage is focused on a mythical enemy, the Jewish conspiracy and those Hitler believed to be in its pay, but his destructive aggression killed millions of real people.

The evidence we have reviewed suggests, first, that from very early childhood, Hitler's actions were determined by unacknowledged shame, alternating between overt and bypassed states. This conjecture is congruent both with his lack of personal relationships and with his most frequent emotional states—abject humiliation, arrogant dominance (what Adler called the "drive for power"), and protracted rage.

Second, the evidence suggests that the combination of insecure social bonds and humiliated fury was endemic among the German masses. Although the particular family in which Hitler's personality was formed was an extreme instance, many Germans, perhaps a majority, were probably raised in similar families, dominated by a harsh, tyrannical father and a "loving" mother who yielded completely to the father. This family system, as Miller (1983) has argued, sets the stage for extreme repression. In the societywide crisis in Germany, beginning with its defeat in World War I and culminating in the Great Depression, both outer and inner conditions were ripe for an explosion of humiliated fury. (To complete our argument, it is necessary to gather evidence of humiliated fury from statements by ordinary Germans during the period under study.)

Third, the evidence suggests that repressed shame and rage were the link between Hitler and the masses. Hitler's statements and manner sanctioned the intense emotional states that existed unexpressed in his public. Although they lack a theoretical framework, Bromberg and Small's analysis comes near to this formulation:

> The abundant, almost unheard-of expression of hate and rageful anger . . . fired [Hitler's] successful orations. . . . [He spoke] the unspeakable for them. His practice of touching off hostile emotions rather than conveying mere critical ideas was wildly successful. (1983: 313)

This summary formulation by Bromberg and Small focuses on rage, ignoring what we consider to be the causal emotion, unacknowledged shame. But an earlier statement concerning the basic source of Hitler's motives include shame:

> Hitler's efforts to *deny his shame* and to avoid situations that would make him feel ashamed pervade much of what he said, wrote, and did. . . .

He inveighed against anything he considered indicative of weakness, inferiority, or defeat. Himself far from his tall, blonde, trim, lithe, tough, ideal German male, he allied himself with the tough image. He who feared to swim or sit in a boat or on a horse boasted of racial, political, and military superiority, superlative courage, and physical excellence. In writing and speeches he denied his awareness of *humiliating weakness* with boasts of his "granite hardness," brutality, mercilessness, and unchangeability, all of which he equated with masculinity. Hardness, brutality, mercilessness, and stubborn perseverance also marked his acts. (184; emphasis added)

In order to explain Hitler's appeal, all that is missing from this statement is that his public was also in a state of chronic shame. Lewis's theory of the shame-rage feeling trap provides a conceptual model for explaining Hitler's behavior, that of the German masses, and the connection between the two. The model is not an abstract one that leaves out the causal chain, the moment-to-moment links between leader and followers, as in the psychoanalytic formulations.

The theory proposed here suggests that Hitler and his public were united by their individual and joint states of emotion, a triple spiral of shame-rage. They were ashamed, angry that they were ashamed, ashamed that they were angry, and so on, without limit. Hitler's hold on the masses: instead of ignoring or condemning their humiliated fury (the mistake that Carter made in the Iran hostage crisis, for example), he displayed it himself. In this way, as Bromberg and Small suggest, he sanctioned their fury.

Our explanation of Hitler's appeal thus goes further than that of psychoanalytic formulations; it explains how Hitler, in justifying the fury of the Germans, would have seemed to them to mitigate it. His rage and his projection of German shame onto the Jews would have temporarily lessened the level of pain of the average German, by interrupting the chain reaction of overt shame and rage: his own behavior and beliefs implied, "You needn't be ashamed of being humiliated and enraged: it's not your fault." The secret of charisma may be that it is not the cognitive content of the message, but the emotional one, that is important. *The leader who is able to decrease the shame level of a group, interrupting the contagion of overt shame, no matter how briefly or at what cost, will be perceived as charismatic.*

For comparative purposes, this conjecture can be used in other, less extreme circumstances, such as to explain Ronald Reagan's charisma in dealing with the Iran hostage crisis, and Jimmy Carter's lack of it. Reagan's response to the crisis was to get angry: he expressed insult and outrage, much like the average voter. Carter, however, refrained from expressing emotion, counseling patience and rationality. To people in the grip of humiliated fury, counsels of this type fail to mitigate pain and may even increase it; they may feel more ashamed of their shame and anger in the face of advice that seems to deny or condemn it.

In his public statements, Carter seemed not only to lack emotion himself but to deny it in others. Early in the hostage crisis, a reporter asked, "How can you satisfy the public demand to end such embarrassment?" (November 28, 1979) In the main, Carter did not respond to the implication that the nation had been embarrassed. Instead, he discussed legal and ethical issues in a detached manner. But toward the end of his statement, he responded to the emotional content of the question in an oblique way, saying that "acts of terrorism may cause *discomfiture* of a people or a government." This distanced response virtually denies all emotion. *Discomfiture* is a genteelism for *shame,* but the hypothetical and abstract nature of the phrasing disguises it out of existence.

The most striking aspect of Carter's stance during the crisis is the absence of anger on his part toward Iran. At no point did he express anger; at most he expressed disappointment and frustration. Like *discomfiture,* these words concern feeling but also disguise and diminish it. Carter seldom expressed emotion, and when he did, it was almost entirely disguised.

Not so his successor. Reagan treated hostile acts by foreign powers as insults not only to the national honor but to his own. He often responded with anger. His tone was set early in his first term. At the press conference of January 29, 1981, he was asked, "Will your policy toward Iran be one of revenge or reconciliation?" Reagan's initial response was not emotional: sounding somewhat like his predecessor, he discussed only

legal considerations. By doing so, he first established his moderation and rationality in the face of the temptation toward an emotional response.

His answer to the next question, however, concerning the possibility of U.S. retribution to future terrorism, struck a different note. After first saying that he would not give a specific answer, he went on:

> People have gone to bed in some of these countries that have done these things to us in the past confident that they can go to sleep, wake up in the morning, and the United States wouldn't take any action. What I mean by that phrase is that anyone who does these things, violates our rights in the future, is not going to go to bed with that confidence.

The emotional style in this passage is quite different from Carter's. Although he made no direct threat, he intimated that he might use fire to fight fire. The references to sleeping and waking seem to threaten night-fears to potential terrorists. This passage also suggests self-righteous anger at enemies, an emotion that Carter always avoided.

Reagan referred explicitly to this emotion—and expressed it—in his statement of September 5, 1983, on the downing of the Korean jetliner by a Russian fighter: "With our horror and our sorrow, there is a righteous and terrible anger. It would be easy to think in terms of vengeance, but that is not a proper answer." This statement shows a pattern similar to that of statements about the hostage crisis; they express righteous anger, but they deny the propriety of acting on the basis of that emotion. With this maneuver, Reagan managed to suggest both that he was forceful (angry) and that he was moral, since he at least gave the appearance of ruling out vengefulness. It is important to note, however, that he did not give the impression of ignoring or condemning the temptation to take revenge.

Carter's response to insult was to express only the second component—moral righteousness. When asked late in his term (November 2, 1980) about the hostages, he spoke of honor: "[O]ur policy is based on two fundamental objectives, protecting the honor and the vital interests of the United States, and working to insure the earliest possible release of the hostages." Carter indicated later in this statement that he would use only those means that would uphold the "national honor . . . and integrity." Carter's idea of honor was quite different from Reagan's. Honor for Reagan meant removing dishonor by meeting force with force, but for Carter it meant prudence and moral virtue.

In this instance, Carter urged restraint rather than yielding to the demands for force and retaliation. His counsel of restraint gave him anticharisma, alienating the majority of the voters. Even though his tactics ultimately proved successful, he got little credit for them. His management of the crisis left an image of weakness and a residue of angry feeling directed toward him. By contrast, when faced with public outcry against Libyan terrorism several years later, Reagan bombed Tripoli. Where Carter had ignored and by implication condemned the feeling trap of the majority of voters (humiliation-rage-aggression), Reagan capitulated to it.

In alienated societies, leaders face the dilemma illustrated by Carter's and Reagan's approaches to the management of emotions. If they resist the shame-anger spiral of the public, they run the danger of losing power, as Carter did. But if they give in to it, they endanger world peace and further the process of self and social alienation, as Reagan did in his actions toward Libya and Iran, and as Hitler did in his whole career. Perhaps the wisest course would be to acknowledge public emotion, as Reagan did, but to avoid acting on it, as Carter did.

. . . To avoid acknowledging shame—both his own and that of the group—the leader may disguise it with anger and aggression.

This chapter outlined the connection between Hitler and the mass of Germans. Both Hitler and his public were in a state of chronic emotional arousal, a chain reaction of shame and anger that gave rise to humiliated fury. The shame component took the bypassed form, which resulted in a cycle generating rage and destructive aggression, since the shame component was not acknowledged.

In seeking to solve the problem of Hitler's appeal to the German masses, this chapter has focused considerable attention on Hitler's personality. We want to emphasize, however, that our analysis does not imply that destructive conflict is solely the product of a unique individual

like Hitler or Stalin, a reduction of historical causation to psychological individualism. On the contrary, Hitler seems to have been only a part in a larger system of causation, one that transcended particular individuals, no matter how depraved. To underscore this point, we briefly review the larger historical setting in which Hitler rose to power.

The foundation for Hitler's rise to power was laid by the treatment Germany received at the end of World War I at the hands of the victors. The terms that the Treaty of Versailles imposed on Germany were not conciliatory but punitive. The punishment took not only a material form but a symbolic one. The blame placed on Germany as the sole originator of the war was a case in point; the exclusion of Germany from the League of Nations as unworthy was another. These two actions served to formally label and stigmatize Germany, isolating it from the world community. If, as Simmel suggested, conflict has its roots in separation, material and symbolic exclusion may generate violence.

Although controversy remains about the details, there is now evidence that France played a considerable role in the instigation of the World War I. Goodspeed (1977), among others, has traced a chain of secret diplomacy before the assassination of Archduke Ferdinand at Sarajevo—the event that triggered the war—that implicates France and Russia. According to Goodspeed, the French president, Poincaré, seems to have told the Russian czar to encourage the Serbian terrorists to an act of violence. He backed up this incitement with the assurance that France would support the Russians "whatever the consequence"—that is, that France would go to war if Germany sought to punish Russia for instigating the assassination.

Goodspeed, like other historians, has argued that France had the most to lose by delaying a war that all the Great Powers thought inevitable. The Poincaré government was particularly concerned about the Germanization of Alsace-Lorraine, the part of France that had been ceded to Germany as a result of the loss of the Franco-German war in 1871. France wished to reclaim the lost provinces before its youth were converted to the German language and culture. In 1913, after forty-two years of German hegemony, time was running out.

To most of the French, the loss of Alsace-Lorraine represented a stain on the national honor—that is to say, it was felt to be shaming. Goodspeed's assessment is widely held among historians: "The French, humiliated and vengeful, could not reconcile themselves to the loss of past glories and were continually reminded of their shame by the "living wound" of the two lost provinces." (1977: 6).

This judgment brings us back to the core of our argument. For much of the period 1871–1914, *revanche* (revenge) was a watchword in French politics, helping to bring about World War I. French aggression and vindictiveness toward Germany, which prevailed over Wilson's advocacy of a conciliatory peace, was an emotional response to their feeling of humiliation in their earlier defeat by Germany. World War II was a result of the Treaty of Versailles, as World War I was a result of the treaty that ended the Franco-German War in 1871. France and Germany were entangled in an interminable conflict driven by unacknowledged shame on both sides.

To the extent that our argument is true, the German aggression that led to World War II was a product not of Hitler's unique personality but of the alienation among nations in the civilization of that time, and the chain reactions of unacknowledged shame and rage that that alienation produced and reflected. The lack of attunement among nations is exemplified by the gross miscalculations of all the contenders in World War I concerning the cost and duration of the war. Both sides were convinced that they would win quickly and easily in less than three months, with little loss of life. The Allies thought they would win because they had more armaments and many more troops; the Central Powers, because they had better armaments and vastly better planning and organization. Each side demonstrated an utter lack of understanding and misunderstanding of the other.

The lack of attunement both among and within nations can be exemplified by the role that England played in the maneuvering that lead to World War I. The leaders of England were apparently uncertain as to whether they would fight in a war between France and Germany until the very moment that mobilization began on the Continent. Although the English and French general staff had been cooperating in planning a war against Germany, this cooperation was kept a secret not only from Germany and the world at large but from the English themselves; not even the English cabinet was informed. Uncertainty as to whether England would fight seems to have been one factor in the German willingness to fight. Had English determination been clear, the German government might have been less aggressive in its demands after Sarajevo.

The European nations in the period 1870–1945 bear a strong resemblance to the dysfunctional families so clearly described by theorists of family systems (like Bowen 1978). Conflicts in such families are interminable because of alienation between and within family members. Each is deceptive toward the other not only out of malice, but more significant, out of self-deception: each family member has disguised or denied his or her own core feelings and needs. The family of nations in our civilization was, and apparently still is, dysfunctional; lack of attunement between and within nations sets the stage for the humiliation-rage-aggression cycle described in this essay.

The analysis in this chapter points to the need for further studies of charisma within a micro-macro, part/whole framework like the one used here. Many studies of World War I are still focused on the single issue of war guilt; a continuing debate on this issue is being waged, particularly in Germany, the United States, and France. Although understanding the role of the various powers in the instigation of the war is a legitimate problem, it is also a very narrow one and ignores many important issues.

A viewpoint that relates parts to wholes in the national-international *system* particularly suggests two large and crucial issues. First, to what extent are studies of war guilt a part of the problem rather than a part of the solution? The blaming that goes on in dysfunctional families is virtually always one of the causes of interminable conflict: each side blames, often in a way that insults (humiliates and angers) the other, continuing the cycle of unconscious vengeance. To what extent are studies of war guilt a continuation, by scholarly means, of the war itself?

This first question raises a broader second question. To what extent do studies which focus on only one party to a conflict (on an individual like Hitler or Poincaré, or on a nation like Germany or France) divert attention from the whole system of which the individual or nation is only a part? It is possible that a narrow focus on individuals or single nations is an unconscious means of protecting the reigning status quo, the overall relationships within and between nations, little changed in the last hundred years.

The present world system is based on carefully regulated relationships within nations and virtual anarchy among them. The framework developed in this chapter, based both on family systems and on Durkheim's theory, suggests that both sets of bonds may be inadequate. The relationships *within* nations seem to be engulfing, involving too much mutual dependency; those *among* nations seem to be too little (isolation). If Simmel and other theorists were right, this system inevitably leads to perpetual conflict. Until we see the system clearly and as a whole, we may continue to repeat the mistakes of the past.

Note

1. Linz was Hitler's birthplace.

References

Bowen, M. 1978. *Family Therapy in Clinical Practice.* New York: J. Aronson.

Bromberg, N., and V. Small. 1983. *Hitler's Psychopathology.* New York: International Universities Press.

Bullock, A. 1964. *Hitler: A Study in Tyranny.* New York: Harper and Row.

Cooley, C. H. 1902. *Human Nature and the Social Order.* New York: Scribner's.

Dahrendorf, R. 1967. *Society and Democracy in Germany.* Garden City: Doubleday.

Davidson, E. 1977. *The Making of Adolf Hitler.* New York: Macmillan.

Feshbach, S. 1971. "The Dynamics and Morality of Violence and Aggression." *American Psychologist* 26: 281–92.

Geen, R. G. 1968. "Effects of Frustration, Attack, and Prior Training in Aggressiveness upon Aggressive Behavior." *Journal of Personality and Social Psychology* 9: 316–21.

Gilbert, G. 1950. *The Psychology of Dictatorship.* New York: Ronald.

Goodspeed, D. 1977. *The German Wars: 1914–1945.* Boston:. Houghton Mifflin.

Hitler, A. 1927. *Mein Kampf.* Boston: Houghton Mifflin. 1943.

Katz, J. 1988. *The Seductions of Crime.* New York: Basic Books.

Kubizek, A. 1955. *The Young Hitler I Knew.* Boston: Houghton Mifflin.

Lansky, M. 1984. "Violence, Shame, and the Family." *International Journal of Family Psychiatry* 5: 21–40.

———. 1989. Murder of A Spouse: A Family Systems Viewpoint. *International Journal of Family Psychiatry* 10, 159–178

———. 1987. "Shame and Domestic Violence." In D. Nathanson, ed. *The Many Faces of Shame.* New York: Guilford.

Lasswell, H. 1960. *Psychopathology and Politics.* New York: Viking.

Lewis, H. 1971. *Shame and Guilt in Neurosis.* New York: International Universities Press.

Miller, A. 1983. *For Your Own Good.* New York: Farrar, Straus, Giroux.

Mitchell, O. 1983. *Hitler Over Germany.* Philadelphia: Institute for the Study of Human Issues.

Retzinger, S. M. 1988. *Marital Conflict: the Role of Emotion.* Unpublished Ph.D. diss., University of California, Santa Barbara.

Sartre, J. 1956. *Being and Nothingness.* New York: Philosophical Library.

Scheff, T., S. Retzinger, and M. Ryan. 1989. "Crime, Violence and Self-Esteem: Review and Proposals." In A. Mecca, N. Smelser, and J. Vasconcellos, eds. *The Social Importance of Self-Esteem.* Berkeley: University of California Press.

Speer, A. 1970. *Inside the Third Reich.* New York: Macmillan.

Stierlin, H. 1976. *Adolf Hitler: A Family Perspective.* New York: Psychohistory Press.

Toland, I. 1976. *Adolf Hitler.* Garden City, N.Y.: Doubleday.

Waite, R. 1977. *The Psychopathic God: Adolf Hitler.* New York: Basic Books

Part II: SOCIAL INEQUALITY AND THE PRODUCTION OF VIOLENCE

The expression of anger is frequently a warning to the recipient that violence is imminent. One of the reasons that much of the research on violence and aggression includes studies of "verbal aggression" is precisely because the conditions that give rise to these verbal expressions are similar to those that give rise to overt acts of physical aggression. In some instances, violence is a product of an explosion of "heated" emotion. In others, the apparent absence of emotion leads the observer to interpret the violence as a product of "cold, calculated rage." Of course, many, if not most, acts of violence do not involve prior warning. Nevertheless, even the cold-blooded execution by a "hit man" occurs in a wider moral context in which the victim somehow "deserved" to die.

Once we understand that anger itself can be understood in its social context, we can understand that violence, as an explicit or implicit expression of anger, is socially constructed. Violence varies with social class, ethnic background, and gender. The chapters in Part II explain how and why this variation occurs; i.e., they describe the social structure of violence. Why are the poor, new immigrants and ethnic minorities more violent than their more affluent counterparts? What role does the industrial economy play in reducing the level of violence of those who have the opportunity to participate? What are the implications of industrial development for groups left out of the expanding opportunities that result? Increasing levels of social inequality that may develop as a result of industrial development, and the resulting increase in social and economic injustice, provide a great reservoir of anger from which violence can result. Moreover, social structures based on racial segregation or gender inequality are maintained through both formal (legal) and informal (social) institutions of violence.

It is possible to explain the social structure of violence without resorting to theoretical assumptions about, or empirical measurements of, anger expression. The chapters in Part II each explore the direct effect of particular social institutions on the production of violence. The discipline of industrial labor and the destruction of traditional community and family life that accompany industrial development play contradictory roles in the production of violence in contemporary society. Industrial development also increases social inequality, which has a direct effect on the production of violence. Roger Lane, in his study of violence in America during the industrial revolution, describes how the participation of white Americans, both "native" and foreign-born, reduced the level of violence in these communities, while the level of violence among African Americans, who were excluded from participating in the industrial labor system, remained high. During the same time, the white majority engaged in acts of violence designed to intimidate the former slave population through lynching and selective enforcement of laws designed to keep them "in their place."

In "Inequality and Community," Elliott Currie attributes the high crime rate in the United States in the 1980s to the "interwoven problems of economic and racial inequality." In the 1990s, we have seen a decline in the violent crime rate in the United States as we experienced an unprecedented economic boom. Currie notes that economic development by itself contributes to declining criminal violence as long as it does not have a deleterious impact on social integration. When traditional community institutions remain strong or alternative institutions develop to provide support for individuals whose lives are disrupted by rapid social change, criminal violence may actually decline.

In the final chapter in Part II, Jane Caputi argues that acts of violence by men against women reflect the patriarchal institutions and cultural values that legitimate continuing patterns of violence against women and girls. Caputi shows how the dynamics of gender inequality play a role in the "sexual politics of murder" in both intimate relations such as murders by husbands and fathers and in situations involving total strangers such as sexually motivated serial murders.

4

Murder in America: 1865–1917

Roger Lane

The years from the later nineteenth century into the early twentieth are in many ways the classic period in American history, as all sections in their own fashion recovered from the Civil War. In the North, East, and Midwest, these were the years of the most rapid industrialization, when almost every index of size and power pointed jaggedly up and the modern physical city began to take shape. In the West, the whole continent between Kansas and California was filled up with new states. In the South, most wracked by the devastation of war, black slavery was replaced by violent intimidation and segregation as forms of racial domination.

Much homicide in every locale was composed of the same familiar elements as always and everywhere: domestic argument, drink, flaring anger, the challenge to honor. But everywhere, too, murder as always both reflected and contributed to social, political, and economic change. Regionally distinctive rates and patterns resulted from racial tension in the South, labor problems in the North, Indian warfare and unsettled conditions in the West. But toward the end of the era these distinctions began to lose some of their earlier force, as a result of the growing power of the urban industrial revolution all over the country, together with the many values and institutions allied with it, from sober behavior to better police work.

In the former Confederate states, the first task of the dominant white majority was to restore as fully and as quickly as possible the power enjoyed before secession. And between 1865 and 1877 they won back much of what they had lost in the formal Civil War by turning, in effect, to an intermittent but ultimately successful guerilla "war of national liberation" based on systematic homicide.

With the Union army on the ground in 1865 and the federal government in charge, reforming northerners wished ideally to remake or "reconstruct" the conquered states in their own image. Many black leaders hoped to break up plantations into smaller units, turning former slaves into small farmers. At minimum, the triumphant Republican party expected to establish itself through friendly governments elected with the support of the new freedmen, white southern allies, and northerners come down either to help reform the region or seize personal advantage in the midst of postwar confusion.

But none of these wishes came true. While the Congress was able to establish Republican rule for varying periods and new state governments struggled to bring the nineteenth century to the benighted Carolinas, the region was simply too poor to support such innovations as penitentiaries, insane asylums, and public schools in addition to the state-supported railroads and other improvements favored by northern capitalists. Belief in the sanctity of private property was too powerful to permit the confiscation of ex-rebel plantations. And while for brief periods it seemed that the white South might accept a black share in political power, the federal government was too divided, inconsistent, and unwilling to commit the money and the manpower needed to ensure real social change.

The two major goals of the resisting southern majority were to get the blacks back to work under conditions as close to slavery as possible and to win back native white rule. The two were related: control of the political and justice systems was essential to uphold "black codes" and "vagrancy laws" designed to keep blacks out of a truly free labor market. And the winning tactic was the same in both cases: armed resistance

---

Selections from "The Civil War to World War I, 1865–1917," pp. 146–213 in *Murder in America: A History,* by Roger Lane (Ohio State University Press 1997). Reprinted by permission.

to Republican state and county governments supported from outside, intimidation of the freedmen through assault and murder.

In the chaos that immediately followed the war, much violence resulted simply from the lack of local law enforcement. But one new trigger for bitter and defeated young men returning home was to find African Americans trying out new roles, defying old rules, and above all voting. During the year following the Confederate surrender in April 1865, federal commanders reported 33 white-black homicides in Tennessee, 29 in Arkansas, at least 70 in Louisiana, all of these figures surely undercounted, at a time when it seemed to some that a black man's life was worth no more "than a stray dog." Murderous race riots, earlier confined to the North, swept into Charleston, Norfolk, and Memphis, where former slaves had taken refuge in unprecedented numbers. On July 30, 1866, as African Americans were holding a political convention in New Orleans' Mechanics Hall, a black man's casual pistol shot at a white newsboy sparked a general assault on the building, and, with the local cops aiding the rioters, some thirty-nine were killed in nearby street fighting before occupying federals arrived.

By that time resistance was taking more organized form. "Patrolers," during slavery a specialized form of night watch, had roamed the countryside in tense times, looking for runaways or simply blacks without passes. After the war this official institution, together with the unofficial "vigilance" tradition, was easily turned to only slightly new, if now illegal, uses. The Knights of the Ku Klux Klan, led by General Nathan Bedford Forrest, the officer responsible for the Fort Pillow Massacre, was only the most famous of the several secret societies that terrorized black and white political opponents across the countryside during the late 1860s.

Intransigent native whites, mostly Democrats, simply refused to recognize the legitimacy of mostly Republican governments elected with black support, and were especially infuriated by armed black state militia. In some states, as in prewar Kansas, two governments claimed the right to rule at the same time, with the outcome in Mississippi, Louisiana, and South Carolina decided by mini-civil wars. And in 1877 the federal government formally surrendered, withdrawing the last blue troops used to support embattled Republican rule, leaving race relations in local white hands. The toll in violent death by then was past counting, with ordinary killings, lynchings, deaths in riots, Klan murders, and casualties inflicted by or on Republican or Democratic militias almost impossible to disentangle.

And under native white rule after 1877, the South remained the most murderous section of the country; in fact, Horace Redfield, writing in 1880, commented that "the number of homicides in the Southern States is proportionately greater than in any country on earth the population of which is numbered as civilized." While there were no reliable statistics across the whole of the South, Redfield counted the number of killings listed in the only states with statewide newspapers, Texas, Kentucky, and South Carolina, a method that almost surely undercounted the number of black deaths, at the hands of members of either race. But even by this flawed measure, during 1878, just after Reconstruction, these three states had a "murder rate" roughly eighteen times that for New England.

The reasons, to a more modern observer, are several. Poverty and desperation are close to the top of the list. Poverty, too, reinforced a tradition of weak government and law enforcement; it had been hard since the seventeenth century for sheriffs and justices to catch and convict local bullies in rural counties, and it was still hard in upcountry Georgia, the hills of Kentucky and Tennessee, and many other jurisdictions where vengeful feuds bypassed the formal system. "Every man should be sheriff on his own hearth," was an old saying in North Carolina.

Blacks, too, now often armed, were no longer valuable property, protected by their masters either from racist whites or from each other. The historian Lawrence Levine has noted that Stagolee, the most celebrated legendary black badman of this period, was a figure "wholly without social purpose or redeeming qualities," who preyed alike on strong and weak, men and women. His place in folklore was an appropriate reflection of a former slave's world in which the justice system in many counties was not protector but predator.

It had always been the hope even of romantic reformers to make convicted prisoners pay for themselves. In the postwar South, states too poor to feed and clothe mostly healthy young men in idleness, the hope seemed more like a necessity. The solution hit upon was the "convict lease system," through which prisoners were in effect sold for a term to the highest bidders. The highest bidders in this era were typically the owners of mines, railroads, or swampy timberland, places where free men would not work. Gangs of prisoners could be held in chains. They didn't drink or show up late, and the price of their labor could be pushed down close to zero if maintenance costs, food and clothes, were kept at a minimum. Death rates ran up to 40 percent a year. And the men were easily replaceable: the opportunities for corruption were obvious, as some counties could turn a profit by sentencing numbers of young black men for small or imagined crimes and then selling them off to the mines.

And if some places invented black crimes, others ignored them entirely, even offenses as serious as homicide, so long as they affected African Americans alone. With every reason to distrust the justice systems in most counties, black men and women then resorted to often murderous ways of settling arguments of every kind, in cabins, barrooms, and work gangs.

And for both races, the old code of honor still held in the minds both of men with grievances and of those called to judge them.

A Louisiana lawyer, Thomas J. Kernan, outlined the "Jurisprudence of Lawlessness" for the American Bar Association in 1906, describing the ways in which southerners could get away with murder. A man was expected to fight, even kill, if a woman's honor was involved; the state of Texas officially adopted the otherwise "unwritten law" that justified, in jurors' eyes, the murder of a wife's lover (but not a husband's) caught in adultery. And if many states had abandoned the old common law "duty to retreat" in order for a killing to qualify as self-defense, in Kernan's South it had long been replaced by something like a duty to advance. Almost any insult, or to an outsider the most trivial challenge to personal respect or reputation, could justify a homicide. In practice dueling had long been above the law, and as the

old formal code decayed, with its elaborate rules, it was enough to shoot a man on sight so long as he—or the community—knew or should have known that it was coming. Any street brawl that a defense lawyer could stretch into anything remotely like a "fair fight" could qualify as a duel of sorts, and win acquittal. In the South, as everywhere, it was the killer, the survivor, whose story was heard, the victim silent as the grave. And unlike the situation in the North, not only the society's bottom rails but also its social and political leaders were often involved in homicide.

When all of these elements came together the result was rural Edgefield Country, South Carolina, around the turn of the century. Former Governor "Pitchfork Ben" Tillman, an Edgefield native, was then serving as senator from the Palmetto State, an unashamedly violent man whose father and an older brother had killed men over card games, and whose nephew, also a politician, shot down a hostile newsman in front of the state capitol early in 1903—successfully pleading self-defense. During the same years the murder rate in Tillman's home county was something over 30 per 100,000, bigger even than the carnage recorded in medieval England.

But while the southern white-on-white murder rate was the highest in the country, it was white-on-black killings that in this era reached their most notorious peak. Lynchings occurred in every state of the Union outside of New England—New Jersey had several—with more than 3,700 incidents recorded between 1889 and 1930, and victims of every color. But the South accounted for well over 80 percent of these, and it was only in the South that murder was used in effect as social policy.

The lynching phenomenon fascinated contemporaries at the time, and has occupied scholars ever since. But while southern lynching took many forms, much of its morbid appeal results from the sheer barbarity of many incidents. As often in the past, racial hatred allowed otherwise ordinary men and some women to gather in mobs—the attendance of women and children at these occasions was often noted—and to treat their victims as less than human. The results included the most barbaric episodes in the history of American homicide: special excursion trains took passengers to Paris, Texas, in 1893, to watch a retarded black man die, over the course of an hour, of red-hot irons thrust into his body and down his throat; in 1911 an accused rapist was tied to a stake on the opera house stage in Livermore, Kentucky, and tickets bought the privilege of shooting at him from the seats.

Mass lynchings of this kind often followed certain communal rituals: a prominent site was selected close to the alleged crime, the victim was given time to pray, hanged, and then shot up or burned after death—more rarely before— with the first match, or shot, ceremonially awarded to the injured person or family. In about one-fourth of the cases the victim was castrated or otherwise mutilated, with body parts or bits of rope then sold off as souvenirs and whatever remained left to swing as a warning to the black community. These sadistic orgies were explained then and later in terms of communal horror at "THE Crime," black rape of a white woman; the participants seem often to have ranged across the whole of the local white social spectrum. Senator Tillman boasted that he would gladly lead a mob to avenge such an outrage. In fact all southern defenses of lynching centered on THE Crime, with much success across the country.

In the late nineteenth and early twentieth century, an era of intense racism fostered by the pseudoscience of Social Darwinism even among the most educated, the brutish inferiority of blacks was an article of faith. The sensational yellow press of the era fed on lynching; although most editorials condemned the bypassing of the court system, and certainly torture, there was much clucking about a natural impatience with the law's delays, and the actual news stories were written by sympathetic southern stringers. Feature writers and illustrators reveled in the opportunity to produce socially acceptable pornography, a one-two punch best involving a first-person account of the alleged crime—"The negro seized me. Then I fainted. God was merciful"—followed by a lurid depiction of its aftermath. Meanwhile even the northern-born Episcopal bishop of Arkansas, in 1903, joined a host of other respectable apologists in declaring, "While I do not justify lynching, I can find no other remedies adequate to repress the crime for which it has been made a punishment by the people of the South."

Later psychologists, too, have concentrated on the rape issue, in arguing that, for example, in an era of repressed sexuality white men projected their own sexual fantasies onto blacks and then punished them savagely out of guilt. But these explanations, like those of contemporary apologists, are at best partial explanations for a complex phenomenon. The offenses for which black men, and some women, earned lynching ran a great gamut, from urging fellow blacks to return to Africa through arson, assault, burglary, and horse theft on to "wild talking." Rape, despite all the furor, accounted for only about one-sixth of the alleged crimes; by far the most usual was murder of a white male.

And only a minority of lynchings involved great mass mobs. A careful study of Georgia, where lynching was common, and Virginia, where it was not, estimates that big crowds accounted for perhaps 30 to 40 percent of all episodes. Many of the others were simply illegal on-the-spot executions carried out by gangs of armed men; given the traditional weakness of law enforcement in rural areas, something like the old medieval institution of hue and cry lived on in the South, and the line between a legal posse, an extralegal search party, and an illegal lynching bee was a thin one, crossed only when a fugitive was either caught or shot down. Often, too, when a black allegedly wronged a white a small number of family or friends of the victim would raid a jail to abduct and execute a man whose crime had otherwise failed to outrage many others. A last form, finally, was "terrorist" lynching, usually carried on at night by organized groups such as the Ku Klux Klan and intended specifically as warning to those who might follow a "troublemaker."

Simple racial prejudice, too, fails as a full explanation for lynching. Prejudice was of course involved—some 85 percent of southern victims were black, including virtually all of those subject to barbaric indignities—but while racial prejudice was nearly universal, lynching was quite unevenly distributed across the South, with some areas virtually immune. (Contemporary white South Africans, too, were among those shocked by the American resort to lynching.) Other simple psychological explanations—such as lynching as an aggressive response to inner frustration—fail for parallel reasons. While this may be accurate, it explains too much: frustration is part of the human experience, and all share the biological capacity for aggression, but only in some places, at some times, did southerners or others react to frustration in this specific way.

While general explanations may have some value, then, the most useful explanations for the *why* of southern lynching look closely at the *where* and *when* for clues to the kinds of historic forces and changes responsible for the phenomenon. Interracial southern lynchings, while never absent earlier, began to rise sharply in the late 1880s, peaked in the 1890s, when they averaged about one hundred a year, and then fell sharply through the early twentieth century. As the great antilynching crusader Ida Wells Barnett pointed out at the time, no explanation that hinges on either black male lust or white male sensitivity to it can explain the timing; white women had often been routinely and calmly left alone on plantations full of black men, notably during the Civil War—why the sudden upsurge in concern more than twenty years after? And no general psychological reason can account, either, for the rapid falloff early in the twentieth century. What does best explain the curve are specific and often turbulent internal changes in southern politics and society.

When the federal government left the South to itself in 1877, the place of African-American men and women had not been fully settled. White domination had been assured, but with slavery gone its forms were not yet clear. Millions of black men still voted; others competed for a variety of jobs; and in cities and countryside men and women jostled with whites, testing the limits of subordination. For both blacks and poor whites, the several economic substitutes for slavery, above all sharecropping and a one-sided tenantry, were being fixed in law, accompanied by much resistance to their specific terms. And the political backing for these legal instruments was still not firmly in place; during the later 1880s and 1890s, the message of the Populist party and other appeals to rebellion against the traditional Democratic elite were directed at black as well as poor white voters. The result was continual tension and violence at the polls, as poor whites feared that plantation owners would order black tenants to vote against

them and rich whites feared an interracial alliance of the dispossessed.

The geography of lynching supports this analysis. Two kinds of areas stood out. One was the counties where staple crops were grown, notably cotton, the one most valued in the international market and above all in the "black belt" where the population of former slaves was thickest. The other was the fastest-growing counties, as in Texas or South Georgia, newly opened by the railroads and filling with both African-American and white in-migrants ready to exploit new lands through raising livestock or lumbering. In both cases the need to draw sharp racial lines, to validate white "honor" and power by demonstrating black impotence or "dishonor," was unusually strong. The fears of whites in the black belt were exaggerated by their minority status, and in the new areas freedmen and women might prove "uppity" in the absence of local traditions, in contrast to Tidewater Virginia, for example, which had long shown them their place.

The solution eventually found was two-sided, political and social. Elite white fears of black voting were put to rest by a variety of non-violent exclusionary tactics widely adopted by the late 1890s. Successfully claiming, before the U.S. Supreme Court, that a political party was a kind of private club, Democratic leaders won the right to restrict primary voting, in many areas all that mattered, to chosen white "members." Poll taxes and literacy requirements, with tests administered by white officials, eliminated hundreds of thousands more freedmen. These last requirements eliminated many poor whites as well—but in some states a "grandfather clause" exempted those who could prove that their ancestors were legally registered—at a time when African Americans were of course still slaves.

The other or social side of this bargain, demanded less by the elite than by poor whites, was legal segregation as a means of showing their own superiority. Racial segregation had long been common in the North as well as the South, but nothing approaching the near-total apartheid dictated by legislation passed around the turn of the century. The goal of absolute separation and physical distance made little sense to the elite, long accustomed to African-American mistresses as well as mammies, and was never in fact achieved in practice. But few objected to it in principle, and it made a nicely symmetrical package when coupled with voting exclusion.

The sharp downturn in lynching that followed the turn of the century had many causes beyond this all-white "bargain." Many southerners of education and standing had long opposed the practice, and their objections strengthened as the region developed a more diversified commercial economy and social structure and the old culture of honor and violence slowly crumbled at the top. Formal dueling died out within a generation of the Civil War, and the homicide rate began to fall not long after that. Individual sheriffs and governors had always fought illegal punishment as an affront to the honor of their own competence, a blot on the reputations of the justice systems of their states, and a discouragement to investors. While prosecutions were rarely attempted and never successful, state militias were called on dozens of occasions to ring local jails or escort black prisoners to trial. Courageous white southerners, men and women, worked for the same ends— but never together with—African-American antilynching crusaders like Ida Barnett and the founders of the National Association for the Advancement of Colored People (NAACP), beginning in 1909.

But the most basic reason for the falling curve was simply that lynching was no longer needed. By the early twentieth century the use of murder as social policy had achieved its ends: southern blacks were tightly fixed in place, economically dependent and politically powerless, and nothing more was needed to hold them down.

. . . the drop in homicide rates that began during the late nineteenth century is far too widespread to be explained in terms of cutting down on riot deaths in American cities. Everywhere it has been studied in the developed world, from Stockholm, Sweden, south to Sydney, Australia, from London across the Atlantic to New York and Philadelphia, then on west to Oakland, the rates of all violent crime, however measured, were declining at the same time. A phenomenon that broad is best explained in terms of the most fundamental economic and social change

in the period: the urban industrial revolution itself.

Before the Civil War, the efforts of reformers and businessmen to create a more orderly workforce . . . had been swamped by the invasion of disorderly Irish immigrants. But the Irish were, or remained, disorderly mostly because of chronic underemployment: during the 1840s and 1850s there was simply too little unskilled or semiskilled work to do in cities. It was in the decades after the war, the most economically expansive in our history, that the urban industrial revolution really took off. This was the era that created the physical city that still exists: high-rise buildings, libraries, ball parks, and museums, all of them enabled by the great manufactories, then new, now all but gone. And at the same time as this upsurge in blue-collar opportunities, the invention of the typewriter, the telephone, and the department store, together with expanding local government, created an explosion in white-collar office jobs as well. The common denominator in all this work was regular, predictable, cooperative behavior, the same kind that made the trains and trolleys run, and kept great crowds of tens or even hundreds of thousands of people moving peacefully to and from work, every day, at the same hours.

Increasing sobriety was essential to the change. Despite much hypocrisy and corruption, liquor control was the biggest single item on the police agenda. Cops arrested drunks in staggering numbers, and were charged by lawmakers with limiting the days, hours, and number of places where liquor might be sold, sometimes to hold off the more extreme reformers, led most famously by the Women's Christian Temperance Union, who legally dried up whole towns, counties, and states. Saloon keepers cooperated with cops by throwing out unruly customers, cooling off potential trouble. By the time of World War I, across the nation, the average yearly alcohol intake had dropped substantially, and the federal government was on the eve of prohibiting the sale of liquor altogether.

Education, with its stress on schoolroom discipline, was almost equally important. While public schools had been established in much of the country during the 1850s, attendance had not usually been required by law. But between 1870 and 1900 the average yearly number of school days per pupil jumped from seventy-eight to ninety-nine, the average number of eligible children attending from 57 to 72 percent. In the context of controlling violence, as important as the three Rs was the continued stress on learning how to do repetitive tasks, cope with boredom and frustration, and curb impulsive behavior and aggression.

Factory and office, finally, reinforced and rewarded this learned behavior and (relative) sobriety. And a measure of the successful change in mass social psychology is provided by the statistics of homicide in Philadelphia, then the city with the broadest industrial base in the United States. Between 1839 and 1859, measured by indictments for homicide . . ., the city's murder rate stood at 3.6 per 100,000 annually. That number dropped between 1860 and 1880 to 3.2, and between 1881 and 1901 to just 2.5, the same downward trend observed in much of the developed world.

But while these homicide figures help describe what was happening, and when, they do not explain why. Two additional sets of clues help provide a psychological explanation for what was happening in the industrial city: the statistics for the other kinds of violent death, suicide and accident.

On the one hand, while the urban industrial revolution created wholly new ways of dying—through electric shock, or falling down elevator shafts—in Philadelphia the rate of old-fashioned or "simple" accidents such as drowning fell dramatically. During 1869–71 the age-standardized rate of drowning was 18.5 per 100,000 a year; by 1899–1901 it had fallen to 8.0. And while the statistics of suicide are notoriously unreliable, as friends and family sometimes cover up what is thought a shameful death, the opposite movement here is even less mistakable. The suicide figures, standardized to account for a slightly aging population, more than doubled between the 5.8 per 100,000 officially recorded in 1868–72 and the 12.2 in 1899–1901.

How to account for these three strong trends in violent death? Social scientists have long noticed that homicide rates are often high in groups whose suicide rates are low, that moving from the bottom toward the top of the scale of income and education the homicide rate falls as suicide rises. An even sharper focus is offered by the suicide-murder ratio, or SMR, the result of dividing the suicide rate by the sum of both rates.

The SMR, invented by the psychologist Martin Gold, is based on the concept that both kinds of death are expressions of extreme frustration, manifested as aggression. Homicide is the result of aggression directed outward, at others; suicide results from aggression directed inward, at the self. Another way of putting it is that homicide is characteristic of people of "honor," suicide of people of "dignity." A low ratio, as among low-income groups, indicates a tendency toward outward aggression; a higher number, as among the educated middle class, indicates a tendency toward inward aggression, and the equation as a whole shows that both rates tend to be higher among groups, such as males, with a stronger tendency toward aggression in either form. The figures for accident, in this model, tend simply to reinforce those for homicide, the accident prone being remarkably similar to the homicidal in their tendency to alcoholic, reckless behavior, to the quick acceptance of physical challenges along the riverbank or on the street.

Put in motion, over time, the SMR explains exactly what was happening to the whole of the urban industrial population, indeed the whole of the United States after the Civil War. Even more important than income, among men, was the nature of occupation and education. American suicide rates, in the late nineteenth century, were lowest among people who did the older kinds of work: merchants and traders as well as farmers and teamsters. The rates were higher among those whose work demanded formal education, close supervision, or both: modest mill workers and clerks as well as higher-status doctors and lawyers. And in Philadelphia as a whole, over time, as the population grew less free-swinging and more sober, regimented, and introspective, suicide rose as murder fell.

The connection between this change and the nature of work is best illustrated by the different histories of three different ethnic groups.

The city's Irish, once infamous for their violence, over the late nineteenth century went to parochial school, got their knuckles rapped when they got rambunctious, and graduated into jobs in factories, offices, and most famously the civil service, where they again learned to stand in line, keep out of trouble, do the job, and wait for promotion. And as they stopped spitting into each other's drinks and settling disputes with fists, feet, and bricks—earlier in the century bricks had been known in some quarters as "Irish confetti," sprinkled freely about on festive occasions—their murder rates dropped. Once the highest of any major group in Philadelphia, toward century's end the rate among those of Irish surnames fell to 1.8 per 100,000, or well below the citywide average.

The direction among African Americans was tragically different. No group in the city, or indeed the nation, made greater strides in education, as the postwar promise of freedom and legal citizenship made schooling the apparent key to opportunity. In Philadelphia, between the 1850s and the 1890s, the black literacy rate soared from about 20 percent to over 80 percent; even in the South, by century's end, the majority at least of young adults could write their names and figure. No period in African-American history witnessed more cultural achievement, as colleges, newspapers, and churches multiplied and knit communities together in mutual support.

Across the whole of the country the number of the highly educated, doctors first, many of them women, and then lawyers, grew at an astonishing pace. But in terms of economic gain, all of that learning, for most, went heartbreakingly for nothing. Few African Americans could afford to hire the professionals who had sacrificed so hard for their degrees, and fewer whites wanted to. And as a result, after reaching a peak in 1910, the proportion of doctors and lawyers in the black population plummeted and did not recover for three generations. There was simply no basis of economic support below the professional level. In an age of truly implacable "scientific" racism, the most qualified of school graduates were unable to ring their dark faces with white collars, to join the new urban army of clerks, typists, and salespeople. Unions and employers combined to keep blacks out of the new factory work, too, for which they were fully qualified, and many were driven out of the older kinds of blue-collar skilled work as carpenters, masons, and plumbers, jobs that they had long held in many cities. They were not only denied

a chance to grab at the fabled American "ladder of opportunity" but in many cases actually kicked off.

The effect of denial and despair, of being confined to medieval jobs in a modern world, was ominous. Many of the most ambitious were driven into dangerous careers in bootlegging, gambling, and prostitution, where business disputes had to be settled physically, without taking them to the courts. African Americans living in high crime areas, still fearful of whites, carried guns, once rare in their communities, more often than whites. And in Philadelphia, inevitably, their rate of indictment for murder, in the antebellum years only moderately high and lower than the Irish, rose raggedly just as the Irish sank, and it had reached 11.4 per 100,000 by the 1890s.

By that time, however, these rates were exceeded by those of a third group, those born in Italy, whose story further underlines the point. Philadelphia's "murder rates" for the early twentieth century are for technical reasons measured not by indictments, as above . . . but by the comparatively lower rate of actual convictions, sentences to death or the penitentiary. Between 1901 and 1907, this rate among non-Italian whites was just 1.3 per 100,000 annually; and among blacks, 12.9. But the Italians, arriving often as single men, came from the nation with the highest homicide rate in Europe; their dispositions not improved by the ocean voyage, their arsenals upgraded by the American gun culture, as newcomers they killed each other and occasional bystanders often enough to reach the truly astonishing homicide conviction rate of 26.5 per 100,000.

But unlike the blacks, the Italians were admitted into factory work, won some security, settled down into lives with legitimate economic futures for themselves and their families. And while the African-American conviction rate stayed high, the Italian rate went down, and by 1908–15 had fallen to about the black level, at 11.4 per 100,000 and dropping fast.

For the whole of the first two decades of the twentieth century, meanwhile, as evidence of the power of the urban industrial revolution to change murderous behavior, the rates among non-Italian whites continued to fall, as they had for decades, reaching 0.7 in 1915–21.

Bibliography

New Orleans race riot in Dennis C. Rousey, *Policing the Southern City: New Orleans, 1805–1889* (Baton Rouge, 1996); Kernan in Ayers, *Vengeance and Justice,* 266–67; Horace V. Redfield, *Homicide, North and South: Being a Comparative View of Crime Against the Person in Several Parts of the United States* (Philadelphia, 1880), quotation on p. 10, statistics on pp. 12–13; hill country in William Lynwood Montell, *Killings: Folk Justice in the Upper South* (Lexington, Ky., 1986); Stagolee quotation in Lawrence W. Levine, *Black Culture and Black Consciousness: Afro-American Folk Thought from Slavery to Freedom* (New York, 1977), 418; Edgefield County, Tillman in Butterfield, *All God's Children,* chaps. 3–4; quotations from rape victim, bishop, in Roger Lane, *William Dorsey's Philadelphia and Ours: On the Past and Future of the Black City in America* (New York, 1991), 43, 51; geography of lynching in W. Fitzhugh Brundage, *Lynching in the New South: Georgia and Virginia, 1880–1930* (Urbana, 1993).

Urban violence, suicide-homicide ratio, Philadelphia stories in Lane, *Violent Death, Roots of Violence,* "Social Meaning of Homicide Trends"; professional law enforcement in Susan C. Towne, "The Historical Origins of Bench Trial for Serious Crime," *American Journal of Legal History* 26, no. 2 (1982): 123–59; Mudgett in Harold Schecter, *Depraved: The Shocking History of America's First Serial Killer* (New York, 1994); Oakland in Lawrence Friedman and Robert V. Percival, *The Roots of Justice: Crime and Punishment in Alameda County, California, 1970–1910* (Chapel Hill, 1981).

5

Understanding Crime: Inequality and Community

Elliott Currie

In 1983, the highest murder rate in the United States among cities with populations above 50,000 was achieved by East St. Louis, Illinois. In that year, the unfortunate citizens of East St. Louis died by violence at the hands of their fellows at the rate of about 100 per 100,000, roughly twelve times the national average. Across the state in Oak Lawn—a Chicago suburb around the same size as East St. Louis—no one was murdered. Three women were raped, giving Oak Lawn a rate of rape about one-fortieth that of East St. Louis.[1]

Also high on the list of particularly violent American cities was Compton, California, an independent enclave of about 80,000 near central Los Angeles. Compton's homicide rate was about 50 per 100,000 in 1983; it also recorded over 1,300 robberies. Out along the freeway to the northwest is the suburb of Thousand Oaks, which, with about as many people, recorded no murders and just 55 robberies.

Or consider the still more striking case of the two Highland Parks. Highland Park, Michigan, lies within inner-city Detroit. Highland Park, Illinois, is a lakeside suburb just north of Chicago. In 1983, Highland Park, Illinois, suffered no murders, 1 rape, and 7 robberies. With a population roughly the same size (less than 30,000), Highland Park, Michigan, endured 27 murders, 55 rapes, and no less than 796 robberies.

What else distinguishes these cities? For one thing, money. Only one family in thirty in Thousand Oaks is poor; close to one in four in Compton. In besieged East St. Louis, things are even worse. There, nearly two out of five families are poor; over in Oak Lawn, just one family in thirty-eight. The two Highland Parks, once again, offer the most extreme contrast—in Highland Park, Michigan, almost one family in three is poor; in Highland Park, Illinois, one in sixty-seven.

And there is a second striking difference. Compton's population is 75 percent black; East St. Louis's, 95 percent. In both Oak Lawn and Thousand Oaks, on the other hand, blacks are less than 1 percent of the population. In Highland Park, Michigan, blacks are 84 percent of the population; in Highland Park, Illinois, 1.5 percent.

A look at the composition of the population of the prisons and jails underscores this point. For years, every effort to determine the economic status of serious criminals who come before the courts or swell the prisons has come up with the same bleak and thoroughly predictable picture. In 1966, the President's Commission on Crime in the District of Columbia found that seven out of ten adult felony offenders in the city had incomes below $3,000.[2] In 1979, the Bureau of Justice Statistics's periodic survey of state prison inmates found more than three-quarters with prearrest incomes below $10,000 a year. Among the inmates of local jails in 1978, the *median* prearrest income was about $3,700. In the United States as a whole, blacks are 12 percent of the population—but nearly half the population of the prisons.

The conclusion that the interwoven problems of economic and racial inequality play a potent role in breeding criminal violence seems hard to avoid. Yet surprisingly, not all criminologists would agree. "The evidence linking income (or poverty) and crime," James Q. Wilson tells us, is "inconclusive"; some criminologists go even further.[3] "Whatever the merits of socioeconomic reform and, specifically, of greater distributive equality," writes Ernest van den Haag, "it could not replace deterrent threats and punishments as means of crime control."[4] Few criminologists at any point on the political spectrum would venture to deny the strong associations between crime and race, but conservatives have often been remarkably reticent about the implications of that connection—and virtually silent on the obviously related question of how we might develop social policies to break it. If anything, conservative writers have been inclined to reject as unworkable, or even dangerous, most of the social programs created in the past two decades to confront racial or economic inequality head-on.

How do we square the evidence of Oak Lawn and East St. Louis, of the two Highland Parks, of Compton and Thousand Oaks, with the argument that inequality has little to do with crime and that increasing equality cannot help us reduce it? The answer is simple: we can't. The evidence for a strong association between inequality and crime is overwhelming. Denying it requires what we might politely describe as a highly selective interpretation of the facts. And we are unlikely to relinquish our status as the most violent of developed societies if we do not confront that hard and uncomfortable reality.

There is no shortage of evidence. Beyond the rough figures offered by places like Compton, East St. Louis, and Highland Park, Michigan, there is an accumulated fund of sophisticated research linking serious crime with social and economic inequality. It is a complicated linkage, because there are different ways of defining and measuring inequality; because a number of potentially confusing sources of bias lurk within both the methods of social science and the workings of criminal justice; and because, especially in the United States, it is frustratingly hard to disentangle the overlapping but partly distinct effects of income and race. Nonetheless, studies of several different kinds,

both in the United States and overseas, show—strongly and recurrently—that economic and racial inequality affect not only the extent of crime but also its seriousness and violence. The relationship tends to be astonishingly linear—the worse the deprivation, the worse the crime.

These associations, which have appeared in criminological research for decades, have been powerfully confirmed in more recent research.[5] Marvin Wolfgang's study of youth crime in Philadelphia . . . found that when the city's youths were divided into two groups of higher versus lower socioeconomic status (SES)—as measured, in this case, by their parents' occupations—the "lower SES" boys committed substantially more crimes, and more serious ones as well.[6] While boys from higher-status backgrounds more often went straight after one offense, the "lower SES" boys were more likely to repeat, even to become what the study called *chronic* offenders—those with at least five arrests by age eighteen.

Cutting across these substantial class differences, however, was the even more powerful factor of race. Black youths, whether of "lower" or "higher" SES, committed more recorded offenses in the first place and were far more likely to commit multiple offenses and serious offenses resulting in bodily injuries. Nonwhite youth were responsible for all the homicides, 86 percent of the rapes, and 89 percent of the robberies, though they represented just 29 percent of the entire youth cohort.

This and later research also drives home another point: the inequality associated with high rates of crime involves more than differences in income alone. The Philadelphia study found that several other characteristics of the youths' lives—school performance, IQ, and how often they had moved—were also related to delinquency. But this was true primarily because these characteristics were themselves so closely associated with racial and class position. For example, boys who were poor achievers in high school were more likely to become delinquent, but then most of the poor achievers were nonwhite. Thus, problems like school failure were best understood as aspects of a larger constellation of adverse social conditions—constituting what the researchers called a *disadvantaged* position—that were inextricable from the overriding problem of racial and class inequality. The more these conditions were combined in the youths' lives, the more they were at risk of becoming delinquent in the first place and of committing serious or repetitive crimes once delinquent. Indeed, the Philadelphia researchers noted, "the recidivists, one-time offenders, and non-offenders lie on a continuum" on all these measures of social disadvantage. Recidivists had the lowest IQ scores and levels of school achievement and the most intracity mobility, while those with no recorded offenses were at the other end of the scale, and one-time offenders fell squarely in the middle.

These general conclusions have appeared again and again in recent research on many different populations in a variety of settings in several countries. Wolfgang's own later study of Philadelphia youths born in 1958 found, for example, that although the second cohort was significantly more violent than the first, racial imbalance remained pervasive and startling.[7] The nearly 6,600 white boys committed 4 homicides, 9 rapes, and 103 robberies; the 7,200 nonwhite boys accumulated 52 homicides, 96 rapes, and over 1,200 robberies. More than a quarter of the nonwhite boys were recidivist delinquents, with one in every nine a "chronic"; among the white boys, only one in nine was a recidivist and one in twenty-eight a "chronic." Similarly, in a 1978 study of violent juvenile delinquents for the Vera Foundation, Paul Strasburg found that black youths accounted for 62 percent of all violent offenses, though they were 49 percent of the study's sample of arrested delinquents.[8] Just over half of the black delinquents in the sample had been charged with a violent crime at least once, compared to just under half of Spanish-speaking delinquents and only 29 percent of whites. More than twice as many blacks as whites—and nearly twice as many blacks as Spanish-speaking youths—had committed three or more violent offenses (though the Spanish-speaking delinquents were slightly more likely than the whites to have committed at least one violent crime). Arrest data from a Rand Corporation study of youth crime and juvenile justice in California uncovered an even more striking racial and ethnic imbalance.[9] In 1980, white youths in Los Angeles were arrested for homicide at a rate of about 15 per 100,000. Among Hispanics, the rate was 103 per 100,000; among

blacks, 292. For robbery, the rate for white youths was a shade under 250 per 100,000; for Hispanics, 918—and for black youths, more than 5,500 per 100,000.

The picture is the same if we look at the racial and economic characteristics of youths who are not just arrested but behind bars. As the California Youth Authority's researchers dryly note, their analysis of the factors distinguishing "chronic" and violent youthful criminals from other delinquents contains "few surprises." Like Wolfgang's research, the CYA study found that the relationship between crime and socioeconomic disadvantage was depressingly linear. The most troubling and dangerous youths—the *chronic violent-aggressive* delinquents who had committed multiple crimes, at least one of which was a murder, manslaughter, rape, or serious assault—were at one end of a spectrum of social deprivation. The nonchronic, less violent delinquents were at the other, while chronic but less violent property offenders were in the middle. "Degree of chronicity and violence-proneness," the Youth Authority researchers concluded, "appears closely paralleled by degree of social deprivation and psychological deviance."[10]

The finding was all the more striking because this was such a tough population to begin with: most of these youths were chronic offenders. But even among them, the less chronic and less violent had several things in common. They were more often white, their parents were much less often of "below-average" socioeconomic level and less likely to have been on welfare, and the boys themselves were likely to have been rated higher on mental ability and to have gone farther in school. Among a sample drawn from one of the institutions in the study, the Preston School for youth, the largest single group was the chronic violent-aggressive offenders. Who were they? Only a fourth had parents who had graduated from high school, versus nearly two-fifths of less chronic or less violent delinquents. Two-thirds of the chronic violent-aggressives came from families of below-average socioeconomic level, versus just two-fifths of the nonchronics. Twice as many chronic violent-aggressives came from families receiving public assistance. Less than half as many had gone past the junior year of high school.

Given America's racial history, it is difficult to sort out exactly how much of the variations in rates of serious crime reflect inequalities of class versus those of race. Where both historical and current forces have kept some minorities disproportionately trapped in the lowest reaches of the economy, the distinction between economic and racial inequality itself is in danger of being uselessly abstract. On balance, however, the evidence suggests that in the United States the effects of class and race on criminal violence in the United States are inextricably intertwined—but that race probably does have an independent effect. In a recent study of the 125 largest American metropolitan areas, for example, Judith and Peter Blau found that greater inequality of family incomes in an urban area "substantially raises its rate of criminal violence"—as does the proportion of blacks in the population.[11] When the Blaus tried to tease out the relative importance of racial versus economic inequalities, they found that most of the influence of race on the crime rate could be accounted for by the fact that blacks were so predictably at the bottom of the socioeconomic ladder—but even when that association was statistically controlled, a significant racial effect remained.

These findings are both remarkably sturdy and remarkably consistent over time and in different countries; their implications for social policy seem transparently obvious. "The high concentration of serious delinquents of the future among children exposed to a characteristic constellation of social deprivation," writes Donald West, "points inexorably to the need to include anti-poverty measures in any coherent policy of delinquency prevention."[12] Yet that seemingly unavoidable conclusion is far from universally accepted. Despite compelling evidence, conservatives have still maintained that the influence of inequality on crime is minimal and that we will prevent little crime by trying to reduce it.

Those who insist that the links between inequality and criminal violence are overstated have offered several different arguments. One is that the commonly observed association is largely spurious, an artifact of the biases of social scientists and of the criminal-justice system itself. A second is that the observed associations are real enough, but they are the result of cultural proclivities or personality deficiencies of some groups, which are regarded as causes rather than consequences of their disadvantaged position in society. In other words, it is not inequality or deprivation that leads to crime, but something about the culture, temperament, or upbringing of a small fraction of the population that leads to both crime and economic disadvantage. This is the most recent variant of the traditional conservative argument that the poor deserve what they get, and that delinquency and violence are merely dramatic expressions of the generally flawed character of those who wind up at the bottom of the social order. A third argument, favored by some of the more extreme proponents of dismantling the welfare states of the Western democracies, goes still further: it is not inequality that generates crime, but our misguided efforts to *reduce* inequality—efforts rooted in a naive egalitarianism and enforced by the political mechanism of the welfare state.

The first argument—that the link between inequality and crime is largely if not entirely spurious—is based on a genuinely important perception: that the statistical evidence on which it rests is subject to powerful biases. For in a society run by the white and the well-to-do, it's argued, the decisions that determine whether individuals who break the law will be channeled through the stages of arrest, conviction, and imprisonment—and thus appear in the official crime statistics—cannot fail to be profoundly affected by racial and class prejudices. Police, in this view, are more likely to stop and arrest minorities and the poor in the first place; judges and juries more likely to convict them and to give them harsher sentences once convicted. Therefore, any apparent relationships between inequality and crime that are derived from official data on arrests, conviction, or the composition of the prison population are at least as much a measure of the behavior of the criminal-justice system as they are an accurate description of variations in the actual behavior of people at different points on the social spectrum.

This case cannot be easily dismissed. No one seriously argues that criminal justice in America has been either color-blind or free of class prejudice. In its more restrained versions, this argument sensitizes us to important pitfalls awaiting researchers who use official criminal statistics. But in its extreme form, the argument requires us to believe not only that the criminal-justice system discriminates against poor and minority offenders, but that it discriminates enough to explain the enormous class and racial variations that appear in the official data on arrest, conviction, and imprisonment. The first belief is doubtless true, at least in some jurisdictions—true enough, at any rate, to warrant serious concern. The second is false.

This is most obvious in the case of racial differences in crime. To take the clearest case, there is no serious argument that the racial disparities in homicide can be credibly attributed to criminal justice biases. And those disparities are stunning indeed. Other things being equal, people in their late adolescence and early adulthood are far more likely to die by violence than infants and young children.[13] But a black infant is more likely to be murdered in the United States than a white person of any age. Similarly, it's a truism that men—other things being equal—are more likely to meet death by violence than women. But other things are *not* equal. At every age until the late forties, a nonwhite woman faces a higher risk of death by homicide than a white man. All this, to be sure, would tell us little about the race of the perpetrators, were it not for the fact that we know the great majority of homicides are intraracial, not interracial.

Public Health Service data on racial differences in death rates tell us the same thing. These figures are subject to uncertainties of their own, but they are not affected by the prejudices of police, prosecutors, or judges. And they too show that, apart from the relatively constant factors of age and gender, race is the most important determinant of the risks of death by violence. Homicide is the leading cause of death for blacks of both sexes between the ages of fifteen and twenty-four: 39 percent of black men and 25 percent of black women who die at these early ages are murdered.[14] At this age, homicide death rates are five times higher for blacks than whites among men and four times higher for women. For men only, homicide is the leading cause of death for blacks aged twenty-five to forty-four as well; black men in this age range are

roughly eight times as likely to meet death by violence as their white counterparts.

These great disparities are also confirmed in *victimization* studies, in which victims are asked to report some characteristics of their attackers, including sex, age, and race. These studies, too, can be biased by victims' misperceptions or even deliberate falsification, but investigations of this problem suggest that victims are in fact reasonably accurate in identifying their attackers. As the criminologist Michael Hindelang has demonstrated, these studies show a remarkable concentration of crimes against the person committed by young black men, a pattern little different from that shown by official police data.[15] Thus, black men aged eighteen to twenty commit personal crimes (rape, robbery, assault, and larceny from the person) at a rate more than five times higher than white men the same age. Indeed, the factor of race is sometimes strong enough to cut across the otherwise definitive effects of age and gender. For example, although violent crime is generally highest for men aged eighteen to twenty, black men over twenty-one have much higher rates of robbery and rape than white men of any age. Among youths under eighteen, black women have slightly higher rates of robbery and assault than white men.

These findings all suggest that, at least for serious crimes of violence, the official criminal-justice statistics are not as far off the mark as critics have sometimes thought. And they are supported by studies that have sought to uncover the extent of racial discrimination in the criminal-justice system. Certainly no one can boast that discrimination has been eliminated. In a recent study of felony offenders in California, Texas, and Michigan, for example, Joan Petersilia of the Rand Corporation found little or no evidence of discrimination by race in arrests, prosecution, or conviction, but did uncover significant and otherwise inexplicable differences at the stage of sentencing in several jurisdictions: both blacks and Hispanics got longer sentences to begin with and served longer stretches in prison.[16]

But the level of discrimination in sentencing found in this and other studies is not nearly great enough to account for the overrepresentation of blacks in prisons (especially since the evidence shows that, if anything, there is still an equally discriminatory countertendency, making for greater leniency in the courts toward blacks who commit crimes against other blacks).[17] The overall incarceration rate for blacks in the state prisons exceeds the white rate by almost seven to one; on an average day, about three out of every hundred black men are behind the walls of a state prison and half that many more in a federal prison or a local jail. Almost one in five black men, versus one in thirty-seven white men, can expect to do time in his lifetime. As Alfred Blumstein has calculated, most of this disparity about 80 percent—can be accounted for by the much higher crime rate among blacks in the first place. That leaves 20 percent unaccounted for, some of which doubtless reflects racial bias.

Unequal treatment in the courts is more likely with somewhat less serious crimes, where there is more room for discretion in sentencing. Thus, Blumstein calculates that the proportion of the racial gap in imprisonment that does not simply reflect higher crime rates may be as high as 33 percent for burglary, but just 5 percent for aggravated assault and less than 3 percent for homicide.[18] This isn't to deny that racial bias may be more severe in some places than others, nor, certainly, to deny the importance of vigorous efforts to eliminate bias from the system wherever it's found. But it does confirm that only a part of the racial differences in incarceration rates can be explained by official bias. And it reminds us that, as Blumstein puts it, "any significant impact on the racial mix in our prisons will have to come from addressing the factors in our society that generate the life conditions that contribute" to the disparity

━━━

The evidence is strong that violence ordinarily *declines* as societies become more prosperous. A familiar sociological argument holds that the transition from the presumably more cohesive communities of the preindustrial era to the more fragmented ones of modern industrial societies *necessarily* involves a decline in social integration and a corresponding rise in crime and other social pathologies. But the record has actually been more complicated—and more encouraging. The best historical evidence shows that interpersonal violence was generally high in preindustrial Europe. It probably increased

temporarily—at least in some places—with the first drastic disruptions wrought by early and harsh industrialization, which threw millions—especially the young—off the land and into the cities, without livelihoods, income, or the traditional supports of family and local community. But then, in most cases, things got better. In much of Europe and, with reservations, the United States, criminal violence seems to have declined in the late nineteenth century as the displaced were gradually, if imperfectly, integrated into stable occupational and communal roles in the industrial order and granted broader access to education and political participation.[19] (One important reservation is that criminal violence remained high in urban black communities in America—another indication that blacks in the United States underwent what the historian Roger Lane describes as a "separate path of development.")

What the historian Ted Robert Gurr calls the "humanizing" effect of industrialization and democratization can also be observed in cross-national studies.[20] As Steven Messner has recently shown in a study of fifty countries, economic development—as measured by the growth of Gross National Product per capita—is associated, on balance, with declining rates of homicide.[21] Why? Economic development ordinarily reduces the level of violence because, over the long run, it reduces economic inequality. As Messner puts it, "The more developed societies do not exhibit especially high levels of homicide, in part because the greater equality in the distribution of income accompanying development serves to deflate the homicide rate."

But it is true that economic growth in some countries *has* been accompanied by increasing criminal violence, even while the general level of affluence has been rising. What this tells us, though, is not that increasing affluence necessarily causes crime, but that something has gone badly awry in the process of growth itself.

━━━

. . . Economic development within the market system tends to undermine traditional institutions of support and mutual obligation; what is most crucial in influencing the pattern of violence and crime is the extent to which these traditional supports manage to survive in the face of that disruption (recall Japan's private mechanisms of social obligation) or are supplanted by new ones (Western Europe's welfare states). Where this happens, the overall effect is to decrease interpersonal violence over time. Where it fails to happen, economic growth may weaken or destroy the supportive relations that existed in more traditional communities without putting anything of substance in their place. The result is an impoverished rural and urban underclass deprived of respectable livelihoods, torn away from personal attachments and informal controls, and dependent on an often inadequate labor market as the exclusive provider of social integration, material welfare, and self-esteem.

. . . the growth of the postwar American economy was unusual among advanced industrial societies in the extent to which it eliminated traditional livelihoods, yet failed to replace them with new opportunities. This helped ensure that the American distribution of income remained highly unequal in spite of the overall rise in the standard of living. To this aspect of economic deprivation must be added the fragmenting impact of a largely unbuffered market economy on less quantifiable but critical dimensions of communal life—local networks of support, traditions of mutual help, values of cooperation, and common provision of basic needs.[22] In particular, the loss of agricultural employment and the large-scale movement from country to city broke older communities apart, while the relative absence of mechanisms to integrate the displaced into new jobs inhibited the development of a stable and supportive urban community life. In a familiar pattern, these transformations brought the unskilled of the rural South, Appalachia, and even the Caribbean and Latin America into American cities just as the capacity of the urban-industrial economy to absorb them was declining, trapping the newcomers in neighborhoods too rapidly changing to sustain strong networks of social support, and placing the marginal and uprooted poor in demoralizing proximity to the prosperous, while saturating them with the lures of an increasingly frenetic consumer culture.[23]

As in the Third World, the combination was (and is) an explosive one—and one that sharply distinguishes the American pattern of economic development. Many other industrial societies suffered similar strains; none suffered them in such extreme form. It is precisely the minimization of inequality and unemployment and the preservation of strong communal institutions that, for example, help account for the experience of two modern industrialized countries noted for their low rates of serious crime—Switzerland and Japan.[24] As the criminologist Marshall Clinard has argued, Swiss economic development was far more decentralized than that in most other countries and took place in the context of a political system strongly based on local self-government and broad community participation. As a result, Switzerland's rise to affluence entailed considerably less disruption of local communal life than occurred in most industrial societies. Similarly, scholars have often pointed to the persistence of strong ties of community and kinship in the face of rapid industrialization in postwar Japan. In both cases, too, economic development was accompanied by a relatively narrow spread of income inequality and very low rates of unemployment, assuring a more egalitarian distribution of the fruits of growth.

It is important to be clear about what this evidence means and doesn't mean. That some forms of economic growth can generate crime doesn't mean that we should romanticize the supposedly harmonious life of poor countries—countries that are often both wretchedly deprived in material terms and ridden with their own forms of institutionalized violence and traditionally accepted brutality. Nor does it suggest that poverty and material deprivation have nothing to do with crime (as comfortable observers in affluent nations sometimes prefer to believe) or justify a less-than-benign neglect of the material needs of the poor at home or overseas. It *does* tell us that if we want to understand the relationships between crime, inequality, and prosperity, we will need a broader conception of what we mean by impoverishment—and prosperity. It tells us that statistics on the growth of Gross National Product or personal income alone are not very precise guides to the extent of social deprivation; that the supports of community and kinship can inhibit violence even where there is little money and few material goods; and that the enforced separation of people from these communal supports in the name of economic growth can be among the worst forms of impoverishment of all. By the same token, it follows that if we wish to mount an effective attack on criminal violence, we cannot be satisfied with simply doling out funds, grudgingly and after the fact, to people who have been stripped of livelihoods and social networks by the dynamics of the private labor market.

Notes

1. City comparisons: crime data from *Uniform Crime Reports, 1983;* demographic data from U.S. Bureau of the Census, *Social and Economic Characteristics of States,* 1980 Census of Population and Housing, volumes for Illinois, California, and Michigan (Washington, D.C.: U.S. Government Printing Office, 1983).

2. President's Commission on Crime in the District of Columbia, *Report* (Washington, D.C.: U.S. Government Printing Office, 1966), p.55; U.S. Bureau of Justice Statistics, *Selected Characteristics of State Prison Inmates, 1979,* p.3.

3. James Q Wilson, "Thinking About Crime" (1983), p. 81.

4. Ernest Van den Haag, "Successful Rehabilitation," p. 1032.

5. Barbara Wootton, *Social Science and Social Pathology* (London: Routledge and Kegan Paul, 1959), pp. 103–106.

6. Marvin Wolfgang et al., *Delinquency in a Birth Cohort,* pp. 245–249.

7. Marvin Wolfgang, "Testimony," pp. 143–145.

8. Paul Strasburg, *Violent Delinquents* (New York: Monarch, 1978), p. 53.

9. Peter Greenwood et al., *Youth Crime and Juvenile Justice in California* (Santa Monica, Calif.: Rand Corporation, 1983), p. 15.

10. Hapaanen and Jesness, *Early Identification of the Chronic Offender.*

11. Judith Blau and Peter Blau, "The Cost of Inequality: Metropolitan Structure and Violent Crime," *American Sociological Review* 47 (February 1982): 121.

12. Donald West, *Delinquency,* p. 147.

13. *Uniform Crime Reports* (1981), p. 341.

14. U.S. Public Health Service, *Health-US, 1982* (Washington, D.C.: U.S. Government Printing Office, 1982), p. 20.

15. Michael J. Hindelang, "Variations in Sex-Race-Age-Specific Incidence Rates of Offending," *American Sociological Review* 46 (August 1981): 466.

16. Joan Petersilia, *Racial Disparities in the Criminal Justice System* (Santa Monica, Calif.: Rand Corporation, 1983).

17. Cassia Spohn et al., "The Effect of Race on Sentencing: A Reexamination of an Unsettled Question," *Law and Society Review* 16, no.1 (1981–82); Gregory Kowalski and John P. Rickicki, "Determinants of Juvenile Postadjudication Decisions," *Journal of Research in Crime and Delinquency* 19, no. 1 (1982).

18. Alfred Blumstein, "On the Racial Disproportionality of United States Prison Populations," *Journal of Criminal Law and Criminology* 73, no.3 (1982): 1260–1281.

19. Ted Robert Gurr, "Development and Decay: Their Impact on Public Order in Western History," and Roger Lane, "Urban Homicide in the Nineteenth Century: Some Lessons for the Twentieth," in *History and Crime,* ed. James Inciardi and Charles Faupel (Beverly Hills: Sage Publications, 1980); John D. Hewitt and Dwight W. Hoover, "Local Modernization and Crime: The Effects of Modernization on Crime in Middletown, 1845–1910," *Law and Human Behavior* 6, no. 3–4 (1982).

20. Gurr, "Development and Decay," p. 43.

21. Steven F. Messner, "Societal Development, Social Equality, and Homicide," *Social Forces* 61, no.1 (September 1982): 238.

22. Edward A. Gargan, "The Downside of Upstate," New York *Times,* September 16, 1984.

23. Robert J. Bursik and Jim Webb, "Community Change and Patterns of Delinquency," *American Journal of Sociology* 88, no. 1 (July 1982); Richard Block, "Community, Environment, and Violent Crime," *Criminology* 17, no. 1 (May 1979).

24. Clinard, *Cities with Little Crime;* Smith, *Japanese Society;* and Ronald P. Dore, *City Life in Japan* (Berkeley: University of California Press, 1958).

6

The Sexual Politics of Murder

Jane Caputi

When is an act sexed? When do you kill, or die, as a member of your gender, and when as whoever else you are? Are you ever anyone else?

—Catharine A. MacKinnon (1982b, p. 703)

Those of us who are . . . so much influenced by violence in the media, in particular pornographic violence, are not some kind of inherent monsters. We are your sons, and we are your husbands, and we grew up in regular families.

—Ted Bundy (Lamar 1989, p. 34)

They made me out to be a monster. . . . but, even my worst enemies admit that I was a good father.

—Joel Steinberg (Gross 1989, p. 72)

In her recent book, *The Demon Lover: On the Sexuality of Terrorism,* Robin Morgan (1989) relates an incident that occurred during a civil rights movement meeting in the early 1960s. A group composed of members of both the Congress of Racial Equality (CORE) and the Student Nonviolent Coordinating Committee (with men outnumbering women three to one) had gathered in the wake of the disappearance of three civil rights workers in Mississippi. The FBI, local police, and the national guard had been dredging local lakes and rivers in search of the bodies. During this search, the mutilated parts of an estimated 17 unidentified bodies were found, all but one of whom were women. Morgan recalls that a male CORE leader, upon hearing that news, agonized: "There's been a whole god-

damned lynching we never even *knew* about. There's been some brother disappeared who never even got *reported.*" When Morgan asked, why only *one* lynching and what about the other 16 bodies, she was told: "Those were obviously *sex* murders. Those weren't political" (pp. 223–24).

Twenty years later, that perception still holds sway. For example, in the spring of 1984, Christopher Wilder raped and murdered a still unknown number of women. About to be apprehended by the police, he shot himself. The *Albuquerque Tribune* (April 14, 1984, p. 2) commented:

Wilder's death leaves behind a mystery as to the motives behind the rampage of death and

Jane Caputi, "The Sexual Politics of Murder," *Gender & Society* Vol. 3, No. 4, pp. 437–456, copyright © 1989 by Sociologists for Women in Society. Reprinted by Permission of Sage Publications, Inc.

I would like to thank Patricia Murphy, Gordene MacKenzie, Elena Ortiz, Mary Caputi, Elizabeth McNamara Caputi, and Shari Weinstein for their help in finding the news stories necessary for researching this essay. Thanks also to Judith Lorber and Pat Miller for editorial suggestions. I dedicate this article to the memory of Elizabeth Ann Landcraft, Frankie Bell, and Althea Oakeley.

terror. With plenty of money, soft-spoken charm, a background in photography, and a part-time career on the glamorous sports car racing circuit, Wilder, 39, would have had no trouble attracting beautiful women.

This man not only murdered women but first extensively tortured them. Although the FBI refuses to release all the details of that abuse, it was revealed that Wilder had bound, raped, repeatedly stabbed his victims, and tortured them with electric shocks. One woman (who survived the attack) had even had her eyelids glued shut. Obviously, Wilder did not wish to date, charm, or attract women; his desire was to torment and destroy. From a feminist perspective, there is no mystery behind Wilder's actions. His were sexually political murders, a form of murder rooted in a system of male supremacy in the same way that lynching is based in white supremacy. Such murder is, in short, a form of patriarchal terrorism.

That recognition, however, is impeded by longstanding tradition, for, as Kate Millett (1970) noted in her classic work, *Sexual Politics:*

> We are not accustomed to associate patriarchy with force. So perfect is its system of socialization, so complete the general assent to its values, so long and so universally has it prevailed in human society, that it scarcely seems to require violent implementation. . . . And yet . . . control in patriarchal societies would be imperfect, even inoperable, unless it had the rule of force to rely upon, both in emergencies and as an ever-present instrument of intimidation. (pp. 44–45)

Early feminist analysts of rape (Brownmiller 1975; Griffin 1983; Russell 1975) asserted that rape is not, as the common mythology insists, a crime of frustrated attraction, victim provocation, or uncontrollable biological urges. Nor is it one perpetrated only by an aberrant fringe. Rather, rape is a direct expression of sexual politics, a ritual enactment of male domination, a form of terror that functions to maintain the status quo. MacKinnon (1982a) further maintains that rape is not primarily an act of violence but is a *sexual* act in a culture where sexuality itself

is a form of power, where oppression takes sexual forms, and where sexuality is the very "linchpin of gender inequality" (p. 533).

The murders of women and children—including torture and murder by husbands, lovers, and fathers, as well as that committed by strangers—are not some inexplicable evil or the domain of "monsters" only. On the contrary, sexual murder is the ultimate expression of sexuality as a form of power. Sex murder (what the FBI also terms "recreational murder") is part of a tradition that Mary Daly first named as gynocide (1973, p. 73). As further defined by Andrea Dworkin (1976), gynocide is "the systematic crippling, raping, and/or killing of women by men . . . the relentless violence perpetrated by the gender class men on the gender class women." She adds that "under patriarchy, gynocide is the ongoing reality of life lived by women" (pp. 16, 19).

It is only through an extraordinary numbing that such a reality can be denied, for the terrible reminders are everywhere: in the ubiquitous posters pleading for information about women who have "disappeared"; in the daily newspaper reports of various public and private atrocities. In January and February 1989, along with all the grimly usual stories, three others demanded my attention. The first was the conviction of Joel Steinberg—the batterer, child killer, familiar family member, and self-proclaimed "good father"—for the death of his illegally adopted daughter. The second was the execution of serial sex killer Ted Bundy, the ultimate stranger and paradigmatic "good son." The third also is related to serial murder: hundreds of women, many of whom police say were working as prostitutes, have been murdered in the past seven years on the West Coast by killers such as Seattle's "Green River Killer" and the Los Angeles "South Side Slayer." Currently, in San Diego County, 39 women who have been categorized as "prostitutes, drug addicts, and street denizens" have been killed since 1985, while in Los Angeles, police are investigating the murders of 69 prostitutes and the killings of 30 other women in what they term "street murders" (Overend and Wood, 1989; Serrano 1989). In this article, I will look at some of the issues raised by these three separate but related gynocidal events.

Mixed Signals[1]

*He was giving me mixed signals. He would
praise me and build my ego. On the other
hand, he was constantly critical. And he
would strike me.*

—Hedda Nussbaum (Hackett 1988, p. 60)

On November 1, 1987, six-year-old Lisa
Steinberg was brought to a hospital emergency
room unconscious and with injuries that led to
her death four days later. The two people who
had been raising her in their Greenwich Village
apartment—Joel Steinberg, a lawyer who had illegally adopted the child, and Hedda Nussbaum,
the former children's book editor he lived with
and battered for some 12 years—were brought
in by the police for questioning. Suspicion was
directed at Steinberg in part because upon being
told that the child had suffered at the very least
"permanent brain damage," he joked that "Lisa
would never be an Olympic athlete." At first,
both Nussbaum and Steinberg were charged
with second-degree murder, but a year later, as
the trial began, the prosecution dropped the
charges against Nussbaum. No longer a defendant, she became the key witness in the state's
case. The trial was televised, and for seven days,
Nussbaum told of her abusive relationship with
Steinberg; videotapes of her extensively and permanently damaged body and face were introduced as evidence. Massive national attention
was focused on the trial, with Nussbaum and
Steinberg continually described as "national
symbols" of domestic abuse. On January 30,
1989, Steinberg was convicted of a lesser charge,
first-degree manslaughter in the death of Lisa
Steinberg.

Steinberg has consistently refused to admit
his guilt; he denies that either Lisa or Hedda was
abused, claims that Lisa's death was accidental or
that Nussbaum killed her, and proclaims himself
to be "a victim." Yet, no matter how reprehensi-
bly Steinberg behaves, he has largely been overshadowed, particularly among feminists, by the
troubling and controversial figure of Hedda
Nussbaum. In part, this is due to the enormous
media attention; millions watched on live television as the disfigured Nussbaum told her story

of their mutual cocaine abuse, his increasingly
bizarre and torturous beatings over a period of
10 years, her desire to protect and remain loyal
to her batterer, and her overwhelming adoration
of him. This case has opened up debate among
feminists as to the culpability of Nussbaum herself, her moral responsibility in the murder of the
child. After beating Lisa into unconsciousness,
Steinberg went out for three hours. During that
time, Nussbaum did not call for emergency help
because, as she testified, she was afraid such an
action would show disloyalty and distrust to
Joel. When he returned, they freebased cocaine
together and did not call for help until the following morning. Some feminists are now asking,
was Nussbaum victim or collaborator?

Steinberg had used not only physical force
but elaborate psychological manipulation to control Nussbaum. In 1982, Nussbaum lost her editor's job; the battering had caused her to miss
too much work. By 1984, eight years after they
began living together, Nussbaum's physical appearance had deteriorated to such an extent that
she rarely left the apartment. Thus isolated, she
was particularly prey to Steinberg's mind games.
Aided by cocaine, he convinced her that her
friends and family (and eventually even the two
children) were part of a hypnotic cult that was
out to get them. Ironically, of course, the only
cult involved was the cult of one that Steinberg
was forming around himself. She later recalled:
"I loved to listen to him talk. Basically, I wor-
shiped him. He was the most wonderful man I
had ever met. I believed he had supernatural,
godlike power" (Hackett 1988, p. 60). As in
other patriarchal cults and religions, the female
supplicant provides fodder for the pornographic fantasies of the empowered, god-identified
men. Nussbaum recalled: "Many days and
nights, Joel would push me to fantasize about the
cults, about the sexual encounters he said I had
with all these people, and about pornographic
videos I had supposedly made. Joel got me to believe these things happened, but I never had
any recollection of them" (Weiss and Johnson
1989, p. 90).

The battering of Nussbaum's body was
clearly recapitulated in Steinberg's simultaneous
battering and disfigurement of her memory and
mind. That psychological manipulation took
shape not only in the bizarre cult delusion but

also in the quotidian mixed signals he consistently sent to her. Many who have studied or experienced abusive men would agree that such behavior is common, perhaps dramatized most vividly in the show of love and affection that often follows a beating. Indeed, contradictory messages—for example, dress glamorously, but if you are raped, you were asking for it—frequently riddle patriarchal communications. Not insignificantly then, one of the most blatant of such mixed messages can be found in the February 13, 1989 issue of *People Weekly.* The cover itself shows a large photo of an unsmiling and clearly disfigured Nussbaum, flanked by two smaller pictures of Joel and Lisa. Underneath, the copy asks the "haunting question. How could any mother, no matter how battered, fail to help her dying child?" In the story, told by a "close friend," Nussbaum is presented as the largely pathetic victim of a sadistic monster. We are told in great detail of the horrors of Steinberg's abuse:

> Steinberg had kicked her in the eye, strangled her, beaten her sexual organs, urinated on her, hung her in handcuffs from a chinning bar, lacerated a tear duct by poking his finger in the corner of her eye, broken her nose several times and pulled out clumps of hair while throwing her about their apartment. "Sometimes he'd take the blowtorch we used for freebasing and move it around me, making me jump. . . . I have burn marks all over my body from that. Joel told me he did this to improve my coordination." (Weiss and Johnson 1989, pp. 89–90)

This last quote from Nussbaum is reiterated in a blown-up section on the left side of a two-page spread. On the right (p. 91) is an advertisement for Neutrogena soap. It features a large photo of a grinning woman, Cathy Guisewite, cartoonist and creator of the strip "Cathy," as well as a highlighted quote from the woman herself:

> I know all about eating a cheesecake after a bad date. People say, "You know exactly how I feel; I'm so relieved that somebody else sits in the closet and eats a cheesecake after a bad date." I think I verbalize for a lot of women

the anxieties and insecurities we live out every day, like I'll buy anything that will promise me a miracle. But, I've bought the 25-step skin care and it's still in the bottom drawer, because I never have the energy even to get to Step Two. I always go back to Neutrogena Soap, because it's so simple. I mean, I stagger into the bathroom, I wash my face, and I can handle it. It's the one thing I don't have to torture myself about.

In order to understand the mode of communication here, it is useful to borrow a concept from television criticism. Raymond Williams (1974) has described a central characteristic of the television experience to be that of *flow*—that is, TV programs are surrounded by commercials and other programs, an uninterrupted following of one thing by another. One result of this flow is a powerful tendency to blur the contents together, a result encouraged by programmers "so that one program leads effortlessly into the next" (Adler 1976, p. 7). Commercial advertisements that accompany programs also participate in this flow pattern.

Cognizant of this media structure, we might consider the basic message that the juxtaposition of article and ad in *People Weekly* delivers. Key themes in each are torture, feminine insecurities, anxieties, and masochism. We move from a graphic description of the torture of a former successful career woman (Nussbaum) to the smiling confession of egregious self-torture by a current career woman (Guisewite). (We might note that Guisewite's "torture" also can be traced to an "abusive" man, the "bad date" for whom she locked herself in a closet.) Moreover, after reading "Hedda's Story," including its mention of the six times Hedda left Joel Steinberg (the lifelong "bad date") only to return, what can we make of these strategically placed and highly resonant words of Guisewite: *"I never have the energy. . . . I always go back . . . because it's so simple. I mean, I stagger into the bathroom, I wash my face, and I can handle it."*

While Nussbaum's torture by a man she continued to live with is appalling (though fascinating enough to rivet the nation), Guisewite's self-torment is pitched as normal, representative, and smilingly cute. Though the article superficially abhors Nussbaum's battering (all the while describing it in titillating detail), the entire media package subtextually attempts to instill in women the very attitudes (insecurity, masochism, self-abuse) that result from abuse. This is a mixed message par excellence, replicating the typical pattern of the batterer.

The patriarchal construction of female victimization is at the heart of the debate over Nussbaum's collusion. Susan Brownmiller, in a *New York Times* editorial (1989a) as well as an article in *Ms.* (1989b), has argued vehemently that feminists should not support "unquestioningly the behaviors and actions of all battered women. . . . The point of feminism is to give women the courage to exercise free will, not to use the 'brainwashed victim's' excuse to explain away the behavior of a woman who surrenders her free will. Victimhood must no longer be an acceptable or excusable model of female behavior" (1989b, p. 61). She condemns Nussbaum as a "narcissist," "empty at the core" (1989a, p. A19) and finds that she was a "participant in her own and Lisa's destruction" (1989b, p. 61). In some ways, particularly if one assumes the perspective of the abused child, such an argument might be compelling. However, this argument collapses in a number of significant ways. First of all, it takes the burden and the focus off Steinberg; once again, the question centers not on how the man could have done this rape, battery, murder, incest, and so on, but on how the woman could have let him. Second, it seeks the reason for battery in the personality of the woman, in this case her "narcissism," and not in male dominance. Finally, Nussbaum's failure to summon emergency aid for Lisa as she lay unconscious was abusive, but an understanding of that behavior must *first* be sought not in Nussbaum's personality, but in her oppression in the nuclear family and in her status as a torture victim (Russell 1982, pp. 273–285).

In her *Times* editorial, Brownmiller (1989a) deplores what she finds to be a common feminine identification with Nussbaum to be both "simplistic and alarming." She further observes: "Significantly, no man of my acquaintance has felt the need to proclaim that he, but for the grace of God, could have been a Joel Steinberg. Decent, honorable men rushed to put a vast distance between themselves and Lisa's convicted

killer" (p. 19). Yet, in some ways, much of women's vituperation against Nussbaum equally might stem from an identification with her, followed by a horrified denial and distancing. Furthermore, and this is my central point, *of course* men both decent and indecent will rush to disassociate themselves from a man who has been publicly shown up as a batterer and murderer. Prior to his public humiliation, or with fictional representatives of the type, some of those very same men frequently gush with admiration for and identification with the sexual criminal. This male rush to disassociate (especially after the fact) is characteristic of a patriarchal culture in which awareness of institutionalized male supremacy is repressed. Thus, in myriad ways, the culture regularly doublethinks a distance between itself and sexual violence, denying the fundamental *normalcy* of that violence in a male supremacist culture and trying to paint it as the domain of psychopaths and "monsters" only (Cameron and Frazer, 1987; Caputi 1987). The career of sex killer Ted Bundy is especially instructive on this point.

The Boys Next Door

Most men just hate women. Ted Bundy killed them.

—Jimmy McDonough (1984, p. 3)

At some point when I was writing my book, *The Age of Sex Crime* (1987), an analysis of the contemporary phenomenon of serial sex murder, I had a dream that I was back living in the white, middle-class, suburban neighborhood I grew up in and that Ted Bundy had moved in a few houses down. This was but one of several such dreams I had while engaged in the writing. Still it made a deep impression on me. Certainly, it meant that my subject was getting closer and closer to my psyche. But it also was significant that the nightmare figure was Ted Bundy, for Bundy is almost universally hailed as the killer who represented the all-American boy, the boy next door who did not marry but, rather, killed the girl next door.

Ted Bundy committed serial murder, and FBI statistics show that this new type of murder has increased drastically in the United States in the last 20 years. In addition, in 1984, the Justice Department estimated that there were at the very least 35 and possibly as many as 100 such killers roaming the country. Justice Department official Robert O. Heck summed up the general situation:

> We all talk about Jack the Ripper; he killed five people [sic]. We all talk about the "Boston Strangler" who killed 13, and maybe "Son of Sam" who killed six. But we've got people [sic] out there now killing 20 and 30 people and more, and some of them just don't kill. They torture their victims in terrible ways and mutilate them before they kill them. Something's going on out there. It's an epidemic. (Lindsey 1984, p. 7)

Although Heck's statement is superficially correct, his language obscures what actually is going on out there, for the "people" who torture, kill, and mutilate in this way are men, while their victims are characteristically females—women and girls—and to a lesser extent younger males. As this hierarchy indicates, these are crimes of sexually political, essentially *patriarchal,* domination. So hidden is this knowledge, however, that criminologist Steven Egger (1984), after first noting that all known serial killers are male, goes on to observe: "This sexual differentiation may lead researchers to study maleness and its socialization as an etiological consideration. However, the lack of this obvious distinction has apparently precluded such study" (p. 351). Yet most researchers have not yet made that so obvious distinction because to do so would inevitably introduce the issue of sexual politics into sexual murder.

Although sexual force against women is endemic to patriarchy, the twentieth century is marked by a new form of mass gynocide: the mutilation serial sex murder. This "age of sex crime" begins with the crimes of "Jack the Ripper," the still unidentified killer who in 1888 murdered and mutilated five London prostitutes. Patriarchal culture has enshrined "Jack the Ripper" as a mythic hero; he commonly appears as an immortal figure in literature, film, television, jokes, and other cultural products. The function of such mythicization is twofold: to terrorize women and to empower and inspire men.

The unprecedented pattern laid down during the Ripper's original siege is now enacted with some regularity: the single, territorial, and sensationally nicknamed killer; socially powerless and scapegoated victims; some stereotyped feature ascribed in common to the victims (e.g., all coeds, redheads, prostitutes, and so on); a "signature" style of murder or mutilation; intense media involvement; and an accompanying incidence of imitation or "copycat" killings. Ripper-type killers include the "Lipstick Killer," the "Boston Strangler," the "Son of Sam," the "Hillside Strangler," the "Green River Killer," and the "South Side Slayer," to name only a few.

The Ripper myth received renewed attention in 1988, the centennial year of the original crimes. That occasion was celebrated by multiple retellings of the Ripper legend. In England, Ripper paraphernalia, such as a computer game, T-shirts, buttons, and cocktails appeared (Cameron 1988). Retellings included a British-produced massively promoted made-for-TV movie, *Jack the Ripper;* an exploitation thriller, called *Jack's Back,* about a killer of prostitutes in contemporary Los Angeles; and scores of new books on the master killer.

Within months of this anniversary celebration for the mythic father of sexual murder, the focus effortlessly and eerily shifted to a figurative son of that very father—a man who himself was portrayed as a paradigmatic American son, the "handsome," "intelligent," and "charming" Ted Bundy. In 1979, he was convicted of three women's deaths and is suspected of being responsible for perhaps 47 more. Bundy, like "Jack the Ripper," is a sex criminal who has spawned a distinctive legend and been attended by a distinctive revelry. In the days preceding his death, his story dominated the mass media, memorializing and further mythicizing a killer who had already been the subject of scores of articles, five books, and a made-for-TV movie (where he was played by Mark Harmon, an actor whom *People Weekly* once gushed over as the "world's sexiest man"). The atmosphere surrounding his execution was repeatedly described as a "carnival" or "circus." On the morning Bundy went to the electric chair, hundreds (from photographs of the event, the crowd seemed to be composed largely of men) gathered across the street from the prison. Many wore specially designed costumes, waved banners proclaiming a "Bundy BBQ" or "I like my Ted well done," and chanted songs such as "He bludgeoned the poor girls, all over the head. Now we're all ecstatic, Ted Bundy is dead." A common journalistic metaphor for the overall scene was that of a tailgate party before a big game. Indications of a spreading Bundy cult continue to appear: a student group at the University of New Mexico in April 1989 offered a program showing a tape of Bundy's final interview. The poster advertising that event displayed a likeness of the killer under the headline: "A Man with Vision. A Man with Direction. A Prophet of Our Times. . . . Bundy: The Man, The Myth, The Legend."

This sort of spontaneous outpouring of folk sentiment regarding Ted Bundy was not without precedent. In the late 1970s, when he was awaiting trial for the murder of Caryn Campbell in Aspen, Colorado, Bundy managed to escape twice. The first time he was caught and returned to custody; the second time he was successful and traveled to Florida. But upon the news of his escapes (particularly the first) a phenomenal reaction occurred. All observers concur: "In Aspen, Bundy had become a folk hero" (Larsen 1980, p. 182); "Ted achieved the status of Billy the Kid at least" (Rule 1980, p. 255); "Aspen reacted as if Bundy were some sort of Robin Hood instead of a suspected mass murderer. A folklore sprang up out of the thin Rocky Mountain air" (Nordheimer 1978, p. 46). T-shirts appeared reading, "Ted Bundy is a One Night Stand." Radio KSNO programmed a Ted Bundy request hour, playing songs like "Ain't No Way to Treat a Lady." A local restaurant offered a "Bundyburger," consisting of nothing more than a plain roll: "Open it and see the meat has fled," explained a sign. Yet after his second escape, the FBI took Bundy seriously enough to name him to their 10 Most Wanted List, seeking him "in connection with 36 similar-type sexual slayings throughout several Western states."

Just as Bundy's white, young, generally middle-class victims were stereotypically (and with marked racist and classist bias) universalized as "anyone's daughters," Bundy himself was depicted as the fatherland's (almost) ideal son—handsome, intelligent, a former law student, a rising star in Seattle's Republican party. And although that idealization falls apart upon close examination (Bundy's photographs show an ordinary face, and he had to drop out of law school due to bad grades), it provided an attractive persona for purposes of identification. As several feminist analysts (Lacy 1982–83; Millett 1970; Walkowitz 1982) have noted, a recurrent and vivid pattern accompanying episodes of sensationalized sex murder is ordinary male identification with the sex killer, as revealed in "jokes, innuendoes, veiled threats (*I* might be the Strangler, you know)" (Lacy 1982–83, p. 61).

After his first escape, the male identification was with Bundy as an outlaw rebel-hero. But subsequently, Bundy did the supremely unmanly thing of getting caught; moreover, at the last moment he confessed to his crimes and manifested fear of death. No longer qualifying as hero, Bundy was now cast into the alternate role of scapegoat. The "bloodthirsty revelers" outside the prison gates, through their objectification of the victims and lust for death, still mirrored Bundy, but now delightedly demanded that the preeminent patriarchal son die as a token sacrifice for his and their sins.

In the final days before his execution, Bundy spoke directly about his cultural construction as a sex killer, telling James Dobson, a psychologist and religious broadcaster, that since his youth he had been obsessed with pornography. Bundy claimed that pornography inspired him to act out his torture and murder fantasies. Five years earlier, another interviewer (Michaud and Aynesworth 1983) had reported a similar conversation with Bundy:

> He told me that long before there was a need to kill there were juvenile fantasies fed by photos of women in skin magazines, suntan oil advertisements, or jiggly starlets on talk shows. He was transfixed by the sight of women's bodies on provocative display. . . . Crime stories fascinated him. He read pulp detective magazines and gradually developed a store of knowledge about criminal tech-

niques—what worked and what didn't. That learning remained incidental to the central thrill of reading about the abuse of female images, but nonetheless he was schooling himself. (p. 117)

Bundy also spoke for himself (although in the third person since he had not yet decided to openly admit his guilt):

> Maybe he focused on pornography as a vicarious way of experiencing what his peers were experiencing in reality. . . . Then he got sucked into the more sinister doctrines that are implicit in pornography—the use, the abuse, the possession of women as objects. . . . A certain percentage of it [pornography] is devoted toward literature that explores situations where a man, in the context of a sexual encounter, in one way or another engages in some sort of violence toward a woman, or the victim. There are, of course, a whole host of substitutions that could come under that particular heading. Your girlfriend, your wife, a stranger, children —whatever—a whole host of victims are found in this literature. And in this literature, they are treated as victims. (p. 117)

Bundy's self-confessed movement from pornography (reportedly introduced to him at an early age by a grandfather who beat his wife, regularly assaulted other people, and tormented animals) to actual sexual assault is consistent with testimony from other sex offenders, including sex murderers, who claim that viewing pornography affected their criminal behavior (Caputi 1987; Einsiedel 1986).

Diana E. H. Russell (1988) has proposed a theoretical model of the causative role of pornography in violence against women. Russell first distinguishes between pornography and erotica, drawing upon a definition of pornography as "sexually explicit material that represents or describes degrading or abusive sexual behavior so as to endorse and/or recommend the behavior as described" (Longino 1980, p. 44). She defines erotica as "sexual representations premised on equality" (Leidholdt and Russell forthcoming; Russell 1988, p. 46). Using the findings from a range of social research from the past decade,

Russell argues that pornography predisposes or intensifies a predisposition in some men to rape women and that it can undermine some men's internal or social inhibitions against acting out sexually violent behavior. Bundy's testimony clearly supports that model.

Bundy's assertions released a wave of scorn, ridicule, and fury in the mainstream press, with some commentators seemingly more angry at his aspersions on pornography than at his crimes. As one columnist (Leo 1989) fulminated: "As Bundy told it, he was a good, normal fellow, an 'all-American boy' properly raised by diligent parents, though one would have liked to hear more about his 'diligent' mother. While nothing of this mother-son relationship is known, a hatred of women virulent enough to claim 50 lives does not usually spring full-blown from the reading of obscene magazines" (p. 53). Once again, normalcy as well as "maleness and its socialization" are vehemently discarded as an etiological consideration for sexual murder; misogynist myth prevails and the finger of blame is pointed unswervingly at a woman. Since Bundy's execution, an extensive article has appeared in *Vanity Fair;* predictably, it absolves pornography and instead condemns Louise Bundy as responsible for the evolution of her son into a "depraved monster" (MacPherson 1989).

A companion chorus of voices suggests that we cannot take Bundy seriously because Dobson, the fundamentalist crusader, led Bundy to his assertions to further his own agenda. Thus, once again, the feminist connection between violence against women and pornography is potentially discredited by its association with fundamentalism. Yet few feminists would agree with the Right that pornography is the sole or root cause of violence against women. Rather, pornography (as well as its diffusions through mainstream culture) is a modern mode for communicating and constructing patriarchy's necessary fusion of sex and violence, for sexualizing torture. Clearly, that imperative has assumed other forms historically: the political operations of military dictatorships, the enslavement of Africans in the "new world," witch-hunting and inquisitions by the Christian church and state, and so on. The basic elements for a gynocidal campaign—an ideology of male supremacy, a vivid imagination of (particularly female) sexual filth, loathing of eroticism, belief in the sanctity of marriage and the family, and the containment of women in male-controlled institutions—structure fundamentalism's very self-serving opposition to pornography.

Finally, it was claimed that Bundy, a characteristic manipulator, was simply manipulating and lying one last time, trying to absolve himself in his eleventh hour by blaming society. Yet a feminist analysis would not accept the equation that to recognize the responsibility of society for sexually political murder is to absolve the murderer. Rather, it would point to the connection between Bundy and his society, naming Bundy as that society's henchman (albeit, like other sex criminals, a freelancer) in the maintenance of patriarchal order through force. Indeed, we might further recognize Bundy as a martyr for the patriarchal state, one who, after getting caught, had to pay for his fervor, the purity of his misogyny, and his attendant celebrity with his life.

Everyone's Sisters

There was wide public attention in the Ted [Bundy] case . . . because the victims resembled everyone's [sic] daughter. . . . But not everybody relates to prostitution on the Pacific Highway.

—Robert Keppel, member of the Green River Task Force (Starr 1984, p. 106)

The victims were universally described as runaways, prostitutes, or drug addicts who "deserved" to die because of how they lived. The distorted portrayal of the girls and women could be expected in a city notorious for its racism, but there was a particular sexist turn, because the victims were not only Black, but female.

—Barbara Smith (1981, p. 68; on a 1979 series of murders in Boston)

Some of the victims were prostitutes, but perhaps the saddest part of this case is that some were not.

—Sir Michael Havers, prosecuting counsel at the trial of Peter Sutcliffe, the "Yorkshire Ripper" (Holloway 1981, p. 39)

There'd be more response from the police if these were San Marino housewives. . . . If you're Black and living on the fringe, your life isn't worth much.

—Margaret Prescod, founder of the Black Coalition Fighting Back Serial Murders (Uehling 1986, p. 28)

Ted Bundy's victims were young white women and were consistently described in the press as "beautiful" with "long, brown, hair." We can recognize some of this description as a fetishization meant to further eroticize the killings for the public. However, while some highly celebrated killers such as Bundy or David Berkowitz, the "Son of Sam," chose victims on the basis of their correspondence to a pornographic, objectifying, and racist ideal, the majority of victims of serial killers are women who, as Steven Egger (1984) noted, "share common characteristics of what are perceived to be prestigeless, powerless, and/or lower socioeconomic groups" (p. 348), that is, prostitute women, runaways, "street women," women of color, impoverished women, single and elderly women, and so on. The Bundy murders consistently aroused not only a unique folklore and ritual revelry but also a public display of mourning because, in the first place, mainstream men could readily identify with Bundy and also because sexual murder, like rape, is understood as a property crime. A far different societal response is forthcoming when the women killed are not white, not "family women," and not middle class. A pattern of police officials waiting an unreasonable amount of time before organizing a concentrated effort to catch a killer, failing to warn a community, refusing to initiate community involvement, prejudicially labeling victims, and ignoring community input has marked nearly all investigations of the murders of "prestigeless" women (Grant 1988a, 1988b; Jones and Wood 1989; Serrano 1989).

In the "Jack the Ripper" crimes, all of the victims were prostitute women. The killer (or, far more likely, someone pretending to be the killer) wrote to the press a letter that not only originated the famous nickname, but also boasted: "I am down on whores and I shan't quit ripping them until I do get buckled." In the late 1970s, a gynocidal killer was active in northern Britain; the first victims were all prostitute women. Perpetuating the myth of the immortal and recurring sex criminal, the men of the press nicknamed him "the Yorkshire Ripper." As in many cases involving the serial murder of prostitute women, including those of the "Green River Killer," the "South Side Slayer," and a current series of murders of "prestigeless" women in San Diego County, a great deal of controversy has attended police handling, or rather, mishandling, of the case (Serrano 1989). In the wake of that controversy in Yorkshire, the British press has claimed that the major problem that the police faced in the early years of that investigation was "apathy over the killing of prostitutes." Police work, it was declared, depends upon public interest, cooperation, and support; and, as the London *Times* noted, "Such was the apathy at the time that it was virtually nil" (Osman and Ford 1981, p. 5). Ironically, in Yorkshire, such open attitudes of hostility to prostitute women and apathy toward their murders were openly expressed not only by the public but also by the police themselves.

Four years after the first mutilation and murder, the killer had begun to target nonprostitute women, and West Yorkshire's Constable Jim Hobson issued an extraordinary statement as an "anniversary plea" to the killer: "He has made it clear that he hates prostitutes. Many people do. We, as a police force, will continue to arrest prostitutes." Here, Hobson matter-of-factly aligns "Ripper" motives and actions to larger social interests as well as police goals. He goes on, shifting voice to a direct appeal to the killer: "But the Ripper is now killing innocent girls. That indicates your mental state and that you are in urgent need of medical attention. You have made your point. Give yourself up before another innocent woman dies" (Smith 1982, p. 11). From such official statements we learn that it is normal

to hate prostitute women; the killer is even assured of social solidarity in this emotion. His deeds, it seems, only become socially problematic when he turns to so-called innocent girls. Over in the Americas, one consultant on the "Green River Killer" case, psychiatrist John Liebert, offered his expert opinion that serial murderers either idealize women or degrade them, seeing women as "'angels or whores,' with no sensible middle ground" (Berger 1984, p. 1). Once again, we are at an utter loss in distinguishing the point of view of the ostensibly deviant sex killer from that of his pursuers or his society. Moreover, the notion that this distinction has any abiding reality in the sex killer's mind is both erroneous and dangerous.

In the mid-1980s, at least 17 women, characterized by the police as prostitutes, were murdered within a 40 mile radius in South Central Los Angeles, a primarily African-American neighborhood; all but 3 of the victims were African-Americans. The police waited until 10 women were killed before notifying the public that a serial murderer was operating and then waited until there were 4 more deaths before forming a task force. In response to police and media neglect, Margaret Prescod, a longtime public spokeswoman for US PROS (a national network of women who work in the sex industry and their supporters) founded the Black Coalition Fighting Back Serial Murders. Rachel West (1987) notes:

> The Black Coalition has stated again and again that they are not convinced that all the women murdered were prostitutes and that the police have offered little evidence to support that claim. When the police could not dig up a prostitution arrest record on victim 17, they immediately said, "but she was a street woman." This statement reflects the attitude of the police toward poor women generally, especially if they are black. We all know only too well that any of us at any time can be labeled a prostitute woman, if we dare step out of line in the way we speak and dress, in the hours we keep, the number of friends we have, or if we are "sexual outlaws" of any kind. (p. 285)

West further observes that in many other instances of serial murder, the killer might begin with prostitute women, but then moves on to women of all types (as in the "Hillside Strangler" killings). When the police or press describe the murdered women as prostitutes, it lulls nonprostitute women into a false feeling of safety. It plays upon sexist and frequently racist prejudices to mute the seriousness of the murders, and—most effectively—it diverts the blame to the victim.

In October 1888, Charles Warren, police chief in charge of the "Jack the Ripper" case, pontificated to the press: "The police can do nothing as long as the victims unwittingly connive at their own destruction. They take the murderer to some retired spot, and place themselves in such a position that they can be slaughtered without a sound being heard" (Cameron and Frazer 1987, p. 20). That sentiment was echoed, one century later, in a piece in the *Los Angeles Times* (Boxall 1989) titled, "Prostitutes: Easy Prey for Killers." It portrays "drug-dazed" women, good daughters gone bad, and contains a quote from Commander William Booth of the Los Angeles police department: "I think that's the highest-risk occupation there is. Mercenaries are way behind prostitutes. . . . There is nothing that carries the risk with it, in peacetime, as streetwalking prostitution" (p. 1). The same article states: "Police sweeps have greatly reduced streetwalking in Hollywood, police say, leaving the gritty main drags of South-Central the city's streetwalking center. Elsewhere in Los Angeles, prostitution tends to take more sophisticated, expensive and less hazardous forms, such as escort services" (p. 23). Thus we can surmise that police actions have contributed toward creating a more dangerous city for South-Central women; moreover, these women, targeted because of their race and class, are in far greater danger than women in moneyed, white areas. Clearly, the illegality of prostitution and institutionalized harassment by the police contributes to making prostitution such a "high-risk" occupation.

Although, as far as I know, there are no national statistics kept on the number of prostitutes murdered annually, the Los Angeles police claim that there have been 69 murders of prostitute women and 30 women killed in what they call "street murders" in the past four years. Assuredly, those numbers register appalling danger. Yet the Steinberg case might remind us that each year 30 percent of all women murdered are killed by their husbands and lovers, about 1,500 women per year (*Uniform Crime Reports,* 1987, p. 11), and that *at least* 1.8 million women are beaten by husbands and lovers annually (Summers 1989, p. 54). Despite blandishments directed toward stereotypical "angels" and "good girls," wifehood seems to rank right up there with prostitution as an endemically unsafe occupation. Faced with such statistics, the invidious distinctions collapse, and we realize with Rachel West (1987) that "the rights of prostitute women are the rights of all women" (p. 285).

As I worked on the conclusion to this piece, I listened to a National Public Radio news program ("Morning Edition," June 7, 1989) reporting that nine women (all of whom were described as prostitutes or drug addicts) had been murdered in the past year in New Bedford, Massachusetts, the site of a notorious gang rape (Chancer 1987). Two other women have been missing for months. A serial killer is suspected; "apathy" is said to be the primary response of the mainstream New Bedford community. Obviously, we have heard this story before. Yet the ascription of "apathy," so common in such cases, is really quite misleading. The reigning, though denied, mood is *hatred,* sexually political hatred. A "hate crime" is conventionally defined as "any assault, intimidation or harassment that is due to the victim's race, religion or ethnic background" (Malcolm 1989, p. A12). That definition obviously must be expanded to include gender (as well as sexual preference). Vast numbers of women are now suffering and dying from various forms of hate crime worldwide, including neglect, infanticide, genital mutilation, battering, rape, and murder. What men might call "peacetime," researcher Lori Heise (1989) truthfully names a "global war on women."

Note

1. Part of this section previously appeared in my review of Susan Brownmiller's *Waverly Place* (Caputi 1989).

References

Adler, Richard. 1976. "Introduction." Pp. 1–16 in *Television as a Cultural Force,* edited by Richard Adler and Douglas Cater. New York: Praeger.

Albuquerque Tribune. 1984. "Blood Trail Ends: Brother Says He's Glad Wilder's Killing Is Over." (April 14):2.

Berger, Joseph. 1984. "Traits Shared by Mass Killers Remain Unknown to Experts." *New York Times* (August 27):1.

Boxall, Bettina. 1989. "Prostitutes: Easy Prey for Killers." *Los Angeles Times* (March 21):1, 23. Copyright 1989, *Los Angeles Times.* Reprinted by permission.

Brownmiller, Susan. 1975. *Against Our Will: Men, Women, and Rape.* New York: Simon & Schuster.

———. 1989a. "Hedda Nussbaum: Hardly a Heroine." *New York Times* (February 2):A19.

———. 1989b. "Madly in Love." *Ms.* (April):56–61.

Cameron, Debbie. 1988. "That's Entertainment? Jack the Ripper and the Celebration of Sexual Violence." *Trouble and Strife* 13:17–19.

Cameron, Deborah and Elizabeth Frazer. 1987. *The Lust to Kill: A Feminist Investigation of Sexual Murder.* New York: New York University Press.

Caputi, Jane. 1987. *The Age of Sex Crime.* Bowling Green, OH: Bowling Green State University Press.

Caputi, Jane. 1989. Review of *Waverly Place.* "Stranger than Fiction." *Women's Review of Books* 6(May):10–11.

Chancer, Lynn S. 1987. "New Bedford, Massachusetts, March 6, 1983–March 22, 1984: The 'Before and After' of a Group Rape." *Gender & Society* 1:239–60.

Daly, Mary. 1973. *Beyond God the Father: Toward a Philosophy of Women's Liberation.* Boston: Beacon Press.

Dworkin, Andrea. 1981. *Pornography: Men Possessing Women.* New York: Perigee.

Egger, Steven A. 1984. "A Working Definition of Serial Murder and the Reduction of Linkage Blindness." *Journal of Police Science and Administration* 12:348–57.

Einsiedel, E. F. 1986. "Social Science Report." Prepared for the Attorney General's Commission on Pornography, U.S. Department of Justice, Washington, DC.

Grant, Jaime M. 1988a. "Who's Killing Us? Part One." *Sojourner: The Women's Forum* (June):20–21.

———. 1988b. "Who's Killing Us? Part Two." *Sojourner: The Women's Forum* (July):16–18.

Griffin, Susan. 1983. "Rape: The All-American Crime." Pp. 39–58 in *Made from the Earth: An Anthology of Writings.* New York: Harper & Row.

Gross, Ken. 1989 "Denying His Guilt. Joel Steinberg Tells How He Cared for the Child He Killed and the Lover He Beat." *People Weekly* (March 13):72.

Hackett, George. 1989. "A Tale of Abuse." *Newsweek* (December 12):60.

Heise, Lori. 1989. "The Global War Against Women." *Washington Post* (April 9): Sec. B, p. 1.

Holloway, Wendy. 1981. "'I Just Wanted to Kill a Woman' Why": The Ripper and Male Sexuality." *Feminist Review* 9:33–40.

Jones, Jack and Tracy Wood. 1989. "Sheriff's Deputy Held in Prostitute's Killings." *Los Angeles Times* (February 25):1.

Lacy, Suzanne. 1982–83. "In Mourning and in Rage (with Analysis Aforethought)." *Ikon* (Fall/Winter):60–67.

Lamar, Jacob V., Jr. 1989. "'I Deserve Punishment.'" *Time* (February 6):34.

Larsen, Richard W. 1980. *Bundy: The Deliberate Stranger.* Englewood Cliffs, NJ: Prentice-Hall.

Leidholdt, Dorchen and Diana E. H. Russell (eds.) Forthcoming. *No Safe Place for Women: Feminists on Pornography.* Oxford: Pergamon.

Leo, John. 1989. "Crime: That's Entertainment." *U.S. News & World Report* (February 6):53.

Lindsey, Robert. 1984. "Officials Cite Rise in Killers Who Roam U.S. for Victims." *New York Times* (January 21):1.

Longino, Helen E. (1980). "What Is Pornography." Pp. 40–54 in *Take Back the Night,* edited by Laura Lederer. New York: William Morrow.

McDonough, Jimmy. 1984. "I Can Teach You How to Read the Book of Life." *Bill Landis' Sleazoid Express* 3 (No. 7):3–5.

MacKinnon, Catharine A. 1982a. Feminism, Marxism, Method, and the State: An Agenda for Theory. *Signs: Journal of Women in Culture and Society* 7:515–44.

———. 1982b. "Toward Feminist Jurisprudence." *Stanford Law Review* 34:703–37.

MacPherson, Myra. 1989. "The Roots of Evil." *Vanity Fair* (May):140–48, 188–98.

Malcolm, Andrew. 1989. "New Efforts Developing against the Hate Crime." *New York Times* (May 12):A12.

Michaud, Stephen G. and Hugh Aynesworth. 1983. *The Only Living Witness.* New York: Linden Press.

Millett, Kate. 1970. *Sexual Politics.* Garden City, NY: Doubleday.

Morgan, Robin. 1989. *The Demon Lover: On the Sexuality of Terrorism.* New York: W. W. Norton.

Nordheimer, Jon. 1978. "All-American Boy on Trial." *New York Times Magazine* (December 10):46 ff.

Osman, Arthur and Richard Ford. 1981. "Lost Chances, Bad Luck and Malice of the Tapes Foiled Untiring Search." *The Times* (May 23):5.

Overend, William and Tracy Wood. 1989. "Deputy 'Devastated' by Arrest in Probe of Prostitute Deaths." *Los Angeles Times* (February 26):CC1, 5.

Rule, Ann. 1980. *The Stranger Beside Me.* New York: New American Library.

Russell, Diana E. H. 1975. *The Politics of Rape: The Victim's Perspective.* New York: Stein and Day.

———. 1982. *Rape in Marriage.* New York: Macmillan.

———. 1988. "Pornography and Rape: A Causal Model." *Political Psychology* 9:41–73.

Serrano, Richard A. 1989. "S. D. Serial-killer Probe Mimics 'Error' Pattern of Green River Slayings." *Los Angeles Times* (San Diego County) (February 26): Part II, 1.

Smith, Barbara. 1981. "Introduction to 'Twelve Black Women: Why Did They Die?'" Pp. 68–69 in *Fight Back! Feminist Resistance to Male Violence,* edited by Frédérique Delacoste and Felice Newman. Minneapolis, MN: Cleis Press.

Smith, Joan. 1982. "Getting Away with Murder." *New Socialist* (May/June):10–12.

Starr, Mark. 1984. "The Random Killers." *Newsweek* (November 26): 106.

Summers, Anne. 1989. "The Hedda Conundrum." *Ms.* (April):54.

Uniform Crime Reports. 1987. FBI, U.S. Department of Justice.

Uehling, Mark D. 1986. "The LA Slayer." *Newsweek* (June 9):28.

Walkowitz, Judith R. 1982. "Jack the Ripper and the Myth of Male Violence." *Feminist Studies* 8:543–74.

Weiss, Naomi with Bonnie Johnson. 1989. "A Love Betrayed: A Brief Life Lost." *People Weekly* (February 13):89–90

West, Rachel. 1987. "US PROStitutes Collective." Pp. 279–89 in *Sex Work: Writings by Women in the Sex Industry,* edited by Frédérique Delacoste and Priscilla Alexander. Pittsburgh, PA: Cleis Press.

Williams, Raymond. 1974. *Television: Technology and Cultural Form.* Glasgow: Fontana/Collins.

Part III: CULTURE: VIOLENCE AND VALUES

In Part III, we see how violence can occur as an expression of support for cultural values. It is somewhat simplistic to argue that America is violent because it has violent values. Instead, we find a willingness to use violence *in defense of values.* Thus, formal and informal mechanisms of social control express support for cultural values through violent means. Clearly, the law is violent; we see this in the criminal justice process from arrest, to imprisonment, to the death penalty. But the process is more complicated than this. Both law and custom legitimate violent responses to norm violations, not only by law-enforcement officials, but by citizens. In other words, the legal establishment, in many ways, legitimates the use of violence by citizens in the defense of cultural norms and values. From "righteous slaughter" to justifiable homicide under Texas law to vigilantism in the Old South, we see how violence in the defense of social order is supported by both law and custom.

In the first chapter in this section, Jack Katz describes how the moral justification for murder resides in the core values of cultural traditions the murderer sees himself or herself as defending in the act itself. Thus, the crying baby is perceived by the father to be defying his authority *at the time of the murder.* Katz's framework helps us to understand many different forms of extreme violence in America today. In a world that supports hypermasculine views of male identity, the "righteous" nature of violence against gay men, from the perspective of the young homophobic male assailant, may result in symbolic acts of mutilation of the victim. When love is defined as a form of "possession," figuratively and literally, betrayal by the lover may lead to homicide as an expression of outrage against the "theft" of the heart and soul of the perpetrator.

The second chapter in this section provides excerpts from anthropologist Henry Lundsgaarde's classic study of the legal and moral justifications for homicide in Texas. In Lundsgaarde's study of murder in "Space City" (Houston), we find an intimate relationship between law and custom in the regulation of homicide. Lundsgaarde reports that "fewer than 50% of the suspects were negatively sanctioned for their acts" in a state that has a record for one of the highest homicide rates in the country and a city that executes more individuals than any other in the nation.

The third chapter in this section, "Crime as Social Control," represents a paradigm shift in our understanding of the role of violence in contemporary society. Donald Black helps us to understand that traditional forms of "self-help" in response to a grievance often take the form of direct acts of aggression against persons or property. Until the publication of Black's article in the *American Sociological Review* in 1983, most criminologists assumed that legal norms had replaced customary forms of social control. Thus, aggressive retaliation for some perceived wrong in defense of personal integrity or destruction of property, in the form of an assault or vandalism, would itself be labeled as a crime. Yet, as Black points out, many acts that are prohibited by law are still supported by traditional values and norms in contemporary society. This theoretical stance helps us to understand the cultural origins of the homicides described in the earlier chapters in this section. To understand the production of violence in contemporary society, we must understand how both law and custom simultaneously encourage and prohibit acts of violence. The murderer who kills his wife's lover may find justification in patriarchal cultural traditions and the laws that support them. At the same time, the premeditated nature of the act may lead to a first-degree murder conviction and, depending on the state, execution by lethal injection.

Nowhere are the points Black makes in the above reading made more cogent than in the Preface to historian Bertram Wyatt-Brown's book, *Honor and Violence in the Old South.* The traditional code of honor in the pre–Civil War South provided "rituals, and even deeds of personal and collective violence" in defense of that code. In this excerpt, we see how violence was essential to the maintenance of slavery and the "humiliation of black people" contributed to the power and prestige of white slaveholders in the Old South. The additional value of this short piece is in the way Wyatt-Brown describes the connection between the slaveholding culture and the rituals of violence that supported that culture.

7

Righteous Slaughter

Jack Katz

What is the killer trying to do in a typical homicide? How does he understand himself, his victim, and the scene at the fatal moment? With what sense and in what sensuality is he compelled to act?

Defining the Problem

Aside from deaths from automobile accidents and murders committed in the course of robberies and other predatory crimes, the modal criminal homicide[1] is an impassioned attempt to perform a sacrifice to embody one or another version of the "Good." When people kill in a moralistic rage, their perspective often seems foolish or incomprehensible to us, and, indeed, it often seems that way to them soon after the killing. But if we stick to the details of the event, we can see offenders defending the Good, even in what initially appear to be crazy circumstances.[2]

To press the point with an extreme example, consider this killing through beating of a 5-week-old infant:

> The victim . . . started crying early in the morning. The offender, the boy's father, ordered the victim to stop crying. The victim's crying, however, only heightened in intensity. The . . . persistent crying may have been oriented not toward challenging his father's authority, but toward acquiring food or a change of diapers. Whatever the motive for crying, the child's father defined it as purposive and offensive.[3]

This scene differed only in degree from everyday, routine events. It is not unusual for parents to demand respect from children and to respond to defiance with beatings. Nor is it unusual to misinterpret an infant's motives. Parents differ widely in the abilities and comprehension that they attribute to children of various ages.[4]

The father just described may have been crazy in some sense but if he was, presumably he had been crazy for some time before he killed; his craziness would not seem to explain the event. Within the situation of the homicide, whatever insanity haunted him was morally shaped. It appears that he did not kill in the course of doing something conventionally considered bad, such as sexually abusing the child, robbing a third party, or sadistically celebrating violence. He did not suddenly explode and kill while irrationally flailing about. Nor was he simply trying to remove an irritation; a more expedient course would have been to put the child out the door, throw him out the window, or abandon him. When parents beat their children, much less kill them, they are using, at best, an indirect, cumbersome way of ridding themselves of the problems the children are causing.

The interpretation that the father defined the crying as defiant and enacted his violence to honor parental authority, is based on few facts. The interpretation becomes more convincing as a way of understanding such events if it is examined in the context of a wide variety of other cases. Thus, it helps to note that in 112 cases of homicides of children in New York, the assailants were primarily parents (especially mothers), and the means of killing were kickings and beatings—extensions of ordinary means of enforcing parental discipline.[5]

Now consider a classic case of homicide caused by sexual jealousy from Henry Lundsgaarde's study of cases in Houston in 1969. For reasons to be explained, I have not removed what may be sensational details, even though the police may have encouraged the surviving seductress, Mrs. Jones, to spice up the account.

> Last night . . . I called Russell at his home. . . . to ask if I could borrow some money from him to pay the rent and the utilities. . . . I guess it was about five minutes to midnight when he got to my house. . . . We were just standing there talking about different things and the troubles me and Jones were having. . . . Russell made some remark about my husband being down at some joint watching the go-go girls. . . . Russell said that I was going to be the talk of the neighborhood because I was standing out front talking to a bachelor. . . . We got in the car. . . . Russell teased me about how my hair looked and he kissed me a few times and then I kissed him back a few times. I kidded him about wrinkling his white shirt and he said that he wasn't worried about his shirt and that it was his tight black pants that were bothering him. . . . I told him to let me see and I felt and he had an erection. This is when he pulled his pants down. . . . [and] told me "It's too late to send me home now!" He reached over and kissed me. About this time I looked over Russell's shoulder and saw my husband. He had a gun. . . . and then Russell said "now listen Jones" or "Wait Jones" and this is when my husband shot him. . . . [I] looked into the car and saw Russell. He was bleeding real bad from the back of his head and he vomited. . . . I grabbed a wet towel from the bathroom and went back to the car and started to wipe stuff off of Russell's face and then I put the rag behind his head. About this time the police arrived and I went back into the house to quiet my children. I told my son to keep the other children in the bedroom.[6]

According to the police, all the participants had been good friends. Mrs. Jones and Russell had been having an affair for two years. Mrs. Jones had suggested divorce to her husband but had not pressed the matter. Mr. Jones had suspected the two and had tried to surprise them in the act. The grand jury refused to bring charges against him. Technically—that is, according to its

official treatment—this homicide was not a crime.

Nor was Francine Hughes judged guilty for the highly publicized killing of her spouse, James. James had frequently beaten her, partly because of his violent opposition to her effort to become independent through education. The day of the killing, Francine's 12-year-old daughter called the police while James was beating Francine, but the police did not arrest him. Francine packed to move out, a decision that had the moral support of her children, and then poured gasoline around the bed in which James had fallen asleep, lit the gas, and drove straight to the sheriff's office to make a hysterical confession. The fact that James was asleep when the fire was set made a finding of self-defense difficult. Instead, the jury found Francine temporarily insane because of James's long-term abuse of her. (There was no indication of a belief in her continuing insanity. Francine was freed soon after the administration of psychological tests.)

Both spouse slayings illustrate that the killer's frequently "self-righteous" attitude (a term used by Lundsgaarde) is not necessarily idiosyncratic. Francine had been repeatedly beaten by James for almost fifteen years. On the day of the murder, she had more at stake than the recurrent issue of physical self-defense. A welfare mother, she had enrolled in business college some months before, and James was now prohibiting her effort to improve herself. The version of the Good she was defending was not simply the right to physical self-defense. It was also a version of the American dream that is widely accepted among people of all political persuasions: to better yourself through education and to escape the welfare rolls by applying yourself to serve business. And although the reaction was not universally favorable, her killing of James was considered righteous and as deserving profound respect by some of the national news commentaries on her case and in the tone of a nationally broadcast television drama.[7]

Likewise, Mr. Jones's killing of Russell was not considered wrong, nor was his Texas grand jury idiosyncratic in understanding that he was upholding the traditional sanctity of the marital union. The defense of *flagrante delicto* has been acceptable for centuries in many societies. If

Mr. Jones and Francine Hughes both experienced an exceptional moment of temporary insanity, they were rational in claiming that their irrationality would be understood by others as righteously inspired.

The presence of children at the scene of the homicide—close to Russell's erotic behavior with Mrs. Jones and as witnesses to James Hughes's beatings of Francine—is also morally significant. Accounts of homicides of spouses often show the killer postured as a defender of the children's moral sensibilities. The following account, from a Canadian study, is taken largely from the husband's construction of the event:

> About two weeks prior to the homicidal act . . . the wife openly told John that he was not wanted anymore and she wanted him to leave home. John begged her to do something and save the marriage for the sake of the children but the wife refused to discuss the matter further. Then John was so upset that he bought a rifle, intending to commit suicide. Just three days prior to the homicide John's wife left home for a lover. . . . When this happened John was crushed emotionally and was looking for ways to hurt himself. . . . After three days (and on Mother's Day) the wife returned home to take the children and go away again. John begged her not to do such a thing to the children but she ignored him. During this argument the children became upset and started crying. Then John turned to his wife and told her what was she doing to the children [sic]. When the wife replied that she "didn't give a damn about the children," John grabbed a knife and stabbed her to death.[8]

The next case of homicide growing out of erotic passions illustrates a different notion of killing in defense of the Good. According to the killer's statement to the police, he and his wife were engaged in sex when she repeatedly called out the name of a fellow he knew to be a former boyfriend. He brought his sexual act to a climax and then shot her. The couple's twin 3-year-old daughters were present.[9]

What is striking in this case is not only the form of the humiliation—the wife's mention of the boyfriend's name is reminiscent of a classic genre of crude jokes—but the husband's claim that he first finished the sex act. On hearing the other fellow's name, he might have lost the will to go on. Attentive to the double entendre, insisting that he would "fuck" her sexually-literally and violently-figuratively, he was transcending the challenge to his virility. Although the legal system was not sympathetic—he was given a life sentence—the killer could consider his act as upholding part of an eternally recognized Good.

The first two killings that were described were among whites, the last was among blacks, and the next occurred in a Mexican-American community. The killer, aged 35, was at home when several people came over to visit his neighbor. One visitor, the neighbor's uncle, aged 50, parked in front of the killer's driveway. After an initial request, the visitor moved his car, but later he again blocked the driveway. The killer, carrying a loaded shotgun, told the visitor that he would kill him if he did not remove his car. The visitor was unarmed and made no response, but he held his ground; then the killer shot him.[10]

In this instance, the killing was formally in defense of property rights, another value that a killer may regard, at the crucial time, as eternal and obviously righteous. In defending his right to control the use of his property, a killer can sense himself upholding the institution of property rights in general. As crazy or foolish as such an incident may appear, it is essential to note that such craziness or foolishness does not occur randomly; the violence erupts in situations that put at stake what the people involved momentarily regard as dimensions of the eternal Good.

That homicidal acts occur in defense of the Good is highlighted by the materially petty, "inconsequential" nature of the conflicts. In the following case, the killer and the victim were black male friends in their twenties. While in a cafe late one Saturday evening, the victim, who had a reputation as a "tough," began picking barbecued food from the killer's plate. The killer complained, but the victim persisted, defiantly splashing hot sauce on the killer. When the fight escalated, the killer pulled out his knife.[11]

To call such fights "childish" may highlight their pathos. But this struggle to control personal property is naturally sensible to all witnesses. Here the killer could expect bystanders to support the defense of his rights, particularly because the victim's reputation as a troublemaker made the issue a community cause.

It is tempting to discount as superficial the claim that such incidents are motivated by morality. There *is* something artificial about the moral explanation. As Peter D. Chimbos noted, in his study of homicides of spouses:

A common technique in arguments is to refer to old grievances or conflicts no longer relevant except as weapons to argue with. . . . Another typical technique is to attack the spouse's deviations from the culturally approved sex role ideal. . . . For example, a wife may accuse her husband of being a poor breadwinner or an incompetent lover. Similarly, a husband may accuse his wife of being "bitchy," "frigid" or promiscuous. Insinuations that the spouse is not a good mother or father to the children are commonly made.[12]

We are accustomed to think that, surely, these people are not *really* killing because they regard a piece of food or a blocked driveway as so important. But it is essential not to overlook the moral form of common homicide. This form does not explain (much less justify) the killing, but it defines the killer's experience and thus sets up the problem so it can be explained.

Frequently, both the killer and the victim agree that "the Good" is at stake, as is illustrated in the following account of a wife's murder of her husband:

A woman, a 35-year-old Black female, had gone to a local cafe to get her husband to come home. . . . She apparently yelled that she was tired of seeing her husband fooling with "them whores" in the cafe and he was overheard to shout that she should remove her eyeglasses. They fought on the sidewalk and during the fight the woman took a .22 caliber pistol from her purse and fired. A witness said that the man tried to raise himself after the first shot had been fired and that the woman then shot him once more. . . . Homicide detectives were able to interview the husband before he died and he stated that he was willing to prosecute the person who had shot him but that he didn't know who had done it![13]

It is not uncommon for victims to refuse to prosecute assailants who are lovers or family members. In this case, the wife was defending the traditional rights of her status. As he was dying, the husband seemed to concede that his wife had a right to shoot him.

Of course, these accounts only sketch the participants at the crucial moments. But it is striking that a "righteous" posture fits such a wide variety of the best sketches available in research on homicide. Consider one final example—a killing recounted by the 15-year-old daughter of the couple involved:

This morning my mother told my stepfather that she was going to cash a check. He told her that he was going to cash the check to pay the car note. Mother told him that he could not pay the car note this week because he had other bills to pay. Mother was sitting on the footstool in the living room reading the paper. My stepfather was sitting in another chair in the same room. He got up and went into the bedroom and got the gun off the bookcase at the head of the bed. He told mother he was tired of this goddamn shit and he said that when he had the gun in his hand. He put the gun in his pocket. Mother told him, "That is what I wanted you to do. Now that you have got the gun, use it!" She told me to go gather up the clothes for the laundry. I left the room and went to get the clothes. I heard three shots. I ran back into the room to see what had happened. My stepfather told me that he had killed my mother and for me to go and call the police.[14]

In many important senses, this killing was not about who would pay which bill; other, more fundamental, sources of tension must have been at work. But in an initially important sense, the fatal fight was literally over which bill would be paid first. In *form,* both the husband and the wife were trying to position themselves to appear to be good people to the world, to creditors—to outsiders—who would think better of them if they paid their bills. Each was trying to defend the Good, not an idiosyncratic value.

One feature of the typical homicide, then, is its character as a self-righteous act undertaken within the form of defending communal values.

The next feature is its lack of premeditation. From a law-enforcement perspective, homicides are relatively easy to solve. The police believe they have grounds to make arrests in from 75 to 90 percent of their homicide cases, compared to perhaps 25 percent of their robbery cases and 15 percent or fewer of their burglary cases.[15] The lack of premeditation in the typical homicide is suggested by the number of killers who make no attempt to escape and wait for the police[16] and by the rapidity with which police "solve" the crime. As Marvin Wolfgang reported in his classic Philadelphia study, "Two-thirds of the offenders in criminal homicide who were taken into custody by the police were arrested on the same day they committed the crime."[17] Even when the offenders run away, their simple and unsuccessful "escapes" indicate that they had not realized that they would become killers until they did.[18]

These homicides are not morally self-conscious acts on the order of calculated political assassinations or coldly executed acts of vengeance. They emerge quickly, are fiercely impassioned, and are conducted with an indifference to the legal consequences. Thus, the second feature of this form of homicide is that the attacks are conducted within the spirit of a quickly developing rage. In addition to explaining how one could come to see one's attack as a defense of the Good, then, I must explain how one becomes enraged.

The third notable feature of these homicidal attacks, which points to a third explanatory task, is suggested by the arbitrary relationship between what the assailants are attempting to do and their practical results. As many researchers have noted, criminal homicides that are not part of a robbery are substantially similar to assaults. It is artificial to take a "killing" as the act to be explained. What the nonpredatory assailant is attempting to do is more accurately captured by the concept of sacrifice: the marking of a victim in ways that will reconsecrate the assailant as Good. The victim's *death* is neither a *necessary* nor a *sufficient* element of the assailant's animating project.

Thus, I arrive at a definition of the problem to be explained as "righteously enraged slaughter," or an impassioned attack through which the assailant attempts to embody in his victim marks that will eternally attest to the assailant's embrace of a primordial Good. The explanation I propose is in three parts:

1. The would-be-killer must interpret the scene and the behavior of the victim in a particular way. He must understand not only that the victim is attacking what he, the killer, regards as an eternal human value, but that the situation requires a last stand in defense of his basic worth.

2. The would-be-killer must undergo a particular emotional process. He must transform what he initially senses as an eternally humiliating situation into a rage. In rage, the killer can blind himself to his future, forging a momentary sense of eternal unity with the Good.

3. The would-be-killer must successfully organize his behavior to maintain the required perspective and emotional posture while implementing a particular project. The project is the honoring of the offense that he suffered through a marking violently drawn into the body of the victim. Death may or may not result, but when it does, it comes as a sacrificial slaughter.

Respectability's Last Stand

The impassioned killers described here were upholding the respected social statuses of husband, mother, wife, father, property owner, virile male, deserving poor/self-improving welfare mother, and responsible debtor. These killers were defending both the morality of the social system and a personal claim of moral worth.

Several patterns in homicide situations indicate that the killers develop a righteous passion against the background of taking a last stand in defense of respectability. First, the behavior of their victims gives them reason to believe that they will no longer be able to ignore a fundamental challenge. David Luckenbill constructed narrative accounts from information in the official files of 71 transactions that culminated in murder in an urban California county over a ten-year period. He found that the roles played by the victims and killers often reversed from the beginning to the end of the event.[19] A study of 159 cases of criminal homicide and assault that were not related to other offenses found that "in most cases, most of the victim's actions were aggressive, indicating that they, [sic] at least partially caused the outcome."[20] This was the most recent in a long line of studies that have provided evidence, in one manner or another, of precipitation by the victims.[21]

Precipitation by victims usually is physical, but the significance of the victim's attack is moral as well. At a minimum, the studies on this phenomenon indicate, in a high percentage of cases, that the person who turns out to be the victim was not trying to escape. To the (eventual) killer, the (eventual) victim, by not trying to brush off or avoid the conflict, is indicating that neither party may escape the implications of what is to transpire.

Thus, in each of the killings described earlier, it may be noted that there were indications that the victim either teased or dared the killer to resolve the conflict. The lurid police account depicts Mrs. Jones teasing her husband to resolve the ambiguous status of their marriage by the openness of her two-year relationship with Mr. Jones's friend Russell; at the fatal moment she and Russell were in a car in front of her house.[22] In the infanticide, the baby was, in the killer's eyes, defying parental orders by persistently crying. In the erotically inspired spouse killing, the killer's wife unwittingly teased him during sex by repeatedly calling out the name of an old boyfriend. In the shotgun, "property rights" killing, the victim, when warned by the killer that he would be shot if he did not clear the driveway, said nothing but held his ground. In the fight in the cafe, the victim teased the killer by "borrowing" his food to the point of daring him to do something about it. In the penultimate case reported here, the husband-victim agreed to fight, telling his wife to take off her glasses. And in the last case in this series, a couple fought over who would pay which bill, and the wife-victim, seeing her husband threaten her with a gun, urged him to use it.

Even the Francine Hughes case, with its strong theme of physical self-defense, involved a dare on other issues in conflict. When Francine Hughes set her sleeping husband on fire, she was reacting to his destruction of her school materials and to his prohibition of her return to school, in essence daring her to defy him and to escape degradation.

From the killer's perspective, the victim either teases, dares, defies, or pursues the killer. In all cases, the victim sustains a sense in the killer-to-be that there is no escape from the issue at hand. In the last case, the wife's urging was not necessarily a narrow demand that her husband kill her, but a means of expressing that she, too, felt that the situation was too awful to bear and that something had to be done immediately to resolve the conflict. Most generally, in all these incidents (except that of the infant), the victim could have tried to escape but did not. That the victims did not try to escape physically indicated to the would-be assailants that they could not escape morally.[23]

That the killer feels compelled to respond to a fundamental challenge to his worth is indicated as well by the frequent presence and the role of an audience. We might expect that homicides would typically occur in private or in circumstances that would give the killer reason not to worry about witnesses. But in the majority of the cases he studied, Luckenbill found that an audience was present, either supporting the violence—urging the combatants on, pointing out an offense, or supplying a weapon—or observing.[24] In no case did the audience oppose or attempt to defuse the situation. When a potentially humiliating conflict occurs in public, an insulted party has grounds to take for granted that he or she cannot simply walk away from the challenge, especially when others are offering such comments as, "Did you hear what he said about you?"; "Are you going to take that?"; and "Here, use this." In any case when bystanders are present, a potential assailant is apt to realize that the audience may develop and carry away its own version of the scene, staining the assailant's reputation beyond any visible limit. What is happening "now," the would-be assailant senses, will determine my identity "then," in the open-ended future. Thus, the killer acts not to affect the image he will have at any envisioned time or place but to escape the premonition of an unbearable "then."

From Humiliation to Rage

When people sense that they have no resort but to confront a challenge to their ultimate personal worth, they need not respond with a violent attack. A common alternative is to turn the challenge against the self and endure humiliation. Transforming humiliation into rage is a second contingency of righteous slaughter.[25]

As with emotions in general, persons who become enraged must create the sensuality that makes them its vehicle. Thus, the analyst must account for a dialectical process in which assailants make themselves the object of forces beyond their control but retain the possibility of abandoning the process.

The situations from which righteous slaughters emerge are either conventionally humiliating, or involve the victim's self-conscious efforts to ridicule or degrade, or include the assailant's perception that the victim's actions are defiant and disrespectful. In some cases, however, the assailant's rage emerges so suddenly and silently that only when it appears does a preceding experience of humiliation become visible. The challenge here is posed not by a lack of evidence but by the subtlety of the phenomenon. Frequently, the assailant does not acknowledge the humiliation to himself until he attempts to transcend it in rage.

Thus, mortal assaults often arise directly from attempts by the killer to deflect the insult with an air of indifference or cool superiority, which is abandoned only in the attack itself. Anger, he realizes, is a concession. That is, the would-be-assailant often anticipates that if he should respond with a display of anger, he would retrospectively acknowledge that the attempted insults of the victim had hit home and that beneath his pretense, he had been on the edge of humiliation. This acknowledgment may itself be humiliating.

When the assailant suddenly drops his air of indifference, he embraces and creates his own humiliation. He then makes public his understanding, not only that he was hurt by the victim, but that he was falsely, foolishly, and cowardly *pretending* not to care. In this double respect, the once-cool but now enraged attacker acknowledges that he has already been *morally* dominated just as he moves to seek *physical* domination. He becomes humiliated at the same time and through the same action in which he becomes enraged.

That humiliation may be constituted in juxtaposition to a simultaneously constituted rage has an important implication for empirical theory. In order to analyze the move from humiliation to rage, we must simultaneously analyze the construction of humiliation *in* rage. That is, we should not err by treating rage as an escape from humiliation. There is an essential link between rage and humiliation. As a lived experience, rage is livid with the awareness of humiliation.

Rage constructs and transforms humiliation so quickly and smoothly that talking and writing about the process can very easily become artificial and obfuscating. In order not to lose sight of the phenomenon, the best approach is to take the rapid and smooth quality of the dynamic as a focus for this analysis.

It is not always easy to move from certain emotional states to certain others, for example to go from sadness to laughter. Humiliation and rage are as opposite as emotions can be, but the switch can be made quickly. How can that be? And how does rage propose to resolve the problems experienced in and through humiliation? How does rage simultaneously recall and transform the experience of humiliation? What is the logic of rage, such that it can grow so smoothly and quickly from humiliation and lead to righteous slaughter as its perfectly sensible (if only momentarily convincing) end?

These questions may appear a bit odd because the process seems so automatic. But it is contingent: not all who experience humiliation become enraged. Moreover, the experience is a personal construction. Although the assailant typically does not perceive himself as having chosen to become humiliated and enraged— although he believes that he was forced into humiliation and carried away by rage—we can unravel the process by which the assailant constructs the sense of logically smooth coherence in the transition from one state of compulsion to another.

The argument is threefold: (1) As experiences, rage and humiliation have certain identical fundamental features. (2) Like images in a mirror, rage and humiliation inversely reflect each other. (3) Righteousness is not the product of rage; it is the essential stepping stone from humiliation to rage. Like a person who passes in front of a cracked mirror and recognizes a reversed and flawed depiction of himself, the would-be assailant needs only the most fleeting encounter with the principle of moral reflection to move from humiliation to rage. The "righteous" thrust of the resulting attack does not develop through discursive reasoning; the attack is not a "statement" of moral superiority. It is the outcome of the embrace of righteousness as a means to the perfect resolution of humiliation through the overwhelming sensuality of rage.

Both humiliation and rage are experienced on a vertical dimension. Dictionaries define humiliation as an experience of being reduced to a lower position in one's own or another's eyes. Humiliation drives you down; in humiliation, you feel suddenly made small, so small that everyone seems to look down on you. Humiliation often moves through the body by warming the top of the head; then moving to the face, where its acknowledgment may create the blush of shame; and then working itself through the self, ultimately to envelope it from top to bottom. Etymologically, humiliation shares roots with "humble." All manner of degrading, debasing, deflating attacks may produce humiliation.

In contrast, rage proceeds in an upward direction. It may start in the pit of the stomach and soon threaten to burst out of your head. "Don't blow your top" and "hold your lid on," we counsel the angry. In Chicago in the late 1960s, one of the most militant youth publications was called *Rising Up Angry*. Members of militant movements understand implicitly that angry people "rise up" and that to affiliate with symbols of sitting down would express a calm resolution in protest.

If one looks back further in etymology, one finds that *humiliation, humble,* and related terms

in English grew out of the Latin for *humus*—the same humus prized by gardeners—the organic, wet, fertile earth that is the most natural foundation for what human beings can grow to sustain life.[26] The wetness of humus is reflected in the liquid character of the experience of humiliation and its family of related feelings. Embarrassment, shame, and humiliation flow through the self. The blush of shame is a sudden wave of blood to the face. Humiliation threatens to drown one's being. When we have made fools of ourselves or have been made fools by others, we may wish or feel we are sinking into the earth. Someone who is completely wrong is "all wet."

Children use water balloons, not balloons with air or helium, to play at humiliation. Practical jokers place water buckets over doors and push victims into swimming pools. One of the most universal conventions for degrading someone is to spit at them. Somehow spitting, which casts a liquid on someone, significantly conveys disrespect; while blowing at someone, though a substantially similar physical act, carries other meanings. To humiliate others in an extreme way, you might urinate on them. You would then expect them to become "pissed off," their response being in opposition to the liquid provocation. An "angry young man" is said to be "full of piss and vinegar," on the understanding that anger is stimulated by the irritating qualities natural to these caustic liquids.

Humiliation as a drowning liquid and rage leaping up like a fiery gas share a boundary-defying holistic quality. Liquids and gases both seep over the edges of containers; neither has any apparent internal divisions. But they are also intrinsically opposed. Rage is a hot gas, a fire; it burns. As fire is to water, so rage is to humiliation. The heat of rage ontologically transforms the liquid of humiliation. Thus, a person "boils" in anger and then, like Yosemite Sam after he has been humiliated by Bugs Bunny, "blows off steam."

Cartoons are useful for understanding the emotional construction of experience. Popular cartoons represent imagery that has proved effective for representing emotions. Like the images of dreams and poetry, cartoon images make sense according to a symbolic logic that operates ubiquitously in everyday life but that somehow resists expression in the conventions of discursive reasoning. So, just as we know automatically that it is appropriate to say that a person might "blow up" in rage and that it is obviously wrong to say that a person might "blow down" in anger, cartoonists naturally illustrate rage as an explosion coming out of a character's head, not his or her foot. In color cartoons, the enraged character might be depicted as progressing from an initially pink irritation through deepening shades of red anger into purple rage and then into an explosion in the hues of a fire.

Tales that children find effective also reveal the symbols that are natural vehicles for emotions in a given culture. That certain patterns make dramatic sense and are persistently fascinating suggests that they fit with the structure of emotions as experienced in everyday life. Metaphoric oppositions, such as those between liquid and gas, cold and hot, and upward and downward movement, are frequently used to juxtapose good and evil.

Take, for example, the death of the evil witch in *The Wizard of Oz*. Dorothy's lethal attack, launched in rage after the witch had snatched one of her silver shoes, consists of throwing on the witch a bucket of water. This is a moral attack, a status-reducing expression of disgust by the young girl from a self-confident stance. Dorothy responds to the witch, whose power is symbolized by the control of fire, by assuming the confident posture of a little princess toward an unspeakably inferior subject, dousing her enemy with a super-spit. The witch then shrinks down to the dirt, ultimately dissolving into nothingness.[27]

Finally, the sexual oppositions. In some social circles, an erection is an "angry" penis. Today, impotence is so fundamentally linked to humiliation that in virtually all modern languages the terms for describing impotence are reliable means of effecting ridicule. If rage is red, hot, and explosive, it is like a penis threatening to ejaculate and it is also like the screaming, red-faced birth of a self. Whichever of these metaphors might be more relevant to a given individual, the language and the symbolic structure of the experience of humiliation is metaphorically the perfect opposite: a return to the womb.[28] The etymology of humiliation points to the centrality of the metaphor of the womb through humus— wet, fertile soil enriched by decayed vegetable

matter—that is the most natural source of all terrestrial life: Gaea, "Mother Earth."

To disparage someone, a contemporary American might readily say that he or she "sucks," a usage that points back to the womb as a reference to the infant's sucking at the breast (as well as to the female in fellatio). Not only what we say but also what we feel in shame and humiliation is symbolically summarized by the metaphor of a return to the womb. In its sensuality, humiliation makes one feel small. In humiliation, one feels incompetent and powerless as if one's stature has been reduced to that of a baby.

Rage is specifically, intensely an oppositional emotion. Thus, humiliation threatens to be end less and diffuse, while rage searches for a target to extinguish itself. In emotional logic, rage has already found its perfect target in humiliation.

When moral attack has us pressed toward humiliation, we may construct rage through a flash recognition of the principle of opposition. The path to rage is right there before us, in the structure of whichever metaphoric features of humiliation may have become most compelling to us long ago, through cartoons, language usage, fairy tales, erotic fantasies, or other regions of popular culture. Along one or the other of the oppositions of upward and downward, static and active, liquid and gaseous, inward and outward, and male and female, we know just where to find an escape route.

Sacrificial Violence: The Embodiment of Righteous Rage

Although those who kill in righteous rage are attempting to settle matters once and for all, they often have tried many times before. The fatal blow is one of a family of acts that form a coherent field of aggressive conduct. To understand the lived experience of homicides committed in everyday settings in defense of the Good, we must understand a range of related phenomena. Why all the shouting and cursing? Why the shoving and pushing? How do the acts that are distinctive to violent attacks—"belting" and "stomping" and "cutting up" the other— seem especially fitting to one who is attempting to transcend humiliation with a righteous passion?

———————

Research on family violence has indicated the hidden or "dark figure" of violent attacks that, but for chance factors, might have ended as homicides. Because victims are reluctant to complain officially, for a variety of reasons ranging from sympathy for the offender to fears of retaliation and self-incrimination, such attacks are notoriously unrepresented in crimes reported to the police. A national survey, whose results were based on what interviewees were willing to admit, found that

> every year about one out of every six couples in the United States commits at least one violent act against his or her partner. . . . The rates for actually *using a knife or gun* on one's spouse are one out of every two hundred couples in the previous year, and almost one out of twenty-seven couples at some point in the marriage. . . . *over 1.7 million Americans had at some time faced a husband or wife wielding a knife or gun, and well over 2 million had been beaten up* by his or her spouse.[29]

That a large percentage of homicides by gun are effected by a single shot has been interpreted as evidence that there is no specific intent to kill: if the first shot misses, another might not be taken.[30] In attacks that result in death, the attack often ceases long before the end of the victim's life, when there is clear evidence of serious injury but equally clear evidence of persistent life: cries of pain, pleas for mercy, moves to retreat. As Philip Cook noted:

> In a large proportion of assaults with deadly weapons, the assailant ceases the attack by choice, rather than because of effective victim resistance. We can infer in unsustained attacks of this sort that the assailant's intent is to injure or incapacitate the victim—that there is no deliberate, unambiguous intent to kill.[31]

In short, there are many indications that the victim's death is not a *necessary* concern in either aggravated assaults or the typical criminal homicide. Perhaps a more striking way to draw attention to the practical perspective animating the assailant is to note the indications that the victim's death may not be a *sufficient* concern. In a "stomping," the attacker may announce to his victim the objective of "kicking your eyes out of your head." The specific practical objective—to remove precisely the condition of the attacker's humiliation, the victim's offending gaze—is more imaginatively related to the project of transcending humiliation than would be the victim's death. Sacrificial violence does not particularly seek the neat end of death; rather, it attempts to achieve the existentially impossible goal of obliteration, of annihilating or wiping out the victim.

To "blow away" or wipe out a person goes beyond death, which only takes life from a body but leaves the body: a wipe out leaves no trace of what was removed. It reflects a specifically transcendent project in which death may be "too good" for the victim, as in the following case:

> I was a good provider for my family and a hard worker. . . . I told her if she stopped with the divorce, and that I would promise to act better and . . . but she wouldn't buy any of it. I got angrier and angrier. . . . I looked at her straight in the face and said, "Well, X, you better start thinking about those poor kids of ours." She said, "I don't care about them: I just want a divorce."
>
> My hate for her exploded then, and I said, "You dirty, no-good bitch", [*sic*] and started pounding her in the face with my fist. She put her arms up and covered her face, so I ran and got my rifle and pointed it at her. I said, "Bitch, you better change your mind fast or I'm going to kill you." She looked up and said in a smart-ass way, "Go ahead then, shoot me." I got so mad and felt so much hate for her, that I just started shooting her again and again. . . [32]

At times the attack persists past death, in a spirit that suggests that the assailant wishes the victim would stay alive or return to life, so the strange joy of killing might be sustained through repetition. It is arbitrary to assume that while the attack persists, the victim's death is the objective. Indeed, the victim's death may frustrate the attacker's purpose.

When the victim's death terminates the violent attack, one should still question whether death was the killer's objective or whether it was a means in a symbolically and emotionally compelling project that transcends death. When one mate slays the other after a series of impassioned fights mobilized by charges of sexual disloyalty, it sometimes seems that the killer specifically wants the victim dead. The relationship had become intolerably humiliating; the killer—like Ruth in the next example—"couldn't take it anymore"; he or she simply wanted to end it.

> Ruth seemed to be secretive about her marital problems because of her pride. She was only separated from her second legal husband and did not want people to know about her common-law relationship [with the victim]. . . . He was teasing her about another woman he met who was nicer and more attractive than Ruth. He also ceased giving any physical affection to Ruth. This bothered Ruth a lot as she started to believe that he was going to leave her for the other woman. The day the homicide occurred. . . . he came back with another woman [and] . . . a bitter quarrel ensued. Ruth could not remember what happened after that. . . . She had stabbed to death the man she had lived with for two years. According to neighbours her last remark before the murder was "If I can't have you, nobody else can!"[33]

The goal of ending the relationship is inadequate to understand the sense of such killings. Ruth's problem, for which the killing was a resolution, could not be solved by her leaving her lover, her suicide, or her lover's death, since the relationship was about to end anyway.

From within the assailant's perspective, killing a deserting lover makes sense as a way of *preserving* a relationship that otherwise would end. If he leaves her or if she leaves him, the relationship they had may well become, in both their romantic biographies, a relatively unremarkable chapter in a series of failed relationships. By killing her mate, Ruth made their relationship last forever; in the most existential-

ly unarguable sense, she made it the most profound relationship either had ever had. Then no one else could have him; no one else could develop a relationship with him that would retrospectively extinguish the special significance they shared. Killing him was her means of honoring and protecting the transcendent significance of their relationship.

Humiliation, Rage, and Sacrificial Violence

In the following account of a fight, the attacker and his brother, after drinking with the victim in a bar, paid for a cab and "a couple of six packs" to take to the home of the victim. On their arrival, the victim announced that the two brothers, who had expected to spend the night, would have to leave. Some curses and threats were exchanged as the brothers moved to leave:

> The dude said, "That's right, get your fucking ass out of here now," and pushed me once more. I said to myself, "Fuck it, that's it, I'm going to fuck him up." I hit him with a right hook, went berserk, and grabbed a lamp and busted him over the head and downed him. I yelled, "You punk motherfucker, I'll kick your eyes out of your head" and stomped him in the face.[34]

After being pushed repeatedly by the victim, the attacker first decided no longer to respect his brother's remonstrations not to attack and began in a relatively civil manner ("with a right hook," as if in a boxing match). Only then did his rage accelerate, generating curses and a wild method of attack. The motions of battle sometimes call up the emotions that would sustain them.

Physical involvement in the style of sacrificial violence commonly precedes the height of rage. In yelling curses, one is deepening the significance of the conflict not only in symbolism but in the physical process as one's whole body is being mobilized for the expression. If anger is a confined experience (for instance, getting red in the face) and rage is a holistic experience (one is in rage or "en-raged"), shouting, screaming, or yelling is a conveniently intermediary step that sensually paves the way for enraged violence.

Family fights often begin in verbal hassling and physical tussling that have an ambiguous status. In such cases, rage does not precede and cause a violent attack; conflictual motions initiated without a source in deep anger may elicit symbolic themes of violent attack that are then taken up in rage. The next quote is from an observer who found himself in the middle of a family battle.

> It started sort of slowly . . . so I couldn't tell for sure if they were even serious. . . . In the beginning they'd push at each other, or shove, like kids—little kids who want to fight but they don't know how. Then, this one time, while I'm standing there not sure whether to stay or go, and them treating me like I didn't even exist, she begins yelling at him like she did.
>
> "You're a bust, you're a failure, I want you out of here, I can always get men who'll work, good men, not scum like you." And they're pushing and poking with their hands, like they were dancing. She pushes him, he pushes her, only she's doing all the talking. He isn't saying a word.
>
> Then all of a sudden, she must have triggered off the right nerve because he lets fly with a right cross that I mean stuns. I mean she goes down like a rock! And he's swearing at her, calling her every name in the book.[35]

Not only does rage sometimes develop after the violence begins, its persistence frequently is contingent on the practical success of violence. If it appears that violence will not succeed, the attacker may put an abrupt stop to rage, anticipating that otherwise he or she risks reverting to a more profound humiliation. In the following case of a fight in a jail cell, the attacker called his victim "crazy" and then was knocked down:

> I really got hot. I just thought I wanted to kill that dirty s.o.b. I jumped up to my feet and pulled out a fingernail file that I had on me. But then I thought, "This file won't stop him, and he's too fucking big to fight without

something more than this. I better back off." After I backed up a few feet, I said, "Motherfucker, don't you ever turn your back near me; you've busted my fucking nose, and I'm going to get you for it." He looked at me and said "Come on, do it right now." I just said, "I'll catch you later" and walked off fast, real fast.[36]

This attacker, however enraged he was, still had the composure to back off with a face-saving curse and a promise of revenge.

Notice how each of the three conditions of righteous slaughter was dismantled in that situation. First, the attacker suddenly realized the practical project of sacrificial violence could not be successfully organized ("he's too fucking big to fight"). His rage then quickly faded, threatening to turn back into humiliation. The further result was a reinterpretation of the situation as no longer calling for a last stand. There will be other opportunities to settle this, the would-be attacker announced with a now-calculated bravado, "I'll catch you later."

In other events, the causal conditions become undone in a different order. The first step back may come when the assailant seizes on grounds to hope for a future acknowledgment of respectability, as in this account:

> I was at home looking for the t.v. guide when I found a note written by my wife. It said that she owed somebody $6 for babysitting for her twelve hours. I thought to myself "Where in the living hell could she have been gone for twelve hours?" My mind then turned to her stepping out with someone behind my back, so I called her. When she came in the room, I said, "What in the hell is this note about?" She grabbed the note out of my hand and said, "Oh, it's nothing." I said, "What in the hell do you mean that it's nothing? Where in the hell were you for twelve hours?"
>
> Then she started giving me some story about going shopping and to the hairdresser's. I said, "Bullshit, that crap doesn't take any twelve hours to do." She said, "Well, maybe the twelve hours that I wrote on the note is a mistake." I said, "Don't hand me that bullshit; you're fucking around with someone." She said, "No, no, I'm not." Then I yelled, "You no-good

tramp, dirty whore, you better tell me where in the hell you have been." She said, "You are acting like nothing but a bum: I'm not going to tell you anything." I thought to myself, "I'm going to beat the damn truth out of that no-good, rotten bitch." I started thinking about tying her up and beating her until she talked, but then I thought that if I went that far, she might leave me, so I dropped it. I was scared that if I did do it, then I would end up losing her.[37]

In this recollection, the alleged adultress denied the accusation ("No, no, I'm not."). There were further curses, but after the denial, the offended spouse did not need to treat the dispute as a last stand, and he turned from being in hell, surrounded by bullshit, to the mundane future—to what life would be like on the other side of a terminal conflict. Then he abandoned the transcendent aspiration of rage. By labeling his accusations as the crude acts of a "bum," his wife threw out a hint of respectability: they should rise above mean suspicions, they are suited to a more refined level of understanding. And, this time anyway, he jumped at that hint and quickly abandoned what he sensed was an even more precarious last stand.

Even when the parties are enraged and are familiar with the ways of sacrificial violence, the interactive character of the relationship with the victim builds a further dimension of uncertainty into the event. The victim may not sustain the pressure of humiliation but back off, redefining the situation as not requiring a last stand.[38] These battles are processes of negotiation over how much is practically required before the pressure to humiliate is over, before the last stand is dismantled, and before an objective reconstruction of offended respectability is deemed accomplished. Rage may seem powerful, both to the enraged person and to analysts, but rage itself does not demand an attack on the body of the humiliating party. If a sacrifice is to be taken, it may be made in the forms of inanimate targets, for example, by punching holes in a wall, smashing chairs on tables, shooting out windows, or throwing about objects that are precious to the offensive party.

There are multiple situational contingencies on the road to righteous slaughter. That there is no inevitability to the event is not due to the defects of methodology or theory or solely to the frequently interactional character of the violence. As experienced by the participants, the event is inherently uncertain in at least two respects.

First, much of the conflict leading to sacrificial violence is conducted not in a controlling attitude but in the stance of prayer. Pushing, shoving, shouting—these characteristic aggressive moves are inadequately understood simply as punitive. Why shove or shout? What damage does that do? Pushing is incomprehensible as "irrational" behavior somehow randomly growing out of "explosive anger." It is pellucid as a way of trying to move the other out of his or her posture to end the humiliation and reverse the pressure to take a last stand. Shouting is loud—not so loud to hurt the other's eardrums but loud enough momentarily to block out one's own openness to the other's definition of the situation. If the other would not shout back, if he or she would "just shut up," perhaps that would be enough. If these moves appear in one light to assume postures of dominance, in another, more obscure way, they are prayers that acknowledge the uncertainty of the evolving moment. These common openings to righteous violence signify a still-engaged moral inclination for peace even as they prepare to honor the Good in blood.

Second, the performance of sacrificial violence is an opening of the self to fate. If the attacker does not know just what the practical result of his attack will be—whether the bullet will hit a vital organ, whether his victim will be strong enough to survive, or how long it will take for medical assistance to arrive—he knows that he does not know. He could know. . . . killers can meditate on and preside over their administration of a coup de grace. They can envision a dead body while they plan an escape and they can arrange corpses after the fact to shape the scene that will greet subsequent discoverers. As can be seen in most modern methods of capital punishment—when carefully balanced chemicals are injected to produce death instantly, painlessly, and without marring the resulting corpse—killing a person can be made the precise, efficient, specific objective of an act.

Notes

1. In some American jurisdictions, the modal homicide has been a killing conducted in the course of other criminal activities, particularly drug marketing. Ronald Heffernan, John M. Martin, and Anne T. Romano, "Homicides Related to Drug Trafficking," *Federal Probation* 46 (September 1982): 3–7. At other exceptional times, "gang warfare" or vendettas have accounted for the single greatest number of criminal killings. It is not possible to state exactly what percentage of officially labeled criminal homicides are righteous slaughters, since such detailed information is not available. However, on the basis of a variety of indicators presented throughout this chapter, it appears that the characterization to follow describes the single most numerous (modal) type of criminal homicide. Insofar as criminal homicide can be identified as a homogeneous experience, this is what, in most times and places, it most often has been. In any case, the validity of the current explanation is independent of the relative frequency of righteous slaughters compared with other forms of homicide.

2. Note that there is no question here of "getting into the offender's mind." The key evidentiary facts are what was said and done, in what order, and what was not said and not done. Neither the evidence nor the theoretical focus is on what is "in the mind" of the subject.

3. David F. Luckenbill, "Criminal Homicide as a Situated Transaction," *Social Problems* 25 (December 1977): 180.

4. Indeed, some would question Luckenbill's gratuitous interpretation that the infant's crying may have been a protest against soiled diapers. It is not clear that 5-week-old infants are as sensitive to cleanliness, or "messes" as are adults.

5. David Kaplun and Robert Reich, "The Murdered Child and His Killers," *American Journal of Psychiatry* 133, no. 7 (July 1976): 810. See also Marvin E. Wolfgang and Margaret A. Zahn, "Homicide: Behavioral Aspects," in *Encyclopedia of Crime and Justice,* ed. Sanford H. Kadish (New York: Free Press, 1983), 2:853. (But Philip J. Resnick, "Child Murder by Parents," *American Journal of Psychiatry* 126 [September 1969]: 328, found that fathers used striking, squeezing, and stabbing, and mothers used drowning, suffocation, and gassing.) That infanticide is typically an extension of routine disciplinary attacks is all the more striking, given the frequency of parental attempts to shoot and stab children. See Murray Straus, Richard J. Gelles, and Suzanne K. Steinmetz, *Behind Closed Doors* (Garden City, N.Y.: Doubleday Anchor Press, 1980), pp. 61–62. See also Murray Strauss and Richard J. Gelles, "Societal Change and Change in Family Violence from 1975 to 1985 as Revealed by Two National Surveys," *Journal of Marriage and the Family* 48 (August 1986): 465–80.

6. Henry P. Lundsgaarde, *Murder in Space City* (New York: Oxford University Press, 1977), pp. 107–8. See also, from the first great qualitative sociological study in the United States, the case of Krupka murdering his wife. William I. Thomas and Florian Znaniecki, *The Polish Peasant in Europe and America* (New York: Dover, 1958), 2:1770–71.

7. The significance of her case in the evolution of the feminist movement is traced in Ann Jones, *Women Who Kill* (New York: Holt, Rinehart & Winston, 1980), pp. 281–95.

8. Peter D. Chimbos, *Marital Violence: A Study of Interspouse Homicide* (San Francisco: R & E Research Associates, 1978), p. 64.

9. Lundsgaarde, *Murder in Space City,* p. 61.

10. Ibid, pp. 109–10. For a similar incident, see Howard Harlan, "Five Hundred Homicides," *Journal of Criminal Law and Criminology* 40 (March–April 1950): 751 (data from Birmingham, Alabama, 1937–44).

11. Lundsgaarde, *Murder in Space City,* p. 111. For a similar incident, see Robert C. Bensing and Oliver Schroeder, Jr., *Homicide in an Urban Community* (Springfield, Ill.: Charles C Thomas, 1960), pp. 72–73 (data from Cleveland).

12. Chimbos, *Marital Violence,* p. 47.

13. Lundsgaarde, *Murder in Space City,* p. 65.

14. Ibid., p. 60. For a similar incident, see Harlan, "Five Hundred Homicides," 746.

15. See, for example, Bensing and Schroeder, *Homicide in an Urban Community,* p. 13, n. 2; Lynn A. Curtis, *Criminal Violence* (Lexington, Mass.: Lexington Books, 1974) (10 percent sample of police offense and arrest reports for 1967 for each of four major crimes in each of the seventeen large U.S. urban areas); and Marvin E. Wolfgang, *Patterns in Criminal Homicide* (Philadelphia: University of Pennsylvania Press, 1958), pp. 289–90 (data from Philadelphia, 1948–52).

16. About 30 percent in Luckenbill's study, "Criminal Homicide as a Situated Transaction." Quantified data on this question have rarely been collected, but widespread qualitative accounts support an impression of generality.

17. Wolfgang, *Patterns in Criminal Homicide,* p. 295.

18. Ibid.

19. Luckenbill, "Criminal Homicide as a Situated Transaction."

20. Richard B. Felson and Henry J. Steadman, "Situational Factors in Disputes Leading to Criminal Violence," *Criminology* 21 (February 1983): 72.

21. For an early formulation of the phenomenon and summaries of ten incidents that parallel those quoted here, see Marvin E. Wolfgang, "Victim-Precipitated Criminal Homicide," *Journal of Criminal Law, Criminology and Police Science* 48 (June 1957): 1–11. See also Curtis, *Criminal Violence,* table 5.1, p. 82; and Harwin L. Voss and John R. Hepburn, "Patterns in Criminal Homicide in Chicago," *Journal of Criminal Law, Criminology and Police Science* 59 (December 1968): 499–508.

22. "Some of the victims so goaded their killers either by provocation in words or deeds, or by incessant nagging that they directly precipitated their own deaths." Terence Morris and Louis Blom-Cooper, *A Calendar of Murder* (London: Michael Joseph, 1964), p. 322.

23. See also John M. Macdonald, *Homicidal Threats* (Springfield, Ill.: Charles C Thomas, 1968). For a broader analysis of the victim's role in killings, see Edwin S. Shneidman, *Deaths of Man* (New York: Jason Aronson, 1983).

24. Luckenbill, "Criminal Homicide as a Situated Transaction." It should be noted, however, that Felson and Steadman, "Situational Factors," 72, claimed that the role of third parties may be exaggerated, since incidents in which no witnesses are present were likely to be excluded.

25. An assertion that the moment of homicidal rage is a "myth" appears in a polemical work directed against gun control. See James D. Wright, Peter H. Rossi, and Kathleen Daly, *Under the Gun: Weapons, Crime and Violence in America* (Chicago: Aldine, 1983), pp. 18–19. No evidence of the emotional character of homicidal behavior is cited; rather, the authors contest the inferences about emotions that others have drawn from statistics on the prior relationship of victim and killer. The intimacy and the legal significance of the emotional experience of homicide systematically block the acquisition of statistically representative, high-quality evidence on the issue. Thus, those who wish to limit their understanding of human experience to what may be documented according to statistical conventions might contest as a myth *any* characterization of the emotional dimension of homicide. Given the indications of qualitative accounts, it is not clear why any serious investigator of the phenomenon would want to do so, outside the context of policy debate or adversarial advocacy. Perhaps part of the confusion is due to the fact that although rage quickly transforms the sense of a situation, that may happen many times in a relationship. Gary Kleck and David J. Bordua, "The Assumptions of Gun Control," in *Firearms and Violence,* ed. Don B. Kates (San Francisco: Ballinger, 1984), pp. 42–43. As a Canadian study of spousal homicide noted, "The lethal act was rarely 'sudden, explosive and unexpected.'" Yet, in each of six cases detailed in this research there is an indicator of rage in the form of a "heated argument" or a "bitter quarrel." See Chimbos, *Marital Violence,* pp. 62–67. Like sexual experience, violence in a relationship may occur repeatedly yet develop in passion each time.

26. Humus then goes back further to a root in *Homo sapiens.* Like shame, whose German root refers to the pubic region, the history of "humiliation" points to a morally sensitive fertility as basic to man's nature. See Eric Partridge, *A Short Etymological Dictionary of Modern English,* 4th ed. (London: Routledge & Kegan Paul, 1966), pp. 292–93.

27. L. Frank Baum, *The Wonderful Wizard of Oz* (Berkeley: University of California Press, 1986), p. 149.

28. People recall, within their experiences of shame, a search for a "hole to crawl into! Let me just cover myself up and nobody can see me." The wish is not exactly to die, but to be in a place where one can exist safely. Janice Lindsay-Hartz, "The Structures of Experience of Shame and Guilt," *American Behavioral Scientist* 27 (July–August 1984): 692.

29. Straus, Gelles, and Steinmetz, *Behind Closed Doors,* pp. 32, 34 (emphasis in original).

30. Zimring, "Gun Control," 721–37. Of course, the fact that so many die with one shot might be interpreted as evidence that there was in fact a specific intention to kill—therefore, once death occurred there was no need for further shots. But many of the gun deaths occur after and outside the scene of the shooting, and even when death occurs in the same scene, there is no evidence in the research literature, qualitative or quantitative, that the killers inspect their victims for signs of life.

31. Cook, "Role of Firearms," p. 249.

32. Lonnie H. Athens, *Violent Criminal Acts and Actors* (Boston, London, and Henley: Routledge & Kegan Paul, 1980), pp. 46, 48.

33. Chimbos, *Marital Violence,* p. 67.

34. Athens, *Violent Criminal Acts and Actors,* pp. 37–38.

35. As quoted by Thomas Cottle, *Boston Sunday Globe,* November 6, 1977, in Straus, Gelles, and Steinmetz, *Behind Closed Doors,* pp. 36–37.

36. Athens, *Violent Criminal Acts and Actors,* pp. 31–32.

37. Ibid., pp. 33–34.

38. Felson and Steadman ("Situational Factors," 67, 72) found that one could predict what an offender would do, not from what he had done earlier in the incident, but only from the behavior of the other.

| 8 |

Homicide as Custom and Crime

Henry P. Lundsgaarde

Nullem crimen sine lege is a basic and universal premise of criminal law. Homicide, accordingly, is only properly viewed as criminal behavior if and when an act of killing is defined as unlawful. In this chapter we will consider and apply those criminal statutes from Texas that discriminate between different kinds of lawful and unlawful homicide pertaining to the judicial outcome for known killers. The high number of Houston homicides, together with the finding that most of the apprehended killers escape any form of legal sanction, will be considered relative to various legal distinctions between murder (with or without malice), homicide by negligence, and justifiable and excusable homicide. The complex connections between social custom and judicial process . . . may be clarified, if only partially, by a careful analysis of the official legal sanctions that apply to an act of killing.

Although nearly 90 percent of all reported homicides in 1969 resulted in the apprehension of the alleged killers, fewer than 50 percent of the suspects were negatively sanctioned for their acts. These notable discrepancies between apprehended suspect and convicted offender can, in part, be explained by pointing to the differences between lawful and unlawful homicide. It is the initial purpose of a criminal proceeding to determine whether a particular act fits into one or the other of these two general categories.

The more general social ends to be served by criminal proceeding are, according to the eminent jurist William L. Prosser, "to protect and vindicate the interests of the public as a whole, by punishing the offender or eliminating him from society, either permanently or for a limited time, by reforming him or teaching him not to repeat the offense, and by deterring others from imitating him."[1] Prosser further notes that a "criminal prosecution is not concerned in any way with compensation of the injured individual against whom the crime is committed, and his [the victim's] only part in it is that of an accuser and a witness for the state. So far as the criminal law is concerned, he will leave the courtroom empty-handed."[2] The victim of a homicide is always a silent and fictitious witness for the state. The separation in modern American law of criminal and tort liability has not only made it exceedingly difficult for a victim's survivors to seek damages from a killer, but it may actually have eliminated a potentially powerful deterrent against homicidal behavior. A tort, which defies precise definition, is generally viewed as a civil wrong. It is an offense against a private individual, as opposed to an offense against the public at large, for which the law may provide a remedy in the form of restitution or financial compensation for damages. Several recent studies of victim compensation programs illustrate both the opportunities for and obstacles against further innovation in this important area of criminal justice. The increasing rate of crimes against the person at the same time reminds us that, as a society, we cannot afford to suppress innovative approaches that may improve the system of criminal justice.[3]

The observation to be made here is that the Texas Penal Code explicitly emphasizes the legal rights of killers. A victim has no rights and his survivors acquire or exercise no rights whatever. This is perhaps best illustrated by the fact that the law of homicide carries no provision for survivorship indemnity or compensation. This is almost the exact opposite of early Anglo-Saxon and English law, and many non-Western legal

Selections from Chapters 6 and 7, pp. 143–192 in *Murder in Space City: A Cultural Analysis of Houston Homicide Patterns*, by Henry P. Lundsgaarde (Oxford University Press 1977). Reprinted by permission.

systems as well, in which the victim's survivors, legal heirs, or relatives received compensation in different kinds of homicide. The modern criminal law has completely transformed the ancient view of homicide as a wrong against a victim and his family to its modern version that views homicide as an offense against the state. The prevalent view of crime as strictly a "social problem" therefore holds no surprise.

The substantive criminal law of Texas is the product of a long common-law tradition that dates back to and is derived from Anglo-Saxon and early English law. The first Texas Penal Code was enacted in 1856 and, except for some minor recodifications, it has survived 117 years without substantial change. The public recognition in 1965 that the Penal Code ought more closely to reflect the changing ideological and socioeconomic conditions of the twentieth century resulted in the enactment of a new Texas Penal Code. This new code (hereafter referred to as the 1974 Code) was enacted by the 63rd Legislature and became effective on January 1, 1974. . . . The most perceptible differences between the old and the new codes pertaining to offenses against the person basically amount to minor semantic changes in terminology and the introduction of Capital Murder as a special category of homicide. It must be noted and emphasized that the 1974 Code, if applied to the 1969 cases, would have produced minor differences, if any, in outcomes for apprehended and convicted killers.

A comparative study of the old and the new penal codes does not reveal any major and significant differences in the homicide statutes other than a change in wording or contextual organization. The 1974 Code, for example, eliminated some 67 different usages associated with the *mens rea* doctrine—which alludes to the medieval notion of an evil-meaning or guilty mind—and substituted four terms to categorize a person's culpability and state of mind. An act is thus deemed lawful or unlawful on the basis of the actor's mentality. Criminal culpability implies that a person behaves *intentionally, knowingly, recklessly* or that he is simply *criminally negligent*. These concepts are graded in terms of their relative magnitude. A person who commits an act *intentionally* is penalized more heavily than a person who is *negligent*. The criterion used to measure the seriousness of a particular act in this scheme is the behavior of a fictional entity characterized as "an ordinary person."[4]

Professor Charles P. Bubany's law review article, "The Texas Penal Code of 1974," illustrates how the new conceptual system may be applied in a homicide prosecution:

> Assume that a defendant strikes a pregnant woman in the abdomen and as a result the baby dies shortly after birth. In a homicide prosecution the evidence might show any of the following: (1) if he struck the woman knowing she was pregnant and for the purpose of killing the child, his conduct was *intentional*; (2) if he knew she was pregnant and that his blows were likely to cause the death, his conduct was *knowing*, even if his only purpose was to cause her pain; (3) if he knew she was pregnant and knew that death of the baby might result, but he did not care, he was only *reckless*; (4) if he knew she was pregnant but did not think his blow was hard enough to hurt the baby, or he did not advert to the fact that she was pregnant although it was plainly observable, he acted with *criminal negligence*; or (5) if he did not know she was pregnant and to the ordinary observer she did not look pregnant, he did not have any culpable mental state, at least with respect to the baby's death as a result (ibid., 1974, p. 306).[5]

The distinctions between lawful and unlawful homicide that emerge from the grading of offenses in accordance with the degree of mental culpability call attention to a basic premise and a fundamental weakness in the criminal law: The classification of an act of killing requires the sanctioning agent—whether a legislature, a district attorney, or a trial judge and jury—to infer *motivation* and *intention* from the killer's behavior. The criminal law is thus almost singularly directed toward the determination of culpability on the basis of psychological variables. The social and cultural implications of a particular act for society at large also are only of tertiary interest to lawyers and judges who are charged with prosecuting and defending killers. The system of criminal justice thus fails to either remedy or in any way resolve "the problem of crime" because it only processes individual offenders in terms of what, at best, must remain uncertain psychological factors resulting in legal culpability or innocence.[6] If a Houston killer can demonstrate the slightest element of "self-defense" (i.e., he did not set out to kill the victim but his response was precipitated by a stimulus from his victim) he downgrades the act to either justifiable homicide or murder without malice. The excessive reliance by the classificatory scheme on such factors as "malice," "state of mind," "intent," and "motive"—which take its ultimate meaningless form in the legal fiction of "the reasonable man"—derives less from the findings of psychology and psychiatry than from prescient and lay presumptions about human behavior.[7] It is, in part, these commonly held presumptions about human behavior that anthropologists and behavioral scientists generally label "custom." Consider for a moment, by way of example, why jurists in Western cultures emphasize such factors as motive and intent rather than stressing the social consequences of an act. A homicide victim is just as dead whether his killer intended to kill him or not and his survivors are just as parentless or childless whether the state absolves the killer of criminal culpability or executes him. Permit me to stretch the example further by contrasting the common-law view of homicide with killing in Eskimo society. The eminent anthropologist E. A. Hoebel has suggested that the Eskimos only developed a form of "rudimentary law" and that they did not collectively punish a killer unless his act, and especially if he repeated it, visibly threatened the survival and welfare of the social unit as a whole. Whether the killer was motivated by passion, wife-stealing, megalomania, or the sadistic pleasure of inflicting pain and suffering upon others was not a deciding factor. The behavior of killing per se, and its social consequences, such as loss of social cohesiveness and cooperation in the interest of survival, were principal factors used to determine the degree of lawfulness or unlawfulness of a killer's homicidal act or acts.[8]

Sir Stephen's distinction between murder and manslaughter squarely demonstrates how psychological rather than sociological considerations dominate the Anglo-Saxon view of relative criminality. He says: "in murder the act or omission by which death is caused is attended by one or more of the states of mind included under the description of malice aforethought, whereas in cases of manslaughter malice aforethought is absent."[9] Justice Holmes (1881) cites an earlier work by Stephen and elaborates the argument for accepting the manslaughter definition that resolves itself into the formula: Murder minus malice aforethought equals manslaughter.[10] Other jurists, who are called upon to develop legislative measures to alleviate many human and social problems, often completely ignore the insights and findings of modern science. If, for example, "the principal end of the law of homicide is the prevention of behavior which may cause death"[11] it should be asked whether simplifying the homicide statutes in fact reduces the number of killings. The following statement from the Foreword to the 1974 Code shows that the legal community is aware of these problems but that significant reforms insofar as the control of interpersonal violence is concerned must await the passing of time:

> The 1856 Penal Code was of course designed for a state much different from the Texas of today. The Texas of a century ago was a rural society with an agricultural economy. The civil war and two world wars had not been fought, the automobile and airplane had not been invented, and no one had heard of Sigmund Freud or Karl Marx. It should come as no surprise, therefore, that the old code punished horse theft more severely than murder without malice, made forgery of land titles a more serious offense than forgery of government bonds, and justified killing the wife's lover (but not the husband's mistress) if taken in the act of adultery. . . . Not all of the new code is appropriate for the 21st century [sic]. Chapter 46 in particular, which deals with weapons, retains too much of the frontier in its treatment of firearms. Chapter 9 (justification), although significantly reducing the amount of violence lawful under the old code, still permits too much force on too many occasions. But these defects pale beside the achievements of the new code in making our penal law responsive and respectable.[12]

Justifiable Homicide

The Texas Penal Code provides that it is lawful and therefore justifiable to kill a human being under any one of the following circumstances: (1) Killing a public enemy, (2) executing a convict, (3) acting in response to a lawful order or directive by a police officer, (4) aiding a police officer, (5) preventing the escape of a person legally apprehended or captured, (6) suppressing a riot, (7) preventing the successful completion of a criminal or felonious act, (8) responding by a husband to provocation by an act of adultery, (9) defending a person or property, (10) defending oneself against an unlawful attack, and (11) defending or upholding property rights.

These 11 justifications can be divided into two general subcategories of justifiable homicide. In one we can include all those killings that result from some form of official law enforcement (1 through 6 above) and, in the other, we include all those killings that result from the act of private citizens who kill in a lawful manner (7 through 11 above). The category of justifiable homicide, which principally concerns killings by private citizens, is, of course, of primary interest in this study.

The statutory problems with those articles that provide individuals great latitude in the use of deadly force are aptly summarized in a comment by William M. Ravkind. He says:

> The provisions of the Penal Code concerning justifiable homicide and their judicial interpretation do not reflect the tempo of our modern-day society, but rather are representative of the code of the "old west." Much of the Penal Code has remained unchanged since the date of its enactment in 1856. Specifically, in the area of justifiable homicide, no significant attempt on the part of the legislature has been made to modernize our law. Our courts have not facilitated the difficulties, but seem to have placed more emphasis upon technical rules of statutory construction than upon the development of a law to meet an everchanging society. Certainly, the legislature could perform no finer service than to reconsider the laws which shelter the violent elements of

our society and which were outdated several decades ago.[13]

We now must look more closely at those articles of the Penal Code that provide private citizens with wide discretionary powers to kill their fellows legally and with impunity. Here we recall the data for the 232 homicide cases. . . . Of these cases or episodes, 50 (22 percent) developed from a quarrel, 28 (12 percent) were the result of victim provocation, 26 (12 percent) were motivated by self-defense, and 47 (22 percent) evolved from domestic quarrels or quarrels over sex. The majority of the homicides in 1969 may therefore be said to qualify for consideration as justifiable homicide. How can this be? The answer, or certainly part of the answer, is to be found in the Penal Code.

Article 1220 of the Texas Penal Code explicitly allows a husband to kill his wife and her paramour if caught in the act of adultery. Although the statute narrowly specifies that the right to kill prevails only as long as the adulterous couple is engaged in intercourse, or while they are still together, it is evident that few if any courts in Texas have interpreted the right to kill *in flagranto delicto* this narrowly. Interestingly enough, a wife does not have the same statutory right to kill her husband and his mistress under similar circumstances.[14]

A man does not forfeit his right of self-defense if caught in the act by a woman's husband. If courts and juries stretch the intent of the statute to include "knowledge of adultery," as opposed to witnessing the spouse in the act of adultery, the way is cleared for husbands to exercise considerable discretion in their treatment of wives. The statute, and the court decisions upholding a husband's right to kill under these circumstances, undeniably finds broad support in the social mores and values of the society. It is of further interest to note that justifiable homicides in this category do not require any legal consideration of intent; that is, whether a husband shoots his wife and her lover in "cold blood" or "in the heat of passion" does not matter. . . . In [one] case the husband quite brutally shot his friend, who was his wife's paramour, without also killing his wife. Since he had suspected that his wife and friend were involved in an adulterous relationship he literally trapped the couple and coolly decided to kill his friend but merely beat his wife. In other states or jurisdictions the husband could conceivably be charged with murder because he manifested not only intent to kill but also his actions were premeditated with malice aforethought. If the events and outcome of this case had been slightly different—if, for example, the wife's lover had seen the husband walking up to his car with a rifle and shot the husband before he shot him—the lover would face a murder charge, but the instructions to the jury, if the case was ever held over by the grand jury for formal indictment, would have necessitated a lesser charge of murder *without malice.*

Professor Stumberg's review of the Texas Penal Code articles on justifiable homicide introduces a phrase that puts the problems in bold relief. He says *"The Texas point of view* is set forth in Articles 1221, 1222, 1224, and 1227 of the Penal Code . . . " (italics added).[15] The "Texas point of view" is, of course, another way of saying Texas custom or Texas culture. It is in these Articles that we see the formalization or institutionalization of cultural values and beliefs. If certain kinds of homicide are culturally defined as lawful it matters very little whether some people more than others benefit or take advantage of the existence of such laws.

Article 1222 makes it justifiable homicide if a person attempts to prevent murder, rape, robbery, maiming, disfiguring, castration, arson, burglary, and theft at night. Of particular interest in this Article is a paragraph that states "If homicide takes place in preventing a robbery, it is justifiable if done while the robber is in the presence of the one robbed or *is flying* [sic] *with the property taken by him*" (italics added).[16] This paragraph, as we can see, permits a person to pursue a fleeing burglar or robber. To kill a fleeing person may be, and here is, viewed as an act in defense of property but it is clearly not a killing precipitated by fear of life or necessitated by self-defense.

The wording of Article 1224 makes it quite explicit that justifiable homicide applies equally to the protection of one's person and property. . . . In [one] case a man "defended" his employer's property ($150) when asked to "Hold it" by a 20-year-old youth who backed

up his verbal threat with a .22 caliber pistol. The killer was no billed by a grand jury. If the case had gone to court the killer's attorney would undoubtedly have moved for a dismissal of the case on grounds that the act was excused by Article 1224. He, after all, had not only acted in self-defense but had actually defended the property in his custody.

Article 1225 helps explain why so many persons kill and get away with it under circumstances that in other states would lead to a murder conviction. *"The party whose person or property is so unlawfully attacked is not bound to retreat in order to avoid the necessity of killing his assailant"* (italics added).[17] In Texas a person can stand this ground and, if he deems it necessary, kill a person who attacks him. In the descriptive case material we witnessed time after time instances in which both killers and victims could easily have de-escalated the seriousness of the situation by retreat. But then, of course, the coward has never been held in very high esteem by frontiersmen or anyone for that matter who equates *macho* with wisdom. The student of Western jurisprudence cannot help seeing the discrepancies here between, say, contract law and the "eye for an eye" element in the Texas Penal Code. Contracts, for example, are negotiated, validated, and subject to arbitration and mediation by third parties. The Texas laws pertaining to justifiable homicide practically eliminate the need for police, judges, juries, and any form of third party authority as long as one can convincingly establish that the killing was a response to a threat against person or property. The qualification added by Article 1226 only truncates the right to kill: "The attack upon the person of an individual in order to justify homicide must be such as produces a reasonable expectation of fear of death or some serious bodily injury."[18] . . . [In one case] a man was provoked by two other men in a cafe. He left the cafe but remained outside. When the two men came out, the provoked killer, who had retreated as far as sitting on the hood of his automobile, had armed himself and was ready to fight off the armed attacks by the two men. The killer certainly had more than a reasonable expectation of being hurt or killed, but why didn't he drive off and call the police?

Article 1224 confers a rather broad privilege to take a human life in defense of person and property. Article 1227 more specifically defines the conditions that must be met if a person exercises his privilege to kill somebody in defense of his property. The brilliant jurist W. W. Hohfeld would have scoffed at the imprecise and muddled language of Article 1227. Hohfeld, as early as 1913 and again in 1917, helped clarify the concept of property by calling attention to the symmetrical nature of all legal relations in terms of jural opposites and correlatives.[19] In brief, one cannot speak of property as either corporeal or incorporeal or of legal relations between people and objects or material possessions. Only people have legal relations, and "things," if you will, merely symbolize these relations. Notice the wording of Article 1227:

> When under article 1224 a homicide is committed in the protection of property, it must be done under the following circumstances:
>
> 1. The possession must be of corporeal property, and not of a mere right, and the possession must be actual and not merely constructive.
> 2. The possession must be legal, though the right of the property may not be in the possessor.
> 3. If possession be once lost, it is not lawful to regain it by such means as result in homicide.
> 4. Every other effort in his power must have been made by the possessor to repel the aggression before he will be justified in killing.

The wording of Article 1227 reflects a parochial understanding of legal concepts—such as confusing the manifestation or exercise of legal rights (possession) with what is called a "mere right"—and it is therefore not surprising that the citizens of Texas generally assume that they simply have a legal right or even a kind of license to kill anyone who tries to take away some of their material belongings. [In one case] the killer . . . , on the basis of hearsay evidence provided by his employee, tracked down the alleged thief and killed him when the man refused to submit to his custody. The employer had clearly lost possession of his money and his killing was not classified as justifiable. He was tried and found to be guilty of homicide *but* released from police custody with a five-year probationary sentence serving as a warning.

The final point to be made is simply this. A variety of statutory provisions exist whereby individual citizens may be justified in the taking of a human life. Few citizens are aware of the legal technicalities that separate criminal from noncriminal homicide. What many Texans do learn as part of the growing-up and socialization process is something closely akin to the principle "a lot of people need killing but no property needs stealing." The person who fails to learn that many people value their "property rights" over a basic human "right to life" is likely to find himself in trouble with "the law." You may justifiably kill because of money or property, but you cannot kill to acquire money or property. If, however, you do kill somebody and the circumstances warrant a trial by judge and jury the probabilities for being penalized and legally punished depend upon cultural views of acceptable and unacceptable homicidal behavior. That killing only rarely is viewed as an unacceptable mode of conduct is shown by the disproportionate number of killers who receive no penalty for the taking of a human life and, generally, in the number of acquittals for the minority population of killers who actually are convicted.

A Cultural Perspective on Homicidal Behavior

In the 232 homicide cases analyzed in this study, 86 percent of the killings resulted from the use of firearms. Nearly eight times as many handguns as rifles and shotguns were used in these killings. Handguns, obviously, are readily concealed and transported. They are as deadly as any other weapon at close range. These facts cast serious doubt on the general applicability of Wolfgang's statement "that few homicides due to shootings could be avoided merely if a firearm were not immediately present, and that the offender would select some other weapon to achieve the same destructive goal."[20] It may very well be true to say that the person who sets out with the single-minded intention of killing somebody else may avail himself of any weapon to achieve his goal. The descriptive case-by-case data presented in this book suggest that the majority of killers often have ambiguous rather than clearly defined motives and that many killings evolve from ambiguous circumstances and myriad different social situations.[21] The only sensible way to determine whether firearms significantly contribute to high frequencies of homicide would be to eliminate all firearms for a specified length of time! The objections to such a test, however, would very likely be as irrational and intellectually stultifying as an editorial comment in the October 1974 issue of *The American Rifleman:*

> More than a few of those who minimize the menace of Communism are loud in their alarms over legitimate gun ownership in the U.S. If you doubt it, just read your daily newspapers and make out a checklist of the public figures who are: (1) soft on Communism and; (2) tough on firearms. . . . Few if any moderates or conservatives, of whatever political party, favor firearms confiscation or anything approaching it. Nearly all of the clamor for more gun control or gun bans comes from those who take a soft attitude toward Communism, toward marijuana and other drugs, and to what many old-time Americans regard as moral laxity. . . . The purpose of such people ought to be painfully obvious by now.

But in a carefully controlled experiment on the role of weapons as aggression-eliciting stimuli, Berkowitz and LePage confirmed their hypothesis that the presence of weapons serves to elicit and escalate aggressive responses in experimental subjects.[22]

The problem is to discover how private and public sanctions, or acts of approval and disapproval, sustain the patterns of interpersonal violence in an urban community. We have looked at many examples of interpersonal violence and our emphasis now must shift to a concern with the conceptual and ideological parts of the culture that ultimately define the phenomenon of killing as either permissible or as a problem that must be brought within the boundaries of social control.

Although far from having explained fully why thousands of Americans annually are homicide victims, the data and findings of this study imply that anything short of a general cultural perspective inevitably fails to explain why so many ordinary citizens find it necessary to use violence against others. The differential treatment, both unofficial and official, accorded known killers shows how a variety of cultural sanctions precipitate and resolve one of the most fundamental problems of social life: the continuous balancing of individual freedoms with the necessities of social order or restraint. The great latitude accorded Texans by statutory law in responding to threats from fellow citizens unquestionably precipitates more violence in the populace than might otherwise be the case. By scaling official sanctions in response to the private and public interest in a particular act, a society manages to negatively sanction aggressive and violent behaviors that directly threaten overall public welfare or that interfere directly with the individual's right to enjoy property. Although various psychological and psychiatric, biological and ethological, or historical and sociological explanations expose many of the variables that correlate with violent behavior (such as intelligence, personality, social environment, and even life-style) none of these has heuristic theoretical value. Killing, as we have seen, when defined in terms of social relationships and punishment, if any, can be explained by referring to cultural values deeply embedded and reflected in formal legal institutions.[23] The cultural perspective, as clumsy and defective as it may appear at times, enables us to incorporate many different explanatory hypotheses into a general and heuristic theoretical framework.

The anthropological and scientific concept of culture is of particular value because it is all-inclusive and neutral. The concept simply refers to "all those historically created designs for living, explicit and implicit, rational, irrational and nonrational, which exist at any given time as potential guides for the behavior of men."[24] The shooting of an innocent victim for "kicks" is as complicated a cultural event as is a carefully planned and executed assassination of a political opponent. The culture concept forces us to shun such tempting ethnocentric and a priori categorizations of killers as hardened criminals, social misfits, psychopathic personalities, or delinquents. The concept allows us to see interpersonal violence as a form of behavior that is not only learned but one that is shaped in many different and subtle ways by cultural values, value orientations, beliefs, attitudes, and everyday norms for interpersonal conduct. The simple fact, so evident in the Houston data, that killers and their victims, in the majority of cases, have a great many things in common should suffice to caution us against the indiscriminate use of labels, such as murderer, that connote psychological attributes and impose a unidimensional perspective on our thinking about different forms of antisocial and anti-life behavior. The critical point here, and the one I shall be principally concerned with explaining, is how cultural guidelines for behavior actually shape the behavior of persons who employ violent means to achieve some personally defined goal.

The principal link between cultural rules, as abstract guidelines for personal conduct, and individual behavior resides in sanctions. On this point, it is difficult to improve upon Radcliffe-Brown's description of how sanctions, both positive and negative, provide the individual members of every culture with a set of prescriptive and proscriptive rules for social interaction:

> In any community there are certain modes of behavior which are usual and which characterize that particular community. Such modes of behavior may be called usages. All social usages have behind them the authority of the society, but among them some are sanctioned and others are not. A sanction is a reaction on the part of a society or of a considerable number of its members to a mode of behavior which is thereby approved (positive sanctions) or disapproved (negative sanctions). Sanctions may further be distinguished according to whether they are diffuse or organized; the former are spontaneous expressions of approval or disapproval by members of the community acting as individuals, while the latter are social sanctions carried out according to some traditional and recognized procedure. . . . The sanctions existing in a community constitute motives in the individual for the regulation of his conduct in conformity with usage.[25]

Radcliffe-Brown further clarifies, as Malinowski concluded in his study, *Crime and Custom in Savage Society* (1926), how sanctions function to ensure a high degree of social conformity and why it is even possible to speak of human behavior as governed largely by cultural norms. Radcliffe-Brown proposes that

> [sanctions] are effective, first, through the desire of the individual to obtain the approbation and to avoid the disapprobation of his fellows, to win such rewards or to avoid such punishments as the community offers or threatens; and, second, through the fact that the individual learns to react to particular modes of behavior with judgments of approval and disapproval in the same way as do his fellows, and therefore measures his own behavior both in anticipation and in retrospect by standards which conform more or less closely to those prevalent in the community to which he belongs. What is called conscience is thus in the widest sense the reflex in the individual of the sanctions of the society (ibid.).

The truly antisocial and deviant person is somebody who either fails to comprehend the rules of his social universe or who consciously rejects community standards in favor of self-defined guidelines. The person who lives outside the normative framework of his society will, if his behavior is defined as threatening or unacceptable to others, be labeled and treated as a misfit and deviant.[26]

It follows that homicide, or any form of interpersonal aggressivity and violence, not only can be viewed as a category of cultural phenomenon but can be studied and analyzed by applying general sanctioning theory. We therefore need to know, for every level of social interaction, how cultural guidelines define and redefine acceptable and unacceptable ways to employ violence in interpersonal relations.

Many Western scholars have come to identify sanctions with the negative organized sanctions of criminal law. This view has led some anthropologists to dispute the applicability of the concept of law to primitive stateless societies and political scientists and jurists to debate whether international relations, which typically lack the sanctioning powers of municipal law, can be effectively regulated with legal rather than economic or military sanctions.[27]

Although the criminal process does indeed represent a very explicit form of sanctioning behavior, it is theoretically unsound to limit the study of sanctions to those situations that most closely represent the criminal process. The general purpose here is to show how almost any kind of well-defined institutionalized sanction, such as the negative sanctions made explicit by criminal law statutes, derive their effectiveness from the complementarity between sanctions and rules of social conduct. The failure of Houston grand juries to indict a sizable number of homicidal offenders must be viewed as public evaluations of some forms of killings as acceptable.

The Danish jurist and sociologist Verner Goldschmidt has conceptualized the distinction between sanction and crime, as follows:

> The term sanction *behaviour* is used instead of merely *sanction* in order to emphasize the fact that sanction constitutes a special type of behaviour characterized by authority and disapproval. In this connection it is important to bear in mind that the deprivation of life implied by a death-penalty, the deprivation of liberty implied by imprisonment or the deprivation of economic values implied by a fine are not in themselves sanction behaviour. Considered separately these interferences might equally well be elements of respectively murder, criminal deprivation of liberty and theft. It is the symbolically meaningful reference to authority combined with disapproval, that makes the decisive difference between sanction and crime.[28]

Similarly, most economic sanctions are ineffective without complementary political or military sanctions and psychological sanctions may be equally ineffective without ritual, moral, or religious sanctions. The analysis of human interaction in terms of sanctions and sanctioning behavior promises to resolve some basic problems relating to cultural stability and change, the maintenance of order together with the protection of individual human freedom, and the resolution of cultural conflicts without recourse to destructive forms of human violence. In these concluding paragraphs it is my purpose to reflect on the Houston data in order to enlarge our perspective on social control.

In the mid-1960s, American society turned "law and order" into a potent political issue. Two major presidential crime commissions, and several new federally supported state crime fighting programs, were established to seek new solutions and to combat the disruptive activities of various protest groups and the "un-American" life-style patterns of hippies and of the drug counterculture. In the 1970s, our society is facing crises of morality, political accountability, and white-collar lawlessness. It is in this rather frantic atmosphere of never-ending crises that the remedies of organized criminal sanctions seem so promising. Yet, the Watergate scandal, which we have all seen or read about, called our attention above all to the relativity of law, as an instrument and source of power, and the profound influence of different values and beliefs on conflicting guidelines for personal and public conduct. The stress placed on the criminal justice system, as a direct result of our desire to cope with presidential misbehavior and ordinary criminality, suggests that some cultural institutions actually have reached a state in which it is possible to speak of an institutional overload.[29]

The treatment of known homicidal offenders in Texas shows us how a society manages to sort out so to speak the "trivial" from the serious. A husband-wife killing, except for very exceptional cases, is not viewed with the same seriousness as the killing of a police officer or gas station attendant. Here, no matter what else one may think of the criminal justice system, the system has a built-in governance mechanism that keeps many potential law cases from clogging the courts and ultimately perhaps generating constitutional issues (and crises) from every unique trespass against law and common morality. These points apply to the current and ongoing debate about the desirability or undesirability of punishing so-called victimless crimes (i.e., prostitution, homosexuality, etc.).

The study of sanctions represents a significant step toward creating a more balanced view of social control and cultural stability. Legal sanctions cannot and should not be expected to perform feats for which they were never designed, feats that tend to ignore the positive side of sanctioning behavior, i.e., the reward of individuals and groups for performance of valued societal duties. These so-called diffuse positive sanctions, although admittedly more illusive than the organized negative sanctions of criminal law, are extremely important to the functioning of a viable social system. The anthropologist and lawyer A. L. Epstein has summarized the relationships between sanctions and social control as follows:

> The sanction is, of course, a concept of fundamental importance in jurisprudence and has played a paramount role in different legal theories. But there seems no good reason why its use should be restricted in this way. The legal sanction, manifested in the form of the penalties, remedies, and modes of redress of the law, represents only one particular means of enforcing conformity to norms and restating their validity when they are breached. Each group and subgroup within a society tends to develop its own distinctive pattern of usages and the means of maintaining them without necessary recourse to the municipal law. Sanctions therefore come to operate within every conceivable set of group relationships: they include not only the organized sanctions of the law but also the gossip of neighbors or the customs regulating norms of production that are spontaneously generated among workers on the factory floor. In small-scale communities, or within segments of a large-scale society, informal sanctions may become more drastic than the penalties provided for in the legal code. Thus the concept of sanctions is not merely of jurisprudential interest; it also has immediate sociological relevance to the analysis of the problem of social control.[30]

We also should examine why it is felt to be necessary to punish a marijuana smoker more severely than a killer and why low income workers often pay higher income taxes than many millionaires. These brief examples may serve to illustrate how criminal sanctions have become the source of what I term the institutional overload. The Houston data illustrate how

a large community can effect social control through a variety of sanctioning processes. One such process, so clearly evident in the cases presented in this book, demonstrates how a community positively rewards private citizens who defend their rights, personal honor, or their property by taking the lives of those who threaten them. The data further show that homicides that result from unsatisfactory interpersonal relationships are not viewed in any way as threatening to the maintenance of social order. Because the vast majority of Texas homicidal offenders are "first offenders," we must acknowledge that the low frequency of punishment for killers effectively pushes "the problem" out of the overloaded criminal justice system and back into the community.

We should clarify the basic conceptual problems here. Sanctioning behavior must be conceptually and analytically separated from other forms of social interaction. The sanctioning concept must be heuristic and universal. It must apply to interpersonal interaction and social group relations. Equal attention must be directed toward clarification of positive or negative and diffuse or organized sanctioning behavior. A general model of this sanctioning process must simultaneously make operational the sanction concept at different levels within each society and be cross-culturally applicable, for scientific purposes only.

Our model specifies that sanctioning behavior, and in turn the sanctioning process, begins with some form of interaction. The interaction involves a sanctioning agent and any number of members of the social system. Systematic description of the kinds of interaction that result in the application of some kind of sanction will, in part, depend on the quality and richness of the ethnographic data. A homicidal episode, an economic transaction, a contractual agreement, or an involved and difficult negotiated settlement between two parties all represent behavioral events leading to empirical inputs into the sanctioning model. The data or interactions, which are essential to a description of how the sanctioning process applies at different levels, and at different historical time intervals, within each society, yield information on different sanctioning thresholds. The sanctioning threshold, which varies between different levels within one society, represents that point in an interaction at which the sanctioning agent either approves or disapproves, overtly or covertly, of a specific act or behavior.[31] The homicides described in this book illustrate how private and public agents decide on the relative seriousness of a particular act. Witnesses to a killing give the police their views on the interactional context of a killing. The police, and in turn the district attorney, make further judgments that affect the outcome for the killer. If, as demonstrated by eyewitness statements and the official interpretation of the homicidal episode, a victim has participated in the release of a sanction against himself, the official response will be quite different from cases in which a killer attacks persons and property without victim provocation.

Once the situation that triggers the release of the sanction has been described, it is possible to observe not only the different kinds of sanctions used within the society but to see the overall sanctioning process at work. The task here is to categorize and understand the particular kinds of sanctioning mechanisms actually in use relative to the context of specific situations and, further, to study the range of sanctioning mechanisms invoked by sanctioning agents (e.g., legal, social, political, economic, religious, psychological, military, ritualistic, moral, or customary). It is not immediately important to classify the different kinds of sanctions as either organized or diffuse or positive or negative. The essential problem is to collectively characterize the kinds of sanctions in relationship to the kinds of situations that invoke the sanctioning processes. . . .

The study of homicide as a form of social interaction permits us to narrow the data base line down to manageable proportions. The study of homicide allows us to scale different sanctions in terms of relative importance, seriousness, and general frequency of expression. It is neither difficult to shift the focus from the analysis of a particular sanctioning subsystem, such as the sanctions that specifically pertain to homicide, to other forms of violent interaction (such as rape, assault, child abuse) nor impossible to extend the analysis to other kinds of social relationships that involve persons in different but less lethal transactional episodes.

We have seen indirectly how such variables as technology or the level of socioeconomic complexity may fail to affect the general outline of sanctioning behavior. It is suspected that cross-cultural differences in sanctioning behavior will reside with individual and cultural usages of different kinds of sanctioning mechanisms rather than with any inherent complexities between simple homogeneous societies and complex heterogeneous ones. Sanctions are clearly more than reactions to breaches of conduct or expressions of approval for conformity. Sanctions must, in some real sense, be part of the cultural ideology and values so that human social action is integrated and coordinated to serve cultural rather than individual ends. Social integration, and in turn cultural stability, must to a large extent result from a compromise between the allocation of authority and social privilege and the preservation of individual choice and action. Societies change, and individuals constantly adjust their motivations and decision-making choices, in response to internal as well as external pressures for change. A clear understanding of sanctioning processes can help us understand how and perhaps even why total cultural systems both sustain and modify their behavioral and ideological guidelines in response to the changing demands of human existence. It is impossible to predict *when* Americans will view the social and private costs of interpersonal violence as parallel in seriousness to the loss of life and happiness to cancer, heart attack, alcoholism, or any form of human experience that prevents the individual, and ultimately society, from maximizing personal and collective achievement. Professor Schneider's insightful study of the punishment for incest in a small Pacific Island society concludes with an important observation that supports the notion that the definition of crime and punishment is relative to the general cultural values and traditions found among the members of any human society. According to Schneider, "The Yap data suggest that it may be useful to separate the problem of why an act is deemed wrong from the question of what is done about it and by whom. It seems that what is done about a particular crime depends very much on who has the right to do something about it. This is essentially a political question and depends on the manner in which the right to use force is distributed throughout the social structure."[32] It is evident from the data presented in this book that Houstonians in particular and Texans in general have maintained a working equilibrium between the rights of private citizens and public officials to negatively sanction disapproved forms of social behavior with death.

Notes

1. Prosser, *Handbook of the Law of Torts* (1964, p. 7).
2. Ibid., p. 7.
3. See, for example, the following studies of victim compensation programs: Brooks' "Compensating Victims of Crime" (1973), Cameron's "Compensation for Victims of Crime" (1963), Edelhertz and Geis' *Public Compensation to Victims of Crime* (1974), Geis' "State Compensation to Victims of Crime" (1967), Lamborn's "Toward a Victim Orientation in Criminal Theory" (1968), Rothstein's "State Compensation for Criminally Inflicted Injuries" (1965), and Sandler's "Compensation for Victims of Crime" (1966).
4. See, for example, *Vernon's Texas Codes Annotated: Penal Code* (1974), Vol. 1, pp. ix–x, 82–90.
5. Bubany, "The Texas Penal Code of 1974" (1974, p. 306). See, also, O'Donnel "Problems with the Texas Penal Code" (1974).
6. Norbert Wiener, *The Human Use of Human Beings* (1954).
7. See, for example, Marshall's *Law and Psychology in Conflict* (1966) and Menninger's *The Crime of Punishment* (1966).
8. Hoebel, *The Law of Primitive Man* (1954) (Chapter 5).
9. Stephen, *A History of the Criminal Law of England* (1883, p. 21).
10. See, Holmes' *The Common Law* (1881, esp. Lecture II).
11. Michael and Wechsler, "A Rationale of the Law of Homicide" (1937, p. 731).
12. *Vernon's Texas Codes Annotated: Penal Code* (1974, Vol. 1, p. xxi). See, also, Baab and Furgeson, "Texas Sentencing Practices" (1967), for a discussion of how analogous criminal offenses result in variable sentences and punishments for offenders.
13. Ravkind, "Justifiable Homicide in Texas" (1959, p. 524). See, also, the 1974 Code, Chapter 9.
14. Chapter 9 of the 1974 Penal Code has omitted adultery as a category of justifiable homicide.
15. Stumberg, "Defense of Person and Property under Texas Criminal Law" (1942, p. 21).
16. *Vernon's Annotated Penal Code* (1961, p. 469).
17. Ibid., p. 547.
18. Ibid., p. 549.
19. Hohfeld, "Some Fundamental Legal Conceptions as Applied in Judicial Reasoning" (1913 and 1917),
20. Wolfgang, *Patterns in Criminal Homicide* (1958, p. 83).
21. For a more detailed view of these arguments see, for example, Seitz, "Firearms, Homicides, and Gun Control Effectiveness" (1972), and Zimring, "Is Gun Control Likely to Reduce Violent Killings?" (1968).
22. Berkowitz and LePage, "Weapons as Aggression-Eliciting Stimuli" (1967).
23. See, for example, Gibbons, *Society, Crime, and Criminal Careers* (1968).
24. Kluckhohn and Kelly, "The Concept of Culture" (1945). See, also, Kroeber and Kluckhohn, *Culture* (1952); Kaplan and Manners, *Culture Theory* (1972); White, "The Concept of Culture" (1959); and Weiss, "A Scientific Concept of Culture" (1973).
25. Radcliffe-Brown, "Social Sanction" (1934, p. 531).
26. See, for example, Cohen, *Deviance and Control* (1966).
27. See, for example, the following general studies in the field of legal anthropology: Hoebel, *The Law of Primitive Man* (1954); Nader, *The Anthropological Study of Law* (1965); Bohannan, "The Differing Realms of the Law" (1965); Friedman, "Legal Culture and Social Development"; and Pospisil, *The Ethnology of Law* (1972).
28. Goldschmidt, "Primary Sanction Behavior" (1966, p. 179).
29. Compare, for example, Packer's book, *The Limits of the Criminal Sanction* (1968).
30. Epstein, "Sanctions" (1968, p. 1).

31. Goldschmidt (ibid., p. 177) defines "sanction-threshold" as *"the total amount of conditions for releasing an organized negative sanction in a given social situation.* The sanction-threshold is not fixed but is assumed to vary like the tolerance limits from situation to situation."
32. Schneider, "Political Organization, Supernatural Sanctions, and the Punishment for Incest on Yap" (1957, p. 800).

References

[Anon.]. *Vernon's Annotated Penal Code of the State of Texas.* Vol. 2A. St. Paul, Minn.: West Publishing Co., 1961.
[Anon.]. *Vernon's Texas Codes Annotated: Penal Code* (Sections 1.01 to 18). St. Paul, Minn.: West Publishing Co., 1974.
Baab, George William, and Furgeson, William Royal, Jr. Texas Sentencing Practices: A Statistical Study. *Texas Law Review* 45:471–503, 1967.
Berkowitz, Leonard, and LePage, Anthony. Weapons as Aggression-Eliciting Stimuli. *Journal of Personality and Social Psychology* 7:202–7, 1967.
Bohannan, Paul. The Differing Realms of the Law. *American Anthropologist* 67:33–42, 1965.
Brooks, James. Compensating Victims of Crime: The Recommendations of Program Administrators. *Law and Society Review* 7:445–71, 1973.
Bubany, Charles P. The Texas Penal Code of 1974. *Southwestern Law Journal* 28:292–339, 1974.
Cameron, Bruce J. Compensation for Victims of Crime: The New Zealand Experiment. *Journal of Public Law* 12:367–75, 1963.
Cohen, Albert K. *Deviance and Control.* Englewood Cliffs, N.J.: Prentice-Hall, Inc., 1966.
Edelhertz, Herbert, and Geis, Gilbert. *Public Compensation to Victims of Crime.* New York: Praeger Publishers, Inc., 1974.
Epstein, Arnold L. Sanctions. In *International Encyclopedia of the Social Sciences,* Vol. 14, edited by David L. Sills. New York: The Macmillan Company and the Free Press, 1968.
Friedman, Lawrence M. Legal Culture and Social Development. In Friedman, Lawrence M. and Stewart Macaulay [comp.]. *Law and the Behavioral Sciences.* New York: The Bobbs-Merrill Co., Inc., 1969.
Geis, Gilbert. State Compensation to Victims of Violent Crime. In The President's Commission on Law Enforcement and Administration of Justice. *Task Force Report: Crime and Its Impact—An Assessment.* Washington, D.C.: U.S. Government Printing Office, 1967, pp. 157–77.
Gibbons, Don C. *Society, Crime and Criminal Careers.* Englewood Cliffs, N.J.: Prentice-Hall, Inc., 1968.
Goldschmidt, Verner. Primary Sanction Behaviour. *Acta Sociologica* 10:173–90, 1966.
Hoebel, E. Adamson. *The Law of Primitive Man.* Cambridge: Harvard University Press, 1954.
Hohfeld, Wesley N. Fundamental Legal Conceptions as Applied in Judicial Reasoning. *Yale Law Journal* 26:710–70, 1917.
Holmes, Oliver W., Jr. *The Common Law.* Boston: Little, Brown, 1881 [Mark DeWolfe Howe, ed. Cambridge: Harvard University Press, 1963].
Kaplan, David, and Manners, Robert A. *Culture Theory.* Englewood Cliffs, N.J.: Prentice-Hall, Inc., 1972.
Kluckhohn, Clyde, and Kelly, William H. The Concept of Culture. In *The Science of Man in the World Crisis,* edited by Ralph Linton. New York: Columbia University Press, 1945, pp. 78–106.
Lamborn, Leroy L. Toward a Victim Orientation in Criminal Theory. *Rutgers Law Review* 22:733–68, 1968.
Malinowski, Bronislaw. *Crime and Custom in Savage Society.* London: Routledge and Kegan Paul, Ltd., 1926.
Marshall, James. *Law and Psychology in Conflict.* New York: The Bobbs-Merrill Co., 1966.
Menninger, Karl. *The Crime of Punishment.* New York: The Viking Press, Inc., 1966.
Nader, Laura. The Anthropological Study of Law. *American Anthropologist* [Special Publication] 67:3–32, 1965.
O'Donnell, James. Problems with the Texas Penal Code. *Houston Law Review* 11:1229–49, 1974.
Pospisil, Leopold. *The Ethnology of Law.* Addison-Wesley Modular Publications, No. 12:1–40, 1972.
Prosser, William L. *Handbook of the Law of Torts.* 3rd ed. St. Paul, Minn.: West Publishing Co., 1964.
Radcliffe-Brown, Alfred R. Social Sanction. *Encyclopaedia of the Social Sciences* 13:531–34. New York: Macmillan Co., 1934.
Ravkind, William M. Justifiable Homicide in Texas [Comment]. *Southwestern Law Journal* 13:508–24, 1959.
Rothstein, Paul F. State Compensation for Criminally Inflicted Injuries. *Texas Law Review* 44:38–54, 1965.

Sandler, Robert A. Compensation for Victims of Crime—Some Practical Considerations. *Buffalo Law Review* 15:645–55, 1966.

Schneider, David M. Political Organization, Supernatural Sanctions, and the Punishment for Incest on Yap. *American Anthropologist* 59:791–800, 1957.

Seitz, Steven T. Firearms, Homicides, and Gun Control Effectiveness. *Law and Society Review* 6:395–613, 1972.

Stephen, Sir James F. *A History of the Criminal Law of England,* Vol. III. London: MacMillan Co., 1883.

Stumberg, George W. Criminal Homicide in Texas. *Texas Law Review* 16:305–34, 1938.

Wechsler, Herbert, and Michael, Jerome. A Rationale of the Law of Homicide (I and II). *Columbia Law Review* 37:701–61, 37:1261–1325, 1937.

Weiss, Gerald. A Scientific Concept of Culture. *American Anthropologist* 75:1376–1413, 1973.

Wertham, Fredric. *A Sign for Cain.* New York: Macmillan Co., 1966.

White, Leslie. The Concept of Culture. *American Anthropologist* 61:227–51, 1959.

Wiener, Norbert. *The Human Use of Human Beings: Cybernetics and Society.* Rev. ed. Garden City, N.Y.: Doubleday and Co., Inc., 1954.

Wolfgang, Marvin E. *Patterns in Criminal Homicide.* Philadelphia, Pa.: University of Pennsylvania, 1958.

Zimring, Franklin, E. Is Gun Control Likely to Reduce Violent Killings? *The University of Chicago Law Review* 35:721–37, 1968.

9

Crime As Social Control

Donald Black

There is a sense in which conduct regarded as criminal is often quite the opposite. Far from being an intentional violation of a prohibition, much crime is moralistic and involves the pursuit of justice. It is a mode of conflict management, possibly a form of punishment, even capital punishment. Viewed in relation to law, it is self-help. To the degree that it defines or responds to the conduct of someone else—the victim—as deviant, crime is social control. And to this degree it is possible to predict and explain crime with aspects of the sociological theory of social control, in particular, the theory of self-help. After an overview of self-help in traditional and modern settings, the following pages briefly examine in turn the so-called struggle between law and self-help, the deterrence of crime, the processing of self-help by legal officials, and, finally, the problem of predicting and explaining self-help itself.

Traditional Self-Help

Much of the conduct described by anthropologists as conflict management, social control, or even law in tribal and other traditional societies is regarded as crime in modern societies. This is especially clear in the case of violent modes of redress such as assassination, feuding, fighting, maiming, and beating, but it also applies to the confiscation and destruction of property and to other forms of deprivation and humiliation. Such actions typically express a grievance by one person or group against another (see Moore, 1972:67–72). Thus, one anthropologist notes that among the Bena Bena of highland New Guinea, as among most tribes of that region, "rather than being proscribed, violent self-help is prescribed as a method of social control" (Langness, 1972:182). The same might be said of numerous societies throughout the world. On the other hand, violence is quite rare in many traditional societies, and at least some of it is condemned in all. What follows is not intended as a representative overview, then, since only the more violent societies and modes of self-help are illustrated. First consider homicide.

In one community of Maya Indians in southern Mexico, for example, any individual killed from ambush is automatically labelled "the one who had the guilt." Everyone assumes that the deceased individual provoked his own death through an act of wrongdoing: "Homicide is considered a *reaction* to crime, not a crime in itself" (Nash, 1967:456). Similarly, it has been observed that in a number of equatorial African societies homicide is rarely predatory—committed for gain—but is nearly always related to a grievance or quarrel of some kind (Bohannan, 1960:256). The Eskimos of the American Arctic also kill people in response to various offenses, including adultery, insult, and simply being a nuisance (see Hoebel, 1954:83–88; van den Steenhoven, 1962: Ch. 4); and, to mention still another example, the Ifugao of the Philippines hold that any "self-respecting man" must kill an adulterer

---

"Crime as Social Control," by Donald Black. *American Sociological Review* 48 (1983), pp. 34–45. Reprinted by permission of the American Sociological Association.

Support for this work was provided by the Program in Law and Social Science of the National Science Foundation. A number of people made helpful comments on an earlier draft: M. P. Baumgartner, John L. Comaroff, Mark Cooney, Jack P. Gibbs, Richard O. Lempert, Craig B. Little, Sally Engle Merry, Alden D. Miller, Calvin K. Morrill, Trevor W. Nagel, Lloyd E. Ohlin, and Alan Stone.

discovered *in flagrante delicto* (Barton, [1919] 1969:66–70). Societies such as these have, in effect, capital punishment administered on a private basis. But unlike penalties imposed by the state, private executions often result in revenge or even a feud, a reciprocal exchange of violence that might last months or years (see, e.g., Otterbein and Otterbein, 1965; Rieder, 1973). Moreover, the person killed in retaliation may not be himself or herself a killer, since in these societies violent conflicts between nonkin are virtually always handled in a framework of collective responsibility—or, more precisely, collective liability—whereby all members of a family or other group are accountable for the conduct of their fellows (see, e.g., Moore, 1972).

Violence of other kinds also expresses a grievance in most instances. Among the Yanomamö of Venezuela and Brazil, for example, women are routinely subjected to corporal punishment by their husbands: "Most reprimands meted out by irate husbands take the form of blows with the hand or with a piece of firewood, but a good many husbands are even more brutal" (Chagnon, 1977:82–83). In parts of East Africa, "Husbands often assault their wives, sometimes with a slap, sometimes with a fist, a foot, or a stick" (Edgerton, 1972:164); and among the Qolla of Peru, a husband may beat his wife "when her behavior warrants it," such as when she is "lazy" or "runs around with other men" (Bolton and Bolton, 1973:64). Another punishment for women in some societies is rape by a group of men, or "gang rape" (e.g., Llewellyn and Hoebel, 1941:202–210). Everywhere, however, it appears that most violence is inflicted upon men by other men.

Property destruction may also be a mode of social control. An extreme form is house burning, a practice quite frequent, for example, in parts of East Africa (Edgerton, 1972:164). Animals, gardens, or other property might be destroyed as well. Among the Cheyenne of the American Plains, a man's horse might be killed (Llewellyn and Hoebel, 1941:117), and in northern Albania, a dog might be killed (Hasluck, 1954:76–78). In one case in Lebanon (later punished as a crime), an aggrieved man cut the branches off his adversary's walnut tree (Rothenberger, 1978:169). Among the Qolla, crops are sometimes damaged as a punishment, such as

"when a man methodically uproots his enemy's potato plants before they have produced any tubers" (Bolton, 1973:234). Netsilik Eskimos may subtly encourage their children to destroy an offender's cache of food, so that what appears to be mischief or vandalism may actually be a carefully orchestrated act of revenge (van den Steenhoven, 1962:74).

Property may also be confiscated as a form of social control, so that what might at first appear to a modern observer as unprovoked theft or burglary proves in many cases to be a response to the misconduct of the victim. Among the Mbuti Pygmies of Zaire, for instance, a seeming theft may be recognized by all as an "unofficial sanction" against a person who has incurred "public disapproval for some reason or another" (Turnbull, 1965:199). Among the Qolla, the moralistic character of a theft is especially clear "when the object stolen has no value to the thief" (Bolton, 1973:233). Lastly, it might be noted that where women are regarded as the property of their fathers or husbands, rape may provide a means of retaliation against a man. This seems to have been involved in some of the gang rapes recorded as crimes in fourteenth-century England, for example, where even a widow might be attacked by a group of men as an act of revenge against her deceased husband (Hanawalt, 1979:109, 153). In some cases, then, rape may be construed as another kind of confiscation.

Modern Self-Help

A great deal of the conduct labelled and processed as crime in modern societies resembles the modes of conflict management—described above—that are found in traditional societies which have little or no law (in the sense of governmental social control—Black, 1972:1096). Much of this conduct is intended as a punishment or other expression of disapproval, whether applied reflectively or impulsively, with coolness or in the heat of passion. Some is an effort to achieve compensation, or restitution, for a harm that has been done. The response may occur long after the offense, perhaps weeks, months, or even years later; after a series of offenses, each viewed singly as only a minor aggravation but together viewed as intolerable; or as an immediate response to the offense, perhaps during a fight or other conflict, or after an assault, theft, insult, or injury.

As in tribal and other traditional societies, for example, most intentional homicide in modern life is a response to conduct that the killer regards as deviant. In Houston during 1969, for instance, over one-half of the homicides occurred in the course of a "quarrel," and another one-fourth occurred in alleged "self-defense" or were "provoked," whereas only a little over one-tenth occurred in the course of predatory behavior such as burglary or robbery (calculated from Lundsgaarde, 1977:237; see also Wolfgang, [1958] 1966: Ch. 10). Homicide is often a response to adultery or other matters relating to sex, love, or loyalty, to disputes about domestic matters (financial affairs, drinking, housekeeping) or affronts to honor, to conflicts relating to debts, property, and child custody, and to other questions of right and wrong. Cases mentioned in the Houston study include one in which a young man killed his brother during a heated discussion about the latter's sexual advances toward his younger sisters, another in which a man killed his wife after she "dared" him to do so during an argument about which of several bills they should pay, one where a women killed her husband during a quarrel in which the man struck her daughter (his stepdaughter), one in which a woman killed her 21-year-old son because he had been "fooling around with homosexuals and drugs," and two others in which people died from wounds inflicted during altercations over the parking of an automobile (Lundsgaarde, 1977). Like the killings in traditional societies described by anthropologists, then, most intentional homicide in modern society may be classified as social control, specifically as self-help, even if it is handled by legal officials as crime. From this standpoint, it is apparent that capital punishment is quite common in modern America—in Texas, homicide is one of the ten leading causes of death—though it is nearly always a private rather than a public affair.

Most conduct that a lawyer would label as assault may also be understood as self-help. In the vast majority of cases the people involved know one another, usually quite intimately, and the physical attack arises in the context of a grievance or quarrel (see, e.g., Vera Institute, 1977:23–42). Commonly the assault is a punishment, such as when a husband beats or otherwise injures his wife because she has not lived up to his expectations. In one case that came to the attention of the police in Boston, for example, a woman complained that her husband had beaten her because supper was not ready when he came home from work (Black, 1980:161), a state of affairs, incidentally, which might have been the woman's own way of expressing disapproval of her husband (see Baumgartner, 1983). Other standards are enforced violently as well. In one instance that occurred in a major northeastern city and that apparently was not reported to the police, a young woman's brothers attacked and beat her boyfriend "for making her a drug addict," and in another a young man was stabbed for cooperating with the police in a burglary investigation (Merry, 1981:158, 180–181). In a case in Washington, D.C., that resulted in an arrest, a boy shot his gang leader for taking more than his proper share of the proceeds from a burglary (Allen, 1977:40–43). Years later, the same individual shot someone who had been terrorizing young women—including the avenger's girlfriend—in his neighborhood. Though he pleaded guilty to "assault with a deadly weapon" and was committed to a reformatory, not surprisingly he described himself as "completely right" and his victim as "completely wrong" (Allen, 1977:62–66, 69–70).

Indigenous people arrested for violence in colonial societies are likely to have a similar point of view: They may be proud of what they have done and admit it quite openly, even while they are being prosecuted as criminals by the foreign authorities. Those apprehended in Europe for the crime of duelling—also a method of conflict resolution—have typically lacked remorse for the same reasons (see Pitt-Rivers, 1966:29–31). Thus, when asked by a priest to pray for forgiveness before being hanged for killing a man with a sword, one such offender in France exclaimed, "Do you call one of the cleverest thrusts in Gascony a crime?" (Baldick, 1965:62). As in duelling, moreover, violence in modern societies is often prescribed by a code of honor. He who shrinks from it is disgraced as a coward (see, e.g., Werthman, 1969; Horowitz and Schwartz, 1974).

Many crimes involving the confiscation or destruction of property also prove to have a normative character when the facts come fully to light. There are, for example, moralistic burglaries, thefts, and robberies. Over one-third of the burglaries in New York City resulting in arrest involve people with a prior relationship (Vera Institute, 1977:82), and these not infrequently express a grievance the burglar has against his victim. In one such case handled by the Boston police, for instance, a woman who had been informed by a neighbor complained that while she was away "her estranged husband had entered her apartment, wrecked it, loaded all of her clothes into his car, and driven away, presumably headed for his new home several hundred miles away" (Black, 1980:115). Though the specific nature of this man's grievance was not mentioned, it seems apparent that his actions were punitive to some degree, and surely his estranged wife understood this as well. In a case in New York City, one resulting in two arrests for burglary, two black women barged into the home of an elderly white woman at midnight to confront her because earlier in the day she had remonstrated with their children for throwing rocks at her window (Vera Institute, 1977:88). A crime may also be committed against a particular individual to express the disapproval of a larger number of people, such as a neighborhood or community, as is illustrated by the report of a former burglar who notes in his autobiography that early in his career he selected his victims partly on moralistic grounds:

> We always tried to get the dude that the neighbors didn't like too much or the guy that was hard on the people who lived in the neighborhood. . . . I like to think that all the places were robbed, that we broke into, was kind of like the bad guys. (Allen, 1977: 39–40)

It should be clear, however, that the victims of moralistic crime may be entirely unaware of why they have been selected, especially when the offender is unknown. Such crimes may therefore be understood as secret social control (compare Becker, 1963:20).

Another possible mode of self-help is robbery, or theft involving violence. Thus, in New York City, where over one-third of the people arrested for robbery are acquainted with their victims, the crime often arises from a quarrel over money (Vera Institute, 1977:65–71). In one case, for example, a woman reported that her sister and her sister's boyfriend had taken her purse and $40 after assaulting her and threatening to kill her baby, but she later explained that this had arisen from a misunderstanding: The boyfriend wanted reimbursement for a baby carriage that he had bought for her, whereas she thought it had been a gift (Vera Institute, 1977:69–70). It seems, in fact, that in many instances robbery is a form of debt collection and an alternative to law. The same applies to embezzlement, though it may also simply express disapproval of the employer who is victimized (see Cressey, 1953:57–59, 63–66).

Conduct known as vandalism, or malicious destruction of property, proves to be a form of social control in many cases as well. Far from being merely "malicious," "non-utilitarian," or "negativistic," with "no purpose, no rhyme, no reason" (Cohen, 1955:25–30, including quoted material in note 4), much vandalism in modern society is similar to the moralistic destruction of crops, animals, and other valuables in traditional societies. But whereas, say, a Plains Indian might kill a horse, a modern agent of justice might damage the offender's automobile. Thus, in one American neighborhood where parking spaces on the street are scarce, the residents have evolved their own distribution system, with its own customary rules and enforcement procedures. In the winter, one such rule is that whoever shovels the snow from a parking space is its "owner," and persistent violators may find that their automobile has been spraypainted or otherwise abused (Thomas-Buckle and Buckle, 1982:84, 86–87). Vandalism may also be reciprocated in a feudlike pattern of mutual destruction: In one case in a northeastern city, a young man found that someone had broken the radio antenna on his automobile, learned from some children who had done it, and thereupon proceeded to slash the tires of the offender's automobile (Merry, 1981:179).

Business places and dwellings may be damaged to punish their owners or inhabitants. Arson, or burning, has a long history of this kind (see, e.g., Hanawalt, 1979:90–91). Less severe sanctions, however, are far more frequent. In a case occurring in a suburb of New York City, for example, a young man drove his car across someone's lawn during a quarrel, and in another incident in the same community several young men spraypainted parts of an older man's house in the middle of the night because he had called the police to disperse them when they were sitting in their cars drinking beer and listening to music (Baumgartner, 1988). If all of the facts were known, then, it seems likely that much seemingly senseless and random vandalism would prove to be retaliation by young people against adults (see Greenberg, 1977:202–204). Some may even be done by children on behalf of their parents, in a pattern analogous to that found among the Eskimos mentioned earlier (for a possible example, see Black, 1980:167–68). If the parents themselves are the offenders, however, other strategies might be followed. Among the Tarahumara Indians of northern Mexico, children with a grievance against their parents often "run away" from home, staying with an uncle or grandparent for a few days before returning (Fried, 1953:291). Qolla children have a similar custom, locally known as "losing themselves" (Bolton and Bolton, 1973:15–16). Modern children do this as well, though like vandalism it is commonly regarded as a form of juvenile delinquency.

Finally, it might be noted that the practice of collective liability—whereby all of the people in a social category are held accountable for the conduct of each of their fellows—occurs in modern as well as traditional societies. This is most apparent during a war, revolution, or riot, when anyone might suffer for the deeds of someone else, but during peaceful times too, seemingly random violence may often be understood in the same way. Today a police officer might become the victim of a surprise attack by a stranger, for example, because of the conduct of one or more fellow officers in the past. Seemingly random crime of other kinds may involve collective liability as well. Thus, for instance, a black rapist described his selection of white victims as a process of vengeance against white people in general:

> It delighted me that I was defying and trampling upon the white man's law, upon his system of values, and that I was defiling his

women—and this point, I believe, was the most satisfying to me because I was very resentful over the historical fact of how the white man has used the black woman. I felt I was getting revenge. (Cleaver, 1968:14)

Similarly, a former burglar and robber remarked that he once selected his victims primarily from a relatively affluent neighborhood, but not simply because this provided a chance of greater material gain: "I really disliked them people, 'cause it seemed like they thought they was better 'cause they had more" (Allen, 1977:32–33). People might be held collectively liable because of their neighborhood, social class, race, or ethnicity. Crime by young people against adult strangers may also have this logic in some cases: All adults might be held liable for the conduct of those known personally, such as police, teachers, and parents. Among young people themselves, particularly in large American cities, rival "gangs" may engage in episodic violence resembling the feud in traditional settings, where each member of a feuding group is liable—to injury or even death—for the conduct of the other members (see, e.g., Yablonsky, 1962). A significant amount of crime in modern society may even resemble what anthropologists describe as "raiding," a kind of predatory behavior often directed at people collectively defined as deserving of revenge (see, e.g., Sweet, 1965; Schneider, 1971:4). And some might properly be construed as "banditry" since it seems to be a kind of primitive rebellion by those at the bottom of society against their social superiors (see Hobsbawm, 1969). In short, although much crime in modern society directly and unambiguously expresses a grievance by one person against another, this may be only the most visible portion of a much broader phenomenon.

Theoretical Considerations

When a moralistic crime is handled by the police or prosecuted in court, the official definition of the event is drastically different from that of the people involved, particularly from that of the alleged offender. In the case of a husband who shoots his wife's lover, for example, the definition of who is the offender and who is the victim is reversed: The wife's lover is defined as the victim, even though he was shot because of an offense he committed against the woman's husband. Moreover, the lover's offense is precisely the kind for which violent social control—by the husband—is viewed as acceptable and appropriate, if not obligatory, in numerous tribal and other traditional societies. Even in modern society, it might be said that the husband is charged with violating the criminal law because he enforced his rights in what many regard as the customary law of marriage. The victim thus becomes the offender, and vice versa. The state prosecutes the case in its own name, while the original offender against morality (if alive) serves as a witness against the man he has victimized—surely a perverse proceeding from the standpoint of the defendant (compare Christie, 1977). It is also enlightening in this regard to consider criminal cases arising from quarrels and fights, where each party has a grievance against the other. Here the state often imposes the categories of offender and victim upon people who were contesting the proper application of these labels during the altercation in question. Whether there was originally a cross-complaint or not, however, in all of these cases the state defines someone with a grievance as a criminal. The offense lies in how the grievance was pursued. The crime is self-help.

It should be apparent from much of the foregoing that in modern society the state has only theoretically achieved a monopoly over the legitimate use of violence (compare, e.g., Weber, [1919] 1958:78; Elias, [1939] 1978:201-202). In reality, violence flourishes (particularly in modern America), and most of it involves ordinary citizens who seemingly view their conduct as a perfectly legitimate exercise of social control. It might therefore be observed that the struggle between law and self-help in the West did not end in the Middle Ages, as legal historians claim (e.g., Pollock and Maitland, [1898] 1968: Vol. 2, 574; Pound, 1921:139–40; see also Hobhouse, 1906: Ch.3). It continues. Many people still "take the law into their own hands." They seem to view their grievances as their own business, not that of the police or other officials, and resent the intrusion of law (see Matza, 1964: Ch.5). They seem determined to have justice done, even

if this means that they will be defined as criminals. Those who commit murder, for example, often appear to be resigned to their fate at the hands of the authorities; many wait patiently for the police to arrive; some even call to report their own crimes (see generally Lundsgaarde, 1977). In cases of this kind, indeed, the individuals involved might arguably be regarded as martyrs. Not unlike workers who violate a prohibition to strike—knowing they will go to jail—or others who defy the law on grounds of principle, they do what they think is right, and willingly suffer the consequences.

Deterrence and Self-Help

To the degree that people feel morally obligated to commit crimes, it would seem that the capacity of the criminal law to discourage them—its so-called deterrent effect—must be weakened. For example, homicides committed as a form of capital punishment would seem to be more difficult to deter than those committed entirely in pursuit of personal gain (on the deterrability of the latter, see Chambliss, 1967). This is not to deny that moralistic homicide can be discouraged to some extent. In fact, one former resident of Harlem has noted that the inhabitants of that unusually violent area appear to debate in their own minds whether or not moralistic homicide is ultimately worth its legal consequences:

> I think everybody was curious about whether or not it was worth it to kill somebody and save your name or your masculinity, defend whatever it was that had been offended—whether it was you or your woman or somebody in your family. (Brown, 1965:220)

He adds that during his years in Harlem this question loomed especially large whenever anyone was executed in prison (Brown, 1965:220). That the desirability of killing another person is entertained at all is remarkable, however, particularly when the death penalty is believed to be a possible result (a belief that appears to be largely unfounded—see below). Furthermore, since other crimes of self-help carry fewer risks of a legal nature, they should be even harder to discourage than homicide. In any event, a theory of deterrence surely should recognize that the power of punishment to deter crime partly depends upon whether a given crime is itself a form of social control (for other relevant variables see, e.g., Andenaes, 1966; Chambliss, 1967; Zimring, 1971).

A related question is the extent to which victimizations are deterred by self-help rather than—or in addition to—law. Although many citizens are entirely dependent upon legal officials such as the police to handle criminal offenders, others are prepared to protect themselves and their associates by any means at their disposal, including violence. It is well known among potential predators in one American neighborhood, for example, that a number of the residents would be dangerous to victimize, in some cases because they enjoy the protection of family members who act as their champions (see Merry, 1981:178–79). Such people are left alone. Entire segments of a community may also be avoided from fear of retaliation. For example, for this reason some thieves and robbers may avoid the poor: "One of the most dangerous things in the world is to steal from poor people. . . . When you steal from the poor, you gamble with your life" (Brown, 1965:214; see also Allen, 1977; 50–52). Moreover, since the deterrent effect of social control generally increases with its severity (see Zimring, 1971:83–90, for qualifications), it should be noted that self-help is often more severe than law. Thus, a burglar or robber might be executed by his intended victim, though burglary and robbery are generally not capital crimes in modern codes of law. Accordingly, to the degree that self-help is effectively repressed by the state, crime of other kinds might correspondingly increase. Among the Gusii of Kenya, for instance, rape dramatically increased after the British prohibited traditional violence against strangers—potential rapists—and, when a rape occurred, violence against the offender and possibly his relatives (Le Vine, 1959:476–77). Perhaps some of the predatory crime in modern society is similarly a result of a decline in self-help.

The Processing of Self-Help

Even while the ancient struggle between law and self-help continues, the response of legal officials to those handling their own grievances by force and violence is not nearly so severe as might be supposed. In fact, crimes of self-help are often handled with comparative leniency. An extreme of this pattern was seen historically, for example, in the generous application of the concept of "self-defense" to justify homicide—otherwise by law a capital offense—in medieval England: In cases in which a killing involved social control, it appears that juries routinely avoided a conviction by fabricating a version of the incident in which the victim had first attacked the defendant, forcing him to resist with violence in order to save his own life (Green, 1976:428–36). Likewise, in more recent centuries European authorities and juries have generally been reluctant to enforce laws against duelling (see Baldick, 1965: Chs.4–7; Andrew, 1980). Earlier in the present century, the same applied to the handling of so-called lynchings in the American South—executions carried out by a group of private citizens, usually against a black man believed to have victimized a white. Typically no one was arrested, much less prosecuted or punished, though the killers frequently were well known and readily available (see, e.g., Raper, 1933). Today, much violent self-help is still tolerated by American officials and juries. Incidents that a lawyer would normally classify as felonious assault, for example—involving severe bodily injury or the threat thereof—are unlikely to result in arrest if the offender and victim are intimately related (Black, 1980:180–85; see also Black, 1971:1097–98). Where an arrest is made, prosecution and conviction are far less likely when the offense entails an element of self-help. Thus, in Houston, people whom the police arrest for homicide are often released without prosecution, and in many cases this seems to be related to the moralistic nature of the killing. In 1969, 40 percent of those arrested for killing a relative (such as a spouse or sibling) were released without prosecution, and the same applied to 37 percent of those arrested for killing a friend or other associate and to 24 percent of those arrested for killing a stranger (Lundsgaarde, 1977:232). And offenses that do initially result in prosecution are likely to be abandoned or dismissed at a later point in the process when self-help is involved, such as when a burglary or robbery is committed in order to collect an unpaid debt (see, e.g., Vera Institute,

1977:69–70, 87–88). At every stage, then, crimes of self-help often receive a degree of immunity from law (but see below).

If the capacity of law to deter crimes of self-help is weak in the first place, surely this leniency, insofar as it is known among the population, makes it weaker still. But it might be wondered why so much self-help occurs in a society such as modern America. Why do so many people criminally pursue their own grievances in a society where law is developed to such a high degree? Why, in particular, are they so violent?

The Theory of Self-Help

Several centuries ago, Thomas Hobbes argued that without a sovereign state—without law—a "war of every one against every one" would prevail, and life would be "solitary, poor, nasty, brutish, and short" [1651] 1962:100). Many stateless societies have since been observed by anthropologists, however, and Hobbes's theory has proven to be somewhat overstated: Life without law does not appear to be nearly as precarious as he believed (see, e.g., Middleton and Tait, [1958] 1970; MacCormack, 1976; Roberts, 1979). Even so, the idea that violence is associated with statelessness still enjoys considerable support. With various refinements and qualifications, an absence of state authority has been used to explain high levels of violence in settings as diverse as the highlands of New Guinea (Koch, 1974: Ch.7), Lake Titicaca in the Andes (Bolton, 1970:12–16), and western Sicily (Blok, 1974:210–12). It has also been used to explain war and other violent self-help in international relations (e.g., Hoffmann, 1968; Koch, 1974: 173–75). A version of the same approach may be relevant to an understanding of self-help in modern society.

Hobbesian theory would lead us to expect more violence and other crimes of self-help in those contemporary settings where law—governmental social control—is least developed, and, indeed, this appears to fit the facts: Crimes of self-help are more likely where law is less available. This is most apparent where legal protection is withheld as a matter of public policy, such as where a contract violates the law. A gambling debt is not legally enforceable, for example, and the same applies to transactions in illicit narcotics, prostitution, stolen goods, and the like. Perhaps for this reason many underworld businesses find it necessary to maintain, in effect, their own police, such as the "strong-arms" of illegal loan operations and the "pimps" who oversee the work of prostitutes (see, e.g., Allen, 1977:100). Furthermore, it appears that social control within settings of this kind is relatively violent (but see Reuter, 1983).

Law is unavailable, or relatively so, in many other modern settings as well, though not necessarily as a matter of public policy. A teenager with a grievance against an adult, for example, will generally be ignored or even reprimanded by the police (Black, 1980:152–55). Lower-status people of all kinds—blacks and other minorities, the poor, the homeless—enjoy less legal protection, especially when they have complaints against their social superiors, but also when conflict erupts among themselves (see Black, 1976: Chs.2–6). To the police and other authorities the problems of these people seem less serious, their injuries less severe, their honor less important. A fight or quarrel among them may even be viewed as itself a "disturbance of the peace," an offense in its own right, regardless of the issues dividing the parties (see Black and Baumgartner, 1983). People in intimate relationships, too, such as members of the same family or household, find that legal officials are relatively unconcerned about their conflicts, particularly if they occur in private and do not disturb anyone else (see Black, 1976:40–44, 1980: Ch.5). In all of these settings neglected by law, crimes of self-help are comparatively common. There are, so to speak, stateless locations in a society such as modern America, and in them the Hobbesian theory appears to have some validity.

Before closing, it is possible to specify the relationship between law and self-help more precisely. The likelihood of self-help is not merely a function of the availability of law, and, moreover, crimes of self-help are not always handled leniently by legal officials. Different locations and directions in social space have different patterns. In other words, the relationship between law and self-help depends upon who has a grievance against whom.

Four patterns can be identified: First, law may be relatively unavailable both to those with grievances and to those who are the objects of self-help, as when people of low status and people who are intimate have conflicts with each other (on the distribution of law, see generally Black, 1976). This pattern has been emphasized above. Secondly, law may be relatively unavailable to those with grievances in comparison to those who have offended them. Should the former employ self-help, they may therefore be vulnerable to harsh treatment by legal officials. This is the situation of people with a grievance against a social superior, such as a teenager with a grievance against an adult, and may help to explain why they tend to develop their own techniques of social control, including, for instance, covert retaliation, self-destruction, and flight (see Baumgartner, 1983). Those with grievances against a social inferior illustrate a third pattern: Law is readily available to them, but not to those against whom they might employ self-help. In this situation, the aggrieved party seemingly has a choice of law or self-help. A man might easily obtain legal help against his teenaged son, for example, but if he simply beats the boy instead—a kind of self-help—he is unlikely to be handled with severity by the police or other officials (see Black, 1980:152–55). The fourth possibility, where law is readily available both to those with grievances and to those who have offended them, is seen where people of high status, and also people who are strangers, have conflicts with each other. Here self-help seems to be relatively infrequent. In sum, law and self-help are unevenly distributed across social space, and each is relevant to the behavior of the other.

Conclusion

The approach taken in this paper departs radically from traditional criminology (as seen, e.g., in Cohen, 1955; Miller, 1958; Cloward and Ohlin, 1960; Sutherland and Cressey, 1960). Indeed, the approach taken here is, strictly speaking, not criminological at all, since it ignores whatever might be distinctive to crime as such (including, for example, how criminals differ from other people or how their behavior differs from that which is not prohibited). Instead it draws attention to a dimension of many crimes that is usually viewed as a totally different—even opposite—phenomenon, namely, social control. Crime often expresses a grievance. This implies that many crimes belong to the same family as gossip, ridicule, vengeance, punishment, and law itself. It also implies that to a significant degree we may predict and explain crime with a sociological theory of social control, specifically a theory of self-help. Beyond this, it might be worthwhile to contemplate what else crime has in common with conduct of other kinds. As remarked earlier (in note 4), for instance, some crime may be understood as economic behavior, and some as recreation. In other words, for certain theoretical purposes we might usefully ignore the fact that crime is criminal at all. The criminality of crime is defined by law, and therefore falls within the jurisdiction of a completely different theory (see especially Black, 1976).

References

Allen, John, 1977, *Assault with a Deadly Weapon: The Autobiography of a Street Criminal.* Edited by Dianne Hall Kelly and Philip Heymann. New York: McGraw-Hill.

Andenaes, Johannes, 1966, "The general preventive effects of punishment." *University of Pennsylvania Law Review* 114:949–83.

Andrew, Donna T., 1980, "The code of honour and its critics: the opposition to duelling in England, 1700–1850." *Social History* 5:409–34.

Baldick, Robert, 1965, *The Duel: A History of Duelling.* London: Chapman & Hall.

Barton, Roy Franklin, [1919], 1969, *Ifugao Law.* Berkeley: University of California Press.

Baumgartner, M. P., 1983, "Social control from below." In Donald Black (ed.), *Toward a General Theory of Social Control.* New York: Academic Press.

———, 1988, *The Moral Order of a Suburb.* New York: Academic Press.

Becker, Howard S., 1963, *Outsiders: Studies in the Sociology of Deviance.* New York: Free Press.

Black, Donald, 1971, "The social organization of arrest." *Stanford Law Review* 23:1087–1111.

————, 1972, "The boundaries of legal sociology." *Yale Law Journal* 81:1086–1100.

————, 1976, *The Behavior of Law.* New York: Academic Press.

————, 1980, *The Manners and Customs of the Police.* New York: Academic Press.

Black, Donald and M. P. Baumgartner, 1983, "Toward a theory of the third party." In Keith O. Boyum and Lynn Mather (eds.), *Empirical Theories about Courts.* New York: Longman.

Blok, Anton, 1974, *The Mafia of a Sicilian Village, 1860–1960: A Study of Violent Peasant Entrepreneurs.* New York: Harper & Row.

Bohannan, Paul, 1960, "Patterns of murder and suicide." Pp. 230–66 in Paul Bohannan (ed.), *African Homicide and Suicide.* Princeton: Princeton University Press.

Bolton, Ralph, 1970, "Rates and ramifications of violence: notes on Qolla homicide." Paper presented at the International Congress of Americanists, Lima, Peru, August, 1970.

————, 1973, "Aggression and hypoglycemia among the Qolla: a study in psychobiological anthropology." *Ethnology* 12:227–57.

Bolton, Ralph and Charlene Bolton, 1973, "Domestic quarrels among the Qolla." Paper presented at the annual meeting of the American Anthropological Association, New Orleans, Louisiana, October, 1973. Published in Spanish as *Conflictos en la Familia Andina.* Cuzco: Centro de Estudios Andinos, 1975.

Brown, Claude, 1965, *Manchild in the Promised Land.* New York: Macmillan.

Chagnon, Napoleon A., 1977, *Yanomamö: The Fierce People.* Second edition; first edition, 1968. New York: Holt, Rinehart & Winston.

Chambliss, William J., 1967, "Types of deviance and the effectiveness of legal sanctions." *Wisconsin Law Review* 1967:703–19.

Christie, Nils, 1977, "Conflicts as property." *British Journal of Criminology* 17:1–15.

Cleaver, Eldridge, 1968, *Soul on Ice.* New York: Dell.

Cloward, Richard A. and Lloyd E. Ohlin, 1960, *Delinquency and Opportunity: A Theory of Delinquent Gangs.* New York: Free Press.

Cohen, Albert K., 1955, *Delinquent Boys: The Culture of the Gang.* New York: Free Press.

Cressey, Donald R., 1953, *Other People's Money: A Study in the Social Psychology of Embezzlement.* Glencoe: Free Press.

Edgerton, Robert B., 1972, "Violence in East African tribal societies." Pp. 159–70 in James F. Short, Jr., and Marvin E. Wolfgang (eds.), *Collective Violence.* Chicago: Aldine.

Elias, Norbert, [1939], 1978, *The Civilizing Process: The Development of Manners.* Vol. 1. New York: Urizen Books.

Fried, Jacob, 1953, "The relation of ideal norms to actual behavior in Tarahumara society." *Southwestern Journal of Anthropology* 9:286–95.

Green, Thomas A., 1976, "The jury and the English law of homicide, 1200–1600." *Michigan Law Review* 74:413–99.

Greenberg, David F., 1977, "Delinquency and the age structure of society." *Contemporary Crises: Crime, Law, Social Policy* 1:189–223.

Hanawalt, Barbara A., 1979, *Crime and Conflict in English Communities, 1300–1348.* Cambridge: Harvard University Press.

Hasluck, Margaret, 1954, *The Unwritten Law in Albania.* Cambridge: Cambridge University Press.

Hobbes, Thomas, [1651], 1962, *Leviathan: Or the Matter, Forme and Power of a Commonwealth Ecclesiasticall and Civil.* New York: Macmillan.

Hobhouse, L. T., 1906, *Morals in Evolution: A Study in Comparative Ethics.* New York: Henry Holt.

Hobsbawm, Eric, 1969, *Bandits.* London: George Weidenfeld & Nicolson.

Hoebel, E. Adamson, 1954, *The Law of Primitive Man: A Study in Comparative Legal Dynamics.* Cambridge: Harvard University Press.

Hoffmann, Stanley, 1968, "International law and the control of force." Pp.34–66 in Karl Deutsch and Stanley Hoffman (eds.), *The Relevance of International Law.* Cambridge: Schenkman.

Horowitz, Ruth and Gary Schwartz, 1974, "Honor, normative ambiguity and gang violence." *American Sociological Review* 39:238–51.

Koch, Klaus-Friedrich, 1974, *War and Peace in Jalémó: The Management of Conflict in Highland New Guinea.* Cambridge: Harvard University Press.

Langness, L. L., 1972, "Violence in the New Guinea highlands." Pp. 171–85 in James F. Short, Jr., and Marvin E. Wolfgang (eds.), *Collective Violence.* Chicago: Aldine.

Le Vine, Robert A., 1969, "Gusii sex offenses: a study in social control." *American Anthropologist* 61:965–90.

Llewellyn, Karl N. and E. Adamson Hoebel, 1941, *The Cheyenne Way: Conflict and Case Law in Primitive Jurisprudence.* Norman: University of Oklahoma Press.

Lundsgaarde, Henry P., 1977, *Murder in Space City: A Cultural Analysis of Houston Homicide Patterns.* New York: Oxford University Press.

MacCormack, Geoffrey, 1976, "Procedures for the settlement of disputes in 'simple societies.'" *The Irish Jurist* II (new series):175–88.

Matza, David, 1964, *Delinquency and Drift.* New York: John Wiley.

Merry, Sally Engle, 1981, *Urban Danger: Life in a Neighborhood of Strangers.* Philadelphia: Temple University Press.

Middleton, John and David Tait (eds.), [1958], 1970, *Segmentary Systems.* New York: Humanities Press.

Miller, Walter B., 1958, "Lower class culture as a generating milieu of gang delinquency." *Journal of Social Issues* 14:5–19.

Moore, Sally Falk, 1972, "Legal liability and evolutionary interpretation: some aspects of strict liability, self-help and collective responsibility." Pp. 51–107 in Max Gluckman (ed.), *The Allocation of Responsibility.* Manchester: Manchester University Press.

Nash, June, 1967, "Death as a way of life: the increasing resort to homicide in a Maya Indian community." *American Anthropologist* 69:445–70.

Otterbein, Keith F. and Charlotte Swanson Otterbein, 1965, "An eye for an eye, a tooth for a tooth: a cross-cultural study of feuding." *American Anthropologist* 67:1470–82.

Pitt-Rivers, Julian, 1966, "Honour and social status." Pp. 19–77 in J. G. Peristiany (ed.), *Honour and Shame: The Values of Mediterranean Society.* Chicago: University of Chicago Press.

Pollock, Frederick and Frederic William Maitland, [1898], 1968, *The History of English Law: Before the Time of Edward I.* Second edition; first edition, 1895. Cambridge: Cambridge University Press.

Pound, Roscoe, 1921, *The Spirit of the Common Law.* Boston: Marshall Jones.

Raper, Arthur F., 1933, *The Tragedy of Lynching.* Chapel Hill: University of North Carolina Press.

Reuter, Peter, 1983, "Social control in illegal markets." In Donald Black (ed.), *Toward a General Theory of Social Control.* New York: Academic Press.

Rieder, Jonathan, 1983, "The social organization of vengeance." In Donald Black (ed.), *Toward a General Theory of Social Control.* New York: Academic Press.

Roberts, Simon, 1979, *Order and Dispute: An Introduction to Legal Anthropology.* New York: Penguin Books.

Rothenberger, John E., 1978, "The social dynamics of dispute settlement in a Sunni Muslim village in Lebanon." Pp. 152–80 in Laura Nader and Harry F. Todd, Jr. (eds.), *The Disputing Process–Law in Ten Societies.* New York: Columbia University Press.

Schneider, Jane, 1971, "Of vigilance and virgins: honor, shame and access to resources in Mediterranean societies." *Ethnology* 10:1–24.

Sutherland, Edwin H. and Donald R. Cressey, 1960, *Principles of Criminology.* Sixth edition; first edition, 1924. Philadelphia: J. P. Lippincott.

Sweet, Louise E., 1965, "Camel raiding of North Arabian Bedouin: a mechanism of ecological adaptation." *American Anthropologist* 67:1132–50.

Thomas-Buckle, Suzann R. and Leonard G. Buckle, 1982, "Doing unto others: disputes and dispute processing in an urban American neighborhood." Pp. 78–90 in Roman Tomasic and Malcolm M. Feeley (eds.), *Neighborhood Justice: Assessment of an Emerging Idea.* New York: Longman.

Turnbull, Colin M., 1965, *Wayward Servants: The Two Worlds of the African Pygmies.* Garden City: Natural History Press.

van den Steenhoven, Geert, 1962, *Leadership and Law among the Eskimos of the Keewatin District, Northwest Territories.* Doctoral dissertation, Faculty of Law, University of Leiden.

Vera Institute of Justice, 1977, *Felony Arrests: Their Prosecution and Disposition in New York City's Courts.* New York: Vera Institute of Justice.

Weber, Max, [1919], 1958, "Politics as a vocation." Pp. 77–128 in *From Max Weber: Essays in Sociology,* edited by Hans Gerth and C. Wright Mills. New York: Oxford University Press.

Werthman, Carl, 1969, "Delinquency and moral character." Pp. 613–32 in Donald R. Cressey and David A. Ward (eds.), *Delinquency, Crime, and Social Process.* New York: Harper & Row.

Wolfgang, Marvin E., [1958], 1966, *Patterns in Criminal Homicide.* New York: John Wiley.

Yablonsky, Lewis, 1962, *The Violent Gang.* New York: Macmillan.

Zimring, Franklin E., 1971, *Perspectives on Deterrence.* Washington, D.C.: Center for Studies of Crime and Delinquency, National Institute of Mental Health.

10

Honor and Violence in the Old South

Bertram Wyatt-Brown

The concept of honor seems inherently and perversely contradictory: comic and tragic, romantic and shrewd, inhumane and magnanimous, brave and hypocritical, sane and mad, like the famous Don in pursuit of the unresponsive Dulcinea. But for all the perplexities that the elusive concept raises, in many regions, especially in slaveholding societies, honor may be seen as a people's theology, a set of prescriptions endowed with an almost sacred symbolism. Under honor's law those who have power to demand, and to hold, esteem and authority are able to do so because the entire social order has sanctioned their rule and called it moral. Whereas in Christian and humanistic ethical systems distinctions are drawn between moral and physical power, honor places them in close proximity.

In these pages, . . . the ethic of honor takes on larger and more socially active meanings than ordinary parlance tends to convey. Honor in the pre–Civil War slave states was an encoded system, a matter of interchanges between the individual and the community to which he or she belonged. Meaning was imparted not with words alone, but in courtesies, rituals, and even deeds of personal and collective violence. In such a system, words could assume particular, and sometimes dangerous, force, as in the case of communicating a challenge to a duel. Likewise, the language of politics was less devoted to rational explanation than to rituals reconfirming shared values; the style of oratory for which the South was famous served to remind listeners of common principles rather than to challenge existing beliefs. Both deeds and words of this character helped to create structure, hierarchy, race control, and social discourse.

Although we prefer to dwell on the individualistic and open-handed side of honor, we must establish its essentially defensive posture. Whites in the antebellum South were a people of honor who would not subject themselves to the contempt of a ruthless enemy, as the Yankee supporters of Abraham Lincoln and abolitionists were thought to be. As early as 1851, secessionist leader James Jones of South Carolina argued that even if the overwhelming power of the North were to defeat a Southern struggle for independence, the Southerners would have at least "saved our honour *and lost nothing.*" The chief aim of this notion of honor was to protect the individual, family, group, or race from the greatest dread that its adherents could imagine. That fear was not death, for dying with honor would bring glory. Neither was it the prospect of damnation in the life hereafter. Judgments of that kind were in the hands of God. Rather, the fear was of public humiliation. This vulnerability was distressing not only in itself, but, and more important, because it forced the humbled party to admit the shame to himself and to accept the full implications. With his loss of autonomy, he had betrayed kinfolk and manhood, in fact, he had betrayed all things held dear.

Thus, honor existed in intimate relation to its opposite: shame. This book describes the fears and projections of ignominy with almost as much attention as it does the usages of honor; one cannot be understood apart from the other. An individual was expected to have a healthy sense of shame, that is, a sense of his own honor. Shamelessness signified a disregard for both honor and disgrace. When shame was imposed by others, honor was stripped away.

In slaveholding cultures, the contrast between the free and the unfree—the autonomy of one, the abjectness of the other—prompts an awareness of moral, as well as political and social stratification. Not all honor societies were slaveholding. Yet no slaveholding culture could casually set aside the strictures of honor. The very debasement of the slave added much to the master's honor, since the latter's claim to self-sufficiency rested upon the prestige, power, and wealth that accrued from the benefits of controlling others.

American planters in the South were far from indifferent to the exigencies of obedience brought about by such a system. While slavery would not have existed without a cash basis, white Southerners spoke more glowingly of the supposed social benefits than they did about the economic advantages of the system. Whatever we may think of their morality, slavery was considered an honorable institution indeed. The assumption of the rightfulness of ownership was a social fact built into the Southern way of life.

Without slavery to sustain the appropriate environment, Southern honor would have died early. But the ethical code that American settlers brought with them from the Old World justified a racial and social bondage that first made temporary chattels of white servants, then made permanent slaves of African imports. From the start, slavery and honor were mutually dependent. After emancipation in 1865, honor, like the labor system that had nourished it, lived on in truncated yet vigorous form, especially with regard to laws and practices that perpetuated the humiliation and subjugation of black people—the imposition of lynch law, Jim Crow, and restrictive education. The most psychologically powerful expression of Southern honor was the sexual dread of black blood in a white womb. In the patriarchal imagination, no humiliation was greater.

For a considerable length of time scholars have concentrated almost exclusively upon the history and meaning of slavery, while the moral underpinnings for the Southern way of life—including slaveholding itself—have received little attention. This book seeks to correct the balance. Honor was neither the romantic fantasy of belles and gallants found in sentimental fiction, nor was it the baseless illusion unworthy of historical notice that some scholars have contended. The ethic cannot be explained as precisely as one can dissect the clauses of a treaty or enumerate the birth and death rates of a New England village. Yet its social force, regardless of how much we admire, loathe, or smile at its manifestations, can be demonstrated as one of the most remarkable features of American cultural history.

Part IV: FAMILY VIOLENCE

Family violence is deeply rooted in American tradition and is sustained by contemporary cultural practices. The first two chapters in this section are taken from *Behind Closed Doors: Violence in the American Family,* the classic work by Murray Straus, Richard Gelles, and Suzanne Steinmetz that made a previously oblivious society aware of just how prevalent family violence is. In the first chapter, "The Marriage License as a Hitting License," we learn that domestic violence is surprisingly commonplace in American families. Although the cultural legitimation of domestic violence has diminished over time, there is still an extraordinary number of men and women who believe that hitting is sometimes "necessary, good, or normal" in a marital relationship.

In the second chapter, "Spare the Rod?," the authors distinguish between extreme violence, beatings that result in visible injury to the child, and more routine forms of violence such as spankings and slaps. The nearly universal support for some form of family violence directed at children is clearly problematic to the authors of this work. They express their concern that a culture that legitimates violence against children on any level encourages some parents to go a step or two further in the means they use to discipline their children. From this perspective, only a position of "zero tolerance" for family violence can reduce the perpetuation of patterns of abusive violence that has continued from one generation to another in too many American families.

The patriarchal tradition that legitimates male violence against women in the family is reflected in little support for women who defend themselves when responding to repeated violent assaults by their partners. Gillespie shows how a battered woman's defense must be constructed from the perspective of the woman. Rather than seeing her defense as an irrational act of the helpless woman, Gillespie shows that her act of self-defense is a rational act given the context in which she lives in fear of her attacker. And that her act of self-defense is justifiable under both law and custom once the gender-specific context is taken into account.

Pleck's powerful description of the history of the legal regulation of family violence shows us how the regulation of violence can be both supported by law at one point in history and condemned at another. These facts in themselves show us how the explanation of the violence itself must be separated from the explanation of how or why it is regulated by law. At the same time, we must be aware that the regulation of violence under law may have an impact on the violence itself. Under certain conditions it may "deter" the violence. Under other conditions it may increase the violence. The article on the impact of mandatory arrest in domestic violence cases demonstrates the complexity of the legal response to family violence. And, finally, we see how, in the Old South, extralegal forms of social control were legitimated by custom and the legal establishment in the lynching of a wife-killer.

11

The Marriage License as a Hitting License

Murray A. Straus
Richard J. Gelles
Suzanne K. Steinmetz

Wife-beating is found in every class, at every income level. The wife of the president of a midwestern state university recently asked one of us what she could do about the beatings without putting her husband's career in danger. Japan's former Prime Minister Sato, a winner of the Nobel Peace Prize, was accused publicly by his wife of many beatings in their early married life. Ingeborg Dedichen, a former mistress of Aristotle Onassis, describes his beating her till he was forced to quit from exhaustion. "It is what every Greek husband does, it's good for the wife," he told her.

What is at the root of such violent attacks? Proverbs such as "A man's home is his castle," go a long way in giving insights into human nature and society. The home belongs to the man. It is the woman who finds herself homeless if she refuses further abuse.

The image of the "castle" implies freedom from interference from outsiders. What goes on within the walls of the castle is shielded from prying eyes. And a modern home, like a medieval castle, can contain its own brand of torture chamber. Take the case of Carol, a Boston woman who called the police to complain that her husband had beaten her and then pushed her down the stairs. The policeman on duty answered, "Listen, lady, he pays the bills, doesn't he? What he does inside of his own house is his business" (*The Real Paper,* February 11, 1976).

The evidence we documented [earlier] suggested that, aside from war and riots, physical violence occurs between family members more often than it occurs between any other individuals. At the same time we also pointed out the limitations of the data. In particular, no research up to now gives information on how often each of the different forms of family violence occurs in a representative sample of American families.

The Over-all Level of Husband-Wife Violence

Violence Rates

A first approach to getting a picture of the amount of violence between the 2,143 husbands and wives in this study is to find out how many had engaged in any of the eight violent acts we asked about. For the year we studied this works out to be 16 percent. In other words, every year about one out of every six couples in the United States commits at least one violent act against his or her partner.

If the period considered is the entire length of the marriage (rather than just the previous year), the result is 28 percent, or between one out of four and one out of three American couples. In short, if you are married, the chances are almost one out of three that your husband or wife will hit you.

When we began our study of violence in the family, we would have considered such a rate of husbands and wives hitting each other very high. In terms of our values—and probably the values of most other Americans—it is still very high. But in terms of what we have come to

"The Marriage License as a Hitting License," pp. 31–50 in *Behind Closed Doors: Violence in the American Family,* by Murray A. Straus, Richard J. Gelles, and Suzanne K. Steinmetz (Anchor Books 1980). Reprinted by permission.

expect on the basis of the pilot studies, this is a low figure. *It is very likely a substantial under-estimate.*

Later in this chapter we will give the reasons for thinking it is an underestimate. But for now, let us examine the violent acts one by one. This is important if we are to get a realistic picture of the meaning of the over-all rate of 28 percent. One needs to know how much of the violence was slaps and how much was kicking and beating up. This information is given in Chart 1.

Slaps, Beatings, and Guns

Chart 1 shows that in almost seven of every hundred couples either the husband or the wife had thrown something at the other in the previous year, and about one out of six (16 percent) had done this at some point in their marriage.

The statistics for *slapping* a spouse are about the same: 7 percent in the previous year and 18 percent at some time.

The figures for pushing, shoving, or grabbing during an argument are the highest of any of the eight things we asked about: 13 percent

had done this during the year, and almost one out of four at some time in the marriage.

At the other extreme, "only" one or two out of every hundred couples (1.5 percent) experienced a *beating-up* incident in the previous year. But a "beating up" had occurred at some time in the marriages of one out of every twenty of the couples we interviewed.

The rates for actually *using a knife or gun* on one's spouse are one out of every two hundred couples in the previous year, and almost one out of twenty-seven couples at some point in the marriage.

We were surprised that there was not a bigger difference between the rate of occurrence for "mild" violent acts (such as pushing and slapping) and the severe acts of violence (such as beating up and using a knife or gun). This is partly because the rates for the more violent acts turned out to be greater than we expected, and partly because the rates for the "ordinary" acts of husband-wife violence were less than expected. Whatever the reasons, it seems that couples are using more than slaps and shoves when violence occurs.

Indeed, the statistics on the number of husbands and wives who had ever "beaten up"

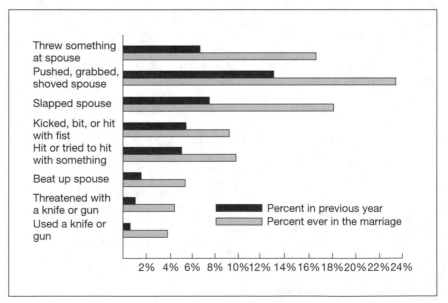

CHART 1 *Rate at Which Violent Acts Occurred in the Previous Year and Ever in the Marriage*

their spouses or actually used a knife or gun are astoundingly high. The human meaning of these most extreme forms of violence in the family can be understood better if we translate the percentages into the total number of marriages affected. Since there were about 47 million couples living together in the United States in 1975, the rates just given mean that *over 1.7 million Americans had at some time faced a husband or wife wielding a knife or gun, and well over 2 million had been beaten up* by his or her spouse.

How Accurate Are the Statistics?

It is difficult to know how much confidence to put in these statistics because several different kinds of error are possible. First, these are estimates based on a sample. But the sample is reasonably large and was chosen by methods which should make it quite representative of the U.S. population. Comparisons with characteristics reported in the U.S. census show that this in fact is the case.

Still, there is the possibility of sampling error. So we computed what is known as the "standard error" for each of the rates in Chart 1. The largest standard error is for the over-all violence index. Even that is low: there is a 95 percent chance that the true percentage of couples *admitting to* ever having physically assaulted one another is somewhere between 26.8 and 28.8 percent of all couples.

"Admitting to" was italicized to highlight a much more serious and more likely source of error, that of an underestimate. The 26.8 to 28.8 percent figure assumes that everyone "told all." But that is very unlikely. Three of the reasons are:

1. There is one group of people who are likely to "underreport" the amount of violence. For this group a slap, push, or shove (and sometimes even more severe violence) is so much a normal part of the family that it is simply not a noteworthy or dramatic enough event always to be remembered. Such omissions are especially likely when we asked about things which had happened during the entire length of the marriage.

2. At the opposite end of the violence continuum, there is another group who fail to admit or report such acts because of the shame involved if one is the victim, or the guilt if one is the attacker. Such violent attacks as being hit with objects, bitten, beaten up, or attacked with a knife or gun go beyond the "normal violence" of family life and are often unreported.

3. A final reason for thinking these figures are drastic underestimates lies in the nature of the sample. We included only couples currently living together. Divorced people were asked only about their present marriage. Since "excessive" violence is often a cause of divorce, the sample probably omits many of the high violence cases.

The sample was selected in this way because a major purpose of the study was to investigate the extent to which violence is related to other aspects of husband-wife interaction. Questions were limited to current marriages because of interview time limits and limits on what people could be expected to remember.

The figures therefore could easily be twice as large as those revealed by the survey. In fact, based on the pilot studies and informal evidence (where some of the factors leading to underreporting were not present), it seems likely that *the true rate is closer to 50 or 60 percent of all couples than it is to the 28 percent who were willing to describe violent acts to our interviewers.*

Men and Women

Traditionally, men have been considered more aggressive and violent than women. Like other stereotypes, there is no doubt a kernel of truth to this. But it is far from the clear-cut difference which exists in the thinking of most people (Maccoby and Jacklin, 1974; Frodi, Macaulay, and Thome, 1977). This is also the case with our survey. About one out of eight husbands had carried out at least one violent act during the course of a conflict in the year covered by the survey, *and* about the same number of wives had attacked their husbands (12.1 percent of the husbands versus 11.6 percent of the wives).

Mutual Violence

One way of looking at this issue is to ask what percentage of the sample are couples in which the husband was the only one to use violence? What percent were couples in which the only violence was by the wife? And in what percentage did both use violence?

The most common situation was that in which both had used violence.

One man who found himself in the middle of a family battle, reported it this way:

> "It started sort of slowly . . . so I couldn't tell for sure if they were even serious. . . . In the beginning they'd push at each other, or shove, like kids—little kids who want to fight but they don't know how. Then, this one time, while I'm standing there not sure whether to stay or go, and them treating me like I didn't even exist, she begins yelling at him like she did.
>
> "'You're a bust, you're a failure, I want you out of here, I can always get men who'll work, good men, not scum like you.' And they're pushing and poking with their hands, like they were dancing. She pushes him, he pushes her, only she's doing all the talking. He isn't saying a word.
>
> "Then all of a sudden, she must have triggered off the right nerve because he lets fly with a right cross that I mean stuns. I mean she goes down like a rock! And he's swearing at her, calling her every name in the book. Jesus, I didn't know what the hell to do.
>
> "What I wanted to do was call the police. But I figured, how can I call the police and add to this guy's misery, because she was pushing him. . . . She was really pushing him. I'd have done something to her myself" (Thomas Cottle in Boston *Sunday Globe,* November 6, 1977).

Of those couples reporting any violence, 49 percent were situations of this type, where both were violent. For the year previous to our study, a comparison of the number of couples in which only the husband was violent with those in which only the wife was violent shows the figures to be very close: 27 percent violent husbands and 24 percent violent wives. So, as in the case of the violence rates, there is little difference between the husbands and wives in this study.

Specific Violent Acts

Chart 2 compares the men and women in our study on each of the eight violent acts. Again, there is an over-all similarity. But there are also some interesting differences, somewhat along the lines of the stereotype of the pot- and pan-throwing wife.

> "I got him good the last time! He punched me in the face and I fell back on the stove. He was walking out of the kitchen and I grabbed that frying pan and landed it square on his head. Man, he didn't know what hit him." (Case reported by the Greater Egypt [Illinois] Regional Planning and Development Commission.)

The number of wives who threw things at their husbands is almost twice as large as the number of husbands who threw things at their wives. The rate for kicking and hitting with an object is also higher for wives than for husbands. The husbands on the other hand had higher rates for pushing, shoving, slapping, beating up, and actually using a knife or gun.

Wife-Beating—and Husband-Beating

Wife-beating has become a focus of increasing public concern in the last few years. In part this reflects the national anguish over all aspects of violence, ranging from the Vietnam war to the upward surge of assault and murder. Another major element accounting for the recent public concern with wife-beating is the feminist movement. Behind that are the factors which have given rise to the rebirth of the feminist movement in the late 1960s and early 1970s.

What Is Wife-beating?

To find out how much wife-beating there is, one must be able to define it in a way which can be objectively measured. When this is tried, it becomes clear that "wife-beating" is a political

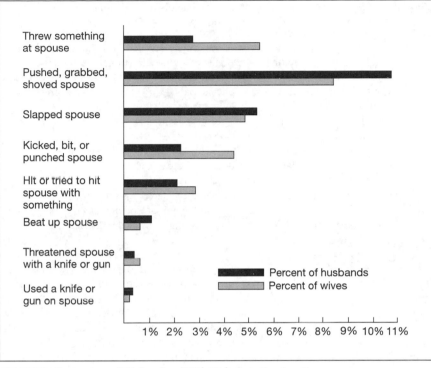

CHART 2 *Comparison of Husband and Wife Violence in Previous Year*

rather than a scientific term. For some people wife-beating refers only to those instances in which severe damage is inflicted. Less severe violence is not considered violence or it is laughed off. A joke one of us heard while driving across northern England in 1974 is no doubt familiar to many readers of this book. It goes like this in the BBC version: One woman asks another why she feels her husband doesn't love her any more. The answer: "He hasn't bashed me in a fortnight." Or take the following letter to Ann Landers:

Dear Ann Landers: Come out of the clouds, for Lord's sake, and get down here with us humans. I am sick to death of your holier-than-thou attitude toward women whose husbands give them a well deserved belt in the mouth.

Don't you know that a man can be pushed to the brink and something's got to give? A crack in the teeth can be a wonderful tension-breaker. It's also a lot healthier than keeping all that anger bottled up.

My husband hauls off and slugs me every few months and I don't mind. He feels better and so do I because he never hits me unless I deserve it. So why don't you come off it?—REAL HAPPY.

Dear Real Happy: If you don't mind a crack in the teeth every few months, it's all right with me. I hope you have a good dentist.

So a certain amount of violence in the family is "normal violence." In fact, most of the violent acts which occur in the family are so much a part of the way family members relate to each other that they are not even thought of as violence.

At what point does one exceed the bounds of "normal" family violence? When does it become "wife-beating"? To answer this question, we gathered data on a series of violent acts, ranging from a slap to using a knife or gun. This allows anyone reading this book to draw the line at whatever place seems most appropriate for his or her purpose.

Measuring Wife-beating

This "solution," however, can also be a means of avoiding the issue. So in addition to data on each violent act, we also combined the most severe of these into what can be called a Severe Violence Index. If these are things done by the husband, then it is a "Wife-beating Index." The Wife-beating Index consists of the extent to which the husband went beyond throwing things, pushing or grabbing, and slapping and attacked his wife by kicking, biting, or punching; hitting with some object; beating her up; threatening her with a gun or knife; or using a knife or gun (the last five behaviors in Chart 1).

Why limit the Wife-beating Index to "only" the situations where the husband went beyond throwing things, pushing, grabbing, and slapping? Certainly we don't want to imply that this reflects our conception of what is permissible violence. None of these are acceptable for relationships between husband and wife—just as they are unacceptable between student and teacher, minister and parishioner, or colleagues in a department. In short, we follow the maxim coined by John Valusek: "People are not for hitting."

What then is the basis for choosing kicking, biting, or punching; hitting with an object; beating up; threatening with a knife or gun; and using a knife or gun for the Wife-beating Index? It is simply the fact that these are all acts which carry with them a high risk of serious physical injury.

What Percentage Are Beaten?

How many husbands and wives experience the kind of attack which is serious enough to be included in the Wife-beating and Husband-beating Indexes? A remarkably large number. In fact, since our survey produced a rate of 3.8 percent, this means that about one out of twenty-six American wives get beaten by their husbands every year, or a total of almost 1.8 million per year.

Staggering as are these figures, the real surprise lies in the statistics on husband-beating. These rates are slightly higher than those for wife-beating! Although such cases rarely come to the attention of the police or the press, they exist

at all social levels. Here is an example of one we came across:

> A wealthy, elderly New York banker was finally granted a separation from his second wife, 31 years his junior, after 14 years of marriage and physical abuse. According to the presiding judge, the wife had bullied him with hysteria, screaming tantrums and vicious physical violence.
>
> The husband wore constant scars and bruises. His ear had once been shredded by his wife with her teeth. She had blackened his eyes, and on one occasion injured one of his eyes so badly that doctors feared it might be lost (Wilmington *Evening Journal*, April 21, 1976, p. 2).

Some 4.6 percent of the wives in the sample admitted to or were reported by their husbands as having engaged in an act which is included in the Husband-beating Index. That works to be about one out of twenty-two wives who attacked their husbands severely enough to be included in this Husband-beating Index. That is over 2 million very violent wives. Since three other studies of this issue also found high rates of husband-beating (Gelles, 1974; Steinmetz, 1977a, b; Straus, 1974), some revision of the traditional view about female violence seems to be needed.

How Often Do Beatings Happen?

Let us look at just the couples for which a violent incident occurred during the year previous to our study. Was it an isolated incident? If not, how often did attacks of this kind occur?

It was an isolated incident (in the sense that there was only one such attack during the year) for only about a third of the violent couples. This applies to both wife-beating and husband-beating. Almost one out of five of the violent husbands and one out of eight wives attacked their partner this severely twice during the year. Forty-seven percent of the husbands who beat their wives did so three or more times during the year, and 53 percent of the husband-beaters did so three or more times. So, for about half the couples the pattern is that if there is one beating, there are likely to be others—at least three per year! In short, violence between husbands and wives, when it occurs, tends to be a recurrent feature of the marriage.

Was There Ever a Beating?

A final question about how many beatings took place can be answered by looking at what happened over the entire length of the marriage. Did something that can be called a beating *ever* happen in the marriage?

There are several reasons why even a single beating is important. First, even one such event debases human life. Second, there is the physical danger involved. Third is the fact that many, if not most, such beatings are part of a struggle for power in the family. It often takes only one such event to fix the balance of power for many years—or perhaps for a lifetime.

Physical force is the ultimate resource which most of us learn as children to rely on if all else fails and the issue is crucial. As a husband in one of the families interviewed by LaRossa (1977) said when asked why he hit his wife during an argument:

> . . . She more or less tried to run me and I said no, and she got hysterical and said, "I could kill you!" And I got rather angry and slapped her in the face three or four times and I said "Don't you ever say that to me again!" And we haven't had any problem since.

Later in the interview, the husband evaluated his use of physical force as follows:

> You don't use it until you are forced to it. At that point I felt I had to do something physical to stop the bad progression of events. I took my chances with that and it worked. In those circumstances my judgement was correct and it worked.

Since greater size and strength give the advantage to men in such situations, the single beating may be an extremely important factor in maintaining male dominance in the family system.

We found that one out of eight couples (12.6 percent) experienced at least one beating incident in the course of marriage. That is approximately a total of 6 million beatings. However, as high as that figure is, the actual statistics are probably higher. This is because things are forgotten over the years, and also because (as was pointed out earlier) the violent acts in question are only about the current marriage. They leave out the many marriages which ended in divorce, a large part of which were marked by beatings.

Wives and Husbands as Victims

This study shows a high rate of violence by *wives* as well as husbands. But it would be a great mistake if that fact distracted us from giving first attention to wives *as victims* as the focus of social policy. There are a number of reasons for this:

1. The data in Chart 2 show that husbands have higher rates of the most dangerous and injurious forms of violence (beating up and using a knife or gun).
2. Steinmetz (1977b) found that abuse by husbands does more damage. She suggests that the greater physical strength of men makes it more likely that a woman will be seriously injured when beaten up by her husband.
3. When violent acts are committed by a husband, they are repeated more often than is the case for wives.
4. The data do not tell us what proportion of the violent acts by wives were in self-defense or a response to blows initiated by husbands. Wolfgang's study of husband-wife homicides (1957) suggests that this is an important factor.
5. A large number of attacks by husbands seem to occur when the wife is pregnant (Gelles, 1975), thus posing a danger to the as yet unborn child. This isn't something that happens only on Tobacco Road:

> The first time Hortense Barber's husband beat her was the day she told him she was pregnant with their first child. "He knocked out my two front teeth and split open my upper lip," the 32 year old honors graduate told a New York Senate Task Force on Women. Later Mrs. Barber's husband regularly blacked her eyes during her pregnancy and threw a knife at her "in jest," cutting her knee (New York *Times*, April 10, 1977, p. 16).

6. Women are locked into marriage to a much greater extent than men. Women are bound by many economic and social constraints, and they often have no alternative to putting up with beatings by their husbands (Gelles, 1976; Martin, 1976; Straus, 1976, 1977). The situation is similar to being married to an alcoholic. Nine out of ten men leave an alcoholic wife, but only one out of ten women leave an alcoholic husband (*Good Housekeeping,* September 1977).

Most people feel that social policy should be aimed at helping those who are in the weakest position. Even though wives are also violent, they are in the weaker, more vulnerable position in respect to violence in the family. This applies to both the physical, psychological, and economic aspects of things. That is the reason we give first priority to aiding wives who are the victims of beatings by their husbands.

At the same time, the violence *by* wives uncovered in this study suggests that a fundamental solution to the problem of wife-beating has to go beyond a concern with how to control assaulting husbands. It seems that violence is built into the very structure of the society and the family system itself. . . . wife-beating is related to other aspects of violence in the family. It is only one aspect of the general pattern of family violence, which includes parent-child violence, child-to-child violence, and wife-to-husband violence. To eliminate the particularly brutal form of violence known as wife-beating will require changes in the cultural norms and in the organization of the family and society which underlie the system of violence on which so much of American society is based.

Norms and Meanings

Just as we need to know the extent to which violent *acts* occur between husbands and wives, parents and children, and brothers and sisters, it is also important to know how family members feel about intrafamily violence. Just how strongly do they approve or disapprove of a parent slapping a child or a husband slapping a wife? To what extent do people see violence in the family as one of those undesirable but necessary parts of life?

It is hard to find out about these aspects of the way people think about family violence. One difficulty is there are contradictory rules or "norms." At one level there are norms strongly opposed to husbands and wives hitting each other. But at the same time, there also seem to be implicit but powerful norms which permit and even encourage such acts. Sometimes people are thinking of one of these principles and sometimes of the other.

Another thing is that violence is often such a "taken for granted" part of life that most people don't even realize there are socially defined rules or norms about the use of violence in the family.

The existence of these implicit norms is illustrated by the case of a husband who hit his wife on several occasions. Each time he felt that it was wrong. He apologized—very genuinely. But still he did it again. The husband explained that he and his wife got so worked up in their arguments that he "lost control." In his mind, it was almost involuntary, and certainly not something he did according to a rule or norm which gives one the right to hit his wife.

But the marriage counselor in the case brought out the rules which permitted him to hit his wife. He asked the husband why, if he had "lost control," he didn't stab his wife! This possibility (and the fact that the husband did not stab the wife despite "losing control") shows that hitting the wife was not just a bubbling over of a primitive level of behavior. Although this husband did not realize it, he was following a behavioral rule or norm. It seems that the unrecognized but operating norm for this husband—and for millions of other husbands—is that it is okay to hit one's wife, but not to stab her.

There is other evidence which tends to support the idea that the marriage license is also a hitting license. For example, "Alice, you're going to the moon," was one of the standard punch lines on the old Jackie Gleason "Honeymooners" skits which delighted TV audiences during the 1950s, and which are currently enjoying a revival. Jokes, plays, such as those of George Bernard Shaw, and experiments which show that people take less severe actions if they think the man attacking a woman is her husband (Shotland and Straw, 1976; Straus, 1976) are other signs.

It has been suggested that one of the reasons neighbors who saw the attack didn't come to the aid of Kitty Genovese in the 1964 Queens murder case was because they thought it was a man beating his wife!

Or take the following incident:

. . . Roy Butler came over to help his bride-to-be in preparations for their wedding, which is why the wedding is off.

Roy, 24, made the mistake of going to a stag party first.

On the way to fiancée Anthea Higson's home, he dropped the wedding cake in the front garden.

In the shouting match that followed, he dropped Anthea's mother with a right cross to the jaw.

Anthea, 21, promptly dropped Roy. She said the wedding was off and she never wanted to see him again.

"If he had hit me instead of my mother, I probably would have married him all the same," [italics added] she said yesterday after a court fined Butler $135 for assaulting Mrs. Brenda Higson.

"But I'm not having any man hitting my mum," Anthea said (Providence *Journal,* September 21, 1976).

Interesting as are these examples, none of them provide the kind of systematic and broadly representative evidence which is needed. That is what we attempted to get in this study.

Measuring the Meaning of Violence

To find out how our sample felt about violence in the family, we used the "semantic differential" method (Osgood, Suci, and Tannenbaum, 1957). For husband-wife violence, we asked subjects to rate the phrase "Couples slapping each other." They were asked to make three ratings: unnecessary . . . necessary; not normal . . . normal; and good . . . bad.

How many of the husbands and wives rated "Couples slapping each other" as "necessary,"

"normal," or "good"? Over all just under one out of four wives and one out of three husbands (31.3 and 24.6 percent) saw this type of physical force between spouses as at least somewhat necessary, normal, or good.

These statistics are remarkably close to those from a national sample studied by the U. S. Violence Commission. The Violence Commission found that about one quarter of the persons interviewed said they could think of circumstances in which it would be all right for a husband to hit his wife or a wife to hit her husband (Stark and Mc Evoy, 1970). This is slightly lower than the percentages for our sample. But if the Violence Commission survey data had been analyzed in the way we examined our data, the results could well have been almost identical.

The separate ratings for violence being necessary, normal, or good are interesting in the contrast they provide with each other and in the way men and women think about violence. On the one hand, there are big differences in the percentage of husbands as compared to wives who could see some situations in which it is necessary for a husband or wife to slap the other (see Chart 3). There is also a larger percentage of husbands who could see some situations in which this would not be a bad thing to do. In fact, for both these ratings, twice as many husbands as wives felt this way.

On the other hand, the percentages for the not normal . . . normal rating are particularly interesting because they are larger and because there is little difference between the men and the women. The figures in the chart show that a large proportion of American husbands and wives see violence as a normal part of married life. It may not be good, and it may not be necessary, but it is something which is going to happen under normal circumstances. The marriage license is a hitting license for a large part of the population, and probably for a much greater part than could bring themselves to rate it as "normal" in the context of this survey.

Summing Up

We are reasonably confident that the couples in the study are representative of American couples in general. But we suspect that not everyone

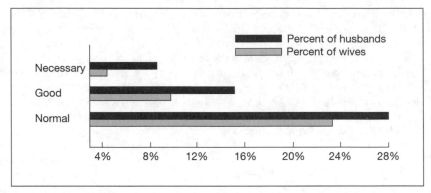

CHART 3 *Percent of Husbands and Wives Who Rated "A Couple Slapping Each Other" as at Least Somewhat Necessary, Good, or Normal*

told us about all the violence in his or her family. In fact, the pilot studies and informal evidence suggest that the true figures may be double those based on what people were willing to admit in a mass survey such as this. If this is the case, then about a third of all American couples experience a violent incident every year, and about two thirds have experienced such an incident at least once in the marriage.

Of course, a large part of these "violent incidents" are pushes and slaps, but far from all of them. A large portion are also actions which could cause serious injury or even death. We know from the fact that so many murderers and their victims are husband and wife that this is not just speculation. For the couples in this sample, in fact, almost one out of every twenty-five had faced an angry partner with a knife or gun in hand.

If the "dangerous violence" is not limited solely to use of a knife or gun, and includes everything *more serious* than pushing, grabbing, shoving, slapping, and throwing things, the rate is three times as high. In short, almost one out of every eight couples admitted that at some point in the marriage there had been an act of violence which could cause serious injury.

Another way of grasping this is to compare the rates for wife-beating and husband-beating in our survey with assaults which are reported in official statistics. The Uniform Crime Reports on "aggravated assault" are given in rate per 100,000. But the rates in this chapter are percentages, i.e., rates per 100, not per 100,000.

We can translate the rates for this survey into rates per 100,000 per year. They are 3,800 per 100,000 for assaults on wives, 4,600 for assaults on husbands, and a combined rate of 6,100 per 100,000 couples. Compare this with the roughly 190 per 100,000 aggravated assaults of all kinds known to the police each year.

Of course, many crimes are not reported to the police. So there have been surveys asking people if they were the victims of a crime. The rate of aggravated assault coming out of the National Crime Panel survey is very high: 2,597 per 100,000. But our rate for wife-beating and husband-beating of 6,100 per 100,000 is almost two and a half times higher. Also, since the Uniform Crime Reports, and especially the National Crime Panel data, include many within-family assaults, the amount by which husband-wife assault exceeds any other type of assault is much greater than these rates suggest.

Leaving aside the fact that our figures on husband-wife violence are probably underestimates, and even leaving aside the psychological damage that such violence can produce, just the danger to physical health implied by these rates is staggering. If any other crime or risk to physical well-being involved almost 2 million wives and 2 million husbands per year, plus a much larger number at some point in the marriage, a national emergency would probably be declared.

References

Frodi, A., J. Macaulay, and P. R. Thome 1977. Are women always less aggressive than men? A review of the experimental literature. *Psychological Bulletin* 84 (July):634–60.

Gelles, R. J. 1974. *The violent home: a study of physical aggression between husbands and wives.* Beverly Hills, Calif.: Sage Publications.

Gelles, R. J. 1975. Violence and pregnancy: a note on the extent of the problem and needed services. *The Family Coordinator* 24 (January):81–86.

Gelles, R. J. 1976. Abused wives: why do they stay? *Journal of Marriage and the Family* 38 (November):659–68.

LaRossa, R. 1977. *Conflict and power in marriage: expecting the first child.* Beverly Hills, Calif.: Sage Publications.

Maccoby, E. E., and C. N. Jacklin 1974. *The psychology of sex differences.* Stanford: Stanford University Press.

Martin, D. 1976. *Battered wives.* San Francisco: Glide Publications.

Osgood, C., G. Suci, and P. Tannenbaum 1957. *The measurement of meaning.* Urbana, Ill.: University of Illinois Press.

Shotland, R. L. and M. K. Straw 1976. Bystander response to an assault: when a man attacks a woman. *Journal of Personality and Social Psychology* 34 (November):990–99.

Stark, R., and J. McEvoy III 1970. Middle class violence. *Psychology Today* 4 (November):52–65.

Steinmetz, S. K. 1977a. Wife-beating, husband-beating—a comparison of the use of physical violence between spouses to resolve marital fights. In *Battered women,* M. Roy, ed., pp. 63–96. New York: Van Nostrand Reinhold.

Steinmetz, S. K. 1977b. *The cycle of violence: assertive, aggressive and abusive family interaction.* New York: Praeger Publishers.

Straus, M. A. 1974. Leveling, civility, and violence in the family. *Journal of Marriage and the Family* 36 (February):13–29, plus addendum in August 1974 issue.

Straus, M. A. 1976. Sexual inequality, cultural norms, and wife-beating. *Victimology* 1 (Spring):54–76.

Straus, M. A. 1977. A sociological perspective on the prevention and treatment of wife-beating. In *Battered women,* M. Roy, ed., pp. 196–239. New York: Van Nostrand Reinhold.

Wolfgang, M. E. 1957. Victim-precipitated criminal homicide. *Journal of Criminal Law, Criminology, and Police Science* 48 (June):1–11. Also reprinted in *Studies in homicide,* M. E. Wolfgang, ed., pp. 72–87. New York: Harper and Row.

| 12 |

Spare the Rod?

Murray A. Straus
Richard J. Gelles
Suzanne K. Steinmetz

"What that kid needs is a good crack in the teeth."

How literally do parents take such phrases? For centuries our society has provided parents with the right and even the mandate to use hitting, slapping, spanking, and other physical force against children.

Parents have been "beating the devil" out of junior since colonial times. Jokes about being taken behind the woodshed or having one's backside warmed by father's razor strap have been around almost as long.

Early colonists, in fact, developed a most effective method of dealing with the unruly child. Many communities enacted "stubborn child laws," which gave parents the right to kill children who were beyond their ability to control.

Our culture is full of reminders of the right of parents to employ violence against their children. Fairy tales, folklore, and nursery rhymes are full of violence against children. Hansel and Gretel's parents, for instance, abandoned their offspring to starve in the forest when money got scarce. The wicked queen told her huntsman to take Snow White into the forest and cut out her heart because the young stepdaughter was so beautiful. Mother Goose's "Old Woman in the Shoe" whipped her children soundly and sent them to bed without any bread.

Today, most parents hit their children at one time or another. Few deny it. And if not proud of it, many honestly believe the slap on the bottom is a just and necessary tool of discipline.

The previous chapter illustrated the fact that there are contradictory rules and attitudes about violence between marriage partners. On the one hand, there are norms which define this kind of violence as wrong. On the other hand, there is a set of attitudes, values, cues, and signals that makes the marriage license a hitting license. This chapter on parental violence reveals an equally contradictory set of rules.

The fact that parents receive the message that using physical force is good, necessary, and beneficial (to them and their children) does not mean that parents have unlimited freedom in their use of physical force. Tradition and now child abuse laws limit parents from inflicting severe or lethal harm. By the end of the 1960s all fifty states enacted legislation which attempted to define illegal acts of physical violence as child abuse and mandated that certain individuals would have to report families in which these acts took place. Presently, American parents have the right to use violence, up to the point of abusing their children.

Unfortunately, the concept of child abuse establishes no precise guide lines to settle what is or is not illegitimate force in the eyes of the law, parents, or communities.

Despite the fact that child abuse has been viewed as a major social problem for the last two decades, a single accepted and acceptable definition simply does not exist. The mother who hits her child with a belt may be praised as a good parent in one community; while in another, the mother who slaps her child's face may risk being reported as an abusive parent.

"Spare the Rod?" pp. 51–75 in *Behind Closed Doors: Violence in the American Family,* by Murray A. Straus, Richard J. Gelles, and Suzanne K. Steinmetz (Anchor Books 1980). Reprinted by permission.

Are Slaps and Spankings Violent?

Let us assume for the moment that, as a society, we take for granted the fact that parents spank their children. Evidence to support this assumption can be drawn from a variety of sources. For example, how many people intervene when an adult spanks or slaps a child in a supermarket?

There is also the tacit and legal approval of corporal punishment in schools, which is based on the belief that schools function as surrogate parents while children are in class. Take, for example, a school district in Oklahoma. There, a rule stating that anyone late for school five times must either submit to a spanking by the principal or be dismissed from school with failing marks had appeared in the student handbook for years. No one ever questioned its use until two parents who didn't believe in spanking threatened to take the school board to court (Boston *Globe,* November 16, 1977, p. 2). Hitting children is so taken for granted that almost all parents view a spanking or a slap as an inevitable part of raising a child.

Given that spankings and slaps are taken for granted, are they violent acts? According to the definition of violence which we presented in the first chapter, our answer is yes. Although violence is a pejorative word and the current thinking about slaps and spankings of children is that they are legitimate parenting tools, our view is that slaps and spankings are simply one end of a continuum of violent acts. When pressed, parents will admit that they slap or spank a child hard enough to get the child to stop doing something the parent does not want done. In one of our early studies we discussed this point with a parent:

> INTERVIEWER: When do you slap or spank your child?
> PARENT: When I want her to stop something . . . like when I want her to get away from the stove.
> INTERVIEWER: How hard do you hit her?
> PARENT: Hard enough to get her to stop.
> INTERVIEWER: You mean if the first slap doesn't get her to stop . . .
> PARENT: I hit her again, a little harder.

We interpret this dialogue to mean that parents will slap their child hard enough to stop the offensive behavior—in other words, the child gets hit hard enough so the "hurt" outweighs the desire to continue the forbidden act.

Over the years our discussions with parents concerning their use of slaps and spankings revealed that most parents do not see these acts as violent, but they do admit that they will spank or slap a child hard enough for the child to be "hurt" and get the message that the parent is angry and wants the child either to change his or her behavior or to learn a lesson. Although parents and the society at large can explain away the hurt by stating that the slaps or spankings were in the best interest of the child, the fact remains that these actions are consistent with the phenomenon we refer to as "violence."

The Ideology of Sparing the Rod

"Spare the rod and spoil the child," "kids need to be hit," "the bamboo stick makes a good child" (message in a fortune cookie)—these phrases all have the same thing in common—they argue that hitting a child is necessary, normal, and good. One question we wanted to answer in our national study of family violence was what proportion of American parents accept the wisdom that spankings and slaps are necessary, normal, and good ways to bring up their children?

We employed the semantic differential technique to measure parents' attitudes toward spanking or slapping a child. We faced a particular problem in creating the exact question which we wanted people to react to. At first we thought of asking a question similar to the one we asked about marital violence—"Couples slapping each other." However, the general question about couples could not be used with children since the term "child" could mean many things to a respondent, ranging from a newborn baby to an eighteen-year-old, six-foot four-inch, two-hundred-pound son. We could have asked numerous questions about spanking and slapping children of various ages, but there simply was not the time in the interview to allow for more than one question. We ultimately decided to ask a specific question about one age group. But what would it be?

Slapping a three-year-old is thought to be different in motivation and consequence than slapping an eighteen-year-old. There were numerous debates over what age child we should select for this question—especially since one of the authors had a "terrible" two-year-old; one had children covering the range from "mouthy" preteen to a "never wrong" teen-ager; and one had children in their late teens, approaching the total independence of adulthood. All could find persuasive reasons for arguing that each child was uniquely "hittable." We settled on twelve-year-old children because, although a difficult age, it is also an age when a parent has alternatives to spankings or slappings (e.g., "grounding," cutting off a child's allowance, early curfew, etc.).

Our results illustrate that most Americans view spanking and slapping a twelve-year-old as necessary, normal, and good. Seventy percent viewed slapping or spanking a twelve-year-old as somehow necessary; 77 percent felt this was normal; and 71 percent viewed these acts as good. The only comparable national statistics come from the study conducted for the National Commission on the Causes and Prevention of Violence in 1968. In this study 86 percent of a national sample agreed that young people needed "strong" discipline by their parents. While not the same as our question, this question lends support to our hypothesis that spankings and slappings are viewed as normal, necessary, and acceptable means of raising children.

How normal is it to slap or spank a twelve-year-old? We did not find a wide distribution of feelings among the people we questioned. Their responses were measured by the average scores reported by the respondents in answering each of the three semantic differential items. The items were measured using a scale that ranged from 1 to 7 (1 = unnecessary, not normal, and bad; 7 = necessary, normal, or good). The average ranking of the necessity of slaps or spankings was 3.5, normality was 4.0, and goodness was 3.6.

Men and Women

Men were found to be slightly more inclined to view slapping and spanking a twelve-year-old as necessary and good, while men and women equally viewed these forms of punishment as normal. Combining all three adjectives, men ranked higher than women in their agreement as to the necessity, normality, and goodness of violence.

Our findings are consistent with most studies on violence and aggression, which indicate that men approve of the use of physical force more than women.

Although there was not a great deal of variation in the perceptions of slaps and spankings, the profile of those most likely to view these acts as necessary, normal, and good, is male, without children, under thirty, and non-white.

Parents and Non-parents

Does having children affect a person's views on whether or not slaps and spankings are normal, necessary, and good? Childless individuals were more likely than parents to view slapping and spanking a twelve-year-old as necessary, normal, and good. The differences were much larger than the differences between men and women.

It is interesting that having a child seems to make people less likely to see slaps and spankings as normal, good, and necessary. Perhaps this is because parents have learned that slaps and spankings do not always get the desired results and other means of training or disciplining children are more effective. Moreover, some parents who spank their children and then see the children turn around and "spank" the family pet or a brother or sister might change their convictions about the "goodness" of a spanking.

Age

One of the clearest and most pronounced differences in people's attitudes toward the use of slaps and spankings appears when we compare people of different ages. Younger Americans are much more likely to view slaps and spankings as necessary, normal, and good. The most agreement with these forms of violence being necessary, normal, and good came from those under thirty. On the other hand, less than two thirds of the people we interviewed who were over fifty years of age saw slaps and spankings of twelve-year-olds as being necessary, normal, and good.

Why were there such pronounced age differences and why is support for slaps and spankings greater among younger Americans? We
must state that we really do not know whether
the age differences are a result of the different experiences each generation faces or if they indicate
that people change their views on slaps and
spankings as they grow older. Since we did not
study our respondents over a period of time, we
cannot answer this point. There are, however,
some possible explanations for the age-related
perceptions of slaps and spankings.

For one, it may be that as parents grow
older they see less necessity, normality, and goodness in using physical punishment. Our comparison of parents and non-parents seems to
bear this out, in that parents are less supportive
of these forms of violence than non-parents.

Second, the younger respondents may be
less likely to have children, and we have seen in
the preceding section that not having children is
related to approving slaps and spankings.

Another explanation is that the older respondents were more likely to have older children and therefore had less recent experience with
actually using slaps and spankings. The farther
people are removed from using a behavior, the
less they may approve of it. This explanation,
however, is less supportable. If true, it would mean
that non-parents would be less approving of slaps
and spankings—and we found just the opposite.

We think the differences between age
groups point to a general cultural ideology which
approves of slapping and spanking children. We
found that more than 80 percent of the individuals under thirty viewed the two forms of hitting
as necessary, normal, and good. Most of these individuals would not be old enough to have
twelve-year-old children. Thus, their approval
of slapping or spanking a preteen could be derived from a general societal support for these
acts rather than actual experience.

All the explanations just offered suggest that
as people grow older and have children, they
experience changes in attitude. But the greater
approval of violence in child rearing by the
younger people in the sample could reflect differences in the learning experiences and beliefs
of different generations. Wars tend to produce an
increase in killing one's fellow citizens as well as
in killing the enemy (Archer and Gartner, 1976).

People in their fifties were born after World War
I and grew up in the Depression, whereas those
in the younger age groups were born after the
Second World War and grew up during the
Korean and Vietnam wars. Moreover, those
under thirty were the first generation to grow
up with high and continuous exposures to TV
violence. The under-thirty generation has seen
violence on both television programming and
television news. They were the first generation to
see a war reported on television (Vietnam), and
to see someone killed on television (Lee Harvey
Oswald in 1963).

So the older groups may always have been
less favorable to violence because they grew up
in a less violent context, and the younger group
may continue to be more favorable to violence
even when they are in their fifties.

Finally, we may be witnessing a change in
the younger generation. New parents in the
1970s may be resorting to an older, more strict
style of child rearing as a reaction to the turmoil,
permissiveness, and "instability" of the 1960s.
Today's parents, facing children going out into a
world of drugs, delinquency, and disorder, might
be using standards and views that their grand-
parents held. Certainly there is rising evidence of
a "new conservatism" emerging in our society.
Newsweek magazine headlines America's "turn
to the right" while the percentage of Americans
supporting capital punishment is higher today
than any time in the last thirty years. Schools
are under pressure to abandon "enrichment" and
return to the three R's, while traditional and fundamental religions are enjoying a new revival.
The high proportion of those under thirty supporting spankings and slappings of children may
be one outcropping of a new era of fundamental and conservative attitudes.

The most important thing we learn from
the analysis of people's attitudes toward using
slaps and spankings is that these acts are generally seen as useful, normal, and acceptable parenting techniques. In fact, it is almost certain
that the figures which are presented in this section underestimate just how much support for
the necessity, normality, and goodness of slaps
and spankings there is in America. Had we chosen to substitute "two-year-old" for "twelve-year-
old" we might have seen proportions close to
100 percent of the population.

Violence Toward Children

"Ordinary" physical punishment and "child abuse" are but two ends of a single continuum of violence toward children. In between are millions of parents whose use of physical force goes beyond mild punishment, but which, for various reasons, does not get identified and labeled as "child abuse." The responses to the questions which asked if slapping or spanking a twelve-year-old was necessary, normal, and good provide us with information on American attitudes about hitting children. But attitudes are not the same as behavior. One could view a slap or a spanking as useful and not slap or spank a twelve-year-old, while, on the other hand, an individual could condemn all hitting, but still slap a child. What one parent may regard as "spanking" may well be considered a brutal beating by others.

We examined the extent, level, and kinds of violence that took place in the homes of 1,146 American couples who had children between the ages of three and seventeen living at home. It would have been too time consuming to ask each respondent about the use of violence on each of the children who were at home (in families with six or more children the interview might have gone on for hours). Instead, we randomly selected one "referent" child in each family. The child was the focal point for the discussion of physical punishment and violence. Thus, our examination of parental violence is not a study of all the violence each parent engaged in, but rather, all the violence a selected child in each family experienced from *one parent.* By using this procedure, we can generalize to how much violence children in the United States experience in one year and over a period of time.

Violence Rates

Seventy-three percent of the respondents report that at some time in their child's life they used some form of violence on the child. Sixty-three percent of the respondents who had children between the ages of three and seventeen living at home mentioned at least one violent episode occurring in 1975.

As might be expected, the milder forms of violence were the most common. Slaps or spankings were mentioned by 58 percent of the parents as occurring in the previous year and by 71 percent as having ever taken place. Forty-one percent of American families report pushing or shoving the referent child in 1975; while 46 percent said pushes or shoves had occurred at some time in the child's life. Hitting with an object was reported by 13 percent of the parents in the previous year and by 20 percent for the years up to the survey year. Throwing an object was less common; approximately 5 percent of the parents did this during the survey year while more than 9 percent admitted that they had thrown something at their child prior to the survey year.

The more dangerous types of violence were the least likely to occur. But even the figures for these extreme forms of violence yield an astoundingly high number of American children who were kicked, punched, bitten, beaten up, threatened with a gun or a knife, or had a gun or a knife used on them in 1975. Let us look first at the number of parents who admitted to having engaged in each type of violence.

Approximately 3 parents in 100 *kicked, bit, or punched* their child in 1975.

Nearly 8 in 100 stated that they had done these things to the referent child prior to the survey year.

Slightly more than 1 percent of the respondents reported beating up the referent child in the previous twelve months, and 4 percent said that they had done this at some point in the child's life. While the term "beat up" was not specifically defined in the course of the interview, the item followed the question on kicking, punching, and biting. Thus, we assume that beating up a child implies more than a single blow.

One child in 1,000 faced a parent who *threatened to use a gun or knife* on him or her in 1975, while nearly 3 children in 100 have grown up facing a parent who at least once threatened them with a gun or knife. The same proportions hold for children who had *guns and knives actually used* on them. Thus, 1 in 1,000 children in

1975 had a parent who shot or tried to shoot him, or stabbed or tried to stab him.

There were nearly 46 million children between the ages of three and seventeen who lived with both parents in 1975 (Bureau of Census, 1975). Extrapolating our findings to these children we estimate that between 3.1 and 4 million children have been kicked, bitten, or punched by a parent at some time in their lives; while between 1 and 1.9 million were kicked, bitten, or punched in 1975. Between 1.4 and 2.3 million children have been "beaten up" while growing up, and between 275,000 and 750,000 American children were "beaten up" in 1975. Finally, our data mean that between 900,000 and 1.8 million children between the ages of three and seventeen have had a parent use a gun or a knife on them at some time. Our figures do not allow for a reliable extrapolation of how many children had guns and knives used on them in 1975, but our estimate (based on an incidence of 1 in 1,000) would be something close to 46,000.

Frequency of Violence

With the exception of being threatened with a knife or gun or having a knife or gun used on them, children who experienced violence in 1975 experienced it more than once. Children who had something thrown at them had it happen an average 4.5 times that one year. Children who were pushed or grabbed or shoved experienced that 6.6 times over a twelve-month period. As we would expect, spankings and slappings were the most frequent—happening 9.6 times. The average for kicks, bites, and punches was 8.9 times in 1975, while children were hit with objects 8.6 times. Beatings occurred less than once every two months—an average of 5.9 times over the year. If a gun or knife was used, it happened "only" once in the survey year.

The figures on how often a form of violence was used must be interpreted with care. For some items these frequencies seem to be low. Most people would expect that if a child is spanked by a parent, this would occur more frequently than once a month. But our data are based on children aged three to seventeen. Thus, the frequencies are the average for all children, three to seventeen, who are spanked by their parents. Obviously, older children might be spanked less often than once a month, while some younger children might be spanked weekly, daily, or in some families, hourly.

We did not expect the more extreme forms of parental violence to be used so frequently. For a child to be kicked, bitten, punched, and beaten up every other month came as a surprise. This finding indicates that the extreme forms of parental violence are not rare, one-shot events. They occur periodically and even regularly in the families where these types of violence are used. If a beating is considered an element of child abuse, then our findings point to the conclusion that child abuse may be a chronic condition for many children, not a once in a lifetime experience for a rare few.

X-ray examinations of suspected child abuse victims have borne this out in recent years. Doctors often find evidence of healed or partially healed broken bones from previous beatings. Physicians were suspicious, for example, when one four-year-old girl told them that "Mama kept hitting me with a big black stick." The little girl, unconscious when brought to the hospital, was suffering from a fractured skull and lacerations of the back, face, arms, and legs. Although her mother indicated there had been an accident, X-rays showed this was not the first time the child had received such injuries (Flato, 1962).

Children at Risk

Our data on parental violence describe what parents did, not the results of these actions. Consequently, we cannot accurately estimate how many children were harmed by their parents while they were growing up, or in 1975. We do not know exactly what respondents meant when they admitted that they "beat up" their child, we do not know what objects they used when they hit a child (a pipe or a paddle?), and we do not know whether children who had guns and knives used on them were wounded. Nevertheless, we can attempt to estimate how many American children were "at risk" of being physically injured. The Child Abuse Index combines all the items which have the highest probability of injuring or damaging a child (kicks, bites, punches, beatings, threats with a gun or knife, use of a gun or knife). Between 3 and 4 out of every 100 parents (3.6 percent) admitted to using at least one of these dangerous forms of violence at least once in 1975. Assuming that any of these acts has a high probability of causing harm to a child victim, between 1.4 and 1.9 million children were vulnerable to physical injury from their parents in 1975.

Granted, being at risk of being injured is not the same as being a victim of child abuse. However, these figures may still be the best available for estimating how many children might be abused each year in the United States. This is because they are the only statistics ever generated from a nationally representative sample using sound scientific measurement procedures. If they are a reasonable estimate of child abuse, then they offer new and surprising information:

First, the estimates are 500,000 to 1 million children higher than previous estimates of the incidence of child abuse.

Second, the figures underestimate the true level of abuse for five important reasons. (1) They are based on self-reports of the parents. Underreporting is quite possible when sensitive questions such as "Did you beat up your child?" are asked. (2) The survey deals with only seven specific forms of violence. Omitted are such things as burning a child, torturing a child, sexual abuse, and other acts which are considered child abuse. (3) The data on violence toward children refer to violent acts of only one of the two parents. (4) The children we studied were only between the ages of three and seventeen. Previous research suggests a large amount of child abuse is directed toward children between three months and three years of age, and these children are not covered in our survey. Had they been included, our figures would certainly be higher. (5) We studied only "intact" families (husbands and wives who were living together). The literature on child abuse suggests that abuse may be more common in families where only one parent lives with the child. Had we studied single-parent families, we might also have uncovered a higher rate of extreme violence toward children. The actual violence children experience is probably much higher than the figures we report here. Thus, while our figures are accurate (in terms of the parent-child relations we investigated) they only hint at a much more extensive incidence of the abuse of children in the United States.

Mothers, Fathers, and Violence

During the survey year, mothers were more likely to have used violence at least once on the referent child and they were more likely than fathers to have used violence on the child in previous years. Sixty-eight percent of the mothers and 58 percent of the fathers engaged in at least one violent exchange with the referent child during the survey year, while 76 percent of the mothers and 71 percent of the fathers had been violent toward the child at another time.

We also found that mothers were more likely to use severe or abusive violence on their children than were fathers.

The finding that mothers are more prone to use severe violence on their children is consistent with the scientific and popular thinking on violence toward children. Research on child abuse often finds mothers to be at least as violent if not more violent than fathers (Bennie and Sclare, 1969; Steele and Pollock, 1974; Gil, 1970).

A simple explanation of mothers' violence is that they spend more time with children than do fathers. The actual explanation of mothers' greater use of violence is probably more complex. In our society, mothers, irrespective of how much time they actually spend with their children, are typically held more responsible for the actions, behavior, and development of their children than are fathers. Thus, frustrations created by children tend to affect the mother more than the father. A problem with the child reflects on her competence as a parent more than the father's.

One woman wrote to Ann Landers stating:

Last night I did something that really frightened me. I was helping our son with his homework and he refused to try to solve the math problem—just kept saying, "I can't get it."

I became so infuriated I started to slap his face as hard as I could and I couldn't stop. Today the little guy was black and blue marked on his cheeks. I was so ashamed I didn't let him go to school.

A second aspect of the explanation is that children interfere with mothers' plans and self-concepts more than fathers'. When a child is born, if a parent has to quit a job or change personal plans and goals, the parent is usually the mother. If a child is sick, the parent who stays home from work is usually the mother. Thus, again, mothers experience more than simply temporal frustration from their children; children affect the total range of their mothers' plans, goals, and expectations.

Carol, a Boston housewife trying to overcome her tendencies toward child abuse, described her feelings this way:

> "I can feel it coming. More or less I think it's depression. I get so damned fed up with the house and knowing that I've gotta watch the kids. I've gotta feed them. I've gotta do dishes. Like you get up in the morning, you cook breakfast, you do dishes, you clean the house. Next thing you know, it's lunchtime. While you're fixing lunch, they're out there messing up two or three rooms. You feed 'em, you do dishes, you clean the rooms, it's suppertime. It's the *same* thing" (*The Real Paper,* February 5, 1975, p. 18).

Undoubtedly, even more factors need to be considered to explain the greater likelihood of mothers using force and violence.

Mothers are more likely than fathers to throw objects at their children, slap or spank them, or hit their children with objects. There is no difference between mothers and fathers for pushing or grabbing; kicking, biting, or punching; or, lastly, beating.

It is interesting to note that mothers are at least as likely as fathers to use even the more serious forms of violence, such as kicks, bites, punches, and beatings. This is important because family violence is probably the only situation where women are as or more violent than are men. If men have a genetic predisposition to be violent, one would expect them to be more violent at home than their wives. Yet, an examination of violence between couples and violence by parents toward children reveals that women are as violent or more violent in the home than are men. This casts a shadow of doubt on the pure genetic theories of violence and points to a need to investigate social and psychological factors associated with family violence.

How Often?

With the exception of using or threatening to use guns and knives (which was admitted only by fathers in the survey), mothers use each type of violence as much or more frequently than their husbands. Children who are kicked, bitten, or punched by their parents encounter these forms of violence twice as frequently from their mothers than from their fathers. While fathers who beat up their children do this on an average of once a year, mothers who beat up their children do it more than once every other month—an average of 7.2 times per year! Mothers and fathers were roughly equal in their frequency of pushing, grabbing, and shoving their children, while mothers more frequently threw objects and slapped and spanked the children.

The final comparison between mothers and fathers reveals that mothers were more likely to use forms of violence which placed their children at risk of physical injury than were fathers. More than 4 percent of the mothers (4.4 percent) compared to "only" 2.7 percent of the fathers had kicked, bitten, punched, or beaten up their child during the survey year. This may seem like a small difference, but it amounts to a 62 percent greater rate of child abuse by mothers than by fathers.

Sons and Daughters as Victims of Violence

We found male children to be the most likely victims of parental violence. Nearly two thirds of the sons (66 percent) and 61 percent of the daughters of the respondents were struck at least once during the year. The greater likelihood of sons becoming victims is linked to parents' use of pushing, grabbing, or shoving their sons more than their daughters. Sons were beaten up somewhat more frequently than daughters were. Also, sons were reportedly the only ones who had guns and knives threatened or used on them.

Although there are few major differences between how violent parents are toward boys and girls when each type of violence is looked at separately, these small differences add up. In addition, the difference between the treatment of boys and girls becomes greater as the seriousness of the violence increases. As a result, the number of boys who are at risk of physical injury is 61 percent greater than for girls (4.5 percent compared to 2.8 percent).

A popular theory to explain boys' greater vulnerability to parental violence is that boys are more difficult to raise and commit more "punishable offenses" than girls. Another hypothesis is that our society accepts and often values boys' experiencing violence because it "toughens them up." Seven out of ten people responding to the 1968 survey conducted for the National Commission on the Causes and Prevention of Violence said that they believed it was important for a boy to have a few fist fights while he was growing up (Stark and Mc Evoy, 1970). Many people might approve of boys being hit more than girls because boys will experience a rougher, more violent world than their sisters. Violence may be approved of and used as a "character builder" for young boys (Straus, 1971).

Age of the Child

There are various hypotheses about what age a child is more vulnerable to being struck or abused by his parents. Some researchers and clinicians propose that the most dangerous period in a child's life is from three months to three years of age (Kempe et al., 1962; Fontana, 1973; Galdston, 1965). Psychologist Urie Bronfenbrenner proposes that the highest rates of child abuse and battering occur among adolescents (1974). David Gil's research on child abuse in America revealed that half of the confirmed cases of child abuse were children over six years of age, while nearly one fifth of the confirmed reports were children in their teens (1970). A recent survey of college students at an eastern

university found that 8 percent of a sample of more than 250 students stated that they had been physically injured by their parents during the last year they (the students) lived at home (Mulligan, 1977).

Our survey indicated younger children were most likely to be victims of some kind of physical force. Since the survey did not include children under three years of age we cannot draw any conclusions about this age group. Eighty-six percent of the three- and four-year-olds had some mode of violence used on them, 82 percent of the children from five years old to nine had been hit, 54 percent of the preteens and early teen-age children (ten to fourteen years old) were struck, and "only" one third of the children fifteen to seventeen years old were hit by their parents.

Younger children were vulnerable to a wide range of forceful and violent acts. Preschoolers and children under nine years old were more likely to be pushed, grabbed, shoved, slapped, spanked, kicked, bitten, hit with a fist, and hit with an object. Teen-age children were more vulnerable to having a gun or a knife used on them, although the differences were not significant.

Younger children are not only more likely to be struck by their parents, they are more likely to be hit frequently. The youngest children in our survey were pushed, grabbed, shoved, slapped, spanked, and hit with an object more frequently than older children. For these modes of violence, each older age group experienced violence less frequently than the younger group. The exceptions to this pattern were beatings, kickings, punches, bitings, and having an object thrown at the child. Children five to nine years of age were kicked, bitten, or punched and had objects thrown at them more frequently than other age groups of children. Older teens were beaten up more frequently than younger children (although this figure is influenced by the fact that one fifteen- to seventeen-year-old was reported beaten up twenty times).

Children under 5 and older teen-age children were the most likely to experience violence that held a high chance of causing physical injury. More than 6 percent (6.7) of children three and four, 2.5 percent of children five to nine, 3 percent of children ten to fourteen, and 4.3 percent of the oldest group of children (fifteen to seventeen) had parents use dangerous forms of violence on them during one year.

The results of our national study of violence toward children tend to confirm both previous theories concerning physical punishment and the abuse of children. Younger children are more likely to be struck by their parents and to be struck more frequently than older children. However, older children, even those in their late teens, experience a wide range of violence (including spankings) and experience it more than once a year. Our data tend to resolve the seeming contradiction which argues that younger children are more vulnerable. If we go by the parents' reports of what they do to their children, we find that preschoolers and children in their late teens are both vulnerable to physical abuse.

The fact that preschoolers and older teenage children share in the risk of being abused is very important. Many parents and social scientists have felt that the abuse of young children was the result of their parents frustration in dealing with them. The "terrible two's," toilet training accidents, touching hot stoves, and getting into mischief are all cited as reasons why younger children are spanked and often beaten. But if, as our data suggest, both preschoolers and older teen-agers are vulnerable to being injured by their parents, then we cannot accept the explanation that many children are abused because they are too young to be reasoned with. Of course, one often hears parents of older teenagers using the same lament as parents of preschoolers. Many parents of children in their late teens bemoan the fact that their children "no longer *listen* to reason." Thus, we find that children too young to reason with and older teen-agers, who refuse to be reasoned with, are both vulnerable to the same resolution of the conflict—violence.

Fathers, Mothers, Sons, and Daughters

We found mothers to be the most frequent users of violence in families and sons the most common victims. We also examined violence toward children by focusing on mothers' and fathers' use of violence on sons and daughters. In no instance were fathers more likely than mothers to strike their children. The general trend of mothers being the more frequent users of violence and sons being the more usual targets persisted.

Fathers were twice as prone to push, grab, shove, slap, or spank their daughters. There was no significant difference in the frequency of mothers and fathers pushing, grabbing, shoving, slapping, or spanking their male children, but mothers were much more likely to do these things to their daughters than were fathers. Mothers also tended to throw things more at their daughters than did fathers.

Sex and Age of Children

Discussions with parents who used violence on their children indicated that perhaps the age of the child influenced which sex child was hit more often or more severely. Some of our early pilot studies (Gelles, 1974) hinted that there was no difference between sons and daughters being struck when they were younger; but, as children got older, boys were the most common victims of frequent and severe parental violence. We did find that for younger children (under nine years old) there were no statistically significant differences between sons and daughters being pushed, grabbed, shoved, slapped, or spanked. However, boys over ten years of age were more likely to experience these forms of violence. In fact, sons fifteen to seventeen were twice as likely as girls to be pushed, grabbed, or shoved.

Summing Up

Most American parents approve of spanking and slapping their children, and almost two out of three American parents slap or spank their children in any given year. Nearly all parents slap or spank their children at least once in their lifetimes.

The total package of information presented in this chapter on attitudes toward violence and violent behavior suggests that children are injured and abused because we as a society are committed to norms which approve of and legitimize using violence as a frequent form of training and punishing children. Given the general attitudes of the society toward using violence and the extent and frequency of parental violence, we should not be surprised to find millions of parents going beyond the "normal violence" permitted to parents and placing children of all ages at risk of being physically injured.

One important point we make in this chapter is that we have demonstrated for the first time, with reliable scientific data on a nationally representative sample, that violence toward children goes well beyond ordinary physical punishment. Millions of children each year face parents who are using forms of violence that could grievously injure, maim, or kill them. In many families these episodes of violence are not merely one-shot outbursts. They are regular patterned ways which parents use to deal with conflict with their offspring. We do not mean to imply that the majority of parent-child exchanges are violent; rather we mean that many children periodically experience severe beatings, kicks, and punches in their homes.

A second point concerns the level of severe violence in families. Our figures do offer some solace since they demonstrate that relatively few parents do use beatings and guns and knives on their children. Nevertheless, although the actual percentage of parents who physically beat their children is small, when you extrapolate the figures to the national population it means that millions of children are involved. Consider how we would react if we found that millions of children faced guns and knives and experienced beatings in schools. If we were talking about smallpox, mumps, or flu, these figures could be interpreted to mean that there is an epidemic of these diseases in the United States. Somehow, people tend to focus on the more dramatic instances of child abuse and exhibit less concern over the mundane and undramatic forms of violence children experience. But violence of any kind is important. The consequences are potentially dramatic, since children who experience violence in their home experience it from those who claim love and affection for them.

One wonders why, when so many have expressed concern about violence in television, no one has ever voiced concern about the consequences of children seeing or being victims of vi-

olence in their own homes. The conventional theory is that the more violence a child sees on television, the more he or she tends to be violent, or is at least tolerant of violence. If this is the case, imagine the consequences of millions of children growing up seeing their parents using violence on each other, and on their children.

Researchers who have studied child abuse continue to find that children who were abused often grow up to be abusing parents (Bakan, 1971; Kempe, et al., 1962; Gil, 1970; Steele and Pollock, 1974). Research on murderers finds that killers experienced more frequent and severe violence as children than their brothers who did not go on to commit a homicide (Palmer, 1962; Gillen, 1946). Examinations of presidential assassins or would-be assassins also find these individuals sharing common histories of violent upbringing. In his diary, Arthur Bremer, Governor George Wallace's would-be assassin, wrote, "My mother must have thought I was a canoe, she paddled me so much." Lee Harvey Oswald, Sirhan Sirhan, and Charles Manson all experienced violent childhoods (Button, 1973).

A study of violent inmates in San Quentin prison found that 100 percent of them experienced extreme violence between the ages of one and ten (Maurer, 1976). Psychologist Ralph Welsh (1976) claims that he has never examined or talked with a violent juvenile delinquent who did not come from an extremely violent background. Moreover, Welsh claims that even if the extreme violence ceases before the child is four years old, the child still is likely to exhibit violent tendencies as a juvenile.

Violence in the streets, violence in the schools, assassinations, murders, assaults, wife abuse, child abuse—are they caused by violence on television, violence in the movies, permissive upbringings? These probably contribute something. But the evidence appears to support the notion that our homes and how we raise our children are the main sources of our violent society.

Surely the pattern is not as simple as "being beaten causes one to beat." A society in which millions of children are kicked, beaten, punished, bitten, shot, and stabbed by their parents has a bigger problem than mere child abuse. Millions of our children are "time bombs" of violence which can explode at home, at school, or in the streets.

References

Archer, D., and R. Gartner 1976. Violent acts and violent times: a comparative approach to postwar homicide rates. *American Sociological Review* 41 (December):937–63.

Bakan, D. 1971. *Slaughter of the innocents: a study of the battered child phenomenon.* Boston: Beacon Press.

Bennie, E. H., and A. B. Sclare 1969. The battered child syndrome. *American Journal of Psychiatry* 125 (July):975–78.

Bronfenbrenner, U. 1974. The origins of alienation. *Scientific American* 231:53ff.

Bureau of the Census 1975. Estimates of the population of the United States by age, sex, and race, *Current population reports,* Series P-25, No. 614. 1970–1975. Washington, D.C.: Government Printing Office.

Button, A. 1973. Some antecedents of felonious and delinquent behavior. *Journal of Clinical Child Psychology* 2 (Fall):35–38.

Flato, C. 1962. Parents who beat children. *Saturday Evening Post* 235 (October 6):30ff.

Fontana, V. J. 1973. *Somewhere a child is crying: maltreatment—causes and prevention.* New York: MacMillan Publishing.

Galdston, R. 1965. Observations of children who have been physically abused by their parents. *American Journal of Psychiatry* 122 (4):440–43.

Gelles, R. J. 1974. *The violent home: a study of physical aggression between husbands and wives.* Beverly Hills, Calif.: Sage Publications.

Gil, D. G. 1970. *Violence against children: physical child abuse in the United States.* Cambridge, Mass.: Harvard University Press.

Gillen, J. L. 1946. *The Wisconsin prisoner: studies in crimogenesis.* Madison: University of Wisconsin Press.

Kempe, C. H., et al. 1962. The battered child syndrome. *Journal of the American Medical Association* 181 (July):17–24.

Maurer, A., 1976. Physical punishment of children. Paper presented at the California State Psychological Convention, Anaheim.

Mulligan, M. A. 1977. *An investigation of factors associated with violent modes of conflict resolution in the family.* Unpublished M.A. thesis, University of Rhode Island.

Palmer, S. 1962. *The psychology of murder.* New York: Thomas Y. Crowell Company.

Stark, R., and J. Mc Evoy III 1970. Middle class violence. *Psychology Today* 4 (November):52–65.

Steele, B. F., and C. B. Pollock 1974. A psychiatric study of parents who abuse infants and small children. In *The battered child,* R. E. Helfer and C. H. Kempe, eds., pp. 89–134. Chicago: University of Chicago Press.

Straus, M. A. 1971. Some social antecedents of physical punishment: a linkage theory interpretation. *Journal of Marriage and the Family* 33 (November):658–63.

Welsh, R. S. 1976. Severe parental punishment and delinquency: a developmental theory. *Journal of Child Clinical Psychology* 35 (1):17–21.

Reasonableness and the Battered Woman

Cynthia K. Gillespie

Physical differences in size and strength, lack of athletic training and self-defense skills, and socialization into passivity and helplessness affect all women in our society to a greater or lesser extent. However, for most women who kill in self-defense, these experiences are only a part of what influences their assessment of danger and the options available to them to counter it because most such women are battered women, and the men they kill are their batterers. Such a woman's past experiences with her assailant and her first-hand knowledge of his violence and his willingness to inflict injury on her, inevitably influence the reasonableness of her assessment of the likelihood that he is about to seriously injure or kill her and whether or not she can prevent that from happening without seriously injuring or killing him first.

The proposition that a battered woman's past experience with her batterer affects the reasonableness of her perception of the peril she is in when he commences to beat her up again would appear so obvious as to hardly require discussion. However, as we shall see, the greatest burdens a battered woman defendant faces at trial are, first, finding a way to explain to the jury how living constantly with violence and the threat of violence affected her view of her situation, and, second, convincing them that her fear of serious injury or death was reasonable.

Fear is a battered woman's constant companion. She wakes up afraid and goes to bed afraid. When she is home alone, she is afraid of what will happen when her man returns—that he will be drunk and angry, that he will beat her for something, often some household chore she has failed to do or for something he has imagined she has been doing in his absence. When he is with her, she is afraid that anything she might do or not do or that something someone else might do that she cannot control—an admiring glance from a man on the street, a phone call from a friend, a whining child—may trigger an episode of violence. Even sleep brings no respite, for she never knows when she might awaken to find herself being raped or beaten. Her sleep is interrupted by nightmares and sudden cold-sweat awakenings. There are women who sleep with their shoes on in case they must run for their lives in the middle of the night.

Everyone has experienced fear at some time, and we all know the feeling of a racing heart, clammy sweat, dry mouth, spinning thoughts and frozen legs that a panic of fear can bring. What we all have difficulty imagining, however, is the effect of living constantly with such fear. In their study of battered women who were referred to a rural mental health clinic, psychiatrist Elaine Hilberman and her colleague Kit Munson described it thus:

> The variety of initial complaints and diagnoses notwithstanding, there was a uniform response to the violence which was identical for the entire sample. The women were a study in paralyzing terror which is reminiscent of the rape trauma syndrome . . . except that the stress was unending and the threat of the next assault everpresent . . . Agitation and anxiety bordering on panic were almost always present: "I feel like screaming and hollering but I hold it in." "I feel like a pressure cooker ready to explode." They talked of being tense and nervous by which they meant "going to pieces" at any unexpected noise, voice or happening. Events even remotely

Selections from "Reasonableness and the Battered Woman," pp. 123–156 in *Justifiable Homicide: Battered Women, Self-Defense, and the Law,* by Cynthia K. Gillespie (Ohio State University Press 1989). Reprinted by permission.

connected with violence, whether sirens, thunder, people arguing or a door slamming, elicited intense fear. A woman who had been shot by her husband panicked at any loud noise. There was a chronic apprehension of imminent doom, of something terrible always about to happen. Any symbolic act or actual sign of potential danger resulted in increased activity, agitation, pacing, screaming and crying. They remained vigilant, unable to relax or sleep. Sleep, when it came, brought no relief. Nightmares were universal, with undisguised themes of violence and danger: "My husband was chasing me up the stairs . . . I was trying to escape but kept falling backwards." "There was a man breaking in the house . . . trying to kill me." "Snakes were after me . . . in my bed."

These women are not experiencing hysteria. There is nothing irrational about their fear. On the contrary, it is all too firmly grounded in reality. A battered woman, by definition, lives with a man who has repeatedly demonstrated both his willingness to inflict pain on her and his ability to do so. The kinds of injury and pain that such women are subject to fairly boggle the imagination.

In their study of 542 women admitted to shelters in the Dallas–Fort Worth area, sociologists William A. Stacey and Anson Shupe tell of women rammed against walls by cars; burned with cigarettes crushed on their backs, necks, faces, and arms; splashed with acid; forced to drink bleach; and burned with butane lighters held to their hair and flesh. ". . . One husband poured a can of drain cleaner into his wife's open palm and forced her to hold her hand under the running kitchen faucet. Another drenched his wife's clothes with gasoline during an argument and stalked her through the house with matches, threatening to 'torch' her."

Lenore Walker tells of women being stomped until their backs are broken; scalded with boiling liquids and hot foods; burned with cigarettes and hot irons; shot; stabbed and mutilated with knives and other sharp objects; and sexually tortured, having objects and substances forced into their vaginas and being made to have sex with animals and, at gunpoint, strangers, as well as suffering vaginal and anal rape.

Even in the more common battering situation, where the man uses "only" his hands and fists and feet in his assaults, as we have seen, the pain and injury that his victim suffers can be devastating. The studies present an endless litany of broken bones, smashed jaws, shattered teeth, yanked out hair, bruises, eyes and mouths swollen shut for days and weeks, chokings, smotherings, damaged internal organs and, over and over, miscarriages and deformed babies caused by kicks and blows to pregnant abdomens.

In 1983, Dr. Angela Browne of the University of New Hampshire did a study which compared a group of forty-two battered women who had killed their mates with a larger sample of two-hundred and five abused women who had not. The purpose of the study was to isolate the variables that seemed most to differentiate the two groups. Looking at the violence that both groups of women experienced, she found that the kinds of violent acts they faced were not significantly different. "Typical battering incidents involved a combination of violent acts and verbal abuse or threats. Types of physical abuse described ranged from being slapped, punched, kicked or hurled bodily, to being choked, smothered or bitten. Women reported attacks in which they were beaten with an object, threatened or injured with a weapon, scalded with hot liquid, or held underwater."

Although the kinds of violence were the same for both groups, several other crucial variables were not. The homicide group reported that the assaults came far more frequently than those suffered by the abuse-only group. Over 63 percent of the women who ultimately killed their husbands reported being beaten more than once a month, compared with 45 percent of the others. Even more telling, nearly 40 percent of the women who committed homicides were (by that point in the relationship) the target of this kind of serious brutality more often than once a week. Only 13 percent of the battered women in the control group reported such frequent assaults.

The women who killed their batterers also suffered significantly more severe and more frequent sexual abuse. Both groups experienced a high incidence of rape (forced sexual intercourse) by their spouses: 76 percent of the homicide group and 59 percent of the control group reported that this happened to them. However, the homicide group suffered a much greater frequency of spousal rape than the comparison group; 40 percent of them reported being raped "often," compared with only 13 percent of the battered women who did not kill. This forced sex often was part of, or the culmination of, a serious beating, inflicted upon a woman who was already injured, bruised, and bleeding. It also tended to be brutal and violent, accompanied by pinching, biting, choking, and bashing the woman's head against solid objects. Apparently intended less for sexual gratification than to inflict pain and humiliation, such episodes often went on for hours and resulted in serious injury to the woman.

Forced intercourse was not the only form of sexual abuse that both groups of women were compelled to endure. Well over half (62 percent) of the women in the homicide group, and 37 percent of the comparison group, reported that their husbands had forced or urged them to perform other sexual acts that the women considered abusive or unnatural. "Sexually abusive acts reported by the women in the homicide group included the insertion of objects into the woman's vagina, forced oral or anal sex, bondage, forced sex with others, and sex with animals. One woman reported being raped with her husband's service revolver, a broom handle, and a wire brush. As with other types of violence, sexual abuse by partners typically involved a variety of assaultive behaviors . . . "

A third significant difference in the nature of the violence suffered by women who killed their mates was in the severity of the injuries that they sustained. They were injured far more seriously than their nonhomicide counterparts.

Injuries to women in the homicide group ranged from bruises, cuts, black eyes, concussions, broken bones, and miscarriages caused by beatings, to permanent injuries such as damage to joints, partial loss of hearing or vision, and scars from burns, bites or knife wounds. Interestingly, although the number of abusive acts reported by women in the homicide group was not significantly higher than the number of acts perpetrated against comparison-group women, these acts were apparently done with much more force.

When asked about four specific incidents, women in the homicide group were much more severely injured in both the second (a typical) and the worst (or one of the most frightening) incidents and, overall, sustained more, and more severe, injuries than did the women in the comparison group.

A woman who is being beaten and tortured and sexually abused several times a week or even several times a month lives a life that is a blur of pain and fear. One injury follows another with no time for healing. New bruises fall on old bruises, stitches are ripped out as old wounds reopen, half-knit bones are broken again. When the man who has proved himself to be so brutal, so inexorable in his cruelty, begins to assault her yet again, it is hard to imagine that anyone could doubt the genuineness and reasonableness of her fear or question whether her belief that she is about to be seriously injured yet again is a reasonable belief. Even so, prosecutors and judges and juries do so over and over again.

A battered woman's fear of her husband springs from her first-hand experience of his violence. Actual injuries suffered, however, are not the only thing that contributes to a woman's fear of her violent mate. Far from being merely the accidental fallout of the batterer's violent behavior, her fear of him is often the intended result of conduct specifically calculated by the man to keep her constantly cowed and terrified. The techniques of psychological abuse that violent men use to intimidate and control the women in their lives are as varied as the human imagination. Verbal harassment is usually a large part of it. The woman is bombarded with constant criticism and deprecation. Everything she does is wrong. Everything she says is stupid. She is a terrible housekeeper, a worse bedpartner, a totally incompetent mother, a whore, a bitch, and a slut. She is so ugly that no other man could possibly want her. Everything that goes wrong is absolutely her fault. If he beats her, she has only herself to blame. Years of this kind of treatment can do devastating damage to a woman's self-esteem and have the insidious effect of bullying her into accepting *his* view of his violence, that it is justified by her own failings as a woman and as a wife.

This is apt to be reinforced by isolation, another common form that psychological abuse often takes. Battered women are frequently intentionally cut off from contact with other people. Sometimes this is the result of the almost pathological jealousy that many battering males exhibit; but it is not only limited to keeping her from having contact with men. Many battered women tell of being cut off from their families and friends, forbidden to socialize with their fellow workers or to work at all, even prohibited from going to church. They often must account for literally every penny of their money and every minute of their time. Their men believe that they have the right to control and monitor every aspect of their women's lives.

The more isolated a woman is from the outside world, the more dependent she must be on her husband. His constant attacks on her competence and value, combined with her ever-diminishing sources of support or help, make the possibility of standing up to him or leaving him unimaginable. His power over her begins to appear invincible.

For some batterers, however, the control over their wives that verbal harassment and social isolation—enforced by sporadic bouts of serious physical violence—gives them is not enough. These are the ones who resort to acts of real terrorism to maintain the upper hand. Angela Browne reports that two of the most commonly reported examples of this kind of behavior are forcing the woman to play Russian roulette with a loaded gun and making her watch while the man tortures or kills a pet animal. Many women tell of being stalked or tormented with guns and knives or splashed with gasoline and threatened with lighted matches or lighters. Much sexual abuse is specifically calculated to cause as much psychological devastation as physical pain. Many batterers seem to delight not merely in making death threats but in detailed and gory descriptions of exactly how the woman will be tortured and killed and how slowly and painfully he will cause her to die.

The pattern that a man's abuse typically follows is also a crucial contributing factor to the reasonableness of a battered woman's fear of death or serious injury at the hands of her abusive husband. There are probably many marriages in which a man resorts to physical violence once and never does so again, perhaps because he is genuinely appalled at his own actions or because his wife makes it absolutely clear that she will leave him if he ever does it again. Much research indicates, however, that once a man develops a pattern of hitting or beating his wife it is highly unlikely that he will ever voluntarily stop. Physical violence, and the threat of physical violence, become for him an increasingly easily resorted-to technique for controlling his wife, imposing his will, getting his way, winning arguments and (some would argue) dealing with stress elsewhere in his life.

Virtually every study shows that the common pattern is for the man's violence to increase steadily over time, both in frequency and severity. Stacey and Shupe found, for example, that "*as the frequency of battering episodes increased, the more severe they became.* [sic] Likewise, the longer that violence continued over months and years, the more serious and dangerous it became. In other words, over time situations usually progressed from verbal abuse to punching the woman often to using weapons. Moreover, such violence began to occur more frequently. Several women told us that they were somehow able to stand back one day and review how the pattern of violence had been intensifying; they then suddenly felt more afraid than at any time during a single beating."

There is more to the usual pattern of violence than repetition and escalation, moreover. Dr. Lenore Walker has pointed out that in the majority of cases in her studies of battered women, the battering followed a distinct three-stage cycle: a tension building phase followed by a major explosion of violence which is followed, in turn, by a period of contrition and attempted reconciliation. It usually does not take a battered woman long to come to recognize the pattern and anticipate its phases. Battering is not just a series of unconnected ordinary arguments that sometimes get out of hand and result in violence. On the contrary, battering is an ongoing, constant phenomenon in a relationship that is merely acted out in different ways at different stages in the cycle. A battered woman's fear is no less acute and her perception of being in serious danger is no less reasonable because she is not being actively beaten at any particular moment.

According to Walker, the first or tension-building stage is characterized by an ongoing series of minor incidents and assaults. He may push or shake or slap her, throw things, dump the dinner on the floor or smash up the furniture. He is likely to accompany this with a barrage of verbal criticism and complaint, berating her for her housekeeping, her cooking, her ability as a mother, her looks, her family and friends. He may begin to make accusations that she is cheating on him with such unlikely partners as the mailman or the carry-out boys at the market or even her own relatives or women friends. If he is one of the many batterers who is most violent when he is drunk, he may start on a round of increasingly heavier drinking. He may also begin to make threats about what he will do to her if she doesn't mend her ways.

These are all things that, taken one by one, tend to seem relatively minor. A woman would feel absurd calling the police, or even her own mother, to complain that her husband had shoved her into a wall or punched her on the arm or thrown a plate of meatloaf at her. So she often copes with these "little batterings" as best she can, denying her anger, soothing and placating and agreeing with her husband's accusations that his rage is caused by her own failures. What she knows, though, after she has seen the whole cycle through a couple of times, is that this first-stage tension-building behavior leads inevitably to stage two, an explosion of serious violence.

The terrifying thing about major battering episodes, where the man is completely out of control and is apt to go on pounding and smashing until his victim is unconscious or he himself drops from exhaustion, is that they are, at the same time, both predictable and unpredictable. A woman who is trapped in such a violent relationship knows she will be beaten again and that the next serious beating may well be worse than the last one. She knows, too, that the commencement of tension-building behavior signals a major explosion's inexorable arrival. She does not know, however, when it will happen or what might trigger it.

One of the most striking characteristics of the stories that battered women tell about their lives is the incredibly trivial nature of the things that often touch off major, even life-threatening, assaults. Del Martin relates:

> In my own conversations with battered women, I have discovered that however a batterer may rationalize his actions to himself, those actions never seem warranted by the actual triggering event. For example, one woman told me she was beaten unmercifully for breaking the egg yolk while cooking her husband's breakfast. Another said her husband blew up because at their child's birthday party she instructed the youngster to give the first piece of cake to a guest, not to him. Another wife was battered because her *husband's* driver's license was suspended. Other women reported these reasons: she prepared a casserole instead of fresh meat for dinner; she wore her hair in a pony tail; she mentioned that she didn't like the pattern on the wallpaper.

Richard Gelles relates two grotesquely similar stories of serious assaults stemming from the issue of who would get the first piece of cake at a child's birthday party. Stacey and Shupe mention beatings set off by such trivialities as "the woman's habit of biting her nails, her particular choice of lipstick, or what happened to be served one night for dinner." Lenore Walker tells of a woman doctor who was beaten so badly she was hospitalized and lost a kidney all because she had been delayed by a patient and arrived home half an hour later than she had said she would.

Frequently, violent assaults are triggered by things that happened only in the batterer's imagination. Many violent men are tormented by sexual jealousy and imagine their wives are unfaithful at every conceivable opportunity with an unbelievable variety of men—landlords, elevator operators, bartenders, store clerks, neighbors, his relatives, her relatives, even total strangers. The most innocent and casual contact with a man can trigger a tirade of accusations of imagined infidelities, embroidered in pornographic detail, while he tries to beat or browbeat her into a confession and then beats her brutally because she finally does confess or because she doesn't.

A battered woman lives in a state that Dr. Elaine Hilberman has described as "constant anticipatory terror." As the tension builds and the danger signals increase, more and more of her energy must go into trying to anticipate what might set him off. She tries to control every minute detail of the household and her own behavior in the desperate hope of avoiding that one unpredictable trigger. Such women talk about walking on eggshells or living life on tiptoe. Everything she does, from frying an egg to expressing an opinion, becomes literally a life and death matter. The strain of it, and the emotional and physical toll it takes, are terrible and are made the more so by the inevitable failure of her efforts. While she knows that her physical safety, and quite possibly her very life, depend on trying to stave off the impending beating as long as possible, she also knows that she cannot ultimately prevent the explosion that her mate is building himself up to. He may blame his beatings on her failures and short-comings, and he may sucker her into assuming that blame herself; but the fact is, what the woman does or does not do has virtually nothing to do with whether or when her husband will beat her.

Once an acute battering episode begins there is nothing she can do to stop it and very little she can do to control it. As Emerson Dobash and Russell Dobash point out, the usual techniques that people resort to, to avoid violent confrontations, do not work for battered women. The two primary techniques that sociologists have identified are withdrawing from the situation and agreement with the accusations that the aggressor is making. Withdrawal, however, as we have seen, is often impossible for an abused woman. Unlike a confrontation in a bar between two strangers, the problem isn't that he is feeling mean and might hit someone. The problem is that he specifically intends to hit *her*. There is seldom any place of refuge in a house or apartment from someone in determined pursuit; and even if she does manage to lock herself in the bathroom, she will eventually have to come out, and he will still be there. Fleeing out the door is seldom an option either. He can easily prevent her from leaving and can and will come after her if she does. Most of these serious assaults take place late at night when the woman has no place to go; and even if she can get away, she will often

be reluctant to leave her children behind in a dangerous situation.

Agreeing with her husband's accusations is no more likely to succeed for, as Dobash and Dobash observe, ". . . there may be circumstances in which acceptance of the potential aggressor's definition of the situation will precipitate a violent reaction. Men described as 'norm enforcers' . . . actually see themselves as acting in a righteous and appropriate manner. They are carrying out justice in their eyes. A woman who agrees, either truthfully or falsely, to her husband's accusations regarding her supposed infidelity or failure to meet his needs may actually guarantee a violent punishment."

Other possible responses seem to be equally ineffective. Richard Gelles points out, in *The Violent Home,* that it seems to make no difference whether or not the assaulted woman fights back. Far from serving to diminish the violence, a woman's failure to fight back can leave her passively at the man's mercy for as long as he has the strength to keep on hitting her. Conversely, if a woman does try to fight back, she is likely to be punished for it with an even more vicious beating. The battered women in Eisenberg and Micklow's study who tried to defend themselves unanimously reported that the more resistance they put up, the more severely they were beaten. Similarly, Walker's subjects indicated that arguing with the man often only enrages him further while, on the other hand, withdrawing into total silence may have exactly the same effect. Screaming or even crying or moaning likewise can make an attack more severe. Even raising her arms or hands to ward off blows may just result in their being twisted or broken. Study after study has revealed that, where escape is impossible, the only thing that a woman can do once a violent assault has begun is passively submit to it, protecting her most vulnerable parts as best she can by rolling herself into a ball, and just try to stay alive until it is over. As Lenore Walker succinctly points out, "According to reports from the battered women, only the batterers can end the second phase."

The third phase of the battering cycle consists, in some relationships, of a kind of honeymoon period, where the man is contrite and apologetic and often attempts to make amends with flowers and gifts and loving behavior. This seems to be particularly characteristic of the earlier years of an abusive marriage, when the man may still be genuinely remorseful and may be afraid that he has really gone too far this time and that his wife will leave him if he cannot manipulate her into forgiving him. Later in these marriages, and from the beginning in many others, the abusive man demonstrates no contrition whatsoever and either justifies his brutality as appropriate or insists that the whole family pretend that it never happens at all. In these relationships, it may be more accurate to characterize the third stage of the battering cycle as "an absence of tension or violence" and a return to apparently normal married life.

The third stage of the battering cycle may provide the woman a respite from immediate danger, but it does not necessarily bring any relief from her fear and anxiety. At the same time that she is trying to convince herself that this time the tranquility, and even happiness, will last she is constantly looking out for warning signs that the tension is beginning to build again toward its inevitable violent climax. Moreover, the fear generated by a serious beating does not just dissipate when the assault is over. It can continue to exist and affect the woman's outlook and behavior for a long time afterwards. She does not have to be facing an imminent second assault or even overtly threatening behavior to be constantly gripped by an utterly reasonable fear of her husband's violence.

Studies have found that battered women are nearly unanimous in their belief that their batterer is capable, physically and psychologically, of killing them. They have no doubt at all that their lives are in danger during serious assaults. For the battered woman who knows she is quite literally in a life or death situation, her very survival depends on her becoming extremely sensitive to cues. She must learn to read the danger signals of an impending attack, so that she can take whatever protective measures the situation permits: getting the children away, stashing a car key where she can grab it quickly, staying out of cul-de-sac rooms where she can be trapped, maneuvering to keep herself on the other side of large pieces of furniture. The earlier she is able to read the danger signals, the greater the likelihood that she will be able to keep herself alive

and uninjured. Unfortunately, what may seem an obvious warning flag to her may later seem to be a lame justification to a jury. It is not at all unusual for a battered woman who kills her husband to explain that she knew that he was about to harm her seriously because he had the same expression on his face or look in his eye that he had when he hurt her badly in the past.

Similarly, a battered woman has no choice but to take her batterer's threats seriously. Threats of violence to come are frequently part of the tension-building period that precedes a serious assault, and she often has had painful first-hand experience of his willingness to carry out those threats. Death threats too must be taken seriously. Despite the arguments frequently made by prosecutors, the fact that he has made them before and has not actually killed her yet does not mean that she can or should assume that such threats are bluffs. She knows that the violence tends to escalate from episode to episode. She knows that he is capable of killing her. A threat to do worse harm to her in the future than he has done to her in the past is, from her point of view, absolutely credible. The death threats that batterers make, unlike the casual ones people sometimes toss into conversations or arguments, are *meant* to be believed. Often taking the form of detailed descriptions of what the man is going to do to her and how, and frequently accompanied by menacing behavior with a knife or gun, these threats are made with the specific intent of causing terror and hence compliance. Many batterers further reinforce the credibility of their death threats by engaging in a terrifying variety of "displaced" homicidal acts, such as killing pets, firing guns into walls and bed pillows, cutting up clothing and other personal possessions, and even digging graves and constructing coffins for their intended victims. The reader may recall Caroline Scott's boyfriend holding her child's teddy bear next to her head and firing a bullet through it. The message of this sort of behavior is always, "You may be next," and a battered woman would be crazy not to take it seriously.

As Hilberman and Munson have observed, "When husbands threaten homicide, they are taken at their word because threats and wishes become a reality with explosive suddenness."

Peter Chimbos, in his study of spousal homicides in Canada, concluded that "threats to kill should especially not be dismissed as 'empty bluffs' or 'drunken ravings.'"

When a defendant who is a battered woman testifies that she was afraid her husband was going to injure or kill her, the fear she is referring to is not just the apprehension generated by the man's immediate actions, as though he were a stranger. Her fear is, rather, a reaction to everything that he has done to her before, the things that he has threatened to do, and the things that her experience has taught her he will likely do. The threats and verbal harangues and "little batterings" of the tension-building stage that lead so inexorably to a major beating may seem relatively trivial in themselves. But when they are recognized as part of a pattern they can be seen for what they are and what the battered woman knows they are: signals that worse violence is to come. Since the woman knows from her own painful experience that the next beating may well be worse than the last and that once it starts she will be powerless to stop it, it is not surprising that it is so often during the tension-building stage, when a severe beating looms but has not yet begun, that the woman seizes a weapon and acts to defend herself. What might appear at first glance to be an overreaction is an entirely reasonable response to the situation she actually faces, and indeed, if she cannot get away, may well be the *only* reasonable one.

A battered woman knows very well what her batterer has done to her in the past, what he has threatened to do, and what he is capable of doing to her now. But this is not the only part of her experience that affects her perception of the situation and the reasonableness of her response. If she is like the overwhelming majority of battered women, she also knows, first-hand, that she cannot rely on the police, the courts, neighbors, relatives, or anyone else for protection against her violent mate. Every attempt to get help is likely only to reinforce her perception that she has no alternative but to protect herself.

Most of us assume, without ever thinking about it, that if there were someone threatening to do us serious harm, we would have only to call for the police and they would come as fast as they could, arrest the wrongdoer and haul him away. Perhaps we would be right if our assailant were a stranger. But if there is one aspect of the battering experience that women report with more consistency than any other when they tell their stories, it is that calling the police seldom does them any good at all.

Getting the police to respond to a call for help is the first problem. "Domestic disturbance" complaints are assigned a very low priority by most police departments. Many battered women report that a call to the police for help may not be responded to for many hours and, alarmingly often, may not be responded to at all. The United States Civil Rights Commission, in its 1982 investigation of the problems that battered women face in the legal system, found this problem to be widespread. In its report, *Under The Rule of Thumb,* the Commission cited one study from Kentucky that found that police failed to respond at all to 17 percent of all calls they received from battered women. Another police officer testified before the Commission that in his department, police would respond in person to only one out of five or six such calls. If the assault appeared to be already over, it was his department's policy merely to inform the caller of the various social agencies that she could contact the next business day and how to get to the courthouse to file a complaint.

In 1973, the Police Foundation conducted a study in Kansas City to explore the relationship between domestic disturbance calls to the police and the crimes of homicide and aggravated assault. The study concluded that "there appears to be a distinct relationship between domestic-related homicides and aggravated assaults and prior police interventions for disputes and disturbances." Indeed, the study found that in the two-year period preceding the homicides that they studied, the police had responded to at least one disturbance call at the address where the killing occurred in 85 percent of the cases. In fully 50 percent of the cases they had responded to five or more such calls in the same two-year period.

Even in such extreme cases, when police failure to protect a battered woman results in her being killed by her batterer, the courts have upheld the right of the police to exercise their discretion not to make arrests or to answer the call at all. Ruth Bunnell, for example, in the year before her death, had called the police no fewer than twenty times for protection against her violent estranged husband. Her calls had resulted in only a single arrest. The night she was killed, Mr. Bunnell telephoned her and told her he was coming over to her house to kill her. She called the police and begged them to come right away. They refused, telling her to call them back when her husband got to the house. She was never able to make the second call. When her husband got there he stabbed her to death.

Ms. Bunnell's estate brought a wrongful death action against the San Jose police department, but the California courts held that California police departments enjoy absolute immunity from such lawsuits. The state Court of Appeals ruled that despite Ruth Bunnell's repeated calls for protection and Mark Bunnell's previous arrest (from which the police ought to have been on notice that a dangerous situation existed), there was no "special relationship" between her and the police that implied any promise on the department's part to protect her.

For a woman to call the police at all when she is the victim of ongoing violence by a brutal mate is an act of enormous courage and defiance. In seeking outside protection, she may very well be putting herself in even greater danger because the risk of her husband's taking violent retribution against her is very real. Indeed, he may quite specifically have threatened to kill her if she ever tried. It sometimes takes a battered woman years to simultaneously find both the opportunity and the nerve to make that call. One can only imagine, then, how devastating it is for a badly beaten woman to call the police for help only to have them fail to arrive or to arrive and do nothing. She is left, alone, having to face or somehow to hide from a man even more enraged than he was when he assaulted her in the first place. And society's message to both of them is clear: a man can beat his woman up all he wants and not suffer any consequences; a woman who is beaten by her man cannot rely on the police to protect her.

If a battered woman perseveres in her quest for protection and prevails upon the police to make an arrest or else goes down to the courthouse and insists on filing a complaint herself, the results are likely to do little more than reinforce this message. The findings of both recent major government studies, by the Civil Rights Commission and the Office of the Attorney General, confirm the conclusions of many other researchers and observers: the criminal justice system fails the battered woman at every turn.

Decisions about whether criminal charges will be brought against the subject of a complaint, what charges to bring, and whether to pursue the case to trial or settle or divert it are made by the prosecutor. He or she has virtually unlimited discretion in these matters, and any number of studies show that this discretion is far more apt to be exercised to keep domestic assault cases out of the courts than to prosecute them. The Civil Rights Commission identified several reasons for this. Many prosecutors, they found, share with the police and the rest of our society the view that wife beating is not a real crime or not important enough for the criminal courts to bother with. Some also believe that women who file complaints are merely seeking to use the criminal justice system vindictively to settle quarrels or manipulate their husbands. Eisenberg and Micklow suggest, in addition, that prosecutors tend to avoid these cases because of the lack of prestige associated with them in criminal trial circles. As we have seen in the area of police willingness to arrest, the likelihood of a prosecutor filing charges and following through in an assault case is much lower if the accused and his victim are married or involved in a present or past romantic relationship.

By far the most common reason that prosecutors give for declining to prosecute wife-beaters is their belief that the women will subsequently change their minds and drop the charges. This does happen, of course, and probably more frequently than in cases where the accused criminal is a stranger to the victim. The battering husband is usually released on his own recognizance pending a trial date which may be weeks or months away. During that period, whether she has gone back to live with him or not, her batterer is apt to bring intense pressure on her, through threats or protestations of remorse, to drop the charges. Especially if she is still trying to keep the marriage together or if she and her children are dependent on his paycheck for food and shelter, she may well decide that pressing the charges through to trial is not really in her interest. But in those cities where vigorous victim advocate programs provide battered women with support and help in negotiating their way through the often baffling and intimidating criminal court system, the number of complaints dismissed by victims declines dramatically. This indicates that the widely shared assumption of prosecutors that battered women will drop charges is very much a self-fulfilling prophecy. As sociologist Murray Straus observed to the Civil Rights Commission, the explanation that battered women will drop the charges provides

> a ready excuse for the police, prosecuting attorney, and judges to follow their "natural" inclinations of treating wife beating as "domestic disturbances" (i.e. not really a crime) rather than as assaults. This in turn sets up a vicious cycle. Since the cases are defined as not really crimes, or as crimes not likely to be successfully prosecuted, women are discouraged from filing charges and encounter foot dragging when they attempt to pursue such charges. As a result, the many who would bring charges if not dissuaded, or who would follow through if obstacles and foot dragging did not occur, do not.

The obstacles and foot dragging can be formidable. Some district attorney's offices require a "cooling off" period of several days or weeks between the assault and the filing of the formal charges. Others have their own "stitch" rules or will only file charges if the man used a weapon or the woman was hospitalized. Many prosecutors require the beaten woman to convince them that she is a "worthy" victim, that she did nothing to provoke the attack, for example, so that *her* behavior rather than the batterer's becomes the key issue. Some refuse to prosecute unless the woman agrees to file for a divorce. Most district attorney's offices require that the woman actually sign a criminal complaint, a legally unnecessary requirement and one not applied to the victims of violent crimes committed by strangers. Cases that could be filed as felonies are often filed as misdemeanors, and serious misdemeanors are reduced to less serious ones such as "disturbing the peace." Batterers are diverted into inappropriate mediation or counselling programs, and in some cities virtually all domestic violence complaints are turned over to family bureaus or domestic divisions for informal settlement and never get to court at all. Charges are dismissed altogether with no notice to, or consultation with, the victim. By far the most common response to a woman's seeking to get charges filed against her violent husband or boyfriend, however, is a flat refusal by the prosecutor to prosecute him at all.

District attorneys, of course, are interested in winning cases, which they tend to define as obtaining both convictions and stiff sentences for those accused. In domestic violence cases, they are likely to obtain neither one because the same attitudes about the noncriminal nature of wife beating and the sanctity of marriage that police and prosecutors exhibit are likely to be shared by the judges who try them. By one estimate, only one domestic violence case in one hundred ever reaches a courtroom. The few that do get there are treated by judges as relatively trivial matters although the cases that manage to make it through the screening, discouragement, and diversion tend to be the most serious ones. If the man is found guilty at all, he is most likely to be given a suspended sentence or fined a small amount and placed on probation. In many places he can avoid any kind of criminal penalty by agreeing to undertake a mediation or counselling program. Many batterers, perhaps most, are released simply on a promise to the judge not to do it again. Although in most jurisdictions the possible jail time for a serious misdemeanor is as much as a year, jail sentences of even a few days are practically unheard of. Mildred Pagelow reports, for example, that in her sample of 350 battered women, not a single one reported filing charges that were carried through to trial, sentencing, and jail. The U.S. Civil Rights Commission concluded that one of the major problems with seeking to get protection for battered women through the criminal courts is the attitude of so many judges that wife beating is not a serious social problem or a serious criminal offense.

All along the line in her search for protection, a battered woman is apt to be told that her problem is really a civil matter; but civil remedies offer her little more protection than criminal ones. Traditionally, the two main noncriminal remedies available to a battered woman have been restraining orders, which require the abuser to leave the woman alone, and peace bonds, which require the abuser to put up a sum of money that he forfeits if he misbehaves again. Both of these remedies have serious drawbacks. Restraining orders in many states are only available to a married woman who files for a divorce. Consequently, battered women who are trying to keep their marriages together, as well as women who are not married or no longer married to their abusers, have no access to them. Restraining orders can seldom be obtained without the assistance and expense of a lawyer, the payment of filing fees and process servers, and a court hearing ten days after the petition for an order is filed—a dangerous delay.

There is a great deal of confusion about the enforcement of restraining orders. Police are frequently unwilling to arrest a man for violating a restraining order unless the violation occurs in the officer's presence. If the woman has no certified copy of the order to show them, for example because her husband has simply torn it up, there is nothing that the police can do; records of such orders are seldom kept on police computers. Many police departments refuse to treat the violation of such an order as a crime, even where state laws make it so. They will advise a battered woman who calls them and produces a copy of an order that they cannot enforce it. They tell her she should call her lawyer to file "contempt of court" charges—which of course involves more expense, more delay, and another hearing which is unlikely to result in any real sanctions against the batterer anyway.

Although peace bonds are apparently still used quite frequently in a few states, they have fallen into disuse in most places because they raise serious questions of constitutional rights. Under most peace bond statutes, a person who has behaved violently in the past and appears likely to behave violently again is required to post a bond guaranteeing his future good behavior. If he is unable to come up with the money for the bond, he can be jailed until he does. This is a scheme that presents any number of constitutional problems involving both due process and equal protection, particularly in the way that it discriminates against impoverished defendants, and no doubt deserves the relative obscurity into which it has lapsed.

In the last few years, the legislatures of almost every state have passed domestic violence legislation in an attempt to provide a civil remedy to battered women that does not suffer from the problems of these more traditional ones. Most states now permit the issuance of a protective order for a victim of domestic violence, requiring the abuser to cease his abuse; and, in some cases, he must move out of the family home and have no further contact with his victim. Such orders are available to women who have not filed for divorce or are not married to their batterers, although the exact kind of relationships covered varies from state to state. These laws also make very clear who has jurisdiction to enforce them and what the penalties are. Most of them provide for an emergency procedure under which a temporary order can be issued by a judge prior to a full-fledged hearing, so that a woman can have immediate protection.

While protective orders are certainly a better remedy than battered women previously have had in the civil courts, they have not yet proved to be a panacea. The U.S. Civil Rights Commission found that, in many states, resistance by judges has undermined the expected functioning of these domestic abuse laws. Judges were found, in particular, to be unwilling to issue eviction orders and emergency orders although the laws clearly provided for them. Punishments imposed for violating protection orders are often light or nonexistent. The whole purpose of the orders—quick action, sure punishment, and placing the onus of leaving the home on the wrongdoer rather than the victim—has frequently been vitiated.

The simple truth is that our society does not protect battered women from their abusers. Every battered woman who has ever called the police only to have them fail to arrive or fail to arrest the man who has beaten her knows this. Every battered woman who has had her husband arrested only to have him be released an hour later and come home in a rage and beat her again knows this. Every battered woman who has tried to have her abuser prosecuted, only to be talked out of it by a district attorney or threatened with death or disfigurement by her abuser if she doesn't drop the charges knows it. Every battered woman who, against all odds, presses assault charges through to trial, only to have her tormentor suffer no penalty at all and be turned loose in exchange for a bare promise not to hit her again, knows it.

A battered woman's attempts to obtain protection from a violent mate often only serve to reinforce her own sense of vulnerability. No one is going to stop the man from hurting her again. No one will stop him from killing her if he wants to. The knowledge that she cannot rely on society to protect her from the violence that occurs in her own home cannot help but affect a battered woman's perception of the danger she is in when another serious attack is imminent. It is hardly unreasonable for her to conclude that if she is to be protected at all, she must seize whatever means is at hand to protect herself.

Bibliography

Books

Browne, Angela. *When Battered Women Kill.* New York: Free Press, 1987.

Chimbos, Peter D. *Marital Violence: A Study of Interspousal Homicide.* San Francisco: R. and E. Research Associates, 1978.

Davidson, Terry. *Conjugal Crime.* New York: Ballantine Books, 1980.

Dobash, R. Emerson, and Russell Dobash. *Violence against Wives.* New York: The Free Press, 1979.

Domestic Violence and the Police: Studies in Detroit and Kansas City. Washington, D.C.: The Police Foundation, 1977.

Gelles, Richard J. *The Violent Home.* Beverly Hills: Sage, 1977.

Giles-Sims, Jean. *Wife-Battering: A Systems Theory Approach.* New York: Guilford, 1983.

Martin, Del. *Battered Wives.* New York: Pocket Books, 1976.

Pagelow, Mildred G.. *Woman Battering: Women and Their Experiences.* Beverly Hills: Sage, 1981.

Stacey, William A., and Anson Shupe. *The Family Secret: Domestic Violence in America.* Boston: Beacon Press, 1983.

Straus, Murray A., Richard J. Gelles, and Suzanne K. Steinmetz. *Behind Closed Doors: Violence in the American Family.* New York: Anchor/Doubleday, 1980.

Walker, Lenore E. *The Battered Woman.* New York: Harper and Row, 1979.

———. *The Battered Woman Syndrome.* New York: Springer, 1984.

Articles

Browne, Angela. "Self-Defense Homicides by Battered Women: Relationships at Risk." Paper presented to the American Psychology and Law Conference, Chicago, October 1983.

Eisenberg, Alan D., and Earl J. Seymour. "The Self-Defense Plea and Battered Women." *Trial* (July 1978): 75.

Eisenberg, Sue E., and Patricia Micklow. "The Assaulted Wife: 'Catch 22' Revisited." 3 *Women's Rights Law Reporter* 138 (1977).

Hilberman, Elaine. "Overview: The 'Wife-Beater's Wife' Reconsidered." *American Journal of Psychiatry* 137 (1980): 1336.

———, and Kit Munson. "Sixty Battered Women." *Victimology* 2 (1977–8): 460.

Howard, Colin. "What Colour is the Reasonable Man?" 1961 *Criminal Law Review* 41.

Lerman, Lisa. "Protection of Battered Women: A Survey." 6 *Women's Rights Law Reporter* 271 (Summer 1980).

Note. "Battered Women and the Equal Protection Clause: Will the Constitution Help Them When the Police Won't?" 95 *Yale Law Journal* 788 (1986).

Rounsaville, Bruce J. "Theories in Marital Violence: Evidence from a Study of Battered Women." *Victimology* 3 (1978): 11.

Sacco, Lynne A. "Wife Abuse: The Failure of Legal Remedies." 11 *John Marshall Journal of Practice and Procedure* 549 (1978).

Taub, Nadine. "Equitable Relief in Cases of Adult Domestic Abuse." 6 *Women's Rights Law Reporter* 241 (Summer 1980).

Truninger, Elizabeth. "Marital Violence: The Legal Solutions." 23 *Hastings Law Journal* 259 (1978).

Miscellaneous

Federal Response to Domestic Violence, The, Washington, D.C.: United States Commission on Civil Rights, 1982.

Glamour, October 1980, 56

Hartzler v. City of San Jose, 46 Cal. App.3d 6 (1975).

New York Times, 15 June 1986, p. E8.

Under the Rule of Thumb: Battered Women and the Administration of Justice, Washington, D.C.: United States Commission on Civil Rights, 1982.

Criminal Approaches to Family Violence, 1640–1980

Elizabeth Pleck

Many people think that family violence was discovered in the 1960s. It is true that the scale of effort on behalf of victims has been greater since that period than ever before. Yet there were earlier periods of reform against family violence in American history. From 1640 to 1680, the Puritans of colonial Massachusetts enacted the first laws anywhere in the world against wife beating and "unnatural severity" to children. A second reform epoch lasted from 1874 to about 1890, when societies for the prevention of cruelty to children (SPCCs) were founded, and smaller efforts on behalf of battered women and victims of incest were initiated. A modern era of interest came into its own in 1962, when five physicians published an article about "the battered child syndrome" in the *Journal of the American Medical Association* (Kempe et al. 1962). In the early 1970s, the women's liberation movement rediscovered wife beating and, somewhat later, marital rape. Since then many other types of family violence, from abuse of the elderly to sibling violence, have come to light.

The history of the criminalization of family violence is contemporaneous with, but not entirely parallel to, the rise (and fall) of these three periods of social interest. In each of them there were significant campaigns to increase the criminal penalties for domestic violence. The most recent period is somewhat mixed since it includes increasing efforts to criminalize incest, wife abuse, and marital rape but also retains persistent doubts about the wisdom of such efforts if they are applied to abused and neglected children. Even in periods when reform against family violence was quiescent, there have been important developments in the American judicial system affecting the handling of family violence criminal cases.

There has always been one necessary (although not sufficient) belief animating reform against domestic violence, namely, that the public interest in enforcement of the law against perpetrators of family violence outweighs the traditional rights of husbands or parents, or respect for domestic privacy. Whereas the state has long possessed the right to punish violators of the criminal law, it has often been claimed that family relationships require or deserve special immunity. Reformers have insisted that outside agencies have the right to intervene in the family and sometimes to take action to remove children from parental custody.

The greater the defense of the rights and privileges of the traditional family, the lower the interest in the criminalization of the family. When family violence is seen as a crime that threatens not only its victims but also the social order, support for criminalization of family violence increases. Thus, the conditions that most impede the criminalization of family violence are increased respect for family privacy, diminished enthusiasm for the state's responsibility to intervene in the family, and vigorous defense of the family ideal, a range of beliefs about the sanctity of the family that serves to shield the home from public view and state intervention. These beliefs include the view that parents have the right to discipline children physically; that a husband possesses the right to have sexual access to his wife; that nagging women or disobedient children often provoke the beatings they receive; that wives and children, as economic dependents, need a male provider; and that the law should not disrupt this traditional pattern of support, except in unusual circumstances.

Some forms of domestic violence have been more likely to be punished as crimes than others. Family murder and infanticide have always been regarded as serious crimes, although they have often been punished as manslaughter, rather than as homicide. Other types of domestic abuse, such as sibling violence and marital rape, have rarely been regarded as crimes. Criminal statutes have been passed to punish specific types of family violence. Many types of family violence have also been prosecuted as assault and battery, disorderly conduct, or breach of the peace. In general, wife abuse has been the type of family violence most likely to appear in court. This is because battered wives have been the victims of domestic violence most willing to complain to the police and to press charges. Sibling violence and marital rape have been the types of family violence least likely to be criminalized because sibling violence is often regarded as normal behavior, and rape laws have often exempted from criminal prosecution a husband's sexual assault on his wife.

Seventeenth-Century American Laws and Courts

Unique features of the Puritan experiment in the New World encouraged the criminalization of family violence. The Puritans of New England believed that the family prepared children for a pious life and that it conveyed their religious values. An institution so necessary to the Puritan mission could not become a sanctuary for cruelty and violence. The Puritans classified verbal or physical assault, whether between strangers or family members, as "wicked carriage." Family

violence was a sin; only if the Puritans maintained their watchfulness against sin would their godly experiment prosper.

The Puritans attacked family violence with the combined forces of community, church, and state. Conformity was expected, and meddling was considered a positive virtue. Neighbors watched each other informally for signs of aberration, which were often reported to the minister or local constable. The political freedom of the Massachusetts Bay Colony from direct English rule during the English Civil War also made it possible for the colony to embed its religious principles in the law.

The colony of New Haven enacted the first American law against family violence in 1639. The law punished incest with death by hanging. If the sexual union had been voluntary, then both parties were to be put to death. No one was ever prosecuted under this statute. Thus this and many other colonial laws, while extremely punitive, had a largely symbolic intent.

Two years later the first law against wife abuse anywhere in the Western world was written into a new criminal code of the Massachusetts Bay Colony. According to one of the provisions of the Massachusetts *Body of Laws and Liberties,* "Everie marryed woeman shall be free from bodilie correction or stripes by her husband, unlesse it be in his owne defence upon her assault" (Massachusetts Colony 1890, p. 51). A few years later, the law was amended to prohibit husband beating as well. Plymouth Colony was probably following Massachusetts Bay in enacting a law against spouse abuse in 1672 (Cushing 1977, p. 48). Wife beating was punished with a five-pound fine or a whipping, and husband beating with a sentence to be determined by the court. The Massachusetts *Body of Laws and Liberties* also protected the "liberties of children." A provision that prohibited parents from choosing their child's mate included a clause that forbade parents from exercising "any unnatural severities" toward children.

Since the Puritans are usually known for their scarlet A's and ducking stools, it may come as a surprise to find that their laws concerned wife beating and child abuse. The Puritans have not received the credit they deserve for their humanitarian ideas. These ranged from outlawing the torture of prisoners to prohibiting cruelty to animals. The *Body of Laws and Liberties* reflected a belief that women and children deserved certain rights; thus, the provision against wife beating was found in a section on the liberties of women; the clause against child abuse was contained in a section on the liberties of children.

New England Puritan attitudes toward wife beating reflected English Puritan ideas. As early as 1599 an English Puritan minister argued that a wife beater should be whipped because "he is worthy to be beaten for choosing no better" (Koehler 1980, p. 19). The English Puritan moral theologian William Gouge, who published a popular manual titled *Domesticall Duties* in 1622, argued that it was immoral for a husband to beat his wife (Stone 1977, p. 179). In his family advice book, the great Puritan preacher William Perkins opposed wife beating, as did another English Puritan writer, Richard Baxter (Stone 1977, p. 179). American Puritans followed English practice in condemning wife beating. In one of his sermons, the famous Boston minister Cotton Mather preached that for "a man to Beat his Wife was as bad as any Sacriledge. And such a Rascal were better buried alive, than show his Head among his Neighbours any more" (Koehler 1980, p. 49).

New England's Puritan laws were in advance of English law and attitudes. Yet English seventeenth-century ecclesiastical courts also punished wife beaters, and some Anglicans in England condemned wife beating. But when the English Puritans came to power under Cromwell, they did not pass legislation against wife beating. The freedom of the Massachusetts Bay Colony from English domination—along with Puritan humanitarian ideas—encouraged the enactment of the *Body of Laws and Liberties*.

The passage of the *Body of Laws and Liberties* occurred during a period of political freedom for the colony. Parliament had granted Massachusetts Bay permission to govern itself, in accordance with English law. When the English Civil War broke out in 1642, the colonies were left on their own. Taking advantage of their freedom from imperial domination, the Puritans set out to draft laws that reflected their religious principles. In the 1630s, freemen, resident stockholders in the investment company backing the colony, demanded a written constitution and a civil and criminal code to protect their liberties.

They were concerned that royally appointed judges might misuse their discretionary powers and infringe on the civil liberties Englishmen had come to expect. Acting on their request, the colony's general court, the equivalent of a colonial legislature, appointed a committee to devise a written legal code that became the law of the colony, even though it was never sent to Parliament for approval. A draft by Puritan minister John Cotton was rejected because it contained too many provisions calling for capital punishment, including one specifying hanging for incest. The general court turned to Reverend Nathaniel Ward, a Puritan minister with English legal training. He pruned some of Cotton's capital provisions and added sections protecting the liberties of women, children, servants, and foreigners. As one of the founders of the New Haven Colony, Cotton was able to achieve enactment of a law against incest there (Haskins 1960, pp. 123–40).

Criminal Justice, 1830–74

No laws against family violence were passed from the time of the Pilgrim statute against wife beating in 1672 until a law against wife beating was enacted in Tennessee in 1850 (State of Tennessee 1850). The whole of the eighteenth and half of the nineteenth century appears to have been a legislative vacuum. Indeed, there is little evidence, aside from an occasional divorce case on grounds of cruelty, to demonstrate even passing interest in this subject during the eighteenth century (Kerber 1980, pp. 170–72, 175–78). Although thinkers of the Enlightenment in the eighteenth century often decried "parental tyranny," they were referring to a parent's denial of a child's right to choose a mate or to a husband's excessive (but not necessarily violent) authoritarianism (Fliegelman 1982). The general lack of interest in family violence can be attributed to the growing distrust of government interference in the family, the increasing respect for domestic privacy, and the waning zeal for state enforcement of private morality (Glenn

1984, pp. 63–83; Pleck 1987, pp. 31–33). The era from 1830 to 1874 was not a period of social concern about family violence. Nonetheless, the criminal approach to family violence progressed gradually during those years, as cities established police, alderman's, or hustings courts. In these general rather than specialized courts, cases of wife beating and child abuse were heard alongside prosecutions of pickpockets and public drunkards.

Because these courts had relatively simple procedures and were located in neighborhoods near the tenements where poor families lived, it was easy for victims and their relatives to bring a complaint to court. The police court was usually located in a small room in a corner of the neighborhood police station. The room reeked of stale cigar smoke and human sweat and was crowded with predatory male bondsmen, messengers, and lawyers soliciting clients. The judge was usually an elected official who had some legal training. A husband who beat his wife might be fined fifty dollars. But if a man could not pay his fine, he might be sent to city jail. Cases of aggravated assault, family murder, or incest were felonies tried in superior court (Steinberg 1981).

While it was relatively easy for women victims to bring a complaint to court, it was much harder to ensure that justice would be meted out. In the police court, on occasion, a brawling husband was fined but his wife was sent to jail! Abused wives who fled their homes, and thereby left their children behind, could be charged with desertion. A wife who decided to drop her complaint against an abusive husband could so enrage a police court judge that he would charge her with contempt of court (*Boston Morning Post* 1837, pp. 81–82, 84–86, 110–11, 121, 137–38, 180, 201–4).

. . . Many writers on family violence decry "the rule of the thumb" that permitted a husband to beat his wife with a stick no thicker than his thumb. In 1783, an English Judge Buller (characterized by a cartoonist as "Judge Thumb") first asserted the rule. But English legal authorities challenged him, and writers and cartoonists lampooned him (May 1978). No American judge ever endorsed the "rule of thumb," and before

the Civil War, two American states passed statutes against wife beating: Tennessee in 1850, and Georgia in 1857 (Pleck 1979). There is no information about the sponsors of this legislation or the reasons why it was passed. It is not known whether the Tennessee law was enforced, although a few severe cases of wife beating were prosecuted under the Georgia law (Wyatt-Brown 1982, p. 281).

The idea that wife beating was not against the law in nineteenth-century America originates with three appellate court rulings issued between 1824 and 1868: one in Mississippi in 1824, and two others in North Carolina in 1864 and 1868 (Pleck 1979). According to these court rulings, a husband had the legitimate right to discipline his wife physically, as long as it was done in a moderate manner. In *Bradley v. State,* 1 Miss. 157 (1824), the Mississippi Supreme Court upheld the right of moderate chastisement, even though Calvin Bradley was found guilty of assault and battery on his wife, Lydia. In *State v. Black,* 60 N.C. 262 (1864), a lower court in North Carolina found Jesse Black guilty of assault and battery on his wife, Tamsey, but the state supreme court, in overturning the ruling and ordering a new trial, upheld the right of a husband "to use toward his wife such a degree of force as is necessary." Jesse Black's actions, they argued, did not constitute assault and battery. After his wife, Tamsey, had taunted him (accusing him of visiting Sal Daly, a prostitute, and calling him a hog thief), he had seized her by the hair and pulled her to the floor and held her there. Since he did not hit or choke her, the court decided he had not committed assault and battery. In *State v. Rhodes,* A. B. Rhodes gave his wife, Elizabeth, three licks with a stick the size of one of his fingers. The North Carolina Supreme Court upheld a lower court ruling that Rhodes was not guilty. Even so, the court rejected the claim "that the husband has the right to whip his wife much or little" but ruled instead that it would "not interfere with family government in trifling cases" (State v. Rhodes, 61 N.C. 453, 353 [1868]). A trifling case, the court seemed to suggest, was one where no permanent injury had been inflicted.

State v. Rhodes has been widely quoted, probably because the North Carolina justices issued a lengthy ruling. But the decision ran contrary to legal opinion of the time, as even they acknowledged. "Our opinion is not in unison with the decisions of some of the sister States," the judges wrote, "or with the philosophy of some very respectable law writers, and could not be in unison with all; because of their contrariety—a decent respect for the opinions of others has induced us to be very full in stating the reasons for our conclusion" (*State v. Rhodes*, pp. 353–54, 1868).

While police courts and state appellate court judges for the most part regarded wife beating as a crime, child abuse appeared to fall within the domain of legitimate parental right. A parent who committed assault and battery on a child could be brought into police court, and charged. But only two cases of child abuse were decided on appeal prior to the beginning of the Civil War. In *Johnson and Wife v. the State of Tennessee*, 21 Tenn. 183 (1840), Mrs. Johnson hit her daughter with a stick or a switch and her fists and slammed her daughter's head against the wall. The case was missing detail about why the Johnsons were beating their daughter or the extent of the injuries they caused. In sending the case back for retrial, the Tennessee court affirmed the Johnsons' right "to chastise their refractory and disobedient" daughter, but it also held that parents must not exceed the bounds of moderation by inflicting cruel and merciless punishment. In retrying the case, a jury decided that the Johnsons had exceeded the bounds of moderation. Their conviction was overturned, however, because the judge in the original trial had improperly instructed the jury.

At about the same time, the North Carolina State Supreme Court put forward an alternative and far more conservative judicial definition of child cruelty. *Pendergrass v. the State of North Carolina*, 19 N.C. 365, 367 (1837), concerned a schoolmistress who hit a misbehaving girl of six or seven on the arm and neck and also beat her with a large (but unidentified) instrument. The girl's marks and bruises disappeared after a few days. The jury found the schoolmistress, Rachel Pendergrass, not guilty. The court upheld the right of a teacher (or a parent) to correct a child moderately. The chastiser's intentions, they argued, had to be considered in deciding whether an act was cruel. In this ruling, cruelty was defined as those acts that endanger life, limbs, or

health, or cause disfigurement or permanent injury. But causing the child only temporary pain was considered legitimate.

Only the most serious and life-endangering cases of child abuse were regarded as criminal in nature. Given these judicial attitudes, it is not surprising to find that very few cases of child abuse were ever brought to court. It is important to note that judges did not necessarily consider the home the best place to raise a child, and thus were not always opposed to removing a child from parental guardianship. In fact, mid-nineteenth-century writers and reformers extolled the virtues of the asylum and the house of refuge as homes for delinquent, orphaned, neglected, or abandoned children (Rothman 1971; Mennel 1973; Schlossman 1977).

Jacksonian era reformers, interested in institutions to house the mentally ill, the insane, and the criminal, established houses of refuge. These were private institutions for children, authorized by laws that permitted courts to commit abandoned, vagrant, destitute, and neglected children to the refuge along with child criminals. Rothman (1971) has traced the origins of the house of refuge to reformers' fears of social unrest and to their desire to impose middle-class morality on the poor, thereby recapturing the Puritans' sense of community watchfulness. In the 1850s, Charles Loring Brace helped to establish the Children's Aid Society in New York City. It sought to rescue children from the city streets and place them with farm families or send them to the West. Most rescued children were presumed to be either runaways, homeless, abandoned, or orphans (Boyer 1978). The lack of inquiry into whether such children had families or relatives with whom they could live suggests a cavalier attitude toward the family life of the poor. But these children were placed, not *because* of parental malfeasance, but because they were believed to be growing up without any parental supervision.

Similarly, though antebellum judges were willing to remove children from homes where drunkenness or neglect occurred, they were unwilling to intervene in instances of physical abuse (Thomas 1972). The desire to respect family privacy and to safeguard the traditional rights of parents to discipline their children was far greater than the fear of social disorder or the desire to control the lives of the poor. There was nothing new in these views; in fact, they represented a continuation of the dominant attitude in most of the eighteenth century.

The High Point of Criminalization, 1875–90

A volcano of moral outrage at domestic abuse and of sympathy for its victims erupted around 1875 and continued for the next fifteen years. The first society to protect children from cruelty was founded in New York in December 1874 (McCrea 1910; Coleman 1924; Hawes 1971; Antler and Antler 1979). By the turn of the century there were more than 300 such societies in the United States. In the same quarter century judges and lawyers campaigned to punish wife beating with the whipping post (Pleck 1983a). Female advocates of temperance helped to pass laws giving tort protection to drunkards' wives and children. Since many drunken men also abused their families, these laws often benefited the victims of domestic violence. One final undertaking was a women's legal aid society in Chicago, which aided victimized women and girls (Pleck 1983b). All these efforts shared the view that family violence was a serious crime.

There were several reasons for the revival of interest in criminal sanctions against family violence that began in 1875. The late nineteenth century resembled the Puritan era in some ways: both were periods of heightened interest in the state's responsibility to enforce public morality. The native-born, middle-class public believed that a society that did not uphold the moral law—a single standard of appropriate behavior —would decay. To stave off calamity, the aroused citizenry looked to the police, courts, and to state legislatures to pass and enforce morals laws. Legislators and voluntary groups sought to prohibit the sale of alcohol, to close saloons on Sundays, to punish violators of the Sabbath, and to eliminate prostitution.

Family violence was also taken seriously because the public was fearful of crime (Boyer 1978, pp. 143–61). The New York millionaires who founded the world's first SPCC worried that neglected and abused boys would, as grown men, "swell the ranks of the dangerous classes," endangering "public peace and security," and that similarly abused girls would soon become young women lost in "body and soul" (New York Society for the Prevention of Cruelty to Children 1876, p. 6). These statements coupled the fear of crime and immorality with the implicit hope that the children of the poor could be molded into respectable citizens. But the fear of crime also reflected a statistical and social reality: after the Civil War, the violent crime rate soared (Pleck 1987, p. 242). Nor was the home spared the turmoil occurring outside it. In the one city for which figures are available, Philadelphia, the rate of husband-wife murders increased from one per million persons between 1839 and 1845 to 4.1 per million between 1874 and 1880 (Pleck 1983b, p. 454).

Middle-class fears of violent crime were joined with a desire to reimpose a rural, Protestant morality on an urban-industrial society. Northerners worried about immigrants, and Southerners about blacks, and the public in all regions looked with suspicion on vagabonds and tramps. Immigrants, blacks, and homeless men were seen as brutish by nature, and unable to control their aggressive and criminal impulses. The enemy of the social order was not the deviant individual, as it had been among the Puritans, but a frightening strata of society, the so-called dangerous classes. Anxieties about the dangerous classes could be marshaled to support the founding of anticruelty societies or the passage of whipping post legislation. At a time of national economic depression, the potential militance of a great army of the unemployed and the threat of a permanent criminal class fueled the demand for criminalizing family violence.

Some scholars attribute the origins of the SPCC to these multiple fears (Hawes 1971; Gordon 1988). As immigration from abroad revived after the Civil War, the American native-born wealthy and middle class worried about violence, depravity, disease, riots, and labor unrest among the urban poor. In the United States these fears were exacerbated by the fact that the poor were largely immigrant and Catholic. But the desire for a well-ordered society was rooted as much in the Civil War as in society's uneasy accommodation to the passing of the agrarian order. After a national bloodbath in which

600,000 men were killed, the public wanted a return to stability. Since strong centralized government had saved the Union, it could be trusted to take on the new responsibilities of enforcing middle-class morality and of punishing the criminal classes.

In addition to these motives, the founders of SPCCs were also genuinely concerned about the suffering of helpless children. The nineteenth century has been termed the "century of the child." Children came to be viewed as individuals, possessing their own rights, rather than as obedient servants to their parents. Children were also regarded as innocent, rather than as innately sinful, beings. The decline of Calvinism and the rise of Romantic thought contributed to this more benign view of the child and to greater concern about children's suffering at parental hands. If the child also had individual rights, then it was the responsibility of the state to help enforce those rights. The state also had a duty to protect the innocent and helpless child (Nelson 1983).

One additional explanation for the origins of the SPCCs (Gordon 1983–84) is that they represented a continuation of the campaigns against corporal punishment that began in the schools and in parental advice literature in the 1830s. Women writers of child-rearing advice and some male school reformers had urged parents to exercise restraint in discipline, using the rod only as a last resort. Less frequent resort to corporal punishment, Gordon has argued, spilled over into greater concern about protecting innocent children. At the same time, rhetoric about children's rights reflected the reality that adolescent children had acquired the right to choose a career or a mate on their own, rather than to await parental approval.

To be sure, while some SPCCs, such as the one in Boston, campaigned against corporal punishment in the home and schools, others, such as the one in New York, advocated corporal punishment of children and carefully distinguished between corporal punishment and cruelty. In city after city, founders of the SPCCs were often millionaires or conservative feminists who had little in common with those who favored milder punishment of children.

There is a similar problem in claiming that the SPCCs reflected a new, more enlightened view of the child. An embarrassingly long interval separates the "discovery of childhood" from the founding of the SPCCs. The idea of the innocence of the child can be traced back to Rousseau. The *Body of Laws and Liberties* had reflected the view that children had certain liberties. Therefore, there must have been some more immediate stimulus to the founding of the SPCCs than changing ideas about children. What was new was the view that the state had a responsibility to protect the innocent child and to guarantee the rights of the child against those of the parent (Nelson 1983, pp. 7–8, 53–56). In the post–Civil War era parents were seen as exercising authority delegated by the state. If they failed to fulfill their responsibilities to their children, then the state had the power and the duty to intervene in order to safeguard the interests of the child.

Decline of Interest in Criminal Approaches to Family Violence during the Progressive Era, 1900–1920

By the 1890s, the perception of family violence as a serious crime began to fade. The last legislative attempt to punish wife beating with the whipping post occurred in 1906. In the period between 1875 and 1890, the view that family violence was a serious crime had coincided with zeal for "law and order." Support for criminalization of family violence had capitalized on fears of violent crime and of the dangerous classes. Those fears could be channeled to support strong punishments, such as the whipping post, to threaten abusive parents with the removal of their children, and, when combined with feminism or temperance, to provide legal assistance to victimized mothers or their daughters. When ideas of rehabilitation and prevention of crime replaced a belief in punitive sanctions, there was less interest in criminal punishment of family violence.

There was no comparable retreat to domestic privacy, as there had been in the 1700s.

But instead, the state's responsibility, while much expanded, was defined in terms of recreating family privacy, rather than in terms of enforcing the criminal law (Rothman 1980). By the early twentieth century, judges of family courts and heads of SPCCs came to view criminal prosecution and police-like methods as unprofessional and outmoded. They believed that social casework methods were more efficient, humane, and better suited to handling the complicated dynamics of abusing families. Ironically, the greater the scrutiny in the family character of domestic violence, the lower the interest in its criminal side.

The juvenile court represented one additional step toward decriminalizing child abuse and strengthening social casework intervention in abusive and neglectful families. A voluminous body of literature has been concerned with either the origins or actual operation of these courts in the early twentieth century (Platt 1969; Schlossman 1977; Ryerson 1978; Rothman 1980; Tiffin 1982). Was it fear of the city, the desire to exert expert control over social problems, or the old middle-class interest in transforming the poor into bourgeoisie that prompted the Progressives to found juvenile courts? Even Schlossman (1977), who finds the juvenile courts similar in many ways to their Jacksonian era predecessors, has identified some unique features, such as the court's emphasis on probation and family-centered treatment for youthful offenders. If the juvenile delinquent could be rehabilitated at home, he or she would not have to be sentenced to reform school. In reality, however, Schlossman found that despite the rhetoric of reformers about cooperating with parents, the day-to-day actions of the juvenile court were often extremely punitive.

While juvenile courts were mainly interested in juvenile delinquency, child neglect was a much lower, but still important, priority. Child neglect was more important to the SPCCs, which, during the Progressive Era, worked closely with the juvenile courts. In terms of the sheer number of cases, child neglect had always been a much larger phenomenon than physical abuse, even in the Victorian era. But SPCCs and the juvenile courts virtually swept aside the problem of physical abuse in favor of child neglect. The category of child neglect fitted with their thinking about social problems and with the remedies they favored.

Progressive Era thought had dual strands: an environmentalism that located social problems in poverty and poor housing, and a eugenicism that rooted the same problems in genetic inferiority. The SPCCs favored social reforms, such as children's playgrounds and mothers' pensions, to remove the social conditions that bred neglect, casework to uplift the family environment through expert (yet friendly) counsel, but also sterilization of the mentally retarded and laws preventing their marriage. They portrayed all of these efforts as preventive remedies, superior to the law enforcement methods of the Victorian SPCCs (Gordon 1988).

The Rediscovery of Family Violence, 1955–80

Family violence persisted from the Progressive Era until the 1960s, but interest in it did not. Social agencies still came across such cases but often classified them as problems of economic hardship, family maladjustment, or mental illness. In the Progressive Era, the etiology of domestic violence was often attributed to moronic tendencies and genetic inferiority, during the Great Depression, to economic hardship, and in the 1940s and 1950s, to family problems or psychiatric illness (Gordon 1988).

The rediscovery of "child cruelty" is usually dated to 1962, when C. Henry Kempe, a Denver pediatrician, and four of his medical colleagues published an article in the *Journal of the American Medical Association* entitled "The Battered Child Syndrome" (Kempe et al. 1962). This landmark publication can be seen more as a result than as a cause of the discovery of child abuse. In the mid-1950s, the specter of violent teenagers menacing the public compelled social workers to abandon their professional offices and reach out to troubled youth. Aiding the neglected child was justified as a means of combating juvenile delinquency. The American Humane Association (AHA), under the leadership of Vincent DeFrancis, pioneered in the development of "aggressive casework," intervention in neglectful families when the caseworker had not been invited. They also surveyed the problem of child neglect. In turn, the AHA alerted the U.S. Children's Bureau to the prevalence of the problem, and the bureau funded the research of Kempe and others. Kempe's survey of the prevalence of severe battering of infants and young children was then used to demonstrate that a new and serious social problem existed (Nelson 1983).

Certainly, the modern era is the first time physicians became major participants in reform against child abuse or neglect. Battered babies were patients of pediatricians and radiologists; the reason for their injuries was uncovered through X-ray evidence. The problem of child abuse and neglect was not confined to hospitalized children, yet their suffering, dependency, and helplessness made a powerful claim on the medical conscience. Stephen Pfohl (1977) has given much of the credit for the rediscovery of child abuse to radiologists. Beginning in the early 1950s, radiologists used X-ray evidence of multiple fractures in young children at various stages of healing in order to cast doubt on parents' explanations that a child had been injured as a result of a single mishap. Pfohl notes that radiology was considered a low-status medical specialty. He attributes the interests of radiologists in child battering to a desire to increase their professional status and to an eagerness to demonstrate that they, too, saved lives.

The social atmosphere of the late 1950s and early 1960s also contributed to the rediscovery of child abuse. Child abuse emerged as a social issue during the height of the civil rights movement, as the nation was prodded by black protest to protect the constitutional rights of minorities. A small but vocal group of advocates of children's rights took up a similar call on behalf of children (Feshbach and Feshbach 1978).

Reform against child abuse led to increased funding for research about its causes, to expanded services to abusive and neglectful families, and to the hiring of additional personnel. The growth of public and professional concern about battered children occurred in the early 1960s, at a time of renewed support for social welfare legislation. National economic prosperity and optimism about government's capacity to solve social problems moved Congress to appropriate large sums for social welfare programs, including those aimed at helping children (Nelson 1983).

The dominance of physicians and social workers in the reform effort against child abuse dampened interest in criminalization of child abuse. Most social workers, doctors, and even many lawyers and judges agreed that imprisoning abusive parents—other than those who had murdered their children—was counterproductive. Police and judges were not qualified to handle family problems, it was claimed. Monrad G. Paulsen, the dean of the University of Virginia Law School, reasoned that "all in all, criminal sanctions can do little to help a child. The major problems concern his care and custody" (Paulsen 1962, p. 43). A legal definition of abuse, Paulsen argued, demanded punishment, rendering the parent's rehabilitation difficult, if not impossible. Prosecution would snuff out any hope of preserving the child's home and would make parents so resentful that casework with them would be imperiled. If charges were brought, it would be difficult to find any witnesses. Fines, it was argued, robbed the family of valuable financial resources. Furthermore, imprisonment would separate the parent from the child (Thomas 1972, p. 341). The law, it was believed, imposed adversarial methods on troubled parents and children in need of counseling.

As a result of media attention and the lobbying efforts of pediatric associations, every state in the nation between 1963 and 1967 passed laws requiring physicians (and sometimes other professionals) to report instances of child abuse to police or social agencies, such as children's protective services (DeFrancis 1966; Costa and Nelson 1978). Reporting laws increased public awareness of child abuse and neglect and led to increased reporting of such cases. Reporting laws were actually criminal statutes since a physician's failure to report child abuse was generally punishable as a misdemeanor under the criminal law (Thomas 1972, p. 331). The Children's Bureau, proposing a model statute, favored mandatory reporting to the police because they were on call twenty-four hours a day. Initially, most reporting statutes designated the police as the agency to receive mandatory reports; subsequent legislation more often designated a child protective service as the reporting agency (Paulsen 1966).

Once cases were reported, the tendency was to rely on civil, rather than on criminal, procedures and on social casework, supplemented by resort to the courts, if necessary. These were the approaches developed during the Progressive Era. The dislike of arrest, prosecution, and punishment of abusive and neglectful parents arose from the objections stated above and from the emphasis of all the parties involved, including the courts and police, on rehabilitating the abusive or neglectful family.

Sociologists and psychiatrists put the spotlight on sibling violence, and social workers, nursing professionals, and psychologists brought elder abuse to light. These were types of family violence that had previously escaped any efforts at reform and had rarely been reported to SPCCs. Of all the types of family violence to receive attention in the period since the mid-1950s, child abuse received the most, followed by wife abuse. Although many women campaigned against child abuse, the problem of child abuse was defined as a public health matter, not a feminist issue. In the early 1970s, the only common ground shared by feminists and advocates of children was concern about victims of incest and sexual molestation.

While reformers against child abuse opposed criminal sanctions against perpetrators, reformers against wife abuse and marital rape favored them and tried to pressure the police and courts to respond adequately to the complaints of women victims. The medical and social work professionals who dominated child abuse reform defined child battering as a psychological illness of the parents requiring social services and psychological treatment. The feminist activists and lawyers who led the campaign against wife beating and marital rape rooted the problem in the inequality of women and in the lack of proper law enforcement.

Wife beating and marital rape were considered crimes, rather than manifestations of mental illness (although many experts emphasized both etiologies). The battered women's movement sponsored legislation to increase the criminal penalties for wife beating, to strengthen civil remedies, and to make it easier for women victims to file criminal charges against their assailants (Schecter 1982). There were no mandatory reporting laws for wife abuse or marital rape similar to those on behalf of child abuse and neglect. But the greater publicity given the problem, the establishment of social service and feminist advocacy groups, and the founding of shelters for battered women encouraged victims to complain to the police and to persist in the arrest, prosecution, and punishment of their assailants.

There were several similarities between the contemporary period of concern about family violence and the two earlier reform epochs. From the sponsors of the *Body of Laws and Liberties* to the founders of the SPCCs, reformers had sought to protect the rights of women and children. Feminists of the Victorian era advocated greater legal rights for married women, along with increased protection in civil and criminal law. The liberation movements for children and women, beginning in the 1960s, also led the way in expanding the legal rights of women and children.

A small, concerned group rather than the public at large has always been the major force behind reform against family violence. The Puritan effort against family violence was not a voluntary social movement as much as a state (and minister-initiated) reform. But in the late nineteenth century and from the mid-1950s through the 1980s, small, private organizations of professionals (mainly lawyers in the late nineteenth century and physicians and social workers in the 1960s and 1970s) championed the children's cause. Similarly, in both of these periods, individual feminists and women's organizations drew attention to "crimes against women" and often found themselves allied with male law enforcement officials, who were desirous of stamping out violent crime.

In all three eras, the fear of violence and of dangerous criminals animated reform. Puritans worried that pirates, heretics, and malcontents would destroy their divinely sanctioned undertaking. Since they did not distinguish between public and private crime, they were as disturbed about violent assaults in the home as they were about theft, corruption, or usury. The late nineteenth-century fear of "the dangerous classes" expressed unease about the new industrial order—the unwelcome presence of Catholic immigrants in cities, tramps in the countryside, and worry about union militants stirring up strikes. The SPCCs hoped to protect young children, so that the future generation could be saved from a life of crime or prostitution. The first reawakening of interest in child abuse and neglect in the mid-1950s came not from pediatricians but from social workers, responding to public fears about an upsurge in juvenile delinquency. In hearings about national legislation against child abuse in 1973, experts pointed out that many violent criminals and assassins had been abused as children (Pleck 1987, p. 177).

In the 1970s as in the 1870s, wife beating began as a women's rights issue and picked up support as a law and order issue. In both centuries, women activists sought to pressure the police and district attorneys to arrest male perpetrators and to prosecute them, and they decried the lenient sentences judges handed down. Feminist organizations accompanied women victims to court and sought to provide them with legal aid. Victorian and some contemporary male law enforcement officials, seeking to strengthen the state's control over violent criminals, recognized that previous criminal efforts to deal with wife beating had not worked. They called for new sanctions (the whipping post in the nineteenth century or court-ordered therapy in the 1970s and 1980s).

If there were many similarities, there were also some important differences. In the modern period, reform was broader, more successful, and national in scope. Puritan reform against domestic violence was confined to the New England colonies. Even at the turn of the century, most cities did not have an SPCC, and the efforts on behalf of abused women were limited to a few places. Moreover, the range of social services to abusive families—from therapy to child care— was far greater in the present than in the past. The numerous self-help groups for victims, former victims, or perpetrators were without precedent.

Nonetheless, as in previous eras of reform, disillusionment began to set in and interest started to wane. In the mid-1970s, influential lawyers and psychiatrists attacked child abuse programs for denying parental rights of due process and for excessive and deleterious removal of children (especially children of the poor and minorities) from their parents (Wald 1975, 1976; Goldstein, Freud, and Solnit 1979). The general argument asserted that abused and neglected children were worse off in foster care or in group homes than they would have been if they had been left with their biological parent(s).

This counterfactual statement was almost impossible to prove or disprove. It must surely have been true in some cases and untrue or mixed in others. But the appearance of this rhetoric can best be read as a sign of disillusionment with the results of state intervention in the family (Ross 1980, pp. 77–81). Once it became clear that child abuse reform also led to greater state intervention in the family (which could mean increasing the number of children removed from the parental home), medical language and good intentions could no longer conceal the controversial nature of the issue.

In the mid-1970s, the controversy was limited to the experts, who disagreed about the merits of child abuse programs. Five years later, it had spread to segments of the general public. In 1980, New Right groups across the country, disturbed about the prevalence of abortion and the "breakdown of the American family," targeted for defeat federal domestic violence legislation. It would have provided federal funds for battered women's shelters, social service and advocacy programs on behalf of battered women, and research (Gelb 1983). New Right groups believed battered women's shelters encouraged women to get divorces and thereby undermined the traditional family. Domestic violence legislation also had to justify itself in light of the desire to reduce the number and size of federal social welfare programs. In 1984, national legislation, funded at drastically reduced levels, was nonetheless enacted.

The resurgence of conservatism targeted not only domestic violence legislation but also child abuse laws. In 1979, one conservative Republican senator, Paul Laxalt of Nevada, introduced a Family Protection Act that had been written by the executive director of a New Right lobbying group, the Moral Majority. Among other provisions, it eliminated federal expenditures specially designated for child abuse prevention and reallocated funding to the states, where such programs would compete with other social service programs. It further proposed to amend the definition of child abuse to exclude corporal punishment of a child by a parent or parental designate. It also stipulated that no federal law, grant, program, or directive would broaden or supersede existing state laws relating to spousal abuse. The Family Protection Act, which never had much chance of being passed, was intended mainly to remind liberal legislators and their sympathizers of the strength of feelings of many conservative groups concerning these issues.

Domestic violence was no longer a "safe" issue. Diminished funding for these programs, including cutbacks in needed personnel, encouraged a lack of public concern. The morning papers and the evening news still carried stories about marital rape, child molestation, sexual abuse at day-care centers, or elder abuse. But attention was more likely to be fleeting.

Yet the ideas that underlay reform implicitly attacked the importance of preserving the family at all costs, of safeguarding domestic privacy, and of allocating special rights to husbands and parents. Legitimate concerns about failures and mistakes in current social policy were mixed with ideological defenses of the traditional family and of domestic privacy. Further, it would cost money to establish battered women's shelters, victim advocacy programs, child protective services, hotlines, and the rest. The national mood favored lower levels of public funding for all social welfare programs and a defense of "the family," namely, parental rights, family autonomy, and domestic privacy. These abstract ideals, however worthy, have always been in conflict with the state's responsibility to protect its weakest and most vulnerable members. The lesson of the past is that the greater the emphasis on the "family" character of domestic violence, the lower the interest and support for criminalization of family violence. This generalization appears to apply equally as well in the 1980s.

References

Antler, Joyce, and Stephen Antler. 1979. "From Child Rescue to Family Protection: The Evolution of the Child Protective Movement in the United States." *Children and Youth Services Review* 1:177–204.

Boston Morning Post. 1837. *Selections from the Court Reports originally published in the "Boston Morning Post" from 1834 to 1837.* Boston: Otis, Broaders.

Boyer, Paul. 1978. *Urban Masses and Moral Order in America, 1820–1920.* Cambridge, Mass.: Harvard University Press.

Coleman, Sydney H. 1924. *Humane Society Leaders in America.* Albany, N.Y.: American Humane Association.

Costa, Joseph J., and Gordon K. Nelson. 1978. *Child Abuse and Neglect: Legislation, Reporting, and Prevention.* Lexington, Mass.: Heath.

Cushing, John D. 1977. *The Laws of the Pilgrims: A Facsimile Edition of the Book of the General Laws of the Inhabitants of the Jurisdiction of New Plymouth, 1672 and 1685.* Wilmington, Del.: Glazier.

DeFrancis, Vincent. 1966. *Child Abuse Legislation: Analysis and Study of Mandatory Reporting Laws in the United States.* Denver: American Humane Association.

Feshbach, Norma D., and Seymour D. Feshbach. 1978. "Toward an Historical, Social and Developmental Perspective on Children's Rights." *Journal of Social Issues* 25:1–7.

Fliegelman, Jay. 1982. *Prodigals and Pilgrims: The American Revolution against Patriarchal Authority, 1750–1800.* Cambridge: Cambridge University Press.

Gelb, Joyce. 1983. "The Politics of Wife Abuse." In *Families, Politics, and Public Policy: A Feminist Dialogue on Women and the State,* edited by Irene Diamond. New York: Longman.

Glenn, Myra C. 1984. *Campaigns against Corporal Punishment: Prisoners, Sailors, Women, and Children in Antebellum America.* Albany: State University of New York Press.

Goldstein, Joseph, Anna Freud, and Albert J. Solnit. 1979. *Before the Best Interests of the Child.* New York: Free Press.

Gordon, Linda. 1983–84. "Child Abuse, Gender, and the Myth of Family Independence: Thoughts on the History of Family Violence and Its Social Control, 1880–1920." *Review of Law and Social Change* 12:523–37.

———. 1988. *Family Violence and Social Control.* New York: Viking Press.

Haskins, George L. 1960. *Law and Authority in Early Massachusetts: A Study in Tradition and Design.* New York: Macmillan.

Hawes, Joseph M. 1971. *Children in Urban Society: Juvenile Delinquency in Nineteenth Century America.* New York: Oxford University Press.

Kempe, C. Henry, Frederic N. Silverman, Brandt F. Steele, William Droegemuller, and Henry K. Silver. 1962. "The Battered Child Syndrome." *Journal of the American Medical Association* 181:17–24.

Kerber, Linda K. 1980. *Women of the Republic: Intellect and Ideology in Revolutionary America.* Chapel Hill: University of North Carolina Press.

Koehler, Lyle. 1980. *A Search for Power: The "Weaker Sex" in Seventeenth-Century New England.* Urbana: University of Illinois Press.

McCrea, Roswell C. 1910. *The Humane Movement.* New York: Columbia University Press.

Massachusetts Colony. 1890. *The Body of Liberties of 1641.* Boston: Rockwell & Churchill.

Mennel, Robert M. 1973. *Thorns and Thistles: Juvenile Delinquents in the United States, 1825–1940.* Hanover, N.H.: University Press of New England.

Nelson, Barbara J. 1983. *Making an Issue of Child Abuse: Political Agenda Setting for Social Problems.* Chicago: University of Chicago Press.

New York Society for the Prevention of Cruelty to Children. 1876. *First Annual Report.* New York: Styles & Cash.

Paulsen, Monrad G. 1962. "The Delinquency, Neglect, and Dependency Jurisdiction of the Juvenile Court." In *Justice for the Child,* edited by Margaret K. Rosenheim. New York: Free Press.

Pfohl, Stephen. 1977. "The Discovery of Child Abuse." *Social Problems* 24:310–21.

Platt, Anthony M. 1969. *The Child Savers: The Invention of Delinquency.* Chicago: University of Chicago Press.

Pleck, Elizabeth H. 1979. "Wife Beating in Nineteenth-Century America." *Victimology* 4:60–74.

———. 1983a. "The Whipping Post for Wife Beaters, 1876–1906." In *Essays on the Family and Historical Change,* edited by Leslie P. Moch and Gary D. Stark. College Station: Texas A & M University Press.

———. 1983b. "Feminist Responses to 'Crimes against Women, 1868–1896.'" *Signs* 8:451–70.

———. 1987. *Domestic Tyranny: The Making of Social Policy against Family Violence from Colonial Times to the Present.* New York: Oxford University Press.

Ross, Catherine J. 1980. "The Lessons of the Past: Defining and Controlling Child Abuse in the United States." In *Child Abuse: An Agenda for Action,* edited by George Gerbner, Catherine J. Ross, and Edward Zigler. New York: Oxford University Press.

Rothman, David J. 1971. *The Discovery of the Asylum: Social Order and Disorder in the New Republic.* Boston: Little, Brown.

———. 1980. *Conscience and Convenience: The Asylum and Its Alternatives in Progressive America.* Boston: Little, Brown.

Ryerson, Ellen. 1978. *The Best-laid Plans: America's Juvenile Court Experiment.* New York: Hill & Wang.

Schechter, Susan. 1982. *Women and Male Violence: The Visions and Struggles of the Battered Women's Movement.* Boston: South End Press.

Schlossman, Steven L. 1977. *Love and the American Delinquent: The Theory and Practice of "Progressive" Juvenile Justice, 1825–1920.* Chicago: University of Chicago Press.

State of Tennessee, 1850. *Acts of the State of Tennessee, Laws, Statutes, etc., for the Years 1849–1850.* Nashville, Tenn.: Kennie & Watterson.

Steinberg, Allen. 1981. "'The Spirit of Litigation:' Private Prosecution and Criminal Justice in Nineteenth Century Philadelphia." Paper read at the annual meeting of the Social Science History Association, Nashville, Tenn., October.

Stone, Lawrence. 1977. *The Family, Sex and Marriage in England, 1500–1800.* New York: Harper & Row.

Thomas, Mason P. 1972. "Child Abuse and Neglect: Historical Overview, Legal Matrix and Social Perspectives." *North Carolina Law Review* 50:327–49.

Tiffin, Susan. 1982. *In Whose Best Interest? Child Welfare Reform in the Progressive Era.* Westport, Conn.: Greenwood.

Wald, Michael S. 1975. "State Intervention on Behalf of 'Neglected' Children: A Search for Realistic Standards." *Stanford Law Review* 27:985–1040.

———. 1976. "State Intervention on Behalf of 'Neglected' Children: Standards for Removal of Children from Their Homes, Monitoring the Status of Children in Foster Care and Termination of Parental Rights." *Stanford Law Review* 28:673–706.

Wyatt-Brown, Bertram. 1982. *Southern Honor.* New York: Oxford University Press.

15

Formal and Informal Deterrents to Domestic Violence: The Dade County Spouse Assault Experiment

Antony M. Pate
Edwin E. Hamilton

The Minneapolis Domestic Violence Experiment examined the relative effectiveness of various police responses to cases of misdemeanor spouse assault (Sherman and Berk 1984a, 1984b). Cases were assigned to three standard methods police use: arrest, attempting to counsel both parties, and sending the suspect away from home for several hours. Based on arrest records and interviews with the victims, the results indicated that cases assigned to the arrest response had the lowest level of recidivism, supporting the hypothesis that arrest has a specific deterrent effect.

Largely because of these results, several police departments adopted a preferred (or mandatory) policy of arrest for cases of spouse assault (Sherman and Hamilton 1984; Sherman, Cohn, and Hamilton 1985; Cohn and Sherman 1987). One legal scholar used the Minneapolis study to justify a proposed model statute requiring police officers to make arrests in cases of misdemeanor domestic assault (Lerman 1984). Furthermore, based on the Minneapolis study, the Attorney General's Task Force on Family Violence (1984, p. 104) recommended that law enforcement agencies establish arrest as the preferred response in cases of family violence.

The Minneapolis experiment has generated considerable debate and criticism (Lempert 1984; Binder and Meeker 1988, forthcoming; Elliott 1989; Meeker and Binder 1990). Critics argued that further studies were needed before making major policy changes based on the Minneapolis results. As a result, the National Institute of Justice funded "replications" of the Minneapolis Domestic Violence Experiment in six additional cities: Atlanta, Georgia; Charlotte, North Carolina; Colorado Springs, Colorado; Dade County (Miami), Florida; Milwaukee, Wisconsin; and Omaha, Nebraska. These studies addressed the criticisms leveled against the Minneapolis study.

The results from five of these replications are now available. Researchers in three sites—Omaha (Dunford, Huizinga, and Elliott 1990),

"Formal and Informal Deterrents to Domestic Violence: The Dade County Spouse Assault Experiment," by Antony M. Pate and Edwin E. Hamilton. *American Sociological Review* 57 (1992), pp. 691–697. Reprinted by permission of the American Sociological Association.

This research was supported by grant 87-IJ-CX-K003 from the National Institute of Justice. Opinions stated herein are those of the authors and do not necessarily represent those of the U.S. Department of Justice. The authors express their appreciation to the Metro-Dade Police Department for their gracious cooperation in conducting this experiment.

Charlotte (Hirschel, Hutchison, Dean, Kelley, and Pesackis 1990), and Milwaukee (Sherman et al., "From Initial Deterrence," 1991)—found no support for an arrest effect with respect to either official records or interviews with victims conducted six months after the presenting incidents. The Colorado Springs study found no deterrent effect of arrest when the analysis was based on official records, but found a strong deterrent effect when victim interviews were analyzed (Berk, Campbell, Klap, and Western 1991, 1992).

The Metro-Dade experiment found several statistically significant deterrent effects of arrest based on both victim interviews and official records (Pate, Hamilton, and Annan 1991). Based on interviews with victims within weeks of the presenting incident, for example, arrest was associated with reductions in the occurrence and number of subsequent assaults by the same suspect on the same victim. Interviews with victims six months after the presenting incident revealed significant deterrent effects attributable to arrest with respect to occurrence and time to a subsequent assault on the original victim; the effect on number of subsequent assaults was only marginally short of significance. Based on reports of subsequent arrests, cases randomly assigned to the arrest response had significantly lower occurrence rates and times to a subsequent assault than those assigned to the no-arrest response. The effect of arrest on subsequent assaults as recorded on official reports completed by officers after responding to calls for police service was not significant.

The conflicting results of the various replications have provoked considerable interest (Sherman 1992). Many of the attempts to explain these differences have suggested that formal sanctions may work differently depending on the mediating effect of informal sanctions (Sherman, Smith, Schmidt, and Rogan 1991; Sherman and Smith 1992; Berk et al. 1992). Even before the replication results were available, Sherman (1984b, p. 270) hypothesized that "more socially bonded people are more deterrable" and therefore employed persons and married persons would be more likely to be deterred by arrest.

Formal and Informal Deterrents

The theory of deterrence rests on the proposition that human behavior is to some degree rational, and thus can be influenced by incentives, particularly the negative incentives inherent in formal sanctions. This leads to the expectation that increases in the severity of penalties and the certainty of their imposition will discourage illegal behavior by increasing its perceived or threatened costs.

Zimring and Hawkins (1971) contended that the deterrent effect of formal sanctions may be enhanced if these sanctions are associated with informal sanctions—"for the majority of people the most degrading aspect of punishment is the social message it conveys" (p. 39). More recently, they argued that "official actions can set off societal reactions that may provide potential offenders with more reason to avoid conviction than the officially imposed unpleasantness of punishment" (Zimring and Hawkins 1973, p. 174). Tittle and Logan (1973) proposed that research on deterrence should consider the possibility that "formal sanctions can be effective only if reinforced by informal sanctions" (p. 386).

Elaborating on this idea, Williams and Hawkins (1986) broadened the conception of the deterrence process and posited that formal sanctions are augmented by the imposition of informal sanctions like *stigma* (e.g., embarrassment); *attachment costs* (e.g., loss of valued relationships); and *commitment costs* (e.g., loss of job or economic opportunities). Commitment costs arise from an individual's "stake in conformity" (Toby 1957; Briar and Piliavin 1965). Williams and Hawkins observed that if informal sanctions are activated by the formal sanction, then informal sanctions should be included in any account of the deterrent effect of formal sanctions.

Few studies have tested this broadened conception of deterrence as it applies to domestic assault. Berk and Newton (1985), alluding to the difficulties, stated:

> It is apparent that deterrence could be operating through a variety of mechanisms. Perhaps offenders are responding to the fear of further

criminal sanctions. Perhaps offenders are responding to the implications of arrest for relationships with friends, family, and neighbors. Perhaps offenders are concerned about what an arrest will do to their employment prospects. . . . Until these and other possible mechanisms are disentangled, theories of deterrence are little more than rhetoric. (p. 262)

Recently, Williams and Hawkins (1989) explored the influence of perceived formal and informal sanctions on arrests for wife assault. They analyzed data from a national survey of married or cohabiting men to determine their perceptions of the likelihood of direct costs (e.g., arrest and going to jail) and indirect costs of committing spouse assault. Based on their earlier work, the authors defined indirect costs as "stigmatic costs (familial and self-humiliation), attachment costs (loss of partner or disapproval from friends and relatives), and commitment costs (loss of job)" (Williams and Hawkins 1989, p. 167). The results indicated that the various indirect costs contributed to a "general sense of fear about arrest" (p. 178) for wife assault. Because these findings were based on men's perceptions of a "hypothetical" arrest for wife assault, it is unclear whether an actual arrest for wife assault would generate similar findings, i.e., that informal processes of social control would influence the deterrent effect of formal sanctions.

The Metro-Dade Spouse Assault Experiment offers an opportunity to test whether arrest is a more effective deterrent to further spouse abuse than alternative police interventions and to examine whether the deterrent effect of arrest is mediated by informal sanctions. We use the data collected during this experiment to examine the effects of two measures of informal control—employment status and marital status—as they interact with the formal sanction of arrest for spouse assault. Three hypotheses on the deterrent effect of arrest for spouse assault are tested: (1) the effect is greater among suspects who are employed (i.e., risk job loss) than for those who are unemployed; (2) the effect is greater among suspects who are married (i.e., risk losing the partner or being humiliated in the eyes of the partner) than

among those who are not married; and (3) the effect is greatest among suspects with the highest level of commitment (i.e., suspects who are both employed and married).

The Metro-Dade Spouse Assault Experiment

The Metro-Dade Spouse Assault Experiment was designed to test the deterrent effect of arrest in domestic violence cases. Conducted by the Police Foundation in cooperation with the Metro-Dade Police Department, the study ran from August 24, 1987 through July 16, 1989. The experiment utilized a randomization procedure to assign cases involving misdemeanor spouse battery that met the following criteria: (1) Probable cause for misdemeanor spouse battery existed, (2) no felony had occurred, (3) victim and subject were both on the scene upon the officers' arrival, (4) the victim was not in immediate danger, (5) the victim was a female 18 years of age or older, (6) the officer was not assaulted by subject or victim, and (7) there were no outstanding arrest warrants, injunctions, or criminal protective orders for victim or subject.

Because of Florida statutory requirements, for the first 13 months of the experiment eligible cases had to involve couples who were married or who had been married.

The Sample

The experimental sample included 907 cases. These cases were contributed by 396 officers. Of the suspects, 36.2 percent were Anglo, 41.7 percent were black, and 22.2 percent were Hispanic. Fifteen percent of the suspects were 18 to 25 years old, 43.8 percent were 26 to 35 years old, 34.3 percent were 36 to 50 years old, and 7.0 percent were over 50 years old. Officers suspected alcohol or drug use by suspects in 69.5 percent of the cases. Approximately 29 percent of the suspects were unemployed at the time of the presenting incident. Most of the couples (78.7 percent) were married at the time of the presenting incident, 2.9 percent were separated,

2.0 percent were divorced, and 16.3 percent had a boyfriend/girlfriend relationship.

Randomization and Treatments

Eligible cases were randomly assigned by the department's Computer Assisted Dispatch system to an arrest or a no-arrest response. Among the 907 eligible cases, 815 (89.9 percent) of the cases received the treatment to which they were randomly assigned; of the 92 misassigned cases, 88 were randomly assigned to the no-arrest condition but actually received an arrest.[1]

Once probable cause was determined, the suspect was told that he was under arrest and read his Miranda rights. The arresting officer then searched the suspect for weapons and contraband and handcuffed the suspect.

Upon arrival at the county jail, the transporting officer and the prisoner(s) were registered and admitted to a holding area. Once admitted to the facility, the transporting officer gave the arrest form to the receiving officer, who searched the prisoner, entered his name in the booking log, obtained his fingerprints, and took photographs ("mug shots").

The prisoner was then taken by the transporting officer back to the booking area and put in the custody of the receiving officer. If the prisoner had not been transported from a district police station, the receiving officer determined whether to release the prisoner on a "promise to appear" (PTA) basis. If a PTA release was offered, the prisoner's personal property was returned and he was released. If a PTA release was not provided, or if the prisoner had been transported from a district station, the receiving officer gave the prisoner the opportunity to post bond. If bond was posted, the prisoner's property was returned and the prisoner released. Although there was wide variation in the time spent under arrest, the average suspect spent 14.6 hours under arrest.

Arrestees were notified by the clerk of the court of the time and place of arraignment, which occurred within 21 days of arrest. At this hearing, the judge could accept a plea of guilty and bind the case over for trial, or release the defendant if probable cause was lacking.

Data Collection

Data concerning subsequent assaults by the suspect against the same victim were gathered from the Domestic Violence Continuation Report form appended to all offense reports involving domestic violence of any type.[2] These data were coded to represent whether a subsequent assault was recorded, the number of such assaults, and the length of time that elapsed until the first subsequent assault.

Analysis

Although analyses of the number of subsequent assaults and elapsed time to a subsequent assault have been conducted, we present here the results of the analysis of whether or not a subsequent assault occurred within six months after the presenting incident. Because this is a binary dependent variable, the distribution is not continuous, and the error variance is not homogeneous (Myers 1990). As a result, ordinary regression analysis or analysis of variance are inappropriate (Amemiya 1981, 1985; Pindyck and Rubinfeld 1991, pp. 248–52). Various approaches to analyzing these types of data have been suggested (Greene 1990, pp. 661–95; Pindyck and Rubinfeld 1991, pp. 254–69). For ease of analysis and interpretation, our analysis uses logistic regression.

Three models were tested using the occurrence of subsequent aggravated battery as the outcome measure. Independent variables included arrest status, prior violence, ethnicity, marital status, and employment status. The prior violence variable was coded 1 if the suspect recorded prior assault involving the same victim and 0 otherwise. Ethnicity was represented by two dichotomous variables, labeled "black" and "Hispanic"; "Anglo" is the deleted category. The marital status variable was coded 1 if the victim and suspect were married at the time of the presenting incident and 0 otherwise. The employment status variable was coded 1 if the suspect was employed (full-time or part-time) at the time of the presenting incident and 0 otherwise. A "commitment" variable was coded 0 for suspects who were unemployed and unmarried,

1 for suspects who were either employed or married, and 2 for suspects who were employed and married.

Results

The results of the logistic regression analyses are presented in Table 1. Model 1 reveals no statistically significant effect of arrest on the occurrence of a subsequent spouse assault. This reflects the similarity between arrested and not-arrested suspects in the occurrence of subsequent reported assaults (9.0 percent and 10.6, respectively).

Model 2 includes all the variables from Model 1 and adds interactions between arrest and employment status and arrest and marital status. The results reveal a statistically significant interaction effect between arrest and employment status, but the interaction effect between arrest and marital status was not statistically significant. This suggests that the deterrent effect of arrest is influenced by the informal sanctions implicit in employment status. The nature of this interaction effect is revealed in analyses of the arrest effect within subcategories of suspects (data not shown). These analyses reveal that this overall lack of effect masks two significant offsetting effects: Arrest had a significant deterrent effect among employed suspects, whereas arrest led to a significant increase in subsequent assaults among unemployed suspects. Figure 1 shows these differential effects graphically. Among unemployed suspects, 7.1 percent of those not arrested had a subsequent assault compared to 16.7 percent

TABLE 1 Logistic Regression Coefficients for Regression of Occurrence of Subsequent Assault on Selected Independent Variables: Metro-Dade Spouse Assault Experiment, 1987 to 1989

Independent Variable	Model 1	Model 2	Model 3
Arrest	−.160 (.228)	.706 (.565)	.922 (.541)
Prior violence	1.280*** (.259)	1.263*** (.263)	1.278*** (.261)
Black	−.228 (.255)	−.255 (.258)	−.219 (.256)
Hispanic	−.372 (.326)	−.329 (.328)	−.334 (.327)
Married	−.118 (.271)	−.343 (.363)	—
Employed	−.232 (.243)	.647 (.382)	—
Commitment	—	—	.168 (.245)
Employed × arrest	—	−1.704*** (.508)	—
Married × arrest	—	.349 (.544)	—
Commitment × arrest	—	—	−.759* (.347)
Constant	−1.965	−2.418	−2.466

*p < .05 ***p < .001
Note: Numbers in parentheses are standard errors; N = 907 for all Models.

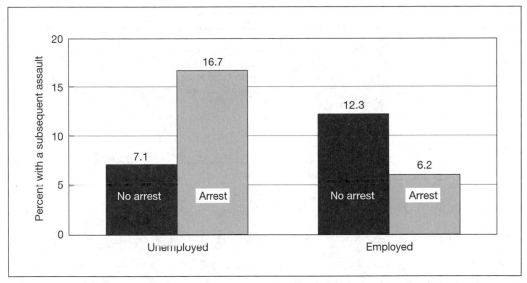

Figure 1 Percent of Suspects with a Subsequent Assault by Employment Status and Arrest Status

of arrestees. Among the employed suspects, however, the results were reversed: 12.3 percent of those assigned to the no-arrest response had a subsequent assault compared to 6.2 percent of arrestees.

Model 3 substitutes the combined commitment variable for the employment status and marital status variables. Results reveal a statistically significant interaction effect between arrest and the composite measure of commitment, indicating that the strong mediating effect of employment status combines with the negligible effect of marital status to produce a moderate effect.

Summary and Discussion

The results of this study provide general support for the hypothesis that the deterrent effect of the formal sanction of arrest for spouse abuse is mediated by the informal sanctions implicit in employment status. Among employed suspects, arrest had a statistically significant deterrent effect on the occurrence of a subsequent assault as

recorded on the Domestic Violence Continuation Report forms. Among unemployed suspects, on the other hand, significant *increases* in subsequent assault were associated with arrest. There were no differences with respect to marital status.

Tests for interaction effects between arrest and employment status revealed significant differences, but the tests for interaction effects between arrest and marital status revealed no significant differences.

As suggested by Sherman (1992) and others, these findings raise serious concerns about the appropriateness and efficacy of universally mandated or preferred arrest for misdemeanor spouse abuse. If arrest deters only those who have something to lose (e.g., a job), that fact must be taken into account when policies are established.

The discrepant findings produced by the various replications of the Minneapolis Spouse Abuse Experiment emphasize the need for further research. When investigating the effectiveness of deterrence strategies, attention must be focused on both formal and informal sanctions and the interactions between them.

Notes

1. In an independent, second-stage experiment, randomly assigned suspects received attention from a specially trained unit of domestic violence detectives. That treatment is not discussed here.
2. Interviews with victims were conducted soon after the presenting incident and six months after that incident. For comparability, only the data from the Domestic Violence Continuation Reports are analyzed here. However, analysis of the victim interviews produced similar results.

References

Amemiya, Takeshi. 1981. "Qualitative Response Models: A Survey." *Journal of Economic Literature* 19(4):483–536.
———. 1985. *Advanced Econometrics*. Cambridge, MA: Harvard University Press.
Attorney General's Task Force on Family Violence. 1984. *Final Report*. Washington, DC: U.S. Government Printing Office.
Berk, Richard A. and Phyllis J. Newton. 1985. "Does Arrest Really Deter Wife Battery? An Effort to Replicate the Findings of the Minneapolis Spouse Abuse Experiment." *American Sociological Review* 50:253–62.
Berk, Richard A., Alec Campbell, Ruth Klap, and Bruce Western. 1991. "A Bayesian Analysis of the Colorado Springs Spouse Abuse Experiment." Department of Sociology and Program in Social Statistics, University of California, Los Angeles. Unpublished manuscript.
———. 1992. "The Deterrent Effect of Arrest in Incidents of Domestic Violence: A Bayesian Analysis of Four Field Experiments. *American Sociological Review* 57:698–708.
Binder, Arnold and James W. Meeker. 1988. "Experiments as Reforms." *Journal of Criminal Justice* 16:347–58.
———. Forthcoming. "Arrest as a Method to Control Spousal Abuse." In *Domestic Violence: The Changing Criminal Justice Response,* edited by E.S. Buzawa and C.G. Buzawa. Westport, CT: Greenwood.
Briar, Scott and Irving Piliavin. 1965. "Delinquency, Situational Inducement, and Commitment to Conformity." *Social Problems* 13:33–45.
Cohn, Ellen G. and Lawrence Sherman. 1987. *Police Policy on Domestic Violence, 1986.* Crime Control Reports, No. 5. Washington, DC: Crime Control Institute.
Dunford, Franklyn, David Huizinga, and Delbert S. Elliott. 1990. "The Role of Arrest in Domestic Assault: The Omaha Experiment." *Criminology* 28:183–206.
Elliott, Delbert S. 1989. "Criminal Justice Procedures in Family Violence Crimes." Pp. 427–80 in *Family Violence,* edited by L. Ohlin and M. Tonry. Chicago: University of Chicago Press.
Greene, William H. 1990. *Econometric Analysis*. New York: Macmillan Publishing Company.
Hirschel, J. David, Ira W. Hutchison III, Charles W. Dean, Joseph J. Kelley, and Carolyn E. Pesackis. "Charlotte Spouse Assault Replication Project: Final Report." National Institute of Justice: Washington, DC. Unpublished manuscript.
Lempert, Richard. 1984. "From the Editor." *Law and Society Review* 18:505–10.
Lerman, Lisa 1984. "A Model Act: Remedies for Domestic Abuse." *Harvard Journal on Legislation* 21:61–143.
Meeker, James W. and Arnold Binder. 1990. "Experiments as Reforms: The Impact of the 'Minneapolis Experiment' on Police Policy." *Journal of Police Science and Administration* 17(2):147–53.
Myers, Raymond H. 1990. *Classical and Modern Regression with Applications,* 2d ed. Boston, MA: PWS—KENT Publishing Company.
Pate, Antony, Edwin E. Hamilton, and Sampson Annan. 1991. "Metro-Dade Spouse Abuse Replication Project: Draft Final Report." National Institute of Justice, Washington, DC. Unpublished manuscript.
Pindyck, Robert S. and Daniel L. Rubinfeld. 1991. *Econometric Models and Economic Forecasts,* 3d ed. New York: McGraw-Hill, Inc.
Sherman, Lawrence W. 1992. *Policing Domestic Violence: Experiments and Dilemmas.* New York: Free Press.
Sherman, Lawrence W. and Richard A. Berk. 1984a. "The Minneapolis Domestic Violence Experiment." Police Foundation Reports, No. 1. Washington, DC: Police Foundation.
———. 1984b. "The Specific Deterrent Effects of Arrest for Domestic Assault." *American Sociological Review* 49:261–72.
Sherman, Lawrence W., Ellen Cohn, and Edwin Hamilton. 1985. *Police Policy on Domestic Violence: A National Survey.* Washington, DC: Crime Control Institute.

Sherman, Lawrence W. and Earl Hamilton. 1984. *The Impact of the Minneapolis Domestic Violence Experiment: Wave 1 Findings.* Washington, DC: Police Foundation.

Sherman, Lawrence W., Janell D. Schmidt, Dennis P. Rogan, Patrick R. Gartin, Ellen G. Cohn, Dean J. Collins, and Anthony R. Bacich. 1991. "From Initial Deterrence to Long-Term Escalation: Short-Custody Arrest For Poverty Ghetto Domestic Violence." *Criminology* 29:821–50.

Sherman, Lawrence W. and Douglas A. Smith. 1992. "Crime, Punishment, and Stake in Conformity: Legal and Informal Control of Domestic Violence." *American Sociological Review* 57:680–690.

Sherman, Lawrence W., Douglas A. Smith, Janell D. Schmidt, and Dennis P. Rogan. 1991. "Ghetto Poverty, Crime and Punishment: Legal and Informal Control of Domestic Violence." Institute of Criminal Justice and Criminology, University of Maryland. Unpublished manuscript.

Tittle, Charles R. and Charles H. Logan. 1973. "Sanctions and Deviance: Evidence and Remaining Questions." *Law and Society Review* 7:371–92.

Toby, Jackson. 1957. "Social Disorganization and Stake in Conformity: Complementary Factors in the Predatory Behavior of Hoodlums." *Journal of Criminal Law, Criminology and Police Science* 48:12–17.

Williams, Kirk R. and Richard Hawkins. 1986. "Perceptual Research on General Deterrence: A Critical Review." *Law and Society Review* 20:545–72.

———. 1989. "The Meaning of Arrest for Wife Assault." *Criminology* 27:163–81.

Zimring, Frank E. and Gordon Hawkins. 1971. "The Legal Threat as an Instrument of Social Change." *Journal of Social Issues* 27:33–48.

———. 1973. *Deterrence: The Legal Threat in Crime Control.* Chicago: University of Chicago Press.

16

Anatomy of a Wife-Killing

Bertram Wyatt-Brown

What occurred in Natchez could, of course, have happened elsewhere—in the semi-rural North or even in some other part of the Western world. Nineteenth-century Southern whites were not unique in upholding the ancient ethic, but they did so with a primal spirit that elsewhere in the transatlantic community was under steady attack. This was a consequence, in part, of their reliance on the institution of slavery and race-based caste proscriptions. In 1834 Natchez, Mississippi, was ethically not very distant from the world that Hawthorne described in his classic story "My Kinsman, Major Molineux."

At seven in the evening on Friday, March 14, 1834, James Foster, Jr. took his wife Susan for a walk near his widowed mother Sarah's house at Foster Fields. The large plantation stretched almost a mile along the winding St. Catherine's Creek, a treacherous stream that eventually runs into the Mississippi River a few miles below the town of Natchez. Though it was only three miles from the Adams County courthouse, those living at Foster Fields considered themselves residents of Pine Ridge, a neighborhood on the Natchez Trace. At ten o'clock Foster ran back to the homestead in a state of agitation. There were twelve adults and a number of small children asleep at the house. But the planter roused only his sister, Nancy A. Wood, a woman old enough to have been his mother, and his niece, Nancy Ligon. Hastily they put on wraps as he stammered out his story. (When under stress, Foster had a tendency to stutter.) He and his wife, he told them, had been down by the bayou, about a thousand feet from the house. There he had "switched" his wife for being "unchaste," and she had confessed her guilt. Somehow, though, the

inflictions had "frightened her into a fit." Grabbing Mrs. Wood by the arm, Foster led the women to the slave quarters. He had carried Susan to one of the cabins.

Inside, Mrs. Wood and Mrs. Ligon found the body laid out on a low bed. Prince, Will, and Bridget, slaves belonging to the widow Sarah, stood by. Prince was a son of Abd al-Rahman Ibrahima, the African ruler whom Thomas Foster, Sr., late owner of Foster Fields, had finally allowed New York colonizationists to transport home to Africa. Both the senior Foster and his aged black servant Ibrahima had been dead some five years. They had not escaped the misery that Thomas Foster, Jr.'s liaison with Ibrahima's daughter Susy had caused, but at least death spared them the disgrace into which the family was plunging in 1834.

Frightened and confused, Mrs. Wood and Mrs. Ligon glanced quickly at Susan's body. Foster excitedly begged the women to apply camphor to her face. But resuscitation was impossible. The body still felt warm, but the hands, Mrs. Wood recalled later, had already turned cold. Susan's dress had been removed, and she was covered only with an underdress that had no bodice. The body had been washed; her hair was still damp. The slave Bridget, Prince's wife, had done her task tenderly, and so well that the women did not notice much evidence of violence. They could only see a small bruise near the temple—or so they later claimed. On Mrs. Wood's orders, Prince and Will, another slave, carried Susan Foster to the main house. They placed her on the bed in the couple's bedroom.

The following day Sarah Foster, Thomas Foster Sr.'s invalid widow, summoned William Foster from his neighboring plantation. William was her husband Thomas's elder brother. A childless but long-married kinsman, he had always taken a special interest in his brother's thirteen children at Foster Fields. Aged though he was, William recognized more signs of violence on Susan's body than a flickering lamp in a slave hovel had revealed the night before. As far as he could tell, "the neck and shoulders from one point to another were all black and blue." On later inspection, he noticed "a grip" on her neck and blood and froth "oozing . . . slowly . . . out of her left nostril." Meanwhile David McIntosh, the husband of Caroline, one of James Foster's nine sisters, hastened over. The McIntosh place was on the opposite bank of the creek, not far away. With Susan lying dead in his own room, James Foster had spent the night at David and Caroline's house. At breakfast on Saturday Foster had told the pair that his wife had died, but had not elaborated on the circumstances. McIntosh came to Foster Fields seeking more information, but could not seem to get a straight story from anybody. The women were too shocked and distracted from the sight they had seen the night before. When Mrs. Ligon and her mother Nancy Wood asked him if Susan should be buried "publickly or privately," McIntosh answered, "Publickly of course as she had died with a Fit there could be no danger." For the first time the two women faced up to the truth, at least partially: they replied, "She did not die in a Fit." Mrs. Frances Ann Wells, another Foster sister in residence, and Mrs. Wood admitted to McIntosh that the night before they had "advised James Foster to escape."

The Pine Ridge neighborhood was shocked that one of its residents had so cruelly killed his wife, a friendless, kinless waif, a mere child. The gentleman who took it upon himself to serve as her guardian *post mortem* was Spence Monroe Grayson, a thirty-one-year-old lawyer just gaining local prominence. In 1839 he was to oppose the passage of the Mississippi Women's Property Act in the state senate, arguing eloquently that woman's purity had to be kept free from the corruption of business transactions. In keeping with these chivalrous views, he volunteered to assist the state's attorney, Daniel Greenleaf. In fact, Grayson had himself listed as the prosecutor of

record in the court docket. Known for his speaking abilities, Grayson no doubt expected to make the chief plea to the jury, leaving to Greenleaf the paperwork and investigation of the circumstances.

Grayson's associations with Pine Ridge ran deep. His uncle and guardian, Beverley R. Grayson, had raised him. William Grayson, congressman, planter, and Revolutionary hero of Prince William County, Virginia, was the head of the clan. Spence Monroe Grayson had lost both parents in 1803 when he was an infant. His uncle Beverley removed to Mississippi, where he hoped to reduplicate the glories and prestige of the family's Virginia forefathers. Beverley Grayson raised his nephew as his own son, and set his young charge a very high example, in the best Southern tradition. Beverley Grayson was long active in civic affairs in Natchez and on the Ridge. With the Foster brothers, James and John, he had helped establish Jefferson College and Elizabeth Female Academy on Pine Ridge. Far from what Southwesterners regarded as the typical Virginia gentleman, impractical and overcivilized, Beverley Grayson operated sawmills, cotton gins, and stores as well as the requisite plantation. Spence Monroe Grayson followed suit. Though just about the same age as James Foster, Jr., whom he must have known since boyhood, Grayson had long before charted his course and knew his mind. He had studied well in school and at Jefferson College, and at age twenty-three he had already joined the Natchez bar through the sponsorship of Senator Thomas Read, his mentor. In 1830, unlike James Foster, Jr., he married a woman with unimpeachable Virginia and Philadelphia connections, Sarah R. Chew, whose father was a leading Natchez nabob. The couple settled down not far from the Fosters' district. It would be interesting to know if there had been bad blood between James Foster, Jr., and his prosecutor when they were growing up together. In any case, Spence Monroe Grayson, as his obituaries in 1839 later attested, was a flower of Southern gentility. Susan Alpha (?) Foster was to have a bold knight after all, though only as avenger of her death.

If Grayson was to serve as representative of Southern civilization, Felix Huston, Foster's attorney, epitomized Southern tradition. Scots-Irish by extraction, Huston was as tall as an ancient Frankish king; the troops in Texas whom he led a few months after Foster's ordeal called him "General Long-Shanks." He and Seargent S. Prentiss, his partner for a time, had the most lucrative practice in Natchez, and Huston's wife, Mary E. Daingerfield, had a plantation directly adjacent to Foster Fields. There Huston entertained lavishly—hunting parties, balls, picnics, shooting matches—but whether the Fosters were ever invited is not known. Sophisticated though he was, Huston was much less genteel than Grayson. Proud of his marksmanship, he fought more than one duel, although his encounter with Albert Sidney Johnston during the Texas Revolution was the most celebrated.

Felix Huston had no second thoughts about taking up the defense of James Foster, Jr. He was already representing him—and many other Foster relations—in the dispute with John Speed over Cassandra's will. Fortunately for Huston's legal strategy, confusions over the impaneling of Mississippi juries under common law were then obstructing judicial procedures. Therefore, Prosecutor Greenleaf quickly responded with a brief upholding the methods by which Woodson Wren, the clerk of court, had established the array. Since no other attorney had utilized the same challenge in that court session, Judge Alexander Montgomery, recently defeated for reelection to the bench, decided to postpone the Foster trial. In the October term Montgomery had felt obliged to throw out all jury cases on the same grounds—that the grand jury that presented the indictments had been improperly convened—and did not wish that to happen again. Therefore he set Foster's trial for the very last day of the term, so that the Foster indictment could be dismissed without cleaning out the docket for the entire term. Although Montgomery did not announce his intentions regarding the Foster trial, its postponement gave a hint that the townspeople did not at all like. It suggested that Huston's motion to quash the venire would probably be accepted. However, they would have to wait until January 2, 1835, the final sitting, to learn whether the wife-killer was to be tried or not.

By the time Montgomery was ready to give his opinion, the Natchez public had been entertained with a full session of cases—four Negro-stealings, an embezzlement, thirteen assault and battery charges, two fornications, and other assorted crimes. Excitement mounted as the only murder trial that term approached. Moreover, there were other tensions in Natchez, indeed in Mississippi and in the nation at large. Devastating cholera attacks had already shocked the region and the country as a whole. Poor weather conditions had unsettled expectations in the Mississippi Valley. In national politics, partisan warfare over President Jackson's determination to destroy the Bank of the United States had grown increasingly bitter. In prior months both Felix Huston and Spence Monroe Grayson had been in fist fights at local rallies of Jacksonians and their opponents, soon to be called Whigs. Still more alarming to friends of the Union was the appearance of organized abolitionism. In October 1833 Northern evangelicals and Quakers had formed the American Anti-Slavery Society in New York, with a local riot to give their efforts national notoriety. At that time, Felix Huston had written to the New York *Courier and National Enquirer,* a fiercely anti-abolitionist paper, saying that if, as a result of the new organization's agitation among slaves, "one female had been violated by that unhallowed union of white and black desperadoes, no man in the State" with antislavery sentiments "would have escaped— they would have perished to a man."

In broad terms, some kind of public sense that moral boundaries and expectations were no longer so precise and sturdy as they once had been seemed to afflict the nation at large. In New York City there were sudden outbreaks of riots, not only against abolitionists and free blacks, but also among political factions. Mobs from Boston burned the Ursuline convent and school at Charlestown, the first of many attacks throughout the northeast in protest against Irish immigration. The epidemic of civil disorders was to grow still worse in 1835. Particularly was this so after the abolitionist postal campaign, which aroused much indignation, North and South, when antislavery pamphlets reached their destinations. Even in 1834, Mississippians feared for public safety when Alonzo Phelps, brigand and murderer, escaped from jail, though he was killed when cornered. The dramatic revelations of Virgil Stewart about a widespread conspiracy of similar highwaymen, "steam doctors," and professional gamblers under John A. Murrell were to reinforce those worries in 1835. White Mississippians readily believed that abolitionists had joined with these villainous elements to overthrow the social order and pillage, murder, and tyrannize law-abiding citizens. There was not a word of truth in the public fantasy. The terror, however, served a customary purpose, notifying all whites of the need for solidarity.

All these eruptions, North and South, were directed toward the reestablishment of traditional popular morality: the supremacy of the Protestant "good" over the Catholic "menace," the white man over the rebellious black, the gentleman of leisure over the lying gamester, the patriot over the subversive abolitionist, the honest citizen over robbers, medical frauds, and anyone else who sought to snatch away the citizen's hard-won cash. These simple themes of alien menace reduced complex circumstances to masterable proportions, so that even the most illiterate yeoman or worker could understand and participate in the rites of exorcism, expulsion, and purification.

James Foster, Jr., it might be said, was one of the early victims in this recurrent but variously motivated "inflammation of the popular mind," as Hawthorne called it. The rituals of sacrifice, by shaming one individual, thereby "proved" the worth, purity of purpose, and security of those beset with evils not so readily apprehended. Such actions thrust the pain of self-recognition upon the victim and what he or she represents. In a sense Foster was to be punished not for his crime alone, but for the anxieties of the citizenry.

There was nothing class-conscious or very modern about any of the mobs of the 1830s, particularly the one that milled about Natchez's handsome, porticoed courthouse on January 2, 1835. The crowd was there to participate in a ritual no less stylized and mythic than that which Hawthorne depicted in his story. Believing that Foster's indictment was likely to be quashed, the citizens told each other, as people had in similar situations in America since the seventeenth century, that the system of justice was defective, unreliable, that technicalities conjured up by the wizards of the law protected rich clients like Foster, leaving the public at the mercy of fiends. The waiting crowd, one of its members later recalled, expected that the judge would soon let

the prisoner "loose upon an outraged community, unscathed, unwhipped of justice." Foster's hands would be "reeking with the blood of his virtuous and butchered wife," and he would be free "to exult and gloat over his infamy, and, like a wild beast *once* fed on human flesh and blood, acquiring an insatiable love for such food, to hunt for other victims." Colonel James Creecy, who later wrote these words, expressed the less grandly articulated feelings of the mob. The ceremony of degradation itself would translate those visceral sentiments into symbolic actions.

Yet, as in all such enterprises, anger was not the sole emotion to sweep that assembly in Natchez. There was also the sense of joy and celebration that a charivari ordinarily elicited. After all, it was January 2, a Saturday in the New Year's holiday. It was a time when, traditionally, bells were rung and noisemakers twirled to scare off a community's old sins and spirits and to welcome in a new beginning, pure and innocent—when ancient Authority, Father Time, was deposed and the new-crowned child was exalted.

Sheriff Gridley and his deputies marched the accused the short distance to the courtroom. Pale and faltering after months of close confinement in shackles, Foster met Felix Huston before the bench. Judge Montgomery, the first native Mississippian to serve as a state common pleas judge, wasted no time. It was his last case before vacating the office. The venire was quashed, he ruled. Foster was free, at least momentarily.

The crowd outside swelled to three hundred or more as word of Montgomery's decision spread. It was as diverse a throng as could be imagined—planters' sons in town to promenade and carouse, Choctaw Indians and their squaws, riverboat men, steamboat passengers, prostitutes, gamblers, town urchins and apprentices, slaves and ordinary white folk visiting on court day. None were dressed for outlandish masquerade. Their regular attire was motley enough, however, according to "Thimblerig," an observer and participant. Thimblerig, who was a professional shell-game artist, later told his story to Colonel David Crockett, whom he joined on a steamboat bound for New Orleans not long afterward. Crockett, on his way to Texas, included the account in his famous autobiography.

Officials of the court and the better sort of folk were not visible. However, they certainly were aware—and tacitly approving—of the events that would ensue. Judge Montgomery, prosecutor Greenleaf, and Sheriff Horace Gridley were nowhere in sight. The Duncans, Holmeses, Quitmans, and others of high station would never have led the rites. The task belonged to upcoming young men not yet weighed down with honors and dignities. Grayson, the prosecutor of record, and Huston, Foster's attorney, remained to accompany him as he stepped into the light of the winter noonday sun. At once "two gentlemen" seized Foster, who fell in the ensuing scuffle. Huston intervened. Urging the pressing throng to move back, Huston helped Foster up and gained permission for them both to pass up the street a hundred yards or so. As they walked away from the catcalls and angry fists, Foster, sobbing abjectly, begged Huston to save him. There was not much the attorney could have done, even if he had wished to do so; by acting like a wheedling coward Foster merely aroused mob disgust all the more. Then, as Huston and the mob had arranged, Huston gave Foster the signal to run. If Foster could have outrun the crowd, he would have gained his freedom. But the prisoner was paralyzed. Depression, shame, and dread sapped his will. The mob grabbed him once again.

According to one account, a line then formed in near silence. "The word 'march' was pronounced finally by the tall man in front," Colonel James Creecy later remembered. He was referring to Felix Huston, who was no longer the prisoner's lawyer but now his chief tormentor. Grayson also joined the head of the procession as it moved toward the ravine near the toll bridge. It was the place where Thomas Foster, Jr., and the slave Susy had met to make their escape together a few years before. The hollow was the customary site for community rituals of this kind in Natchez. The leaders lashed Foster to a tree. For the next several hours—from about noon to sundown—the citizens laid on the strokes with a cowhide whip, "until," said Thimblerig, "the flesh run in ribands from his body." Each lash was a reminder of the agony that Foster had perpetrated upon Susan, a biblical retribution indeed.

As the sun began to set, the lynchers heated up the tar, while debating whether Foster should be branded on both cheeks, have his ears

slit, or be scalped. (The first two choices were penalties current on the state's statute books. Not for another decade did the penitentiary mode replace corporal exactions in Mississippi.) The decision was for a partial scalping; a complete one would have been fatal. After this was done, tar was poured over Foster's head, shoulders, and back, followed by a dousing with the traditional feathers. Dressed in this manner and otherwise wearing only "a miserable pair of breeches," Foster was led back to town. On the way he fainted several times. As he lay groaning, no one attended him. He was, recalled Thimblerig simply, "an object of universal detestation." After Foster was seated backwards to the cart's tail, the lynchers accompanied the "common dray" with the sounds of pots banging, lids clashing, boys whistling, and drummers beating unrhythmically—the "rough music" of the antique "rogue's march."

By this time the crowd was a happy thoroughly drunken New Year's throng. As Sheriff Gridley helped Foster climb the jail steps, a howl went up. "Take him to the river, tie him to a log, and set him adrift," some yelled. "Hang the villain!" "Never turn such a fellow loose to butcher another wife," cried others. These bowdlerized threats from Colonel Creecy's account do not capture the gutter language that was no doubt really used. But Grayson, who addressed the mob from the steps, was probably accurately quoted. He was said to have replied, "My friends, we have *done* our duty as good citizens, and I now propose that we all go quietly to our homes!" The "common dray" was rolled off. The bulk of the mob dispersed. Gridley took Foster inside, for Foster's own protection. Only a few stragglers remained, but they had murderous intentions. Some were muttering that Foster should have been branded and his ears cut off, back at the hollow. They were waiting for a chance to act on their own.

James Creecy, in his memoir, claimed that he had not seen Foster clearly until the victim was led up the steps. In awe and fear, he exclaimed, "Almighty Father, what a picture! He was more like a huge shapeless fowl, covered with masses of feathers, all turned the wrong way, than anything else." Thimblerig also described him: "The blood oozing from his stripes had become mixed with masses of feathers and tar, and rendered his aspect still more horrible and loathsome." Finally, the editor of the Natchez *Courier* aptly remarked, "So far from recognizing Foster" as he had appeared in court that morning, "we could scarcely realize that he was a man. The mob believed he was a monster at heart, and were determined that his external appearance should correspond with the inner man."

The mob had sought to purge the community of a deviant judged so beneath human attribute that tar—a kind of representational excrement—was fitting apparel. Instead of acting as the protector of his wife (who was also a child), he had had no "fear of God before his eyes" and, as the common-law indictment read, had been "moved and seduced by the instigation of the Devil" to slay her maliciously. In a patriarchal world, one might chastise a loved one, but few crimes were worse than intrafamilial killings. In addition, Foster was a gamester—in debt, accused of fraud, and so addicted to gambling that his habits aroused contempt even in that gambling-obsessed age and region. Like an alcoholic who could not hold his liquor, Foster repelled other men who were drinkers and gamblers themselves. His excesses caricatured their own inclinations in frightening ways. He was the mirror of what they might become. For these reasons Foster had to be transformed from what he was, an ordinary, even physically attractive young man, into a creature with whom no one needed to identify himself. Clad in feathers, he became the male-turned-female, a humiliated cowbird, the symbol of the cuckoldry that he had sought to escape in his furious assault upon his wife. From a superhuman beast "hunting for other victims," to borrow from Creecy, Foster was translated into a puny-brained, two-legged, feather-covered capon, as harmless as the bird whose neck was habitually wrung for Sunday dinner.

One may be sure that such humiliations had the desired psychological effect on the victim. Hawthorne's description of Major Molineux's reaction was very accurate. Foster's state of mind was even more abject. His agony can best be compared with the violation felt by a man or woman subjected to unremitting gang rape. Later that night, at about two in the morning, two men on horseback led an unmounted horse to the jail. Thimblerig, who watched, recalled

that "Foster was with difficulty placed astride." The mob's lookouts tried to grab him, but Foster found strength enough to shake them loose. One fired a pistol, but the shot only grazed Foster's hat, and the three rode off into the night. The party stopped at Foster Fields, only a few miles away.

One of the two men who rescued Foster was one of his brothers-in-law, Daniel MacMillan of neighboring Franklin County, Mississippi, a justice of the peace and a hard-driving man. Perhaps the other horseman was MacMillan's son. On May 21, 1835, almost five months later, Foster had sufficiently recovered to assign his share of whatever remained of Thomas Foster, Sr.'s, estate to that son, Calvin MacMillan, his nephew. No doubt this was the reward for the rescue. The Foster clan of James, Jr.'s, generation, it would seem, seldom did much for each other without some monetary exchange. Once his signature was on that indenture, Foster disappeared.

The Fosters seldom spoke of him again, but one member of the clan thought that he had gone to Texas. Allegedly, he never remarried and died at the close of the century. According to the same unsubstantiated report, he left a large estate in Houston town lots to his grandnephew, Governor Murphy Foster, the grandson of James's former partner in Franklin, Louisiana, Levi Foster. The legacy, so the story goes, would have been a public embarrassment during the reform governor's reelection campaign against the infamous Louisiana Lottery gang, then a powerful political machine, and so Murphy Foster, fearing that the ancient murder would hurt his election chances, refused the inheritance. The whole tale seems implausible.

Nevertheless, it appears that Foster did survive, as Grayson and Huston had intended. Certainly recuperation from some 150 lashes required a strong constitution, but Foster owed his life to the attorneys who had allowed his humiliation but had prevented a sentence of death. The reasons for this mercy were several. First, Grayson was a gentleman who took the title seriously. It would have been barbarous for a Virginian and Christian to let him die after a court had rendered a contrary verdict. Second, both Grayson and Huston were lawyers sworn to uphold the sanctity of the court with which they were affiliated. Third, they were members of the planter class, and Foster had once been so regarded, too. Though his rank had been lost, it could not be forgotten. To let a mob of the poor and powerless kill someone of superior original standing would violate convention and order. The ordinary cheating gamester, the rebellious slave, the lowly ne'er-do-well were fit objects for a death sentence under lynch law. But a planter, even a wife-killer, was not to be hanged summarily. The second generation of Fosters might have forfeited their place in local estimation with two divorce cases, adulterous miscegenation, and then murder. Nevertheless James Foster, Jr., reasoned Huston and Grayson, should be allowed to survive.

Yet these factors do not explain why the crowd so promptly obeyed Grayson's call for a return to order. All but the handful who lingered in hopes of more excitement accepted his plea and left the scene. The reason they did so was that Grayson and Huston had also served another purpose. As leaders of the mob, they had given sanction to what was done. For the duration of the charivari they were exploited by the crowd as much as they used it for their own ends: the punishing of a planter who had violated the class code and the code of honor attached to it. The attorneys lent legitimacy to deeds that were clearly illegal, even reprehensible if undertaken by a single actor. Through them the rite became "holy aggression," in contrast to Foster's distinctly unholy offense. Someone had to initiate the action in the name of all, and at once such an individual became more than a leader: he was regarded as a hero by those following him, as one whose strength of will and sense of rightfulness could set aside all doubts and fears. The crowd shared in his glory even as they were the instruments by which the hero acquired it. If the individual who instigated the first acts against the scapegoat had no prior prestige but arose from the mob itself, matters could quickly get out of hand. But leaders like Huston and Grayson were men already held in respect. They had the authority to control both the beginning and the ending of the episode, so that studied "misrule" did not degenerate into wild disorder. If that had occurred, Foster would doubtless have perished. To folk ill equipped for deeds of special courage, the power of the respected leader assumed almost a magical character. He made possible, as Ernest Becker put it, "the expression of forbidden impulses, secret wishes, and fantasies." As father and elder brother in the phalanx of honor and heroics, individuals such as the two attorneys condoned and supervised the appetites of conventional men for power, or rather the semblance of it. If anything went wrong, the leaders, not the anonymous participants, would have to bear the burden.

Yet it was important for the leaders' own self- and group esteem to restrict the action, much as a father would in dealing with a child dangerously close to a frightening loss of control. Too much power makes men afraid. It opens floodgates of passion not easy to shut. It destroys the crowd's unanimity, beneath which hide the ever-present anxieties of life and of death. Grayson thus demanded what the crowd really wanted: release from their own dreams of omnipotence, dreams too intense to sustain for very long. At the same time, his words of restraint implicitly reminded the listeners that those who initiated such awesome proceedings had the authority, derived from the crowd and from their own local prominence, to end them. The fantasy of heroism that fellowship evoked had to cease. The squeaks of Foster's empty cart, receding into the night, signaled the return to mundane human concerns and transiencies.

It was therefore hardly surprising that the Foster affair led to no reexamination of public policy. No journalist or judge called for the strengthening of the police and judicial systems. No preachers—Adams County boasted very few anyhow—climbed the rostrum to denounce the charivari or the ethic that made it so serviceable a device. The very opposite occurred: the launching of lynch law crusades throughout the state to hunt down other deviants from conventional standards of behavior. Even the Fosters may have thought it all had turned out for the best. The wastrel son relinquished his legal claims to Cassandra's fortune and whatever else might come to him from his father and mother's estates in future. The succeeding generations buried the memory of his disgrace as they had Susan, who still lies in the sod of Foster Fields, without a marker. People who rely upon oral tradition have very selective memories.

What was true of the clan's amnesia about James was also true for the South as a whole. The darker aspects of honor were seldom to be questioned, then or for many years to come. Individuals and sometimes groups spoke out against popular forms of injustice and honor—duels, summary hangings, mob whippings. These efforts at reform seldom received public acclamation and support. Even historians, whether native to the South or not, have not seen these expressions of public will and private esteem as part of a total cultural pattern. Instead they have been labeled tragic aberrations, or techniques by which the planter class manipulated lesser, more virtuous folk. Gentility, the nobler, brighter feature of Southern ethics, has been a more congenial topic. Certainly it was the model that Southerners have publicly revered and exalted. The selectivity was natural. Nonetheless, the higher claims of chivalry, Stoic and Christian, were put to the service of primal honor. Gentlemen like Spence Monroe Grayson often found themselves carried along on the tides of multitudes, or were driven to silent acquiescence with no chance of guiding the public into calmer moods. The choice that Grayson made in standing at the head of Foster's enemies was exactly the same one that many others would later make when "honor" cried out for secession. The prudent man was wise to stand aside, saving doubts for afterthoughts when passions died away. Thus the "innocence" of primal values, as Faulkner made clear, was an imperfect shield against misperceptions, contradictions, and thoughtless cruelty. It could even be their very source. As Hawthorne had observed, men had many voices, and more than one mask. Honor had always had many faces.

Part V: SEXUAL VIOLENCE

As we saw in the preceding discussion of the social structure of violence, gender plays a major role as a status variable in explaining how violence contributes to the maintenance of unequal patriarchal relations. In Part V, we explore the role that gender inequality plays in explaining *sexual* violence, including rape and sexual harassment. Although there are women perpetrators of sexual violence and male victims, most of the perpetrators are male and its victims female. Once we understand that sexual violence occurs in the context of gender inequality and the cultural values that support them, we can understand why, for example, the very idea of rape and its legal construction have legitimated sexual violence against women when they "deserve it" by violating gender norms. Changing legal standards both reflect and contribute to increasing standards of equal treatment in the wider social context. But Horney and Spohn show that only systematic, holistic rape law reform is likely to have any impact on the reality of rape in America.

Sexual Assault

There is little question that sexual violence occurs within a framework of gender inequality and the patriarchal cultural values that support it. But, the established *psychologically*-oriented feminist explanation of rape is problematic. The argument that "power rape" and "anger rape" are motivated by male desires to overpower and punish women by virtue of their gender is tautologous, i.e., true by definition. While we may observe that men indeed overpower women when they engage in forcible sexual intercourse and punish them by virtue of the infliction of physical and emotional pain that rape involves, this does not in itself explain why men engage in these acts. The readings in this section demonstrate how the eroticizing of aggressive sexual conduct as an expression of patriarchal values must be understood as a separate cultural source of sexual aggression against women. In the first piece, Richard Felson maintains that the *primary* motive for rape is sexual gratification. Rapists are typically sexually active individuals who use sexual coercion to obtain their objective when other approaches fail. Although many men in America may find violent sexual imagery sexually stimulating, the lack of inhibition and opportunity may play a greater role in the actual incidence of rape than the willingness to do so.

The next three chapters describe the specific cultural codes that legitimate date rape and marital rape, respectively. The literature suggests that "hypermasculine" men are attracted to women who have been socialized to accept the extremes of traditional gender-stereotyped roles. Men are supposed to be strong and overpowering, but also romantic lovers who are expected to take care of and protect "their" women. This "chivalry" has its counterpart in the socialization of women to be dependent and weak. Women who accept the code are likely to find themselves in situations in which they become vulnerable to sexual victimization. Should a woman violate the code, she is viewed as someone who "deserves" to be raped because she "asked for it." She, in turn, blames herself because she accepts the view that nice girls don't get raped, so she must have done something to "deserve it." Kanin describes how men who are socialized to accept "hypererotic" cultural perspectives concerning gender roles are likely to justify rape under a variety of conditions, especially in environments where there is strong peer support. In their study of campus fraternity life, Martin and Hummer describe how these all-male social institutions "create a sociocultural context" that "commodifies" women and legitimates sexual aggression through a code that reinforces loyalty, group protection, and secrecy.

According to the common law, marriage was a traditional defense to rape. Upon marriage, control over a woman's life transferred from her father to her husband. Thus, a woman's body became the property of her husband available to him "on demand." The chapter on marital rape examines the cultural and legal issues surrounding the historical shift in attitudes toward marital rape. Only recently has there been a significant change in the legal protection afforded women in choosing when and how to relate sexually with their spouse. Many states have changed their statutes since the Gelles article was first published in 1979. Some states now prohibit marital rape under all circumstances, but many others still allow some exemptions from prosecutions for marital rape. As recently as July 1998, the National Clearinghouse on Marital and Date Rape reported that 32 states still have some exemptions from prosecuting husbands for forcible rape. Typically, these states restrict the definition of marital rape to overt acts of violence, exempting husbands from the charge of rape in situations when a woman is physically or mentally unable to consent, for example, when she is asleep, under the influence of alcohol or drugs, or disabled. In effect, in those states, she must be a victim or threatened victim of domestic violence in order to be defined as a victim of marital rape.

In the final chapter in this section, we see how efforts to reform rape law in the United States have largely failed. In their seminal article on rape law reform, Julie Horney and Cassia Spohn argue that most rape law reform has been more symbolic than real. Part of the problem is that the very meaning of rape in both law and custom includes defenses that provide a wide array of justifications within the framework of patriarchal assumptions concerning the roles of men and women. In many jurisdictions, the burden of proof shifts to the woman to prove that she indeed "resisted" his "naturally" aggressive sexual advances, and to do so requires some sort of physical injury. The authors describe how rape law reform in the state of Michigan provides a unique case of relatively effective change as the crime of rape was changed to "criminal sexual conduct" and elements of the crime, such as the use of force and the degree of injury, could be proven separately. Prosecutions (indictments) increased and convicted rapists went to prison for longer sentences as a result. Although there were no increases in the percent of indictments that ended in conviction, the total number of rapists who went to prison increased.

Sexual Harassment

To fully comprehend its impact on its victims, sexual harassment must be understood as a form of violence against women. Although males are occasional victims of sexual harassment by women and other males, as in the case of rape and the sexual victimization of children, the vast majority of victims are female and the perpetrators are male. Sexual harassment is often overtly physical, and even when it is not, it is intimidating to its victims and coercive in the way it limits both physical and social mobility. The clearest example of this is in "quid pro quo" sexual harassment when harassers use their power to coerce their victims to submit to sexual demands.

The topic of sexual harassment is included in a separate section in the discussion of sexual violence because it is qualitatively different from other forms of sexual violence. As Catharine MacKinnon showed in her work on the sexual harassment of working women, sexual harassment is a form of sex discrimination and thus violates the fundamental civil rights of women. We begin this section with two excerpts from her classic work, *The Sexual Harassment of Working Women: A Case of Sex Discrimination* (1979).

The first chapter describes the social causes of sexual harassment, beginning with the culturally based assumption that sexual aggression by men is a natural product of biologically based gender differences. MacKinnon explores the cultural myths and legal assumptions based upon the presumed links between physical differences, gender identification, and sex-role behaviors. Sexuality, she points out, reflects a combination of all three and is not simply a "biological determinate."

In the next chapter, "The Legal Regulation of Sexual Harassment: From Tort to Sex Discrimination," MacKinnon reviews the historical shift in the legal regulation of sexual harassment from a private harm to an individual under tort law to a recognized form of discrimination that contributes to the continuing subordination of women as a group. As a private harm, women had little legal recourse unless their harasser went beyond the boundaries of what was assumed to be "natural" sexual aggression directed at attractive women. "Boys will be boys," after all. MacKinnon's work has been instrumental in bringing to public consciousness and to the courts the recognition that sexual harassment in the workplace is a form of sex discrimination.

In the final chapter, Beth Quinn summarizes the literature concerning the social causes of sexual harassment and recent changes in the legislation and case law concerning sexual harassment in the workplace.

17

Motives for Sexual Coercion

Richard B. Felson

The study of rape tends to be segregated from the study of other forms of harm-doing. Although rape is a violent crime, general theories of aggression, violence, and crime are rarely applied to rape. In this chapter, I use a social interactionist approach to aggression to examine the possible motives for rape and other forms of sexual coercion. That theory interprets coercive behavior as instrumental behavior designed to compel and deter others, to punish people for perceived misdeeds, and to obtain desired identities. Following social learning theory (from social psychology) and control theory (from criminology), I also discuss the role of inhibitions (see Malamuth, 1986). For a man to engage in sexual coercion, he must not only have a goal that would be satisfied by such behavior but must lack the inhibitions that would prevent the behavior.

Sexual coercion involves the use of contingent threats or bodily force to compel a person to engage in sexual activity. The offender, or "source," in the language of social influence theory, is almost always a male, whereas the victim or "target" is usually a female.[1] When the offender uses contingent threats, he threatens to harm the target unless she engages in sexual relations. For example, a man may threaten a woman with a weapon, an employer may threaten to fire an employee, or a spouse may threaten to seek outside companionship or leave the marriage.[2] In the case of bodily force, a man may use his superior strength to force sexual activity on a woman, or he may impose sexual relations when she is unconscious or in a condition in which consent is impossible.

It is important (although sometimes difficult) to distinguish sexual coercion from the noncoercive means that a source may use to influence a target who is unwilling or hesitant to engage in sexual relations (e.g., persuasion, deception, self-presentation, reward, sexual stimulation, arranging conducive circumstances, or encouraging the target to become intoxicated). This distinction is sometimes blurred by researchers in their attempts to demonstrate high frequencies of sexual coercion (see Gilbert, 1991).

The three major outcomes of sexual coercion are sexual behavior, harm to the target, and domination of the target. It is unclear which one of these outcomes is the goal of the action and which outcomes are incidental. Although an incident can have multiple goals, in this chapter I assume for simplicity that for a given incident of sexual coercion, one goal (and one motive) predominates. I consider these outcomes in discussing the role of social influence, retributive justice, and social identity—three social processes involved in coercive acts generally—in sexual coercion.

The model depicted in Figure 1 attempts to clarify the argument regarding social motives. It suggests that contingent threats and bodily force, if successful, produce three proximate outcomes in an incident of sexual coercion. Any of these outcomes could be the actor's proximate goal. Each proximate goal is associated with a distal goal, and each can also be considered a means to that distal goal. In other words, attainment of the proximate goal satisfies some motive. I shall refer to the diagram as I discuss each of the motives.

Sexual Compliance

Females tend to be more selective than males in their sexual behavior, restricting their sexual activity to partners with whom they have positive

---

"Motives for Sexual Coercion," by Richard B. Felson. Pp. 233–253 in *Aggression and Violence: Social Interactionist Perspectives,* edited by Richard B. Felson and James T. Tedeschi. Copyright © 1993 by the American Psychological Association. Reprinted with permission.

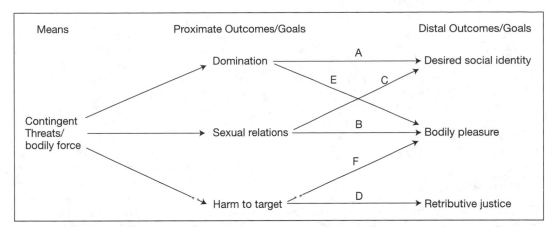

Figure 1 Alternative goals and motives for sexual coercion. Path A: Power motive. Path B: Sexual motive. Path C: Socio-sexual motive. Path D: Grievance motive. Paths E and F: Coercive-sexual motive

feelings (Ellis, 1989; Shields & Shields, 1983; Thornhill & Thornhill, 1983). They are more likely than males to interpret sex in terms of romance rather than recreation (Gagnon, 1977). The fact that people with sexual fetishes are almost exclusively male also indicates a strong sex difference in the ability to disassociate sexual response from interpersonal relationships (Gregor, 1990).[3]

As a result of sex differences in selectivity, it is not surprising that males are much more likely to attempt to influence females to have sex than the reverse, using a variety of techniques (Sorenson, Stein, Siegel, Golding, & Burnam, 1987). Furthermore, given that there can be conflict over sexual relations (e.g., a man may desire sex and a woman may be unwilling) and given that some people use force to get what they want, it would seem obvious that at least some sexual coercion is sexually motivated.

According to this point of view, the offender's immediate goal is to have sexual relations. He dominates the victim and accepts the victim's suffering as a consequence of his actions even though domination and punishment are not his goals. In other words, coercion is a means to an end, not an end in itself. He uses coercion for strategic reasons—to obtain compliance and to avoid apprehension.

Since the 1970s, most researchers have rejected sexual motivation as an explanation for rape and other forms of sexual coercion. This counterintuitive idea has been stated repeatedly and in the strongest possible terms without any reasonable evidence to support it (see Felson, 1991, for an explanation of the popularity of this idea).

Palmer (1988) reviewed and criticized the arguments against the sexual motivation for rape (see also Hagen, 1979; Shields & Shields, 1983; Symons, 1979; Thornhill & Thornhill, 1983). In general, these arguments are based on spurious reasoning and the misreporting of evidence in those few instances in which evidence is reported. For example, the facts that force is used, that some rapes are premeditated, that some rapists experience sexual dysfunction, and that the victims are not always young have all been cited as evidence against sexual motivation. As Palmer pointed out, these facts say little or nothing about the motivation for sexual coercion. Furthermore, the age distribution of victims, as I discuss later, supports a sexual explanation.

Part of the confusion arises because of the failure to recognize that sexual motivation has social psychological as well as biological elements. It does not simply reflect the pursuit of physical pleasure nor is it the product of uncontrollable biological urges. Clearly, sexual behavior satisfies other goals as well. In other words, sexual behavior—whether coercive or consensual—is partly based on nonsexual motives (Gagnon, 1977). Both could ultimately reflect quests for power, status, or self-esteem. And sexual activity can bring these rewards for women as well as for men. These complexities led Felson and Krohn (1990) to describe the motivation for some rapes as "socio-sexual" rather than sexual. In Figure 1, Path B represents the relation between sexual relations and bodily pleasure, whereas Path C represents concerns for power. Note that this is different from the feminist approach, which suggests that domination is the immediate goal of the offender.

Sexual Aspirations

If sexual motivation involves social psychological processes, it should not be related in any simple way to sexual deprivation or satiation. Kanin (1965, 1967, 1985) argued that sexual aspirations or relative deprivation is a more important factor in sexual coercion. He found subjective sexual deprivation rather than actual sexual deprivation to be positively correlated with the use of sexual coercion by college men. College men who were dissatisfied with the frequency of their sexual activity, or who indicated that a higher frequency of orgasms was necessary for them to be sexually satisfied, were more likely to engage in coercive sexual behavior. In addition, college men who used sexual coercion were likely to have more sexual experience, presumably because they engaged in greater effort to obtain partners. Similarly, rapists who have been married reported a high frequency of marital intercourse and extramarital affairs (Gebhard, Gagnon, Pomeroy, & Christenson, 1965; Goldstein, 1973; Le Maire, 1956).

Access to willing, attractive females, even in a permissive sexual atmosphere, is restricted for most males. Kanin's research suggests that young men devote considerable effort to finding women who will engage in sexual relations. The fact that some men are willing to pay a high price to engage a prostitute also indicates that there are strong barriers to sexual access. Coercion gives males a very wide choice of sexual partners.

Situational Context

Another way to examine the motivation for sexual coercion is to examine the social interaction that immediately precedes coercive behavior. This is primarily relevant to coercion involving men and women who know each other. For example, it is important to determine whether coercion is used only with other techniques and whether it is used as a first or last resort. One would expect a male whose motive is to dominate or punish his victim to prefer coercive sex to consensual sex and to use coercive methods as a first resort. On the other hand, if sexual coercion is sexually motivated, then one would expect males to use coercion as a last resort with females they know, after other methods of influence have failed.

Evidence for sexual motivation is provided by Kanin's (1967, 1985) research on high school and college-aged men. He found that males who used sexual coercion were much more likely to use other methods to encourage sexual relations such as falsely professing love or attempting to get a female intoxicated. One assumes that these behaviors preceded coercive behavior. This evidence suggests that sexual coercion is used along with noncoercive techniques, that it is more likely to be used as a last resort, and that coercion itself has no special attraction for these men.

Sexual motivation is also apparent in incidents of rape among the Mehinaku Indians of Brazil (Gregor, 1990). There is a high level of promiscuity in the tribe. As in other societies, men show a much stronger proclivity to engage in sexual activity—they describe unwilling women as "stingy with their genitals"—and they initiate most sexual interactions. The men attempt to encourage women to engage in sexual relations frequently by offering fish in exchange. On occasion, when women refuse, the men use some level of coercion, described vaguely as "pulling," to force the women into the bush.

The nature of sexual scripts may also increase the use of coercion among sexually motivated males. The typical consensual encounter involves an implicit request by the male and compliance by the female. Rather than making an explicit verbal request, the male initiates intimate activity and proceeds to the next level of intimacy unless he meets resistance. Misunderstandings may result because males may misread ambiguous sexual signals (Goodchilds & Zellman, 1984; Muehlenhard, Friedman, & Thomas, 1985; Muehlenhard & Linton, 1987) or because of a general tendency for men to overestimate women's sexual interest (Abbey, 1982;

Shotland & Craig, 1988). Females may also avoid expressing a firm refusal to avoid an embarrassing scene. When a female refuses a sexual overture, it implies rejection and violates rules of politeness (Goffman, 1955).

As a result of the sexual script, males may treat initial resistance as an opening bargaining position rather than as a final offer. This interpretation is not necessarily inaccurate as indicated by reports from college women that they sometimes engage in "token resistance" (i.e., they resist initially when they are actually interested in sexual activity; Muehlenhard & Hollabaugh, 1988). In these instances, females may believe that they decrease their power and status by giving in too easily.

There is also evidence that females are sometimes ambivalent about whether they want to engage in sexual activity or about the level of intimacy they desire (Muehlenhard & Hollabaugh, 1988). Knowing this, males may use persuasion or attempt to sexually stimulate females to influence them. Males may not view these tactics as aggressive or inappropriate and, as a result, their inhibitions may not be activated. Furthermore, during the "negotiation process," sexually aroused males may have lower inhibitions about using coercion and other techniques that violate their moral standards.

The role of sexual motivation was demonstrated in a study of 71 college students who had committed rape (Kanin, 1985). In every case, the rape occurred during a date after an intensive consensual sexual encounter, most commonly involving oral–genital sex. If date rapes occur when males are sexually aroused, it is likely that sexual motivation is involved.

Attractiveness

If sexual coercion is sexually motivated, then one would expect that those who are physically attractive would be more likely to be victimized. This issue has been examined indirectly in research on the age of rape victims. There is clearly a negative association between age and physical attractiveness if one excludes the very young for whom there are sexual taboos. The attraction of men for young women in consensual sex is apparently found in every culture (Thornhill & Thornhill, 1983). Homosexual men

also show a preference for young men (Bell & Weinberg, 1978).

There is clear evidence of a very strong relation between age and rape victimization. According to the National Crime Survey, only 11% of the rape victims are 35 or older, and only 4% are 50 or older (Bureau of Justice Statistics, 1985). This same pattern is apparent in the rape of male victims. One could argue that this is related to the activity patterns of youth (Cohen & Felson, 1979). Young women are more likely to go out at night and to date, and their greater contact with a variety of men may put them at greater risk. In fact, they are more likely to be victims of crime generally (Bureau of Justice Statistics, 1985).

Although differential opportunity may be a factor, the evidence suggests that it is only a partial explanation of the age–victimization relation. Felson and Krohn (1990) attempted to control for differential opportunity by comparing crimes of robbery with crimes in which rape was committed in conjunction with robbery. During the robbery of a woman, the offender often has the opportunity to rape her as well. The evidence suggests that during a robbery involving a male offender and a female victim, a rape is more likely to occur if the victim is young. The average age of robbery victims is 35, whereas the average age of robbery–rape victims is less than 28. This suggests that rapists have a strong preference for youth, which suggests that they prefer physically attractive victims.

Interviews with rapists also suggest that attractiveness is an important factor in their selection of victims (Ageton, 1983; Queen's Bench Foundation, 1978). Additional evidence comes from a study of sexual violence in a prison for men (Lockwood, 1980). Lockwood found that most victims were young, slim White men. Interviews with inmates suggested that men who were young and slim were preferred because they were viewed as more attractive and as most highly resembling women. It is difficult to explain this pattern in terms of differential opportunity.

Sexual Coercion in Prison

Because heterosexual sexual access is either forbidden or severely restricted in prison and because many inmates are young and at the height of their sexual interest, it is not surprising that homosexual relations occur. The use of sexual coercion in part reflects the fact that prisons are filled with men who lack inhibitions about using violence. It may also reflect the reluctance of many heterosexual men to take the "passive role" in homosexual sex. In other words, there are many inmates willing to play the active role and relatively few willing to play the passive role. As a result, it is probably difficult to find partners to engage in consensual sexual activity. Powerful inmates who seek sexual satisfaction are likely to force weaker inmates to play the passive role. This is similar to the situation outside prison wherein there is a surplus of males and a scarcity of females interested in casual sex.

That a man's role in coercive encounters affects his power and status in prison does not necessarily imply that power and status are the goals of these actions. If power is the goal, then one would expect inmates to prefer unwilling over willing targets, and one would expect inmates to brag about incidents of sexual coercion to others. On the other hand, a sexually motivated offender is likely to prefer consensual to coercive sex and to use coercion as a last resort. Evidence that inmates use noncoercive as well as coercive techniques to influence other inmates to engage in sexual activity suggests a sexual motive (Lockwood, 1980).

Sexual Arousal and Violence

Some rape offenders may be sexually aroused by the use of coercion. This is represented in Figure 1 by Paths E and F, which suggest that harming the victim or dominating her may be associated with bodily pleasure. However, evidence from laboratory research on sexual arousal of rapists suggests that rapists are generally not more stimulated by violent sex than they are by nonviolent sex (e.g., Abel, Barlow, Blanchard, & Guild, 1977; Quinsey, Chaplin, & Varney, 1981). In these studies, films of violent and consensual sex were shown to rapists and to control groups, and penile tumescence was measured. The studies consistently showed that convicted rapists were no more likely to be sexually aroused by depictions of rape than they were by depictions of consensual sexual acts. Nonrapists, on the other hand, were less aroused by depic-

tions of rape than by depictions of consensual sex. This pattern suggests that rapists differ from other men in terms of their inhibitions, not in terms of any preference for sexual violence. Unlike other men, the arousal of rapists is not inhibited by viewing sexual violence.[4]

In sum, there is some evidence to support the idea that many acts of sexual coercion are sexually motivated. Young men with high sexual aspirations are more likely to use sexual coercion as well as noncoercive techniques to obtain sexual compliance. In addition, sexual coercion tends to be used as a last resort in incidents involving people who know each other, after other techniques have failed. The ambiguity of consensual sexual scripts may also lead males to misread female resistance and to fail to realize that their behavior is offensive to females. Finally, the targets of sexual coercion tend to be young, and youth is associated with attractiveness. Age differences in opportunity for victimization can only explain part of this pattern.

Sexual Coercion as an Expression of Grievances

Sexual coercion, like other forms of coercion, could reflect the expression of a grievance. Knowing the humiliation the victim will experience, some men may use sexual coercion as a form of punishment. The offender may be angry at the victim for some perceived misdeed, and he may believe that she deserves to be punished. In this case, the punishment is an act of retributive justice, and the harm to the victim is "just dessert" (see Path D in Figure 1).

This explanation suggests that males who engage in sexual coercion have been involved in a conflict with the victim beforehand and that they feel aggrieved. The social interaction is likely to be similar to homicides and assaults in which verbal conflict escalates, culminating in physical and sexual attacks. Another possibility is that males feel aggrieved when females resist their noncoercive attempts to encourage sexual activity and use sexual coercion as punishment. If men expect sexual relations for whatever reason and women refuse, the former may feel aggrieved.

One would expect that grievances are much more likely to be involved in incidents involving people who know each other (Black, 1983).[5] In particular, one might expect sexual coercion to be associated with conflicts between couples who are married, estranged, or involved in some other romantic or sexual relationship. Sexual coercion may be particularly common among estranged couples when the woman is no longer receptive to a sexual relationship. Men may use sexual coercion to punish women for insults, rejection, refusing to engage in consensual sex, infidelity, or some petty grievance. If homicides and assaults can involve petty grievances, so can rapes.

Nonstrategic Punishment

The strategic use of coercion is oriented toward compliance.[6] If men punish victims during incidents of sexual coercion for nonstrategic reasons (e.g., if they use gratuitous violence), it suggests that their immediate goal is to harm. An offender who values harm is likely to harm the victim in a variety of ways: He may insult or humiliate the victim, and he may physically attack the victim even when she complies.[7] On the other hand, one would expect sexually motivated offenders to use enough threatening language to obtain compliance but otherwise treat their victims relatively well. They might even engage in acts of tenderness normally associated with consensual sex. Although such behaviors have been reported by rape victims, the frequency is unclear (MacDonald, 1971). No one has ever studied in a systematic way how men who engage in sexual coercion otherwise treat their victims.

There is evidence that physical violence tends to be used sparingly in incidents of sexual coercion (Amir, 1971). For example, Ageton (1983) found that only a small proportion of young men use much physical force during incidents of sexual coercion. Results from the National Crime Survey also indicate that there are relatively few injuries not related to the rape itself (Bureau of Justice Statistics, 1985). Finally, sexual coercion among college students rarely involves a physical attack (Koss, Gidycz, & Wisniewski, 1987).

Gratuitous violence sometimes does occur, however. If nonstrategic coercion reflects an expression of grievances, one would expect it to be more frequent in acts of coercion involving estranged couples and others who know each other. A number of studies suggest that this is the case (Amir, 1971; Koss, Dinero, & Seibel, 1988). For example, Felson and Krohn (1990) found that victims were more likely to be physically injured in instances in which the offender and victim were an estranged couple. This effect is observed even when offenders have a weapon (and thus a credible threat) and when victims do not resist. Presumably, in many of these instances, the offender rapes and beats up his exwife or exgirlfriend as an act of punishment.

Felson and Krohn (1990) provided evidence that rapes involving older offenders and victims are more likely to involve gratuitous violence and therefore a punishment motive and are less likely to involve sexual motivation. Using National Crime Survey data, they found that victims were more likely to be physically injured during a rape when offenders and victims were older. The positive association between age and violence was striking given that youths are much more violent during other crimes and in other contexts (Gottfredson & Hirschi, 1990). This pattern is consistent with evidence that sexual motivation declines for men as they get older (Gagnon, 1977) and with the fact that youths are perceived as more sexually attractive. It suggests that incidents involving offenders with lower sexual interests and less sexually attractive victims tend to involve more gratuitous violence.

Grievances Against Groups

Another possibility is that some men are angry at women generally and that they express this anger through sexual coercion. In this case, the act of coercion involves a grievance against the general category of which the victim is a member. The evidence is mixed concerning the relation between sexual coercion and hostility toward women (Buss & Durkee, 1957; Koss & Dinero, 1987; Rada, Laws, & Kellner, 1976; Scully & Marolla, 1985). However, even if one were to find a relation between hostility toward women and rape, it would not necessarily imply that sexual coercion is an expression of this general hostility. It is also possible that negative attitudes toward women reduce men's inhibitions concerning the use of sexual coercion. For example, a sexually motivated man might use coercion if he lacks concern for women (Malamuth, 1986). This will be discussed further.

There are reasons to be skeptical of explanations of interpersonal violence that emphasize hatred for groups. Most incidents of homicide and assault are directed against individuals for whom the offender has a grievance. In spite of recent emphasis on "bias crimes" (i.e., crimes based on group prejudice), such incidents are quite rare. For example, in the United States, one might expect a high level of interracial crime based on group prejudices. Most crimes, however, including rape, are intraracial (e.g., Amir, 1971). In spite of the prejudice that some Whites feel toward Blacks, the incidence of Whites raping Blacks is extremely rare (South & Felson, 1990).

Interracial rapes committed by Blacks have sometimes been interpreted in terms of the perpetrator's hatred for Whites. It has been argued that some Blacks rape White women to obtain vengeance against White men (LaFree, 1982). The evidence does not support this point of view. First, South and Felson (1990) found that during robberies of female victims, Blacks were slightly less likely to rape the woman if she was White than if she was Black. If rapes by Blacks reflect their grievances against Whites, there should be a preference for White victims. Furthermore, they found no evidence that interracial rapes were more frequent in metropolitan areas in which there was greater interracial conflict or inequality (see also O'Brien, 1987). Although Lockwood (1980) found that Blacks tended to rape White men in prison, he found no evidence that it reflected grievances against Whites.[8]

Deviant Targets

There is some evidence that men are more likely to use sexual coercion against women they consider deviant. For example, Amir (1971) found that about 20% of the rape victims he studied had "bad reputations," whereas another 20% had police records, many of them for sexual misconduct. Supporting evidence also comes from Kanin's (1985) study of the effect of date rape on the reputations of male college students.

Relatively few of these young men (7–9%) believed that their best friends would respond favorably if they knew that the respondent attempted to coerce a "more or less regular date" to have sexual intercourse. On the other hand, the percentages were much higher for "bar pickups," "known teasers," "economic exploiters," and women with "loose reputations." For example, 81% of rapists and 40% of the control group indicated that they would get a positive response from their friends if the woman was a "known teaser." This suggests that some men believe that rape is justifiable against women who violate certain moral standards. Amir's evidence suggests that these women tend to be selected as targets.

There are at least two interpretations of these results. First, some men may feel personally aggrieved against these women and may attempt to punish them for their alleged wrongdoings. Second, it may be that men are sexually motivated but are disinhibited from using sexual coercion with women whom they perceive as deviant. In other words, they use the target's bad reputation as a justification for their behavior. This seems more likely given the evidence that men do not usually engage in nonstrategic violence and the evidence supporting sexual motivation. Furthermore, neither a "bar pick-up" nor a woman with a "loose reputation" is likely to cause the respondent or his friends to feel personally aggrieved.

In summary, there is indirect evidence that some acts of sexual coercion involve the expression of grievances. The use of gratuitous or nonstrategic violence during some of these incidents implies that men seek to punish the victim and not just gain compliance. That most incidents do not involve gratuitous violence suggests that punishment is not usually the motive for sexual coercion. However, some males may feel justified using coercion against females they perceive as not worthy of respect.

Power and Domination

By definition, power and domination are involved in all acts of coercion, sexual or otherwise. The issue is whether, as some feminists claim, power is the goal of sexual coercion, that is, whether men use sexual coercion *because* it allows them to feel dominant over female victims (Deming & Eppy, 1981).[9] Because there is no clear theoretical statement of this approach, it is difficult to imagine how it might be tested (e.g., Brownmiller, 1975).[10]

The aggression literature suggests a way that the power motive can be reconceptualized to make it testable and to connect it to a broader literature. That literature examines the role of social identities and impression management and suggests that those who engage in coercion are sometimes seeking to appear more powerful to themselves or others (Felson, 1978; Luckenbill, 1977; Toch, 1969). Some acts of sexual coercion could also reflect this motive. A man may seek to dominate a woman by compelling her to engage in sexual relations, thereby attaining a social identity as powerful (see Path C in Figure 1). He may demonstrate power to the woman he is bullying, to himself, or to some third party. He may also view his ability to control the target as an accomplishment.[11]

The emphasis of the literature on social identities and aggression, however, is on retaliation (Felson, 1978). It suggests that people retaliate when they perceive that they have been attacked to avoid appearing weak. Males may feel that they have been attacked when females reject their sexual requests. Because a female generally requires positive feelings before having sexual relations, her decision about whether to have sexual relations has identity implications for the male. By complying or turning him down, she communicates her evaluation of him. Her consent grants him special status, whereas her refusal denies him that status. (On the other hand, a male's decision to have sexual relations with a female does not necessarily imply anything about his feelings for her.) For this reason, males may view sexual noncompliance as an attack on their identity and may retaliate. They may also feel aggrieved and may punish females out of a sense of justice.

Some of the incidents involving estranged couples described previously may reflect this process. For example, a man whose wife has become involved with another man may feel that he has been made to appear weak and may attack his wife in retaliation. The "jilted lover" may use sexual coercion as well as other forms of coercion to save face. In general, sexual relations have profound status implications for men and women and are therefore a significant source of conflict.

If offenders are oriented toward power, then they should prefer coercive sex to consensual sex. To coerce the victim to do something he or she would not do otherwise demonstrates power. Thus, the power/identity explanation predicts that men who commit sexual coercion prefer resistance, whereas the socio-sexual explanation predicts that men who commit sexual coercion prefer compliance. For example, according to the power explanation, sexually coercive men prefer to date women who are uninterested in sexual relations. They do not attempt to influence women to have consensual sex using noncoercive techniques but use coercive techniques as a first resort. This profile is not consistent with Kanin's (1985) evidence, described earlier.

If some acts of sexual coercion involve impression management, then one would expect them to be affected by the perceived reaction of third parties, as are other forms of coercion (see Felson, 1978, for a review). For most audiences, however, men who use coercion against women are likely to be viewed negatively by an audience. Men who attack women are sometimes called cowardly, indicating that they are perceived as low in power.[12] Furthermore, evidence suggests that coercive incidents involving men and women (unlike intragender incidents) are less likely to escalate if there is an audience present (Felson, 1982).

The only direct evidence regarding the effect of third parties on sexual coercion comes from Kanin's (1985) study of the effect of date rape on the reputations of college students. Recall that relatively few rapists or nonrapists believed that they would enhance their reputation by using sexual coercion against a "more or less regular date." On the other hand, many rapists and, to a lesser extent, other men, indicated that they would get a positive response if the woman was some sort of deviant target. In general, it appears that there are some audiences that respond favorably to the use of sexual coercion, at least against a deviant target.

Individual Differences

Most males have sexual interests, most have at least an occasional grievance with a female, and most would like to avoid appearing weak. However, most males do not use sexual coercion. Therefore, there must be some individual characteristics that distinguish males who use sexual coercion from those who do not. In part, males may vary in the strength of goals satisfied by this behavior. Thus, Kanin's (1985) work suggests that men who use sexual coercion tend to have high sexual aspirations. However, social learning theory and control theory suggest that learned inhibitions and disinhibitions are also important. Men who engage in sexual coercion are less likely to have certain inhibitions that would discourage this behavior.

One can conceive of two types of inhibitions (or disinhibitions): those related to women specifically (i.e., sexist attitudes) and those related to the use of coercion and exploitative behavior generally.

Sexist Attitudes

Considerable attention has been paid to the effect of sexist attitudes or "rape myths" on the use of sexual coercion. It has been argued that men who use sexual coercion tend to lack concern for women, view women as sex objects, believe that women want to be raped, or have some other attitude related to women. This reflects the feminist argument that sexual coercion is produced by sexism.

The evidence that sexist attitudes correlate with sexual coercion is mixed (Ageton, 1983; Howells & Wright, 1978; Rapaport & Burkhart, 1984; for reviews, see Koss & Leonard, 1984; Malamuth, 1981). However, even if cross-sectional correlations between certain attitudes and coercive sexual behavior could be demonstrated, their causal interpretations are unclear. It may be that men express these beliefs to justify their use of coercion (Koss, Leonard, Beezley, & Oros, 1985). For example, a rapist may report that the woman enjoyed the incident to justify his behavior. The issue is a general one in the attitude/behavior literature. The causal interpretation of correlations between attitudes and behaviors is unclear. Longitudinal research would be useful to examine whether such beliefs in fact have a causal impact on coercive sexual behavior.

If attitudes toward women do have causal effects on sexual coercion, it must still be determined whether attitudes toward women act as instigators or disinhibitors of sexual coercion. As indicated earlier, a man who is hostile toward a woman (or toward women generally) may use sexual coercion to punish her. In this case, his hostility instigates the attack, and his goal is to express his grievance. On the other hand, a man may have some other goal, but his hostility toward women may reduce his inhibitions about harming them.

There are at least two ways to determine whether hostility instigates or disinhibits sexual coercion. First, if a man engages in nonstrategic attacks against a woman, it would suggest that his goal is to punish her and that hostility is an instigator rather than a disinhibitor of his attack. Second, if attitudes are disinhibitors one would expect them to interact statistically with goals in their effect on behavior. For example, one might predict that the relation between sexual aspirations and sexual coercion to be stronger when men have negative attitudes toward women. A statistical interaction between hostility toward women and sexual aspirations would suggest that hostility removes inhibitions. On the other hand, if hostility toward women has only main effects on sexual coercion, it would suggest support for the punishment model. Supporting evidence for the inhibition argument comes from work by Malamuth (1986), who found interactions between sexual arousal to rape scenes and various attitudes in their effects on sexual coercion.

General Inhibitions

General inhibitions refer to inhibitions that are not specific to females; males who lack these inhibitions may not treat males any better than they treat females. According to this point of view, men who engage in sexual coercion are likely to be the same men who engage in other forms of coercion and in other exploitative behaviors. The argument is consistent with evidence that those who commit crime rarely specialize (Gottfredson & Hirschi, 1990).[13] The evidence regarding rape offenders reveals the same pattern: Few men specialize in rape. The criminal records of those who have been convicted of rape tend to be similar to the criminal records of those who have been convicted of other crimes (Alder, 1984; Wolfgang, Figlio, & Sellin, 1972).[14] Rapists are usually versatile offenders, committing property crimes as well as violent crimes. In addition, there is evidence that convicted rapists are similar to men convicted of other offenses in their attitudes toward women and toward women's rights (Howells & Wright, 1978).

If rapists are versatile offenders, then one would expect the characteristics of individuals that predict sexual coercion to be the same ones that predict involvement in crime and deviant behavior generally. Those who commit crime tend to have similar goals as the rest of us, but they lack certain internal and external controls (Gottfredson & Hirschi, 1990; Hirschi, 1969). Either they have failed to internalize certain moral inhibitions, or they lack self-control, or they do not have the social bonds to conventional society that increase the costs of engaging in criminal or deviant behavior. There is evidence that the same external controls that predict criminal behavior in general also predict sexual coercion (Ageton, 1983).

Conclusion

There is substantial evidence that many acts of sexual coercion are sexually motivated. For example, the evidence that offenders have high sexual aspirations, that they also use noncoercive methods to encourage sexual relations, and that they usually choose young women all point to a sexual motive. The use of coercive and noncoercive influence techniques may in part be based on sex differences in sexuality (whether learned or innate). That females are more selective than males creates conflict between the sexes and leads some males to use coercion to produce compliance. Similarly, strong sexual interests among prison inmates but a scarcity of inmates willing to play a passive role in homosexual encounters leads to the use of sexual coercion in prison.

Sexual coercion, like other forms of coercion, undoubtedly has a variety of motives, however. There is evidence that in some instances, the offender is motivated by a desire to punish the victim. This is suggested by findings that incidents of sexual coercion involving estranged couples or older offenders and victims are more likely to involve gratuitous violence. Although there is no convincing evidence that sexual coercion is motivated by power concerns, this seems a reasonable hypothesis given the importance of social identities in other forms of aggression.

The evidence is also clear that men who engage in sexual coercion engage in other forms of coercion, crime, and deviance. Explanations of sexual coercion must therefore incorporate insights from the general study of crime and deviance. If men who use sexual coercion are versatile offenders, we must examine those general factors that disinhibit their behavior.

There may also be situational factors that disinhibit the use of sexual coercion. In particular, it appears that some men justify sexual coercion against women whom they perceive as deviant. These women are viewed as "fair game." In addition, because of the nature of sexual scripts, men sometimes mistakenly believe that women are interested in sexual relations. They may treat initial resistance as an opening bargaining position rather than a final offer. They may pressure women if they sense any ambivalence. If men do not view their behavior as aggressive, then their inhibitions are not likely to be activated. In general, the negotiation process involved in consensual sexual relations is likely to result in at least some degree of coercive behavior.

In conclusion, a social interactionist theory provides a promising approach to the understanding of sexual coercion. Most important, it clarifies some theoretical arguments in the literature and suggests some testable hypotheses. Sexual coercion will be better understood when we apply general knowledge about coercion and crime to this behavior and avoid a narrow, ideological approach.

Notes

1. According to the National Crime Survey, 7.3% rapes of people living in the community involved men raping other men.

2. Note that some acts of coercion are legal and may be viewed as morally appropriate (e.g., when someone threatens to leave their spouse because of the lack of a sexual relationship).

3. These sex differences in sexuality may have a biological basis (e.g., Ellis, 1989; Thornhill & Thornhill, 1983). Because sex differences in sexual response have obvious reproductive consequences, one would expect them to have evolutionary significance.

4. It is possible, however, that a small percentage of rapists are aroused by violence but that their preferences are not detectable in the relatively small samples that form the basis of this research.

5. Grievances are possible between strangers, however (Wolfgang, 1958).

6. The offender may also use coercion to discourage the victim from going to the police. Also, some rape victims report that the offender used violence to force them to take a more active role during the sex act (MacDonald, 1971).

7. It is possible, however, that men who seek to punish the victim use sexual coercion but no other type of punishment. Still, one would predict that gratuitous violence is more likely when the offender values punishment rather than compliance.

8. White targets were preferred, in part, because they were viewed as vulnerable; they lacked support from third parties.

9. Some feminists favor a more sociological version of the power thesis (e.g., Brownmiller, 1975). They argue that the function of sexual coercion is to control women and to keep them in traditional roles. Rape is attributed to a patriarchal social context that encourages coercive behavior against women. This approach does not focus on the goals of individuals but views offenders as acting unwittingly as agents of social control. Gregor (1990) described a form of group rape in a Brazilian Indian tribe that fits this description. The threat of rape is used to prevent women from observing certain male rituals. Because of their fear, the women complied with the rule, and a group rape had not occurred for 40 years. That such a pattern is rarely observed in other societies suggests that rape is generally not a social control mechanism developed by societies to control women.

10. Groth, Nicholas, Burgess, and Holmstrom (1977) classified 65% of their sample of convicted rapists as motivated by power, but their classification scheme seems arbitrary. In particular, they give no evidence to distinguish power from sexual motivation. For a critique of their classification, see Palmer (1988).

11. Some rapists report that they enjoy the power they exercise over their victims (Scully & Marolla, 1985).

12. If retaliation reflects an attempt to recover self-esteem, it would not be affected by the presence of an audience.

13. Not only do they commit many different types of crimes, they also tend to drink and smoke heavily and be involved in traffic accidents. Gottfredson and Hirschi (1990) argued that low self-control is the common element in these behaviors.

14. In addition, the social–demographic characteristics of rapists tend to be similar to those of other types of offenders (Alder, 1984).

References

Abbey, A. (1982). Sex differences in attributions for friendly behavior. Do males misperceive females' friendliness? *Journal of Personality and Social Psychology, 42,* 830–838.

Abel, G. G., Barlow, D. H., Blanchard, E. B., & Guild, D. (1977). The components of rapists' sexual arousal. *Archives of General Psychiatry, 34,* 895–903.

Ageton, S. (1983). *Sexual assault among adolescents.* Lexington, MA: Lexington Books.

Alder, C. (1984). The convicted rapist. A sexual or a violent offender? *Criminal Justice and Behavior, 11,* 157–177.

Amir, M. (1971). *Patterns in forcible rape.* Chicago: University of Chicago Press.

Bell, A. P., & Weinberg, M. S. (1978). *Homosexualities: A study of diversity among men & women.* New York: Simon & Schuster.

Black, D. (1983). Crime as social control. *American Sociological Review, 48,* 34–45.

Brownmiller, S. (1975). *Against our will: Men, women and rape.* New York: Simon & Schuster.

Bureau of Justice Statistics. (1985). *The crime of rape*. Washington, DC: U.S. Department of Justice.

Buss, A. H., & Durkee, A. (1957). An inventory for assessing different kinds of hostility. *Journal of Consulting Psychology, 21*, 343–349.

Cohen, L. E., & Felson, M. (1979). Social change and crime rate trends: A routine activity approach. *American Sociological Review, 44*, 588–608.

Deming, M. B., & Eppy, A. (1981). The sociology of rape. *Sociology and Social Research, 64*, 357–380.

Ellis, L. (1989). *Theories of rape: Inquiries into the causes of sexual aggression*. New York: Hemisphere.

Felson, R. B. (1978). Aggression as impression management. *Social Psychology, 41*, 205–213.

Felson, R. B. (1982). Impression management and the escalation of aggression and violence. *Social Psychology Quarterly, 45*, 245–254.

Felson, R. B. (1991). Blame analysis: Accounting for the behavior of protected groups. *American Sociologist, 22*, 5–24.

Felson, R. B., & Krohn, M. (1990). Motives for rape. *Journal of Research in Crime and Delinquency, 27*, 222–242.

Gagnon, J. H. (1977). *Human sexualities*. Glenview, IL: Scott, Foresman.

Gebhard, P. H., Gagnon, J. H., Pomeroy, W. B., & Christenson, C. V. (1965). *Sex offenders: An analysis of types*. New York: Harper & Row.

Gilbert, N. (1991). The phantom epidemic of sexual assault. *Public Interest, Spring*, 54–65.

Goffman, E. (1955). On face-work: An analysis of ritual elements in social interaction. *Psychiatry, 18*, 213–231.

Goldstein, M. J. (1973). Exposure to erotic stimuli and sexual deviance. *Journal of Social Issues, 29*, 197–219.

Goodchilds, J. D., & Zellman, G. L. (1984). Sexual signaling and sexual aggression in adolescent relationships. In N. M. Malamuth & E. Donnerstein (Eds.), *Pornography and sexual aggression* (pp. 233–243). San Diego, CA: Academic Press.

Gottfredson, M., & Hirschi, T. (1990). *A general theory of crime*. Stanford, CA: Stanford University Press.

Gregor, T. (1990). Male dominance and sexual coercion. In J. W. Stigler, R. A. Shweder, & G. Herdt (Eds.), *Cultural psychology: Essays on comparative human development* (pp. 477–495). Cambridge, MA: Cambridge University Press.

Groth, A. N., Burgess, A. W., & Holmstrom, L. L. (1977). Rape: power, anger, and sexuality. *American Journal of Psychiatry, 134*, 1239–1243.

Hagen, R. (1979). *The biosexual factor*. New York: Doubleday.

Hirschi, T. (1969). *Causes of delinquency*. Berkeley: University of California Press.

Howells, K., & Wright, E. (1978). The sexual attitudes of aggressive sexual offenders. *British Journal of Criminology, 18*, 170–173.

Kanin, E. J. (1965). Male sex aggression and three psychiatric hypotheses. *Journal of Sex Research, 1*, 227–229.

Kanin, E. J. (1967). An examination of sexual aggression as a response to sexual frustration. *Journal of Marriage and the Family, 3*, 428–433.

Kanin, E. J. (1985). Date rapists: Differential sexual socialization and relative deprivation. *Archives of Sexual Behavior, 6*, 67–76.

Koss, M. P., & Dinero, T. E. (1987, January). *Predictors of sexual aggression among a national sample of male college students*. Paper presented at the New York Academy of Sciences Conference, Human Sexual Aggression: Current Perspective, New York City.

Koss, M. P., Dinero, T. E., & Seibel, C. A. (1988). Stranger and acquaintance rape: Are there differences in the victim's experience? *Psychology of Women Quarterly, 12*, 1–24.

Koss, M. P., Gidyez, C. A., & Wisniewski, N. (1987). The scope of rape: Incidence and prevalence of sexual aggression and victimization in a national sample of students in higher education. *Journal of Consulting and Clinical Psychology, 55*, 162–170.

Koss, M. P., & Leonard, K. E. (1984). Sexually aggressive men: Empirical findings and theoretical implications. In N. M. Malamuth & E. I. Donnerstein (Eds.), *Pornography and sexual aggression* (pp. 213–232). San Diego, CA: Academic Press.

Koss, M. P., Leonard, K. E., Beezley, D. A., & Oros, C. J. (1985). Non-stranger-sexual aggression: A discriminate analysis classification. *Sex Roles, 12*, 981–992.

LaFree, G. D. (1982). Male power and female victimization: Toward a theory of interracial rape. *American Journal of Sociology, 88*, 311–328.

Le Maire, L. (1956). Danish experiences regarding the castration of sexual offenders. *Journal of Criminal Law, Criminology, and Police Science, 47*, 294–310.

Lockwood, D. (1980). *Prison sexual violence*. New York: Elsevier.

Luckenbill, D. F. (1977). Criminal homicide as a situated transaction. *Social Problems, 25*, 176–186.

MacDonald, J. M. (1971). *Rape offenders and their victims*. Springfield, IL: Charles C Thomas.

Malamuth, N. M. (1981). Rape proclivity among males. *Journal of Social Issues, 37,* 138–157.

Malamuth, N. M. (1986). Predictors of naturalistic sexual aggression. *Journal of Personality and Social Psychology, 50,* 953–962.

Muehlenhard, C. L., & Hollabaugh, L. C. (1988). Do women sometimes say no when they mean yes? The prevalence and correlates of women's token resistance to sex. *Journal of Personality and Social Psychology, 54,* 872–889.

Muehlenhard, C. L., & Linton, M. A. (1987). Date rape and sexual aggression in dating situations: Incidence and risk factors. *Journal of Counseling Psychology, 34,* 186–196.

O'Brien, R. M. (1987). The interracial nature of violent crimes: A reexamination. *American Journal of Sociology, 92,* 817–835.

Palmer, C. T. (1988). Twelve reasons why rape is not sexually motivated: A skeptical examination. *Journal of Sex Research, 25,* 512–530.

Queen's Bench Foundation. (1978). *Rape prevention and resistance*. San Francisco: Queen's Bench Foundation.

Quinsey, V. L., Chaplin, T. C., & Varney, G. A. (1981). A comparison of rapists' and non-sex offender's sexual preferences for mutually consenting sex, rape, and physical abuse of women. *Behavioral Assessment, 3,* 127–135.

Rada, R. T., Laws, D. R., & Kellner, R. (1976). Plasma testosterone levels in the rapist. *Psychosomatic Medicine, 38,* 257–268.

Rapaport, K., & Burkhart, B. R. (1984). Personality and attitudinal characteristics of sexually coercive college males. *Journal of Abnormal Psychology, 93,* 216–221.

Scully, D., & Marolla, J. (1984). Convicted rapists' vocabulary of motive: Excuses and justifications. *Social Problems, 31,* 530–544.

Scully, D., & Marolla, J. (1985). Riding the bull at Gilley's: Convicted rapists describe the rewards of rape. *Social Problems, 32,* 251–263.

Shields, W. M., & Shields, L. M. (1983). Forcible rape: An evolutionary perspective. *Ethology and Sociobiology, 4,* 115–136.

Sorenson, S. B., Stein, J. A., Siegel, J. M., Golding, J. M., & Burnam, M. A. (1987). The prevalence of adult sexual assault: The Los Angeles Epidemiologic Catchment Area Project. *American Journal of Epidemiology, 126,* 1154–1164.

South, S. J., & Felson, R. B. (1990). The racial patterning of rape. *Social Forces, 69,* 71–93.

Symons, D. (1979). *The evolution of human sexuality*. New York: Oxford University Press.

Thornhill, R., & Thornhill, N. W. (1983). Human rape: An evolutionary analysis. *Ethology and Sociobiology, 4,* 137–173.

Toch, H. (1969). *Violent men: An inquiry into the psychology of violence*. Chicago: Aldine.

Wolfgang, M. (1958). *Patterns in criminal homicide*. Philadelphia: University of Pennsylvania Press.

Wolfgang, M., Figlio, R. M., & Sellin, T. (1972). *Delinquency in a birth cohort*. Chicago: University of Chicago Press.

18

Date Rapists: Differential Sexual Socialization and Relative Deprivation

Eugene J. Kanin

Introduction

There is a long tradition among a number of academic disciplines of attributing sexual deviance to a paucity of legitimate sexual outlets. The central theme is that deviance is an adaptation to the frustration of the "normal" sex drive. For example, the hoboes' homosexual activities and their association with prostitutes have been seen as the consequence of a nonmarital existence (Anderson, 1923). Cohen (1961) observed that Jamaican girls can turn to homosexuality when deprived of heterosexual intercourse for prolonged periods. Others have depicted deviant sexual adaptations in sex-segregated penal institutions (Fishman, 1934; Clemmer, 1958; Sykes, 1958; Lockwood, 1980) and in areas having distorted sex ratios (Wheeler, 1960). Perhaps the most frequently heard justification for legalized prostitution focuses on its ability to curtail rape. Bonger (1916) long ago viewed unemployment and the resultant inability to marry as conditions precipitating rape. Psychiatrists have also held that sexual frustrations can result in explosive sexual expressions (Cohen et al., 1971; Guttmacher, 1951; Karpman, 1954). Recently, some criminologists have strongly implied that rape is the consequence of the male's inability to acquire sexual activity legitimately (Clark and Lewis, 1977). And lastly, trying to explain the differential rape rates of Boston and Los Angeles, sociologists have applied the concept of relative frustration (Chappell et al., 1977). Essentially, they contend that it is sexually less frustrating to be rejected by a woman in a sexu-

ally restrictive society than in a sexually permissive setting, thereby hypothesizing higher rates for the latter.

It seems in order to acknowledge that the most influential perspective today largely opposes the idea that sexual frustration is a cause of rape; this is particularly so when sexual frustration is ascribed a primary role. Thio (1983), for example, has little trouble with this issue, blanketly stating, without supporting empirical evidence, that "the assumption that *sexual* frustration causes rape is hardly tenable because *nonsexual* frustration has much more to do with rape"[1] (p. 156). This issue will certainly not be resolved in this paper, but we will introduce an analysis of a variant rapist population, admittedly biased but probably no more so than any other studied rapist population, and make an effort to demonstrate that intellectual parochialism arising from the study of those who officially become labeled as rapists seems hardly appropriate.

In this paper we will study a group of self-disclosed rapists in order to determine whether these men are encountering difficulties in obtaining heterosexual outlets by more conventional means. Our principal objective, then, is to examine the sexual histories of rapists and nonrapists and attempt to determine if the former are more sexually deprived. It is apparent here that rape is *primarily* being examined from a sexual perspective rather than from one that views it as an expression of power and aggression. The assumption of a sexual perspective has its genesis in the nature of these acts and is not an expression of a polemic to cover all rape. Our study of

"Date Rapists: Differential Sexual Socialization and Relative Deprivation," by Eugene J. Kanin. *Archives of Sexual Behavior* 14 (Plenum Press 1985), pp. 219–231. Reprinted by permission.

this particular sample reveals all the offenses to have been date rapes and to have occurred only after intensive consensual sexual encounters between the rapists and their victims. We have argued elsewhere that a sexual framework is more appropriate to the facts regarding these men, acknowledging, of course, that in rape the power-aggression component is, in one form or another, *ipso facto* present (Kanin, 1984) and, in some cases, dominant.

Method

In this paper we will report on 71 self-disclosed rapists. These 71 men are all white, unmarried college undergraduates who came to our attention as solicited volunteers during the past decade from university classes and campus organizations where this writer has lectured. In all instances, these men voluntarily presented themselves as possible rapists who were amenable to study by interview and questionnaire. Anonymity of response and the option to terminate participation at any time were emphatically stressed.

An arresting issue here concerns the validity of these disclosures and the subsequent attachment of the rape label. For these volunteers to be accepted as rapists, it was necessary to conform to the legal criterion that penetration was accomplished on a nonconsenting female by employing or threatening force. In every case, a validity check was exercised by having the respondent give two accounts of the assaultive incident, one at the beginning and one at the end of the interview. All 71 cases reported here satisfied these conditions. Fifteen additional volunteered cases were rejected for inclusion in this study because they either failed to conform to the foregoing criterion (13) or decided to discontinue the interview (2). Not one case was excluded on the basis of mendacity. This should be no surprise, since the events reported here could hardly be considered ego enhancing, particularly since they are not being related to select peers.

A short profile of these men and the nature of their assaults is in order to appreciate the assumption of a sexually dominant perspective rather than the currently more popular power-aggression stance. First, these were all cases of date rape. The majority of the pairs had two to five dates together prior to the rape, and most of these pairs had sexually interacted on a prior date(s) in a fashion comparable to the sexual interaction that immediately preceded the rape. Every case of rape followed a fairly intensive bout of sex play, the most common activity being orogenital. Only six men were reported to the police, and in every case the charges were dropped. Thus, these date rapists are not represented in any official tally of rapists. Also crucial to an understanding of these rapists is that only six volunteered that they were recidivists, and all these admitted to but a single prior rape, all under comparable circumstances.

Since there was a conspicuous absence of the use of weapons and fists, it is virtually impossible, in any objective sense, to evaluate realistically the amount of force necessary to have brought these females to victimization. This is due to the fact that the rape interaction would have to take into account the male's execution of force, which usually includes both a physical and verbal dimension, and his companion's interpretation of that force which would result in the victim's determining if sexual compliance were the most judicious adaptation. It was not unusual for some of these men to report that they had exerted greater efforts on dates with other women but were clearly successfully rebuffed, and for some men to express surprise that their partners were so readily intimidated.[2] There is a strong fortuitous factor contributing to these rapes, namely, the interaction stemming from the unique characteristics and perspectives of both the aggressor and the victim.

The control group consists of 227 white, undergraduate, unmarried college males from 15 assorted university classes. The age composition of this group was comparable to that of the rapists. Every male in class at the time of the administration of the schedule cooperated. Eleven schedules were deemed incomplete, and eight others were eliminated because the respondent identified himself as a homosexual. Thirty-six others were excluded from the control group because they indicated that they had engaged in heterosexual encounters with dates where they either tried to gain coitus by employing force or threats or did, in fact, succeed in "forcing" a female to have intercourse. Considering the chance element involved in date rape, viz., that the degree of force necessary to rape successfully may be less important than the nature of the particular victim involved, it was assumed that a high proportion of these men had probably engaged in behavior comparable to our rapists. Therefore, their inclusion would introduce an undesirable bias in the controls. In other words, what we wanted to avoid in our control sample was including men who had been involved in heterosexual performances that could very well have precipitated a rape of the type with which we are dealing.[3]

Results and Discussion

Sexual Histories

Rape is clearly only one facet of a wide range of erotic activities engaged in by these men. These rapists have had, comparatively speaking, considerably more heterosexual experience, have engaged in a more persistent quest for heterosexual encounters, and have utilized more exploitative techniques in their efforts to gain sexual expression. To be specific, the rapist appears considerably more sexually successful and active. Regarding the incidence of coitus exclusive of the rape experiences, inspection of these data show that the rapists are more experienced than the controls, 100% and 59%, respectively. It is worth noting that this 100% incidence characterized these men at the time of the rape. In addition, the frequency of consensual heterosexual outlets as estimated by the respondents

for the past year are overwhelmingly in favor of the rapist. Heterosexual orgasms resulting from coitus, fellatio, and masturbation average 1.5 per week for the rapists, while the mean for the controls is 0.8 per month. It is obvious that these rapists represent a very sexually active group of young men.

Much of this success can probably be attributed to the fact that these men are sexually predatory, that is, they are much more apt to attempt to precipitate new sexual experiences and to employ a variety of surreptitious seductive techniques. For example, when our respondents were asked the frequency with which they attempt to seduce a new date, 62% of the rapists and 19% of the controls responded "most of the time." The rapists' quests for heterosexual engagements largely borders on a no-holds-barred contest. To illustrate, these men were asked about efforts to gain coital access by employing such methods as trying to intoxicate their companions, threatening to terminate the relationship, falsely promising some sort of relationship permanence, i.e., "pinning," engagement, or marriage, falsely professing love, and threatening to abandon their dates, e.g., make them walk home. Table 1 rather cogently portrays these rapists as most apt to pursue their sexual goals by employing drugging, extortion, fraud, and lying: 93% of the rapists, compared to 40% of the controls, used at least one of these techniques while in college. Crucial to the central argument of this paper is the finding that 93% of the rapists, but only 37% of the controls, said that their best friends would "definitely approve" of

TABLE I Incidence of Sexual Exploitation Techniques Employed by Rapists and Controls since College Entrance, by Percentage

	Rapist (N = 71)	Controls (N = 227)
Attempt to intoxicate female with alcohol	76[a]	23[b]
Falsely profess love	86	25
Falsely promise "pinning," engagement, or marriage	46	6
Threaten to terminate relationship	31	7
Threaten to leave female stranded	9	0

[a]28% also involved marijuana.
[b]19% also involved marijuana.

such tactics for *certain* women. Furthermore, 91% of the rapists, in contrast to 32% of the controls, have had such procedures seriously suggested to them by their best friends as functional for sexual success. Sexual exploitation of the female largely permeates their entire male-female approach. The foregoing is compelling testimony to the fact that those who have been most successful in obtaining heterosexual outlets are also those who resort to deviant means.

Regarding the question of assessing sexual frustration by the criterion of sexual experience, it has usually been assumed on *a priori* grounds that a comparative lack of sexual encounters can be roughly translated into proportional increases of frustration. However, it is necessary first to aspire to a goal in order to experience frustration. If the controls should demonstrate a comparatively lesser interest in sex for whatever reasons, then it would be questionable simply to attribute frustration to those with less experience and sexual satisfaction to those with greater experience. It is plausible, of course, that a male with few, if any, heterosexual outlets can still assess himself as not sexually frustrated. The sexually more successful male, on the other hand, may be experiencing frustration if his aspirations exceed his achievements. Asking the respondents to indicate the degree of satisfaction with which they view their sexual activities of the past year, the rapists with their more extensive experience are more apt to report dissatisfaction than the controls with their comparative lack of sexual activity, 79% and 32%, respectively. These findings suggest that satisfaction with one's sexual activity might be only casually related to one's sexual activities. It will be argued here that the dissatisfaction manifested by the rapists is due to a differential socialization in a hypererotic male culture, a culture where sexual success is of paramount importance in the maintenance of self-esteem, and the inability to achieve sexual success can, on a select occasion, result in an expression of violence sufficient to achieve rape.

Differential Sexual Socialization: Peer Groups

In trying to conceptualize a socialization process that would increase the likelihood of date rape, it became very apparent from the study of these data that direct tutelage or example, for all practical purposes, be totally excluded. However, it is feasible to think in terms of a sexual socialization that not only would make sex a highly valued and prestigious activity but also would provide justifications for directing sexual efforts toward specific targets. More specifically, sexual socialization can be thought to comprise influences positive to sexual predation, including providing stereotypes of ideal victims, and of the absence of negative definitions that serve to counteract or insulate against the positive "pulls." Agents that could be considered central to providing such definitions would be an individual's peers and family.

An attempt was made to gauge the degree that one's current peer group would condone aggressive and offensive sexual efforts by obtaining the *imputed* reputational consequences of such behavior. The respondents were asked what they thought would be the reputational consequences in the eyes of their best friends "if they found out that you offended a woman by *trying* to force her to have sexual intercourse, during the course of which you used physical force and/or threats." It is patently implicit here that these are not successful efforts and, therefore, that these acts do not constitute forcible rape. The question was phrased so as to apply to aggressions committed against five hypothetical women, each possessing a significant characteristic that might affect her attractiveness as an aggression target. Table II shows the percentage of rapists and controls who believe that their

TABLE II Imputed Positive Reputational Consequences of Aggressively Offending Five Select Hypothetical Women, by Percentage

	Rapists (N = 71)	Controls (N = 227)
Bar "pick-up"	54	16
Woman with "loose" reputation	27	10
Known "teaser"	81	40
Economic exploiter	73	39
A more or less regular date	9	7

reputations would be enhanced by aggressing against a woman playing a role with a stereotyped sexual significance in the male world. Although it is apparent that the "teaser" and economic exploiter are prime targets for both groups, positive reputational consequences are dramatically seen as forthcoming from the friends of the rapists. Their erotic subculture has adequately conferred the label of legitimate sexual targets on certain "deviant" females. In a substantial segment of the male culture, four of these women qualify as social deviants by violating expectations in the dating encounter. Essentially, the "pick-up," the "loose woman," and the "teaser" are viewed as upending sexual expectations after "flaunting," "advertising," and "promising" sexual accessibility. The economic exploiter, although less sexually explicit, earns her deviant label by violating reciprocity norms held by some segments of the male culture. In short, these women are seen as not playing by the rules of the game, and, therefore, the man feels justified in suspending the rules regarding his dating conduct. It should be noted that these men are aware that frequent encounters with "rough sex" would evoke suspicion of derangement, even from their close friends. Only a minority, about 25%, would tell their friends about such encounters. There is, additionally, an anxiety that these aggressions could be status detracting in that they highlight sexual failure and the inability to succeed by more sophisticated means. Essentially, their friends are not seen as rewarding violence; the offensive sexuality that receives acclaim—or at least does not draw opprobrium—is largely due to the "provocative" conduct of the victim.

Not only do these males have associates who they believe would condone aggressive behavior, but they are also subjected to peer influences to be sexually active. Responses to the question, "What degree of pressure do your best friends exert on you to seek sexual encounters?" shows that the rapists are indeed the recipients of such spheres of influence. Table III clearly portrays the rapists as receiving such peer enticements, whereas the controls are overrepresented as receiving little or no pressure from their friends. The evidence thus far shows that the rapists have a differential association with close friends who encourage and reward sexual

TABLE III Degree of Pressure Exerted by Current Friends for Sexual Activity, by Percentage

	Rapists (N = 71)	Controls (N = 227)
Great deal and considerable	40	9
Moderate	45	28
Little and none	15	63
Totals	100	100

experience and who will also support sexual transgressions on select females.

It is crucial to note that these men did not acquire their aggressive sexuality in college. Although they definitely tended to immerse themselves in an erotic culture that served normative reference-group functions for them, this current culture functioned as a reference group primarily by supporting and sustaining values acquired prior to college entrance. Of course the newly acquired collegiate friendship groups did serve reference-group functions in that they embellished old values, provided new vocabularies of adjustment, altered old norms, and introduced new norms. If we look at the behaviors of these men while they were still in high school, we find the same peer group phenomenon operating, only in an exaggerated fashion. For example, 85% of the rapists, in contrast to 26% of the controls, reported high school friendships where pressure for heterosexual expression was "great and considerable."

It seems appropriate here to raise the question as to the nature of the perceptions of these respondents regarding their peer group influences. Specifically, it may be charged that these perceptions are largely defensive and, therefore, represent distortions. Our evidence, however, does not lend support to such a hypothesis but rather bolsters the position that the sexual socialization of these rapists was substantially influenced by a supportive hypererotic male culture. This is particularly the case when we examine some of the more concrete behavioral aspects involving the rapists and their close associates. For example, it can be pointed out that the rapists are much more apt to have a history of collaborative sex. Fully 41% of the rapists, but only 7% of the controls, were ever involved in either a "gang-bang" or a sequential sexual sharing of a female with a male friend. Furthermore, over 67% of the rapists had had intercourse with a female whom a friend had recommended as sexually congenial. Only 13% of the controls indicated that they were ever recipients of such a friendship referral network. Lastly, 21% of the rapists reported that their first female-genital contact, whether manual, oral, or coital, was the direct consequence of having been "fixed-up" by a friend(s). This contrasts rather sharply with the 6% of the controls who reported that such third-party arrangements had entered into their premier episode. All these data tend uniformly to confirm these respondents' perceptions that their close associates do indeed represent an active hypererotic influence.

Differential Sexual Socialization: Family Influences

A basic socialization role could also be played by the fathers of these men. Fathers are observed to exhibit a wide spectrum of attitudes toward their sons' sexual activities, ranging from severely proscribing such conduct to virtually condoning and even encouraging "manly" pursuits. Although some fathers were reported to have urged their sons to go out and "get some," this attitude was quite the exception; very few men reported paternal sexual encouragement. In fact, in order to compose a working category of fathers whose attitudes were not unequivocally unfavorable to premarital sex, as checked on a 5-point Likert-type scale, it was necessary to combine the categories "very favorable," "favorable," and "neutral." Even here we find only 21% of our total sample, and the rapists are only represented about 4% more than the controls, a negligible difference.

However, when we inspect the unfavorable attitude categories, a very striking contrast appears only in the "very unfavorable." Approximately equal representation of rapists and controls are found with fathers whose attitudes are "unfavorable," 46% and 54%, respectively. But in the case where the father's attitude toward premarital sex is perceived to be "very unfavor-

able," we find 72% of the controls and only 28% of the rapists. It may well be that the father's major influence on his son's sexual activities is not to be found in encouragement and support but rather in a very strong posture of disapproval. In other words, the nature of paternal influence on a son's sexual orientation is more the product of a strong proscriptive position than a positive encouraging one.

Differential Sexual Socialization: Justifications

An integral aspect of the variety of differential sexual socialization with which we are dealing should involve the provision for a vocabulary of adjustment, a means of justifying behavior. It has been shown that these rapists see their prestige as being enhanced for sexually exploiting select women. It would seem to follow that their associates, those who encourage them to deviate, would provide them with—or reinforce—appropriate vocabularies of adjustment so that they can continue to maintain their conception of themselves as beings of worth and esteem while continuing to exploit and degrade. Such a process would be an essential prerequisite for the maintenance and perpetuation of group values. Approximately 86% of these rapists believe that rape, in the abstract, and not necessarily in their own behavior, can be justified under certain conditions. This contrasts rather sharply with the 19% of the controls who believe in the justifiability of rape. These justifications, as one would expect, are almost completely made up of women viewed as "teasers," economic exploiters, and "loose." The more extensive information gathered through the interviews with the rapists seems to point to a composite of teaser-exploiter-loose as the quintessential deviant dating companion. She is seen as the one who financially extends the man, who enters into sex play with sufficient enthusiasm to convey a presupposition of having "been around," and who insists on stabilizing the sexual aspect of the relationship short of coitus. It should be pointed out, however, that in reality victims only seldom qualify, even under student standards, as economic exploiters but eminently qualify as "teaser-loose" because of the nature of their role in the sexual encounter, namely, one that is consensual and active.

Considering again peer group influence on the ability to perceive a deviant act as justified, it is found that 93% of the rapists who indicated they were recipients of great, considerable, or moderate peer group pressure for sexual activity indicated that rape can be justified. The rapists who reported that their peers exerted little or no pressure for sexual involvement were considerably less apt to believe in the justification of rape, only 45%.

Relative Deprivation

Now that it has been established that these rapists were the recipients of strong social pressures for sexual achievement, it is time to return to the finding that these more experienced men reported a greater incidence of sexual dissatisfaction than the sexually less experienced controls. As previously stated, more extensive sexual experience could readily be associated with greater dissatisfaction if one's peers highly value sexual accomplishment and confer prestige rewards for success. In effect, an exaggerated level of sexual aspiration is introjected from one's erotically oriented significant others, a level that, at best, will be difficult for the majority of college males to maintain continually. Aspiration levels may be reflected in the subjective estimates held by these men regarding their sexual needs. When asked, "How many orgasms (ejaculations) per week, from any source, do you think you would require in order to give you sexual satisfaction?", the rapists report a mean number of 4.5, in contrast to 2.8 for the controls. It could be inferred that these men are experiencing relative deprivation in that dissatisfaction largely stems from their inability to achieve ambitious goals (see Kanin, 1967).

Evidence supporting this position comes from demonstrating that the degree of the rapists' sexual satisfaction with their sexual accomplishment for the previous year appears strongly related to the degree of pressure their friends exert for sexual experience. The rapists show the most pronounced inclination to report sexual satisfaction when little or no group pressure is applied, 71%, while satisfaction is less frequently indicated by the recipients of great, consider-

able, and moderate pressures, 40%. Although this finding does not prove a causal nexus exists here, it is compatible with "reference group theory."

Conclusions

The purpose of this paper was to show that these date rapists experienced a differential sexual socialization that resulted in the development of an exaggerated sex impulse and the placing of an inordinately high value on sexual accomplishment. Consequently, a frustration of the aroused impulse led these men to undergo an acute sense of goal deprivation that can best be understood in the context of relative deprivation. Specifically, it is sexually less frustrating to encounter rejection when one's socialization has provided for a lower level of aspiration than when one's socialization has instilled a high expectancy of sexual success (see Kanin, 1967; Chappell et al., 1977). The female's rejection of coital intimacy after rather intensive advanced sexual interaction is primarily the expression of her need to stabilize intimacy for personal reasons, and not to exploit or to be fashionably provocative.[4] The male fails to recognize this. Instead, he focuses on whether her rejection is genuine and/or on the adequacy of his sexual powers, a very likely manifestation of a perceptual defense process. This results in his bewilderment and anxiety. The disregard for her rejection behavior and the subsequent display of aggressive presentations, verbal and physical, intended and/or unintended, readily led to the rape episode on this occasion. The inflicting of punishment or suffering through the rape appears incidental in the vast majority of cases and, at best, serves a secondary function. There is very little evidence here that violence functioned as a sexual stimulant for these men (see Barbaree et al., 1979). The coital experience, the manifest and anticipated benefit, and the accompanying reaffirmation of self-worth, not entirely lost to consciousness, appear to be prime movers for these rapes.

Although this paper imputes a prime role to reference groups, there exists a possibility that these exaggerated levels of sexual aspiration and the accompanying aggressive behaviors have their genesis in other than positive reference groups. Early familial and other primary group influences might have affected aspects of personality development of (1) a generalized hostility toward the female world, (2) an aggressive component and (3) a hypererotic orientation. The foregoing could have the effect of prompting one to seek out membership groups holding sexually congenial perspectives. However, the reference group interpretation is favored since it is grounded in a substantial body of research that has consistently demonstrated the significance of peer influence on sexually aggressive behavior (Reiss, 1960; Polk *et al.,* 1981; Kanin, 1967; Ageton, 1983).

Notes

1. Italics are in the original.
2. None of this is to imply that these women were merely being respectably reluctant. All cases where the female metamorphosed into an active participant were discarded, along with cases where she apparently showed no traumatic consequences.
3. In view of the nature of the accidental samples of rapists and controls, all percentages were rounded off, and no tests of statistical significance were employed. Instead, we relied exclusively on the pronounced differences between the rapists and the nonrapists.
4. The great majority of our respondents concurred with this interpretation at the time of the interview.

References

Ageton, S. S. (1983). *Sexual Assault among Adolescents.* D. C. Heath, Lexington, Massachusetts.

Anderson, N. (1923). *The Hobo.* University of Chicago Press, Chicago.

Barbaree, H. E., Marshall, W. L., and Lanthier, R. D. (1979). Deviant sexual arousal in rapists. *Behav. Res. Ther.* 17: 215–221.

Bonger, W. A., (1916). *Criminality and Economic Conditions.* Little, Brown, Boston.

Chappell, D., Geis, G., Schafer, S., and Siegel, L. (1977). A comparative study of forcible rape offenses known to the police in Boston and Los Angeles. In Chappel, D., Geis, R., and Geis, G. (eds.), *Forcible Rape,* Columbia University Press, New York.

Clark, L., and Lewis, D. (1977). *Rape: The Price of Coercive Sexuality.* The Woman's Press, Toronto.

Clemmer, D. (1958). *The Prison Community.* Rinehart and Co., New York.

Cohen, Y. A. (1961). *Social Structure and Personality.* Holt, Rinehart, and Winston, New York.

Cohen, M. L., Garofalo, R. B., Boucher, R. B., and Seghorn, T. (1971). The psychology of rapists. *Sem. in Psychiat.* 3: 307–327.

Fishman, J. F. (1934). *Sex in Prison.* Podell, New York.

Guttmacher, M. S. (1951). *Sex Offenses.* Norton, New York.

Kanin, E. (1967). Reference groups and sex conduct norm violations. *Soc. Quart.* 8: 495–504.

Kanin, E. (1984). Date rape: Unofficial criminals and victims. *Victimology,* 9: 95–108.

Karpman, B. (1954). *The Sexual Offender and His Offenses.* Julian Press, New York.

Lockwood, D. (1980). *Prison Sexual Violence.* Elsevier, New York.

Polk, K., Adler, C., Bazemore, G., Blake, G., Cordray, S., Coventry, G., Galrin, J., and Temple, M. (1981). Becoming adult: An analysis of motivational development from age 16 to 30 of a cohort of young men. *Final Report of the Marion County Youth Survey.* University of Oregon, Eugene, Oregon.

Reiss, A. J. (1960). Sex offenses: The marginal status of the adolescent. *Law Contemp. Prob.* 25: 309–333.

Sykes, G. (1958). *The Society of Captives.* Princeton University Press, Princeton, New Jersey.

Thio, A. (1983). *Deviant Behavior.* Hougton-Mifflin, Boston.

Wheeler, S. (1960). Sex offenses: A sociological critique. *Law Contemp. Prob.* 25: 258–278.

19

Fraternities and Rape on Campus

Patricia Yancey Martin
Robert A. Hummer

Rapes are perpetrated on dates, at parties, in chance encounters, and in specially planned circumstances. That group structure and processes, rather than individual values or characteristics, are the impetus for many rape episodes was documented by Blanchard (1959) 30 years ago (also see Geis 1971), yet sociologists have failed to pursue this theme (for an exception, see Chancer 1987). A recent review of research (Muehlenhard and Linton 1987) on sexual violence, or rape, devotes only a few pages to the situational contexts of rape events, and these are conceptualized as potential risk factors for individuals rather than qualities of rape-prone social contexts.

Many rapes, far more than come to the public's attention, occur in fraternity houses on college and university campuses, yet little research has analyzed fraternities at American colleges and universities as rape-prone contexts (cf. Ehrhart and Sandler 1985). Most of the research on fraternities reports on samples of individual fraternity men. One group of studies compares the values, attitudes, perceptions, family socioeconomic status, psychological traits (aggressiveness, dependence), and so on, of fraternity and nonfraternity men (Bohrnstedt 1969, Fox, Hodge, and Ward 1987; Kanin 1967; Lemire 1979; Miller 1973). A second group attempts to identify the effects of fraternity membership over time on the values, attitudes, beliefs, or moral precepts of members (Hughes and Winston 1987; Marlowe and Auvenshine 1982; Miller 1973; Wilder, Hoyt, Doren, Hauck, and Zettle 1978; Wilder, Hoyt, Surbeck, Wilder, and Carney 1986). With minor exceptions, little research addresses the group and organizational context of fraternities or the social construction of fraternity life (for exceptions, see Letchworth 1969; Longino and Kart 1973; Smith 1964).

Gary Tash, writing as an alumnus and trial attorney in his fraternity's magazine, claims that over 90 percent of all gang rapes on college campuses involve fraternity men (1988, p. 2). Tash provides no evidence to substantiate this claim, but students of violence against women have been concerned with fraternity men's frequently reported involvement in rape episodes (Adams and Abarbanel 1988). Ehrhart and Sandler (1985) identify over 50 cases of gang rapes on campus perpetrated by fraternity men, and their analysis points to many of the conditions that we discuss here. Their analysis is unique in focusing on conditions in fraternities that make gang rapes of women by fraternity men both feasible and probable. They identify excessive alcohol use, isolation from external monitoring, treatment of women as prey, use of pornography, approval of violence, and excessive concern with competition as precipitating conditions to gang rape (also see Merton 1985; Roark 1987).

The study reported here confirmed and complemented these findings by focusing on both conditions and processes. We examined

Patricia Yancey Martin and Robert A. Hummer, "Fraternities and Rape on Campus," *Gender & Society* 3 (4), pp. 457–473, copyright © 1989 by Sociologists for Women in Society. Reprinted by Permission of Sage Publications, Inc.

We gratefully thank Meena Harris and Diane Mennella for assisting with data collection. The senior author thanks the graduate students in her fall 1988 graduate research methods seminar for help with developing the initial conceptual framework. Judith Lorber and two anonymous *Gender & Society* referees made numerous suggestions for improving our article and we thank them also.

dynamics associated with the social construction of fraternity life, with a focus on processes that foster the use of coercion, including rape, in fraternity men's relations with women. Our examination of men's social fraternities on college and university campuses as groups and organizations led us to conclude that fraternities are a physical and sociocultural context that encourages the sexual coercion of women. We make no claims that all fraternities are "bad" or that all fraternity men are rapists. Our observations indicated, however, that rape is especially probable in fraternities because of the kinds of organizations they are, the kinds of members they have, the practices their members engage in, and a virtual absence of university or community oversight. Analyses that lay blame for rapes by fraternity men on "peer pressure" are, we feel, overly simplistic (cf. Burkhart 1989; Walsh 1989). We suggest, rather, that fraternities create a sociocultural context in which the use of coercion in sexual relations with women is normative and in which the mechanisms to keep this pattern of behavior in check are minimal at best and absent at worst. We conclude that unless fraternities change in fundamental ways, little improvement can be expected.

Methodology

Our goal was to analyze the group and organizational practices and conditions that create in fraternities an abusive social context for women. We developed a conceptual framework from an initial case study of an alleged gang rape at Florida State University that involved four fraternity men and an 18-year-old coed. The group rape took place on the third floor of a fraternity house and ended with the "dumping" of the woman in the hallway of a neighboring fraternity house. According to newspaper accounts, the victim's blood-alcohol concentration, when she was discovered, was .349 percent, more than three times the legal limit for automobile driving and an almost lethal amount. One law enforcement officer reported that sexual intercourse occurred during the time the victim was unconscious: "She was in a life-threatening situation" (*Tallahassee Democrat,* 1988b). When the victim

was found, she was comatose and had suffered multiple scratches and abrasions. Crude words and a fraternity symbol had been written on her thighs (*Tampa Tribune,* 1988). When law enforcement officials tried to investigate the case, fraternity members refused to cooperate. This led, eventually, to a five-year ban of the fraternity from campus by the university and by the fraternity's national organization.

In trying to understand how such an event could have occurred, and how a group of over 150 members (exact figures are unknown because the fraternity refused to provide a membership roster) could hold rank, deny knowledge of the event, and allegedly lie to a grand jury, we analyzed newspaper articles about the case and conducted open-ended interviews with a variety of respondents about the case and about fraternities, rapes, alcohol use, gender relations, and sexual activities on campus. Our data included over 100 newspaper articles on the initial gang rape case; open-ended interviews with Greek (social fraternity and sorority) and non-Greek (independent) students (N = 20); university administrators (N = 8, five men, three women); and alumni advisers to Greek organizations (N = 6). Open-ended interviews were held also with judges, public and private defense attorneys, victim advocates, and state prosecutors regarding the processing of sexual assault cases. Data were analyzed using the grounded theory method (Glaser 1978; Martin and Turner 1986). In the following analysis, concepts generated from the data analysis are integrated with the literature on men's social fraternities, sexual coercion, and related issues.

Fraternities and the Social Construction of Men and Masculinity

Our research indicated that fraternities are vitally concerned—more than with anything else—with masculinity (cf. Kanin 1967). They work hard to create a macho image and context and try to avoid any suggestion of "wimpishness," effeminacy, and homosexuality. Valued members display, or are willing to go along with, a narrow conception of masculinity that stresses competition, athleticism, dominance, winning, conflict, wealth, material possessions, willingness to drink alcohol, and sexual prowess vis-à-vis women.

Valued Qualities of Members

When fraternity members talked about the kind of pledges they prefer, a litany of stereotypical and narrowly masculine attributes and behaviors was recited and feminine or woman-associated qualities and behaviors were expressly denounced (cf. Merton 1985). Fraternities seek men who are "athletic," "big guys," good in intramural competition, "who can talk college sports." Males "who are willing to drink alcohol," "who drink socially," or "who can hold their liquor" are sought. Alcohol and activities associated with the recreational use of alcohol are cornerstones of fraternity social life. Nondrinkers are viewed with skepticism and rarely selected for membership.[1]

Fraternities try to avoid "geeks," nerds, and men said to give the fraternity a "wimpy" or "gay" reputation. Art, music, and humanities majors, majors in traditional women's fields (nursing, home economics, social work, education), men with long hair, and those whose appearance or dress violate current norms are rejected. Clean-cut, handsome men who dress well (are clean, neat, conforming, fashionable) are preferred. One sorority woman commented that "the top ranking fraternities have the best looking guys."

One fraternity man, a senior, said his fraternity recruited "some big guys, very athletic" over a two-year period to help overcome its image of wimpiness. His fraternity had won the interfraternity competition for highest grade-point average several years running but was looked down on as "wimpy, dancy, even gay." With their bigger, more athletic recruits, "our reputation improved; we're a much more recognized fraternity now." Thus a fraternity's reputation and status depends on members' possession of stereotypically masculine qualities. Good grades, campus leadership, and community service are "nice" but masculinity dominance—for example, in athletic events, physical size of members, athleticism of members—counts most.

Certain social skills are valued. Men are sought who "have good personalities," are friendly, and "have the ability to relate to girls" (cf. Longino and Kart 1973). One fraternity man, a junior, said: "We watch a guy [a potential pledge] talk to women . . . we want guys who can relate to girls." Assessing a pledge's ability to talk to women is, in part, a preoccupation with homosexuality and a conscious avoidance of men who seem to have effeminate manners or qualities. If a member is suspected of being gay, he is ostracized and informally drummed out of the fraternity. A fraternity with a reputation as wimpy or tolerant of gays is ridiculed and shunned by other fraternities. Militant heterosexuality is frequently used by men as a strategy to keep each other in line (Kimmel 1987).

Financial affluence or wealth, a male-associated value in American culture, is highly valued by fraternities. In accounting for why the fraternity involved in the gang rape that precipitated our research project had been recognized recently as "the best fraternity chapter in the United States," a university official said: "They were good-looking, a big fraternity, had lots of BMWs [expensive, German-made automobiles]." After the rape, newspaper stories described the fraternity members' affluence, noting the high number of members who owned expensive cars (*St. Petersburg Times,* 1988).

The Status and Norms of Pledgeship

A pledge (sometimes called an associate member) is a new recruit who occupies a trial membership status for a specific period of time. The pledge period (typically ranging from 10 to 15 weeks) gives fraternity brothers an opportunity to assess and socialize new recruits. Pledges evaluate the fraternity also and decide if they want to become brothers. The socialization experience is structured partly through assignment of a Big Brother to each pledge. Big Brothers are expected to teach pledges how to become a brother and to support them as they progress through the trial membership period. Some pledges are repelled by the pledging experience, which can entail physical abuse; harsh discipline; and demands to be subordinate, follow orders, and engage in demeaning routines and activities, similar to those used by the military to "make men out of boys" during boot camp.

Characteristics of the pledge experience are rationalized by fraternity members as necessary to help pledges unite into a group, rely on each other, and join together against outsiders. The process is highly masculinist in execution as well as conception. A willingness to submit to authority, follow orders, and do as one is told is viewed as a sign of loyalty, togetherness, and unity. Fraternity pledges who find the pledge process offensive often drop out. Some do this by openly quitting, which can subject them to ridicule by brothers and other pledges, or they may deliberately fail to make the grades necessary for initiation or transfer schools and decline to reaffiliate with the fraternity on the new campus. One fraternity pledge who quit the fraternity he had pledged described an experience during pledgeship as follows:

> This one guy was always picking on me. No matter what I did, I was wrong. One night after dinner, he and two other guys called me and two other pledges into the chapter room. He said, "Here, X, hold this 25 pound bag of ice at arms' length 'til I tell you to stop." I did it even though my arms and hands were killing me. When I asked if I could stop, he grabbed me around the throat and lifted me off the floor. I thought he would choke me to death. He cussed me and called me all kinds of names. He took one of my fingers and twisted it until it nearly broke. . . . I stayed in the fraternity for a few more days, but then I decided to quit. I hated it. Those guys are sick. They like seeing you suffer.

Fraternities' emphasis on toughness, withstanding pain and humiliation, obedience to superiors, and using physical force to obtain compliance contributes to an interpersonal style that de-emphasizes caring and sensitivity but fosters intragroup trust and loyalty. If the least macho or most critical pledges drop out, those who remain may be more receptive to, and influenced by, masculinist values and practices that encourage the use of force in sexual relations with women and the covering up of such behavior (cf. Kanin 1967).

Norms and Dynamics of Brotherhood

Brother is the status occupied by fraternity men to indicate their relations to each other and their membership in a particular fraternity organization or group. Brother is a male-specific status; only males can become brothers, although women can become "Little Sisters," a form of pseudomembership. "Becoming a brother" is a rite of passage that follows the consistent and often lengthy display by pledges of appropriately masculine qualities and behaviors. Brothers have a quasi-familial relationship with each other, are normatively said to share bonds of closeness and support, and are sharply set off from nonmembers. Brotherhood is a loosely defined term used to represent the bonds that develop among fraternity members and the obligations and expectations incumbent upon them (cf. Marlowe and Auvenshine [1982] on fraternities' failure to encourage "moral development" in freshman pledges).

Some of our respondents talked about brotherhood in almost reverential terms, viewing it as the most valuable benefit of fraternity membership. One senior, a business-school major who had been affiliated with a fairly high-status fraternity throughout four years on campus, said:

> Brotherhood spurs friendship for life, which I consider its best aspect, although I didn't see it that way when I joined. Brotherhood bonds and unites. It instills values of caring about one another, caring about community, caring about ourselves. The values and bonds [of brotherhood] continually develop over the four years [in college] while normal friendships come and go.

Despite this idealization, most aspects of fraternity practice and conception are more mundane. Brotherhood often plays itself out as an overriding concern with masculinity and, by extension, femininity. As a consequence, fraternities comprise collectivities of highly masculinized men with attitudinal qualities and behavioral norms that predispose them to sexual coercion of women (cf. Kanin 1967; Merton 1985; Rapaport and Burkhart 1984). The norms of masculinity are complemented by conceptions of women and femininity that are equally distorted and stereotyped and that may enhance the probability of women's exploitation (cf. Ehrhart and Sandler 1985; Sanday 1981, 1986).

Practices of Brotherhood

Practices associated with fraternity brotherhood that contribute to the sexual coercion of women include a preoccupation with loyalty, group protection and secrecy, use of alcohol as a weapon, involvement in violence and physical force, and an emphasis on competition and superiority.

Loyalty, group protection, and secrecy. Loyalty is a fraternity preoccupation. Members are reminded constantly to be loyal to the fraternity and to their brothers. Among other ways, loyalty is played out in the practices of group protection and secrecy. The fraternity must be shielded from criticism. Members are admonished to avoid getting the fraternity in trouble and to bring all problems "to the chapter" (local branch of a national social fraternity) rather than to outsiders. Fraternities try to protect themselves from close scrutiny and criticism by the Interfraternity Council (a quasi-governing body composed of representatives from all social fraternities on campus), their fraternity's national office, university officials, law enforcement, the media, and the public. Protection of the fraternity often takes precedence over what is procedurally, ethically, or legally correct. Numerous examples were related to us of fraternity brothers' lying to outsiders to "protect the fraternity."

Group protection was observed in the alleged gang rape case with which we began our study. Except for one brother, a rapist who turned state's evidence, the entire remaining fraternity membership was accused by university and criminal justice officials of lying to protect the fraternity. Members consistently failed to cooperate even though the alleged crimes were felonies, involved only four men (two of whom were not even members of the local chapter), and the victim of the crime nearly died. According to a grand jury's findings, fraternity officers repeatedly broke appointments with law enforcement officials, refused to provide police with a list of members, and refused to cooperate

with police and prosecutors investigating the case (*Florida Flambeau,* 1988).

Secrecy is a priority value and practice in fraternities, partly because full-fledged membership is premised on it (for confirmation, see Ehrhart and Sandler 1985; Longino and Kart 1973; Roark 1987). Secrecy is also a boundary-maintaining mechanism, demarcating in-group from out-group, us from them. Secret rituals, handshakes, and mottoes are revealed to pledge brothers as they are initiated into full brotherhood. Since only brothers are supposed to know a fraternity's secrets, such knowledge affirms membership in the fraternity and separates a brother from others. Extending secrecy tactics from protection of private knowledge to protection of the fraternity from criticism is a predictable development. Our interviews indicated that individual members knew the difference between right and wrong, but fraternity norms that emphasize loyalty, group protection, and secrecy often overrode standards of ethical correctness.

Alcohol as weapon. Alcohol use by fraternity men is normative. They use it on weekdays to relax after class and on weekends to "get drunk," "get crazy," and "get laid." The use of alcohol to obtain sex from women is pervasive—in other words, it is used as a weapon against sexual reluctance. According to several fraternity men whom we interviewed, alcohol is the major tool used to gain sexual mastery over women (cf. Adams and Abarbanel 1988; Ehrhart and Sandler 1985). One fraternity man, a 21-year-old senior, described alcohol use to gain sex as follows: "There are girls that you know will fuck, then some you have to put some effort into it. . . . You have to buy them drinks or find out if she's drunk enough. . . ."

A similar strategy is used collectively. A fraternity man said that at parties with Little Sisters: "We provide them with 'hunch punch' and things get wild. We get them drunk and most of the guys end up with one." "'Hunch punch,'" he said, "is a girls' drink made up of overproof alcohol and powdered Kool-Aid, no water or anything, just ice. It's very strong. Two cups will do a number on a female." He had plans in the next academic term to surreptitiously give hunch punch to women in a "prim and proper" sorority because "having sex with prim and proper sorority girls is definitely a goal." These women are a challenge because they "won't openly consume alcohol and won't get openly drunk as hell." Their sororities have "standards committees" that forbid heavy drinking and easy sex.

In the gang rape case, our sources said that many fraternity men on campus believed the victim had a drinking problem and was thus an "easy make." According to newspaper accounts, she had been drinking alcohol on the evening she was raped; the lead assailant is alleged to have given her a bottle of wine after she arrived at his fraternity house. Portions of the rape occurred in a shower, and the victim was reportedly so drunk that her assailants had difficulty holding her in a standing position (*Tallahassee Democrat,* 1988a). While raping her, her assailants repeatedly told her they were members of another fraternity under the apparent belief that she was too drunk to know the difference. Of course, if she was too drunk to know who they were, she was too drunk to consent to sex (cf. Allgeier 1986; Tash 1988).

One respondent told us that gang rapes are wrong and can get one expelled, but he seemed to see nothing wrong in sexual coercion one-on-one. He seemed unaware that the use of alcohol to obtain sex from a woman is grounds for a claim that a rape occurred (cf. Tash 1988). Few women on campus (who also may not know these grounds) report date rapes, however; so the odds of detection and punishment are slim for fraternity men who use alcohol for "seduction" purposes (cf. Byington and Keeter 1988; Merton 1985).

Violence and physical force. Fraternity men have a history of violence (Ehrhart and Sandler 1985; Roark 1987). Their record of hazing, fighting, property destruction, and rape has caused them problems with insurance companies (Bradford 1986; Pressley 1987). Two university officials told us that fraternities "are the third riskiest property to insure behind toxic waste dumps and amusement parks." Fraternities are increasingly defendants in legal actions brought by pledges subjected to hazing (Meyer 1986; Pressley 1987) and by women who were raped by one or more members. In a recent alleged gang rape incident at another Florida university, prosecutors failed to file charges but the victim filed a civil suit against the fraternity nevertheless (*Tallahassee Democrat,* 1989).

Competition and superiority. Interfraternity rivalry fosters in-group identification and out-group hostility. Fraternities stress pride of membership and superiority over other fraternities as major goals. Interfraternity rivalries take many forms, including competition for desirable pledges, size of pledge class, size of membership, size and appearance of fraternity house, superiority in intramural sports, highest grade-point averages, giving the best parties, gaining the best or most campus leadership roles, and, of great importance, attracting and displaying "good-looking women." Rivalry is particularly intense over members, intramural sports, and women (cf. Messner 1989).

Fraternities' Commodification of Women

In claiming that women are treated by fraternities as commodities, we mean that fraternities knowingly, and intentionally, *use* women for their benefit. Fraternities use women as bait for new members, as servers of brothers' needs, and as sexual prey.

Women as bait. Fashionably attractive women help a fraternity attract new members. As one fraternity man, a junior, said, "They are good bait." Beautiful, sociable women are believed to impress the right kind of pledges and give the impression that the fraternity can deliver this type of woman to its members. Photographs of shapely, attractive coeds are printed in fraternity brochures and videotapes that are distributed and shown to potential pledges. The women pictured are often dressed in bikinis, at the beach, and are pictured hugging the brothers of the fraternity. One university official says such recruitment materials give the message: "Hey, they're here for you, you can have whatever you want," and, "we have the best looking women. Join us and you can have them too."

Another commented: "Something's wrong when males join an all-male organization as the best place to meet women. It's so illogical."

Fraternities compete in promising access to beautiful women. One fraternity man, a senior, commented that "the attraction of girls [i.e., a fraternity's success in attracting women] is a big status symbol for fraternities." One university official commented that the use of women as a recruiting tool is so well entrenched that fraternities that might be willing to forgo it say they cannot afford to unless other fraternities do so as well. One fraternity man said, "Look, if we don't have Little Sisters, the fraternities that do will get all the good pledges." Another said, "We won't have as good a rush [the period during which new members are assessed and selected] if we don't have these women around."

In displaying good-looking, attractive, skimpily dressed, nubile women to potential members, fraternities implicitly, and sometimes explicitly, promise sexual access to women. One fraternity man commented that "part of what being in a fraternity is all about is the sex" and explained how his fraternity uses Little Sisters to recruit new members:

> We'll tell the sweetheart [the fraternity's term for Little Sister], "You're gorgeous; you can get him." We'll tell her to fake a scam and she'll go hang all over him during a rush party, kiss him, and he thinks he's done wonderful and wants to join. The girls think it's great too. It's flattering for them.

Women as servers.
The use of women as servers is exemplified in the Little Sister program. Little Sisters are undergraduate women who are rushed and selected in a manner parallel to the recruitment of fraternity men. They are affiliated with the fraternity in a formal but unofficial way and are able, indeed required, to wear the fraternity's Greek letters. Little Sisters are not full-fledged fraternity members, however; and fraternity national offices and most universities do not register or regulate them. Each fraternity has an officer called Little Sister Chairman who oversees their organization and activities. The Little Sisters elect officers among themselves, pay monthly dues to the fraternity, and have well-defined roles. Their dues are used to pay for the fraternity's social events, and Little Sisters are expected to attend and hostess fraternity parties and hang around the house to make it a "nice place to be." One fraternity man, a senior, described Little Sisters this way: "They are very social girls, willing to join in, be affiliated with the group, devoted to the fraternity." Another member, a sophomore, said: "Their sole purpose is social—attend parties, attract new members, and 'take care' of the guys."

Our observations and interviews suggested that women selected by fraternities as Little Sisters are physically attractive, possess good social skills, and are willing to devote time and energy to the fraternity and its members. One undergraduate woman gave the following job description for Little Sisters to a campus newspaper:

> It's not just making appearances at all the parties but entails many more responsibilities. You're going to be expected to go to all the intramural games to cheer the brothers on, support and encourage the pledges, and just be around to bring some extra life to the house. [As a Little Sister] you have to agree to take on a new responsibility other than studying to maintain your grades and managing to keep your checkbook from bouncing. You have to make time to be a part of the fraternity and support the brothers in all they do. (*The Tomahawk*, 1988)

The title of Little Sister reflects women's subordinate status; fraternity men in a parallel role are called Big Brothers. Big Brothers assist a sorority primarily with the physical work of sorority rushes, which, compared to fraternity rushes, are more formal, structured, and intensive. Sorority rushes take place in the daytime and fraternity rushes at night so fraternity men are free to help. According to one fraternity member, Little Sister status is a benefit to women because it gives them a social outlet and "the protection of the brothers." The gender-stereotypic conceptions and obligations of these Little Sister and Big Brother statuses indicate that fraternities and sororities promote a gender hierarchy on campus that fosters subordination and dependence in women, thus encouraging sexual exploitation and the belief that it is acceptable.

Women as sexual prey. Little Sisters are a sexual utility. Many Little Sisters do not belong to sororities and lack peer support for refraining from unwanted sexual relations. One fraternity man (whose fraternity has 65 members and 85 Little Sisters) told us they had recruited "wholesale" in the prior year to "get lots of new women." The structural access to women that the Little Sister program provides and the absence of normative supports for refusing fraternity members' sexual advances may make women in this program particularly susceptible to coerced sexual encounters with fraternity men.

Access to women for sexual gratification is a presumed benefit of fraternity membership, promised in recruitment materials and strategies and through brothers' conversations with new recruits. One fraternity man said: "We always tell the guys that you get sex all the time, there's always new girls. . . . After I became a Greek, I found out I could be with females at will." A university official told us that, based on his observations, "no one [i.e., fraternity men] on this campus wants to have 'relationships.' They just want to have fun [i.e., sex]." Fraternity men plan and execute strategies aimed at obtaining sexual gratification, and this occurs at both individual and collective levels.

Individual strategies include getting a woman drunk and spending a great deal of money on her. As for collective strategies, most of our undergraduate interviewees agreed that fraternity parties often culminate in sex and that this outcome is planned. One fraternity man said fraternity parties often involve sex and nudity and can "turn into orgies." Orgies may be planned in advance, such as the Bowery Ball party held by one fraternity. A former fraternity member said of this party:

> The entire idea behind this is sex. Both men and women come to the party wearing little or nothing. There are pornographic pinups on the walls and usually porno movies playing on the TV. The music carries sexual overtones. . . . They just get schnockered [drunk] and, in most cases, they also get laid.

When asked about the women who come to such a party, he said: "Some Little Sisters just won't go. . . . The girls who do are looking for a good time, girls who don't know what it is, things like that."

Other respondents denied that fraternity parties are orgies but said that sex is always talked about among the brothers and they all know "who each other is doing it with." One member said that most of the time, guys have sex with their girlfriends "but with socials, girlfriends aren't allowed to come and it's their [members'] big chance [to have sex with other women]." The use of alcohol to help them get women into bed is a routine strategy at fraternity parties.

Conclusions

In general, our research indicated that the organization and membership of fraternities contribute heavily to coercive and often violent sex. Fraternity houses are occupied by same-sex (all men) and same-age (late teens, early twenties) peers whose maturity and judgment is often less than ideal. Yet fraternity houses are private dwellings that are mostly off-limits to, and away from scrutiny of, university and community representatives, with the result that fraternity house events seldom come to the attention of outsiders. Practices associated with the social construction of fraternity brotherhood emphasize a macho conception of men and masculinity, a narrow, stereotyped conception of women and femininity, and the treatment of women as commodities. Other practices contributing to coercive sexual relations and the cover-up of rapes include excessive alcohol use, competitiveness, and normative support for deviance and secrecy (cf. Bogal-Allbritten and Allbritten 1985; Kanin 1967).

Some fraternity practices exacerbate others. Brotherhood norms require "sticking together" regardless of right or wrong; thus rape episodes are unlikely to be stopped or reported to outsiders, even when witnesses disapprove. The ability to use alcohol without scrutiny by authorities and alcohol's frequent association with violence, including sexual coercion, facilitates rape in fraternity houses. Fraternity norms that emphasize the value of maleness and masculinity over femaleness and femininity and that elevate the status of men and lower the status of women in members' eyes undermine perceptions and treatment of women as persons who deserve consideration and care (cf. Ehrhart and Sandler 1985; Merton 1985).

Androgynous men and men with a broad range of interests and attributes are lost to fraternities through their recruitment practices. Masculinity of a narrow and stereotypical type helps create attitudes, norms, and practices that predispose fraternity men to coerce women sexually, both individually and collectively (Allgeier 1986; Hood 1989; Sanday 1981, 1986). Male athletes on campus may be similarly disposed for the same reasons (Kirshenbaum 1989; Telander and Sullivan 1989).

Research into the social contexts in which rape crimes occur and the social constructions associated with these contexts illumine rape dynamics on campus. Blanchard (1959) found that group rapes almost always have a leader who pushes others into the crime. He also found that the leader's latent homosexuality, desire to show off to his peers, or fear of failing to prove himself a man are frequently an impetus. Fraternity norms and practices contribute to the approval and use of sexual coercion as an accepted tactic in relations with women. Alcohol-induced compliance is normative, whereas, presumably, use of a knife, gun, or threat of bodily harm would not be because the woman who "drinks too much" is viewed as "causing her own rape" (cf. Ehrhart and Sandler 1985).

Our research led us to conclude that fraternity norms and practices influence members to view the sexual coercion of women, which is a felony crime, as sport, a contest, or a game (cf. Sato 1988). This sport is played not between men and women but between men and men. Women are the pawns or prey in the interfraternity rivalry game; they prove that a fraternity is successful or prestigious. The use of women in this way encourages fraternity men to see women as objects and sexual coercion as sport.

Today's societal norms support young women's right to engage in sex at their discretion, and coercion is unnecessary in a mutually desired encounter. However, nubile young women say they prefer to be "in a relationship" to have sex while young men say they prefer to "get laid" without a commitment (Muehlenhard and Linton 1987). These differences may reflect, in part, American puritanism and men's fears of sexual intimacy or perhaps intimacy of any kind. In a fraternity context, getting sex without giving emotionally demonstrates "cool" masculinity. More important, it poses no threat to the bonding and loyalty of the fraternity brotherhood (cf. Farr 1988). Drinking large quantities of alcohol before having sex suggests that "scoring" rather than intrinsic sexual pleasure is a primary concern of fraternity men.

Unless fraternities' composition, goals, structures, and practices change in fundamental ways, women on campus will continue to be sexual prey for fraternity men. As all-male enclaves dedicated to opposing faculty and administration and to cementing in-group ties, fraternity members eschew any hint of homosexuality. Their version of masculinity transforms women, and men with womanly characteristics, into the out group. "Womanly men" are ostracized; feminine women are used to demonstrate members' masculinity. Encouraging renewed emphasis on their founding values (Longino and Kart 1973), service orientation and activities (Lemire 1979), or members' moral development (Marlowe and Auvenshine 1982) will have little effect on fraternities' treatment of women. A case for or against fraternities cannot be made by studying individual members. The fraternity qua group and organization is at issue. Located on campus along with many vulnerable women, embedded in a sexist society, and caught up in masculinist goals, practices, and values, fraternities' violation of women—including forcible rape—should come as no surprise.

Note

1. Recent bans by some universities on open-keg parties at fraternity houses have resulted in heavy drinking before coming to a party and an increase in drunkenness among those who attend. This may aggravate, rather than improve, the treatment of women by fraternity men at parties.

References

Allgeier, Elizabeth. 1986. "Coercive Versus Consensual Sexual Interactions." G. Stanley Hall Lecture to American Psychological Association Annual Meeting, Washington, DC, August.

Adams, Aileen and Gail Abarbanel. 1988. *Sexual Assault on Campus: What Colleges Can Do.* Santa Monica, CA: Rape Treatment Center.

Blanchard, W. H. 1959. "The Group Process in Gang Rape." *Journal of Social Psychology* 49:259–66.

Bogal-Allbritten, Rosemarie B. and William L. Allbritten. 1985. "The Hidden Victims: Courtship Violence among College Students." *Journal of College Student Personnel* 43:201–4.

Bohrnstedt, George W. 1969. "Conservatism, Authoritarianism and Religiosity of Fraternity Pledges." *Journal of College Student Personnel* 27:36–43.

Bradford, Michael. 1986. "Tight Market Dries Up Nightlife at University." *Business Insurance* (March 2): 2, 6.

Burkhart, Barry. 1989. Comments in Seminar on Acquaintance/Date Rape Prevention: A National Video Teleconference, February 2.

Burkhart, Barry R. and Annette L. Stanton. 1985. "Sexual Aggression in Acquaintance Relationships." Pp. 43–65 in *Violence in Intimate Relationships,* edited by G. Russell. Englewood Cliffs, NJ: Spectrum.

Byington, Diane B. and Karen W. Keeter. 1988. "Assessing Needs of Sexual Assault Victims on a University Campus." Pp. 23–31 in *Student Services: Responding to Issues and Challenges.* Chapel Hill: University of North Carolina Press.

Chancer, Lynn S. 1987. "New Bedford, Massachusetts, March 6, 1983–March 22, 1984: The 'Before and After' of a Group Rape" *Gender & Society* 1:239–60.

Ehrhart, Julie K. and Bernice R. Sandler. 1985. *Campus Gang Rape: Party Games?* Washington, DC: Association of American Colleges.

Farr, K. A. 1988. "Dominance Bonding Through the Good Old Boys Sociability Network." *Sex Roles* 18:259–77.

Florida Flambeau. 1988. "Pike Members Indicted in Rape." (May 19):1, 5.

Fox, Elaine, Charles Hodge, and Walter Ward. 1987. "A Comparison of Attitudes Held by Black and White Fraternity Members." *Journal of Negro Education* 56:521–34.

Geis, Gilbert. 1971. "Group Sexual Assaults." *Medical Aspects of Human Sexuality* 5:101–13.

Glaser, Barney G. 1978. *Theoretical Sensitivity: Advances in the Methodology of Grounded Theory.* Mill Valley, CA: Sociology Press.

Hood, Jane. 1989. "Why Our Society Is Rape-Prone." *New York Times,* May 16.

Hughes, Michael J. and Roger B. Winston, Jr. 1987. "Effects of Fraternity Membership on Interpersonal Values." *Journal of College Student Personnel* 45:405–11.

Kanin, Eugene J. 1967. "Reference Groups and Sex Conduct Norm Violations." *The Sociological Quarterly* 8:495–504.

Kimmel, Michael, ed. 1987. *Changing Men: New Directions in Research on Men and Masculinity.* Newbury Park, CA: Sage.

Kirshenbaum, Jerry. 1989. "Special Report, An American Disgrace: A Violent and Unprecedented Lawlessness Has Arisen Among College Athletes in all Parts of the Country." *Sports Illustrated* (February 27): 16–19.

Lemire, David. 1979. "One Investigation of the Stereotypes Associated with Fraternities and Sororities." *Journal of College Student Personnel* 37:54–57.

Letchworth, G. E. 1969. "Fraternities Now and in the Future." *Journal of College Student Personnel* 10:118–22.

Longino, Charles F., Jr., and Cary S. Kart. 1973. "The College Fraternity: An Assessment of Theory and Research." *Journal of College Student Personnel* 31:118–25.

Marlowe, Anne F. and Dwight C. Auvenshine. 1982. "Greek Membership: Its Impact on the Moral Development of College Freshmen." *Journal of College Student Personnel* 40:53–57.

Martin, Patricia Yancey and Barry A. Turner. 1986. "Grounded Theory and Organizational Research." *Journal of Applied Behavioral Science* 22:141–57.

Merton, Andrew. 1985. "On Competition and Class: Return to Brotherhood." *Ms.* (September): 60–65, 121–22.

Messner, Michael. 1989. "Masculinities and Athletic Careers." *Gender & Society* 3:71–88.

Meyer, T. J. 1986. "Fight Against Hazing Rituals Rages on Campuses." *Chronicle of Higher Education* (March 12):34–36.

Miller, Leonard D. 1973. "Distinctive Characteristics of Fraternity Members." *Journal of College Student Personnel* 31:126–28.

Muehlenhard, Charlene L. and Melaney A. Linton. 1987. "Date Rape and Sexual Aggression in Dating Situations: Incidence and Risk Factors." *Journal of Counseling Psychology* 34:186–96.

Pressley, Sue Anne. 1987. "Fraternity Hell Night Still Endures." *Washington Post* (August 11):B1.

Rapaport, Karen and Barry R. Burkhart. 1984. "Personality and Attitudinal Characteristics of Sexually Coercive College Males." *Journal of Abnormal Psychology* 93:216–21.

Roark, Mary L. 1987. "Preventing Violence on College Campuses." *Journal of Counseling and Development* 65:367–70.

Sanday, Peggy Reeves. 1981. "The Socio-Cultural Context of Rape: A Cross-Cultural Study." *Journal of Social Issues* 37:5–27.

———. 1986. "Rape and the Silencing of the Feminine." Pp. 84–101 in *Rape,* edited by S. Tomaselli and R. Porter. Oxford: Basil Blackwell.

St. Petersburg Times. 1988. "A Greek Tragedy." (May 29):1F, 6F.

Sato, Ikuya. 1988. "Play Theory of Delinquency: Toward a General Theory of 'Action.'" *Symbolic Interaction* 11:191–212.

Smith, T. 1964. "Emergence and Maintenance of Fraternal Solidarity." *Pacific Sociological Review* 7:29–37.

Tallahassee Democrat. 1988a. "FSU Fraternity Brothers Charged" (April 27):1A, 12A.

———. 1988b. "FSU Interviewing Students About Alleged Rape" (April 24):1D.

———. 1989. "Woman Sues Stetson in Alleged Rape" (March 19):3B.

Tampa Tribune. 1988. "Fraternity Brothers Charged in Sexual Assault of FSU Coed." (April 27):6B.

Tash, Gary B. 1988. "Date Rape." *The Emerald of Sigma Pi Fraternity* 75(4):1–2.

Telander, Rick and Robert Sullivan. 1989. "Special Report, You Reap What You Sow." *Sports Illustrated* (February 27):20–34.

The Tomahawk. 1988. "A Look Back at Rush, A Mixture of Hard Work and Fun" (April/May):3D.

Walsh, Claire. 1989. Comments in Seminar on Acquaintance/Date Rape Prevention: A National Video Teleconference, February 2.

Wilder, David H., Arlyne E. Hoyt, Dennis M. Doren, William E. Hauck, and Robert D. Zettle. 1978. "The Impact of Fraternity and Sorority Membership on Values and Attitudes." *Journal of College Student Personnel* 36:445–49.

Wilder, David H., Arlyne E. Hoyt, Beth Shuster Surbeck, Janet C. Wilder, and Patricia Imperatrice Carney. 1986. "Greek Affiliation and Attitude Change in College Students." *Journal of College Student Personnel* 44:510–19.

20

Power, Sex, and Violence:
The Case of Marital Rape

Richard J. Gelles

The Women's Movement in the 1970s has increased the sensitivity of women and society to two major crimes which women fall victim to: sexual assault and physical assault by their husbands. Victims of rape and battered wives have a great deal in common. For years these two crimes have been the most underreported crimes against persons in the criminal justice system. Additionally, battered wives and rape victims are often accused of "asking for," "deserving," or "enjoying" their victimization. Finally, in most cases of rape or physical assault by their husbands, women who turn to the criminal justice system for assistance or relief are often maltreated or ignored by police, lawyers, and judges.

The purpose of this essay is to examine rape and physical violence together by analyzing the case of marital rape. The entire subject of marital rape, or sexual assault of wives by husbands, opens up a host of controversies. First, the concept of marital rape is one which has not existed legally. By legal tradition, a woman could not be raped by her husband, since the "crime" of rape was ordinarily and legally defined as forcing sexual intercourse on someone other than the wife of the person accused (Brownmiller, 1975; Gallen, 1967; Griffen, 1971; New York Radical Feminists, 1974).[1] Second, labeling sexual intercourse forced on a wife by a husband "marital rape" implies a major value judgment by the labeler concerning appropriate interpersonal relations between family members. Finally, if husbands force wives to have sexual relations, even accompanied by physical violence, do the wives or the husbands consider this behavior problematic or "rape"?

The essay begins by examining the controversies surrounding the study of marital rape. Next, the literature on rape is reviewed in order to summarize the facts known about rape which could be applied to the case of marital rape. The third section summarizes two sources of data which we use to shed some light on the incidence and social context of marital rape. The final section discusses further issues in the study of marital rape.

Does Marital Rape Exist?

The major question which must be addressed at the outset is, Can we or should we investigate a phenomenon which, by legal definition, has not even existed? Rape has been defined conceptually as "any sexual intimacy forced on one person by another" (Media and Thompson, 1974: 12). A less objective and more culturally relative definition of rape is provided by Levine in his study of rape in the Gussi tribe. Levine defines rape as "culturally disvalued use of coercion by a male to achieve the submission of a female to sexual intercourse" (1959: 969). The dictionary definition of rape is "sexual intercourse with a woman by a man without her consent and chiefly by force or deception" (Webster's New Collegiate Dictionary, 1975). Thus, by dictionary definition, conceptual definition, and cultural definition, any woman can theoretically be raped by any man. Media and Thompson's definition (1974) implies that a man can also be the victim of rape by a woman, and research on homosexual assault in prison documents that men are raped by men (Davis, 1970). The criminal justice system modifies these definitions by not viewing forced sexual intercourse between husbands and wives as rape. The rationale for this appears to be that the courts view the marriage contract as requiring wives (and husbands) to have sexual relations with their spouses (Cronan, 1969). While the "duty" of sex is, in a legal sense, equally distributed in marriage, the compulsory nature of sexual relations in marriage works chiefly to the advantage of the male (Gillespie, 1971) because men are typically able to muster more physical, social, and material resources in their relations with their wives.

Given that marital rape has not existed legally, should we examine it as part of family behavior and as an aspect of marital violence? We believe that we should. The legal prescriptions which imply that the wife is the "property" of her husband (Griffen, 1971) and which give the husband the permanent right to sexual relations once the wife says "I do" (New York Radical Feminists, 1974) are a reflection of an ideology, not a portrait of reality. The law is a reflection of what behavior ought to be, not what behavior actually is. The fact that the criminal justice system is largely populated by males partially explains the fact that legal statutes reflect a "male dominant" view of family behavior. A case in point is the California Penal Code, which requires that a woman be more injured than is commonly allowed for battery in order to press an assault charge against her husband (Calvert, 1974). The fact that the courts do not accept the concept of marital rape does not, in our opinion, mean that wives are not being raped by their husbands.

Because forced sexual relations between a husband and wife have traditionally not legally been considered cases of rape, the question arises whether or not a wife herself views the incident as a rape. This is an empirical question which we will take up in detail in a later section of the essay, but it is likely that the majority of women who are physically forced into having sexual intercourse with their husbands do not consider this to be an incident of rape, a violent act, or a deviant act. Thus, if the victim herself is unlikely to view the behavior as rape, how can we discuss the phenomenon of marital rape? In order to answer the question it would be wise

to briefly analyze why a woman would not view physically coerced sex as rape. Our research on marital violence suggests that many victims of family violence (including abused children) do not view these acts as violence or as problematic. Women who have been beaten severely by their husbands often state that they "deserved to be hit," that they "needed to be hit," or that "husbands are supposed to hit their wives" (see Gelles, 1974; 1976; and Parnas, 1967). The fact that women are socialized to believe that violence between spouses is expected and normative does not diminish the fact that women are often injured by their husbands in trying to redress these acts (see Field and Field, 1973; Truninger, 1971; Gelles, 1976). In analyzing forced sexual relations between spouses, we believe that the pervasive ideology of "women as men's chattel" has served to deny women the opportunity to perceive their own sexual victimization. We have chosen to discuss the issue of marital rape, irrespective of the wife's subjective perceptions of the behavior, because we believe this is a phenomenon which needs to be questioned and studied.

The discussion of the wife's perceptions of forced sexual intercourse and our rationale for choosing to investigate this phenomenon despite the fact that many women do not perceive themselves as rape victims raises the issue of the value implications involved in labeling the phenomenon as rape. Rape is a perjorative term which connotes repulsive and violent deviance. Webster's New Collegiate Dictionary states that rape can also be defined as "an outrageous violation" (Webster's New Collegiate Dictionary, 1975). We have chosen to use the term rape in this essay for the same reasons we have decided to title our investigation "Studies of Violence Between Family Members" and for the same reasons we have chosen to study abused wives. We believe that the area of violence between family members has long suffered from selective inattention (Dexter, 1958) at the hands of both social scientists and society in general. The plight of victims of violence between family members has been overlooked by students of the family, agencies of social control and social services, and the public at large. In order to rectify this situation, it often requires using an emotionally charged word to draw attention to this phenomenon. The history of research on abused children reveals that battered children were largely ignored until Henry Kempe labeled the phenomenon as "The Battered Child Syndrome" (Kempe et al., 1962). We have decided to label this essay as an investigation of marital rape partly as a reaction to the discriminatory practice of not allowing a woman to protect herself from violent or physically coercive sexual intercourse at the hand of her husband, and in an attempt to draw scholarly and public attention to this issue.

Research on Rape

Because the law views rape as an act of sexual penetration of the body of a woman *not one's wife,* there are virtually no official statistics available on the subject of marital rape. Brownmiller alludes to the depiction of a marital rape on a television episode of the series "The Forsythe Saga" (Brownmiller, 1975) and Russell (1975) devotes a chapter of her book to a description of marital rape. Beyond these descriptive data and illustrations, there is little else one can locate which bears directly on the incidence or nature of marital rape. The lack of official statistical data is a direct result of the law not viewing marital rape as a crime. Peters (1975), for example, reports that none of the patients he treated for incestuous rape reported their assaults.[2]

There are two areas of rape research which bear on the case of marital rape. The first area is the study of victim-offender relations and the second considers the element of "power" as a component of sexual assault.

Victim-Offender Relations

The conventional wisdom concerning rape suggests that women are typically assaulted in dark alleys by strangers. The research which has been carried out on patterns of rape indicates that this conventional wisdom may be more myth than reality. Amir's research (1971) on patterns of victimization revealed that 48% of the rape victims knew the offender. Pauline Bart's (1975) examination of 1,070 questionnaires filled out by victims of rape found that 5% of the women were raped by relatives, .4% by husbands, 1%

by lovers, and 3% by ex-lovers. Thus, a total of 8.4% of the women were raped by men with whom they had intimate relations. Bart's survey also found that 12% of rape victims were raped by dates and 23% were raped by acquaintances. Less than half of the victims (41%) were raped by total strangers.

Additional research on rape also reveals a pattern where victims were likely to know the offender or be related to the offender. Of the 250 victims of rape studied by the Center for Rape Concern at Philadelphia General Hospital, 58% of the rape victims under the age of 18 were assaulted by a relative or acquaintance. When the victim is a child, she is likely to be sexually attacked by her father—six of the 13 children were raped by their fathers (Peters, 1975).

The research on victim-offender relationships dispels the myth that the majority of women are raped by strangers. For the purposes of our focus on marital rape, the research results indicate that intimacy and sexual assault are frequently related. The women who are raped by boyfriends, dates, lovers, ex-lovers, husbands, relatives, and other men that they know *might* represent the tip of an iceberg which reveals a more extensive pattern relating intimacy with forced sexual relations.

Power and Rape

A theme in much of the literature on rape is that rape is less a sexual act and more an act of power in the relations between men and women. Bart concludes, based on her analysis of questionnaires filled out by rape victims, that rape is a power trip, not a passion trip (1975). Brownmiller also perceives rape as a power confrontation. She views rape as an act of hostility toward women by men—rape is an attempt by a man to exercise power over a woman (1975). Seites (1975) agrees that rape is a sexual power confrontation. She postulates that marital rape is an act where a husband can assert his power and control over his wife.

If rape is viewed more as an act of power than a sexual act, then we can examine marital rape by focusing on the power dynamics of the family. Goode (1971) has stated that all social systems depend on force or its threat, and that the family is no exception. Goode goes on to propose that the more resources individuals have, the more force they can command, but the less they will use that force. On the other hand, the fewer resources individuals have, the less force they can command, but the more they will use the force. Goode theorizes that men who lack sufficient resources to hold the socially prescribed dominant role in the family will use physical force to compensate for the lack of resources.

If Goode's resource theory of family violence is correct, then we can predict that men who command limited social/psychological and verbal resources are likely to use more force on their wives than men who are well educated, hold prestigious jobs, and earn a respectable income (see O'Brien, 1971, and Gelles, 1974, for empirical data on this hypothesis). If rape is viewed as an act of violence and an act of power, we could deduce that men who have few social and psychological resources are likely to use an act such as marital rape to intimidate, coerce, and dominate their wives. Rape of wives might grow out of a husband's lack of verbal skills and an inability to argue equally with his wife, or it might be a means of the husband demonstrating how he can dominate his wife despite the fact that he is poorly educated or unemployed. In addition, because rape can be a degrading experience, some husbands may use this act to humiliate their wives and thus gain a degree of power and control over their spouses.

Research on Marital Rape

While the research on victim-offender relationships, on victims of rape, and on family violence allows us to speculate about marital rape, the research carried out to date allows no direct insights into the incidence or nature of the phenomenon. In order to provide some direct information on the topic of marital rape we attempted to gather data which would shed light on this phenomenon. This section reports on two investigations. The first was a survey of Rape-Crisis Centers which asked the centers to provide us information on the number of cases of marital rape they encounter and on specific

aspects of these cases. The second investigation was part of a larger study of physical violence between husbands and wives (see Gelles, 1974, 1975b, 1976). The second investigation analyzed transcriptions of interviews with women who had been beaten by their husbands to see what information could be gleaned on the sexual aspects of the beatings.

The increased attention on the plight of victims of sexual assaults led to the establishment of Rape-Crisis Centers throughout the nation which provide legal, medical, and social services to victims of rape. In the spring of 1975 Joan Seites (1975) contacted 40 Rape-Crisis Centers which were chosen from a listing compiled by the Center for Women Policy Studies.[3] From the centers 16 completed questionnaires were returned (one questionnaire was returned because of insufficient address), a response rate of 40%.

The purpose of the survey was to determine whether or not cases of marital rape are reported to Rape-Crisis Centers, and if so, how many cases are reported. Of the 3,709 reported calls dealing with rape and attempted rape received by the 16 centers, 12 calls dealt with marital rape (.3%). This figure is low and comparable with Bart's finding (1975) that .8% of the victims of rape reported being attacked by their husbands.

Because Rape-Crisis Centers do not always record the offender-victim relationship, we cannot be sure that the 12 reported marital rapes fully represent the proportion of husband-wife rapes in the 3,709 calls which were handled. However, the data do reveal that at least some women are reporting instances of marital rape despite the fact that the law does not view forced marital sexual intercourse as rape and despite the fact that few women would view physically coerced sex at the hands of their husbands as requiring a call to a Rape-Crisis Center.

The questionnaires also asked the centers to discuss some of the aspects of the calls they received about marital rape. One agency reported that women complained that their husbands were coming home drunk and hitting them and then raping them. These callers were not asking for rape counseling, they asked for information about divorce. It would appear that because there are few agencies which are capable of providing counseling and assistance to battered wives (there were 6 Battered Wife Centers in the United States as of March 1976), that women who were beaten by their husbands seek help from the best known women's agency—Rape-Crisis Centers. Thus, wives may report rape and battering to centers in order to get some help in solving problems of marital violence.

The agencies which did provide information about cases of marital rape reported that raped wives were likely to be fearful of future assaults and were angry with their husbands. One agency provided a personal account of a woman whose husband attempted to rape her.

> Almost 14 years ago, my first husband attempted to rape me. At the time, we were very close to being separated and I think he wanted to attempt to bring us closer, back together through a sexual act—he always maintained that that was his prime means of communication, how he felt the closest. At first I fought and when he attempted to smother me with a pillow, I panicked and became only concerned with how to get him to stop—I was afraid he was going to kill me. So I became totally unresponsive to him—wouldn't talk or anything and he eventually stopped tearing my clothes and pulling me and there was no intercourse. Because it happened in the context of a whole lot of bad things in our marriage (he had been violent to me once or twice before, but not sexually so), I didn't have any particular feelings at the time except relief that it was over. Very shortly thereafter, I left him. I never thought of the incident as attempted rape until almost 10 years later when I was walking away from a session of a women's group I was in wherein we had been talking about specific rape incidents that had occurred to some of the members. Until that time, I think I felt rape was of the stereotypic type of the stranger leaping out of the bushes and never thought of an incident like that occurring between people who knew each other—especially husband and wife, as rape. I think this is true of many married women—they have accepted society's dictum that a man has sexual access to his wife whenever he wants, whether she does or not. Thus, it never occurs to them that this could be a crime, a felonious assault, that this is, indeed, rape.

The questionnaires from the Rape-Crisis Centers provide some additional information on marital rape. First, although forced sexual intercourse may take place frequently between husbands and wives, most women do not view this as rape.

> I know personally, not professionally, many women who have been raped by their husbands. Some file for divorce. Few consider the act rape, since they themselves consider themselves property.

> Most women probably do not realize, or classify such actions as "rape" because they have been infused with cultural myths surrounding rape.

Many wives view themselves to blame for the incidents of forced sexual intercourse. The woman raped by her husband who was interviewed for Russell's book (1975) indicated that she thought the incident was partially her fault because she should have known not to get into the situation which led to her victimization. This kind of victim-blaming is common in incidents of rape where victims are thought to have brought on the assault through provocative behavior and being "in the wrong place at the wrong time." Victim-blaming by the victim is found in instances of marital rape and marital violence (Gelles, 1974; 1976) as victims of deviance in the family try to neutralize the stigma of the deviance by blaming themselves for their husbands' behavior.

Lastly, as in cases of marital violence, women who are forced into having sexual relations with their husbands are ashamed to tell other people about this problem.

> The biggest issue we've noticed is that married women don't talk to each other about their sex lives to any extent and especially not about rape!

In-Depth Interviews

Interviews with 80 family members on the subject of violence between husbands and wives elicited some discussions about the relation between sex and violence. A number of wives reported being beaten by their husbands as a result of their husbands becoming jealous over a suspected incident of infidelity. Husbands also reported that their wives struck them over suspicions about extramarital affairs (see Gelles, 1974: 82–85, 147–148).

Although the questions asked in the course of the interviews did not specifically pertain to the subject of marital rape, an analysis of the transcriptions of the interviews identified four women who discussed sex-related violence which could be viewed as instances of marital rape or attempted marital rape. The most consistent pattern found in the interviews with the four women was that they felt that they were coerced or forced into having sex with their husbands and that the husbands criticized the wives for not being affectionate.

> Well, uh, he used to tell everybody that I was cold . . . he (came home) drunk or he had been out half the night. I didn't really feel like it (sexual intercourse). But we never argued about it. Usually he got his way because I wasn't about to go up against it.

> He was one of those—he liked to strike out a lot and hit you and a lot of that was based on sex . . . he thought that I was a cold fish—I wasn't affectionate enough. . . . Sometimes he took a shotgun to me.

> He was drinking . . . I know that was the problem—he said as far as he was concerned I wasn't affectionate enough—it (sexual intercourse) was anytime he felt like it—whatever time he came home—it was crazy . . . different hours.

What emerged from the interviews was that wives frequently did not want to have sex with their husbands because of the fact that their husbands were drunk, came home at odd hours, or were critical of their wives' sexual responsiveness. The husbands, however, appeared to believe that their wives should have intercourse with them on demand and that if they refused it was because they (the wives) were frigid. Moreover, husbands seemed to view a refusal of intercourse as grounds for beating or intimidating their wives.

In all four cases, the wives gave in to their husbands' demands rather than be physically forced into having sexual intercourse. Thus, the review of the in-depth interviews did not find an instance of a woman being violently forced into having sex, as in the case discussed previously in this essay or the case discussed by Russell (1975).

We have stated previously that one reason why so little attention has been directed toward forced sexual intercourse in marriage is the theory that this is not viewed as a problem by most wives. One interview indicated that forced sex was, indeed, viewed as problematic by at least one woman in the study. This woman explained that she often provoked her husband into physical fights by verbally taunting him after he came home intoxicated and demanding sex. She went on to state that her husband would beat her after these verbal assaults, she would cry, and he would drop his demands for sex. Thus, she viewed being beaten up as a more acceptable alternative to marital rape.

An analysis of the literature on rape, the survey of Rape-Crisis Centers asking about marital rape, and the examination of transcripts of interviews on marital violence only begins to scratch the surface of the topic of marital rape. There are numerous issues which ought to be considered in detail in further investigations of marital rape. We shall briefly discuss five issues where further consideration is needed.

1. It is claimed that the family predominates in acts of violence ranging from slaps to murder and torture (Straus, Gelles, and Steinmetz, 1976). Although the official statistics on rape do not bear us out, we believe that a woman is most likely to be physically forced into having sexual intercourse by her own husband. Previous studies of marital violence (Gelles, 1974; Straus, 1974a, 1974b, 1976; Steinmetz, 1975) have not examined sexual violence in marriage. We think that an important aspect of future research on violence in the family would be a focus on acts of marital rape and acts of violence which involve the sexual suppression of women.

2. A second issue which we feel needs to be discussed is the nominal and operational definitions of marital rape. The central question which needs elaboration is whether marital rape is an

act which must be accompanied by physical force and violence, or whether the act *itself* is violent? Interviews with women who had been victims of violence indicate that most of these women submitted to sexual intercourse without being physically beaten. Because the intercourse was not accompanied by violence, these women did not view the behavior as rape, and instead focused on their husbands' drinking or staying out late as the main problems in the marriage. Because marital rape is technically legal and because women have traditionally been socialized to believe they are the property of their husbands, we would speculate that the only instances of marital rape which would be reported to Rape-Crisis Centers, social service agencies, or social scientists would be those cases where physical violence is involved. Thus, the full extent of how many women are verbally coerced or intimidated into having sex against their wills with their husbands may remain an unknown.

3. We have been able to glean some insights on marital rape from the research on victim-offender relations in cases of rape. One area where the research on nonmarital rape can provide no help in understanding marital rape is the consequences of the attack. Much of the research on rape goes into great detail on the aftermath of the attack and the effects on the victim. We believe that the consequences of being raped by a stranger or even a boyfriend are far different from being raped by one's husband. Peters (1975) who studied a number of cases of incestuous sexual assault, proposes that rape by a family member or relative produces different emotional consequences than rape by a stranger. Peters states that rape by a stranger might be physically dangerous, but rape by a relative or friend may be more disillusionary. Russell's presentation of a case of marital rape (1975: 71–81) illustrates this point. Mrs. Michel, who was raped by her husband in front of bystanders, stated that she felt the rape was partially her fault. She broke out in hives the next day and felt humiliated by the incident. While we know about the reactions of women who were raped by non-family members, and we have some data on battered wives, we know little about women who are sexually assaulted by their husbands. The available data suggest that raped wives are nei-

ther masochists nor do they enjoy being sexually assaulted by their husbands (see Russell, 1975: 75).

4. A discussion of rape or marital violence almost inevitably raises the question of whether there is an association between acts of violence and acts of sex. Faulk (1977) suggests that marital violence may sometimes be sexually stimulating in itself. He states that some wives report that their husbands want sexual intercourse soon after a violent outburst. Faulk goes on to report that it is uncertain whether the violence itself is sexually stimulating or whether husbands are trying to use sexual intercourse as a means of reconciliation. In addition:

> Some wives report that their clothes were partly torn off during the violence, and a few saw this as sexually motivated. It seems likely, however, that in many cases the clothes were torn off to prevent women from escaping [Faulk, 1977].

The little empirical research and theoretical discussion which focuses on the relationship between sex and violence support Faulk's contention that sex is not an intrinsic component of marital violence. An analysis of TAT responses of college students to ambiguous pictures reveals little association between sexual thema and violent thema in the stories produced (Gelles, 1975a). While women did not associate sex with violence in their fantasy production, there was a slight association in the stories produced by men. Steinmetz and Straus (1974) argue that there is little evidence for a *biological* association between sex and violence and postulate that sex antagonism and sex segregation in this society might explain the tendency to use violence in sexual acts.

The analysis of marital rape suggests that the association of sex and violence are means which husbands can use to dominate and intimidate their wives without fear of outside intervention. Because women cannot legally charge their husbands with marital rape and because acts of marital violence rarely result in successful prosecution of the husband, forced sexual intercourse and marital violence are two unsanctioned methods which husbands can invoke to establish dominance in their families.

5. The final point for consideration concerns the nature of the law which denies women the right to charge or seek prosecution of their husbands for acts of marital rape. An obvious question which arises is, if marital rape exists, and it is a problem, should the law be changed to provide women avenues of legal recourse for redress in acts of marital rape? If we argue that yes, the laws should be changed, there are two problems which arise. First, if all wives could take their husbands to court for forcing them into having sexual intercourse, this might flood the court with intrafamily litigations. The already overburdened criminal justice system probably could not handle the large number of cases which it might have to process. Second, arguing for changing the law somehow implies that such a change would provide women with legal rights. The case of marital violence serves as a good reminder that giving a woman the *de jure* legal power to charge her husband with an illegal act does not necessarily mean that the police and courts will provide her with relief and protection. Although women can charge their husbands with physical assault, the chances of the courts intervening and helping them are quite slim (Gelles, 1976; Truninger, 1971; Field and Field, 1973). Any legal change in the area of marital rape would also have to be accompanied by social, attitudinal, and moral changes whereby society views the issue of marital rape seriously, refrains from viewing victimized wives as being masochists or really enjoying the rape, and conveys a willingness to intervene in family matters and provide real protection for victims of marital rape.

Conclusion

The available evidence on marital violence indicates that a number of women are forced into having sexual relations with their husbands through intimidation or physical force. Faulk's research (1977) identified cases where sexual intercourse was forced on a wife after her husband beat her. Other data point to the fact that despite the fact that marital rape is not possible in a strict legal sense, some women are talking about and reporting incidents of marital rape.

From a research point of view, we believe that the topic of marital rape is an important area of investigation for social scientists. Investigations of marital rape and subjective perceptions of forced sexual relations between husbands and wives (including instances where wives are forced into having sexual acts that they find repugnant) will provide valuable insights into the family, power relations in the family, and the range and nature of sexual activities in marriage. A focus on marital rape also tends to move this subject from the taken for granted into the problematic. This transition might serve to call into question the legal position of women and whether women ought to have broader legal rights in terms of dealing with their husbands. We conclude that the head in-the-sand approach to marital rape is no longer acceptable for social scientists, members of the criminal justice system, or for women in this society.

Editor's Note: This chapter was originally published in the *Family Coordinator,* volume 26(1977): 339–347, an official publication of the National Council on Family Relations.

Notes

1. South Dakota became the first state to eliminate the spousal exclusion from the statute on rape. The 1975 Rape Law reads: "Rape is an act of sexual penetration accomplished by any person." Other states, such as Florida, do not specifically exempt married persons from rape prosecution (Silverman, 1976:10). NB: As of January 1, 1979, Oregon, Iowa, Delaware, Massachusetts, and New Jersey had removed the spousal exclusion from their Rape Laws. South Dakota placed the spousal exclusion back in the Rape Law in 1977.

2. Incestuous sexual assaults are not reported for other reasons, among which might be the victims' embarrassment.

3. A sample of 40 crisis centers was chosen from the listing. A questionnaire was sent to Rape-Crisis Centers in each state represented in the listing. If more than one Rape-Crisis Center was listed in a state, then a single center was selected based on the degree of professionalism

and organization indicated by the name of the center. The sample, while geographically broad, is *not* a representative sample of Rape-Crisis Centers. Each center was sent a questionnaire with a self-addressed, stamped envelope. Only a one-wave mailing was used in this survey.

Update

The Extent of Marital Rape

Our discovery of marital rape was a serendipitous finding of an exploratory research project aimed at examining violence toward women (Gelles, 1974).

Since the publication of "Power, Sex, and Violence: The Case of Marital Rape," there have been three major research efforts aimed at discovering the extent and patterns of marital rape. The sociologists David Finkelhor and Kersti Yllo interviewed 323 Boston-area women for their book, *License to Rape: Sexual Abuse of Wives* (1985). In their book, 10% of the women said they had been forced to have sex with their husbands or partners. Violence accompanied the rape in about half of the instances. This rate of rape compares to the 3% of the women who reported being raped by strangers. Finkelhor and Yllo conclude that rape by intimates is by far the most common form of rape.

Diana Russell surveyed more than 930 women in San Francisco for her book, *Rape in Marriage* (1982). Of the 644 women who had been married, 14% reported one or more experiences of marital rape.

The sociologists Nancy Shields and Christine Hanneke have also been investigating marital rape and its relation to wife battering (1983). They have found that a significant number of battering victims are also victims of marital rape. Their data suggest that when sexual violence occurs in a marriage it is not an isolated event. Most of the victims in the Shields and Hanneke study were raped more than once or twice.

Legal Changes

At the time of the initial research on marital rape, there had been little public attention focused on the problem. Only one state had removed the marital exclusion from the rape laws (South Dakota). At the time of the initial publication of "Power, Sex, and Violence: The Case of Marital Rape" the case of John and Greta Rideout was making headlines across the country. Greta Rideout had charged her husband, John, with marital rape; and the case was about to go to trial in Oregon. The case received significant media attention for weeks and ended with John's acquittal and the couple's reconciliation.

There has been a national debate over whether marital rape should be criminalized. Arguments against criminalizing marital rape include the position that outlawing marital rape would lead to frivolous claims, that the private nature of the "crime" would make it impossible to prove, that such a law would have a negative effect on the family and pave the road to divorce, that such a law is a violation of privacy, and that the law is superfluous (Finkelhor and Yllo, 1985).

Nevertheless, those arguing that marital rape is a crime and needs to be outlawed if women are to be protected and the crime is to be deterred have made inroads in nearly every state. At this writing [1987], according to the National Clearinghouse on Marital Rape in Berkeley, California, 28 states and the District of Columbia allow a husband to be prosecuted for rape even while he lives with his partner; 21 states allow prosecution of the partners if they are living apart; and 1 state, Alabama, retains the marital exclusion for married partners, irrespective of where they live.

References

Amir, M. (1971) *Patterns of Forcible Rape.* Urbana, IL: University of Chicago Press.
Bart, P. (1975) "Rape doesn't end with a kiss." *Viva* 39–42: 100–102.
Brownmiller, S. (1975) *Against Our Will: Men, Women and Rape.* New York: Simon & Shuster.

Calvert, R. (1974) "Criminal and civil liability in husband-wife assaults," pp. 88–90 in S. Steinmetz and M. Straus (eds.) *Violence in the Family*. New York: Harper & Row.

Cronan, S. (1969) *Marriage*. New York: Feminist Press.

Davis, A. (1970) "Sexual assaults in the Philadelphia prison system," pp. 107–124 in J. Gagnon and W. Simon (eds.) *The Sexual Scene*. Chicago: Aldine.

Dexter, L. (1958) "A note on selective inattention in social science." *Social Problems* 6 (Fall): 176–182.

Faulk, M. (1977) "Sexual factors in marital violence." *Medical Aspects of Human Sexuality* 11 (October): 30–38.

Field, M. and H. Field (1973) "Marital violence and the criminal process: neither justice nor peace." *Social Service Review* 47, 2: 221–240.

Finkelhor, D. and K. Yllo (1985) *License to Rape: Sexual Abuse of Wives*. New York: Holt Rinehart, & Winston.

Gallen, R. (1967) *Wives' Legal Rights*. New York: Dell.

Gelles, R. (1974) *The Violent Home: A Study of Physical Aggression between Husbands and Wives*. Newbury Park, CA: Sage.

Gelles, R. (1975a) "On the association of sex and violence in the fantasy production of college students." *Suicide* 5 (Summer): 78–85.

Gelles, R. (1975b) "Violence and pregnancy: a note on the extent of the problem and needed services." *Family Coordinator* 24 (January): 81–86.

Gelles, R. (1976) "Abused wives: why do they stay?" *Journal of Marriage and the Family* 38 (November): 659–668.

Gillespie, D. (1971) "Who has the power? The marital struggle." *Journal of Marriage and the Family* 33 (August): 445–458.

Goode, W. (1971) "Force and violence in the family." *Journal of Marriage and the Family* 33 (November): 624–636.

Griffen, S. (1971) "Rape: the all-American crime." *Ramparts* (September): 26–35.

Levine, R. (1959) "Gussi sex offenses: a study in social control." *American Anthropologist* 61: 965–990.

Media, A. and K. Thompson (1974) *Against Rape*. New York: Farrar, Straus, & Giroux.

New York Radical Feminists (1974) *Rape: The First Sourcebook for Women*. New York: New American Library.

O'Brien, J. (1971) "Violence in divorce prone families." *Journal of Marriage and the Family* 33 (November): 692–698.

Parnas, R. (1967) "The police response to domestic disturbance." *Wisconsin Law Review* 914 (Fall): 914–960.

Peters, J. (1975) "The Philadelphia rape victim study," pp. 181–199 in I. Drapkin and E. Viano (eds.) *Victimology: A New Focus*, Vol. 3. Lexington, MA: D. C. Heath.

Russell, D. (1975) *The Politics of Rape: The Victim's Perspective*. New York: Stein and Day.

Russell, D. (1982) *Rape in Marriage*. New York: Macmillan.

Seites, J. (1975) "Marital rape: dispelling the myth." (Unpublished).

Shields, N. M. and C. R. Hanneke (1983) "Battered wive's reactions to marital rape," pp. 132–150 in D. Finkelhor et al. (eds.) *The Dark Side of Families: Current Family Violence Research*. Newbury Park, CA: Sage.

Silverman, S. (1976) "Rape in marriage: is it legal?" *Do It Now* (June): 10.

Steinmetz, S. (1975) "Intra-familial patterns of conflict resolution: husband/wife; parent/child; sibling/sibling." Ph.D. dissertation, Case Western Reserve University.

Steinmetz, S. and M. Straus (1974) *Violence in the Family*. New York: Harper & Row.

Straus, M. (1974b) "Cultural and social organizational influences on violence between family members," pp. 53–69 in R. Prince and D. Barrier (eds.) *Configurations: Biological and Cultural Factors in Sexuality and Family Life*. Lexington, MA: D. C. Heath.

Straus, M. (1974c) "Leveling, civility, and violence in the family." *Journal of Marriage and the Family* 36 (February): 13–29.

Straus, M. (1976) "Sexual inequality, cultural norms, and wife beating." *Victimology* 1 (Spring): 54–76.

Straus, M., R. Gelles, and S. Steinmetz (1976) "Violence in the family: an assessment of knowledge and research needs." Paper presented at the annual meetings of the American Association for the Advancement of Science.

Truninger, E. (1971) "Marital violence: the legal solutions." *Hastings Law Review* 23 (November): 259–276.

Webster's New Collegiate Dictionary (1975) Springfield, MA: Merriam.

21

Rape Law Reform and Instrumental Change in Six Urban Jurisdictions

Julie Horney
Cassia Spohn

During the past twenty years there has been a sweeping effort to reform rape laws in this country. Reformers questioned the special status of rape as an offense for which the victim, as well as the defendant, was put on trial. They suggested that the laws and rules of evidence unique to rape were at least partially responsible for the unwillingness of victims to report rapes and for the low rates of arrest, prosecution, and conviction (Batelle Memorial Institute 1977; Loh 1980; McCahill, Meyer, and Fischman 1979; Vera Institute of Justice 1981). They cited evidence that these laws and rules of evidence resulted in pervasive skepticism of the victim's claims and allowed criminal justice officials to use legally irrelevant assessments of the victim's status, character, and relationship with the defendant in making decisions regarding the processing and disposition of rape cases (Bohmer 1974; Estrich 1987; Feild and Bienen 1980; Feldman-Summers and Lindner 1976; Holmstrom and Burgess 1978; Kalven and Zeisel 1966; LaFree 1981, 1989; McCahill et al. 1979; Reskin and Visher 1986).

Concerns such as these sparked a nationwide, grass-roots movement in which women's groups lobbied for rape law reforms. Their efforts resulted in changes in the rape laws of all fifty states. The overall purpose of the reforms was to treat rape like other crimes by focusing not on the behavior or reputation of the victim but on the unlawful acts of the offender. Advocates of the new laws anticipated that by improving the treatment of rape victims the reforms would ultimately lead to an increase in the number of reports of rape (Cobb and Schauer 1974; Marsh, Geist, and Caplan 1982; Sasko and Sesek 1975). They also expected that the reforms would remove legal barriers to effective prosecution and would make arrest, prosecution, and conviction for rape more likely (Cobb and Schauer 1974; Marsh et al. 1982; Robin 1982).

In this study we address these expectations. Using time-series data on more than twenty

From "Rape Law Reform and Instrumental Change in Six Urban Jurisdictions," by Julie Horney and Cassia Spohn. *Law and Society Review* 25 (1991), pp. 117–153. Reprinted by permission of the Law and Society Association.

This mansucript is based on work supported by the National Institute of Justice under Grant No. SES 8508323 and by the National Science Foundation under Grant No. 85-IJ-CX-0048. Points of view are those of the authors and do not necessarily represent the position of the U.S. Department of Justice or the National Science Foundation.

Numerous people made important contributions to this research effort over a period of several years. We would especially like to thank our project associates who supervised the data collection at the study sites: James Gibson, University of Houston; Kathryn Newcomer, George Washington University; Karen O'Connor, Emory University; Joseph Peterson, University of Illinois at Chicago; and David Rauma, University of Michigan. We would also like to thank our data collectors, who coded data on thousands of cases from court records.

thousand rape cases in six major urban jurisdictions, we examine the impact of rape reform legislation on reports of rape and the outcome of rape cases.

Rape Law Reform

States enacted reform statutes that vary in comprehensiveness and encompass a broad range of reforms. The most common changes were (1) changes in the definition of rape; (2) elimination of the resistance requirement; (3) elimination of the corroboration requirement; and (4) enactment of a rape shield law. We briefly describe each of these reforms below.

1. Many states replaced the single crime of rape with a series of offenses graded by seriousness and with commensurate penalties. Historically, rape was defined as "carnal knowledge of a woman, not one's wife, by force and against her will." Thus, traditional rape laws did not include attacks on male victims, acts other than sexual intercourse, sexual assaults with an object, or sexual assaults by a spouse. The new crimes typically are gender neutral and include a range of sexual assaults.

2. A number of jurisdictions changed the consent standard by modifying or eliminating the requirement that the victim resist her attacker. Under traditional rape statutes, the victim, to demonstrate her lack of consent, was required to "resist to the utmost" or, at the very least, exhibit "such earnest resistance as might reasonably be expected under the circumstances" (Tex. Penal Code 1980). Reformers challenged these standards, arguing not only that resistance could lead to serious injury but also that the law should focus on the behavior of the offender rather than on that of the victim. In response, states either eliminated resistance of the victim as an element of the crime to be proved by the prosecutor or attempted to lessen the state's burden of proving nonconsent by specifying the circumstances that constitute force—using or displaying a weapon, committing another crime at the same time, injuring the victim, and so on.

3. The third type of statutory reform was elimination of the corroboration requirement—the rule prohibiting conviction for forcible rape on the uncorroborated testimony of the victim. Critics cited the difficulty in obtaining evidence concerning an act that typically takes place in a private place without witnesses. They also objected to rape being singled out as the only crime with such a requirement.

4. Most states enacted rape shield laws that placed restrictions on the introduction of evidence of the victim's prior sexual conduct. Under common law, evidence of the victim's sexual history was admissible to prove she had consented to intercourse and to impeach her credibility. Reformers were particularly critical of this two-pronged evidentiary rule and insisted that it be eliminated or modified. Critics argued that the rule was archaic in light of changes in attitudes toward sexual relations and women's role in society. They stressed that evidence of the victim's prior sexual behavior was of little, if any, probative worth (Ireland 1978). Confronted with arguments such as these, state legislatures enacted rape shield laws designed to limit the admissibility of evidence of the victim's past sexual conduct. The laws range from the less restrictive, which permit sexual conduct evidence to be admitted following a showing of relevance, to the more restrictive, which prohibit such evidence except in a few narrowly defined situations. The laws also usually specify procedures for determining the relevance of the evidence; most states require an *in camera* hearing to determine whether the proffered evidence is admissible.

The Impact of Rape Reform

Proponents of rape law reform predicted that the various statutory changes would produce a number of instrumental results. They expected the reforms, particularly the rape shield laws, to improve the treatment of rape victims and thus to prompt more victims to report the crime to the police. They believed that elimination of resistance and corroboration requirements would remove major barriers to conviction; as a result, prosecutors would be more likely to indict and fully prosecute rape cases, and juries and judges would be more likely to convict in rape trials. They expected that conviction would also be facilitated by the enactment of rape shield laws that restricted admission of evidence of the complainant's sexual history. Finally, reformers believed that definitional changes would make it easier to prosecute cases that did not fit traditional definitions of rape, would prevent jury nullification by having penalties commensurate with the seriousness of the offense, and would lead to more convictions through plea bargaining because appropriate lesser offenses would be available to prosecutors in their negotiations.

Reformers clearly had high hopes for the rape law reforms, but their expectations may have been unrealistic. In fact, the literature on legal impact, which abounds with examples of "the remarkable capacity of criminal courts to adjust to and effectively thwart reforms" (Eisenstein, Flemming, and Nardulli 1988:296), should lead us to predict that the rape law reforms would have only limited effects on reports of rape and the outcome of rape cases.

The chronic failure of reforms aimed at the court system suggests that reformers have misperceptions about the nature of the judicial process (Nimmer 1978). Most reform proposals "assume that we have a hierarchic, centralized, obedient system of courts that will automatically and faithfully adhere to new rules" (Eisenstein et al. 1988:296). These misperceptions cause reformers to overestimate the role of legal rules in controlling the behavior of decisionmakers and to underestimate the role of discretion in modifying the legal rules. Statutory changes like the rape law reforms must be interpreted and applied by decisionmakers who may not share the goals of those who championed their enactment and who therefore may not be committed to their implementation. Numerous studies have demonstrated limited impact of reforms when officials' attitudes were at odds with reformers' goals (e.g., Ross and Foley 1987; Loftin, Heumann, and McDowall 1983).

Even if criminal justice officials agree with the legal change in principle, they may resist if it impinges on interests protected by the courtroom workgroup (Eisenstein and Jacob 1977). Officials may modify or ignore reforms that threaten the status quo by impeding the smooth and efficient flow of cases or that require changes in deeply entrenched and familiar routines. Studies have shown that reforms that interfere with plea bargaining and the production of large numbers of guilty pleas (Carter 1974; Nimmer and Krauthaus 1977) or that attempt to alter the "going rates" established by the workgroup (Church 1976; Heumann and Loftin 1979) are especially at risk of being undermined.

There are other explanations for the failure of court reforms to produce the instrumental results anticipated by reformers. Some reforms are doomed to failure because "the limits altered by the reform are nonessential or irrelevant in practice" (Nimmer 1978:189). Nimmer (1977), for example, found no change in sentences imposed for importation of heroin after a federal statute lowered the minimum and maximum sentences that could be imposed; plea bargaining had been used before the legal change to circumvent the minimum, and the maximum sentence was seldom imposed, so the statutory change was irrelevant to sentence outcomes.

Other reforms may have limited impact because their passage was primarily symbolic. Faced with a vocal constituency demanding action, decisionmakers might adopt a policy with little bite to provide "symbolic reassurance that needs are being attended to, problems are being solved, help is on the way" (Casper and Brereton 1984:124). Policymakers might, for example, placate constituents by enacting a very weak version of the legal change being sought, by adopting a law that differs very little from other laws on the books or from case law, or by adopting a reform that they know full well will not be enforced.

All the foregoing suggest that the advocates of rape law reform may have been overly optimistic about the effects of the reforms. It also suggests that we should approach the task of interpreting the outcomes of the reforms with great care. It obviously is important to consider not only the specific provisions of the laws themselves but also the comprehensiveness of the reforms, the contexts in which the reforms are to be implemented, and the consequences for decisionmakers charged with enforcing the reforms.

Previous Research on Rape Law Reform

Despite the fact that most states have enacted rape law reforms, there has been little empirical research on the effect of these laws. The studies that have been conducted have yielded mixed results. Two studies examined the impact of the 1974 Michigan criminal sexual conduct statute, the most sweeping rape law reform in the country. In an interrupted time-series analysis, Marsh et al. (1982) found increases in the number of arrests for rape and in convictions on the original charge but no change in the number of rapes reported to the police. Caringella-MacDonald (1984) compared postreform attrition and conviction rates in a Michigan jurisdiction with rates from three jurisdictions with more traditional rape laws and concluded that the differences in these rates provided "indirect" evidence that the Michigan law had had an effect.

Studies of other jurisdictions found some changes in officials' attitudes (Largen 1988) but very limited effects on case outcomes. Loh (1981) examined the effect of the Washington state rape reform statute on the prosecution of rape cases in King County (Seattle) and found no change in charging decisions or in the overall rate of conviction, although convictions for rape rather than for other offenses such as assault increased. In a study of California reforms, Polk (1985) analyzed statewide yearly data and found no significant change in the police clearance rate or the conviction rate, but slight increases in the rate of filing felony complaints and in the rate of incarceration for those convicted of rape. Gilchrist and Horney (1980) found no evidence of an increase in indictments or convictions after rape law reforms were implemented in Nebraska.

These empirical studies provide some evidence of the impact of rape law reforms in four jurisdictions but leave many unanswered questions about the nationwide effect of the reforms. Design limitations in each study also limit the conclusiveness and generalizability of their results. None of the designs included controls for the history threat to internal validity—that is, for the possibility that events other than the legal changes could have produced the effects noted. Furthermore, none of the studies collected data for more than three years following the reforms, so it is possible that the effects detected may have been transient ones or that delayed effects may have gone undetected (Casper and Brereton 1984). Finally, some studies used simple before-and-after designs, which cannot take long-term trends into account.

Perhaps the most serious problem for interpretation of the studies described above is that, with the exception of Largen's (1988) study of officials' perceptions, each was conducted in only one state and each used a somewhat different design and different measures. Thus we don't know whether the disparate results reflect the varied research strategies or jurisdictional differences in the reforms enacted. Individual states adopted relatively strong or weak reforms; even by the reformers' own expectations, we should anticipate finding greater impact in the jurisdictions with stronger versions of the reform laws. The apparently greater impact of reforms in Michigan would be consistent with the widespread characterization of the Michigan changes as the model for rape law reform. It might also reflect the fact that Michigan adopted a broad, sweeping reform at a single time rather than making changes in a piecemeal fashion as some jurisdictions did. A serious test of the impact of rape law reforms requires a multijurisdiction study.

The Current Study

In this study we assess the impact of rape law reform in six urban jurisdictions. The jurisdictions—Detroit, Michigan; Cook County (Chicago), Illinois; Philadelphia County (Philadelphia), Pennsylvania; Harris County (Houston), Texas; Fulton County (Atlanta), Georgia; and Washington, D.C.—represent states that enacted different kinds of rape law reforms. As Berger, Searles, and Neuman (1988) showed with a factor analysis of reform variables, there is significant variability in the extent to which individual states have reformed their statutes along the different dimensions of the law. Any ranking of jurisdictions in terms of strength of reforms is thus bound to be imprecise because of the difficulty of evaluating the relative importance of the different kinds of reforms. Nevertheless, to be able to make general comparisons of outcomes across jurisdictions, we selected Detroit, Chicago, and Philadelphia to represent jurisdictions with relatively strong reforms and Atlanta, Washington, D.C., and Houston to represent jurisdictions with weaker reforms. The reforms enacted in the six jurisdictions are summarized below and presented in detail in Table 1.

The Michigan law, considered by many to be the model rape law reform, included all the

TABLE 1 Summary of Rape Law Reforms Evaluated in Six Jurisdictions

	Definition	Law States Resistance Not Required	Law States Corroboration Not Required	Shield Law
Michigan 4-1-75	Four degrees of criminal sexual conduct defined by penetration vs. contact and by presence or absence of aggravating circumstances (e.g., personal injury, force, coercion, armed with weapon, victim incapacitated)	Yes	Yes	Sexual conduct evidence admissible only if with defendant or to show source of semen, pregnancy; disease; and, in each case, only if prejudicial nature does not out weigh probative value. Written motion required; *in camera* hearing may be held.
Pennsylvania 6-17-76		Yes	Yes	Sexual conduct evidence admissible only if with defendant where consent is issue and only if admissible pursuant to other rules of evidence. Written motion and *in camera* hearing required.
Illinois[a] 1-4-78		No	No	Sexual conduct evidence admissible only if with defendant. *In camera* hearing required to determine if defense has evidence to impeach in the event conduct denied by complainant.
Georgia 7-1-76				Past sexual behavior (including marital history, mode of dress, sexual reputation) admissible if it supports inference that accused could reasonably have believed victim consented; sexual behavior involving the accused admissible. Motion and *in camera* hearing required.
7-1-78		No	Yes	
District of Columbia 5-3-76[b]		No	Yes	
9-2-77[b]				Reputation evidence admissible only in unusual cases where probative value outweighs prejudicial effect; behavior with defendant admissible if consent is issue. No procedural requirements.
Texas[c] 9-1-75		No	No	Specific acts of sexual activity, opinion evidence, reputation evidence admissible if prejudicial nature does not outweigh probative value. Notice and *in camera* hearing required.

[a] Illinois adopted a statute stating that resistance is not required, but we were not able to evaluate this reform, which occurred in 1984.
[b] Changes in case law.
[c] Texas adopted rather minor definitional changes in 1983; we did not evaluate the impact of this reform.

changes described above. The Michigan statute redefines rape and other forms of sexual assault by establishing four degrees of gender-neutral criminal sexual conduct based on the seriousness of the offense, the amount of force or coercion used, the degree of injury inflicted, and the age and incapacitation of the victim. The law states that the victim need not resist the accused and that the victim's testimony need not be corroborated.

Michigan also enacted a very restrictive rape shield law. Evidence of prior sexual activity with persons other than the defendant is admissible only to show the source of semen, pregnancy, or disease. Evidence of the victim's past sexual conduct with the defendant can be admitted only if a judge determines that it is material to a fact at issue (generally consent) and that its inflammatory or prejudicial nature does not outweigh its probative value.

Although we categorized the reforms adopted in Illinois and Pennsylvania as "strong" reforms, they are neither as broad nor as comprehensive as those enacted in Michigan. The Illinois reforms were incremental; in 1978 the state implemented a strong rape shield law very similar to the law enacted in Michigan, but it was six years later before definitional changes were adopted and the resistance requirement was repealed. In 1976 Pennsylvania passed a strong rape shield law and repealed the corroboration and resistance requirements. Although these are significant changes, Pennsylvania retains Model Penal Code definitions of rape and involuntary deviate sexual intercourse, which many reformers believe still place undue focus on the circumstances that define nonconsent.

The reforms adopted in Washington, D.C., Georgia, and Texas are much weaker. Although corroboration requirements have been eliminated or weakened in each jurisdiction, all three jurisdictions continue to require resistance by the victim. Georgia and Texas passed very weak rape shield laws that give judges considerable discretion to admit sexual conduct evidence. Washington, D.C., has not amended its rape statutes since 1901, but case law restricts the introduction of evidence of the victim's prior sexual conduct. Washington, D.C., and Georgia have traditional carnal knowledge definitions of rape, as did Texas until relatively minor definitional changes were made in 1983.

Hypotheses

In this study we evaluate the impact of rape law reform on reports of rape and the outcome of rape cases. We test reformers' expectations that the reforms would result in increases in (1) the reporting of rapes to the police, (2) the indictment of rape cases by prosecutors, and (3) the conviction of offenders. Although most of the reform laws did not deal explicitly with sentencing, we consider the possibility that the attention focused on the seriousness of the crime of rape would lead judges to incarcerate more offenders and to impose more severe sentences on those incarcerated.

We noted earlier that there are a number of reasons for suggesting that reformers' expectations for the rape law reforms were unrealistic. If the resistance to change inherent in the criminal justice system is to be overcome, strong reforms will be required. We therefore hypothesize that the stronger reform laws of Michigan, Illinois, and Pennsylvania will have greater impact than those of Georgia, Texas, and Washington, D.C.

We also consider whether impact is greatest with comprehensive reform or incremental change. Reformers viewed the Michigan reform as a model for other states; the Michigan legislature addressed reformers' concerns in one far-reaching revision of the statutes. The Michigan reform was so dramatic and broad in scope that a powerful message was sent to decisionmakers in the criminal justice system. If the attitudes of system participants are to change, this kind of strong statement might be necessary. Yet Nimmer (1978:181) has asserted that "the probability of system change is inversely related to the degree of change sought by a reform" and that "a series of limited reforms is more likely to generate systemic change than a single, far-reaching reform."

We compare outcomes in Detroit, where the reforms were enacted at a single time, with outcomes in Chicago and Philadelphia, where rape shield laws of comparable strength were enacted, but where fewer of the other reforms were adopted at the same time. If Nimmer is correct, we should find greater impact in Chicago and Philadelphia than in Detroit. If, however, it takes dramatic, comprehensive change to overcome the predisposition to resist change, then we should find the greatest impact in Detroit.

Research Design and Methodology

Jurisdictions

As noted above, we selected six jurisdictions to represent states that enacted various types of law reforms. Other factors also influenced our choice of these six cities. To control for the threat of history to the design . . . , we chose jurisdictions in which reforms were implemented at several different times. Also, to obtain an adequate number of cases for the statistical analysis, we selected major urban jurisdictions.

Case Selection

We gathered court records data on rape cases processed from 1970 through 1984 in the six jurisdictions. We collected data on rapes reported to the police during the same time period from the FBI's Uniform Crime Reports (UCR). In each jurisdiction we collected data on forcible rape cases and on other sexual assaults that were not specifically assaults on children. We performed all analyses for both forcible rape and total sexual assaults. Because the pattern of results did not differ with the inclusion of other sexual assaults (and because the types of offenses included varied from jurisdiction to jurisdiction), we present here only the results for forcible rape cases since they are the most comparable. In Michigan, where the reforms included definitional changes, we selected the closest equivalent crimes for the forcible rape analysis (details described below).

Dependent Variables

The dependent variables include the number of reports of forcible rape; the indictment ratio (indictments divided by reports); the percentage convicted (convictions divided by indictments); the percentage convicted on the original charge (convictions for rape divided by indictments); the percentage incarcerated (incarcerations divided by convictions); and the average sentence (average maximum sentence—in months—for

defendants incarcerated after a conviction for rape).

Interviews with Criminal Justice Officials

To more fully evaluate the rape law reforms, in 1985 and 1986 we interviewed criminal justice officials in the six jurisdictions. We conducted lengthy, structured, face-to-face interviews with a sample of 162 judges, prosecutors, and defense attorneys (Spohn and Horney 1991). We selected officials who had experience with rape cases before and after the legal reforms went into effect or who had handled a substantial number of rape cases in the postreform period. We also interviewed police officers and rape crisis center personnel in each jurisdiction.

Results

The results of our analyses indicate that, contrary to reformers' expectations, the reforms had little effect on reports of rape or the processing of rape cases. The only clear impact of the laws was in Detroit, and even there the effects were limited. Below we discuss the results for Detroit in detail and then briefly summarize the results for the other five jurisdictions.

The statutory changes adopted by Michigan in 1975 produced some of the results anticipated by reformers. There was an increase in the number of reports of rape and in the ratio of indicted to reported cases. Additionally, the maximum sentence for those incarcerated increased. On the other hand, there was no change in the percentages of indictments resulting in conviction or in conviction on the original charge or in the percentage of convictions resulting in incarceration.

Our analysis of monthly reports of rape revealed that the new law produced a significant increase of about twenty-six reports per month. Because our measure of reports did not allow us to separate changes in reporting from changes in crime rates, we compared reports of rape with reports of robbery and felony assault for the period 1970 through 1980. If the increase in reported rapes reflected a general trend in violent crimes, we should have seen similar increases for these other crimes. Such increases were not evident. The pattern for felony assault reports was much like that for reported rapes, but the time-series analysis indicated no significant change coincident with changes in the rape laws. The pattern for reported robberies was quite different, and there was no significant change at the time when reporting of rapes increased.

Our results also indicate that the reforms had some effects on case processing in Detroit. The case processing variables are measured for the offenses of rape, sodomy, and gross indecency before the 1975 legal changes and for the offenses of first- and third-degree criminal sexual conduct after the changes. The time-series analysis of these data indicated that the indictment ratio increased by .18. Thus, not only were there more indictments simply because of an increase in the number of cases reported, but prosecution of these cases was more likely following the legislative changes.

The likelihood of conviction, on the other hand, did not change as a result of the reforms. With the increase in reports and indictments, however, the steady conviction rate indicates that prosecutors were obtaining more *total* convictions in the postreform period. This was confirmed by a statistical analysis of the absolute number of convictions. We also found that the reforms did not change the likelihood of incarceration but that the average sentence received by those incarcerated increased by about sixty three months.

Some reformers predicted that the definitional reforms would lead to an increase in plea bargaining, since the graded criminal sexual conduct offenses would make it possible to reduce original charges to charges still within the sexual offense category. When we examined the percentage of cases convicted on original charges, we found no evidence of a decrease that would correspond to a greater reliance on plea bargaining. In fact, the percentage of cases convicted on the original charge increased after the new laws went into effect, although the increase was not statistically significant.

Michigan's strong and comprehensive reforms produced some, but not all, of the effects anticipated by reformers. The strong evidentiary changes enacted in Illinois (1978) and Pennsylvania (1976), in contrast, had no effect on reports of rape or the processing of rape cases in Chicago or Philadelphia.

The three cities with weaker reforms also showed almost no evidence of impact for the changes in rape laws. The only significant effect found for Washington, D.C., was a decrease in reported rapes after the elimination of the corroboration requirement. We have no theoretical rationale to explain such a decrease; we suspect that it was merely coincidental with the new law. In Atlanta there were some changes in the processing of rape cases but none that could be attributed to the legal reforms.

We found a number of changes in Houston, but most occurred years after implementation of the new laws, suggesting that they were due to other causes. Still, some changes occurred at the time of the rape law reform. The number of reported rapes increased by an average of 17.25 reports per months, and the indictment ratio *decreased* by .08. The average sentence for those incarcerated for rape increased by almost eighty-five months.

To test whether the trend might simply be part of a general increase in crime in Houston during those years, we looked at the monthly data for reported robberies and reported assaults for the same period. The long-term trends [are] similar to the trend for reported rapes, but without the increase in level apparent for reported rapes immediately after the law reforms. That slight increase in reported rapes thus might have been produced by the publicity surrounding the reforms.

The significant decrease in the indictment ratio was not what reformers predicted. We suspect that it was a result of the increase in the number of rape reports; as reports of rapes increased in Houston, the number of indictments did not keep pace. Similarly, the impact on sentences probably follows from the decrease in the indictment ratio. As more cases came into the system and as prosecutors became more selective, it is quite likely that the average case being prosecuted was more serious, producing an increase in average sentence length.

Discussion

Our analysis of the impact of rape law reforms in six major urban jurisdictions revealed that legal changes did not produce the dramatic results anticipated by reformers. The reforms had no impact in most of the jurisdictions. While the greatest, albeit limited, impact was found in Detroit, where a single reform dramatically changed all the rape laws, a simple strong reform–weak reform distinction cannot explain the pattern of results. We found no greater impact in two jurisdictions with relatively strong reforms—Chicago and Philadelphia—than in the three jurisdictions with relatively weak reforms.

As noted earlier, many reforms have failed because reformers assumed that the behavior of decisionmakers in the criminal justice system is controlled by legal rules. A failure to appreciate the role of discretion in case processing often leads to reforms that do not include adequate incentives for changing behavior. In order to understand our results, we look first at the specific provisions of the rape law reforms, considering how they actually affected decisionmakers.

Definitional Changes

Reformers anticipated that replacing the single crime of rape with a series of gender-neutral graded offenses with commensurate penalties would lead to an increase in convictions. They predicted that the availability of appropriate lesser charges would enable prosecutors to obtain more convictions through plea bargaining and would discourage jury nullification by providing other options to juries reluctant to convict for forcible rape.

We found no evidence of an increased likelihood of convictions in Detroit, where definitional changes took effect, or in any of the other jurisdictions. The fact that we found no decrease in the proportion of cases resulting in convictions on the original charge indicates that there was no increase in plea bargaining. Our interviews led us to believe that the reforms' implicit focus on the seriousness of the crime of rape may have created an unwillingness to plea bargain that counteracted the facilitative effects of

the definitional changes. In Detroit, in fact, the Wayne County Prosecutor's office has an explicit policy restricting plea bargaining. The policy requires the complainant's approval prior to reducing charges. In addition, the policy provides that charges of criminal sexual conduct in the first degree may only, except in unusual circumstances, be negotiated down to criminal sexual conduct in the third degree (CSC3) and that CSC3 charges may not be reduced.

Reformers also expected that the new laws would encourage juries to convict on lesser charges in cases that might otherwise have produced an acquittal for forcible rape. This assumes that prosecutors will ask for instructions on lesser included charges. Prosecutors in Detroit, however, said they were reluctant to ask for these instructions because they feared that jurors would be hopelessly confused if given definitions for criminal sexual conduct in the first, second, third, and fourth degrees. Thus the complexity of the law, considered important for its inclusiveness, may have undermined one of the reformers' goals.

Elimination of Corroboration and Resistance Requirements

Reformers predicted that eliminating the requirements for corroboration and resistance would make it easier to prosecute cases and therefore more likely that prosecutors would file charges and obtain convictions. We believe that reformers were overly optimistic about the effects of these largely symbolic changes. For one thing, court decisions over the years had already considerably loosened both requirements. Officials in every jurisdiction reported that a prompt report or physical evidence of intercourse could corroborate the victim's testimony; thus, it was almost always possible to get past a motion for a judgment of acquittal. As one judge stated, "The case law was so broadly interpreted that a scintilla of corroboration was satisfying." Similarly, courts had ruled that a victim was not required to put her life in jeopardy by resisting an attack, and that evidence of force on the part of the offender was tantamount to proof of nonconsent by the victim. By the mid-1970s the corroboration and resistance requirements could be viewed as minor hurdles if prosecutors wanted to proceed with a case, and formal elimination of the statutory requirements was therefore irrelevant in practice.

More important, elimination of the requirements does nothing to constrain the discretion of decisionmakers. As Nimmer (1978:176) observed, reformers often assume that removing alleged legal obstacles will allow decisionmakers to behave in the "correct" way, when in fact "problems are typically not the product of artificial barriers or constraints but of conscious behavioral choices made both individually and as a group by professionals within the system." As one of our respondents explained, the law may no longer require corroboration, but that does not mean that the prosecutor will file charges when the complainant's story is totally uncorroborated.

Prosecutors often make charging decisions based on their estimates of whether cases could be won before a jury; if they believe a jury will look for corroboration and resistance, they will continue to require them for charging. Many prosecutors we interviewed believed, in fact, that jurors are unlikely to convict in the absence of these factors. As one prosecutor noted, "Juries still expect some resistance or some explanation as to why there was none. This is especially true if it was a date gone sour; if we can't show some resistance in this case we're in a lot of trouble." Concerning corroboration, another stated, "If you're talking about consent defenses, jurors are still looking for corroborating evidence—physical injury, a weapon, a hysterical call to the police; old habits and old attitudes die hard, and we can change the law but we can't necessarily change attitudes."

Juries might be influenced if instructed that the victim need not resist her attacker and that her testimony need not be corroborated. Many officials we interviewed believed, in fact, that it could be very important for jurors to hear this, not from the prosecutor, but from the judge. Even when a statute explicitly states the lack of a need for resistance or corroboration, however, such instructions are given at the discretion of the judge and the prosecutor. Some judges routinely give the instruction; others instruct only if requested to do so by the prosecutor. Some judges reported that the prosecutor always asks

for the instruction; some said that prosecutors never do. Thus, the potential for impact of the reforms is again diminished by the discretionary nature of the criminal justice system.

Analysis of elimination of corroboration and resistance requirements, then, suggests that reformers had unrealistic expectations concerning their impact. Although these reforms may have sent an important symbolic message, they did not significantly alter the decisionmaking context. Neither requirement was an insurmountable hurdle before the reforms, and the reforms themselves did not constrain the discretion of prosecutors or jurors. In the postreform period, as in the prereform period, corroboration and resistance evidence may still be important to the successful prosecution of at least some kinds of rape cases.

Rape Shield Laws

Reformers predicted the rape shield laws would have a greater impact on the processing and disposition of sexual assault cases than would the other reforms. They anticipated that the restrictions on evidence damaging to the complainant would prompt more victims to report rapes to the police and would lead directly to an increase in convictions and indirectly to an increase in arrests and prosecutions.

Effects of Weak Shield Laws

We did not expect the weak shield laws of Washington, D.C., Georgia, and Texas to have a significant impact on case processing. The laws adopted in each of these states continue to allow judges considerable discretion in deciding whether to admit sexual history evidence. Case law in Washington, D.C., for example, excludes evidence of the victim's prior sexual conduct with parties other than the defendant but allows evidence of the victim's reputation for chastity if the judge determines that its probative value outweighs its prejudicial effect. The Georgia law allows evidence of the victim's sexual reputation or sexual conduct with third parties if the judge finds it supports an inference that the accused reasonably could have believed the victim consented. And the Texas law is often cited as an example of the most permissive kind of law (Berger 1977; Galvin 1986). Texas does not categorically exclude any sexual conduct evidence; rather, such evidence can be admitted if the judge finds that the evidence is relevant.

By leaving so much to the judge's discretion, the shield laws enacted in these jurisdictions did little to alter the "rules" for handling rape cases. Weddington (1975–76) observed that the Texas shield law in essence made no change. The motion *in limine* had always been available to prosecutors to exclude irrelevant evidence, and the judge always determined relevance. Prosecutors in Atlanta suggested that Georgia's rape shield law was actually weaker than the case law in effect prior to the law's passage. In both states, much stronger reforms had been presented to legislators. The weak shield laws that were passed can be viewed as symbolic policies designed to placate the interest groups lobbying for change.

Effect of Strong Shield Laws

The rape shield laws enacted in Michigan, Illinois, and Pennsylvania are much stronger. The laws in all three states generally prohibit the introduction of evidence of the victim's past sexual conduct. The prohibition includes evidence of specific instances of sexual activity, reputation evidence, and opinion evidence. There are only very narrow exceptions to the shield. All three jurisdictions permit introduction of the victim's past sexual conduct with the defendant, but only if the judge determines that the evidence is relevant. The shield laws enacted in these states, then, sent a strong message to defense attorneys, prosecutors, and judges. They clearly stated that certain types of sexual history evidence are inadmissible. Unlike the laws adopted in Texas, Georgia, and the District of Columbia, they also attempted to place meaningful limits on judges' discretion to admit certain kinds of evidence.

One important procedural aspect of the rape shield laws is the requirement of an *in camera* hearing for determining admissibility of evidence relating to the victim's sexual history. Our interviews with judges, prosecutors and defense attorneys, however, revealed that *in camera* hearings are rarely if ever held, especially if the evidence concerns sexual conduct between the victim and the defendant. Prosecutors reported that they generally concede the relevance of evidence of a prior sexual relationship between the victim and the defendant and do not challenge defense attorneys who attempt to introduce the evidence without requesting a hearing. Similarly, judges use their discretion to overlook the *in camera* requirement or to overrule prosecutors' objections to the introduction of the evidence.

It is not surprising that criminal justice officials have found ways to circumvent the formal procedural requirements of the shield laws. As Casper and Brereton (1984:123) note, "implementors often engage in adaptive behavior designed to serve their own goals and institutional or personal needs." *In camera* hearings are time consuming and would be a waste of time if judges routinely rule that evidence of a prior relationship between the victim and the defendant is relevant. Rather than going through the motions of challenging the evidence and perhaps alienating other members of the courtroom workgroup, prosecutors concede the point.

Noncompliance might also be attributed to agreement among prosecutors and judges that evidence of a prior sexual relationship between the victim and the defendant is always relevant to the issue of consent. Reformers believed that the relevance of this kind of evidence would depend on factors such as the nature and duration of the sexual relationship or the separation in time from the alleged rape. We believe decisionmakers have developed a much simpler rule based on shared norms of relevance and fairness in evidentiary issues. Their "admissibility rule" states that if the sexual conduct was with the defendant, it is relevant. Like "going rates" in sentencing (Feeley 1979; Loftin et al. 1983) or "normal crime" categories in charging (Mather 1974; Sudnow 1965), the rule routinizes and simplifies the decisionmaking process.

The disregard of the requirement for hearings contradicts Nimmer's (1978) assertion that legal rules are most effective when they specify procedural steps in case processing. The *in camera* hearings required by rape shield laws, however, differ from other procedural requirements in one important way. While the laws mandate hearings in certain situations and clearly specify the procedures to be followed, they do not provide for review or sanction of judges who fail to follow the law. Moreover, if a defendant is acquitted because the judge violated the law and either admitted potentially relevant evidence without a hearing or allowed the defense attorney to use legally inadmissible evidence, the victim cannot appeal the acquittal or the judge's decisions. If, on the other hand, the judge followed the law and refused to admit seemingly irrelevant sexual history evidence, the defendant can appeal his conviction. All the consequences, in other words, would lead judges to err in favor of the defendant.

The avoidance of *in camera* hearings clearly undermines the reforms to the extent that issues of relevance are not debated if the sexual conduct was between the victim and the *defendant*. Their absence does not mean legally prohibited evidence of sexual conduct between the victim and *third parties* is being admitted. To the contrary, it appears that hearings are avoided on these issues because the members of the workgroup agree that such evidence cannot be admitted. The other side of the admissibility rule, in other words, is that sexual conduct between the victim and parties other than the defendant is not relevant. Judges in every jurisdiction stated that defense attorneys don't even attempt to introduce the more questionable kinds of sexual history evidence. As one judge in Chicago explained, "Attorneys are warned that I will interpret the law strictly and they don't even try to bring it up unless it concerns the victim and the defendant."

If evidence clearly proscribed by the law is effectively excluded, we must consider other explanations for the lack of impact of the strong rape shield laws. Why is it that even these strong laws did not produce the types of changes envisioned by reformers? For one thing, the shield laws primarily affect cases that go to trial and, particularly, the small percentage of cases tried before a jury. Moreover, sexual history evidence is only relevant in cases where the defense is consent. Since it is unlikely that consent will be the defense when a woman is raped by a total stranger, this means that sexual history evidence

will be relevant only when the victim and the defendant are acquainted. The shield laws, then, have the potential to affect directly only the relatively few rape cases in which the victim and the defendant are acquainted, the defendant claims the victim consented, and the defendant insists on a trial.

Unfortunately, no data are available on how often a complainant's sexual history entered into cases before the rape shield laws were enacted. Although reformers cited horror stories regarding harassment of victims in court, most respondents in jurisdictions we studied could recall few, if any, prereform cases in which defense attorneys used this tactic. If testimony regarding the victim's sexual history with third parties was rarely introduced, then restricting the use of such evidence would produce little change. Respondents in several jurisdictions reported, in fact, that previous case rulings had accomplished much of what the rape shield laws were designed to do.

We have discussed the weaknesses of the individual reforms and have explained why the reforms did not produce the instrumental results anticipated by reformers. These results might also be due to the fact that the reforms had the potential to affect only certain types of cases. Estrich (1987) has emphasized the importance of the distinction between aggravated rape and "simple" rape. Aggravated rapes are those that involve strangers, multiple assailants, or armed force; simple rapes are committed by unarmed acquaintances, acting alone. She has suggested that traditional rape law provisions represented "a set of clear presumptions applied against the woman who complains of simple rape" (Estrich 1987:28). She has also asserted (ibid., p. 29) that historically the processing of rape cases has not been characterized by indiscriminate sexism, but that there has been and still is

a far more sophisticated discrimination in the distrust of women victims: all women and all rapes are not treated equally. As the doctrines of rape law were developed in the older cases, distinctions were drawn, explicitly and implicitly, between the aggravated, jump-from-the-bushes stranger rapes and the simple cases of unarmed rape by friends, neighbors, and acquaintances. It was primarily in the latter cases that distrust of women victims was actually incorporated into the definition of the crime and the rules of proof.

Estrich maintains that resistance and corroboration requirements were loosened in aggravated rape cases and that evidence of a victim's past sexual conduct was only considered relevant in simple rape cases.

If Estrich is correct, then it follows that most of the rape law reforms have been directed at simple rape cases, and thus the greatest impact should have been seen in these cases. If, as we argue above, the laws fail to place meaningful constraints on the discretion of decisionmakers, then impact could only be achieved by modifying decisionmakers' basic distrust of victims of simple rape. Further research should address this issue.

Evidence of Impact

Two sites did show some evidence of impact. In Detroit we found increases in reports of rape, in the ratio of indictments to reports, and in the length of the maximum sentence. In Houston also we found some evidence of increases in reporting and sentence length, but they were accompanied by a decrease in the indictment ratio.

The Effect of System Variables

To understand the impact of a reform it is important to understand not only the characteristics of the reform itself but also the structure of the system on which it is imposed. The jurisdictions we studied differed in a number of ways. They varied, for example, by method of judicial selection, by whether prosecutors screened arrest charges, by whether charging was by grand jury or preliminary hearing, by the predominance of trials versus plea bargaining, and by whether the prosecutor's office had a special unit for handling rape cases. Because the rape law reforms were directed toward trial proceedings, we might have expected that the jurisdiction with a much higher rate of trials (Philadelphia) would have

shown more impact. This was not the case. Similarly, we might have predicted greater change in that same city because of the special rape prosecution unit. Our primary finding was the overall lack of impact of rape law reforms in spite of these differences.

Detroit, however, differs from the other five jurisdictions in a number of ways that might be relevant to the effectiveness of the reforms in that jurisdiction. First, although every jurisdiction had a rape crisis center, only in Detroit is the Rape Counseling Center run through the Police Department. This close association gives the Counseling Center earlier and greater access to victims than in many cities and thus potentially greater influence in encouraging reporting and pressing for prosecution.

A second noteworthy difference is the centralized policy orientation of the Wayne County Prosecutor's office. The Wayne County Prosecutor was unusual in requiring formal training of new prosecutors, having formal policies on practices such as plea bargaining, and having supervisors carry out formal review of assistant prosecutors' decisions. These factors may be more important than having a special unit for rape cases in ensuring that the goals of rape law reform are met. We suspect that such centralized control serves to greatly weaken the kind of courtroom workgroup effects that operate to resist change. In fact, a sensitivity to the role of courtroom workgroups led the Wayne County Prosecutor, in 1984, to implement a policy of rotating deputies to different courtrooms every four months. Defense attorneys had always been assigned to cases rather than courtrooms. Rather than a typical public defender system, Detroit has a private defender corporation that handles about 25 percent of the indigent cases, while the rest are handled by private attorneys. With less chance for workgroups to develop and function autonomously, reforms may have a greater chance to effect instrumental change.

The fact that the rape law reforms had an impact on case processing in Detroit but not in the other five jurisdictions, then, can be attributed to a combination of factors. The strong and comprehensive laws enacted in Michigan were more than a symbolic response to a vocal constituency clamoring for change. The laws defined new crimes, mandated new procedures, and limited the discretion of criminal justice officials. Although, as we argue above, individual components of the reform package had limited potential to affect case outcomes, the comprehensive nature of the reform may have overcome resistance to change inherent in the criminal justice system. Coupled with the weaker workgroups and other contextual factors which distinguish Detroit from the other jurisdictions, this comprehensive approach to reform may explain our results.

References

Battele Memorial Institute Law and Justice Study Center (1977) *Forcible Rape: Final Project Report.* National Institute on Law Enforcement and Criminal Justice. Washington, DC: Government Printing Office.

Berger, Ronald J., Patricia Searles, and W. Lawrence Neuman (1988) "The Dimensions of Rape Reform Legislation," 22 *Law & Society Review* 329.

Berger, Vivian (1977) "Man's Trial, Woman's Tribulation: Rape Cases in the Courtroom," 77 *Columbia Law Review* 1.

Bohmer, Carol (1974) "Judicial Attitudes Toward Rape Victims," 57 *Judicature* 303.

Caringella-MacDonald, Susan (1984) "Sexual Assault Prosecution: An Examination of Model Rape Legislation in Michigan," 4 *Women and Politics* 65.

Carter, Lief (1974) *The Limits of Order.* Lexington, MA: D.C. Heath.

Casper, Jonathan D., and David Brereton (1984) "Evaluating Criminal Justice Reforms," 18 *Law & Society Review* 121.

Church, Thomas W., Jr. (1976) "Plea Bargains, Concessions and the Courts: Analysis of a Quasi-Experiment," 10 *Law & Society Review* 377.

Cobb, Kenneth A., and Nancy R. Schauer (1974) "Legislative Note: Michigan's Criminal Sexual Assault Law," 8 *University of Michigan Journal of Law Reform* 217.76

Eisenstein, James, Roy B. Flemming, and Peter F. Nardulli (1988) *The Contours of Justice: Communities and Their Courts.* Boston: Little, Brown.

Eisenstein, James, and Herbert Jacob (1977) *Felony Justice: An Organizational Analysis of Criminal Courts.* Boston: Little, Brown.

Estrich, Susan (1987) *Real Rape.* Cambridge, MA: Harvard University Press.

Feeley, Malcolm M. (1979) *The Process Is the Punishment: Handling Cases in a Lower Criminal Court.* New York: Russell Sage Foundation.

Feild, Hubert S., and Leigh B. Bienen (1980) *Jurors and Rape: A Study in Psychology and Law.* Lexington, MA: Lexington Books.

Feldman-Summers, Shirley, and Karen Lindner (1976) "Perceptions of Victims and Defendants in Criminal Assault Cases," 3 *Criminal Justice and Behavior* 135.

Galvin, Harriet R. (1986) "Shielding Rape Victims in the State and Federal Courts: A Proposal for the Second Decade," 70 *Minnesota Law Review* 763.

Gilchrist, Karen, and Julie Horney (1980) "Assessing the Impact of Changes in the Nebraska Rape Statutes: Effect on Prosecution." Presented at the annual meeting of the Western Society of Criminology, Newport Beach, CA.

Heumann, Milton, and Colin Loftin (1979) "Mandatory Sentencing and the Abolition of Plea Bargaining: The Michigan Felony Firearm Statute," 13 *Law & Society Review* 393.

Holmstrom, Lynda Lytle, and Ann Wolbert Burgess (1975) "Rape: The Victim and the Criminal Justice System," 3 *International Journal of Criminology and Penology* 101.

———— (1978) *The Victim of Rape: Institutional Reactions.* New York: Wiley-Interscience.

Ireland, Marilyn J. (1978) "Rape Reform Legislation: A New Standard of Sexual Responsibility," 49 *University of Colorado Law Review* 185.

Kalven, Harry, and Hans Zeisel (1966) *The American Jury.* Boston: Little, Brown.

LaFree, Gary D. (1980) "Variables Affecting Guilty Pleas and Convictions in Rape Cases: Toward a Social Theory of Rape Processing," 58 *Social Forces* 833.

———— (1981) "Official Reactions to Social Problems: Police Decisions in Sexual Assault Cases," 28 *Social Problems* 582.

———— (1989) *Rape and Criminal Justice: The Social Construction of Sexual Assault.* Belmont, CA: Wadsworth.

Largen, Mary Ann (1988) "Rape-Law Reform: An Analysis," in A. W. Burgess (ed.), *Rape and Sexual Assault II.* New York: Garland.

Loftin, Colin, Milton Heumann, and David McDowall (1983) "Mandatory Sentencing and Firearms Violence: Evaluating an Alternative to Gun Control," 17 *Law & Society Review* 287.

Loh, Wallace D. (1980) "The Impact of Common Law and Reform Rape Statutes on Prosecution: An Empirical Study" 55 *Washington Law Review* 543.

Marsh, Jeanne C., Alison Geist, and Nathan Caplan (1982) *Rape and the Limits of Law Reform.* Boston: Auburn House.

Mather, Lynn M. (1974) "Some Determinants of the Method of Case Disposition: Decision-Making by Public Defenders in Los Angeles," 8 *Law & Society Review* 187.

McCahill, Thomas W., Linda C. Meyer, and Arthur M. Fishchman (1979) *The Aftermath of Rape.* Lexington, MA: Lexington Books.

Nimmer, Raymond T. (1977) "The System Impact of Criminal Justice Reforms," in J. L. Tapp and F. J. Levine (eds.), *Law, Justice, and the Individual in Society: Psychological and Legal Issues.* New York: Holt, Rinehart & Winston.

———— (1978) *The Nature of System Change: Reform Impact in the Criminal Courts.* Chicago: American Bar Foundation.

Nimmer, Raymond T., and Patricia Ann Krauthaus (1977) "Plea Bargaining: Reform in Two Cities," 3 *Justice System Journal* 6.

Polk, Kenneth (1985) "Rape Reform and Criminal Justice Processing," 31 *Crime and Delinquency* 191.

Reskin, Barbara F., and Christy A. Visher (1986) "The Impacts of Evidence and Extralegal Factors in Jurors' Decisions," 20 *Law & Society Review* 423.

Robin, Gerald D. (1982) "Forcible Rape: Institutionalized Sexism in the Criminal Justice System," in B. R. Price and N. J. Sokoloff (eds.), *The Criminal Justice System and Women: Offenders, Victims, Workers.* New York: Clark Boardman.

Ross, H. Laurence, and James P. Foley (1987) "Judicial Disobedience of the Mandate to Imprison Drunk Drivers," 21 *Law & Society Review* 315.

Sasko, Helene, and Deborah Sesek (1975) "Rape Reform Legislation: Is It the Solution?" 24 *Cleveland State Law Review* 463.

Spohn, Cassia, and Julie Horney (1991) "'The Law's the Law, But Fair Is Fair': Rape Shield Laws and Officials' Assessments of Sexual History Evidence," 29 *Criminology* 137.

Sudnow, David (1965) "Normal Crimes: Sociological Features of the Penal Code in a Public Defender Office," 12 *Social Problems* 255.

Vera Institute of Justice (1981) *Felony Arrests: Their Prosecution and Disposition in New York City's Courts.* New York: Longman.

Weddington, Sarah (1975–76) "Rape Law in Texas: H.B. 284 and the Road to Reform," 4 *American Journal of Criminal Law* 1.

Statute Cited

Texas Penal Code Ann. sec. 21.02 (Supp. 1980).

22

The Social Origin of Sexual Harassment

Catharine A. MacKinnon

. . . In the biological view, sexual expression seems presumed to derive from a biological need or genital drive or to be deeply rooted in a natural order that connects biological differences with expressions of mutual attraction. The idea is that biology cannot be questioned or changed, and is legitimate, while society can be, and may be "artificial." Perhaps this presumption underlies the clear doctrinal necessity, if sexual harassment is to be considered sex discrimination under existing conceptions, to establish sexual harassment as less a question of "sexuality" than of gender status: an implicit legal presupposition that sexuality is buried in nature, while gender status is at least in part a social construct. . . . In an attempt to justify legal nonintervention, sexual harassment is implicitly argued to be an inevitable and integral part of the naturally given, not socially contingent or potentially changeable, sexual relations between women and men.

Upon closer scrutiny, these presumptions about sex have little to do with the occurrence of sexual harassment. Women possess a physical sex drive equal to or greater than that of men,[1] yet do not systematically harass men sexually. Some men, who have nothing wrong with them sexually, seem able to control their behavior. Not all women experience sexual attraction to all men, nor all men to all women. These factors suggest that something beyond pure biology is implicated. Usually, the last thing wanted in these incidents is species reproduction, which removes any connection with a natural drive in that direction. Moreover, not everything deemed natural by defining all sexual behavior as biological is thereby made socially acceptable. If economically coerced intercourse is biological, rape must be also, but it is not legally allowed for that reason.

The image of codetermination in sexual matters by men and women is scrupulously maintained in these cases. But for the unwilling woman, no "attraction" is involved, and little power. Even if the "attractiveness of the sexes for one another" were inevitable, that would not make its expression indiscriminate. Calling sex "natural" means here, in effect, that women are to be allowed no choice of with whom and under what conditions to have sexual relations. In these cases, we are dealing with a male who is allegedly exercising his power as an employer, his power over a woman's material survival, and his sexual prerogatives as a man, to subject a woman sexually. One would have to argue that sexual power is by nature asymmetrical, and hence that it is biological for males to threaten, force, blackmail, coerce, subject, exploit, and oppress women sexually, to conclude that sexual harassment is natural.

More likely, it is only under conditions of women's social inequality (conditions which Congress responded to by the passage of Title VII and other legislation) that sexual harassment is presented as a social inevitability mystified as a natural one.[2] In this view, it is only under conditions in which men systematically hold superior positions to women and are not only willing but able to abuse their position with impunity, and in which women have so few practical alternatives, that so natural an occurrence persists. This is not to deny the existence of social and biological differences, but to question whether the economic subordination of women by sexual means is an inevitable consequence of those differences. Arguably, we are here confronting an inequality in social power rationalized as a biological difference, specifically with a society that rigidly defines role opportunities in terms of sex, and then sanctifies those roles by at- tributing to them a basis in nature. This is as true for the fact that women are inferiors on the job as it is for the sexual relations that male su- periors coercively initiate.

What is Sex?

The legal interpretation of the term *sex,* as illus- trated by the foregoing, has centered upon the gender difference between women and men, which the law views as a biological given. "Gen- der *per se*" is considered to refer to an obvious biological fact with a fixed content. Factors "other than gender *per se,*" but correlated with it, may also ground a discrimination claim. These factors are treated in legal discourse as accre- tions—some biological, some social—upon the biological foundation. These presuppositions about sex and gender have been so widely as- sumed that it has seldom been considered whether they are appropriate foundations for a social policy directed toward women's equality, or even whether they are, to the best of our cur- rent knowledge, true.

One major contradiction within the legal conception of sex as gender was posed by the *Gilbert* analysis. The plaintiff argued that preg- nancy was a gender distinction per se because only women become pregnant. The majority of the Supreme Court argued that pregnancy was other than gender per se, in part because it is vol- untary, while gender is not; in part because not all women become pregnant, so it is not a char- acteristic of the sex; and in part because no men become pregnant, so women and men were not being *treated* discriminatorily, they merely *are* different. Defining sex with reference to gender was inadequate to resolve the issue of whether, in order for a classification such as pregnancy to be considered sex-based, all women must be ac- tually or potentially so classified, or whether it is sufficient that all those so classified are women, with no men even potentially included, or whether the fact that no men can be so affected means that the exclusion *cannot* discriminate against women.

To generalize beyond the explicit terms of the Supreme Court's holding, its resolution of this issue could be stated as follows: for differ- ential treatment of the sexes to be considered sex-based, it must occur, or potentially occur, to all members of a group defined by biological gender, but not for reasons unique to that biol- ogy. That is, to be sex-based, a treatment (or classification or factor) must be universal to women but not unique to women. It must affect all women and, in some sense, not only women. Pregnancy was considered both not universal to women and unique to women, thus not a gen- der classification. On this level, the logic of the *Manhart* and *Gilbert* results are reconcilable. *Manhart* presents the mirror image of *Gilbert:* al- though "extra" longevity is not universal to women, the challenged rule was universally ap- plied to set all women's pension fund contribu- tions; nor is "extra" longevity unique to women, since some men also experience it. So, since the rule affects all women and is based upon a char- acteristic not of women only, the policy of dif- ferential contributions was found to be a gender classification.

Several empirical presumptions are implic- it in this approach. It is assumed that a solid physical underpinning exists for the sex differ- ence and that sex is dimorphic. The sexes are un- derstood in terms of their differences and these differences are considered physical and bipolar. It is assumed that a clear, known line can be drawn between those attributes of gender which are biological and those which are other than biological. The relevant referent for the legal meaning of sex is supposed to be primarily in bi- ology rather than society.

The particular place of "sexuality" as one index to maleness or femaleness has never been firmly located in this legal scheme of sex as gen- der and gender as biology. Other than in the few sexual harassment cases, the question has rarely been posed. One recent EEOC case, justifying the lack of protection for homosexuals under Title VII, distinguished "sexual practice" from "gender as such," the latter defined as "an im- mutable characteristic with which a person is born."[3] Sexuality, or at least homosexuality, seemed to mean something one does, gender something one is. Similarly, the *Harvard Law Re- view* implicitly distinguished between sexuality and sex as gender under Title VII as follows: "Although jobs which require sex appeal may exploit their occupants as sex objects, [Title VII] was not designed to change *other* views that society holds about sexuality"[4] (emphasis added). A series of interconnected propositions emerges: "sex" in the legal sense is primarily a matter of gender status; gender status is a matter of innate biological differences; homosexuality is a "practice," not a matter of gender status, hence not within the ambit of sex discrimination. But what exactly is heterosexuality? What is its relationship to the gender difference? How do gender and heterosexuality interrelate in what discrimination law means by "sex"?

The relationship of sexuality to gender is the critical link in the argument that sexual harassment is sex discrimination. Empirically, gender is not monolithic. Three dimensions can be distinguished: physical characteristics, gender identification, and sex role behavior. Contrary to legal presumptions, current research shows that none of these dimensions is perfectly intercorrelated with, nor strictly predetermines, any other. Gender, then, is not as simple as the biological difference between women and men, nor is that difference itself purely or even substantially a biological one. Sexuality as a complex interaction of (at least) all three is even less simply biologically determinate. It is neither simply a matter of gender status nor a practice without reference to biological differences. Perhaps most significantly, social and cultural factors, including attitudes, beliefs, and traditional practices—quite proper targets for legal change, compared with biological facts—are found to have a substantially broader and more powerful impact upon gender, even upon its biological aspects, than legal thinking on the sex difference has recognized.

Physical characteristics which provide indices of gender include internal and external reproductive organs and genitalia, gonads, hormone balance, and genetic and chromosomal makeup.[5] Strictly speaking, in several of these physical senses gender is not immutable, merely highly tenacious. A transsexual operation, with hormone therapy, can largely transform gender on the physical level, with the major exception of reproductive capacity. But then many born males and females do not possess reproductive capacity for a variety of biological and social reasons. Aside from these characteristics, some evidence of physical differences between the sexes in the aggregate exists in the following areas: body shape, height and weight, muscularity, physical endurance, possibly metabolic rate, possibly some forms of sensory sensitivity, rate of maturation, longevity, susceptibility to certain physical disorders, and some behaviors at birth (irritability, type of movement, and responsiveness to touch).[6] The scientific research stresses the wide, if not complete, mutability of even these differences by social factors such as psychological reinforcements, type of customary physical activity, and career patterns.[7] Moreover, on the biological level, the sex difference is not a polar opposition, but a continuum of characteristics with different averages by sex grouping.

> Most characteristics are found in both sexes: the more common difference is in the positive or negative value attached to a characteristic, depending on who has it. . . . [W]hile it need not and cannot be argued that the individual human being is a biological *tabula rasa* at birth, the slate of *a priori* assumptions concerning the social-biological characteristics should be blank.[8]

Most sexual behaviors which differ by sex or within sex groupings have been found to lack any known biological basis. Choice of sexual object in terms of sex preference for the same or opposite sex is one; intensity of sexual desires and needs is another. Masters and Johnson's research has decisively established that women's sexual requirements are no less potent or urgent than those of men.[9] "There is little factual basis for the belief that males need sex more than do females. It is more likely that men do not exercise so much control over sexual behavior. Male sexual behavior is condoned, even encouraged, whereas females are taught restraint in sexual expression."[10] Social factors rather than biological differences are seen to shape observed differences in sexual needs and patterns of their expression.[11] For example, in spite of physiological differences between women and men, there is no physiological basis for male aggressiveness and female passivity in sexual initiation. Without changing biology, "a woman can be aggressive-ly receptive and a man be motivationally passive in the sexual act."[12] Some scholars locate sexu-al excitement itself more in society than in na-ture. "The very experience of sexual excitement that seems to originate from hidden internal sources is in fact a learned process and it is only our insistence on the myths of naturalness that hides these social components from us."[13] Sex-ual feeling and expression are seen as a form of "scripted" behavior[14] which is as powerfully de-termined by sexism as by sex.[15] Gagnon and Simon note that "many women's . . . participa-tion in sexual activity, has often—historically, possibly more often than not—had little to do with their own sense of the erotic."[16] The social facts of sexual inequality increasingly appear to define this fact of the meaning of sex, rather than the facts of sex differences providing an ir-refutable argument against their existence.

Nor is gender *identity* primarily determined by physical attributes, according to current thought and research. Gender identification, de-fined as the sense one has of being a man or a woman and the presentation of self and accep-tance by others as such, is neither a fact nor a sense "with which one is born." Rather, it is as-signed and learned.

The effect of biology on the behavior of the sexes, so often accepted as primary, has been found to be largely secondary. In its place, a vast body of research documents the powerful and pervasive impact of social sex roles on attitudes and behavior, including sexual ones. A "sex role" is a widely held, learned, acted upon, and so-cially enforced definition of behaviors, attitudes, or pursuits as intrinsically more appropriate or seemly for one sex than for the other. It refers to the cultural practice of allocating social roles ac-cording to gender. Socialization is the process by which men and women are socially created to correspond to each society's definition of its "masculine" and "feminine" sex roles. Although scholars differ in their views and evaluations of the origins, social functions, exact transmission processes, contents, and impact upon individual personality of sex roles, the existence of strong-ly sex-typed social patterns within most cultures is barely disputed.

Choice of occupation, activities, goals, and feelings are strongly associated with masculine or feminine roles in virtually all cultures. The con-tent of these categories varies sufficiently across cultures to suggest that the institutionalization of specific sex role conceptions derives from the specific history and development of each society, rather than from anything intrinsic to the sex difference—even including dimorphism itself.[17] Some societies, for example, have more than two genders.[18] On the whole, sex roles reproduce themselves and tend to describe sex groups in the aggregate, which is not surprising, since people have been molded in their image. As with biol-ogy, however, individual characteristics vary as much within sex groups as between them, and sex groups overlap to a considerable extent.[19]

What hermaphrodism does to the concept of biological gender, transsexuality does to the concept of sex roles. The rigid exclusivity of each sex of the other is undercut in the clear presence of some of both. Transsexuals experi-ence a sense of sex identity cruelly trapped in a nonconforming body. Whatever the cause of this sense, it cannot be biological gender, since sex identity stands opposed to the body; nor can it be sex role conditioning alone, since sex identity is also opposed to that. The source of such a thorough rejection of standard sex role conditioning as well as physiology is obscure. But it is testimony to the power of the social correlation of sexual identity with physiology that, in order to pursue the desired behavior patterns fully, transsexuals consider it necessary to alter their *bodies* to accord with their gender identity. A final observation captures both mean-ings: first, gender identification may be better understood as a social definition of biology than as a biological definition of society, and, sec-ond, the power of that definition. Commenting upon the justice of a proposed chromosome test for determining the femaleness of the transsex-ual tennis player Dr. Renee Richards, one woman observed: "I think nature is not always correct. . . . She looks like a woman, plays like a woman. She *is* a woman. Chromosomes make things scientific, but nature is not always a hun-dred percent correct."[20]

Socially as well as biologically, gender is not as rigidly dimorphic as it is commonly supposed to be in legal discussions of equality. It is, instead, a range of overlapping distributions with different median points. The majority of women and men are located in the area of overlap. If for most characteristics the majority of women and men fall in the area where the sexes overlap, to premise legal approaches to the sexes on their differences requires the exclusion of those persons whose characteristics overlap with the other sex—that is, most people. The extremes, the tails of both curves, which apply only to exceptional women and men, are implicitly used as guidelines for sex specificity. They become norms, ideals for emulation, and standards for judgments when they are not even statistically representative.

There is a real question whether it makes sense of the evidence to conceptualize the reality of sex in terms of differences at all, except in the socially constructed sense—which social construction is what the law is attempting to address as the *problem*. To require that a given characteristic, in order to be considered a sex characteristic, be universal to the sex grouping is to require something that is not uniformly true even of most of the primary indices of gender. To then require (as the *Gilbert* approach does) that that same characteristic be comparable to, while remaining different from, the corresponding characteristic of the opposite sex, tends to exclude those few characteristics that approach being truly generic to a sex group.

While the biological sex difference has been both exaggerated and used to justify different treatment, sex inequality as a social force has been reflected in the substantive content of sex roles. Sex roles shape the behavior and express the relative position of the sexes. Although social differences between the sexes are far more pronounced than biological differences, to the extent they have been seen as differences they have not been seen as inequalities. It is not at all a distortion of the evidence to characterize the *social* situation of the sexes as largely dimorphic. In fact, the sexes are, and have been, far more dimorphic socially than they are, or have been, biologically. Much of the specific content of sex roles in American culture are those stereotypes that the law prohibits as overt job qualifications: women are weak, good with their fingers, bad at numbers, unable to stand long hours, too emotional for high seriousness. Male sex roles encourage

men to be strong, aggressive, tough, dominant, and competitive. These values, which come to be considered "male," do describe conforming and common male behavior in many spheres, including the sexual.[21] Interpreting sexual behavior in sex role terms, Diana Russell argues that rape should be viewed not as deviance but as overconformity to the male sex role.[22] In support, one recent study found that convicted rapists were "sexually and psychologically normal" according to male social norms.[23] Another study quotes a parole officer who worked with rapists in prison facilities: "Those men were the most normal men there. They had a lot of hangups, but they were the same hang-ups as men walking out on the street."[24] Although intending to exonerate men as a sex rather than to criticize male sex roles as socially defined, Lionel Tiger makes a corroborative observation that implicitly links rape findings to sexual harassment: "[It] is relatively 'normal' for males to seek sexual access to females who are their subordinates."[25]

As the examples suggest, such behaviors are almost never observed in women. Powerful social conditioning of women to passivity, gentleness, submissiveness, and receptivity to male initiation, particularly in sexual contact, tends effectively to constrain women from expressing aggression (or even assertion) sexually, or sexuality assertively, although there probably is no biological barrier to either. The constraints appear linked to women's relative social position.

> [It is] males who are supposed to initiate sexual activity with females. Females who make "advances" are considered improper, forward, aggressive, brassy, or otherwise "unladylike." By initiating intimacy they have stepped out of their place and usurped a status prerogative.[26]
>
> Women are considered synonymous with sex, yet female sexuality is seen as valid only under certain conditions, such as marriage. Even in more permissive ages like our own, there are still limits. One of these is the point where a female can be labeled promiscuous. Another is the point where she attempts to exercise any power: women who initiate and direct sexual activity with male partners find that they have gone too far and are feared and rejected as "castrators."[27]

Implicit in these observations is the view that sexual expression shaped by sex roles prescribes appropriate male and female conduct, defines normalcy, designs sexual rituals, and allocates power in the interest of men and to the detriment of women. In this respect, there definitely is a "difference" between the sexes:

> The value of such a prerogative [to initiate intimacy] is that it is a form of power. Between the sexes, as in other human interaction, the one who has the right to initiate greater intimacy has more control over the relationship. Superior status brings with it not only greater prestige and greater privileges, but greater power.[28]

> [The] fantasy world that veils [women's] experience is the world of sex as seen through male eyes. It is a world where eroticism is defined in terms of female powerlessness, dependency and submission.[29]

The substance of the meaning of sex roles, in sexuality as in other areas, just as with the social roles allocated to the races, is not symmetrical between women and men. Rather, male and female sex roles complement each other in the sense that one function of the female sex role is to reinforce the impression, and create the social actuality, of male dominance and female subordination. Ellen Morgan describes this asymmetry in sexual relationships as one means through which gender inequality is expressed and maintained in American society:

> We have a sexual situation in which the humanity and personhood of the woman, which make her seek autonomy and action and expression and self-respect, are at odds with her socially organized sexuality. We have a situation in which the dominant male sexual culture aggrandizes the male ego whereas the subordinate female style damages the female ego. Sex means different things to women and men by this time.[30]

. . . The implications of these roles for interpersonal behavior on the one hand and systemic powerlessness on the other are drawn in the following quotation:

> The "trivia" of everyday life—using "sir" or first name, touching others, dropping the eyes, smiling, interrupting and so on . . . are commonly understood as facilitators of social intercourse but are not recognized as defenders of the status quo—of the state, the wealthy, of authority, of those whose power may not be challenged. Nevertheless, these minutiae find their place on a continuum of social control which extends from internalized socialization (the colonization of the mind) . . . to sheer physical force (guns, clubs, incarceration).[31]

This examination suggests that the legally relevant content of the term *sex,* understood as gender difference, should focus upon its *social meaning* more than upon any biological givens. The most salient determinants of sexuality, much like those of work, are organized in society, not fixed in "nature." As might be expected, sex role learning, inseparably conjoined with economic necessity when the sexual aggressor is both a man and an employer, tends to inhibit women's effective resistance to "normal" male intrusions and claims upon women's sexuality, whether they come as a look or a rape. In this perspective, sexual harassment expresses one social meaning that sex roles create in the sex difference: gender distributes power as it divides labor, enforcing that division by sexual means.

Editor's Note: This chapter is changed only slightly from the way it appeared under the title, "The Social Causes of Sexual Harassment," pp. 121–136 in *Sexual Harassment: Confrontations and Decisions,* edited by Edmund Wall. Buffalo, NY: Prometheus Books (1992).

Notes

1. "It can hardly be claimed any longer that men have greater 'sex drives' and therefore, a lesser expression of sex must be attributed to an inhibition on the part of women to display sexual interest in this manner." Nancy Henley, "Power, Sex and Nonverbal Communication," in Thorne and Henley, eds., *Language and Sex: Difference*

and Dominance (Rowley, Mass.: Newbury House, Publishers, 1975), p. 193. G. Schmidt and V. Sigusch in a study entitled "Women's Sexual Arousal" reported little gender difference in physiological or self-ratings of sexual arousal in response to erotic stimuli, in J. Zubin and J. Money, *Contemporary Sexual Behavior: Critical Issues in the 1970s* (Baltimore: Johns Hopkins University Press, 1973), pp. 117–43. Such differences are widely attributed to cultural factors. See, for example, W. J. Gadpaille, "Innate Masculine-Feminine Differences." *Med. Asp. Hum. Sexuality* (1973): 141–57.

2. Vivien Stewart in "Social Influences on Sex Differences in Behavior" notes, "the contemporary feminist movement has made us so aware of the malleability of what were once considered 'eternal verities' that the impact of social forces on sex differences in behavior hardly seems to require documentation," in M. Tietelbaum, ed., *Sex Differences: Social and Biological Perspectives* (Garden City, New York: Anchor Press, Doubleday, 1976), at 138. The article summarizes research on social mechanisms and processes by which "babies born with male and female physical characteristics *are transformed into* 'masculine' and 'feminine' adults." *Id.,* at 138 (emphasis added). Reviewing the mass of evidence in his chapter entitled "Biological Influences on Sex Differences in Behavior," Ashton Barfield comes to a similar conclusion about sexual behavior in particular. "Adult androgen [male hormone] levels may contribute to libido, but so can experience and attitude. . . . Cultural factors influence the types of stimuli which cause arousal and the choice of sex object." Tietelbaum, at 108. See also references in chap. 6, *infra,* note 106.

3. 2 Empl. Prac. Guide (CCH) Par. 6493 (1976).

4. 84 *Harvard Law Review* (1971); 1109, 1184 (emphasis added). . . .

5. John Money, "Developmental Differentiation of Femininity and Masculinity Compared," in Farber and Wilson, eds., *The Potential of Woman* (New York: McGraw-Hill, 1963), p. 56; John Money and Patricia Tucker, *Sexual Signatures: On Being A Man or A Woman* (Boston: Little, Brown, 1975); R. Stoller, *Sex and Gender: On the Development of Masculinity and Femininity* (London: Hogarth, 1968); R. Green and J. Money, *Transsexualism and Sex Reassignment* (Baltimore: Johns Hopkins University Press, 1969); Edward S. David, "The Law and Transsexualism: A Faltering Response to a Conceptual Dilemma," *Connecticut Law Review* 7 (1975): 288; J. Money and A. Erhardt, *Man and Woman, Boy and Girl* (Baltimore: Johns Hopkins University Press, 1972); J. Money, *Sex Errors of the Body* (Baltimore: Johns Hopkins University Press, 1968); Note, *Transsexuals in Limbo, Maryland Law Review* 31 (1971): 236.

6. Ashton Barfield, "Biological Influences on Sex Differences in Behavior," in M. Tietelbaum, ed., *Sex Differences: Social and Biological Perspectives* (Garden City, N.Y.: Anchor Press, Doubleday, 1976), 107. Bibliography of research supporting this summary, ibid., p. 110–21.

7. Eleanor F. Maccoby, ed., *The Development of Sex Differences* (Stanford: Stanford University Press, 1966).

8. Barfield, *supra,* note 18, at 109, 110.

9. Robert Masters and Virginia Johnson, *Human Sexual Response* (Boston: Little, Brown, 1966).

10. R. Staples, "Male-Female Sexual Variations: Functions of Biology or Culture," *Journal of Sexual Response* 9 (1973): 11–20.

11. A. C. Kinsey et al., *Sexual Behavior in the Human Male* (Philadelphia: W. B. Saunders Co., 1948). Kinsey's famous studies of sexual arousal in women and men in the 1930s and 1940s seemed to confirm that the sexes differed substantially in this respect. Culturally, his results were used to endow men with animal lust, women with demure passionlessness. (Demonstrating that obscure ability of racism to survive evidence, the stereotype of the black woman as sex-crazed was never apparently confronted by these findings purporting to represent the sexuality of all biological females.) A recent replication of Kinsey's studies suggests that cultural repression of women's sexuality largely accounts for his findings. Sigusch and Schmidt conclude that sexual arousability "is as strongly and quite similarly structured for both women and men." They explain the difference between their results and Kinsey's as follows:

> His findings cannot serve as evidence for a lesser capacity for women to become sexually aroused by pictoral and narrative stimuli. They reflect one aspect of the cultural desexualization of women in western societies which 20 to 30 years ago, when Kinsey collected his data, was more extensive than today.

V. Sigusch and G. Schmidt, "Women's Sexual Arousal," in Zubin and Money, *Contemporary Sexual Behavior: Critical Issues in the 1970s* (Baltimore: Johns Hopkins University Press, 1973), pp. 118–19.

12. J. Marmor, "Women in Medicine: The Importance of the Formative Years," *Journal of American Medical Women's Association* (July 1968), 621.

13. John H. Gagnon and William Simon, *Sexual Conduct: The Social Sources of Human Sexuality* (Chicago: Aldine Publishing Company, 1973), p. 9.

14. Ibid., pp. 19–26.

15. See Judith Long Laws and Pepper Schwartz, *Sexual Scripts: The Social Construction of Female Sexuality* (Hinsdale, Ill.: The Dryden Press, 1977), who apply Gagnon and Simon's concept to women's sexuality specifically.

16. John H. Gagnon and William Simon, eds., *The Sexual Scene* (Chicago: Aldine Publishing Company, 1970), p. 4.

17. Margaret Mead, *Sex and Temperament in Three Primitive Societies* (New York: Dell, 1935); Margaret Mead, *Male and Female: A Study of the Sexes in A Changing World* (New York: William Morrow & Co., 1975, pp. 7–8; Michele Rosaldo and Louise Lamphere, eds., *Woman, Culture and Society* (Palo Alto, Calif.: Stanford University Press, 1974); Rayna R. Reiter, ed., *Toward an Anthropology of Women* (New York: Monthly Review Press, 1975).

18. See Anna S. Meigs, "Male Pregnancy and the Reduction of Sexual Opposition in A New Guinea Highlands Society," *Ethnology: An International Journal of Cultural and Social Anthropology* 15, no. 4 (October 1976): 393–407; C. S. Ford and F. Beach, *Patterns of Sexual Behavior* (New York: Harper, 1951) provides background and several illustrative examples.

19. There are numerous excellent reviews and collections of sex role research. A classic in the field is Eleanor E. Maccoby, ed., *The Development of Sex Differences* (Stanford, Calif.: Stanford University Press, 1966). A bibliography of research conducted from 1973 to 1974 can be found in *Women's Work and Women's Studies, 1973–4, A Bibliography* (The Barnard College Women's Center, 1975), pp. 285–302, and a list of bibliographies on the subject at ibid., pp. 321–22. Recent books on varying levels include Carol Tavris and Carole Offir, *The Longest War: Sex Differences in Perspective* (New York: Harcourt, Brace Jovanovich, 1977); Nancy Reeves, *Womankind: Beyond the Stereotypes* (Chicago: Aldine Publishing Company, 1977); Shirley Weitz, *Sex Roles: Biological, Psychological and Social Foundation* (Oxford University Press, 1977). For a political perspective on sex roles in terms of power, see, e.g., Nancy Hartsock, "Political Change: Two Perspectives on Power," *Quest: A Feminist Quarterly* (Summer 1974): 10–25. An application to the law is Barbara Kirk Cavanagh, "A Little Dearer Than His Horse: Legal Stereotypes and the Feminine Personality," 6 *Harv. C.R.C.L. Review* (1970): 260–87.

20. *New York Times,* August 22, 1976, (Sports Section), p. 3. See also the discussion by Germaine Greer of transsexual April Ashley, *The Female Eunuch* (New York: McGraw Hill, 1970), pp. 54–55, *but cf.* the legal decision in the same case, *Corbett v. Corbett,* [1971], p. 83 (P. P. Div'l Ct.) (England).

21. A very different approach to analyzing sexuality for legal purposes can be found in the psychoanalytic interpretations collected in Ralph Slovenko, *Sexual Behavior and the Law* (Springfield, Ill.: Charles C. Thomas, 1965).

22. Diana E. H. Russell, *The Politics of Rape* (New York: Stein & Day, 1975), p. 260.

23. Andrea Medea and Kathleen Thompson, *Against Rape* (New York: Farrar, Straus & Giroux, 1974), pp. 29–30.

24. Susan Griffin, "Rape: The All-American Crime," *Ramparts,* 10 (September 1971): 25–35, reprint in Jo Freeman, ed., *Women: A Feminist Perspective* (Palo Alto, Calif.: Mayfield Publishing Co., 1975), p. 26.

25. Lionel Tiger, *Men in Groups* (New York: Random House, 1969), p. 271. Lynn Wehrli, "Sexual Harassment at the Workplace: A Feminist Analysis and Strategy for Social Change," (M.A. Thesis, Massachusetts Institute of Technology, December 1976) makes the same connection, p. 86.

26. Nancy Henley and Jo Freeman, "The Sexual Politics of Interpersonal Behavior," in Freeman, ed., *Women: A Feminist Perspective* (Palo Alto, Calif.: Mayfield Publishing Co., 1975), pp. 393–94.

27. Linda Phelps, "Female Sexual Alienation," in Freeman, *Women: A Feminist Perspective,* p. 20.

28. Henley and Freeman, in Freeman, *Women: A Feminist Perspective,* pp. 393–94.

29. Phelps, in Freeman, *Women: A Feminist Perspective,* p. 19.

30. Ellen Morgan, "The Erotization of Male Dominance/Female Subordination," University of Michigan, Papers in Women's Studies 2 (1975): 112–45, reprint by Know, Inc., p. 20. See also Nancy M. Henley, *Body Politics: Power, Sex and Nonverbal Communication* (Englewood Cliffs, N.J.: Prentice-Hall, 1977), pp. 94–123.

31. Henley, "Power, Sex and Nonverbal Communication," in Barrie Thorne and Nancy Henley, eds., *Language and Sex: Difference and Dominance* (Rowley, Mass.: Newbury House, Publishers, 1975), p. 184.

Cases Cited

City of Los Angeles, Department of Water and Power v. Manhart, 98 S. Ct. 1370 (1978).
Gilbert v. General Electric, 429 U.S. 125 (1976).

23

The Legal Regulation of Sexual Harassment: From Tort to Sex Discrimination

Catharine A. MacKinnon

Standard legal doctrine in the areas of tort, labor, and crime, which could have moderated the extremes of conventional role expectations when they restrained and damaged women, has, on the whole, institutionalized them. The law has tended to internalize and reflect, and thereby legitimize and enforce, traditional male and female norms. For example, the *act* of rape can be criticized as one expression of the male role of assertive sexual initiation, heedless of women's wishes. To the extent the *crime* of rape is defined to reflect rather than counter this role definition, allowing rape to be *legally normal* as well, rape as women experience it will not be effectively prohibited. Because sexual harassment, too, has appeared so much a part of the normal and expectable behavior between the sexes, the law has fallen short of women's needs and aspirations in similar ways. Prior to the recent cases, the law had failed to grasp the whole configuration of sexual harassment as a distinct theory. Perhaps this is too much to have expected. The greater criticism may be its consistent failure to take the shorter step of recognizing that the constituent acts of sexual harassment were actionable all along if existing doctrines had been applied to them. Contract doctrine, as the *Monge* case illustrates, did not have to be changed to prohibit sexual harassment in employment; it merely had to be applied.[1]

With a little more creativity and a little less sexism, sexual harassment might long have been a recognized tort. But it is even more interesting that without going very far out of mainstream thinking, many of the acts that comprise incidents of sexual harassment, if properly construed (this, after all, is what lawyers do), arguably fit into the traditional torts of assault and battery, with corollary dignitary harm, or, if sufficiently extreme, the tort of intentional infliction of emotional distress. This application has not commonly been made. In the labor area an explicit contractual prohibition of sexual harassment could be bargained over; but incidents could also be arbitrated as grievances—for example, under those clauses in most collective agreements that require "just cause" for termination—but apparently have not been.[2] The Occupational Safety and Health Act could forbid sexual harassment in so many words; sexual harassment could also be—but, again, seems not to have been—interpreted as a workplace "stress" under the existing code, which forbids systematic threats to worker goals, integrity, or well-being.[3]

Examination of the criminal law reveals an arsenal of potential, if partial, approaches that have not been applied to the facts of sexual harassment. Sexual harassment often includes criminal acts such as rape, sexual assault, sexual imposition, deviate sexual intercourse, solicitation, or adultery.[4] Often involved, in addition, are more esoteric or antiquated crimes which still exist in some form in some jurisdictions: lewdness, criminal conversation, fornication, insult, bribery, oppression, exploitation, and blackmail. In the absence of the legitimate employment relation, sexual submission in exchange for material survival is conventionally considered prostitution, which remains illegal in most jurisdictions. A great many instances of sexual harassment in essence amount to solicitation for prostitution. Reported cases and commentaries do not disclose that acts comprising sexual harassment have been prosecuted on any of these criminal grounds, any more than on the foregoing civil grounds. Such a fact of administration confronts the legal system at a point at which its theory and practice converge.

Before a systemic critique is launched, another possible explanation for the lack of legal response to facts amounting to sexual harassment should be considered: sexual incidents in the employment context might not have been reported to those who could initiate legal action. It makes sense that women would not complain to authorities. The threat and potential for direct reprisals upon exposure, women's precarious position in the labor market, and the previously slim chance of success mean that most women, in order to complain officially, would have to take risks that most women are not in an economic position to take. Such an explanation also exposes the social circularity, from women's standpoint, of nonreporting as a justification for legal nonresponse. The law participates in constructing the balance of risks run in reporting. One reason for a lack of complaints may be the lack of legitimation of these injuries *as injuries* which an effective legal prohibition would give. Concretely, when nothing helpful is known to be done, complaint becomes an integral part of the social pathology of the problem, a further aggravation of the injury of the incident itself, instead of a potential solution to it. Together with the psychological impact of sexual harassment upon women's socialized sense of self-worth and the confirmation that a legal nonresponse gives to women's apprehensions about the reactions of others, it seems reasonable that incidents might not be reported. But this indicts more than exonerates the legal system.

Complaints may also have been made but not heard. Wife beating provides a direct analogy. The constituent acts of domestic battery are obvious criminal violations; they are regularly grounds for arrest and, if proven, for conviction in contexts other than husband and wife. Women's attempts to gain legal redress and protection from domestic victimization are infamously ineffectual.[5] This suggests that intimate assaults on women by men are ignored even when they are reported—even when there is an unambiguous doctrinal receptacle for the complaint. The guarantee of impunity seems to be particularly firm when incidents involve either sexuality or violence within a relationship presumed to have a sexual dimension. With the beating of women in the home as well as with the sexual harassment of women on the job (acts which occur when women and men are involved in a relation which is presumptively sexualized, as both home and workplace are) even acts that have been objectively illegal are systematically tolerated.

The legal profession, in addition, has probably seen the nexus between work and sex presented by sexual harassment to introduce "complications" in bringing suits or prosecutions. A clean approach through *either* employment, tort, criminal, or labor law may have appeared impracticable or cumbersome. Neither a quick fix, rich clients, nor a good prospect of large money damages has made such suits attractive. In light of this analysis, the lack of documented legal response to facts amounting to sexual harassment, much less to the totality of the problem, seems less justified by the lack of reports than the lack of reports seems explained by those factors which make sexual harassment a women's problem. The same factors, in turn, begin to explain the effective acquiescence of the legal system.

A more fundamental reason than the absence of reports for the legal system's lack of response to sexual harassment is the conceptual inadequacy of traditional legal theories to the social reality of men's sexual treatment of women. It is no accident that no recognized legal category has been applied with any regularity to the entire fact pattern of sexual harassment. No legal doctrine except sex discrimination, which is relatively new, comfortably accommodates the entire configuration of facts, places them in broad social perspective, or approaches the appropriate relief. Although the facts of sex discrimination have a long history in women's suffering, the prohibition on sex discrimination as such lacks a common law history. Other and older areas of law can contribute the experience, analogues, applicable concepts, and additional avenues for partial or supplementary relief that such a history might have supplied. They illustrate how the law has approached women's sexuality. They provide, moreover, a point of comparison that clarifies the distinctive contribution of sex discrimination as a legal concept and assists in its interpretation. Exploring some illustrative common law attempts to treat intimate violations of women as illegal recaptures and recasts an ongoing history—its contributions and its limitations.

Criminal Law

Many acts of sexual harassment are technically crimes and should be prosecuted. The criminal law has not, however, been generally sympathetic to sexual injuries as women experience them. Unlike most other crimes, and like no other crimes against the person,* corroboration is often required and juries are instructed to be especially careful in evaluating the testimony "in view of the emotional involvement of the witness and the difficulty of determining the truth with respect to alleged sexual activities carried out in private."[6] "In private" means more than "while alone." Many crimes are committed in the absence of nonparticipant eyewitnesses. Privacy sanctifies the sphere of the sexual. Because these events so often occur in private, they are safe from public witness. In part because they feel so alone, women are disabled from effective resistance. Such a conception of the "private" becomes a special legal caution that women who accuse men of sexual injury cannot be judged by ordinary standards of credibility. It turns men's "right to be let alone"[7] into a shield behind which isolated women can be sexually abused one at a time.

The Model Penal Code defines sexual assault as subjecting "another not his spouse to any sexual contact" including those circumstances in which "he knows that the contact is offensive to the other person." Sexual contact is defined as "any touching of the sexual or other intimate parts of the person of another for the purpose of arousing or gratifying sexual desire of either party."[8] This suggests that sexual assault, in common with ordinary sexual contact, is motivated by sexual desire. Sexual assault is distinguished from sexual nonassault only by the fact that a wrong person—in this example, a person known to be offended by it—is its object: At what point sexual assault is distinguishable from permissible sexual intimacy is a good question. Here, sexual assault differs from most (if not all) other forms of assault: the proscribed act and the allowed act are the same act. Ultimately, only the meaning to the acted-upon distinguishes them.

Sexual assault as experienced during sexual harassment seems less an ordinary act of sexual desire directed toward the wrong person than an expression of dominance laced with impersonal contempt, the habit of getting what one wants, and the perception (usually accurate) that the situation can be safely exploited in this way—all expressed sexually. It is dominance eroticized. The sense that emerges from incidents of sexual harassment is less that men mean to arouse or gratify the women's sexual desires, or often even their own, and more that they want to know that they can go this far this way any time they wish and get away with it. The fact that they can do this seems itself to be sexually arousing. The practice seems an extension of their desire and belief that the woman is there *for them,* however they may choose to define that. The factors of advantage, the quality of presumption, and the manipulation of occasion may participate in motivating heterosexual contact in ordinary course; they may be constituents or stimuli of ordinary male sexual desire. But to define the crime in the terms of the perpetrator's misplacement of otherwise fine feelings begins the process of distinguishing the sexual from other

---

*The proof requirements for sexual injuries are most like those for treason.

forms of violation, a process which then extends to an inquiry into what the victim did to arouse this desire and whether she found the assault gratifying.[9] It may be that the normal sexual interactions to which sexual assault is assimilated should be examined in light of the difficulty of distinguishing the two.

An earlier version of the Model Penal Code's sexual assault provision prohibited sexual contact without consent. The requirement was deleted with the following justification: "This seems too strict a standard of criminality, considering the frequency with which tentative sexual advances are made without explicit assurance of consent."[10] The statute prohibits subjection to sexual contact, which presumably should be distinguishable in practice from "tentative sexual advances." At least, advances which subject one to sexual contact, as defined, are not very tentative. More bluntly, this statement reflects the belief that since men so frequently initiate sexual contact without determining whether women want it or not, such acts should not be considered criminal. This approach eviscerates the entire conception of a sexual assault when the unwanted offensiveness of the contact is the only feature that divides it from the noncriminal.

Exactly the conditions that make sexual harassment pernicious may tend to disqualify it as sexual assault. For example, the economic threats that sanction sexual coercion, as well as women's social conditioning to seek men's approval, may prevent women from being sufficiently explicit about the offensiveness of the man's behavior to meet the statutory requirement. Further, it is overwhelmingly clear that male perpetrators do not as a rule experience sexual episodes as the assaults that the victims feel them to be. This must be one reason they can continue to do it. Men who sexually harass women are commonly dumbfounded that the women resent it, even when the women have declined flatly from the beginning and resisted explicitly throughout. Assuming that men's bafflement is sincere, it not only measures monumental insensitivity but also indicates the difficulty of showing that the perpetrator "knew the contact would be offensive." Apparently, men are responsible only if they know they are sexually offensive, and nothing in the law requires (or

even strongly encourages) them to know what their conduct means to women.

The rape law is similarly inadequate as a guide to a work-related, gender-specific abuse. It more shows the ambivalence of the law, often its misogyny. Rape ordinarily has referred to a male having "sexual intercourse with a female not his wife" by force or threats to life or physical integrity.[11] "Gross sexual imposition" is the lesser crime for the same act when the woman is under compulsion "to submit by any threat that would prevent resistance by a woman of ordinary resolution."[12] Apparently threat of loss of subsistence has not been found within this prohibition. Consent is a defense. If a woman is threatened with loss of her job if she resists sexual relations, and then does not resist for that reason, she is legally considered to have consented. Menachem Amir summarizes this view: "Threats which may be urgent in terms of the personality and social needs of the victim are known to exist; for example, the threat of loss of a job. . . . Generally, the law refuses to deal with such threats as anything more than reasons for giving consent, which thereby bars conviction of rape."[13] Since the woman's participation has been forced by coercing her consent rather than by coercing the act itself, the intercourse is not considered forced. With the law taking this stance, imagine a complaining witness testifying as follows: "I didn't want to sleep with him but I wanted the job so much and he was holding it over my head, that *I was willing,* right then, to sleep with him, in order to get the job."[14] Because of his power as an employer, the perpetrator gains legal immunity as a man.

Tort Law

Women's bodies, particularly the conditions and consequences of men's sexual access to them, are not a novel subject for the law, as the foregoing examination reveals. The law of torts, or private harms, historically provided civil redress for sexual invasions at a time when social morality was less ambiguous in defining a woman's sexuality as intrinsic to her virtue, and her virtue as partially constitutive of her value, hence as capable of compensable damage. Perhaps with this tradition in mind, several recent sexual harassment cases have suggested—usually as a reason for holding sexual harassment not to be sex discrimination—that sexual harassment should be considered tortious. The federal court in *Tomkins,* implicitly finding that since sexual harassment is a tort it is not discrimination, stated that Title VII "is not intended to provide a federal tort remedy for what amounts to physical attack motivated by sexual desire on the part of a supervisor and which happened to occur in a corporate corridor rather than a back alley."[15] One appellate judge, concurring in the judgment in *Barnes* that sexual harassment is sex discrimination, observed, "An act of sexual harassment which caused the victim, because of her rejection of such advances, to be damaged in her job, would constitute a tort."[16] Which tort is not specified, although "[t]here is no necessity whatever that a tort must have a name."[17] It is, however, necessary that the definition of the legal wrong fit the conceptual framework of tort law. Brief examination of traditional tort views of sexual wrongs against women illustrates that tort law is not simply wrong, and is partially helpful, but is fundamentally insufficient as a legal approach to sexual harassment.

Sexual touching that women do not want has historically been considered tortious under a variety of doctrines, usually battery, assault, or, if exclusively emotional damage is done, as the intentional infliction of emotional distress. A battery is a harmful or offensive contact which is intentionally caused. While contact must be intentional, hostile intent, or intent to cause all the damages that resulted from the contact, is not necessary. Variously formulated, "taking indecent liberties with a woman without her consent,"[18] "putting hands upon a female with a view to violate her person,"[19] or "intentional touching of a woman by a man without excuse or justification"[20] have been considered battery. Battery is said to include instances in which a compliment is intended, "as where an unappreciative woman is kissed without her consent."[21]

Battery, the actual touching, is often combined with assault, the fear of such a touching. The tort of assault consists in placing a person in *fear* of an immediate harmful or offensive con-

tact. It is "a touching of the mind, if not of the body."[22] The invasion is mental. The defendant must have intended at least to arouse apprehension, and actually have done so. The fear-producing event must be more than words alone, but words can clarify an otherwise equivocal act. Defenses include consent, but only to those acts consented to; consent to a kiss, for example, does not extend to anything further. Nor are provocative words a defense.

Kissing a woman without her consent has been considered actionable under a combination (or confusion) of assault and battery doctrines. In 1899, a husband and wife recovered $700 for assault on the wife for forcible hugging and kissing "against her wish and by force."[23] In 1921, a railroad was found responsible for the embarrassment and humiliation of a woman passenger caused when a drunken man, of whose boisterous conduct and inebriated condition the railroad was aware, fell down on top of her and kissed her on the cheek.[24] In 1895 in Wisconsin, a twenty-year-old schoolteacher recovered $1,000 from the employer of a railroad conductor who grabbed and kissed her several times despite her clear attempts to discourage and repel him.[25]

Other early cases finding sexual incursions actionable reveal that little has changed in men's sexual behavior, although something seems to have changed in the social and legal standards by which it is evaluated. In a case in 1915, a woman recovered damages for assault and battery against a man who squeezed her breast and laid his hand on her face. The defendant denied the whole incident, then characterized the touching as "nothing more than a harmless caress."[26] In a similar case in 1921, a woman recovered for the mental anguish arising from an indecent assault, defined as "the act of a male person taking indecent liberties with the person of a female, or fondling her in a lewd and lascivious manner without her consent and against her will." The judge found it unnecessary for the assault to be made in an angry or insolent manner: "Indecent assaults are not made in that way."[27] Sexual assault—whether or not it was done with bad feeling—is still assault.

Contemporary sexual mores make it difficult to imagine such cases in court. Women are, it seems, supposed to consider acts in this tradition harmless, and litigation in this area is now relatively uncommon.* As recently as 1961, however, an Arizona woman was granted $3,500 actual damages and $1,500 punitive damages in a full-fledged case of sexual harassment in employment brought under the tort theory of assault and battery. The complaint alleged indecent assault by force and violence for an employer's efforts to seduce and offend the dignity of a sixty-five-year-old woman he employed as a caretaker in a trailer park. The situation included the "defendant placing his hand upon the private parts of the plaintiff."[28] The woman resisted the advances for two years and was finally discharged. Although this case holds hope for the tort approach, perhaps the desexualization of older women made more than usually credible her assertions that the man's acts were neither desired nor provoked, and that her dignity was violated.

Sexual propositions in themselves have not generally been considered torts where there is no physical incursion upon or trespass against the person, or no physical injury. In Magruder's famous formulation: "Women have occasionally sought damages for mental distress and humiliation on account of being addressed by a proposal of illicit intercourse. This is peculiarly a situation where circumstances alter cases. If there has been no incidental assault or battery, or perhaps trespass to land, recovery is generally denied, the view being apparently, that there is no harm in asking."[29] Expressing attitudes toward women's assertions of sexual injury which have remained largely unchanged to the present day, the court in one case of solicitation of sexual intercourse found the injury of a sexual proposition "generally considered more sentimental than substantial . . . vague and shadowy" and "easily simulated and impossible to disprove." Without physical "impact," the injury of a sexual proposition is considered "remote" and to have a "metaphysical character."[30] It is not an injury *in itself*.[31]

Most broadly considered, tort is conceptually inadequate to the problem of sexual harassment to the extent that it rips injuries to women's sexuality out of the context of women's social circumstances as a whole. In particular, short of developing a new tort for sexual harassment as such, the tort approach misses the nexus between women's sexuality and women's employment, the system of reciprocal sanctions which, to women as a gender, become cumulative. In tort perspective, the injury of sexual harassment would be seen as an injury to the individual person, to personal sexual integrity, with damages extending to the job. Alternatively, sexual harassment could be seen as an injury to an individual interest in employment, with damages extending to the emotional harm attendant to the sexual invasion as well as to the loss of employment. The approach tends to pose the necessity to decide whether sexual harassment is essentially an injury to the person, to sexual integrity and feelings, with pendent damages to the job, or whether it is essentially an injury to the job, with damages extending to the person. Since it is both, either one omits the social dynamics that systematically place women in these positions, that may coerce consent, that interpenetrate sexuality and employment to women's detriment because they are women.

Unsituated in a recognition of the context that keeps women secondary and powerless, sexual injuries appear as incidental or deviant aberrations which arise in one-to-one relationships gone wrong. The essential purpose of tort law, although it has policy assumptions and implications, is to compensate individuals one at a time for mischief which befalls them as a consequence of the one-time ineptitude or nastiness of other individuals. The occurrence of such events is viewed more or less with resignation, as an inevitability of social proximity, a fall-out of order which can be confronted only probabilistically. Sexual harassment as understood in this book is not merely a parade of interconnected consequences with the potential for discrete repetition by other individuals, so that a precedent will suffice. Rather, it is a group-defined injury which occurs to many different

---

*Such causes of action may also have been pretexts for racial repression. Black men may have been prosecuted and white men not for the same sexual conduct. This hypothesis requires investigation.

individuals regardless of unique qualities or circumstances, in ways that connect with other deprivations of the same individuals, among all of whom a single characteristic—female sex—is shared. Such an injury is *in essence* a group injury. The context which makes the impact of gender cumulative—in fact, the context that makes it injurious—is lost when sexual harassment is approached as an individual injury, however wide the net of damages is cast. Tort law compensates individuals for injuries while spreading their costs and perhaps setting examples for foresightful perpetrators; the purpose of discrimination law is to change the society so that this kind of injury need not and does not recur. Tort law considers individual and compensable something which is fundamentally social and should be eliminated. . . .

All of this is not to say that sexual harassment is not both wrong and a personal injury, merely that it is a social wrong and a social injury that occurs on a personal level. To treat it as a tort is less simply incorrect than inadequate. The law recognizes that individual acts of racism could be torts in recognizing that the dignitary harm of racist insults can be compensated like any other personal injury.[32] This does not preclude a finding that the same acts of racial invective on the job are race discrimination.[33] Although racial insults impact upon blacks on a personal level, they are systematically connected to the "living insult" of segregation.[34] Although reparations may be due,[35] the stigma is not eradicable by money damages to one black person at a time. As with sexual harassment, the reason these acts can occur and recur, and the source of their sting, is not the breaking of a code of good conduct, but the relegation to inferiority for which they stand.

To see sexual harassment as an injury to morality is to turn it into an extreme case of bad manners, when the point is that it is the kind of bad manners almost exclusively visited upon women by men with the power to get away with it. One can see the social invisibility of blacks as white rudeness, but it makes more sense to see it as racism. The major difference between the tort approach and the discrimination approach, then, is that tort sees sexual harassment as an illicit act, a moral infraction, an outrage to the individual's sensibilities and the society's cherished but unlived values. Discrimination law

casts the same acts as economic coercion, in which material survival is held hostage to sexual submission. . . .

Sexual Harassment as Sex Discrimination: An Inequality Argument

Practices which express and reinforce the social inequality of women to men are clear cases of sex-based discrimination in the *inequality* approach. Sexual harassment of working women is argued to be employment discrimination based on gender where gender is defined as the social meaning of sexual biology. Women are sexually harassed by men because they are women, that is, because of the social meaning of female sexuality, here, in the employment context. Three kinds of arguments support and illustrate this position: first, the exchange of sex for survival has historically assured women's economic dependence and inferiority as well as sexual availability to men. Second, sexual harassment expresses the male sex-role pattern of coercive sexual initiation toward women, often in vicious and unwanted ways. Third, women's sexuality largely defines women as women in this society, so violations of it are abuses of women as women.

Tradition

Sexual harassment perpetuates the interlocked structure by which women have been kept sexually in thrall to men and at the bottom of the labor market. Two forces of American society converge: men's control over women's sexuality and capital's control over employees' work lives. Women historically have been required to exchange sexual services for material survival, in one form or another. Prostitution and marriage as well as sexual harassment in different ways institutionalize this arrangement.

The impact of these forces, which affect all women, often varies by class. Exclusion of moderately well-off women (that is, women attached to moderately well-off men) from most gainful occupations was often excused by fears that virtuous women would fall victim to sexual predators if they were allowed to work.[36] This exclusion, however, insured their dependence for survival upon bartering attractiveness and sexuality for subsistence, only from different men. Deprived of education and training in marketable skills, excluded from most professions, and disdaining as unsuitable the menial work reserved for their lower-class sisters, such women's adequacy was traditionally measured in large part by sexual allure. As they entered the paid labor force in increasing numbers, the sexual standard they were judged by accompanied them; the class status they held as adjuncts to middle-class men did not. Working-class and poor women did not have the choice between the home and the workplace. And they have always maintained an even more precarious hold on jobs than their male counterparts, with chronically lower wages, and usually without security or the requisites to claim advancement. Because they were women, these factors put them at the mercy of the employer sexually[37] as well as economically. Once in the work force, usually in women's jobs, the class distinctions among women were qualified by their common circumstance, which was sex defined. "Sometimes the employer's son, or the master himself, or the senior stablehand, would have taken them. Men didn't always use brute force, the physical coercion or the threat of it that is the standard definition of rape. Often the threat of dismissal was sufficient."[38]

This point is illustrated in the following excerpt from Olive Pratt Rayner's *The Typewriter Girl* (dated by Margery Davies as late nineteenth century):

Three clerks (male), in seedy black coats, the eldest with hair the color of a fox's, went on chaffing with one another for two minutes after I closed the door, with ostentatious unconsciousness of my insignificant presence. . . . The youngest, after a while, wheeled around on his high stool and broke out with the chivalry of his class and age, "Well, what's your business?"

My voice trembled a little, but I mustered up courage and spoke. "I have called about your advertisement . . . "

He eyed me up and down. I am slender, and, I will venture to say, if not pretty, at least interesting looking.

"How many words a minute?" he asked after a long pause.

I stretched the truth as far as its elasticity would permit. "Ninety-seven." I answered. . . .

The eldest clerk, with the foxy head, wheeled around, and took his turn to stare. He had hairy hands and large goggle-eyes. . . . I detected an undercurrent of double meaning. . . . I felt disagreeably like Esther in the presence of Ahasuerus—a fat and oily Ahasuerus of fifty. . . . He perused me up and down with his small pig's eyes, as if he were buying a horse, scrutinizing my face, my figure, my hands, my feet. I felt like a Circassian in an Arab slavemarket.[39]

Millett generalizes this observation: "A female is continually obliged to seek survival or advancement through the approval of males as those who hold power. She may do this through appeasement or through the exchange of her sexuality for support and status."[40]

The generality of "women" and "men" must be qualified by recognizing the distinctive effect of race. Racism does not allow black men to share white men's dominance of economic resources. Black women have not tended to be economically dependent upon black men to the degree white women have been upon white men. To the extent black women are employed by white men, as most have been from slavery until the present, the foregoing analysis applies directly to them, intensified, not undercut, by race. There is little indication that this statement by an anonymous black woman in 1912 is significantly outdated.

I remember very well the first and last work place from which I was dismissed. I lost my place because I refused to let the madam's husband kiss me. . . . he took it as a matter of course, because without any love-making at all, soon after I was installed as cook, he walked up to me, threw his arms around me, and was in the act of kissing me, when I demanded to know what he meant, and shoved him away. . . . I believe nearly all white men take, and expect to take, undue liberties with their colored female servants. . . . where the girl is not willing, she has only herself to depend upon for protection. . . . what we need is present help, present sympathy, better wages, better hours, more protection, and a chance to breathe for once while alive as free women.[41]

Moreover, when black women enter the labor market of the dominant society, they succeed to the secondary place of white females (remaining, in addition, under the disabilities of blacks), while black men succeed at least to some of the power of the male role. Indeed, many of the demands of the black civil rights movement in the 1960s centered upon just such a recovery of "manhood."

Similar to the way in which the status of American blacks of both sexes encompasses personal and economic exploitation, sexual harassment deprives women of personhood by relegating them to subservience through jointly exploiting their sexuality and their work. As women begin to achieve the minimum material conditions under which equality with men can concretely be envisioned, and increasingly consider their skills worth a wage and their dignity worth defending, the necessity to exchange sex for support becomes increasingly intolerable. It is a reminder of that image of a deprived reality in which sexuality and attractiveness to men were all a woman had to offer—and she had very little control over either. The history of the role of sexuality in enforcing women's second-class economic status, sketched only very briefly here, makes sexual requirements of work "uniquely disturbing to women."[42]

> It is a reminder, a badge or indicia [sic] of the servile status she suffered . . . and which she is now trying to shake off. . . . To make her advancement on the job depend on her sexual performance is to resurrect her former status as man's property or plaything.[43]

But is such status really a thing of the past? The sexual harassment cases and evidence suggest that it is not. Emma Goldman's analysis has no less vitality now than in 1917:

> Nowhere is a woman treated according to the merit of her work, but rather as a sex. It is therefore almost inevitable that she should pay for her right to exist, to keep a position in whatever line, with sex favors. Thus it is merely a question of degree whether she sells herself to one man, in or out of marriage, or to many men.[44]

A guarantee against discrimination "because of sex" has little meaning if a major traditional dynamic of enforcement and expression of inferior sex status is allowed to persist untouched. A guarantee of equal access to job training, education, and skills has little substance if a requirement of equality in hiring, promotion, and pay can legally be withheld if a woman refuses to grant sexual favors. A man who is allowed to measure a woman's work by sexual standards cannot be said to employ her on the basis of merit. If a woman must grant sexual consideration to her boss in exchange for employment benefits, her material status still depends upon her sexual performance, and the legal promise of equality for women is an illusion.

Notes

1. See the discussion of *Monge v. Beebe Rubber,* 316 A.2d 549, 551–2 (N.H. 1974).

2. Of course, this requires that women be unionized; few are. See chap. 2, *supra,* note 37. See also, *Gates v. Brockway Glass,* 93 L.R.R.M. 2367 (C.D. Cal. 1976).

3. The Occupational Safety and Health Act of 1970 mandates that the National Institute of Occupational Safety and Health conduct research into the psychological factors involved in worker safety and health. 29 U.S.C. §§669, 671.
It does not appear that sexual harassment has been studied in this connection, although suggestive work has been done in the field of occupational stress generally. See, for example, Alan McLean, ed., *Occupational Stress* (Springfield, Ill.: Charles C. Thomas, 1974). One article therein notes in passing that "racial prejudice, felt or real, can be a source of stress for the worker, independent of the requirements or nature of the job." Bruce K. Margolis and William H. Kroes, "Occupational Stress and Strain," *id.,* at 17. See also *id.,* at 94, and Alan McLean, *Mental Health and Work Organizations* (Chicago: Rand McNally, 1970).

4. See, for example, *Model Penal Code* (1962), §251.1 (lewdness); §213.1 (1) (rape); §213.2 (deviate sexual intercourse by force or imposition); §213.3 (seduction); §213.4 (sexual assault); §5.02 (solicitation); §213.1(2) (gross sexual imposition), and the discussion of views of the criminal law on women's sexuality at 161–64, *infra.*

5. *Carmen Bruno et al. v. Michael Codd, Commissioner of New York City Police Department et al.*: "For too long, Anglo-American law treated a man's physical abuse of his wife as different from any other assault, and, indeed as an acceptable practice." 90 Misc. 2d 1047, 1048, 396 N.Y.S.2d 974, 975 (Sup. Ct. 1977). The favorable result to the complaining women in this case was recently reversed. *Bruno v. Codd,* 407 N.Y.S. 2d 165 (App. Div. July 20, 1978).

6. *Model Penal Code,* §213.6(6).

7. The phrase "the right of a person to be let alone" is the classic definition of the right to privacy, usually attributed to T. Cooley, *A Treatise on the Law of Torts,* §135 (2d ed., 1888), and cited to *Roberson v. Rochester Folding Box Co.,* 171 N.Y. 538, 64 N.E. 442 (1902). See also Warren and Brandeis, *The Right to Privacy,* 4 *Harv. L. Rev.* 193 (1890).

8. *Model Penal Code,* §213.4(1) and §213.4.

9. For a similar, but not identical, analysis of rape, see Susan Brownmiller, *Against Our Will: Men, Women and Rape* (New York: Bantam Books, 1976). For discussion, see chap. 7, *infra,* at 218–20, and works referenced.

10. *Model Penal Code,* at 149.

11. *Model Penal Code,* §213.1(1).

12. *Model Penal Code,* §213.1(2)(a).

13. Menachem Amir, *Patterns in Forcible Rape* (Chicago: University of Chicago Press, 1971), at 21.

14. Working Women United Institute, "Speak-Out on Sexual Harassment," Ithaca, N. Y., May 4, 1975 (typescript).

15. *Tomkins v. Public Service Electric & Gas Co.,* 422 F. Supp. 553, 556 (D.N.J. 1976) *rev'd,* 568 F.2d 1044 (3d Cir. 1977).

16. *Barnes v. Costle,* 561 F.2d 983, 995 (D.C. Cir. 1977) (MacKinnon, J., concurring).

17. W. Prosser, *The Law of Torts,* 3.

18. *Id.,* at 36.

19. *Hough v. Iderhoff,* 69 Or. 568, 139 P.931, 932 (1914).

20. *Gates v. State,* 110 Ga. App. 303, 138 So.2d 473, 474 (1964). This was a criminal battery, the quotation taken from another criminal battery case, *Goodrum v. State,* 60 Ga. 509 (1878). "If to put the arm, though tenderly, about the neck of another man's wife, against her will, is not an assault and battery, what is it? . . . There was nothing to excite rapture or provoke enthusiasm. Why should he embrace her? Why persist in caressing her? . . . He took the risk of not meeting with a responsive feeling in her, and must abide all the consequences of disappointment" *id.,* at 510, 511. On the question of what is and is not a sexual touching, see *People v. Thomas,* 91 Misc. 2d 724 (1977).

21. Prosser, *supra,* note 62, at 36, n. 85.

22. *Kline v. Kline,* 158 Ind. 602, 64 N.E. 9, 10 (1902), cited in Prosser, *supra,* note 62, at 38.

23. *Ragsdale v. Ezell,* 20 Ky. 1567, 49 S.W. 775, 776 (1899).

24. *Liljegren v. United Rys. Co. of St. Louis,* 227 S.W. 925 (Mo. Ct. App. 1921). She was awarded $500, which corrected for inflation is $1,684 in 1977. Similarly corrected for inflation to 1977, the damage awards for sexual harassment tort cases, *infra,* are as follows. The actual awards are in parentheses. *Skousen* (1961), $7,350 ($3,500) actual, $3,015 ($1,500) punitive, for $10,065 ($5,000) total damages; *Hatchett* (1915), $2,969 ($500); *Martin* (1920), $1,354 ($450); *Kurpgeweit* (1910), $9,670 ($1,500); *Ragsdale* (1899), $5,051 ($700); *Craker* (1895), $7,220 ($1,000); *Davis* (1905), $26,740 ($4,000) (note that the *Davis* jury award was overruled).

25. In a situation familiar to sexually harassed women, the perpetrator simply did not believe her when she told him she wanted him to leave her alone. Their dialogue reportedly ended as follows: "'Look me in the eye, and tell me if you are mad.' I said, 'I am mad.'" *Craker v. The Chicago and Northwestern Railway Company,* 36 Wis. 657, 659, 17 Am. Rep. 504 (1895). She apparently was. Her report precipitated his immediate firing; she proceeded criminally (for criminal assault and battery) and won, and then sued the employer for civil damages. The *Craker* decision is notable in several respects. The treatment of the size of the damage awarded—which amounts to an inquiry into how much this woman's bodily integrity and sexual feelings are worth—is incisive and sympathetic: "who can be found to say that such an amount would be in excess of compensation to his own or his neighbor's wife or sister or daughter?" 36 Wis., at 679. The judge's refusal to separate the woman's sense of wrong at the injustice done her from her mental suffering and pain, holding both proper objects of *compensatory* damages, would be considered pathbreaking had it been more widely followed:

And it is difficult to see how these are to be distinguished from the sense of wrong and insult arising from injustice and intention to vex and degrade. The appearance of malicious intent may indeed add to the sense of wrong; and equally, whether such intent be really there or not. But that goes to mental suffering, and mental suffering to compensation. . . . What human creature can penetrate the mysteries of his own sensations, and parcel out separately his mental suffering and his sense of wrong—so much for compensatory, so much for vindictive damages? 36 Wis., at 678.

The decision further held the employer responsible for this intentional tort by the employee, an unusual departure. The standard view is that employers are only responsible for employee negligence.

One employing another . . . would be as little likely to authorize negligence as malice. . . . [T]he true distinction ought to rest . . . on the condition whether or not the act of the servant be in the course of his employment. . . . If we owe bread to another and appoint an agent to furnish it, and the agent of malice furnish a stone instead, the principal is responsible for the stone and its consequences. In such cases, negligence is malice. 36 Wis., at 668–69.

26. *Hatchett v. Blacketer,* 162 Ky. 266, 172 S.W. 533 (1915).
27. *Martin v. Jensen,* 113 Wash. 290, 193 P. 674 (1920). By analogy with the law of trespass to property, recovery for mental anguish alone was allowed where suffering "is the result of a wanton or intentional trespass on the person of a woman." 193 P., at 676.
28. *Skousen v. Nidy,* 90 Ariz. 215, 367 P.2d 248 (1961).
29. Magruder, "Mental and Emotional Disturbance in the Law of Torts," 49 *Harv. L. Rev.* 1033, 1055 (1936). It is interesting that the cases commonly cited in support of Magruder's proposition do not squarely support it. Some hold that the facts were improperly pleaded. *Prince v. Ridge* states that an attempt by words of persuasion to induce a female to have sexual intercourse does not constitute an assault, but finds that the instant case presents sufficient acts for a battery, an assault, or both. 32 Misc. 666, 66 N.Y.S. 454, 455 (Sup. Ct. 1900). It would seem usual that more than simply asking would be involved.

Other cases referenced to support the formulation require that a physical *injury,* not merely an *act,* must be alleged to make out an assault. As is often the case where sex is involved, this requirement confuses the basic doctrine. The doctrine of assault requires only an act, not an injury. An example of a correct application of assault doctrine requiring physical acts, not physical injuries, is one 1880 Vermont case, in which a blind traveling music teacher, sleeping overnight in the defendant's house, was propositioned. "During the night he stealthily entered her room, sat on her bed, leaned over her person, and made repeated solicitation to her for sexual intimacy, which she repelled." *Newell v. Witcher,* 53 Vt. 589 (1880), quoted in *Reed v. Maley,* 115 Ky. 816, 74 S.W. 1079, 1081 (1903). The defendant was found liable for trespass and assault on the person for sitting on the bed and leaning over her. (Although it was the defendant's property, the sleeping room was considered exclusively the plaintiff's for the night.) The assault finding meant that the plaintiff was found in fear of sexual touching from the proposition; the cited physical acts were sufficient to ground actionable assault, while the proposition alone would not.

Davis v. Richardson, 76 Ark. 348, 89 S.W. 318 (1905), by contrast, required physical *injury.* In this case, a fifteen-year-old girl was seized and embraced "in a rude and indecent manner" by a man who kissed her with "violent and indecent familiarity" and "acted like he was going to do something else." The damage award of $4,000 ($26,740 in 1977) was overturned because an instruction allowed the jury to conclude that the mere proposal was actionable, although acts sufficient for both assault and battery were evidenced. *Bennett v. McIntire,* 121 Ind. 231, 23 N.E. 78 (1889) similarly took the approach of requiring some physical invasion of itself actionable before any recovery could be allowed for sexual propositions. In a case for seduction and debauching of his wife, the plaintiff pleaded a cause of action in trespass. Defendant was argued to have gained permission to come upon plaintiff's property by fraud, then seducing his wife. It was held that since he was on the property by permission, albeit fraudulent, no damages were recoverable. Trespass was the only cause of action apparently considered, with seduction as aggravation of damages.

Similarly, in *Reed v. Maley,* 115 Ky. 818, 74 S.W. 1079 (1903), in which a man solicited a woman to have sexual intercourse, no cause of action was held to exist.
30. 74 S.W., at 1080 (referring to several other cases).
31. The judge posed a reverse familiar to readers of the early sexual harassment cases:

Suppose a bawd should solicit a man upon a public street to have sexual intimacy with her; he certainly could not maintain a civil action against her. If an action could be maintained by a woman against a man for such solicitation, the same right to maintain one would exist in his favor. Whilst he might not suffer the same anguish and humiliation on account of such solicitation as the woman, yet the right of recovery would be the same. The amount of it would only be determined by reason of the difference in effect such a solicitation would have upon one or the other. 74 S.W., at 1081.

Although a proposition would have a different impact upon the sexes, it is nevertheless argued that because a man "certainly could not maintain a civil action" for a proposition by a woman (why not is not considered), a woman should be similarly precluded.

The dissenting judge in this case urged that a sexual proposition should be actionable as solicitation to commit adultery. It should be prohibited not because it preys upon women, but because "if unsuccessful, it is liable to lead to violence and bloodshed at the hands of the [one supposes male] relatives of the woman; and if successful it defeats the end for which marriage is intended, and destroys the woman." 74 S.W. 1079, 1083. He thought punitive damages appropriate for reasons that combined solicitude for the woman's shattered virtue with an eye toward her undone housework: "The purity of woman and the sanctity of the marriage relation lie at the basis of our whole social fabric. . . . The natural effect of an indecent proposal of this character to a virtuous woman would be to upset her nerves and unfit her for discharging for the time her domestic duties." 74 S.W. 1074, 1083–1084.

32. See, for example, *Alcorn v. Ambro Engineering, Inc.,* 468 P.2d 216, 36 Cal. Rptr. 216 (Sup. Ct. 1970); *Wiggs v. Coursin,* 355 F. Supp. 206 (S.D. Fla. 1973); *Gray v. Serruto Builders,* 110 N.J. Sup. 297, 265 A.2d 404 (1970).

33. See EEOC cases discussed at 210, *infra.*

34. *Brunson v. Board of Trustees,* 429 F.2d 820, 826 (1970).

35. See Boris Bittker, *The Case for Black Reparations* (New York: Random House, 1973).

36. See Mary Bularzik, "Sexual Harassment at the Workplace: Historical Notes," *Radical America,* vol. 12, no. 4 (July-August 1978), at 25–43, especially the discussion at 29–31; Robert Smuts, *Women and Work in America* (New York: Schocken Books, 1971), at 88; Louise A. Tilly, Joan W. Scott, Miriam Cohen, "Women's Work and European Fertility Patterns," *Journal of Interdisciplinary History,* vol. 6, no. 3 (1976), at 463–470.

37. See William Sanger, *A History of Prostitution* (New York: Medical Publishing Co., 1858), repr. in Rosalyn Baxandall, Linda Gordon, and Susan Reverby, *America's Working Women* (New York: Random House, 1976), at 96; Richard B. Morris, *Government and Labor in Early America* (New York: Columbia University Press, 1946), repr. at *id.,* at 26–29.

38. Edward Shorter, "On Writing the History of Rape," *Signs: Journal of Women in Culture and Society,* vol. 3, no. 2 (Winter, 1977), at 475.

39. Bliven, *Wonderful Writing Machine,* at 75–76 (no date given), repr. in Margery Davies, *Woman's Place Is At the Typewriter: The Feminization of the Clerical Labor Force* (pamphlet), at 13, repr. from *Radical America,* vol. 8, no. 4 (July-August 1974).

40. Kate Millett, *Sexual Politics* (New York: Avon, 1969), at 54.

41. Gerda Lerner, *Black Women in White America* (New York: Vintage Books, 1973), at 149–150.

42. Memorandum in Opposition to Defendant Company's Motion to Dismiss Plaintiff's Title VII Claim at 10, *Tomkins v. Public Service Electric & Gas Co.,* 422 F. Supp. 553 (D.N.J. 1976).

43. *Id.,* at 14–15.

44. Emma Goldman, *The Traffic in Women* (New York: Times Change Press, 1970), at 20.

24

Sexual Harassment—Adult Workplace

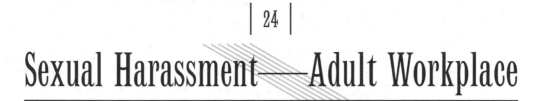

Beth A. Quinn

Sexual harassment "is a problem with a long past but a short history" (Fitzgerald and Shullman 1993:23). The behavior has been around for a long time (for example, Bularzik 1978); yet widespread awareness of sexual harassment as harmful and deviant is relatively recent. Not until 1986 did the U.S. Supreme Court recognize it as a form of sex discrimination, and widespread public concern has emerged only since the high-profile cases of the early 1990s.

Sexual harassment is unusual in that it has been constructed as a social problem primarily through the workings of the courts rather than through a concerted social movement, the actions of moral crusaders, or powerful and self-interested actors. Initial recognition of sexual harassment as a social rather than personal problem emerged out of feminist "consciousness raising" in the 1970s (Farley 1978; MacKinnon 1979). Yet sexual harassment gained legitimacy as a social problem only when the courts began to recognize it as a form of sex discrimination. Public recognition has developed more from media coverage of high-profile cases and legally mandated workplace training than from feminist activism.

The Equal Employment Opportunity Commission (EEOC), the federal agency responsible for promulgating sexual harassment regulations, defines two primary forms of sexual harassment: quid pro quo and hostile work environment. Quid pro quo harassment is:

> Unwelcome sexual advances, requests for sexual favors, and other verbal or physical conduct of a sexual nature . . . when (1) submission to such conduct is made either explicitly or implicitly a term or condition of

an individual's employment, (2) submission to or rejection of such conduct by an individual is used as the basis for employment decisions affecting such individual. (29 C.F.R. §1604.11, a 1–2)

Behavior is considered quid pro quo if an individual is required to submit to sexual conduct lest they suffer some negative employment consequence. The infamous Hollywood "casting couch" is a classic example.

The second form, hostile work environment harassment, includes unwelcome sexual behavior that "has the purpose or effect of unreasonably interfering with an individual's work performance or creating an intimidating, hostile, or offensive working environment" (29 C.F.R. §1604.11, a.3). Of the two forms, the latter draws the most criticism, primarily because of the supposed difficulty in determining when an environment has become "hostile." Nonetheless, a classic example is a situation where male workers engage in a barrage of sexist and sexual comments to demean or degrade female workers. This can include placing pornography (sometimes "individualized") in their work spaces, and making overt sexual come-ons. This form differs from quid pro quo since there need not be any tangible job loss. The hostile actions themselves form the basis of the harm.

There is some controversy over the meaning of *sexual* in the term sexual harassment. That is, does harassment have to be *sexual* to count as harassment? Can an environment pervasive with sexist remarks and literature, for example, be considered "hostile" when the remarks lack sexual content? The EEOC (1999) has recently clarified that "gender harassment" is implicit in the definition of illegal harassment, although it has failed to change the language of its regulations to reflect this. The courts, on the other hand, have tended to dismiss sexual harassment claims when they lack sexual content (Colker 1995; Schultz 1998). Social science research reflects this emphasis in that most studies focus on inappropriate sexual behavior rather than gender harassment.

Role of the Law

The first cases brought under discrimination law were all instances of quid pro quo harassment. Women lost jobs, were denied jobs, or submitted to coerced sexual activity to keep their jobs. Even so, initial attempts in the 1970s to have the law recognize the harm of sexual harassment failed (MacKinnon 1979).

These cases floundered on the shoals of an interesting ambivalence about the deviance of these behaviors. On the one hand, plaintiffs' arguments were rejected because the behaviors were seen as a "personal proclivity" (*Corne v. Bausche & Lombe* 1975) or as an "isolated incident" (*Miller v. Bank of America* 1976). The events were viewed as acts of individualized deviance, and thus outside the purview of discrimination law and employer liability. On the other hand, these same judges worried that to accept sexual harassment as prohibited sex discrimination would result in a flood of cases. This fear ironically reveals an acceptance of sexual harassment as normal and even pervasive. In either case, sexual harassment remained something that was "isolated and idiosyncratic, or . . . natural and universal, and, in either case, inappropriate for legal intervention" (Rhode 1989:233).

The D.C. Court of Appeals set the stage for the gradual acceptance of sexual harassment as sex discrimination in its rulings in *Barnes v. Costle* (1977) and *Williams v. Bell* (1978), two classic quid pro quo cases. Although the lower courts rejected the plaintiff's claims, the court of appeals accepted the argument that the women had been subjected to the propositions and subsequent retaliations *because of* their sex. The behavior constituted illegal sex discrimination, the court reasoned, because it imposed conditions of employment that would not have been applied to men; thus the conditions of employment were impermissibly grounded in gender.

The EEOC first issued regulations covering sexual harassment in 1980, effectively codifying sexual harassment as sex discrimination. The guidelines included a definition of hostile work environment (along with one of quid pro quo harassment), although few courts had yet to accept it as a form of sex discrimination.

In 1986, the Supreme Court visited the subject for the first time in *Meritor Savings Bank v. Vinson*. A hostile work environment harassment case, *Vinson* solidified the legitimation of sexual harassment as prohibited sex discrimination, accepting the EEOC's interpretation of hostile work environment harassment as discrimination. In this case, the Court left many issues unresolved, but subsequently has clarified its position in a string of cases in the 1990s. Beginning with its 1993 decision in *Harris v. Forklift Services, Inc.,* the Court held that sexual harassment need not result in psychological harm or impaired job performance for it to be actionable as sex discrimination. The Court ruled that an environment is hostile when it is "permeated with discriminatory intimidation, ridicule, and insult that is sufficiently severe or pervasive to alter the conditions of the victim's employment and create an abusive working environment." In 1998, the Court ruled in *Oncale v. Sundowner Offshore Services* that same-sex harassment also constitutes prohibited sex discrimination.

Patterns of Sexual Harassment

Given the current state of research, four conclusions about sexual harassment may be drawn with some certainty. First, it is a pervasive harm. Second, although some women sexually harass, men are by far the most likely perpetrators. Third, men are much less likely to label behavior as harassing than are women. And last, many victims never explicitly identify sexually harassing behavior as such, and of those who do, most never make formal complaint.

Sexual Harassment is Pervasive

That sexual harassment is pervasive is supported by hundreds of prevalence surveys conducted over the last 20 years. Rates of sexual harassment of women range from 20 percent to 80 percent, depending on how the question is asked and the time frame given (Fitzgerald 1990).

Conducted in 1981, the U.S. Merit Service Protection Board (MSPB) survey was one of the first to explore sexual harassment. The survey of 23,000 federal employees revealed that 47 percent of the women (and 15 percent of the men) had experienced some form of sexually harassing behaviors at their jobs in the previous two years. A follow-up survey published in 1987 found similar levels of harassment (12 percent and 14 percent). In telephone interviews of a sample of 832 working women, Barbara Gutek (1985) found that about one-half had been subject to sexual harassing behavior at some time in their working lives.

Based on prevalence rates, women are two to five times more likely to be harassed than men. Of the roughly 15,000 sexual harassment complaints filed with the EEOC in 1998, 87 percent were filed by women. Among women, those in occupations that are traditionally male and in numerically male-dominated work contexts are more likely to be sexually harassed. For example, in a recent survey by the navy, 64 percent of women reported experiencing sexual harassment in their work or training; surveys of women in policing show similarly high rates of reported harassment (Gruber 1998). In a survey of Canadian women, Gruber (1998) found support for the "contact hypothesis," which posits that the likelihood of being sexually harassed is dependent more on the level of contact with men than on the type of job a woman holds.

There is some evidence that women who are organizationally more vulnerable (for example, low rank, lack of access to institutional support, young) also are more likely to be harassed (Gutek and Koss 1993; MSPB 1981, 1988). Similarly, Rogers and Henson's (1997) qualitative study of temporary workers showed sexual harassment to be a startlingly pervasive condition of work and that effective resistance was difficult if not impossible because of the workers' structural location.

Although harassed at a much lower rate than women, men who are harassed usually are employed in occupations or organizations dominated by women (giving weight to a parallel version of the "contact hypothesis") or are in disempowered positions in their organizations (MSPB 1981, 1988). However, given the paucity of research, conclusions are difficult to draw.

Men are the Usual Perpetrators of Sexual Harassment

Most information about perpetrators, thus far, comes from victim surveys. The MSPB surveys found the typical perpetrator to be older than the victim, married, had harassed other women, and was *not* the victim's immediate supervisor. Gutek (1985) found a similar pattern. Women in her study, however, were more likely to have been harassed by supervisors, a discrepancy most likely because of Gutek's gathering perpetrator data for only the most severe forms of harassment. Most disturbing is the implication of Gutek's "perpetrator profile": It varied little from the demographics of the random sample of working men in the same study.

There is a growing body of experimental work on men's likelihood to harass. Noting that sexual harassment, at least in its most severe forms, is similar to rape, Pryor (1987) created the Likelihood to Sexually Harass (LSH) scale by adapting Malamuth's Propensity to Rape scale. The LSH presents subjects with 10 scenarios of sexual exploitation and asks them to rate the likelihood that they would engage in the act, provided they would experience no adverse consequence. High scores on the scale have been shown to be positively correlated with negative attitudes toward women, adversarial sexuality beliefs, sex role stereotyping, rape myth acceptance, and high scores on authoritarianism, and negatively correlated with empathy and feminine personality characteristics (Fitzgerald and Weitzman 1990; Pryor 1987). "The profile of a male who is likely to initiate severe sexually harassing behavior," notes Pryor (1987:277), "is one that emphasizes sexual and social male dominance." Thus far, little research has been conducted exploring the perpetrators of hostile work environment harassment (but see Quinn 1996).

Women and Men Perceive Sexual Harassment Differently

The question of interpreting harassing behavior has produced a large body of experimental research. Subjects are presented with vignettes of various interactions and asked whether sexual harassment has occurred. Vignette details (for example, level of coercion, power differences, the type of workplace), as well as the demographics (for example, gender) of the raters, are varied to assess the impact on subjects' ratings. That women often see sexual harassment where men see compliments, harmless seduction, or "horseplay" is one of the most consistent findings (Bursik 1992; Cohen and Gutek 1985; Jaschik and Fretz 1991). In addition, research finds that the more one subscribes to traditional notions of gender, the less likely one is to identify behavior as sexual harassment (for example, Gutek and Koss 1993). However, Saperstein, Triolo, and Heinzen (1995) found that being a feminist did not increase the likelihood of formal complaint. The implication is that acceptance of sexual harassment as deviant rather than normative varies with gender and patterns of traditional sex stereotypes. That is, traditional masculine socialization works to normalize sexually harassing behaviors.

Victims Seldom Take Direct Action

Contrary to popular media accounts of "runaway" settlements and overly sensitive women, very few individuals who are sexually harassed take any action against their harassers. Faced with harassing behavior, women are very unlikely to use direct confrontation (Gruber 1989; Gutek and Koss 1993), or report to an authority (Lach and Gwartney-Gibbs 1993; MSPB 1981, 1988; Riger 1991).

A comparison of population totals to EEOC complaint rates is illustrative. The Department of Labor estimates that in November of 1999, 58 million women were employed in the American workforce. Assuming the most conservative two-year prevalence rate of 20 percent and arbitrarily assuming that only 20 percent of those incidents are severe enough to move beyond the immediate organization, we would expect 2,320,000 cases of harassment over two years, or 1,160,000 cases per year. In marked contrast, the EEOC received only 9,574 sexual harassment complaints from women in 1998, more than 100 times less than would be expected.

When compared with what we know about disputing in general, this is not all that surprising. Most people "lump it" when they lack social or institutional means for resolving disputes (for example, Bumiller 1988; Felstiner, Abel, and Sarat 1980–1981, 1974; Merry 1979). This does not render the issue unproblematic but shifts the focus to finding an explanation for the lack of meaningful avenues of resolution.

Recent qualitative research is beginning to shed some light on the matter. Quinn (forthcoming) proposes that requirements for complaint often run contrary to the everyday organizational tactics of power for many women. To complain of hostile work environment harassment, for example, is to make more visible one's own powerlessness, and it lets the harasser know that he is "getting to you." In the case of quid pro quo, women realize that, as in rape, a complaint often looks worse for the victim than for the accused, given that women who engage in any sort of sexuality (consensual or coerced) are open to stigmatizing labels (for example, whore, tease). Clair's (1993) analysis of the way in which sexual harassment incidents are framed in everyday discourse, as well as other work in the discursive model (for example, see Bingham 1998), offers valuable insight into victims' failure to complain.

Models of Causation

Theories of causation can be broken into two broad categories: the feminist or sociocultural approach, and the organizational approach. Perhaps the most influential feminist theory has been offered by Catharine MacKinnon (1979). For MacKinnon, sexual harassment is "the unwanted imposition of sexual requirements in the context of a relationship of unequal power" (1979:1). MacKinnon also notes that "central to the concept is the use of power derived from one social sphere to lever benefits or impose deprivations in another" (MacKinnon 1979:1). In the classic quid pro quo scenario, harassers borrow power from the organizational sphere to force a subordinate woman to submit to sexual demands. In hostile work environment harassment, the sphere from which power is leveraged is gender; sexual harassment works to enhance the harasser's organizational power by calling attention to a woman's sexuality or gender, both potentially disempowering sociocultural positions. The two types of sexual harassment are conceptually connected in a continuum of sex and power. In the first case, organizational power begets sex; in the second, sex (gender) begets organizational power.

Within this feminist framework sexual harassment is symptomatic and productive of the systematic subordination of women to men, sustained through various forms of violence and through the social construction of sexuality and gender. For MacKinnon and other radical feminists, sexual harassment is the expression of this gender hierarchy within the work world, with the function and effect of keeping women "in their place" (MacKinnon 1979; Schultz 1998). Thus sexual harassment is another form of violence against women, akin to rape. It can be, as *Mother Jones* entitled it in 1978, "The Executive's Alternative to Rape."

The most potent critique of the radical feminist theory of sexual harassment is its inability to explain women's sexual harassment of men (Rospenda, Richman, and Nawyn 1998). Although rare, the EEOC estimates that 10 percent of all complaints it receives are men claiming to be victims of women's harassment.

The organizational model posits that sexual harassment is but a side effect of the use of hierarchical power in organizations, rather than something that men do to women per se. That women are the most common victims is the result of women's lack of organizational power rather than the direct effect of the use of sexualized and gendered power. This organizational stratification is, of course, at least partially a result of sex discrimination, but the organizational model posits that harassment is but an indirect effect of these social processes. The MSPB survey, as well as Gruber's early work on differences in

sexual harassment rates by type of job and organization, reflect this theoretical framework.

Given this frame, one would predict an increase in women's harassment of men as women rise to more positions of power in organizations. The EEOC does report an increase in the number of men lodging complaints of sexual harassment from 1992 ($n = 958$) to 1998 ($n = 2,015$), yet this still represents less than 13 percent of the total claims filed.

The primary weakness of the organizational perspective is that it fails to account for both coworker harassment, the most common form of sexual harassment, and "contrapower harassment," where those higher in the hierarchy are harassed by organizational subordinates. Studies of harassment of faculty members, for example, reveal high rates of sexually harassing behaviors from male students toward female faculty members (Grauerholz 1989; Rospenda, Richman, and Nawyn 1998). From the organizational perspective, it is difficult to see how coworkers, who by definition hold equivalent formal organizational power, or subordinates who hold less power, would be motivated and successful in pursuing sexual harassment. Both forms are counterintuitive if sexual harassment is simply the misuse of institutional power.

A variation of the organizational model is Gutek's sex-role spillover model (1985). Gutek proposes that sexual harassment is the result of women's traditional roles, especially their sexual roles, "spilling over" into the workplace. This assumption also is evident in Lyn Farley's work in which she defines sexual harassment as any "unsolicited nonreciprocal male behavior that asserts a woman's sex role over her function as a worker" (Farley 1978:14–15).

Gutek suggests that there are two forms of spillover. For women in nontraditional fields, the role spillover applies to the individual woman. As a minority in the field, she is more visible as a woman and, as such, will experience sexual harassment because of men's confusion about her role. For women in traditionally female-dominated fields, spillover occurs in the field as a whole, and, thus, women are more likely to be subjected to sex role stereotypes that may include expectations of sexualized behavior. Interestingly, given the pervasive gendering of work, many women in traditional jobs may fail to recognize the behavior as harassment; it is "just what happens" to women.

Sex role spillover theory falters in leaving traditional gender norms underexamined and uncriticized. Although it offers a rudimentary explanation of sexual harassment in the workplace, it fails to explain the logic (or justice) of sexual harassment as a way that men normatively treat women. It addition, the term "spillover" implies that gender norms are somehow "smuggled" into the workplace (Rogers and Henson 1997) ignoring the ways in which organizations and jobs are already gendered for both women and men (Connell 1995; Kanter 1977).

The most likely explanation for sexual harassment is that it originates from interactions between various forms of sociocultural power (gender as well as race and class), and formal and informal organizational power. The most promising theoretical direction is an elaboration of these interactions. Rather than simply looking to the effect of workplace hierarchy, Gruber (1989), for example, suggests that the behavior and attitudes of organizational leaders produce local norms that may alternatively foster sexual harassment or help control it. Conrad and Taylor (1998) integrate broader organizational theory with sociocultural/feminist analyses of power differentials between men and women to account for the subtleties and variations of harassment. In explaining cases of contrapower sexual harassment, Rospenda et al. (1998) elegantly demonstrate the ways in which various sources of power come into play in sexual harassment. The common thread in these emerging theories is their framing of sexual harassment as embedded in multiple discourses of power and in focusing attention on the processes of harassment (Cleveland and Kerst 1993; Quinn 1996). As Bingham (1998:9) explains,

> a discursive approach elucidates how cultural discourses create frames—material, psychological, and social—within which sexual harassment and responses to it transpire. It illuminates how sexual harassment is enacted, interpreted, and especially how it is normalized and challenged through discursive practices.

Conclusion

The behaviors that make up the concept "sexual harassment" are now recognized—at least in the abstract—as inappropriate, deviant, and illegal in the workplace and in institutions of education (Quinn 1996). As a form of sex discrimination, sexual harassment is seen to be harmful and deserving of prevention, remediation, and punishment. On the other hand, sexual harassment continues to be accepted, especially at the level of the everyday and the particular, as normative masculine behavior. Although it might not be "proper," it is often simply accepted as what men do (Connell 1995). Entangled in these contradictory discourses and as an emerging social problem, sexual harassment offers a unique view of the simultaneous production of deviance and the maintenance of normative conditions.

References

Bingham, S. G. ed. 1998. *Conceptualizing Sexual Harassment as Discursive Practice.* Westport, CT: Praeger.

Bularzik, M. 1978. "Sexual Harassment at the Workplace: Historical Notes." *Radical America* 124:25–43.

Bumiller, K. 1988. *The Civil Rights Society: The Social Construction of Victims.* Baltimore, MD: Johns Hopkins University Press.

Bursik, K. 1992. "Perceptions of Sexual Harassment in an Academic Context." *Sex Roles* 27(7–8):401–12.

Clair, R. P. 1993. "The Use of Framing Devices to Sequester Organizational Narratives: Hegemony and Harassment." *Communications Monographs* 60:1–24.

Cleveland, J. N., and M. E. Kerst. 1993. "Sexual Harassment and Perceptions of Power: An Underarticulated Relationship." *Journal of Vocational Behavior* 42(1):49–67.

Cohen, A. G. and B. A. Gutek. 1985. "Dimensions of Perceptions of Social-Sexual Behaviors in a Work Setting." *Sex Roles* 13(5–6):317–27.

Colker, R. 1995. "Whores, Fags, Dumb-Ass Women, Surly Blacks and Competent Heterosexual White Men: The Sexual and Racial Morality Underlying Anti-Discrimination Doctrine." *Yale Journal of Law and Feminism* 7:195–225.

Connell, R. W. 1995. *Masculinities.* Berkeley: University of California Press.

Conrad, C. and B. Taylor. 1998. "The Contexts of Sexual Harassment: Power, Silences, and Academe." Pp. 45–58 in *Conceptualizing Sexual Harassment as Discursive Practice,* edited by S. Bingham. Westport, CT: Praeger.

Equal Employment Opportunity Commission (EEOC). 1999. "Enforcement Guidelines: Vicarious Employer Liability for Unlawful Harassment by Supervisors." *Compliance Manual,* §915.002. Washington, DC: U.S. Government Printing Office.

Farley, L. 1978. *Sexual Shakedown: The Sexual Harassment of Women on the Job.* New York: McGraw-Hill.

Felstiner, W., R. Abel, and A. Sarat. 1980–1981. "The Emergence and Transformation of Disputes: Naming, Blaming, Claiming. . . ." *Law and Society Review* 15(3–4):631–54.

Fitzgerald, L. F. 1990. "Sexual Harassment: The Definition and Measurement of a Construct." Pp. 21–44 in *Ivory Power: Sexual Harassment on Campus,* edited by M. Paludi. Albany: State University of New York.

Fitzgerald, L. F. and S. Shullman. 1993. "Sexual Harassment: A Research Analysis and Agenda for the 1990s." *Journal of Vocational Behavior* 421:5–27.

Fitzgerald, L. F. and L. M. Weitzman. 1990. "Men Who Harass: Speculations and Data." Pp. 125–40 in *Ivory Power: Sexual Harassment on Campus,* edited by M. Paludi. Albany: State University of New York.

Grauerholz, E. 1989. "Sexual Harassment of Women Professors by Students: Exploring the Dynamics of Power, Authority, and Gender in a University Setting." *Sex Roles* 21:789–801.

Gruber, J. E. 1989. "How Women Handle Sexual Harassment: A Literature Review." *Sociology and Social Research* 74:3–9.

———. 1998. "The Impact of Male Work Environments and Organizational Policies on Women's Experiences of Sexual Harassment." *Gender and Society* 123:301–20.

Gutek, B. 1985. *Sex and the Workplace.* San Francisco, CA: Jossey-Bass.

Gutek, B. and M. P. Koss. 1993. "Changed Women and Changed Organizations: Consequences of and Coping with Sexual Harassment." *Journal of Vocational Behavior* 421:28–48.

Jaschik, M. and B. Fretz. 1991. "Women's Perceptions and Labeling of Sexual Harassment." *Sex Roles* 25(1–2):19–23.

Kanter, R. M. 1977. *Men and Women of the Corporation.* New York: Basic Books.

Lach, D. H. and P. Gwartney-Gibbs. 1993. "Sociological Perspectives on Sexual Harassment and Workplace Dispute Resolution." *Journal of Vocational Behavior* 421:102.

MacKinnon, C. A. 1979. *The Sexual Harassment of Working Women.* New Haven, CT: Yale University Press.

Merry, S. E. 1979. "Going to Court: Strategies of Dispute Management in an American Urban Neighborhood." *Law and Society Review* 13:891.

Pryor, J. B. 1987. "Sexual Harassment Proclivities in Men." *Sex Roles* 17(5–6):269–90.

Quinn, B. A. Forthcoming. "The Paradoxes of Complaining: Law, Humor, and Harassment in the Everyday World." *Law and Social Inquiry.*

———. 1996. "Sexual Harassment in the Everyday World: The Power of Sex/The Power of Law." Ph.D. dissertation, Department of Criminology, Law and Society, University of California Irvine.

Rhode, D. 1989. *Justice and Gender: Sex Discrimination and the Law.* Cambridge, MA: Harvard University Press.

Riger, Stephanie. 1991. "Gender Dilemmas in Sexual Harassment Policies and Procedures," *American Psychologist* 46:497–505.

Rogers, J. K. and K. D. Henson. 1997. "Hey, Why Don't You Wear a Shorter Skirt? Structural Vulnerability and the Organization of Sexual Harassment in Temporary Clerical Employment." *Gender and Society* 12:215–27.

Rospenda, K. M., J. A. Richman, and S. J. Nawyn. 1998. "Doing Power: The Confluence of Gender, Race, and Class in Contrapower Sexual Harassment." *Gender & Society* 121:40.

Saperstein, A., B. Triolo, and T. E. Heinzen. 1995. "Ideology or Experience: A Study of Sexual Harassment." *Sex Roles* 32(11–12):835–42.

Schultz, V. 1998. "Reconceptualizing Sexual Harassment." *Yale Law Journal* 1076:1683–805.

U.S. Merit Systems Protection Board (MSPB). 1981. *Sexual Harassment in the Federal Workplace: Is It a Problem?* Washington, DC: U.S. Government Printing Office.

———. 1988. *Sexual Harassment in the Federal Government: An Update.* Washington, DC: U.S. Government Printing Office.

Part VI: CRIMINAL VIOLENCE

In this section, we continue to explore the structural and cultural correlates of social violence. The tendency in contemporary criminology, especially applied criminology, is to "pathologize" the behavior of the individual offender, ignoring the wider social context that produces the violence. Each of the readings in this section contributes to the development of a systematic sociology of violence that does not rely on detecting amorphous individual motivations in order to explain criminal conduct.

The definition of specific forms of violence as criminal is a consequence of many of those very processes that produce the violence in the first place. Thus, predatory acts of working-class individuals, offenses against property and persons, have been criminalized by a political process that frequently ignores similar acts by higher-status persons. Criminal violence, then, is distinguished from other forms of violence by the fact that it is subject to governmental social control; i.e., it is made illegal and subject to official sanctions such as arrest and incarceration. Thus, criminalizing violence defines such behavior as immoral (evil) predatory conduct, whereas similar conduct may, under different circumstances, be treated as morally justified. Thus, paraphrasing the words of President Reagan during the Iran-Contra controversy of the 1980s, "one man's terrorist" becomes "another man's freedom fighter." We should also understand that subjecting violence to legal regulation may have an impact on the frequency and nature of that violence.

We begin this unit with Eric Hickey's seminal work on the "cultural development" of the serial killer. What do we mean when we identify a killing as pure "evil"? From the perspective of the victim of a terrorist attack or a multiple sexual offender, evil is perceived in terms of the cultural framework of the target of the violence. From the perspective of the perpetrator, a terrorist act may be perceived as moralistic in nature, part of a "holy war" against some perceived enemy. Yet, when an act of violence is committed by someone from within one's own society, it is hard to understand how that society may produce the very act that it prohibits. Nevertheless, even serial murderers are products of their own society. I include the chapter on the "Hillside Strangler" precisely because it describes the world from the perspective of the serial killer and why his actions make sense to *him*. The serial killer comes from a world in which sexual gratification occurs in a context of eroticized power over a depersonalized object. Although this behavior may be framed in psychobiological terms—the killer is seen as mentally deranged and/or genetically predisposed to violence—such individualistic explanations of the behavior of the serial killer fail to recognize its origin in the patriarchal cultural values of contemporary society (see, for example, Caputi's discussion of the sexual politics of murder, pp. 66–78). Nowhere is the normative aspect of predatory behavior more evident than in the case of serial murder.

Charles Horton Cooley, in his classic work on the primary group, described the "we-feeling" that comes from identification with the rules of the game that govern intimate relationships. Pride and shame are emotions that derive from the successes and failures of the actor's conduct in connection with the normative order of the primary group. Thus, we have seen how Hitler's rage against Jews can be understood as a response to the humiliation he experienced at the hands of an authoritarian father, whose authoritarian values were part of a wider, deeply anti-Semitic culture. Just as Hitler transformed his unacknowledged shame into rage at an available target, European Jewry, the sexual predator in America turns his rage against available, powerless targets, typically women and children. On occasion, gay men and boys are targeted by sexual predators such as Jeffrey Dahmer, whose victims were usually low-income males who were members of minority ethnic groups. In the next chapter in this section, Scheff and Retzinger describe the psychosocial process by which unacknowledged shame is transformed into predatory sexual violence. As in the case of sexual aggression in general, the authors conclude that predatory sexual violence derives from "hyperidentification" with the norms and role expectations associated with "masculinity" as it is defined in the wider societal context.

The next set of readings focus on organized forms of violence, each of which expresses some degree of opposition to the existing social order. Banditry, i.e., organized assaults on dominant economic institutions, involves great planning and skill, supported by an antiauthoritarian ideology. James Inciardi demonstrates how the existence of a boundary or "frontier" between those outside and inside the established social order sets the stage for armed assaults on cargo-laden ships by Caribbean pirates, on banks and stagecoaches by Western frontier bandits such as Jesse James, and on banks by Depression-era bank robbers such as John Dillinger. In many cases, contemporary bandits are demobilized soldiers whose skills in armed assaults derive from their military experience. Such was the case following the U.S. Civil War. Many of the Western bandits of the late nineteenth century had been members of Quantrill's Raiders, a guerrilla warfare unit of the Confederate army. It is today's "urban frontier" that provides a breeding ground for organized armed robbery in the United States.

In order to capture the normative aspects of the world of organized crime, this section includes an article on the role of the professional "hit man," the key to enforcing the will of organized crime networks. According to the author, the professional hit man, or contract killer, can be distinguished from "made" members of organized crime syndicates who kill out of loyalty to the group. Levi describes how the contract killer learns to perform his role according to a set of professional norms. These norms, like other similar "subcultural" value systems, enable the killer to "neutralize" dominant cultural norms. An important part of this framework is that the target is someone whose elimination is justified according to a code that distinguishes between insiders who are justifiable targets and outsiders who are not. The hit man who violates these rules may find himself without the ordinary protections and payoffs that keep him out of prison. What is more significant is that he may experience "guilt," or self-punishment, for violating both the norms of his profession and the norms of the wider society. Thus, he loses the ability to rationalize his behavior and escape the moral implications of his conduct. In this particular case, Levi describes the guilt of a hit man who kills his adversary in an ordinary barroom brawl. A similar experience can be expected should a hit man kill an innocent civilian who is not part of the crime network.

Harold Vetter and Gary Perlstein describe the origins of domestic terrorism in the United States in terms of its history of racial injustice in a context of rapid social change. Left-wing terrorism by black militants and their sympathizers arose in the 1960s and 1970s in response to the promise of equal justice and continued obstacles to full achievement of that equality. As we have seen in the earlier chapters of this book, injustice produces rage, and structural inequality produces violence. Terrorism, as organized violence intended to undermine or destroy the core institutions of society, is a response to injustice and inequality, whether perceived or real. Right-wing terrorism, usually by white racists or separatists, has similar origins. In the 1980s, these groups' hatred of established institutions were fueled by perceived advances in opportunities for minorities, old anti-Semitic ideologies, and economic disaster for many Midwestern farmers and members of the working class as American jobs and markets moved overseas. In the absence of widespread support for both left-wing and right-wing terrorists in the general population, and with little outside support, it should not be surprising that many of these groups resorted to ordinary banditry to fund their political objectives. The cultural roots of the radical right-wing movement in the United States was similar to the frontier, antigovernment ideology that gave rise to the Western bandits in the late nineteenth century. The bombing of the federal Murrah Building in Oklahoma City by Timothy McVeigh, an apparent follower of the antigovernment, neo-Nazi Aryan Nations' ideology, was followed by a period of decline in support for right-wing "militias" in the United States.

The final chapter of the book examines the social origins of violence in the American prison system and the impact the violent world of the American prison has on the wider society. The violence that results from the structural inequality of the wider society is reproduced in the American prison system. Racial and ethnic conflicts that occur on the outside appear in prison as racially motivated sexual assaults and prison gangs organized along racial lines. In the 1960s and 1970s, the American prison system became a breeding ground for the antiwhite racism of the Black Muslim movement, also known as the Nation of Islam. By the 1980s, the American prison was a fertile environment for the expansion of white supremacist ideology and organization. The Aryan Nations, right-wing militia groups, and others began to recruit some of its hard-core membership from the Aryan Brotherhood prison gang and disaffected ex-military men, such as Timothy McVeigh. For the "ordinary" prisoner, survival in this "world of violence" meant joining a racially oriented prison gang and accepting violence as a way of life in order to survive. These violent convicts then returned to society frequently more dangerous than when they entered prison. Silberman shows that the American prison system plays a role in reproducing the structural conditions and ideological beliefs that contribute to violence in the wider society.

25

Cultural Development of Monsters, Demons, and Evil

Eric W. Hickey

Halloween, Friday the 13th, Nightmare on Elm Street, and other "splatter" movies remind us that evil, dangerous beings reside in our communities. The notion of evil monsters, demons, ghouls, vampires, werewolves, and zombies roaming the earth can be traced back to early civilization. In the past, explanations for mass and serial murders were often derived from demonology or the belief that life events were controlled by external forces or spirits. The notion that life on earth was primarily controlled by forces of good and evil has its origins in the belief in the existence of gods and devils.

In many past cultures—and in some modern ones—mental illness was generally viewed as a distinct form of possession, the controlling of a human by an evil spirit. The Gospel of St. Matthew in the Bible refers to two persons possessed with devils who were "exceedingly fierce," and when Christ bade them come out they went immediately and entered the bodies of swine. In turn the "swine ran violently" to the sea and perished in the waters (Matthew 8:28–32). In the Gospel of St. Mark a similar experience occurs except the man is described as a lunatic possessed with a devil. The devil, discovered to be many devils, was thus called Legion and consequently cast out into a herd of swine. In turn, the swine again "ran violently" into the sea and perished (Mark 5:1–14). In the modern-day world, David Richard Berkowitz, the "Son of Sam" or "44-Caliber Killer," who hunted 13 victims over a period of 13 months in New York City, first claimed he did the killings because his neighbor's demonically possessed dogs com-manded him to do so. Later he admitted he concocted the story to get back at his neighbor and his noisy dogs.

There seems to have been some confusion in the past in distinguishing insane persons from those who were "possessed." Sometimes those who were mentally ill were identified as being possessed and vice versa, at least in the Middle East, and sometimes mentally ill or possessed people were revered as the oracles of a deity or a soothsayer. In other times and places, similarly afflicted people were stoned to death or subjected to trephining, an early form of treatment of illnesses whereby holes were drilled in the skull to allow the evil spirits to leave (Suinn, 1984, p. 32).

Some cultures also believed that a person could be "invaded" by more than one spirit at a time. In modern days we might call such a manifestation a case of "multiple personalities," as described in Thigpen and Cleckley's *The Three Faces of Eve* (1957) and Flora Schreiber's *Sybil* (1973). The notion of multiple personalities has been sometimes used as a defense by serial killers. For example, Kenneth Bianchi, one of the "Hillside Stranglers" in California and also Washington, claimed he was involved in killing 12 women because he was controlled by multiple personalities. Convincing for a while, Bianchi's defense finally came apart under close scrutiny by psychiatric experts.

People have also believed that evil spirits can inhabit the bodies of animals, causing them to act wildly. Just as many cultures have long entertained the notion that criminals can be possessed by demons, they have identified particular animals that are most likely to be possessed as well. In many legends and much folklore wolves are singled out as being the most likely animal to have dealings with the devil. The natural enmity between wolf and man has existed for centuries, and consequently wolves have been hunted relentlessly. Given the belief that humans and animals can be demonically possessed, it is not surprising the belief also exists that a possessed human could become a wolf. A person able to command such a metamorphosis became known as a werewolf (*were* was an old English term for *man*). The belief in "lycanthropy," or the transformation of persons into wolves, can be traced back to at least 600 B.C., when King Nebuchadnezzar believed he suffered from such an affliction. Jean Fernal (1497–1558) of France, a physician, believed lycanthropy to be a valid medical phenomenon. Many societies around the world have a term for "werewolf": France, *loup-garou;* Germany, *Werwolf;* Portugal, *lob omen;* Italy, *Lupo mannaro.* In Africa stories abound of "were-leopards" and "were-jackals," whereas "were-tigers" are common in India (Hill & Williams, 1967, p. 185).

To those living in the sixteenth and seventeenth centuries witches were similar to werewolves in that one was able to experience the transformation only if a pact was made with the Prince of Darkness, or Satan. In the sixteenth century, Paracelsus wrote that violent, wicked men may have the opportunity to return after death as an animal, usually a wolf. The purpose of this human-to-wolf transformation was the inevitable killing of humans, particularly children, in order to eat their flesh. Recurrent throughout werewolf literature is the theme of anthropophagy, or the enjoyment of eating human flesh. Jean Grenier, a young seventeenth-century Frenchman, claimed to be a werewolf and confessed that he had devoured the flesh of many young girls. Another notorious werewolf was Germany's Peter Stubb, or Stump, of the sixteenth century. After completing a "pact" with the devil he simply donned a wolfskin belt and was able to transform himself whenever he had the urge to kill. Naturally he murdered those who offended him along with several women and girls, whom he raped and sexually tortured before cannibalizing. Stubbs, who fathered a

child by his daughter and then ate his own son, managed to murder 13 young children and two expectant mothers by some of the most perverse and cruel methods imaginable (Hill & Williams, 1967, pp. 189–190).

Lycanthropy was also viewed as a form of madness in which a person believed him- or herself to be an animal, usually a wolf, and expressed a desire to eat raw meat, experienced a change in voice, and had a desire to run on all fours. To ensure the perpetuation of werewolf lore, stories of those possessed usually included reminders of how difficult it was to destroy such monsters. The werewolves were believed to be extraordinarily powerful creatures who could change back to human form at will or at the break of day. Belief in these terrifying creatures was often fueled by the occasional discovery of a mutilated corpse along a highway or brought in with the tide. Consider the story of the Sawney Beane family and how their behavior may have reinforced the belief in werewolves and other similar monsters.

> Born under the reign of James I of Scotland, in east Lothian near Edinburgh, Sawney Beane, described as idle and vicious, took up with a woman of equally disreputable character. They relocated to a large cave that was difficult to detect because the sea tide covered the entrance. Sawney and his wife took shelter in this cave and began robbing and murdering unsuspecting travelers. To avoid detection they murdered every person they robbed, and to satisfy their need for food they resorted to cannibalism. Each time they killed someone they carried him or her to their den, quartered the victim, and salted the limbs and dried them for later consumption. Each family member played a specific role in capturing and killing their victims. To ensure that no one escaped, precautions were taken to attack no more than six people on foot or two on horses. This arrangement lasted several years, during which time they sired six sons and six daughters, eighteen grandsons and fourteen granddaughters, most the offspring of incest.
>
> Frequently the Beane family would dispose of surplus legs and arms by throwing them into the sea. In due course many of these body parts were carried by the tides to other

shores, where they were discovered by townspeople. Search parties failed to uncover any new information; they just cast suspicion on innocent travelers and innkeepers. Although dozens of persons were arrested, people continued to disappear regularly. Following several years of searching, soldiers finally discovered the cave, but they were not prepared for what they found inside. Aside from many boxes of jewels and other valuables, arms, legs, and thighs of men, women, and children hung in rows while other body parts were soaking in pickling. The family was arrested and executed without trial, the men suffering death by extreme mutilation and the women burned at the stake [Kerman, 1962, pp. 11–15].

Vampires also took their place in the showcase of horror but not until they received the attention of writers in the nineteenth century. Bram Stoker's *Dracula* (1897) was modeled on the fifteenth-century Wallachian nobleman Vlad Tepes, also known as "Vlad the Impaler" and "Drakul" (Dragon). He was particularly known to be a "vicious and depraved sadist" who enjoyed torturing and murdering peasants who lived within his jurisdiction. Stories circulated about the secret horror chambers in the depths of his castle and how he was believed to be the devil or at least one of his emissaries (Hill & Williams, 1967, p. 195). Tales evolved suggesting that some vampires could also transform themselves into werewolves. However, vampires usually had but one goal—to drink human blood—whereas werewolves mutilated and cannibalized. Vampires were also believed to be sexually involved with their victims, albeit discreetly, because of (for some people) the erotic nature of sucking human blood. In his book *Man Into Wolf* (1951), Robert Eisler described a British "vampire" who in 1949 murdered nine victims and drank blood from each of them. By 1995, any erotic subtleties in vampirism had been replaced with direct expressions of sexual arousal, gratification, and their fusion with violence and death. In the film *Interview with a Vampire: The Vampire Chronicles,* vampires dine upon the blood of female victims, who experience orgasmic arousal and, immediately following, terror and death. Thus, the repeated implications of

sexual mania in the role-creation of the vampire throughout history are clear.

Werewolves and vampires are joined by a host of other sinister monsters all bent on the destruction of humankind, especially young women and children. Among them are zombies, or walking "corpses," and ghouls who reportedly feast on both live and dead bodies. The sexual connotation of these acts is pervasive.

Some of the early European serial killers who were thought to have been vampires or other "creatures of the night" in reality were nothing more than depraved murderers. Following are brief descriptions of two such people:

Gilles de Rais, born in 1404, became heir to the greatest fortune in the whole of France. After fighting alongside Joan of Arc and being awarded the title Marshall of France, his beloved Joan of Arc was captured and put to death. Apparently he never recovered from the loss and soon lost his great wealth. Convinced that he needed to make a pact with the Devil himself in order to regain his fortunes, he murdered a young boy by slitting his throat, severing his wrist, cutting out his heart, and ripping out his eyes from their sockets. He then saved the boy's blood to write out his pact with the Devil. Having discovered his enjoyment for torturing and killing children, he began to recruit them in large numbers for his own murdering pleasure. Although documentation is not available, it is believed he killed several hundred children, drinking their blood and engaging in necrophilia. One of his many perverted pleasures was to have the heads of his child victims stuck on upright rods. De Rais would then have their hair curled by a professional beautician and have their lips and cheeks made up with rouge. A beauty contest was then held, and the "winner" was used for sexual purposes.

Countess Elizabeth Bathory of fifteenth-century Hungary became heavily involved in sorcery, witchcraft, and devil worship. Although she married and bore children, she maintained a predilection for young girls. With her husband off to the wars, she began to indulge herself in the torture and slaying of young girls and women. Stimulated by sado-eroticism, the countess bathed in the blood of her victims in order to maintain her fair complexion. She was believed to have been responsible for the deaths of more than a hundred victims.

Such people appear to be the forerunners of the modern serial killer. Their acts are no more disgusting or cruel than those of their twentieth-century counterparts. We have kept their legends alive by scapegoating the wolf and perpetuating the tales of vampires, witches, ghouls, and zombies.

A function of the early European church was to find ways to eradicate the problems attributed to witchcraft and sorcery. Under guidance from Pope Innocent VIII, two Dominicans, Heinrich Institor (Kramer) and Jakob Sprenger produced the first encyclopedia of demonology, the *Malleus Maleficarum* (*Witch's Hammer*), in 1486. This compendium of mythology would be used for centuries to identify and destroy witches, wizards, and sorcerers. Thousands of people were "identified" through torturous means and then promptly burned at the stake (Marwick, 1970, pp. 369–377). The latent or unintended function of the great witch hunt, or the Grand Inquisition, was the creation of a witch "craze" that cost many innocent lives. Sanctioned by government, the witch hunt took on new meaning, and practically overnight witches were to be found everywhere. The efforts of the church and state probably did more to perpetuate the belief in sorcerers, werewolves, vampires, witches, and so on, than any other single force in society.

One more type of historical "monster" bears mentioning: In Jewish medieval legend a *golem* was a robot, or an artificial person (*golem* means a "clay figure supernaturally brought to life"). Golems were given "life" by means of a charm; occasionally they ran amok and had to be destroyed. Dr. Joshua Bierer (1976) uses the term *golem* to describe a case in which a man and his wife were having serious marital problems due primarily to his inability to develop any kind of meaningful relationship. His extramarital affairs were frequent, always in search of something he could not find. His mistresses did not sense that he was actually without love, commitment, or a desire for meaningful relationships. In reality he hated all women and wanted to kill them. To avoid this psychological truth he moved quickly from one affair to another. Dr. Bierer explained

that this client had had a difficult childhood during which his mother was incapable of showing him any affection. Both parents were absent for long periods of time, leaving him to the whims of a cruel nanny who apparently forced him into frequent, emotionally stressful situations. Dr. Bierer concluded that everybody needs love, affection, and attention. Without these one can become emotionally truncated and run the risk of developing into a golem (1976, pp. 197–199).

Although we cannot assume that people suffering from the "golem syndrome" will become murderers, the golem profile does appear to capture the essence of many serial killers. A person who can orchestrate the destruction of another human being and have no remorse, no feeling for his or her victim or external need to defend his or her actions exemplifies the term golem.

For example, the present author had the opportunity of working with a patient during the late 1970s who was confined to a state mental hospital for the criminally insane. As a young man, rather alienated from others, he had dropped out of school but was still living with other students. His feelings of inferiority and fear of others fueled his journey into loneliness. Fantasy replaced reality, and soon he began indulging himself in morbid literature while his disdain intensified for those around him. He began reading a work by Dr. David Abrahamsen, *The Murdering Mind,* and quickly identified with the main character. He also began to fantasize about death and how it might feel to kill another person. One night after quarreling with a roommate over a box of detergent, this young man drifted into his fantasy world. He decided it was now time to realize his ultimate fantasy. He went to a closet and removed and loaded a shotgun and then went into his roommate's bedroom. He carefully placed the shotgun next to the head of his intended victim, and a moment later another roommate across the hall was jolted awake by the blast. The killer calmly propped the shotgun against the wall, called the police, and informed them that he had just killed his roommate and that he would be waiting for them to come and get him. People were appalled by his "coolness," his lack of remorse, his lack of feeling for what had taken place. He appeared to be void of emotions entirely. He was finally found guilty but mentally ill and confined to the state hospital.

Although the monsters we have discussed have their origins in demonology, witchcraft, belief in the supernatural, and folklore, modern "monsters," of course, are no longer attributed to transcendental sources. The mutilated corpses strewn in pieces along highways in California and the bodies left to rot in secluded wooded areas of Washington state or secreted under the floorboards of someone's home in Chicago are not the victims of fictional beings. Instead, they are the victims of the David Hills, the Ted Bundys, and the John Gacys of our society. Monsters in their own right, but the monster lives within and is unleashed only when the intended victim has entered his or her area of control. Are the men and women who commit such atrocities today possessed of the devil, or are they simply evil people, devils unto themselves who make their conscious choice for evil, just as others choose good? The answer may become difficult and complicated as we explore the possible explanations for serial murder.

Serial Murder, Cults, and The Occult

Closely tied to the notions of evil and demonology are cult-related activities. In the United States it is not a crime to belong to a cult—the term means "a system of religious worship; devotion or homage to person or thing." Nor is it a crime to practice beliefs of the occult—things that are "kept secret, esoteric, mysterious, beyond the range of ordinary knowledge; involving the supernatural, mystical, magical" (Sykes, 1976, pp. 249, 755)—provided those practices occur within an accepted legal framework.

Satanic cults in the United States appear to have attracted a growing number of followers interested in the worship of Satan. The problem does not stem from the fact that people join satanic organizations but from the belief that such cults may indeed practice human sacrifices. Anton La Vey, a one-time rock musician and actor consultant for the movie *Rosemary's Baby,* founded the Church of Satan on the witches'

feast day of Walpurgis Night (Walpurgisnacht), April 30, 1966, which reportedly has a membership of 20,000 (Holmes, 1990). LaVey wrote *The Complete Witch, The Satanic Rituals,* and *The Satanic Bible.* According to La Vey's bible (1969), members worship the trinity of the devil—Lucifer, Satan, and the Devil—including the nine pronouncements of the devil:

1. Satan represents indulgence, instead of abstinence!
2. Satan represents vital existence, instead of spiritual pipe dreams!
3. Satan represents undefiled wisdom instead of hypocritical self-deceit!
4. Satan represents kindness to those who deserve it, instead of love wasted on ingrates!
5. Satan represents vengeance, instead of turning the other cheek!
6. Satan represents responsibility, instead of concern for the psychic vampires!
7. Satan represents man as just another animal, sometimes better, more often worse, than those who walk on all fours, who because of his divine and intellectual development has become the most vicious of all!
8. Satan represents all of the so-called sins, as they lead to physical, mental or emotional gratification.
9. Satan has been the best friend the church has ever had, as he has kept it in business all these years! [La Vey, 1969, p. 25]

Holmes (1990), who interviewed two high priests and several coven members of satanic cults, noted that members are encouraged to fulfill their potential by advancing through different levels of "actualization" via magic, spells, rituals, and so on. They progress by holding membership in the Church of Satan and participating in traditional worship services similar to the rituals, hierarchy, and organization of other churches. They may then progress to other levels within the church. Members learn from their Satanic Bible various "invocations," including the Invocations Employed toward the Conjuration of Lust and Destruction. One chapter carries the title "On the Choice of a Human Sacrifice." Those who are proven devotees and have advanced in the levels of "personal affiliation" are invited to participate in human and animal sacrifices that include the use of various devices and rituals. It is important to understand that membership involvement in satanic churches depends on factors common to any church, including loyalty, knowledge, and understanding of doctrines and oaths and the degree of commitment to these covenants. Indeed, many satanic cults operate independently of the main church. For example, in 1971 the Satanic Orthodox Church of Nethilum Rite was established in Chicago in an occult bookshop. As a competitor to La Vey's church, members of the Chicago church believe in God as the creator of the universe and that Satan, as the holder of all knowledge, created God.

In the late 1960s, Charles Manson and his followers gave new meaning to the word *cult*. Each member was believed to have paid homage to Manson and to have carried out his ritualistic death sentences. Allegedly, Manson was affiliated with the Process, or Church of the Final Judgement, a satanic cult. In the late 1980s a voodoo cult in Matamoros, Mexico, heavily involved in drug smuggling into the United States, was believed to have killed 15–20 victims, executing them with machetes, guns, and knives. The group had come to believe that through certain forms of witchcraft the drug smugglers could gain protection from police, bullets, and other threats to their drug trade. By cutting out and burning the brains of a victim and then mixing them with blood, herbs, rooster feet, goat heads, and turtles, the cult members believed they could operate with impunity.

Voodooism predates La Vey's Church of Satan by hundreds if not thousands of years and varies considerably in rituals, spells, and hoaxes. Rather than a formal organization, voodoo is the use of or belief in religious witchcraft. Persons trained in the practice of voodoo cast spells on or bewitch others as a means of protection, vengeance, and so forth. In this particular case the secret charms and hoaxes of voodoo were practiced to meet the "special" needs of the smugglers. The group, led by a "godfather" and a female witch, killed and mutilated anyone for their own reasons, including greed and vengeance.

Most serial murderers who are involved in cult-related homicides do not appear to be particularly advanced in satan worship. Several appear to be self-styled satanists who dabble in the occult, but the extent of their involvement is difficult to measure. Donald Harvey, believed to have methodically murdered 58 victims in at least three different hospitals, had books on satan worship in his possession but refused to comment about the material. Richard Ramirez, the Night Stalker in California, ardently proclaimed his ties to satanism by displaying his pentagram* tattooed on his left palm, shouting "hail Satan!" when leaving court, and listening incessantly to the AC/DC *Highway to Hell* album. Part of his ritualistic attacks included inscribing satanic symbols in the homes of victims. Henry Lucas, a serial killer who roamed the southern states and killed hitchhikers, confessed his involvement with satan worship. Allegedly he and his partner Otis Toole were paid to kidnap children to be used for human sacrifices, prostitution, and black-market sales. The duo were believed to be members of the satanic group Hand of Death. Robin Gecht and three other young men terrorized Chicago in the early 1980s by abducting, mutilating, and killing several young women. In a form of satan worship they were believed to have cut up animal and human body parts for sacrifice on a makeshift altar and then cannibalized some of the remains. Robert Berdella of Kansas City publicly admitted in 1989 to the ritual tortures and homosexual murders of several young men but denied any connection to satan worship even though evidence indicated otherwise.

Steve Daniels (1989), a specialist in ritual/cult groups reasons that

> one can see that if a serial killer picks and chooses beliefs that fit his aberrant needs, mixes this with signs, symbols, and machinations of satanism, conceives personal rituals and adds to all of this a liberal use of drugs, a

---

*five-pointed star formed by intersecting lines

frightening picture emerges: an evil, drug-lubricated butchering machine who justifies his behavior by exalting Satan.

Assessing the degree of influence of satanic worship among serial killers has begun to attract both law-enforcement and academic researchers. It is premature to state that serial killers in general have ties to satanic cults even though what the offenders *do* is satanic in nature. The fact remains that many serial killers have had no ties to satan worship before or during their murder careers. Perhaps offenders mention satanism when they are captured simply to add to the already sensational nature of the homicides. Perhaps the police and the media overreact and refer to satanism when they are confronted by the work of a serial killer. Perhaps there are certain types of serial killers who can be described as cult-driven, whereas others are influenced only superficially by satanism. In the cases of those who do become involved in satanic worship and serial killing, we should determine which behavior started first. Does satanic worship stimulate individuals or groups of people to kill, or were they already murderers when they found satanism to be attractive? For whatever reasons, it appears that reports of cult-related homicides continue to persist—which may provide researchers with useful research data.

The Notion of Evil

Levin and Fox (1985) refer to multiple murderers as evil people (p. 210). In the "hard sciences" such as chemistry and physics, exactness and quantification are necessary requirements; however, the notion of evil is intangible and unmeasurable, and it is often used as a misnomer for inappropriate behavior. In Western culture the closest we come to quantifying good or evil is by observing that someone is a really good person or a really bad person. We have a tendency to judge people in terms of their goodness or badness, but seldom do we refer to others as being "evil." Instead, evil is a label we reserve for those worse than bad. "Badness" we expect to find in many people, but evil relegates individuals to a special classification that suggests some form of

satanic affiliation. Interestingly, both bad and evil persons may engage in similar types of undesirable behaviors yet be categorized with different labels. Part of the problem in assigning such labels is determining exactly what constitutes good or evil. Some people believe that gambling is "of the devil," whereas others see it more as a benign form of entertainment or recreation. The same can be said of drinking alcohol, committing fornication, or illegal use of drugs.

But homicide is another matter. Killing for recreation is not only unacceptable, it elicits some of our deepest anxieties about being alone and meeting strangers. We can understand to some degree the typical "domestic" homicide—a husband and wife, or other family members, find themselves in altercations that end in someone being killed. One can even understand why a person with a grudge may finally lash out at his or her tormentor or why an individual dying of an incurable disease is killed by a friend or a family member to halt the suffering. We may not agree in any way with the act of killing—most people believe that killing another human being is wrong. We do, however, understand to some degree the reason for killing and are able to place such homicides in context with everyday life. We consider them to be domestic, "crimes of passion" or situational killings that can be explained away as marital problems, family disputes, or acts of mercy. These types of crimes are illegal and wrong in the eyes of society. However, we know that most of these offenders will not kill again. They have freed themselves from their intimate entanglements and most then want, at some point, to get on with their lives. Domestic homicides, however, are in stark contrast to serial murder.

Multiple-homicide offenders, especially serial murderers, are incomprehensible to society. If someone has murdered children because he enjoys killing, that raises serious questions about the offender's rationality. Surely no one in his or her "right" mind could rape and murder a dozen children simply for recreation. We find it disgusting to imagine such crimes and disturbing to hear words such as "enjoyment" and "recreation" associated with the taking of human life. For many, evil then becomes the appropriate label for those who apparently enjoy controlling and destroying human life. What greater crime exists than to deny another person his or her free agency, the right of self-determination?

The quest for power and control over the lives of others is exemplified by the case of Josef Mengele, a physician and geneticist recruited into the Nazi ranks to direct the processing of concentration camp prisoners at Birkenow and Auschwitz during World War II. While Hitler stepped up his campaign for his "Final Solution," Mengele also promoted his own bizarre agenda for thousands of camp victims. Posner and Ware (1986), in their book *Mengele,* examine the depths to which one person is willing and able to descend, once given unbridled control over the lives of others.

Mengele was an intelligent, articulate individual who appeared dedicated to his work. Married, with a family, he managed to compartmentalize his life in and out of the camps. Under the guise of science he masqueraded as a medical researcher, but his rationalizations could not hide the truth. But do all people have such propensities? What, if anything, keeps most of humanity from such diabolical practices? Martin Buber, a noted Jewish theologian, examined the myths and notions of evil and found that some people are in a process of moving toward evil whereas others have been consumed by it. This may be analogous to a continuum along which we are constantly moving toward increasing degrees of goodness or increasing degrees of badness or, ultimately, evil. Some religions, such as Christianity, refer to the temptations people must endure and overcome in order to achieve a state of goodness; those who succumb become slaves to their own vices and passions. The ultimate notion of evil may be defined by those individuals who appear to have progressed past worldly temptations and have become devils unto themselves, completely without guilt, remorse, or compassion for their victims.

Erich Fromm (1973) refers to human evil as a process that includes the principle of agency or choice.

> Our capacity to choose changes constantly with our practice of life. The longer we continue to make the wrong decisions, the more our heart hardens; the more often we make the right deci-
> sion, the more our heart softens—or better perhaps, comes alive.... Each step in life which increases my self-confidence, my integrity, my courage, my conviction also increases my capacity to choose the desirable alternative, until eventually it becomes more difficult for me to choose the undesirable rather than the desirable action. On the other hand, each act of surrender and cowardice weakens me, opens the path for more acts of surrender, and eventually freedom is lost. Between the extreme when I can no longer do a wrong act and the extreme when I have lost my freedom to right action, there are innumerable degrees of freedom of choice. In the practice of life the degree of freedom to choose is different at any given moment. If the degree of freedom to choose the good is great, it needs less effort to choose the good. If it is small, it takes a great effort, help from others, and favorable circumstances [pp. 173–178].

Dr. M. Scott Peck refers to evil people as the "people of the lie": They are constantly engaged in self-deception and the deception of others. He goes on to say that "the lie is designed not so much to deceive others as to deceive themselves. They cannot or will not tolerate the pain of self-reproach. The decorum with which they lead their lives is maintained as a mirror in which they can see themselves reflected righteously" (1983, pp. 66–75). Peck observed that although it might be difficult to define evil people by the illegality of their actions, we can define them by the "consistency of their sins" (p. 71).

The notion of evil may best be understood if one perceives evil to be both a characteristic of an individual and a behavior. Men and women who commit evil acts are often perceived to possess evil characteristics. Thus serial killers not only *do* evil, but they also possess various developmental characteristics that may contribute to the evil. This differentiation between behavior and characteristics may depend on the type of serial killer. For example, some serial murderers possess highly developed narcissistic, or self-centered qualities. Fromm, discussing the pathology of narcissism, refers to people who exhibit "malignant narcissism." Many of these offenders display an unrelenting will to promote their own wants and needs over everyone else's. As Peck (1983) observes, "they are men and women of obviously strong will, determined to have their own way. There is remarkable power in the manner in which they attempt to control others" (p. 78). The epitome of narcissism may well be the total domination of others.

For example, the present author researched a case in which the offender is believed to have murdered 12–14 victims during a series of robberies on the West Coast. He usually stalked and attacked dark-haired, attractive women working in stores and other places of business. After robbing his victims he would bind them with tape and force them to engage in sexual acts. This entailed the victim assuming a kneeling position and being forced to perform fellatio on her attacker. During these encounters he held a gun to the victim's head. Sometimes he forced the woman to look him in the eyes until he climaxed, at which point he fired a bullet into her brain. Usually those whom he executed were victims who became hysterical, cried, and begged for mercy. Those who survived had complied with his demands but remained calm, some even joking with their assailant. The killer sought total domination and submission over his victims before pulling the trigger. The victim's death symbolized the attacker's signature on a completed act of total control over another human being.[1] In 1996, this author contacted one of the victims who had survived being attacked. A prominent magazine in England wanted to do a story on a female survivor. I was impressed with the inner strength possessed by this woman determined not only to survive, but to live without fear.

When Evil Embraces Good

The notion of evil becomes complicated by the generally accepted belief that those who commit sins can repent and virtually turn their lives around. The Christian Bible is replete with exhortations to repent. Whether or not we accept the Christian principle of repentance, the fact remains that people can and do stop committing sins and crimes. This "change of heart" may precipitate in some a desire to correct the wrong they have done and to become productive rather than destructive members of society. Prisons seem to breed religious conversions, which

sometimes do appear to effect a change in attitude and behavior.

Is it possible for convicted and incarcerated serial killers to experience this "change of heart," experience remorse for their crimes and never engage in them again? The scope of this research does not provide concrete answers to this question, but a few brief observations can be made.

Frequently in the processing of offenders a judge is influenced in sentencing by the display of remorse. The general public is incensed when a convicted criminal displays no remorse for his or her crimes. Many people do not or can not fathom homicide beyond the realm of television and expect those who commit such crimes to have some degree of remorse. We tend to equate remorse with the recognition that a terrible wrong has been committed and that the offender, recognizing his or her wrong, feels sorrow.

Recognizing words such as "sorrow" and "remorse" as qualitative terms and difficult to quantify, we are faced with the task of determining sincerity. Many serial murderers, some who have killed dozens of victims and are now in prison, profess a sincere conversion and deep commitment to God and/or Christian principles.

In one case an offender killed at least 12 victims. Some of those murdered were children whom he tortured and sexually attacked for hours before finally taking their lives. He recalled during an interview that on one occasion a young woman he attacked died too quickly. He was outraged that she had not lived longer for him to torture. In his anger he hung her from a ceiling and for several minutes bludgeoned and kicked the corpse. Later that day he found another young woman, who died much more slowly. This killer is now a converted Christian who is confident that God has forgiven him for his crimes and that he eventually will be set free.

Another offender killed 11 children over a period of one and one-half years in the early 1980s. Seven of the eleven boys and girls were raped or sodomized. Some he bludgeoned to death with a hammer, others he strangled or stabbed to death. Apprehended for only the last missing child, he made a deal with the authorities. In return for money he would be willing to take authorities to the grave sites of other missing children, but without the money there would be no bodies. The parents of the missing children in the area naturally wanted to know if it was their son or daughter killed by this mass murderer or whether their child was still alive somewhere. The authorities, without public knowledge, agreed to the exchange, and the killer began locating the dead children. Each time a body was recovered, $10,000 was placed in an account bearing the offender's wife's name. After ten bodies had been exchanged, the offender terminated the deal. He now resides in an isolation unit in a maximum-security facility and as a result of public outrage, his wife was forced to return the $100,000.

This author has corresponded and spoken with the offender on several occasions. He clearly understands what he has done is wrong, but now claims no remorse for his deeds. When asked about his victims, he responded, "I have put this whole matter behind me now. They are my brothers and sisters in Christ. All the children are with our Lord Jesus Christ now, and some day I shall be there with them." Claiming to have always been a Christian, the offender enrolled at a divinity college, where he pursued coursework in religious studies. He has written essays condemning abortion and capital punishment (a reversal of his previous stance) and supporting the power and importance of prayer.

A third offender sodomized and murdered five young boys over the course of several months. Once caught and sentenced to die, he expressed great remorse for his actions. He desperately wanted the families of his victims to forgive him. He sought forgiveness from God. He wrote letters to the victims' families. He cried bitterly over his crimes and to prove his remorse he stopped his appeals process. He stated that he deserved to die for what he had done. However, he also stated that despite his deep remorse, he knew that if he was ever again returned to society that he would start killing again because he had been consumed by powerful urges to destroy children.

These are only three of many cases of serial killers who ardently embrace God. Whether the embracing of God and/or Christianity will in-

evitably lead to productive rather than destructive lives remains to be seen.

When Good Embraces Evil

The more perversely and obscenely some murderers tend to behave or are depicted by the media to have acted, the greater the interest by the general public. Most persons are simply fascinated and shocked with the innovative destructiveness of multiple murderers. Most serial killers, especially those males viewed as attractive and charming, quickly draw a following of women, mostly young. These women attend the trial, write letters, and send photographs of themselves hoping to receive some attention from the killer. Some wish to help the offender recover from his aberrant behavior or are simply interested in having contact with someone so dangerous, but from a safe distance. We have yet to adequately explore the impact of media and public attention on serial killers and future offenders. We do know serial murders elicit an immediate response from some people who otherwise would in all probability never have contact with the offender. The relationship between the public and the offender is shaped to some degree by the amount of publicity, the types of victims, and the personality of the offender.

Inevitably some people are drawn to the offender because they have a desire to befriend and understand the person. Every serial killer whom this author has known always has a group of followers. They are, themselves, a most fascinating group of people. They come from a variety of backgrounds, but most are female. In one instance a woman met an offender after he had been convicted and sentenced to prison for killing children. She came to believe that it was God's will that she devote herself to the betterment of this man's life and has every intention of remaining faithful to him. She understands the nature and the extent of his crimes but is convinced that the offender is salvageable. After 15 years of devotion, she married the offender, who is never expected to be released. This type of involvement by a convicted killer with morally "straight" members of the community raises several questions. What influence, if any, do such offenders have over members of the community? What factors create attraction between someone who has ritualistically killed children and another person who abhors violence? Is there an attraction between people who strive to do good and those who commit acts of evil? It is easy to ascribe naiveté to those who align themselves with offenders, but we fall short in understanding the dynamics of such relationships.

Note

1. Some of this information was gathered from interviews with the offender and surviving victims in December 1988.

References

Abrahamsen, D. (1973). *The Murdering Mind.* New York: Harper and Row.

Bierer, J. (1976). Love-making—An act of murder. *International Journal of Social Psychiatry, 22*(3), 197–199.

Daniels, S. (1989). Satanic beliefs, criminal actions. *The Training Key,* International Association of Chiefs of Police, 390.

Eisler, R. (1951). *Man into Wolf.* New York: Greenwood Press.

Fromm, E. (1973). *The Anatomy of Human Destructiveness.* New York: Holt, Rinehart and Winston.

Hill, D., and P. Williams (1967). *The Supernatural.* New York: Signet Books.

Holmes, R. M. (1990). *Profiling Violent Crimes.* Newbury Park, CA: Sage.

Kerman, S. L. (1962). *The Newgate Calendar.* New York: Capricorn Books.

La Vey, A. (1969). *The Satanic Bible.* New York: Avon.

Levin, J., and J. A. Fox (1985). *Mass Murder: The Growing Menace.* New York: Plenum Press.

Marwick, M. (1970). *Witchcraft and Sorcery.* Baltimore: Penguin Books.

Peck, M. S. (1983). *People of the Lie.* New York: Simon and Schuster.

Posner, G. L., and J. Ware (1986). *Mengele.* New York: Dell.

Schreiber, F. R. (1973). *Sybil.* New York: Warner Books.

Suinn, R. M. (1984). *Fundamentals of Abnormal Psychology.* Chicago: Nelson-Hall.

Sykes, G. (1976). *The Concise Oxford Dictionary* (6th ed.). Oxford: Clarendon Press.

Thigpen, C., and H. Cleckley (1957). *The Three Faces of Eve.* New York: McGraw-Hill.

26

The Hillside Strangler

Jack Levin
James Alan Fox

It had been six years since the "Hillside Strangler" was on the loose. The people of Los Angeles were trying to forget the string of brutal murders that occurred in their city between October 1977 and February 1978; but the slow wheels of justice in the trial of Angelo Buono kept the memories alive. During a two-year period, nearly four hundred witnesses had taken the stand to describe or to defend Buono's alleged deeds of viciousness, before his guilt was finally determined.[1]

Only one real question now remained to be decided surrounding the famous Hillside Strangler case. Would Angelo Buono, who with his adoptive cousin Kenneth Bianchi had raped, tortured, sodomized, and strangled ten young women discarding their bodies on hillsides and roadsides, be condemned to die in the gas chamber? All that was left now, mercifully, was the final stage—the penalty phase—of the longest trial in the history of this country.

Judge Ronald M. George stared from his bench down at Angelo Buono, who had just been convicted of nine counts of murder. Judge George tried hard to hide his impatience as he waited for what seemed an eternity for Buono to respond to a very simple inquiry.

"Do you wish to testify?" asked Judge George, looking directly at the defendant. Buono sat calmly and coldly, in a navy blue jump suit inscribed "Los Angeles County Jail" on the back, rather than in a suit and tie as he had worn prior to the guilty verdicts. Destined for either the gas chamber or at least life imprisonment without the possibility of parole, Buono chose not to play the role of the humble defendant. The judge waited for Buono to speak, but nearly half a minute of total silence passed.

The judge then repeated, "Do you wish to testify?" The gallery of spectators leaned forward, straining to catch any words that Buono might mutter. The press took notes to back up their tape recorders, which, contrary to courtroom regulations, were turned on, capturing the long spaces of silence.

The courtroom was filled with an air of anticipation. After all, Angelo Buono had sat motionless and without emotion or expression for over two years. His only gesture reported by some court observers had been that of disdain toward Kenneth Bianchi, Buono's accomplice and cousin whose confession had implicated him.

Finally, Buono answered the judge; he wanted to speak to the court. Some observers predicted that Buono would now plead his innocence or maybe plead for mercy; others speculated that he would ask for the death sentence as an ultimate act of martyrdom. Whatever his intention, a few words from Buono would surely be a fitting conclusion to a drama that had lasted for over six years since the death of a Hollywood prostitute in late 1977.

The first of the Hillside Stranglings, which would come to paralyze Los Angeles, was discovered on October 18, 1977. The nude body of a woman was found perversely sprawled alongside of Forest Lawn Drive, near the famous Forest Lawn Cemetery, resting place of "the stars." Homicide detectives conducted their routine search of the area for evidence and questioned nearby residents about any peculiar sights or sounds they might recall. With close to nothing to go on except an obvious cause of death—strangulation, probably manual—the body was sent for an autopsy.

The body was easily identified: Yolanda Washington, a 19-year-old part-time waitress and part-time prostitute, was well known to the vice squad working the Hollywood streets. For Yolanda, prostitution was simply a profitable business. A "good night" could bring in over three hundred dollars which would go farther than any legitimate job in helping to support her 2½-year-old daughter Tameika. Unfortunately for her, she was not a high-class call girl. She worked the fast and cheap streets of Hollywood, where drugs and commercial sex overshadowed the starlet images. Yolanda knew the risks involved. There was always the chance of injury from some crazy john who liked violence. But the kinkier and the more violent the man's fantasies and desires, the greater was the payoff. While such were the occupational hazards, Yolanda never bargained for murder.

The streets were hardly shaken by the news of the murder. While Washington's death was a top item of conversation at the Howard Johnson's at the corner of Hollywood and Vine, where the pimps and hookers usually hung out, ate, and relaxed, the death of a streetwalker did not come as a surprise, but simply was a reminder to be careful.

The newspapers downplayed the strangling too. Unlike a simultaneous mass slaughter as bloody as that perpetrated by the Manson family or a murder of someone of high position, Washington's death was hardly newsworthy. A brief, well-hidden, back-page report of a body found on a hillside would be the first page of the Hillside Strangler saga.

Nearly two weeks later, on October 31, another body was discovered along a roadside in Glendale, just a few miles from Hollywood. It too was nude and bore ligature or rope marks around the wrists, ankles, and neck. Subsequent examination revealed evidence of rape and sodomy. The victim was identified as 15-year-old Judith Lynn Miller, and her story is sad indeed.

Unlike streetwise Yolanda Washington, Judy Miller was an unhappy runaway living in a run-down Hollywood motel who sought from the streets and her makeshift family of other runaways the love and support she apparently felt she lacked at home. We may never know if her parents even grieved her death; her mother was wanted by the police for welfare fraud and her father jumped probation on unemployment fraud. As in life, she was alone in death. Her body remained in the morgue unclaimed for ten days following her murder.

The details of Judy Miller's killing and the torturous last few hours of her life are similar to the horror suffered by eight more women to follow, though Kenneth Bianchi admits remembering most vividly the terror in Miller's eyes. Indeed, she was the first "child" subjected to Buono's house of unspeakable tortures.

With the exception of Washington who was killed in an automobile, each of the other nine victims of the Hillside Strangler was kidnapped and brought to Buono's home. In order to avoid their involuntarily urinating right after death—like Washington's body had done—Buono and Bianchi first forced each of the victims to go to the bathroom. Each was then tied by the arms, legs, and neck to a special chair in Buono's spare bedroom. Each was brutally raped, sodomized with various instruments, and strangled to death. The nude and bruised bodies were tossed, like refuse, along roadsides and hillsides in Los Angeles and Glendale, hence the name "Hillside" Stranglings. (Cindy Hudspeth, the last victim, was an exception; her body was put in the trunk of her car and pushed down a ravine.)

The murders began shortly after Kenneth Bianchi moved at the age of 26 to Los Angeles from Rochester, New York where he was raised. "I came [to California] hoping to find a better job," Bianchi later explained to psychiatrists; "I always wanted to go to California—the sun, the girls, the beaches, you know, the dreams."[2] Bianchi had also looked up his cousin Angelo Buono, who took him in.

The question of why Buono and Bianchi embarked on their spree of murder is complex. But once they tried it, they found killing exciting and fun.

Up to the point of Washington's murder, neither Buono nor Bianchi had a history of violent crime. Their initiation into murder emanated not out of a psychotic need to taste the blood of another, not out of the frustration of divorce or unemployment, but out of a spirit of adventure rooted in their friendship. By one account, Bianchi and Buono reportedly were sitting around Buono's house one day, when they began talking about what it must feel like to kill someone. Almost as a lark, they went out and tried it.

While some of us might find the act of killing abhorrent, Buono and Bianchi apparently found it to their liking. Characteristic of sociopaths generally, they felt neither guilty nor remorseful about the deed, seeing the prostitute as merely a tool for their personal gratification. In any case, they could always rely on each other to help justify their crimes to themselves, no matter how dastardly.

After the first time, killing gets easier. Just as the addict requires increasing doses of a drug to satisfy his craving, the serial killer who kills for sexual pleasure typically requires more and more perversity to satisfy his sadistic libido.

Though all the Hillside Stranglings were heinous, they grew more brutal, true to form, as the victim count rose. Victim seven, Kristina Weckler, was "for the fun of it" injected with cleaning solution causing her body to convulse and then was gassed with a bag connected by a hose to the oven. Victim eight, Lauren Wagner, was tortured and burned with an electric cord on her hands and body.

Another pattern of change that emerged in the killings played an important role in the development of the Hillside Strangler story. While the early victims were women of the night or of the street, Buono and Bianchi began branching out to suburban neighborhoods for more "innocent" prey.

The deaths of Washington and Miller were considered, by those who even considered them at all, as part of the subculture of the streets. Among the streetwalkers of Hollywood there sprung a new and understandable fear following these murders, yet this was only enough to prescribe greater caution. Coping with the dangers and the role of the automobile in the culture of Los Angeles, hookers worked in pairs; one would write down the license plate number of another's trick as the other hopped into his car. All were quick to be alarmed by johns who were into pain—inflicting it, that is.

It was easy at first for most citizens to distance themselves from the murders, since they were happening just to "common prostitutes." But then came November 20, 1977, the day when the bodies of victims five and six—Dolores Cepeda, age 12, and Sonja Johnson, 14—were discovered together near Dodger Stadium, a week following their disappearance.

Unlike Washington and Miller, these two young friends were schoolgirls who did not understand or anticipate danger as they got off the bus on their way home from shopping. That day Sonja's father, Tony Johnson, had refused to pick them up by car. (His guilt about the refusal later drove Tony to an aborted suicide attempt, excessive drinking, and a fatal liver disease.) Bianchi and Buono, on the other hand, did offer to drive them home, but it was to Buono's home instead.

The news of the brutal deaths of the two girls sparked fear and anger all around the Los Angeles area. For the first time, the citizens of Los Angeles were warned that an unknown serial killer might be responsible for a number of recent unsolved murders, linked by the similar manner in which the victims' bodies were discarded. The extensive media coverage of the case both fueled and reflected public anxiety. Not only were citizens demanding that the police do something about the Hillside Stranglings, but most changed their own life-styles in significant ways. Women frantically enrolled in self-defense courses which sprang up in response to the pervasive and intense levels of fear. One physical education professor announced a special six-hour course in self-defense designed for up to sixty-seven students, and as many as a thousand people called for information on the offering. Residents were not only taking active steps to protect themselves, they also began avoiding any dark street or even going out whenever unnecessary. They were, above all, suspicious of strangers.

The situation worsened with the discovery of one important clue. Witnesses who had seen some of the victims on the nights of their deaths reported that two men posing as police had "arrested" the victims. The police ruse was consistent with the autopsies' strange absence of evidence of struggle. Ordinarily, one would find traces of skin or hair underneath the fingernails of victims who had clawed at their attackers. The police charade explained why the girls—especially the two youngsters—had apparently gone willingly with the killers.

After reading in the papers that the stranglers posed as officers, the public trusted no one. How could one be certain of the authenticity of a man wearing a blue uniform with a shield? Could the strangler be, in fact, a cop gone astray? All rules of order consequently broke down. One high school girl from the San Gabriel Valley, for example, refused to stop for a police officer who had spotted her for a traffic violation; instead she sped home to safety with the police in hot pursuit. Others showed the same caution of the police. Eventually, police officials, understanding the cause for panic, were forced to allow motorists not to stop immediately for the police but to continue driving to a police station where it would be safe. As might be expected, speeding motorists "were getting away with murder" under the new set of rules.

Aside from fear of being the next victim, there was always the chance of being the one to discover another nude and mangled body discarded around the city. Marcia Chaiken of the Brentwood section of L.A., for instance, had planned for a long time to take girl scout troop 1139 on a hiking trip to scenic Griffith Park. After the discovery in that vicinity of three bodies believed to be victims of the strangler, Marcia canceled the excursion.

The citizens were not alone in their state of frenzy. The press wrote strong editorials criticizing the police force for its inability to catch the killer. A Hillside Strangler Task Force was formed, and a reward of over $140,000 was offered for information leading to the arrest of the strangler. The Task Force, a combined effort of the Glendale Police, the Los Angeles Police, and the Los Angeles Sheriff's Department, grew to eighty-four officers, and would frantically follow any lead available. And the apprehensive community gave them plenty of leads to investigate, over 10,000 of them. Chief of Police Daryl F. Gates later admitted that this effort was probably too broad and decentralized, a case of too many cooks spoiling the broth. Lt. Edwin Henderson who headed the Task Force agreed, "When you expand a task force to the size it was, you lose a lot of control."[3]

Astonishingly, at one point, for example, an investigator had questioned Kenneth Bianchi about one of the victims, Kimberly Martin, a call girl whose last assignment sent her to Bianchi's apartment building. But this lead got lost in the shuffle and was never relayed to the proper individuals.

As suddenly as the murders had begun on October 17, 1977 with Washington's murder, they ended after Cindy Hudspeth's body was found in her trunk; ten homicides in five months, and then nothing. As the spring and summer months passed without recurrence of the stranglings, the people of Los Angeles slowly recovered and began to relax. Still the investigation and the work of the Task Force forged ahead toward more and more dead ends.

It was not until almost a year after the killings had stopped that the case broke. It broke, not in Los Angeles, but in a small, industrial, seaport town of 50,000 in Washington, just 20 miles from the Canadian border, as far northwest as one can get in the continental United States.

In January 1979, Bellingham, Washington experienced a double homicide—the only killings they would have that entire year. The bodies of Karen Mandic and Diane Wilder, college roommates, were found strangled, raped, yet clothed in the trunk of Mandic's car, following a report of their disappearance. An investigation of their recent whereabouts uncovered that Mandic had been hired by a man from a security firm to housesit for $100 per hour while the home security system was out for repair. Karen asked her friend along as company during the job; neither was seen alive again. Bellingham police immediately suspected Kenneth A. Bianchi, the man who had hired Mandic; and maneuvered for his arrest. Bianchi's California driver's license prompted a call to authorities there.

Lt. Phillip Bullington of Los Angeles, who received the call from the Bellingham police, will always remember the date: January 13, 1979, the day after his wedding anniversary when his wife had tried to boost his spirits by suggesting that maybe "the call" would come tomorrow. It had been almost a year since the last body was found, a year full of frustration and fruitless clues. The strangler was no longer on everybody's lips, and some suggested that the expensive Task Force should be declared a failure and be disbanded, leaving the case of the Hillside Strangler in the "permanently" unsolved category.

But when this new lead surfaced, Bullington jumped at the bait. The similarities were so strong. The two victims in Bellingham were described as two young coeds from Western Washington University who were lured by "a real smooth talker" and then raped and strangled. The check on Bianchi's driver's license uncovered that he lived in the same apartment building in Glendale where Kristina Weckler had once lived, where Kim Martin was last known to have been, and across the street from where Cindy Hudspeth had lived and been abducted. Investigators from L.A. left immediately for Bellingham.

Though the similarities in the crimes were many, the effects on the communities were hardly comparable. Bellingham, a usually peaceful and quiet community, was stunned by the murder of two young coeds, but the police were led quickly to an arrest, so panic did not result.

The arrest of Kenneth Bianchi on suspicion of murder was a surprise to everyone in Bellingham who had known him. Kelli Boyd, Ken's girlfriend and the mother of his baby, always thought of him as a gentle man who was kind to her and to his friends. "The Ken I knew couldn't ever have hurt anybody or killed anybody—he wasn't the kind of person who could have killed somebody," she explained.[4] Friends who knew him during the nearly eight months he lived in Bellingham described Ken as an "all-around nice guy." His boss at the security firm knew him as a hard worker, an excellent security guard with a bright future. Even Bellingham's Chief of Police Terry Mangan considered Ken a fine prospect for his own police force. Indeed, character references just didn't seem to jibe with circumstantial evidence that implicated Ken.

While Ken calmly insisted on his innocence, and his friends confidently awaited his clearance of the charges, detectives were arduously combing the scene of the crime for clues. A microscopic search of the carpet on the stairs in the Bellingham house where the murdered girls had been housesitting unearthed long blond head hairs probably belonging to Karen Mandic and pubic hairs matching those of Ken Bianchi. Ken's position suddenly worsened. His attorney, Dean Brett, decided to resolve the inconsistency between Ken's claims and the extant evidence by seeking the opinion of psychiatric specialists.

Brett consulted with psychiatrist Donald Lunde of the Stanford University Medical School. Lunde saw striking inconsistencies between Bianchi's recollections during interviews and information contained in various medical and psychiatric records from his childhood. Ken had been raised in Rochester, New York by his adoptive parents, Nicholas and Frances Bianchi, who had received custody of him when he was three months old. Generally, Kenneth Bianchi presented a description of his childhood as one filled with love, joy, and tranquility. Psychiatric records, however, described Ken as an extremely troubled boy who had been completely and pathologically dependent on his adoptive mother. Mrs. Bianchi, who herself was portrayed as psycho-logically imbalanced and paranoid, had dealt with Ken by unconsciously giving a "double-message," a combination of overprotectiveness and excessive punitiveness. On the one hand she would drag Ken to the doctor for the mildest of ailments, but, on the other hand, would discipline him by holding his hand over a stove burner. Dr. Lunde was forced to conclude that Ken was repressing much of his past, and possibly might not remember the stranglings.

As the physical and circumstantial evidence mounted against Bianchi, his attorney became increasingly skeptical not only of Ken's stories and alibis, but of his very sanity. Still, Ken resisted Brett's wish to enter an insanity plea, so Brett decided to probe further into the possibility of amnesia for the crimes. He called in an expert in hypnosis who might be able to restore Ken's repressed memory.

Dr. John Watkins of the Department of Psychology at the University of Montana undertook a series of lengthy sessions with Bianchi, many of which were facilitated by hypnosis. Watkins uncovered a startling revelation which would dramatically change the entire character of the case. During one session of hypnosis, Ken became suddenly agitated, as if his entire being was instantly transformed.

"Are you Ken?" questioned Watkins.[5]

"Do I look like Ken?" his patient replied sarcastically. Hypnosis had produced the emergence of a second personality—"Steve Walker." Steve Walker was crude, sadistic, impatient, and proudly boasted of his crimes in both L.A. and Bellingham.

"Killing a broad doesn't make any difference to me," bragged Steve. "Killing any-fuckin'-body doesn't make any difference to me."

Steve continued to describe in detail the murders in California and in Bellingham. He also named his cousin Angelo Buono as his accomplice in the L.A. killings, explaining "Angelo is my kind of man—there should be more people in the world like Angelo." Yet Steve admitted that Ken knew nothing about the crimes, adding "I hate Ken."

The "multiple personality" theory—that Ken possessed two different personalities, one who did the killing, and another who knew nothing of it—was a way out of the dilemma. The puzzle seemed so clear now, at least to some people. If he had multiple personalities, the loving father, kind friend, and reliable worker could make up one of his characters, and the vicious murderer another.

When Ken was a boy, Dr. Watkins surmised, he had invented Steve as a repository for all his hateful feelings toward his mother. In this way, Ken could remain a loving and devoted son. The Ken personality would stay the affectionate man whom everyone knew, while Steve—unbeknownst to Ken—would periodically emerge with vengeance. Hence, it seemed that Kenneth Bianchi was clearly not legally sane at the time of the murders. Ken himself viewed videotapes of Steve's hypnotic appearances, and reluctantly and despondently accepted his illness and his role in the murders. With his permission, Dean Brett changed the plea to "not guilty by reason of insanity" for the Bellingham murders of coeds Mandic and Wilder.

Judge Jack Kurtz, disturbed by the sudden change in plea, called in an independent advisor to the court, Dr. Ralph Allison, renowned expert on multiple personalities and altered ego states. Dr. Allison also hypnotized Bianchi and confronted the vicious personality of Steve who angrily described the murders.

"I fuckin' killed those broads," Steve boasted, ". . . Those two fuckin' cunts, that blond-haired cunt and the brunette cunt."[6]

"Here in Bellingham?" checked Allison.

"That's right."

"Why?"

"'Cause I hate fuckin' cunts!"

Steve also detailed proudly the killings in L.A., beginning with the murder of Yolanda Washington.

"She was a hooker. Angelo went and picked her up. I was waiting on the street. He drove her around to where I was. I got in the car. We got on the freeway. I fucked her and killed her. We dumped her body off and that was it. Nothin' to it."

Allison also explored Bianchi's childhood, taking him back through hypnosis to the age of 9. There he found the climate of fear and hurt from which the alter ego had been invented.

While entranced, 9-year-old Ken explained, "I ran away once, hid under my bed. Mommy was hitting me so bad. I met Stevie."

Allison probed a bit further. "How did you first meet him?"

In a child-like squeal, Ken replied, "I closed my eyes. I was crying so hard and all of a sudden, he was there. He said hi to me, told me I was his friend. I felt really good that I had a friend that I could talk to."

Allison was convinced, and reported his conclusion to the court: Ken Bianchi was a dual personality, was not aware of his crimes, and therefore incompetent to stand trial.

To others, besides Watkins and Allison, the multiple personality theory was just a bit too neat. Many were not convinced, particularly in view of the benefits of such a conclusion. The County Prosecutor, David McEachran, conjectured, for example, that if Bianchi could "con" the psychiatrists into thinking he was insane, then following a not guilty due to insanity disposition, he could possibly "con" them into believing he regained his sanity, and go free. At the strident request of the prosecutor, one further expert was called in, Dr. Martin Orne of the Department of Psychiatry of the University of Pennsylvania Medical School.

Orne, understanding the benefits to Bianchi in possibly faking a multiple personality, set out to analyze not so much Ken's personality, but the assumption of "multiple personality" itself. Orne carefully and expertly devised "tests" of the authenticity of Ken's hypnotic trance; if he could fake hypnosis, he could fake the multiple personalities.

Orne mentioned in passing, just prior to hypnotizing Bianchi, that it was rare in the case of a multiple personality for there to be just two personalities.[7] A few minutes later once Bianchi was hypnotized, out came "Billy," personality number three. On another occasion, Orne asked Ken, under hypnosis, to sit and talk with his attorney who actually was not present in the room. Ken overplayed his part, going so far as to shake the hand of the absent Brett. Then Orne had Brett come into the room. Bianchi immediately shifted his attention to the real Brett, remarking "How can I see him in two places?" This was significant because a hypnotized subject ordinarily doesn't question the existence of two of the same people.

Other tests also suggested strongly that the hypnosis was feigned. Prosecution psychiatrist

Saul Faerstein summarily argued "Bianchi was almost a caricature of a hypnotized person, with eyes closed and head bobbing—a pseudo trance."[8] Furthermore, books on psychology were found in Bianchi's home—including one on hypnotic techniques, further endorsing the theory that this was all a well-planned method to escape guilt. However, there was no real proof one way or the other concerning the dispute over the validity of both the hypnosis and the existence of a multiple personality. How one interpreted the evidence and even Orne's tests, which themselves were subjective, depended on one's predisposition in the case.

The police and in particular the detectives in the Hillside Strangler Task Force were dead set against the insanity claim. Los Angeles Police had no real evidence against Angelo Buono except for the testimony of Bianchi. If Bianchi were found to be legally insane, or even if his testimony were determined to have been stimulated by hypnosis, then under California law none of what Bianchi had to say about the crimes could be used in court. Thus, not only might Bianchi escape the death penalty, but Buono might even go free.

What was the truth of Bianchi's mental state? This was either a classic case of a multiple personality, which someday might become the basis for an engrossing piece of nonfiction like *The Three Faces of Eve* or *Sybil,* or just a top-notch job of acting.

The key discovery that convincingly refuted the "multiple personality" theory came from investigators in L.A. as they followed up on Ken's life there. They found a suspicious looking copy of a transcript from Los Angeles Valley College, showing Bianchi's academic record. Not only was the date of Ken's birth wrong, but the transcript listed courses that were taken even before Bianchi had ever moved to Los Angeles. Upon the request of the investigators, the registrar at Valley College produced the authentic transcript. Prior to alteration of the name, it had belonged to a Thomas Steven Walker.

Bianchi was a very good con man. He, in fact, had once convinced a North Hollywood psychologist to give him space in his counseling office until he got his own practice on its feet. Ken had displayed his phony diploma from Columbia University, a master's degree in psychology, and he conversed convincingly about psychology.

As part of his plan to assemble the needed credentials, Ken had placed a job advertisement in the *Los Angeles Times* to hire a counselor, requesting that applicants send a resume as well as a college transcript. When the real Steve Walker responded to the ad, Ken substituted his own name on Walker's credentials and used them to further his own career. An altered ego could presumably mimic a real identity, such as that of Steve Walker. But Bianchi first saw Walker's name as an adult, whereas "Stevie Walker" had appeared under hypnosis when Bianchi was regressed back to the age of 9. It is, of course, possible that by coincidence two Steve Walkers appeared in Bianchi's life—one a childhood fantasy and the other a person who answered an ad years later. More likely, Bianchi was faking hypnosis.

Now that it was clearly a hoax—the multiple personalities, the hypnotic trance, the diplomas, and the "nice guy" facade—Bianchi retracted his insanity plea, and entered a plea of guilty. Part of the deal with the prosecutor—in order to avoid a death sentence—required him to testify against his cousin Angelo. Before the judge in Washington, Bianchi tearfully vowed[9]:

> I can't find the words to express the sorrow I feel for what I've done. In no way can I take away the pain that I've given to others. In no way can I expect forgiveness from anybody. To even begin to try to live with myself I have to take responsibility for what I have done. And I have to do everything I can to get Angelo Buono and to devote my entire life to do everything I possibly can to give my life so that nobody else will hopefully follow in my footsteps.

Regardless of the claim of some court observers that Bianchi was faking the tears and the remorse, as he had faked hypnosis, the stage was set for the next chapter in the Hillside Strangler saga, the ordeal of *State of California vs. Angelo Buono, Jr.* After a hearing in California affirmed Bianchi's sanity and clarity of memory, Bianchi's testimony could be used in Los Angeles against his cousin. . . .

Notes

1. Information in this chapter was drawn mainly from various reports in the *Lost Angeles Herald Examiner,* many of which were written by Frank Candida; from issues of the *Los Angeles Times,* particularly a November 15, 1983 feature by Bella Stumbo; from Public Broadcasting Service's *Frontline,* #206, "The Mind of a Murderer", March, 1984; from Ted Schwarz, *The Hillside Strangler: A Murderer's Mind* (Garden City, New York: Doubleday, 1981); and from personal interviews with Judge Ronald M. George, attorneys Roger Boren, Michael Nash, Alan Simons, author Neville Frankel, reporter Frank Candida, and an anonymous court-watcher. Finally, some of the courtroom events described were observed by the authors.
2. "I came hoping . . . " PBS, *Frontline.*
3. "When you expand . . . " *Daily News,* Los Angeles, November 15, 1983.
4. "The Ken I . . . " PBS, *Frontline.*
5. "Are you Ken?" and ensuing conversation between Bianchi and Dr. John Watkins, *ibid.*
6. "I fuckin' killed . . . " and ensuing conversation between Bianchi and Dr. Ralph Allison, PBS, *Frontline* and Ted Schwarz, pp. 170–175.
7. Conversation between Bianchi and Dr. Martin Orne, PBS, *Frontline.*
8. "Bianchi was almost . . . " *Time,* January 14, 1980.
9. "I can't find . . . " *State of Washington v. Kenneth A. Bianchi.* See also PBS, *Frontline.*

Reference

Schwarz, Ted, *The Hillside Strangler: A Murderer's Mind.* Garden City, New York: Doubleday, 1981.

27

Shame, Anger and the Social Bond: A Theory of Sexual Offenders and Treatment

Thomas J. Scheff
Suzanne M. Retzinger

There is a large literature on the causes of sexual assault and the treatment of sex offenders, summarized in Marshall et al. (1990) and Hall et al. (1993). Both summaries make it clear that there is no agreement on the causes of sexual assault, nor on its treatment: there is no theory that explains sexual assault, and no treatment that has been effective in treating sex offenders. Here we propose that the main reason for their inconclusiveness is that these studies have not dealt directly and extensively with relationships and emotion, which we take to the main elements in causation and cure. Instead, they focus on behavior, thoughts, and beliefs.

However, there is one reoccurring finding which involves the offender's emotions in an indirect way. Studies have repeatedly shown that sex offenders seek to humiliate their victims, as summarized in Darke (1990). Typically, the authors of these studies interpret the intent to humiliate as an interest in power. The theory of shame-rage loops, to be described below, suggests a more elaborate interpretation: being ashamed of themselves in general, assaultive men are also ashamed of their sexual desires. Experiencing women as haughty and rejecting, sex offenders reject the women they see as rejecting them. Feeling humiliated and powerless (a shame state), they humiliate and dominate in return. But since their shame is unacknowledged, it leads to shame-rage loops that produce compulsive violence against women.

Since unacknowledged shame is common among human beings, it is necessary to construct a more specific theory that formulates the elements that produce sexual aggression. As already indicated, one element is the inability to deal with recurring shame. To explicate that idea:

1. Sex offenders are hypothesized to be quick to take offense or feel insulted and humiliated.
2. They are unable to extricate themselves from continuous loops of shame.
3. For offenders, these loops do not take the form of being ashamed of being ashamed (shame-shame loops), which lead to withdrawal and passivity, but shame-anger, which lead to continuous *humiliated fury,* the emotional basis for contempt and hatred.
4. Finally, these men have no secure social bond to which they can turn to share their pent-up feelings; they are in the zero bond condition. This combination, continuous shame-anger loops and zero bonds, will produce either madness, suicide-homicide, or sexual assault. Since all of the elements in this formulation are counterintuitive, it will be necessary to review each in turn.

A Theory of Social Bonds

Since sexual assault often takes the form of gang rape (Dark 1990), one would assume that at least offenders in this category would have strong social bonds with their gang. But we propose that gang bonds are not secure, indicating true solidarity, but based on unquestioned loyalty to the gang and to its code of behavior. We argue that a social relationship can be so close and demanding as to be suffocating, and therefore not a secure bond, just as a relationship can be distant and rejecting, also not a secure bond. Gang members, by this definition, can be just as alienated as lone individuals are from others.

We believe that a secure bond strikes a balance between being too close (engulfment) and too far (isolation). Following Elias's (1987) idea of the "I-We" balance, the three states of the bond can be identified by the disposition of pronouns in discourse.

To give the idea of the I-We balance an empirical basis, language can be an indicator of the state of the social bond between two people, by focusing on the use of pronouns, particularly *I, you, we, and it*. The disposition of these pronouns within a sentence, and the relative weight accorded them, can be used as cues to three different states of the bond—solidarity, and the two opposite forms of alienation, isolation and engulfment. As discussed below, this analysis can be backed up with a study of emotion cues, showing how pride cues signal solidarity, and shame cues signal alienation.

Our approach draws upon and overlaps with Buber's (1958) discussion of I-thou, and many other formulations. What we call solidarity language, (I-I) corresponds exactly to his I-thou. What we call the language of isolation (I-you) corresponds exactly to his I-it. We use different terms because Buber, like most philosophers and social scientists, did not consider the other form of alienation, what Bowen (1978) called fusion (me-I). The idea of engulfment is centrally important in family systems theory (sometimes called enmeshment or fusion) but is absent elsewhere in the human sciences. Social scientists usually confound engulfment with solidarity. In engulfed relationships, one or both parties subordinate their own thoughts and feelings to those of the others(s). In solidarity, each party recognizes the sovereignty of the other, but balances respect for the other's position with respect for one's own.

Our use of I and me is quite different than Mead's (1934). His social psychology seems to assume perfect solidarity, without considering the possibility of alienation. In Mead's scheme, the me is made up of the internalized represen-

tation of the roles of others. For example, the citizen utilizing a criminal court is prepared by already knowing the role of the judge, the jury, the policeman, jailer, etc.

Mead didn't consider the accuracy with which each member of a society knows the roles of the other members. By ignoring this issue, he evades the issue of imperfect relationships, of alienation. Consider the doctor-patient relationship. Obviously the patient has only a superficial knowledge of the doctor's role, and superficiality of her knowledge can cause impediments to cooperation. For instance, since the patient understands very little of what the doctor knows of the relationship between the patient's illness and the medication that the doctor has prescribed for treatment, the patient might fail to follow the doctor's orders. The relationship is asymmetric in this way.

The relationship is also asymmetric the other way round. Although the patient has never learned the role of the doctor, the doctor should certainly know the role of the patient, since she has been a patient before becoming a doctor, and will continue to be a patient as a doctor. We would expect, therefore, that the doctor would understand patients. But as it turns out, there are impediments to such understanding. As part of their training, and as part of their management of their roles, many doctors seem to "forget" the patient's experience; they do not understand their patients, not because of lack of knowledge, but because of emotional barriers which doctors erect against them.

This process of forgetting also occurs in the teacher's role. Most teachers call very little upon their own role as students to guide their teaching. Rather their teaching seems to conform to the way other teachers teach. Once we have learned a body of knowledge, we seem to repress the difficulties we had in learning it, which erects a wall between us and our students. In the language we will use here, in our role as teachers, we are engulfed with other teachers, and isolated from our students. Bimodal alienation, as we call it, seems to be the most common form of social relationship in the modern world (Scheff and Retzinger, 1991; Scheff, 1994). In this format, individuals or groups are engulfed within, isolated without, as in sects, cults and academic schools of thought. In the social sciences it has been customary to refer to this system of relationships in terms of ethnocentrism, but this concept is imprecise and static.

The theoretical approach to social integration most similar to the one advocated here is found in Elias's (Introduction, 1987) discussion of the "I-self" (isolation) and the "we-self" (engulfment). Elias discusses the "I-we balance" (solidarity) in a way that is quite similar to our usage, but he doesn't apply it to actual instances. Elias proposed a three-part typology of what he called social figurations: independence (lack of cooperativeness because of too much social distance), interdependence (a balance between self and other that allows for effective cooperation), and dependence (lack of cooperativeness because of too little social distance). Although this typology grows out of Elias's long-standing commitment to the concept of interdependence, his attention was usually limited to this concept, rather than to the other two components of the typology. In this paper, we give equal theoretical and empirical weight to all three types.

The concept of the I-We balance is oriented largely to the verbal components of interaction, ignoring the nonverbal. An approach devised by Retzinger and I (Scheff and Retzinger, 1991; Scheff, 1994) is oriented to both verbal and nonverbal elements. We argue that the emotions of pride and shame are directly related to the state of social relationships, and can serve as indicators of the nature of that relation from moment to moment. In our scheme, pride is the emotional cognate of a secure, unalienated bond, and shame signals threat to the bond.

It would appear that careful analysis of the state of social relationships might require using both the I-We and the pride-shame approaches. The first is simpler, the second more subtle and complex, requiring use of a technique developed by Retzinger (1991) to identify cues to shame. The limitation to determining the I-We balance is that human beings often use language in a less than straightforward way, disguising their own motives and goals. Word choice is largely voluntary and intentional; we can easily hide our motives and goals in our verbal expressions. Since shame signals are, for the most part, stereotyped and out of awareness, the analysis of nonverbal cues can detect strains in relationships even when they are covert and hidden. The two

approaches can be used to complement each other in determining the state of the bond.

Elias's scheme comes closest to what seems to be needed, if we are to connect the micro and macro worlds. Many other theories are closely related to this scheme, but contain only two of the three types. Durkheim (1897), Doi (1971) and Seeman (1975) considered only the two forms of alienation that we are calling isolation and engulfment, but didn't relate them to the third, solidarity. Buber's typology contains isolation and solidarity, but not engulfment, as do Marx and Braithwaite (1989).

Braithwaite's theory of reintegrative shaming in crime control (1989), which he has applied to the practice of community "conferences" in Australia, excludes one of the types of alienation, engulfment. One case that we observed when consulting in Australia illustrates engulfment, rather than reintegrative shaming (solidarity) or stigmatization (isolation). The offender was an adult male in a case of driving under the influence, with three previous arrests on this charge. With the help of most of the other participants (except for the arresting officer), he successfully denied his responsibility. Even the facilitator, a male, colluded with his defense, that because of the extenuating circumstances in this instance, drinking a six-pack, apparently a norm among working class men, and driving was not morally wrong. Rather than being overshamed, often the case with juvenile offenders, this offender was undershamed, because of engulfment between him and most of the other participants in the conference. This outcome was unusual, in that the outcome of most of the conferences is closer to reintegrative shaming than to either engulfment or isolation (stigmatization).

All three types of relationships are implied in the work of Satir (1971), who contrasts defensive postures that we would call isolated (blaming, computing) or engulfed (placating, distracting) with what she calls leveling. By leveling she seems to have meant communication which is direct but respectful. Being direct without being respectful involves isolation, just as being respectful but not direct implies engulfment, as we use these terms here. Leveling involves balancing the claims of the individual with those of the relationship, an I-We balance as we have suggested.

The scheme proposed here suggests that most earlier discussions of social alienation and solidarity and related concepts are misleading, since they ignore one of the three types of relationships described above, or confound one with another. Most classic Western studies which compare Asian and Western societies seem to have valorized Western isolation and individualism by confounding it with solidarity based on rational outcomes (Durkheim's [1895] description of organic solidarity), as Markus and Kitayama (1991) have charged. But from the point of view proposed here, it seems likely that Markus and Kitayama have made an equal and opposite error, valorizing Asian (unity-based) societies by confounding engulfment with interdependence. A similar confusion seems to exist in classical studies of autonomy, which feminist scholarship has shown to be male oriented, or in Elias's terminology, oriented toward independence rather than interdependence. But again, most feminist scholarship may be making the equal and opposite error, confounding engulfment with interdependence or solidarity.

Shame as the Master Emotion

Because of limitations of the concept of shame in Western societies, it is difficult to convey the importance of shame dynamics for understanding both normal and pathological behavior. In earlier publications (Scheff 1990; Retzinger 1991; Scheff and Retzinger 1991; and Scheff 1994), we have argued that shame is subject to extensive repression in modern societies. This repression is both caused by and gives rise to rampant individualism.

These ideas are documented in Elias's magisterial study (1978; 1982; 1983) of the historical development of modern civilization in the West. Elias used excerpts from European advice manuals over the last five hundred years to show the gradual but implacable repression of shame. (For a detailed discussion of one of Elias's examples, 19th century advice to mothers on controlling their daughter's sexual knowledge

through shame, and *shame about shame,* see Scheff and Retzinger 1991, pp. 10–12.) The idea that one can be ashamed of being ashamed leads to the concept of continuous loops of shame, which is our explanation of the mechanism of repression.

One obvious indicator of repression is the difference between the treatment of shame in the languages of modern and traditional societies. In European languages, and especially in English, the concept of shame is extremely narrow, and extremely negative. In the English language shame has the meaning of disgrace and profound emotional pain. But in other European languages, there is both a shame of disgrace (as in the French *honte*), and a positive, everyday shame (as in the French *pudeur*), which refers to modesty, shyness, and (at least in classic Greek) awe. The possibility that there was once a positive shame in English is suggested by the word *humility* (because of its relation to humiliation), but humility has lost its relationship to shame in modern English.

The narrowness and negativeness of the concept of shame in modern societies is still more strongly suggested by comparison with the shame lexicon in the languages of traditional societies. It has been shown that the shame lexicon in Mandarin Chinese is much larger than those of modern societies (Shaver et al. 1992). The Mandarin emotion lexicon also contains a large number of shame-anger combinations unknown in English, but parallel to the Scheff-Retzinger usage (see below). The shame lexicon is rich in traditional societies because its members are sensitive to social relationships, requiring awareness of shame and embarrassment, as contrasted with the individualism of modern societies. The small and narrow lexicon of shame in Western languages, especially English, suggests that most forms of shame are being overlooked or avoided.

In order to understand shame dynamics, it is necessary to recover the positive facets of shame, and to recover the breadth of the shame concept from the maws of repression and silence. The positive aspects of shame have been explored by Lynd (1958), Tompkins (1963, V. 2) and in great detail, by Schneider (1977). Here is a representative statement (Lynd 1958,

p. 66): "The very fact that shame is an isolating experience also means that if one can find ways of sharing and communicating it, this communication can bring about particular closeness with others. . . ." The idea expressed in this passage is crucially significant for our theory of treatment: if the offender can come to the point of "sharing and communicating" his shame *instead of hiding or denying it,* the damaged personality of the offender can begin to be repaired.

Recovering the actual breadth of the shame concept is also of crucial importance for repairing the damaged bond between the offender and others, because shame is a Protean presence among all of the relevant parties. The offender will be ashamed because he has been publicly condemned for wrongdoing. The offender's supporters will be ashamed because of their relationship to him. The victim will be ashamed in the sense of feeling betrayed, violated, and/or impotent. The victim's supporters, in so far as they identify with her, will share this kind of shame. The public at large will be inclined to shame or humiliate the offender, seeking not only justice but also, in some cases, revenge.

So long as shame is disguised and denied, it inhibits the participants from repairing the bonds between them. The vast domain of shame was discovered in modern psychology by Helen B. Lewis, a psychoanalyst and research psychologist. In her ground-breaking study (1971) she found shame to be omnipresent but almost never mentioned in psychotherapy sessions. Instead it was ignored, disguised, or denied. The sociologist Goffman (1967) implied that shame (he called it embarrassment), actual or anticipated, was a haunting presence in all human contact, not just in psychotherapy. According to Goffman, social relationships are haunted not just by actual embarrassment, but much more frequently, by the anticipation of embarrassment. Retzinger (1991) has developed a systematic procedure for identifying anger, shame and embarrassment, no matter how hidden or disguised, by reference to visual, verbal, and nonverbal cues. Members of modern societies require retraining in shame language, especially the language of gesture and innuendo, in order to become aware of shame in themselves and others.

In our earlier articles and books (Scheff 1990; Retzinger 1991; Scheff and Retzinger 1991; Scheff 1994), we have treated shame as a large family of emotions and affects, drawing upon the work of Lynd (1958), Tomkins (1963), Goffman (1967), Lewis (1971) and many others. Our definition includes the positive aspects of shame, such as what Schneider called "a sense of shame," as well as embarrassment, humiliation, shyness, modesty, and feelings of discomfort, awkwardness, inadequacy, rejection, insecurity and lack of confidence. In our usage, we give particular emphasis to shame/anger sequences, as in Mandarin Chinese. Our concept is much, much broader than the way shame is used in vernacular English. We have reason to believe that our definition of shame recovers the broadness of the concept that is in use in traditional societies.

The most detailed treatment of shame in traditional societies can be found in a discussion of *whakamaa,* the conception of shame in Maori society (Metge 1986). According to this study, whakamaa means shy, embarrassed, uncertain, inadequate, incapable, afraid, hurt, depressed, or ashamed (pp. 28–29). Only the inclusion of afraid (fear) would seem to differ from our usage. But the examples that Metge uses for afraid suggest not the emotion of fear (danger to life or limb), but social fear, that is, anticipation of shame. As in our usage, whakamaa concerns not only feelings, but also relationships. Maori usage, like ours, also stresses the importance of acknowledging shame, and the disruptive consequences when shame is not acknowledged. Although we did not know about whakamaa when we developed our conception of shame, it is exactly parallel to Maori usage.

Most traditional societies, like the Maoris, have a subtle and wide-ranging language of emotions and relationships which we in the West have lost. The understanding of shame in its positive, broad, and relational sense might be a crucial issue in understanding the causation and treatment of sex offenders.

A theoretical issue of great importance for this article is the difference between pathological and normal shame. Like Braithwaite (1989), we think that effective crime control requires normal (re-integrative) rather than pathological shame. By paying close attention to the particular way shame is manifested, it is possible to distinguish, moment by moment, between the two forms of shame as they occur in social interaction.

According to our theory, manifestations of normal shame, although unpleasant, are BRIEF, as little as a few seconds. Shame, anger, and other related emotions which persist for many minutes are pathological. We propose that shame is a highly reflexive emotion, which can give rise to long-lasting feedback loops of shame: one can be ashamed of being ashamed, and so on, around the loop, resulting in withdrawal or depression. Another loop is being angry that one is ashamed, and ashamed that one is angry, and so on around the loop. Furthermore, shame-anger loops can occur between, as well as within, participants. Indignation can be contagious, resulting in mutual and counter-indignation. Both individual and social emotional loops can last indefinitely. Persistent, relentless emotions such as continuing embarrassment, indignation, resentment and hatred are always pathological.

Finally, we argue that shame plays a crucial role in normal cooperative relationships, as well as in conflict. We show that shame signals a threat to the social bond, and is therefore vital in establishing where one stands in a relationship. Similarly, pride signals a secure bond. Shame is the emotional cognate of a threatened or damaged bond, just as threatened bonds are the source of shame. This equation allows one to translate shame language into relationship language, and vice versa.

If, as Goffman (1967) and others have argued, normal shame and embarrassment are an almost continuous part of all human contact, we can see why the visible expression of shame by the offender looms so large in symbolic reparation. When we see signs of shame and embarrassment in others, we are able to recognize them as human beings like ourselves, no matter the language, cultural setting, or context. The central role of shame in human contact has long been recognized in the scientific-humanist tradition, as expressed by Darwin, Nietzsche, Sartre, and many others. We think that the difficulty in overcoming the Western views of

shame is the principle impediment to success in understanding and treating sex offenders.

The Theory of Shame-Rage Loops

In her study of shame in psychotherapy, Lewis (1971) uncovered a mechanism linking unacknowledged shame to anger and verbal aggression. Using hundreds of transcripts of psychotherapy sessions, she applied the Gottschalk-Glaser scale (1969) to the words in each transcript for emotions. Although her study yielded other emotions such as grief and fear, the only pattern she found to repeat itself in all sessions was shame followed by anger and aggression. When a patient felt distant from, rejected or criticized by the therapist, or inadequate, rather than mentioning the feeling (shame or embarrassment), the patient would either withdraw or show anger toward the therapist. Since the shame that was elicited by the coding procedure was seldom explicitly mentioned by the patient or the therapist, Lewis called it *unacknowledged* shame.

Lewis proposed that the patient's shame could take three principal routes. It could be discharged harmlessly through discussion or laughter, it could lead to withdrawal or termination of therapy, or it could lead to verbal aggression (Lewis 1987). Because of this last route, Lewis suggested that there is a strong affinity between shame and anger.

In her study of marital quarrels, Retzinger (1991) investigated the affinity between shame and anger reported by Lewis. Using the Gottman (1979) method for eliciting quarrels, Retzinger analyzed the emotions in videotapes of four marital quarrels. She found that unacknowledged shame always preceded anger in the 16 escalations of the quarrels she studied, confirming Lewis's earlier study.

On the basis of the Lewis, Retzinger, and other studies, Scheff and Retzinger (1991) proposed a theory of shame/rage loops leading to verbal or physical violence. We suggested that when shame is not acknowledged and discharged, it refuses to subside; one can be ashamed of being ashamed, and so on, a shame-shame loop, which leads to withdrawal. But an alternative route is a shame/anger loop: one can be angry one is ashamed, and ashamed that one is angry. This is the loop which occurred most frequently in Lewis's (1971) and in Retzinger's (1991) studies. Tracing back from anger or angry escalation, these studies invariably found an incident of unacknowledged shame.

The idea of emotion loops provides new meaning to the familiar idea that pathological emotions are reactive, rather than being primary emotions (Greenberg and Safran 1987). Most theories of emotions in psychotherapy have long suggested that anger is usually not the primary emotion in quarrels, but is a reaction to some other emotion. Such theories, however, have not been specific about the name of the underlying primary emotion, referring to it by a generic name like "hurt." In our theory we propose that the major component in "hurt" is shame, that is, feelings of rejection and/or inadequacy. Nor have earlier theories specified the mechanism relating primary and reactive emotions, or pointed to empirical indicators. This article seeks to fill in these missing elements.

Drawing upon her findings, Lewis (1971; 1976; 1987) devised a type of shame therapy. When she detected anger toward herself, she encouraged the patient to first acknowledge their anger, then trace back from it to see if they could find a moment of shame or humiliation. Her patients discovered that instead of revealing their feelings of inadequacy or humiliation, they were instead masking them by verbally attacking the therapist or withdrawing. Apparently feelings of humiliation, even in therapy, are so painful that they are usually not revealed, even to self. Instead the humiliated person often seeks to humiliate the person who they feel humiliated them: *humiliation leads to counter-humiliation.*

The humiliation–counter-humiliation sequence is well known in the world of everyday life. Most sports coaches, for example, seem aware of it. When one's team is winning by a large margin, the knowing coach will substitute heavily, not only to give the second and third teams practice, but also to avoid, if possible, "rubbing in" the defeat to the point that the other coach plots revenge. The defeated coach may experience an overwhelming defeat as an insult, and vow to insult the other coach in return, giving rise to shame/anger sequence within and between the coaches. Shame/anger loops may also be the emotional basis for institutionalized conflict between individuals and between groups, as in duels, feuds, vendettas, and wars (Scheff and Retzinger 1991; Scheff 1994).

Causation of Sexual Assault: A Theory

To understand the role of shame in sexual assault, it will be necessary to briefly review relevant aspects of the shame literature. One major finding of gender differences in emotionality involves studies of what has come to be called "field dependence and independence" (For a summary of some of the findings selected from a very large corpus, see Wapner and Demick 1991). It was Lewis (1971; 1976) who called attention to emotional elements in what until then had been construed as a perceptual phenomenon.

The concept of field dependence grew out of the work on conformity by Asch and others. Persons who yielded to group opinion in making perceptual judgments (such as lengths of lines) were said to be field dependent. Those who did not yield, field independent. Lewis (1971; 1976) showed a correlation between field dependence and the experience of shame. Those who were field dependent also showed an inclination toward a certain type of shame, which Lewis called overt, undifferentiated shame. This type of shame involves the experience of emotional pain and unwanted bodily symptoms, such as sweating, blushing and rapid heartbeat. This type corresponds to the vernacular meaning of a shame experience, which is painful, visible, and conscious.

But in the same study (Lewis 1971) also uncovered a different, less overt type of shame, which she called *bypassed*. This type is completely outside of awareness, but is indicated by repetitive, obsessive thoughts and rapid, slightly off-key speech. Lewis identified this emotion as shame because it occurred in the kind of context which sometimes resulted in overt shame, the patient experiencing the therapist as distant, critical, or rejecting.

Lewis showed that bypassed shame was characteristic of persons who were field independent. The relevance to this article is that she and others also showed a strong relationship between gender and field dependence: women strongly tend toward field dependence, men toward field independence. If, as Lewis's studies suggest, men tend toward bypassed shame, women toward overt shame, these findings would have implications for differences in male and female sexual shame.

The concepts of overt and bypassed shame correspond closely to central aspects of Adler's (1956) theory of personality. Adler thought that if children were denied love during critical stages of maturation, they would develop either one of two types of adult personality. The first type he called the inferiority complex, which seems to be an exact parallel to what we would call chronic overt shame. The second direction he called the drive for power, which parallels what we are calling bypassed shame. His whole theory implies a shame dynamic, since we expect that children to whom love was denied would suffer from feelings of rejection (shame).

In the language of our theory, overt shame is correlated with shame-shame loops, of being ashamed of being ashamed. This idea is exemplified by shy people who blush: when they become aware they are blushing, they experienced a self-perpetuating self-consciousness: they are ashamed of being ashamed, and so on. Since women tend more than men to experience shame in the overt mode, we would expect to find women tending toward shame-shame loops more than men. This loop is associated with passivity, shyness or withdrawal. Real or imagined distance, criticism or rejection by men may be expected, therefore, to lead to passivity or withdrawal in shame-prone women.

Men are more likely than women to experience shame in the bypassed mode. This mode is much less available to consciousness than the overt mode, and associated with shame-anger loops. Men may bypass the painful experience of shame by becoming angry. But they are ashamed of their anger (in the bypassed mode), and angry that they are ashamed, and so on. Unacknowledged shame in this mode gives rise to what Lewis (1971) called "humiliated fury."

Male and Female Sexual Shame

Although there are few empirical studies, we will assume that shame about sexuality is quite prevalent in modern societies, and that it is particularly obvious in adolescents and young adults. In his study of the civilizing process, Elias (1978; 1982) used excerpts from European advice and etiquette manuals from the 12th through the 19th centuries to show that there has been a rapidly accelerating rise in shame in many areas of life, especially shame about the body, emotions, and violence. He specifically points to sexuality as one of the areas of increasing shame (1978, pp. 169–190). It seems clear that virtually all children in modern societies learn to be embarrassed and ashamed about their bodies and body functions, including their sexuality. What happens to their sexual shame as they grow to adults?

Again following Elias's lead, we propose that sexual shame does not disappear for most adults, but goes underground. Elias (1978, pp. 180–181) suggests that women are especially shamed into silence about their sexuality. Contrary to Elias, who did not have the concept of bypassed shame available to him at the time he wrote (the original text was written in 1939), we argue that most adults continue to be ashamed of their sexuality, but that men and women manage their shame differently. The theory of shame loops, in conjunction with the studies of gender differences described above, suggests that there should be a substantial difference between the way in which men and women experience shame about sexuality.

Our theory would help to explain differences in male and female sexuality. If women tend toward shame-shame loops in reaction to their shame about sexuality, this process would explain the direction that sexuality often takes with women: lack of sexual interest, withdrawal, passivity, or late-blooming interest, since shame-shame loops lead to silence and withdrawal.

Shame about sexuality would lead men in a different direction, however. Since shame-anger loops are associated with the way in which men tend to manage shame, through bypassing (denial, which, in psychoanalytic terms, leads to a reaction formation), we would expect male sexual shame to lead to boldness, anger and aggression. The shame-anger loop can be seen as the emotional basis of machismo, the hyper-masculinity that is explicitly named in Spanish-speaking societies, but is prevalent in most current and past cultures. To the extent that male shame is bypassed in any society, we would expect a generalized shame-proneness, manifested by sensitivity to insults, real or imagined, hostility and aggressiveness. Although counter-intuitive, the theory of shame loops provides a testable theory of male aggressiveness, which posits that machismo rests upon personal and social insecurity, which translated into our language, means shame-proneness.

There is some indirect evidence that links sex offenses with insecurity (shame) about one's masculinity. This evidence comes from a series of studies of the self-esteem of sex offenders. Before discussing it, some comments are needed concerning the measurement of self-esteem.

The measure that comes nearest to uncovering emotions are self-esteem scales. It seems likely that high self-esteem is based on persistent pride in self, and low self-esteem, on persistent shame. But these scales do not take into account the subject's defenses against their emotions (Scheff et al. 1989). All self-esteem scales confound exaggerated confidence in self as a defense against shame, with true self-respect.

There is one series of studies of rapists which strongly supports this inference (Marshall and Marshall 1981; Marshall and Turner 1985; and Lawson et al. 1979). In their investigation of the self-esteem level of rapists, these studies found that most of them scored either very low or very high. But these investigators then took a step that is quite unusual in self-esteem studies, they sought external corroboration of self-esteem levels from persons who knew the subjects.

For those rapists who scored well above the mean of non-offenders, we had prison staff who were acquainted with them provide their evaluations of the offenders using the same scale. These staff reported that high-scoring offenders were low in self-esteem, but compensated for that with a bravado style that reflected hyperidentification with the traditional male role (Lawson, et al. 1979)

This study suggests support for our argument, that the most powerful component of self-esteem is shame and pride, and that existing self-esteem scales confound exaggerated self-confidence with pride. The exaggerated masculinity and aggressiveness of sex offenders may be produced by unacknowledged shame.

A Theory of the Cause and Treatment of Sex Offenders

The discussion above leads to the following propositions:

1. The compulsion to assault women is a product of unacknowledged shame about sexuality, which has taken the path of shame-rage loops. Men, much more than women, tend to bypass their shame, making it less accessible to consciousness. Bypassed shamed about sexuality is the hidden cause of sexual compulsions.

2. A treatment procedure based on this theory would seek to interrupt hidden shame cycles, bring them into consciousness, and to teach social skills which would avert the generation of new shame.

1. **Uncovering hidden shame.** As already indicated above, the technique that Lewis (1971; 1977; 1987) used to uncover shame in psychotherapy was to first note the occurrence of anger and hostility, no matter how subtle, toward herself, the therapist. She then encouraged the client to first acknowledge the hostility, then trace it back to earlier events. Invariably she found that the patient had experienced feelings

of rejection or inadequacy earlier, which were expressed, however, as hostility. (This mechanism may lead to male hostility to women, discussed above: the man feels rejected by women, does not acknowledge this feeling, but rejects them in retaliation). Lewis then helped the client to explore the feeling of shame or embarrassment verbally, leading to the uncovering and discharge of shame.

2. The latter step, the actual experiencing of shame during verbal discussions of it, requires the most effort on the part of the client and therapist. Detection of hostility by the therapist is straightforward. The client usually needs to learn to trace back from anger to shame, requiring patience from both participants, but most clients learn the skill. Finding and experiencing the client's actual feeling of shame through discussion may require considerable cooperation between patient and therapist. (For other approaches to shame therapy, see Broucek 1991; Goldberg 1991; Kaufman 1980; and Wurmser 1981).

3. To apply the type of shame therapy developed by Lewis to male sex offenders, it would probably be focused on their unacknowledged shame in general, as well as the emotions aroused by the client's sexuality, and by women. If a man feels ashamed of his sexuality and/or rejected by, or inadequate with, women, but does not acknowledge these feelings even to himself, a likely outcome is the kind of hostility toward women that can lead to assault. If the buried feelings of sexual rejection or inadequacy can be uncovered in therapy, they can be experienced and discharged.

4. **Communication skills.** If the theory outlined here is correct, sex offenders need to learn new skills in communicating with others, particularly women. Friction in close relationships is unavoidable, including feelings of inadequacy and/or rejection. Learning to level (Satir 1972), to be direct but respectful, with others, particularly with women, can forestall the creation of new shame and hostility, by teaching offenders to acknowledge shame, rather than denial.

Summary

This article proposes a new theory and treatment of male sexual violence, which focuses on a new idea, that hyperidentification with masculinity is based on carefully hidden shame and insecurity, rather than on true self-respect. The theory leads to a type of treatment for sex offenders leading to the uncovering of repressed shame, and learning of communication techniques which decrease the arousal of shame.

References

Adler, A. 1956. *The Individual Psychology of Alfred Adler.* New York: Basic Books.

Bowen, M. 1978. *Family Therapy in Clinical Practice.* New York: J. Aronson.

Bowen, M. and M. Kerr. 1988. *Family Evaluation.* New York: Norton.

Braithwaite, J. 1989. *Crime, Shame and Reintegration.* Cambridge: Cambridge U. Press.

Broucek, F. 1991. *Shame and the Self.* New York: Guilford.

Buber, M. 1958. *I-Thou.* New York: Scribners.

Darke, J. 1990. Sexual Aggression: Achieving Power through Humiliation. Pp. 55–72 in W. L. Marshall et al. (Eds.), *Handbook of Sexual Assault.* New York: Plenum.

Doi. T. 1971. *The Anatomy of Dependence.* Tokyo: Kodansha International.

Durkheim, E. 1895. *Rules of Sociological Method.* London: Macmillan. (1982).

———. 1897. *Suicide.* London: Routledge (1952).

Elias, N. 1978. *The History of Manners.* New York: Vintage.

———. 1982. *Power and Civility.* New York: Vintage.

———. 1987. *Involvement and Detachment.* Oxford: Blackwell.

Goldberg, C. 1991. *Understanding Shame: Theoretical and Clinical Implications.* New York: Jason Aronson.

Goffman, Erving. 1967. *Interaction Ritual.* New York: Anchor.

Gottman, J. 1979. *Marital Interaction* New York: Academic Press.

Gottschalk, L. and G. Gleser. 1969. *Manual for the Gottschalk-Gleser Scales.* Berkeley: U. of California Press.

Hall, G. C., R. Hirschman, J. Graham, and M. Zaragoza. 1993. *Sexual Aggression*. Washington, D.C.: Taylor and Francis.

Kaufman, G. 1989. *The Psychology of Shame: Theory and Treatment of Shame-based Syndromes*. New York: Springer.

Lawson, J. S., W. L. Marshall, and P. McGrath. 1979. The Social Self-Esteem Inventory. *Educational and Psychological Measurement* 39: 803–811.

Lewis, H. 1971. *Shame and Guilt in Neurosis*. New York: International Universities Press.

———. 1976. *Psychic War in Men and Women*. New York: NYU Press.

———. 1987. *The Role of Shame in Symptom Formation*. Hillsdale: LEA.

Lynd, Helen. 1958. *On Shame and the Search for Identity*. New York: Harcourt; New York: Plenum.

Markus, H. and S. Kitayama. 1991. Culture and the self: implications for cognition, emotion, and motivation. *Psychological Review* 98: 224–253.

Marshall, W. L., D. Laws, and H. Barbabee. 1989. *Handbook of Sexual Assault*. New York: Plenum.

Marshall, W. L. and P. Marshall. 1981. *Social Functioning in Penitentiary Inmates*. Unpublished MS.

Marshall, W. L. and B. Turner. 1985. *Life Skills Training in Penitentiary Inmates in Canada*. Report to the Solicitor General of Canada, Ottawa.

Mead, G. H. 1934. *Mind, Self and Society*. Chicago: U. of Chicago Press.

Metge, Joan. 1986. *In and Out of Touch: Whakamaa in Cross Cultural Perspective*. Wellington: Victoria U. Press.

Retzinger, S. 1991. *Violent Emotions*. Newbury Park: Sage.

Satir, V. 1971. *Peoplemaking*. Palo Alto: Science and Behavior Books.

Scheff, T. 1990. *Microsociology*. Chicago: U. of Chicago Press.

———. 1994. *Bloody Revenge*. Boulder: Westview Press.

Scheff, T. and S. Retzinger. 1991. *Emotions and Violence*. Lexington: Lexington Books.

Scheff, T., S. Retzinger, and M. Ryan. 1989. Crime, Violence and Self-Esteem. In A. Mecca, N. Smelser, and J. Vasconcellos (Eds.). *The Social Importance of Self-Esteem*. Berkeley: U. of California Press.

Schneider, Carl. 1977. *Shame, Exposure, and Privacy*. Boston: Beacon Press.

Seeman, M. 1975. Alienation Studies. *Annual Review of Sociology* 1:91–124.

Shaver, Philip, et al. 1992. Cross-cultural similarities and differences in emotions. In M. Clark (Ed.), *Review of Personality and Social Psychology* 13: 175–212.

Tomkins, Silvan. 1963. *Affect, Imagery, Consciousness, V. 2*. New York: Springer.

Wapner, S. and J. Demick. 1991. *Field Dependence-Independence: Cognitive Style Across the Life Span*. Hillsdale: LEA.

Wurmser, L. 1981. *The Mask of Shame*. Baltimore: Johns Hopkins U. Press.

28

The American Bandit

James A. Inciardi

Reflections on the general nature of professional "heavy" crime have tended to be limited and arbitrary. The specific criminal patterns of this behavior system have seemingly eluded ordering into any concise theoretical structure. The parameters of professional "heavy" crime have emerged on continuums, in combination or close proximity with numerous alternative levels of criminality, or in variable and overlapping contexts. These are reflected in the works of many criminologists. Although the ideal concept for professional "heavy" crime will probably not be attained here, a basis for the application and use of this label, as well as an analysis of the subsumed orders of behavior, are offered.

As contrasted with professional theft, "heavy" crime employs the skillful and proficient use of coercion, force, and the threat of violence. Typically, organization and planning occur prior to the commission of offenses, and the elements of speed and surprise are introduced for reducing the risk of apprehension. The participants are economically motivated, and pursue their activities in an occupational or career frame of reference, with socialization into and professionalization within their world of crime normally occurring through a differential association process. Organization and cooperation in the effective execution of crimes are bounded by a limited group of individuals. Although "lone-wolf" operators are indigenous to the profession, the majority of efforts are group oriented.

Unlike that of the traditional professional thieves, the label of *professional heavy crime* was not of ingroup origin. Rather, it emerged through the combined enterprises of the underworld and the upperworld. *Heavy* appears throughout both early and later professional criminal and hobo argots, referring to *that which is dangerous and risky or involves force or violence.* Since 1925, *heavy* has carried the connotation of *tough* in popular slang usage; by 1930 the term had begun to fall into disuse within the underworld. References to the "heavy" as a "professional" do not appear in criminals' human documents; by contrast, professional thieves view "heavy" behavior as that of the amateur. That the "heavy" was a "professional" seemingly emerged within the discipline of criminology on the part of theorists who recognized the unique stature of the "professional thief," yet wished to highlight the expertise and occupational context of specific aggressive behavior. As such the term was useful only to the extent that it delineated the full range of one diverse field.

The history of crime suggests that central to a conceptualization of professional "heavy" crime is the notion of *banditry.* In its purest form, banditry is the practice of marauding by organized or semiorganized groups. It emerges on the frontiers of organized society, and is characteristic of segments of the outcast or oppressed. Methods are highly visible and pitiless, while goal orientations are occupational and economic. Banditry endures until such time as its effective arena is encroached upon by civilization, and is suppressed or dispersed when the advancing society can no longer contain it. The specific action patterns of banditry vary, as the "frontier" or "civilization" varies; implicit in the closing of old frontiers is the emergence or expansion of newer ones.

Banditry, or professional "heavy" crime, is tangibly manifest in piracy in the grand manner of Blackbeard and Henry Morgan. Piracy was banditry on a maritime frontier. After the Spanish discovery of America in 1492, the West Indies became a frontier of Europe and remained

From "Professional 'Heavy' Crime . . . Notes on the Career of the American Bandit," pp. 85–101 in *Careers in Crime,* by James A. Inciardi (Rand McNally College Publishing Co. 1975). Reprinted by permission.

so for some three hundred years. The buccaneers and pirates of the Caribbean were the counterparts of the notorious highwaymen of seventeenth- and eighteenth-century England, the desperados of the American West, the public enemies of the depression-ridden 1930s, and the billion-dollar cargo hijackers of the contemporary era. Each had its own unique frontier, miscreant population, and intruding civilization, yet common to all were patterns of social change that defined the context of their genesis, rise, and decline.[1]

Piracy

Piracy emerged in the Western Hemisphere in response to a unique interaction of many natural and social events. The voyages of Columbus provided Spain with an early start in seeking the treasures of the New World. The ensuing territorial conquests gave that nation an almost total claim on the Americas, as well as the financial strength to construct the most powerful navy in Europe. France and England became allied against this domination, and the growing hostilities were further stimulated by a Spanish colonial policy prohibiting non-Spanish traders in Spanish America. Trade, with cargoes often in excess of $100 million per ship, found a natural right-of-way through the Caribbean, made highly navigable by the Gulf Stream currents, prevailing winds, and sheltering islands of the West Indies.[2]

The topography of these islands was well suited for piracy. Located along the heavily traveled Gulf Stream routes, the islands provided landside strongholds close to the illicit maritime ventures. The endless number of coves offered natural opportunities for ambush, and with only scattered habitation and development, these marine bandits could swiftly retreat to the security and sanctuary of unobserved seclusion.

During the seventeenth and eighteenth centuries the West Indies became a repository for the transported convict and the social, political, economic, and religious displacements from Great Britain, France, and Spain, and a sanctuary for the runaway indenture and the unemployed "free willer" who had sold himself under an indenture agreement. The island of Tortuga off the coast of Haiti was well situated for the fugitive sailors from the wreck of *La Rochelle,* for groups of exiled French Calvinists already embittered by Spanish religious persecution, and for the English, French, and Dutch sea tramps who had been denied entry to the Spanish colonies. Finally, the Treaty of Utrecht in 1713, which put an end to the War of the Spanish Succession, pushed throngs of vagrant sailors from the disbanded fighting fleets into the seaport towns of the Indies.

The grand era of piracy began in 1714 when Captain Henry Jennings and three hundred seamen descended upon the salvage crew of a grounded Spanish galleon, looting the vessel of some three hundred thousand pieces of eight. News of the event proved inspirational to the social pariah and displaced mariner on the Caribbean waterfronts, and ships were seized, manned, and turned pirate. The initial efforts of these seafaring robbers focused on the highly loathed Spanish, but in time their armed plunder recognized few national differences.

The decline of piracy began with the march of civilization into the maritime frontier in the West Indies. The peace of Utrecht brought only a brief armistice, followed by almost uninterrupted warfare in the following century. England fought with France and Spain for supremacy of the seas, including the West Indies. The vagrant seamen, who had manned the colors of the *Jolly Roger,* dwindled as the Royal Navy employed inducements and press-gangs for meeting the growing need for crew. Individual pirate vessels represented only minimal opposition to the newer wartime fleets, and naval maneuvers were often subjoined with penetrating amphibious operations. With a final British victory in the West Indies, new legal codes and sanctions were adopted to reduce the existing violence and corruption of the islands' drunken and brawling youth, thus making systematic colonization more attractive.

Thus, piracy was maintained only to the extent that the maritime frontier endured. The West Indies had been the fountainhead of the pirates who vexed shipping not only in the Caribbean, but in the seas surrounding Africa, India, and the East as well. As the source diminished and the frontier was transformed, piracy died in the waters of both hemispheres.

...from Jesse James to John Dillinger

"Heavy" crime as it existed a century ago can be conceptualized as a composite of natural and social events generating temporally concurrent and operationally similar offense patterns. The outlaws of the American West—the organized groups of cattle thieves and rustlers, the bank bandits, and the train and stage robbers— emerged from a common nexus, were stimulated by a shared ethos, and pursued parallel criminal careers. They grew in part from discontinuity and rebellion in an expanding nation disorganized by a civil war, and in part from the pioneer spirit of the frontier, one both attracting and engendering strength, self-sufficiency, and rugged individualism.

The Frontier West

The American frontier was Elizabethan in its quality—simple, childlike, and savage. It was a land of wilderness to be approached afoot, on horseback, in barges, or by wagon by only the most durable with a readiness for adventure. It was a land of riches where swift and easy fortunes were sought by the crude, the lawless, and the aggressive, and where written law lacked form and cohesion.

The professional outlaws emerged during the period following the surrender at Appomattox in 1865. Many were Union and Confederate veterans who wandered the country as penniless vagabonds searching for excitement. Many of them drifted to the Southwest when Congress opened millions of acres there for settlement and development. In these free lands were herds of cattle, left untended and free to roam during the war years. Much of this stock was also unbranded, proof of ownership was practically impossible, and "possession was nine points of the law." Branding these mavericks provided a natural opportunity for rapid economic security for the newly arrived homesteader, as it was considered legitimate cow hunting.

But there were those who claimed a prior right to this public domain in Texas, Oklahoma, and Wyoming, which had been staked by them decades before the war. Their relentless and violent persecution of the homesteader and small rancher made cattlemen in general the common enemy of many settlers, and the mavericking of random steers evolved into rustling as an organized business. To this new collective of frontier predators were added the miscreant soldiers of fortune—the thieves, prostitutes, and whiskey peddlers—who sought refuge in the territory west of Fort Smith, Arkansas. This seventy-four-thousand square miles of Indian country from Texas and Kansas to Colorado had "rights of sanctuary," for there was no court or formal law under which a fugitive could be extradited.

Surpassing the efforts of the cattle thieves and adding to professional organized banditry were the robbers of stage, train, and bank. The first "regular" stagecoach service in the West began during the autumn of 1849 in California; it became a recognized mode of travel soon after the first Concord coach was brought by clipper ship around Cape Horn to San Francisco in 1850. Although stagecoach robbery began in 1852, its boldest exploits occurred during the 1870s. Stagecoach robbery became a regular trade during that decade in California, Wyoming, Montana, and the Dakotas, made profitable by the gold dust and moneyed investors carried through mountainous and secluded mining regions.[3]

The Great Train Robberies

Train robbery began on October 6, 1866 when John and Simeon Reno took $13,000 from the safe aboard an Ohio & Mississippi Railway express car near Seymour, Indiana. The Renos were seemingly the founders of this typically American institution, which endured for nearly a half century. Following the Reno gang, train robbery spread to Missouri and Nevada in 1870, and flourished during that decade.[4]

Jesse Woodson James was among the more celebrated of the train robbers. He was a product of the hardships and embitterment of the Civil War and the Kansas-Missouri border wars, and began his outlaw career as a bank robber with the aid of Cole, Jim, John, and Bob Younger. Jesse and his troupe became known nationally on July 21, 1873 with the holdup of a Chicago, Rock Island & Pacific train near Adair, Iowa. Their estimated $4,000 theft was small when contrasted with other efforts of the period, but the James-Younger technique of wrecking the train prior to its robbery made a new and daring contribution to outlawry.

In general, few lines of demarcation separated the train robbers from the bank bandits of the post–Civil War decades, for the same individuals invariably pursued both avenues of theft. Yet, while organized posses of lawmen and townspeople actively pursued the bank bandits, making their work risky, train robbery survived with only limited opposition. Country sidings were often secluded and unsecured, but there was also a widespread apathy toward the railroad industry. Building of the railroad networks in the eastern United States started in the 1830s, and a total of 35,085 miles of track had been laid by 1865. At the close of the Civil War, however, only 3,272 track-miles traversed all of the trans-Mississippi West, and it was not until late in the Reconstruction Era that railroad transportation began to play a significant role in Western expansion.

Bitterness and hatred for the railroads reached its peak in the late 1860s, resulting from the policies of the Southern Pacific, combined with conflicts over the Kansas land grants from 1854 to 1890. The Southern Pacific had induced settlers to invest in and develop the areas proposed for its route; later it disclaimed these settlers' legal title to their lands. The settlers also claimed that many companies bypassed prosperous communities as a penalty for not cooperating with the railroad's objectives. Federal land policies, furthermore, allowed many companies to grab millions of acres, which they then sold at exorbitant prices. Finally, political and advertising patronage enabled the railroads to engage in rate discrimination and monopolistic practices.

Farmers, laborers, and other settlers felt cheated in land deals, freight rates, and wildcat stocks and bonds, and worried little when others preyed on the railroads. Thus, criminals in the tradition of Jesse and Frank James and the Younger brothers continued to operate with what, in retrospect, appeared to have been comparative ease and safety. Indeed, the James-Younger gang and others, such as Chris Evans, John Sontag, Bill Doolin, the Dalton brothers,

Sam Bass, Black Bart, and Henry Starr, became celebrated heroes.

Outlaw Sanctuaries

Folklore often depicts the bandits of the American West as ribald, hysterical, and contorted humans in a playground of idle masculinity. The outlaw followed little of this tradition. Rather, rustlers and robbers were the functionaries of a highly developed business made profitable by the skillful use of their natural and social environments. The successful planning and execution of their crimes were made possible by the topography of confusing ranges of high mountains, segmented by wide deserts, and creviced with inaccessible canyons. An intimate knowledge of the dim trails and widely spaced waterholes that bridged the wilderness from Mexico to Canada defined the boundaries of an impregnable area.[5]

This domain, spanning five states and intersecting the borders of three nations, was known as the *Outlaw Trail* (Figure 1). Positionally significant along the trail was *Brown's Hole,* an inaccessible mountain-walled valley lying partially in the states of Utah, Colorado, and Wyoming. It offered security and sanctuary since any attempt to capture a fugitive or recover stolen stock would require the unlikely cooperation of officers from three adjoining states. Brown's Hole was the headquarters for most of the cattle and horse thieves in Utah and Wyoming, including the legendary Butch Cassidy and the Wild Bunch. It had its own routine, social life, and codes of conduct, with permanent settlements where children grew into young men trained as expert rustlers, bank robbers, and stagecoach predators.

To the north of Brown's Hole, the Outlaw Trail passed through the *Hole-in-the-Wall* en route to its uppermost point above the Little Rockies of Montana. Located in Johnson County, Wyoming, adjacent to vast and protected grazing lands, and just west of Deadwood, South Dakota, the explosive boom town of the 1870s celebrated as a junction city for robbers, gamblers, and bounty hunters, the Hole-in-the-Wall was also a lure for the territory's illicit cow hunters, and accepted such fugitives as Jesse and Frank James and the Younger brothers.

South of Brown's Hole was the most isolated hideout in the west—*Robbers' Roost.* A plateau

Figure 1 The Outlaw Trail, the Western Cattle Trails, and Western Bandit Country

based at the summit of the San Rafael Swell, it was a natural rock fortress and endured from 1870 to 1895. Other bandit sanctuaries were similarly arranged: *Robbers' Cave* in the San Boise Mountains of Oklahoma; *Jackson Hole* in Wyoming; the *Dakota Badlands;* the *Cookson Hills,* an outthrust of the Ozark Mountains in northeast Oklahoma; and the *Osage Hills,* just west of the Cookson range. These fail-safe asylums along the Outlaw Trail and its neighboring regions not only extended protection to the fleeing bandit and outlaw, but, of greater impact, provided the organized rustlers with positional access to the established cattle trails that reached northward from Texas to the railhead cow towns of the Great Plains.

The Passing of the Western Bandits

Heavy crime in the American West declined as social and technological changes brought civilization to the frontier. The outlaw era began with the close of the Civil War and endured for some fifty years. Yet almost immediately after it reached its peak during the 1870s, the phenomena that would cause its deterioration and ultimately limit its duration grew rapidly. The long cattle drives, for example, which had allowed the rustler to raid the slow-moving herds, diminished rapidly during the 1880s. The beef magnates of the previous decade had foreseen the end of free grazing on public lands, and had purchased the better pasture areas for fencing. Barbed wire, given rather reluctant support in an effort to contain the growing numbers of sheep, ultimately blocked the efforts of drovers. Railroads were piercing deeper into the Texas range lands with offers of better facilities and more favorable rates for stock shipment. By 1890, the old cattle trails had been almost totally abandoned.[6]

The stagecoach robber was similarly driven to search for more opulent horizons. The discomforts of the stagecoaches limited their usefulness as a mode of travel, and the hazards of highway robbery forced many shippers to seek alternate methods of transport. The building of the Central Pacific and Virginia and Truckee Railroads virtually eliminated the stage lines to California in 1870, and similar rail growth drained much of the profit from the stage industry during the 1880s.

The decline in cattle and stagecoach theft and the resulting shift of "heavy" criminality to bank and train robbery cannot be totally attributed to the revolution in transportation. Similar patterns of evolution were also occurring in the nation's criminal justice machinery and private law-enforcement bodies. In 1875, for example, a United States District Court was established at Fort Smith, Arkansas, and given jurisdiction and enforcement powers in that seventy-four-thousand square mile territory once regarded as a virtual sanctuary. In addition, the Texas Rangers, first equipped by Stephen Austin in 1823 as a settlers' protection against Indians and later organized as a corps of irregular fighters at the outbreak of the Texas Revolution in 1835, evolved into an effective opponent of the outlaws after 1870.

Stage and express lines, banks, and railroads were afforded protection by private organizations, such as the Rocky Mountain Detective Association, The Pinkerton National Detective Agency, and Wells, Fargo & Company. Public, private, and railroad-owned enforcement groups were successful in increasing the risks and diminishing the profits of train robbery: baggage cars were equipped with ramps and stalls containing fast horses for the immediate pursuit of bandits; detectives and guards rode unobtrusively in coaches; single locomotives were kept ready on sidings to speed alarms and transport posses; express cars were made with finer precision and strength; substantial rewards were offered; and federal involvement extended investigations beyond county and state boundaries. Technology joined the law-enforcement effort through more efficient communication and transportation, and forensic science made identification and apprehension less difficult.

The legal, economic, social, and technological changes that caused the decline of the outlaw raiders of the trans-Mississippi rail systems also defined the limits of bank robbery. All forms of Western barbarism had been contained by the county and town vigilance committees, representing quasi-public efforts to adapt self-government to the special conditions of the frontier. The vigilante (watchman) was first described in Victor Prudon's *Vigilantes de Los Angeles, 1836,* and received unusually great attention in the pulp journalism that often glorified the vigilante committees of post–gold rush California. Similar self-appointed enforcement bodies emerged in frontier Montana, Idaho, Nevada, Nebraska, Wyoming, and North Dakota as local efforts to limit the activities of rustlers, horse thieves, bank robbers, and road agents. Finally, the mountainous hideaway of the professional bandit was transformed by the westward expansion of civilization. America's urbanization had gained momentum following the Civil War, reaching farther inland with rival trading centers to serve each frontier outpost. Industrialization, exploitation of new resources, and transoceanic migrations created new settlements, competing cities, and metropolitan centers.

> . . . The bandits had been born of the wilderness: its thickets and swamps had been the background and its lonely trails the scene of all their operations. And now the wilderness itself was vanishing; the scene had shifted,

and like actors on a vacant stage, they were left with no background for the consummation of their plotting (Coates, 1930:301).

With the beginning of the twentieth century, the West appeared conquered. Train robberies dropped from twenty-nine in 1900 to seven in 1905, and never increased significantly. The Outlaw Trail had also disappeared—laid waste, barren, and eroded by the endless thousands of woolly sheep that tore at the roots of its landscape, devouring even the hoary sagebrush. Only a limited number of the old-style Western bandits survived, such as Al Spencer, Henry Starr, and Matt Warner.

The Dillinger Days

The modern bandits of the Depression Era were the ideological descendants of the earlier outlaw breed. Their frontier was more social than natural—public apathy and rapid social change. The crash of 1929 severed the national income, hundreds of banks collapsed, and thirteen million Americans were jobless; radicalism was prominent and endorsements for a Communist presidential candidate in 1932 were heard from Dos Passos, Dreiser, and other notable opinion-makers. Urban centers had grown so large that local law enforcement had become unwieldy and inefficient, and areas of vice and corruption were unbounded. The changes in law, science, and community organization, although they led to the demise of the rustler and robber of stage, bank, and train a few decades previously, failed to adjust to the new criminality. Armed with machine guns, the new professional "heavies" re-created the frontier pattern of rapid assault, followed by immediate and elusive retreat. Fast cars and intricate highways replaced the desert and canyon escape routes. Like commuters, now the outlaws shuttled between distant cities or to adjoining states for sanctuary. Local police were helpless: they had few modern weapons; their patrol vehicles were old and often disabled; they were understaffed and poorly paid, many times having to provide their own guns and transportation. New political administrations frequently changed police chiefs at the cost of morale and efficiency. County officials were equally ineffective, state police were little more than paper organizations, and federal authority was subject to local political pressure and states' rights.

Such was the setting for the crime wave of the 1930s, with principals like John Dillinger, Frank Nash, Wilbur Underhill, "Pretty Boy" Floyd, Bonnie Parker and Clyde Barrow, "Machine Gun" Kelly, "Ma" Barker, Alvin Karpis, and "Baby Face" Nelson. Bank robbery was their primary objective, undertaken openly and insolently as in the days of the outlaw West. Every detail was organized. All operations were carefully planned; methods and routes for escape were predetermined. Gangs were closely knit to insure loyalty and cohesion. Contacts were formalized in the vice areas and underworld *cooling-off-joints,* where criminal money could always find safety. The towns of Joplin, Missouri, St. Paul, Minnesota, and Hot Springs, Arkansas were popular. One could always find the fences for stolen goods, the physicians who never reported the gunshot wounds, the lawyers who knew how to evade the law, the police who could be bribed, the tailors who made clothes with concealed pistol pockets, the mechanics who constructed bulletproof cars, and the *tipsters* and *markers* who advised where to rob. Kidnappers were similarly organized; many were meshed in the professional bank-robbery operations.[7]

Yet this era of professional banditry was short lived. The criminals who had chosen organized bank robbery and kidnapping as a vocational pursuit endured for less than a decade, essentially because of the Federal Bureau of Investigation. This new force of special agents, trained in the use of rifles, pistols, shotguns, and submachine guns, had been developing since 1924. Each of its enforcement officers was equipped with a knowledge of fingerprint identification, scientific crime detection, and the preservation of evidence at crime scenes. The effectiveness of this Bureau was demonstrated immediately following a series of national crime bills authored by U.S. Attorney General Homer S. Cummings, passed by Congress during May and June of 1934, and signed into law by President Franklin D. Roosevelt. Under this new legislation it became a federal offense to assault or cause the death of a federal officer, to rob a national bank, to flee across state boundaries to avoid prosecution or giving testimony in federal criminal cases, to transport stolen property valued at $5,000 or more across state lines, to use interstate communications in extortion attempts, and to carry hostages or kidnap victims from one state to another. Furthermore, Bureau agents were authorized to carry weapons at all times and were given full police powers in all jurisdictions throughout the nation. The effect was to provide the F.B.I. with the authority and methods not previously held by any enforcement body, thus preventing the professional robbers and kidnappers from interstate flight into undisputed sanctuary. Within a few years, most of the known outlaws and "public enemies" were apprehended.

In retrospect, the professional "heavy" offenders and their prototypes from the early West were more than ideationally similar in activity and operation. Rather, the frontier outlaw was succeeded by the depression bandit, often forming a continuing criminal heritage and tradition handed down from generation to generation through unbroken personal connections. Geographical proximity and social legacy were well suited for this. John Dillinger, "Baby Face" Nelson, the Barker family, Alvin Karpis, "Machine Gun" Kelly, Bonnie Parker, and the Barrow brothers were fourth- and fifth-generation Americans. Several came from the Ozarks and the Osage and Cookson Hills, as did Jesse and Frank James and the Younger brothers. And these areas, even early in the new century, were not altogether a closed frontier. Oklahoma was a territory until 1907, and statehood was withheld from Arizona and New Mexico until 1912. The rugged hills west of Fort Smith, Arkansas, cut with narrow valleys, steep watercourses, picturesque bluffs, and natural caves, remained without paved roads as late as the 1930s and served as a rest and refuge place for outlaws of both periods.

Population, too, was limited, for urban growth had been slow in these regions and metropolitan expansion was yet to come. The pioneer traditions endured. Personal and community conflicts were handled arbitrarily by the permanent settlers; respect for Eastern legislators did not dominate, and contempt for subservience and obedience was characteristically strong. It was within this setting that *both* generations of outlaws were socialized and matured into the criminal world. Jesse James, the Youngers, Billy the Kid, and the other notorious agents of the road and rail were not forgotten; as ancestral and legendary heroes they were very much a part of the local folklore. Ma Barker, for example, who became twenty-one in 1893, had spent her youth and adolescent years as a contemporary of the Dalton brothers, the Doolin gang, and the James-Younger troupe. And Henry Starr was still to prey on banks for some two decades when John Dillinger was born.

The connection between William Clark Quantrill and Charles "Pretty Boy" Floyd was characteristic of the outlaw lineage. Theirs was a seventy-year line, beginning in the mid-nineteenth century. Quantrill had been the cornerstone of an organized band of guerrillas that emerged from the Kansas-Missouri border wars and became prominent during the Civil War. Jesse James and Cole Younger were among these outlaw raiders; and John Shirley, an innkeeper from Carthage, Missouri and a Confederate sympathizer, had always extended hospitality to the marauding group. It was from Cole Younger and John Shirley that "Pretty Boy" Floyd's criminal heritage descended. Shirley was the father of Belle Starr, the notorious "bandit queen." Belle had been the mistress of Cole Younger, and the alleged wife of Sam Starr, a Cherokee Indian. During her outlaw reign, which spanned the 1880s, Henry Starr was among her active followers. Henry's career extended far beyond that of Belle into the twentieth century to merge finally with the efforts of Frank Nash and Al Spencer. Spencer, Nash, and Starr were transitional outlaws, and linked the past to the later operations of "Pretty Boy" Floyd. Floyd had spent his youth in Sallisaw, Oklahoma, deep within the Cookson Hills. He migrated to Wichita, Kansas in the early 1920s and was introduced to John Callahan, who schooled him in the dynamics of robbery and acquainted him with some of his underworld affiliates. Callahan had been a fence for Al Spencer, and an associate of Frank Nash and Eddie Adams. It was in Wichita that Adams and Nash became known to Floyd. Adams and Nash remained Floyd's allies for the duration of his career, less than a decade.

Contemporary "Heavy" Crime

The end of the Western outlaw and the violent warfare between the F.B.I. and the hoodlums only altered the types of professional "heavy" crime. Bank raids declined with federal involvement in the investigation and prosecution of such robberies, which reached a low of only 24 during 1943. Yet, by 1950, bank robberies had increased to 81, to 346 in 1959, and the number escalated over 400 percent to over 2,000 by 1970.[8]

This dramatic increase, however, seemingly involved more nonprofessional offenders. A comprehensive F.B.I. review of 238 bank holdups, which occurred during the summer of 1964, indicated:

> Many of the violations . . . revealed that the robbers seldom made any well-defined plans as to their methods of operation or getaway. . . . One pair of armed robbers jumped from their car and dashed up to the doors of a bank only to find they were locked. Seven robbers were arrested inside by the bank guards or police officers who were summoned while the teller stalled. Twenty-four who attempted robberies were thwarted by bank employees who either refused to comply with their demands, screamed, or merely ducked behind their cages or calmly walked away. In one of these cases, the bandit fled when the teller fainted, and in another, the teller advised the would-be bandit that she was going to faint and he told her to go ahead, then calmly walked out (F.B.I., 1970c:289).

This unsophisticated type of bank robbery is also evident in high rates of clearance. Of the 332 offenders involved in the 238 cases surveyed by the F.B.I., 63 percent (210 persons) were apprehended. Furthermore, of those arrested by the F.B.I. for bank robbery, almost half had no prior records or a history of only minor offenses. A lack of professionalism in their behavior has also been noted by Blackie Audett (1954), a "heavy" of some import whose forty-year career included more than twenty-seven robberies, beginning with a $1.5 million theft from a Canadian mail train. Similarly, Camp (1967) found that many bank robberies were precipitated by overdue installment payments.

Professional Armed Robbery

Other sources suggest that the skillful bank bandit has managed some degree of survival. Typical contemporary robberies occur at branch banks in rural areas where escape is more likely or where architectural design has reduced risk of capture. The robbers, acting both alone and in concert with others, draw heavily on the underworld's resources, using its network of information, its hideouts, and its experienced car thieves, drivers, and gunmen. Patience is demanded of the successful bank robber, for thorough observation of banking routines, study of traffic conditions and roads in and around the bank to be raided, and later meetings with the handlers of stolen money are required. During the 1960s Montreal became the leading city in North America for bank robbery. As many as 93 cases occurred during 1968 with only 25 percent clearance by arrest. Gartner (1968:77–78) described these robberies:

> Robbers work in teams . . . heavily armed. . . . Their planning is careful and their timing precise. Knowing that it takes police about three minutes to respond to an alarm, the robbers usually take no more than a minute to leap over the counters and clean out the cash drawers.

The social organization and occupational techniques of professional bank robbery are also reflected in the wider spectrum of *armed robbery*. Professional "heavy" crime exists more frequently in store robbery and hijacking. The engineering of any operation or job is a group decision. The strategy decided on determines the role of each gang member according to an assessment of individual strengths and weaknesses. Although there is some variation from group to group, the vast majority of professional robberies manifest these procedural characteristics: (1) there is a definite target assuring a profitable outcome; (2) the target is fully studied several weeks in advance; (3) mock or practice trials are made; (4) timetables are established and escape routes charted; (5) there is a getaway car with a special driver; (6) there is a lookout man, and a gunman with an accomplice for inside operations; and (7) there is a planned time, place, and method for division of the money. Willie Sutton described his general preparations for robbing a bank:

> . . . I studied the habits of the employees and the guards and the cops on the beat. I learned the complete layout of the bank, and drew a plan. . . . I learned the location of every burglar alarm and safeguard. . . . I rehearsed my men thoroughly in their parts (Reynolds, 1953:19).

In contrast to the traditional professional thieves, such as safe burglars, pickpockets, or confidence operators, whose criminal pursuits require manual and/or verbal dexterity, only the *planning* of an armed robbery demands talent; its *commission* does not. Skill limits the style and amount of planning, and these determine the nature of the three levels of robbery tactics (Einstadter, 1969:76):

1. *The Ambush*—little planning; participants attack an establishment in guerrilla fashion; random selection of victim; high incidence of violence.
2. *The Selective Raid*—some planning; limited analysis of site conditions; tentative plan of approach.
3. *The Planned Operation*—well planned and well structured in every aspect; risks held to a minimum

Hijacking

Precision hijacking falls within the level of a planned operation, and requires acute organization to gain a substantial profit. During 1966, for example, in the United States an estimated $120 million worth of merchandise was hijacked from more than 10,000 trucks, increasing to some $750 million in 1968, and $880 million in 1969. Such expansion has occurred seemingly as a result of single-product cargoes, which are much easier to dispose of. More and

more, bargain-hunting consumers and financially pressed retailers and wholesalers create black markets by seeking stolen items. Finally, the relative ease of stealing unguarded trucks or intercepting transport vehicles on poorly patrolled highways carries a low risk when compared with other robbery operations. A high degree of professionalism is exhibited by the precision and efficiency of the predators—merchandise is stolen to order, specialized equipment is employed, and goods are catalogued. For example:

> Or look at a 16-man gang in Illinois . . . the hijackers used "consultants" to tip them on movements of valuable cargos; custom-built "work cars" equipped with police radios, racing engines and switches to turn off rear lights; and a "crash car" containing gunmen, instructed to "take out any heat" caused by police during any operation (Surface, 1968:116).

Diamond Theft

Diamond theft also reflects precision of operation and high profitability, although robberies of this type occur with limited frequency. Diamonds have always represented prized targets due to their small size and concentrated value. Furthermore, since only the diamond cutter who has divided a stone can identify it, these gems have the additional quality of being virtually untraceable. Data from the late 1960s indicate that five or six major diamond robberies occur per year among the more than four hundred salesmen who travel throughout the world carrying as much as $1 million in diamonds on their person. In terms of organization, one diamond thief indicated that the illicit operators work with patience, often staking out salesmen's homes and hiring assistants to monitor airport arrivals. In addition, a diamond setter and part-time carrier and salesman commented that merchants, unguarded and unarmed, often transport $25 thousand to $100 thousand worth of these precious stones on local trips within New York City's diamond center. Since only one robbery can net the potential holdup man a handsome sum, he can afford to spend more time and be more systematic in making his plans. Due to the infrequency of these offenses, it is difficult to understand the structure and process of diamond theft, allowing only limited and tentative generalizations.

Accurate data and conceptual notes are similarly unavailable for the professional arsonist. Descriptions of the skilled *torch* who employs elaborate devices for setting fires on contract as a service for overinsured businessmen have appeared. Yet the few studies of the incendiary firesetter have failed to locate such professionals in treatment or incarcerated populations. Descriptive reports have indicated that these seemingly profit-motivated types fall within the ranks of amateur offenders and pyromaniacs.

Career Aspects

In general, the rationale of these career "heavies" dictates a conscious choice of targets where only agent-victims are present. All persons in and around the preferred targets: banks, loan companies, supermarkets, groceries, liquor and drug stores, and gas stations, are considered as an amorphous mass, and confrontations with employees become an impersonal matter. In addition to this denial of the victims, they rationalize any face-to-face behavior as "not *too* dishonest." On a more pragmatic level, victims with no personal stake in the place to be robbed are preferred since the risks of retaliation are reduced.

The typical professional "heavy" crime career usually involves early experiences with a juvenile gang where techniques and rationalizations for the deviant behavior are gradually and continuously learned. Individuals move from petty offenses to auto theft, burglary, and robbery. As young adults their experiences with police, courts, and reformatories add to their sophistication in criminality and to deviant self-conceptions. Living on the fringes of society, members of the "heavy" rackets view robbery as a way to "get rich quick," to become socially mobile, and to start anew, rather than as a vocation or career. Yet, with this life-style and social milieu, having an ethos of "easy come, easy go," such offenders often fail to advance economically or to translate gains into conventional worth, thus locking themselves more firmly into a criminal career.

Future Directions of Heavy Crime

As a final note, contemporary professional "heavy" offenders are appearing in fewer and fewer numbers as the frontiers for their effective operations continue to decline. Bank robbery has been all but totally thwarted by integrated law-enforcement systems, by scientific advances in safeguarding mechanisms, and by architecturally superior physical plants. Similar gains have not been extended to the alternative robbery targets—the drug and liquor stores, and the gas stations—yet their lower cash yields require more repeated activities, increasing risk potential and reducing professional involvement.

. . . History documents the professional "heavies" as emerging from the fringes of organized society into frontiers with few obstacles to prosperous banditry. And they persisted until law, technology, and growth circumscribed, enveloped, and finally conquered their frontiers. Yet the killers, thieves, and oppressors, the more exhibitionistic criminals, became America's folk heroes. Although less altruistic than myth might relate, they were challengers of an encroaching *lex loci.* Captain Kidd fought the hated Spanish fleets; the James-Younger gang battled the despised rail entrepreneurs; Clyde Barrow provided a depression-stricken rural America with vicarious revenge against banks; and Willie Sutton escaped three times from a highly criticized correctional institution. Further, they robbed institutions, not people. Indeed, they regarded themselves as modern Robin Hoods. The almost outworn pattern repeatedly pictured them as robbing the rich to give to the poor. Minor mythology has described them as men of action, fighting their way through regions often stagnant with despair or apathy, forfeiting their option to be free men, pitting themselves against the harsh and hostile worlds of authority and orthodoxy. The era of the nomadic bandit of the frontier has passed; that of the free-lance robber-gunman has begun to fade. Yet this response to outlaw daring continues to be vital in public reaction. Charles Starkweather, the Nebraska teenage killer of eleven in 1958, was an adolescent protagonist, and for a period was a teenage hero and idol. More recently, D. B. Cooper, the skyjacker who jumped from a commercial jet with the airline's $200,000 ransom, became a folk hero not unlike Jesse James, John Dillinger, and Robin Hood.

Notes

1. The concepts of banditry are descriptive of the era of the English highwaymen, which spanned the major portion of the seventeenth and eighteenth centuries. Highway robbery was encouraged and supported by advances in handgun development, the existence of secluded country byways, and a large number of wealthy travelers on a frontier characterized by England being the only country in the civilized world without a paid police force. The highwayman and his frontier disappeared with the start of interlocking banking systems, the building of the railroad, the enclosure of the wild country heaths, and the establishment of armed police patrols (see Hayward, 1735; Colquhoun, 1806; Pike, 1873–76a, 1873–76b; Ribton-Turner, 1887; Lee, 1901; Honore, 1923; de la Torre Bueno, 1947; Pringle, 1958, 1963, 1965).

2. The historical discussion of piracy has been based on Burney (1816), Froude (1895), Gosse (1924, 1932), Means (1935), Rusche and Kirchheimer (1939), de la Torre-Bueno (1947), and Woodbury (1951).

   Corresponding patterns of banditry and piracy characterized the evolution and disintegration of the pirates of the Natchez Trace, the Hudson River, and numerous other inland waterways and harbors during eighteenth- and nineteenth-century America (see Martin, 1868; Sutton, 1873; Coates, 1930; Daniels, 1962; Albion, 1967; Richardson, 1970).

3. The historical spectrum of cattle rustling can be found in Raine (1929), Adams (1948), Kelly (1958), Wallis (1964), and Drago (1969). The term *maverick,* referring to any unbranded animal running loose on the open range, descends from Colonel Maverick, a Texas rancher made wealthy by branding the unmarked occupants of the free lands (see Hough, 1918:146–47; Williamson, 1930:177).

   Stagecoach robbery for the period 1850–1880 is discussed by Cook (1882) and Loomis (1968). For an interesting narrative description of the coaching era, see Wilson (1922), Harlow (1934), and Earle (1938).

4. Train robbery began in 1866 and its beginning is explored by Harlow (1934:331–37) and Holbrook (1962:269–71); the Jesse James era is examined in the works of Triplett (1882) and Settle (1966). Considerable analysis has been undertaken of the development of the railroad and its social and economic effects on the West. My examination of material on these processes and their relationship to the persistence of train robbery and the glorification of the numerous train bandits included Warner and King (1940), Horan (1949), Hungerford (1949), Block (1959), Wellman (1961), Holbrook (1962), Gates (1966), Drago (1968), and O'Connor (1973).

5. The Outlaw Trail and the numerous outlaw sanctuaries are discussed in the works of Cook (1882), Mercer (1894), Warner and King (1940), Dunham and Dunham (1947), Le Fors (1953), Gard (1954), Kelly (1958), Huntington (1959), Wellman (1961), Crawford (1962), Drago (1964, 1965), and Hawgood (1969).

6. The passing of the Western bandits was attributed to many independent and interrelated events. The appropriate literature sources for these events include: changes in the beef and sheep industry (Gard, 1954:206–12; Hawgood, 1969:338); abandonment of cattle trails (Gard, 1954:259–64; Drago, 1965:243–52); the problems associated with stagecoach travel (Bunn, 1853:240; Cook, 1882; Harlow, 1934:341; Hawgood, 1969:234–72); the establishment of a federal district court at Fort Smith, Arkansas (Shirley, 1957); the Texas Rangers (Webb, 1935; Castleman, 1944); the Rocky Mountain Detective Association (Cook, 1882); the Pinkerton National Detective Agency (Rowan, 1931; Horan, 1969); Wells, Fargo & Co. (Hungerford, 1949; Loomis, 1968; Lake, 1969); public, private, and railroad-owned enforcement groups (Hubbard, 1945; Block, 1959; Wellman, 1961; Holbrook, 1962); and vigilante groups (Dimsdale, 1866; Simpson, 1893; Williams, 1921; Homsher, 1960; Myers, 1966; Bean, 1968:136–37).

7. The machine-gun bandits of the 1930s are discussed by Sullivan (1932), Kirkpatrick (1934), Cooper (1936, 1937), Hoover (1938), Wellman (1961), and Toland (1963). The development of the F.B.I. and its epic "war" on these public enemies appears in the works of Corey (1936), Hoover (1938), Cooper (1939), Look Magazine (1947), Lowenthal (1950), Colby (1954), Reynolds (1954), Whitehead (1956), Cook (1964), and Turner (1970).

8. Materials on armed robbery can be found in Reynolds (1953), Audett (1954), Varna (1957), Camp (1967), Gartner (1968), and F.B.I. (1970c). Specific robbery organizations and operations appear in DeBaun (1950), Roebuck and Cadwallader (1961), Roebuck (1967:106–17), and Einstadter (1969). Hijacking is discussed by Gartner (1968), Surface (1968), and Williams (1970).

Diamond theft is examined by Stringer (1923) and Gartner (1968). These authors suggest that knowledge of the victims' daily routines, exploited by the thieves, is typical in many large diamond thefts. This seemed to be the case in a robbery of more than five dozen diamonds during late 1969. The victim reported to me that a team of bandits entered his premises at a time when he usually had no customers, they indicated a knowledge of his personal history, and were aware of the extent of the valuables kept in his vault. This informant also said that Providence, Rhode Island and Revere, Massachusetts were the major habitats of diamond thieves. Providence is a center for jewelry manufacturing and Revere is a resort-amusement suburb of Boston. This point was corroborated (in a confidential personal communication) in 1972 by an insurance investigator and a private detective working in the Boston-Somerville-Revere-Lynn area of Massachusetts.

The professional arsonist as a "heavy" criminal is commented on in Lewis and Yarnell (1951), Bloch and Geis (1970:296), and Inciardi (1970).

The career aspects of "heavy" criminals are examined by Reynolds (1953), Audett (1954), Camp (1967), and Einstadter (1969).

References

Adams, Ramon F. 1948. *The Old Time Cowhand*. New York: Macmillan.

Albion, Robert. 1967. *The Rise of New York Port (1815–1860)*. New York: Scribner's.

Audett, Blackie. 1954. *Rap Sheet: My Life Story*. New York: William Sloane.

Bean, Walton. 1968. *California: An Interpretive History*. New York: McGraw-Hill.

Bloch, Herbert A., and Gilbert Geis. 1970. *Man, Crime and Society*. Second Edition. New York: Random House.

Block, Eugene B. 1959. *Great Train Robberies of the West*. New York: Avon.

Bunn, Alfred. 1853. *Old England and New England*. Philadelphia: Hart, Carey & Hart.

Burney, James. 1816. *The History of the Buccaneers of America*. New York: Norton (1950 edition).

Camp, George N. 1967. "Nothing to lose: a study of bank robbery in America." Ph.D. dissertation, Yale University.

Coates, Robert M. 1930. *The Outlaw Years*. New York: Literary Guild.

Cook, D. J. 1882. *Hands Up*. Norman: University of Oklahoma Press (1958 edition).

Cook, Fred. 1964. *The F.B.I. Nobody Knows*. New York: Macmillan.

Cooper, Courtney R. 1936. *Ten Thousand Public Enemies*. Boston: Little, Brown.

———. 1937. *Here's to Crime*. Boston: Little, Brown.

———. 1939. *Designs in Scarlet*. Boston: Little, Brown.

Corey, Herbert. 1936. *Farewell Mr. Gangster: America's War on Crime*. New York: Appleton-Century.

Crawford, T. E. 1962. *The West of the Texas Kid*. Norman: University of Oklahoma Press.

Daniels, Jonathan. 1962. *The Devil's Backbone*. New York: McGraw-Hill.

de la Torre-Bueno, Lillian (ed.) 1947. *Villainy Detected*. New York: Appleton-Century.

Drago, Harry Sinclair. 1964. *Outlaws on Horseback*. New York: Dodd, Mead.

———. 1965. *Great American Cattle Trails*. New York: Dodd, Mead.

———. 1969. *Notorious Ladies of the Frontier*. New York: Dodd, Mead.

Dunham, Dick, and Vivian Dunham. 1947. *Our Strip of Land*. Manila, Utah: Daggett County Lions Club.

Earle, Alice Morse. 1938. *Stagecoach and Tavern Days*. New York: Macmillan.

Einstadter, Werner J. 1969. "The social organization of armed robbery." *Social Problems* 17 (Summer):64–83.

Federal Bureau of Investigation (F.B.I.). 1970. "Profile of a bank robber," in Herbert H. Bloch and Gilbert Geis, *Man, Crime, and Society*. Second Edition. New York: Random House.

Froude, James Anthony. 1895. *English Seamen in the Sixteenth Century*. New York: Scribner's.

Gard, Wayne. 1954. *The Chisholm Trail*. Norman: University of Oklahoma Press.

Gartner, Michael (ed.) 1968. *Crime and Business*. Princeton: Dow Jones.

Gates, Paul Wallace. 1966. *Fifty Million Acres: Conflicts over Kansas Land Policy, 1854–1890*. New York: Atherton Press.

Gosse, Philip. 1924. *The Pirates' Who's Who*. Boston: Lauriat.

———. 1932. *The History of Piracy*. New York: Tudor.

Harlow, Alvin F. 1934. *Old Waybills*. New York: Appleton-Century.

Hawgood, John A. 1969. *America's Western Frontiers*. New York: Knopf.

Hayward, A. L. 1735. *Lives of the Most Remarkable Criminals*. New York: Dodd, Mead (1927 edition).

Holbrook, Stewart H. 1962. *The Story of American Railroads*. New York: Bonanza Books.

Homsher, Lola M. (ed.) 1960. *South Pass, 1868*. Lincoln: University of Nebraska Press.

Honore, Paul. 1923. *Highwaymen*. New York: Robert M. McBride.

Hoover, J. Edgar. 1938. *Persons in Hiding*. Boston: Little, Brown.

Horan, James D. 1949. *Desperate Men*. New York: Bonanza Books.

———. 1969. *The Pinkertons: The Detective Dynasty That Made History*. New York: Crown.

Hough, Emerson. 1918. *The Passing of the Frontier*. New Haven: Yale University Press.

Hubbard, Freeman H. 1945. *Railroad Avenue*. New York: McGraw-Hill.

Hungerford, Edward. 1949. *Wells Fargo*. New York: Bonanza Books.

Huntington, William. 1959. *Bill Huntington's Both Feet in the Stirrups*. Billings, Mont.: Western Livestock Reporter.

Inciardi, James A. 1970. "The adult firesetter: a typology." *Criminology* 8(August):145–155.

Kelly, Charles. 1958. *The Outlaw Trail*. New York: Bonanza Books.

Kirkpatrick, E. E. 1934. *Crime's Paradise*. San Antonio, Tex.: Naylor.

Lake, Carolyn (ed.). 1969. *Under Cover for Wells Fargo: The Unvarnished Recollections of Fred Dodge*. Boston: Houghton Mifflin.

Lee, W. L. Melville. 1901. *A History of Police in England*. London: Metheun.

Le Fors, Joe. 1953. *Wyoming Peace Officer*. Laramie: Laramie Ptg. Co.

Lewis, Nolan D. C., and Helen Yarnell. 1951. *Pathological Firesetting*. New York: Nervous and Mental Disease Monographs.

Look Magazine. 1947. *The Story of the F.B.I.* New York: E. P. Dutton.

Loomis, Noel M. 1968. *Wells Fargo*. New York: Bramhall House.

Lowenthal, Max. 1950. *The Federal Bureau of Investigation*. New York: Sloane.

Martin, Edward Winslow. 1868. *Secrets of the Great City*. Philadelphia: National.

Means, P. A. 1935. *The Spanish Main*. New York: Scribner's.

Mercer, A. S. 1894. *The Banditti of the Plains; or, the Cattlemen's Invasion of Wyoming in 1892*. Norman: University of Oklahoma Press (1954 edition).

Myers, John Myers. 1966. *San Francisco's Reign of Terror*. Garden City, N.Y.: Doubleday.

O'Connor, Richard. 1973. *Iron Wheels and Broken Men: The Railroad Barons and the Plunder of the West*. New York: Putnam.

Pike, Luke Owen. 1873–76a. *A History of Crime in England; vol. 1, from the Roman Invasion to the Accession of Henry VII*. London: Smith, Elder.

———. 1873–76b. *A History of Crime in England; vol. 2, from the Accession of Henry VII to the Present Time*. London: Smith, Elder.

Pringle, Patrick. 1958. *The Thief Takers*. London: Museum Press.

———. 1963. *Highwaymen*. New York: Roy.

———. 1965. *Hue and Cry: The Story of Henry and John Fielding and Their Bow Street Runners*. New York: William Morrow.

Raine, William Macleod. 1929. *Famous Sheriffs and Western Outlaws*. Garden City, N.Y.: Doubleday, Doran.

Reynolds, Quentin. 1953. *I, Willie Sutton*. New York: Farrar, Straus & Young.

———. 1954. *The F.B.I.* New York: Random House.

Ribton-Turner, J. C. 1887. *A History of Vagrants and Vagrancy and Beggars and Begging*. London: Chapman & Hall.

Richardson, James F. 1970. *The New York Police: Colonial Times to 1901*. New York: Oxford University Press.

Roebuck, Julian B. 1967. *Criminal Typology*. Springfield, Ill.: Thomas.

Roebuck, Julian B., and Mervin L. Cadwallader. 1961. "The Negro armed robber as a criminal type." *Pacific Sociological Review* 4(Spring):21–28.

Rowan, Richard W. 1931. *The Pinkertons, a Detective Dynasty*. Boston: Little, Brown.

Rusche, George, and Otto Kirchheimer. 1939. *Punishment and Social Structure*. New York: Columbia University Press.

Settle, William A., Jr. 1966. *Jesse James Was His Name*. Columbia: University of Missouri Press.

Shirley, Glenn. 1957. *Law West of Fort Smith*. New York: Henry Holt.

———. 1965. *Henry Starr: Last of the Real Badmen*. New York: David McKay.

Simpson, C. H. 1893. *Life in the Far West*. Chicago: Rhodes & McClure.

Stringer, A. 1923. *The Diamond Thieves*. Indianapolis: Bobbs-Merrill.

Sullivan, Edward Dean. 1932. *The Snatch Racket*. New York: Vanguard Press.

Sutton, Charles. 1873. *The New York Tombs: Its Secrets and Mysteries*. New York: United States Publishing Co.

Toland, John. 1963. *The Dillinger Days*. New York: Random House.

Triplett, Frank. 1882. *The Life, Times and Treacherous Death of Jesse James*. Chicago: Chambers.

Turner, William W. 1970. *Hoover's F.B.I.—The Men and The Myth*. Los Angeles: Sherbourne.

Varna, Andrew. 1957. *World Underworld*. London: Museum Press.

Wallis, George A. 1964. *Cattle Kings of the Staked Plains*. Denver: Swallow Press.

Warner, Matt, and Murray E. King. 1940. *The Last of the Bandit Riders*. New York: Bonanza Books.

Webb, Walter Prescott. 1935. *The Texas Rangers: A Century of Frontier Defense*. Boston: Houghton Mifflin.

Wellman, Paul I. 1961. *A Dynasty of Western Outlaws*. Garden City, N.Y.: Doubleday.

Whitehead, Don. 1956. *The F.B.I. Story*. New York: Random House.

Williams, John D. 1970. "Highway robbery." *Wall Street Journal* March 24:1.

Williams, Mary Floyd. 1921. *History of the San Francisco Committee of Vigilance (of 1851)*. Berkeley: University of California Press.

Williamson, Jefferson. 1930 *The American Hotel*. New York: Knopf.

Wilson, Violet A. 1922. *The Coaching Era*. New York: Dutton.

Woodbury, George. 1951. *The Great Days of Piracy in the West Indies*. New York: Norton.

29

Becoming a Hit Man: Neutralization in a Very Deviant Career

Ken Levi

Our knowledge about deviance management is based primarily on behavior that is easily mitigated. The literature dwells on unwed fathers (Pfuhl, 1978), and childless mothers (Veevers, 1975), pilfering bread salesman (Ditton, 1977), and conniving shoe salesmen (Friedman, 1974), bridge pros (Holtz, 1975), and poker pros (Hayano, 1977), marijuana smokers (Langer, 1976), massage parlor prostitutes (Verlarde, 1975), and other minor offenders (see, for example, Berk, 1977; Farrell and Nelson, 1976; Gross, 1977). There is a dearth of deviance management articles on serious offenders, and no scholarly articles at all about one of the (legally) most serious offenders of all, the professional murderer. Drift may be possible for the minor offender exploiting society's *ambivalence* toward his relatively unserious behavior (Sykes and Matza, 1957). However, excuses for the more inexcusable forms of deviant behavior are, by definition, less easily come by, and the very serious offender may enter his career with few of the usual defenses.

This article will focus on ways that one type of serious offender, the professional hit man, neutralizes stigma in the early stages of his career. As we shall see, the social organization of the "profession" provides "neutralizers" which distance its members from the shameful aspects of their careers. But for the novice, without professional insulation, the problem is more acute. With very little outside help, he must negate his feelings, neutralize them, and adopt a "framework" (Goffman, 1974) appropriate to his chosen career. This process, called "reframing," is the main focus of the present article. Cognitively, the novice must *reframe his experience* in order to enter his profession.

The Social Organization of Murder

Murder, the unlawful killing of a person, is considered a serious criminal offense in the United States, and it is punished by extreme penalties. In addition, most Americans do not feel that the penalties are extreme enough (Reid, 1976:482). In overcoming the intense stigma associated with murder, the hit man lacks the supports available to more ordinary types of killers.

Some cultures allow special circumstances or sanction special organizations wherein people who kill are insulated from the taint of murder. Soldiers at war, or police in the line of duty, or citizens protecting their property operate under what are considered justifiable or excusable conditions. They receive so much informal support from the general public and from members of their own group that it may protect even a sadistic member from blame (Westley, 1966).

Subcultures (Wolfgang and Ferracuti, 1967), organizations (Maas, 1968), and gangs

Ken Levi, "Becoming a Hit Man: Neutralization in a Very Deviant Career," *Journal of Contemporary Ethnography* (formerly *Urban Life*) Vol. 10., No. 1, pp. 47–63, copyright © 1981 by Sage Publications, Inc. Reprinted by Permission of Sage Publications, Inc.

I would like to thank Sharon Barnartt, Jack Douglas, Edgar Mills, Daniel Rigney, and two anonymous reviewers for their helpful criticisms and suggestions.

(Yablonsky, 1962) that unlawfully promote killing can at least provide their members with an "appeal to higher loyalties" (Sykes and Matza, 1957), if not a fully developed set of deviance justifying norms.

Individuals acting on their own, who kill in a spontaneous, "irrational" outburst of violence can also mitigate the stigma of their behavior.

> I mean, people will go ape for one minute and shoot, but there are very few people who are capable of thinking about, planning, and then doing it [Joey, 1974:56].

Individuals who kill in a hot-blooded burst of passion can retrospectively draw comfort from the law which provides a lighter ban against killings performed without premeditation or malice or intent (Lester and Lester, 1975:35). At one extreme, the spontaneous killing may seem the result of a mental disease (Lester and Lester, 1975:39) or dissociative reaction (Tanay, 1972), and excused entirely as insanity.

But when an individual who generally shares society's ban against murder, is fully aware that his act of homicide is (1) unlawful, (2) self-serving, and (3) intentional, he does not have the usual defenses to fall back on. How does such an individual manage to *overcome his inhibitions* and *avoid serious damage to his self-image* (assuming that he does not share society's ban)? This is the special dilemma of the professional hit man who hires himself out for murder.

Research Methods

Information for this article comes primarily from a series of intensive interviews with one self-styled "hit man." The interviews were spread over seven, tape-recorded sessions during a four-month period. The respondent was one of fifty prison inmates randomly sampled from a population of people convicted of murder in Metropolitan Detroit. The respondent told about an "accidental" killing, involving a drunken bar patron who badgered the respondent and finally forced his hand by pulling a knife on him. In court he claimed self-defense, but the witnesses at the bar claimed otherwise, so they sent him to

prison. During the first two interview sessions, the respondent acted progressively ashamed of this particular killing, not on moral grounds, but because of its "sloppiness" or "amateurishness." Finally, he indicated there was more he would like to say. So, I stopped the tape recorder. I asked him if he was a hit man. He said he was.

He had already been given certain guarantees, including no names in the interview, a private conference room, and a signed contract promising his anonymity. Now, as a further guarantee, we agreed to talk about him in the third person, as a fictitious character named "Pete," so that none of his statements would sound like a personal confession. With these assurances, future interviews were devoted to his career as a professional murderer, with particular emphasis on his entry into the career and his orientation toward his victims.

Was he reliable? Since we did not use names, I had no way of checking the veracity of the individual cases he reported. Nevertheless, I was able to compare his account of the hit man's career with information from other convicted murderers, with police experts, and with accounts from the available literature (Gage, 1972; Joey, 1974; Maas, 1968). Pete's information was generally supported by these other sources. As to his motive for submitting to the interview, it is hard to gauge. He apparently was ashamed of the one "accidental" killing that had landed him in prison, and he desired to set the record straight concerning what he deemed an illustrious career, now that he had arrived, as he said, at the end of it. Hit men pride themselves on not "falling" (going to jail) for murder, and Pete's incarceration hastened a decision to retire—that he had already been contemplating, anyway.

A question might arise about the ethics of researching self-confessed "hit men" and granting them anonymity. Legally, since Pete never mentioned specific names or specific dates or possible future crimes, there does not seem to be a problem. Morally, if confidentiality is a necessary condition to obtaining information about serious offenders, then we have to ask: Is it worth it? Pete insisted that he had retired from the profession. Therefore, there seems to be no "clear and imminent danger" that would justify the violation of confidentiality, in the terms set forth by the American Psychological Association (1978:40). On the other hand, the *possibility* of danger does exist, and future researchers will have to exercise their judgment.

Finally, hit men are hard to come by. Unlike more lawful killers, such as judges or night watchmen, and unlike run-of-the-mill murderers, the hit man (usually) takes infinite care to conceal his identity. Therefore, while it is regrettable that this paper has only one case to report on, and while it would be ideal to perform a comparative analysis on a number of hit men, it would be very difficult to obtain such a sample. Instead, Pete's responses will be compared to similar accounts from the available literature. While such a method can never produce verified findings, it can point to suggestive hypotheses.

The Social Organization of Professional Murder

There are two types of professional murderers: the organized and the independent. The killer who belongs to an organized syndicate does not usually get paid on a contract basis, and performs his job out of loyalty and obedience to the organization (Maas, 1968:81). The independent professional killer is a freelance agent who hires himself out for a fee (Pete). It is the career organization of the second type of killer that will be discussed.

The organized killer can mitigate his behavior through an "appeal to higher loyalties" (Sykes and Matza, 1957). He also can view his victim as an enemy of the group and then choose from a variety of techniques available for neutralizing an offense against an enemy (see, for example, Hirschi, 1969; Rogers and Buffalo, 1974). But the independent professional murderer lacks most of these defenses. Nevertheless, built into his role are certain structural features that help him avoid deviance ascription. These features include:

(1) *Contract.* A contract is an unwritten agreement to provide a sum of money to a second party who agrees, in return, to commit a designated murder (Joey, 1974:9). It is most often arranged over the phone, between people who have never had personal contact. And the victim, or "hit," is usually unknown to the killer (Gage, 1972:57; Joey, 1974:61–62). This arrangement is

meant to protect both parties from the law. But it also helps the killer "deny the victim" (Sykes and Matza, 1957) by keeping him relatively anonymous.

In arranging the contract, the hired killer will try to find out the difficulty of the hit and how much the customer wants the killing done. According to Pete, these considerations determine his price. He does not ask about the motive for the killing, treating it as none of his concern. Not knowing the motive may hamper the killer from morally justifying his behavior, but it also enables him to further deny the victim by maintaining his distance and reserve. Finally, the contract is backed up by a further understanding.

> Like this guy who left here (prison) last summer; he was out two months before he got killed. Made a mistake somewhere. The way I heard it, he didn't finish filling a contract [Pete].

If the killer fails to live up to his part of the bargain, the penalties could be extreme (Gage, 1972:53; Joey, 1974:9). This has the ironic effect that after the contract is arranged, the killer can somewhat "deny responsibility" (Sykes and Matza, 1957), by pleading self-defense.

(2) *Reputation and Money.* Reputation is especially important in an area where killers are unknown to their customers, and where the less written, the better (Joey, 1974:58). Reputation, in turn, reflects how much money the hit man has commanded in the past.

> And that was the first time that I ever got 30 grand … it's based on his reputation. … Yeah, how good he really is. To be so-so, you get so-so money. If you're good, you get good money [Pete].

Pete, who could not recall the exact number of people he had killed, did, like other hit men, keep an accounting of his highest fees (Joey, 1974:58, 62). To him big money meant not only a way to earn a living, but also a way to maintain his professional reputation.

People who accept low fees can also find work as hired killers. Heroin addicts are the usual example. But, as Pete says, they often receive a bullet for their pains. It is believed that people who would kill for so little would also require little persuasion to make them talk to the police (Joey, 1974:63). This further reinforces the single-minded emphasis on making big money. As a result, killing is conceptualized as a "business" or as "just a job." Framing the hit in a normal businesslike context enables the hit man to deny wrongfulness, or "deny injury" (Sykes and Matza, 1957).

In addition to the economic motive, Pete, and hit men discussed by other authors, refer to excitement, fun, game-playing, power, and impressing women as incentives for murder (Joey, 1974:81–82). However, none of these motives are mentioned by all sources. None are as necessary to the career as money. And, after awhile, these other motives diminish and killing becomes only "just a job" (Joey, 1974:20). The primacy of the economic motive has been aptly expressed in the case of another deviant profession.

> Women who enjoy sex with their customers do not make good prostitutes, according to those who are acquainted with this institution first hand. Instead of thinking about the most effective way of making money at the job, they would be doing things for their own pleasure and enjoyment [Goode, 1978:342].

(3) *Skill.* Most of the hit man's training focuses on acquiring skill in the use of weapons.

> Then, he met these two guys, these two white guys . . . them two, them two was the best. And but they stayed around over there and they got together, and Pete told [them] that he really wanted to be good. He said, if [I] got to do something, I want to be good at it. So, they got together, showed him, showed him *how to shoot.* . . . And gradually, he became good. . . . Like he told me, like when he shoots somebody, he always goes for the head; he said, that's about the best shot. I mean, if you want him dead then and there. . . . And these two guys showed him, and to him, I mean, hey, I mean, he don't believe nobody could really outshoot these two guys, you know what I mean. *They know everything you want to know about guns, knives, and stuff like that* [Pete].

The hit man's reputation, and the amount of money he makes depends on his skill, his effective ability to serve as a means to *someone else's ends.* The result is a focus on technique.

> Like in anything you do, when you do it, you want to do it just right. . . . On your target and you hit it, how you feel: I hit it! I hit it! [Pete].

This focus on technique, on means, helps the hit man to "deny responsibility" and intent (Sykes and Matza, 1957). In frame-analytic terms, the hit man separates his morally responsible, or "principal" self from the rest of himself, and performs the killing mainly as a "strategist" (Goffman, 1974:523). In other words, he sees himself as a "hired gun." The saying, "If I didn't do it, they'd find someone else who would," reflects this narrowly technical orientation.

To sum up thus far, the contract, based as it is on the hit man's reputation for profit and skill, provides the hit man with opportunities for denying the victim, denying injury, and denying responsibility. But this is not enough. To point out the defenses of the professional hit man is one thing, but it is unlikely that the *novice* hit man would have a totally professional attitude so early in his career. The novice is at a point where he both lacks the conventional defense against the stigma of murder, *and* he has not yet fully acquired the exceptional defenses of the professional. How, then, does he cope?

The First Time: Negative Experience

Goffman defines "negative experience" as a feeling of disorientation.

> Expecting to take up a position in a well-framed realm, he finds that no particular frame is immediately applicable, or the frame that he thought was applicable no longer seems to be, or he cannot bind himself within the frame that does apparently apply. He loses command over the formulation of viable response. He flounders. Experience, the meld of what the current scene brings to him and

what he brings to it—meant to settle into a form even while it is beginning, finds no form and is therefore no experience. Reality anomically flutters. He has a "negative experience"—negative in the sense that it takes its character from what it is not, and what it is not is an organized and organizationally affirmed response [1974:378–379].

Negative experience can occur when a person finds himself lapsing into an old understanding of the situation, only to suddenly awaken to the fact that it no longer applies. In this regard, we should expect negative experience to be a special problem for the novice. For example, the first time he killed a man for money, Pete supposedly became violently ill.

When he [Pete], you know, hit the guy, when he shot the guy, the guy said, "You killed me" . . . something like that, cause he struck him all up here. And what he said, it was just, I mean, *the look right in the guy's eye,* you know. I mean he looked like: *why me?* Yeah? And he [Pete] couldn't shake that. Cause he remembered a time or two when he got cut, and all he wanted to do was get back and cut this guy that cut him. And this here. . . . No, he just could not shake it. And then he said that at night-time he'll start thinking about the guy: like he shouldn't have looked at him like that. . . . I mean actually [Pete] was sick. . . . He couldn't keep his food down, I mean, or nothing like that. . . . [It lasted] I'd say about two months. . . . Like he said that he had feelings . . . that he never did kill nobody before [Pete].

Pete's account conforms to the definition of negative experience. He had never killed anyone for money before. It started when a member of the Detroit drug world had spotted Pete in a knife fight outside an inner city bar, was apparently impressed with the young man's style, and offered him fifty dollars to do a "job." Pete accepted. He wanted the money. But when the first hit came about, Pete of course knew that he was doing it for money, but yet his orientation was revenge. Thus, he stared his victim in the *face,* a characteristic gesture of people who kill enemies for revenge (Levi, 1975:190). Expecting to see

defiance turn into a look of defeat, they attempt to gain "face" at the loser's expense.

But when Pete stared his victim in the face, he saw not an enemy, but an innocent man. He saw a look of: "Why me?" And this *discordant* image is what remained in his mind during the weeks and months to follow and made him sick. As Pete says, "He shouldn't have looked at him like that." The victim's look of innocence brought about what Goffman (1974:347) refers to as a "frame break":

Given that the frame applied to an activity is expected to enable us to come to terms with all events in that activity (informing and regulating many of them), it is understandable that the unmanageable might occur, an occurrence which cannot be effectively ignored and to which the frame cannot be applied, with resulting bewilderment and chagrin on the part of the participants. In brief, a break can occur in the applicability of the frame, a break in its governance.

When such a frame break occurs, it produces negative experience. Pete's extremely uncomfortable disorientation may reflect the extreme dissonance between the revenge frame, that he expected to apply, and the unexpected look of innocence that he encountered and continued to recall.

Subsequent Time: Reframing the Hit

According to Goffman (1974:319), a structural feature of frames of experience is that they are divided into different "tracks" or types of information. These include, "a main track or story line and ancillary tracks of various kinds." The ancillary tracks are the directional track, the overlay track, the concealment tracks, and the disattend track. The disattend track contains the information that is perceived but supposed to be *ignored.* For example, the prostitute manages the distasteful necessity of having sex with "tricks" by remaining "absolutely . . . detached. Removed. Miles and miles away" (1974:344). The existence of different tracks allows an individual to define and redefine his experience by the strategic placement of information.

Sometimes, the individual receives outside help. For example, when Milgram in 1963 placed a barrier between people administering electric shocks, and the bogus "subjects" who were supposedly receiving the shocks, he made it easier for the shockers to "disattend" signs of human distress from their hapless victims. Surgeons provide another example. Having their patients completely covered, except for the part to be operated on, helps them work in a more impersonal manner. In both examples, certain crucial information is stored away in the "concealment track" (Goffman, 1974:218).

In other cases help can come from guides who direct the novice on what to experience and what to block out. Beginning marijuana smokers are cautioned to ignore feelings of nausea (Becker, 1953:240). On the other hand, novice hit men like Pete are reluctant to share their "experience" with anyone else. It would be a sign of weakness.

In still other cases, however, it is possible that the subject can do the reframing *on his own*. And this is what appears to have happened to Pete.

> And when the second one [the second hit] came up, [Pete] was still thinking about the first one. . . . Yeah, when he got ready to go, he was thinking about it. *Something changed.* I don't know how to put it right. Up to the moment that he killed the second guy now, he waited, you know. Going through his mind was the first guy he killed. He still seeing him, still see the *expression on his face.* Soon, the second guy walked up; I mean, it was like just his mind just *blanked out* for a minute, everything just blanked out. . . . Next thing he know, he had killed the second guy. . . . *He knew what he was doing,* but what I mean, he just didn't have nothing on his mind. Everything was wiped out [Pete].

When the second victim approached, Pete says that he noticed the victim's approach, he was aware of the man's presence. But he noticed none of the victim's personal features. He did not see the victim's face or its expression. Thus, he did not see the very thing that gave him so much trouble the first time. It is as if Pete had *negatively*

conditioned himself to avoid certain cues. Since he shot the victim in the head, it is probable that Pete saw him in one sense; this is not the same kind of experience as a "dissociative reaction," which has been likened to sleepwalking (Tanay, 1972). Pete says that, "he knew what he was doing." But he either did not pay attention to his victim's personal features at the time of the killing, or he blocked them out immediately afterward, so that now the only aspect of his victim he recalls is the victim's approach (if we are to believe him).

After that, Pete says that killing became *routine.* He learned to view his victims as "targets," rather than as people. Thus, he believes that the second experience is the crucial one, and that the disattendance of the victim's personal features made it so.

Support from other accounts of hit men is scant, due to a lack of data. Furthermore, not everything in Pete's account supports the "reframing" hypothesis. In talking about later killings, it is clear that he not only attends to his victims' personal features, on occasion, but he also derives a certain grim pleasure in doing so.

> [the victim was] a nice looking women. . . . She started weeping, and [she cried], "I ain't did this, I ain't did that" . . . and [Pete] said that he shot her. Like it wasn't nothing . . . he didn't feel nothing. It was just money [Pete].

In a parallel story, Joey, the narrator of the *Killer,* also observes his victim in personal terms.

> [The victim] began to beg. He even went so far as to tell us where he had stashed his money. Finally, he realized there was absolutely nothing he could do. He sat there quietly. Then, he started crying. I didn't feel a thing for him [1974:56].

It may be that this evidence contradicts what I have said about reframing; but perhaps another interpretation is possible. Reframing may play a more crucial role in the original redefinition of an experience than in the continued maintenance of that redefinition. Once Pete has accustomed himself to viewing his victims as merely targets, as "just money," then it may be less threatening to look upon them as persons, once again. Once the "main story line" has been established, discordant information can be presented in the "overlay track" (Goffman, 1974:215), without doing too much damage. Indeed, this seems to be *the point* that both hit men are trying to make in the above excerpts.

The Heart of the Hit Man

For what I have been referring to as "disattendance" Pete used the term "heart," which he defined as a "coldness." When asked what he would look for in an aspiring hit man, Pete replied,

> See if he's got a whole lot of heart . . . you got to be cold . . . you got to build a coldness in yourself. It's not something that comes automatically. Cause, see, I don't care who he is, first, you've got feelings [Pete].

In contrast to this view, Joey (1974:56) said,

> There are three things you need to kill a man: the gun, the bullets, and the balls. A lot of people will point a gun at you, but they haven't got the courage to pull the trigger. It's as simple as that.

It may be that some are born with "heart," while others acquire it in the way I have described. However, the "made rather than born" thesis does explain one perplexing feature of hit men and other "evil" men whose banality has sometimes seemed discordant. In other aspects of their lives they all seem perfectly capable of feeling ordinary human emotions. Their inhumanity, their coldness, seems narrowly restricted to their jobs. Pete, for example, talked about his "love" for little children. Eddie "The Hawk" Ruppolo meekly allowed his mistress to openly insult him in a public bar (Gage, 1972). And Joey (1974:55) has this to say about himself:

> Believe it or not, I'm a human being. I laugh at funny jokes, I love children around the house, and I can spend hours playing with my mutt.

All of these examples of human warmth indicate that the cold heart of the hit man may be less a characteristic of the killer's individual personality, than a feature of the professional framework of experience which the hit man has learned to adapt himself to, when he is on the job.

Discussion

This article is meant as a contribution to the study of deviance neutralization. The freelance hit man is an example of an individual who, relatively alone, must deal with a profound and unambiguous stigma in order to enter his career. Both Pete and Joey emphasize "heart" as a determining factor in becoming a professional. And Pete's experience, after the first hit, further indicates that the inhibitions against murder-for-money are real.

In this article "heart"—or the ability to adapt to a rationalized framework for killing—has been portrayed as the outcome of an initial process of reframing, in addition to other neutralization techniques established during the further stages of professionalization. As several theorists (see, for example, Becker, 1953; Douglas *et al.*, 1977; Matza, 1969) have noted, people often enter into deviant acts first, and then develop rationales for their behavior later on. This was also the case with Pete, who began his career by first, (1) "being willing" (Matza, 1969), (2) encountering a frame break, (3) undergoing negative experience, (4) being willing to try again (also known as "getting back on the horse"), (5) reframing the experience, and (6) having future, routine experiences wherein his professionalization increasingly enabled him to "deny the victim," "deny injury," and "deny responsibility." Through the process of reframing, the experience of victim-as-target emerged as the "main story line," and the experience of victim-as-person was downgraded from the main track to the disattend track to the overlay track. Ironically, the intensity of the negative experience seemed to make the process all the more successful. Thus, it may be possible for a person with "ordinary human feelings" to both pass through the novice stage, and to continue "normal relations" thereafter. The reframing hypothesis has implications for other people who knowingly perform stigmatized behaviors. It may be particularly useful in explaining a personal conversion experience that occurs despite the relative absence of deviant peer groups, deviant norms, extenuating circumstances, and neutralization rationales.

References

American Psychological Association (1978). *Directory of the American Psychological Association.* Washington, DC: Author.

Becker, H. (1953). "Becoming a marijuana user." *Amer. J. of Sociology* 59:235–243.

Berk, B. (1977). "Face-saving at the singles dance." *Social Problems* 24, 5:530–544.

Ditton, J. (1977). "Alibis and aliases: some notes on motives of fiddling bread salesmen." *Sociology* 11, 2:233–255.

Douglas, J., P. Rasmussen, and C. Flanagan (1977). *The Nude Beach.* Beverly Hills: Sage.

Farrell, R., and J. Nelson (1976). "A causal model of secondary deviance; the case of homosexuality." *Soc. Q.* 17:109–120.

Friedman, N. L. (1974). "Cookies and contests: notes on ordinary occupational deviance and its neutralization." *Soc. Symposium* (Spring):1–9.

Gage, N. (1972). *Mafia, U.S.A.* New York: Dell.

Goffman, E. (1974). *Frame Analysis.* Cambridge, MA: Harvard Univ. Press.

Goode, E. (1978). *Deviant Behavior: An Interactionist Approach.* Englewood Cliffs, NJ: Prentice-Hall.

Gross, H. (1977). "Micro and macro level implications for a sociology of virtue—case of draft protesters to Vietnam War." *Soc. Q.* 18, 3:319–339.

Hayano, D. (1977). "The professional poker player: career identification and the problem of respectability." *Social Problems* 24 (June):556–564.

Hirschi, T. (1969). *Causes of Delinquency.* Berkeley: Univ. of California Press.

Holtz, J. (1975). "The professional duplicate bridge player: conflict management in a free, legal, quasi-deviant occupation." *Urban Life* 4, 2:131–160.

Joey (1974). *Killer: Autobiography of a Mafia Hit Man.* New York: Pocket Books.

Langer, J. (1976). "Drug entrepreneurs and the dealing culture." *Australian and New Zealand J. of Sociology* 12, 2:82–90.

Lester, D., and G. Lester (1975). *Crime of Passion: Murder and the Murderer.* Chicago: Nelson-Hall.

Levi, K. (1975). *Icemen.* Ann Arbor, MI: University Microfilms.

Maas, P. (1968). *The Valachi Papers.* New York: G. P. Putnam.

Matza, D. (1969). *Becoming Deviant.* Englewood Cliffs, NJ: Prentice-Hall.

Pfuhl, E. (1978). "The unwed father: a non-deviant rule breaker." *Soc. Q.* 19:113–128.

Reid, S. (1976). *Crime and Criminology.* Hinsdale, IL: Dryden Press.

Rogers, J., and M. Buffalo (1974). "Neutralization techniques: toward a simplified measurement scale." *Pacific Soc. Rev.* 17, 3:313.

Sykes, G., and D. Matza (1957). "Techniques of neutralization: a theory of delinquency." *Amer. Soc. Rev.* 22:664–670.

Tanay, E. (1972). "Psychiatric aspects of homicide prevention." *Amer. J. of Psychology* 128:814–817.

Veevers, J. (1975). "The moral careers of voluntarily childless wives: notes on the defense of a variant world view." *Family Coordinator* 24, 4:473–487.

Verlarde, A. (1975). "Becoming prostituted: the decline of the massage parlor profession and the masseuse." *British J. of Criminology* 15, 3:251–263.

Westley, W. (1966). "The escalation of violence through legitimation." *Annals of the American Association of Political and Social Science* 364 (March) 120–126.

Wolfgang, M., and F. Ferracuti (1967). *The Subculture of Violence.* London: Tavistock.

Yablonsky, L. (1962). *The Violent Gang.* New York: Macmillan.

30

Domestic Terrorism U.S.A.

Harold J. Vetter
Gary R. Perlstein

Although American diplomats, military personnel, business executives, and even tourists have been the targets of terrorism abroad, the continental United States has been comparatively free from much of the violence that seems to be endemic to other parts of the world. This is not to deny, however, that the 1960s and 1970s were turbulent decades dominated by extremist political activity and violence. It was a period during which the nation experienced major social and cultural changes. The civil rights revolution broke up the caste system and changed relationships among racial and ethnic groups; there was a decline in respect for tradition and a weakening of informal social controls; and there was growing disenchantment with, if not outright rejection of, authority (Silberman, 1980).

Blacks made some progress in their efforts to achieve full equality in American society. In 1954, the Supreme Court's landmark *Brown v. Board of Education* decision struck down the "separate but equal" doctrine. The growing size of the northern black vote made civil rights a primary issue in national elections and ultimately resulted in the establishment of the Federal Civil Rights Commission in 1957.

Martin Luther King, Jr., rose to national prominence and achieved a great deal of support for the civil rights movement through his nonviolent but direct action protests against segregation and discrimination. His successes included the Montgomery city bus boycott of 1955 and 1956, the 1963 march on Washington, and the battle that same year for voting rights in Selma, Alabama. But these victories also intensified blacks' expectations and made them more dissatisfied with their current circumstances. This resulted in a rising tempo of nonviolent action that culminated in the student sit-ins of the 1960s and the birth of the civil rights revolution.

By 1963, the protest movement had achieved a new sense of urgency. Blacks were no longer willing to wait, but began to demand complete "freedom now." The National Advisory Commission on Civil Disorders (1968) suggests that the meteoric rise of the Black Muslims to national prominence during this period was a major factor in awakening black protest. Black people made their demands known through massive protests in northern cities against inequities in housing, education, and employment and also through demonstrations in the South. But it became evident by 1964 that nonviolent direct action was of limited usefulness. At this point, despite major victories, most blacks were still treated as second-class citizens, were relegated to separate and inferior schools and slum housing, suffered disproportionately high unemployment and underemployment, and still experienced discrimination within the criminal justice system. Feeling as though the nation was moving toward two societies—one black and one white—that were separate and unequal, blacks took to the streets to express dissatisfaction with their circumstances.

For a period of three years, beginning with the Watts riot in Los Angeles in the summer of 1965 and continuing to the disturbances that were touched off by the murder of Martin Luther King, Jr., our cities, particularly during the summer, exploded on a regular basis. Forty-three disorders and riots were reported during 1966; in 1967, 164 civil disorders were reported, of which twenty-five percent were labeled either serious or major in terms of violence and damage. In examining the causes of these disturbances, the National Advisory Commission on Civil Disorders (1968) suggests that, in addition to pervasive segregation, discrimination, and poverty, which had served to catalyze the volatile nature of this mixture, other factors included frustration over unfulfilled expectations engendered by major judicial and legislative victories; an atmosphere created by white terrorism directed against nonviolent protests in which violence was approved and encouraged; the open defiance of federal and judicial authority by state and local officials resisting desegregation; frustrations of powerlessness that led some blacks to believe there was no other effective alternative to violence as a means of expressing and redressing grievances; and a new mood among blacks, particularly the young, in which apathy and submission to the system were replaced by enhanced self-esteem and racial pride.

Also, during the 1960s, our country experienced both violent and nonviolent reactions to the Vietnam War. This opposition was without precedent because it involved such a wide variety of individuals and social groups, including youths and students, prestigious leaders, academic and literary figures, radical groups, and segments of various ethnic and racial and religious groups. Resistance to the war began with questions about the need for tactics such as the use of napalm, saturation bombing, and defoliation, but it escalated to a point where a large minority of the population began to question the justice of the war itself. Some of the more radical opponents began to question the legitimacy of the political system that was conducting the war and to manifest willingness to use violence to oppose it. This group went on to be critical of our society in general and, particularly, of certain types of social arrangements such as those involving racism and sexism. Composed of New Left activists, racial minorities, middle-class and middle-aged liberals, and even some upper-class "radical chic" patrons, the group constituted an assertive, active, and, in some instances, aggressive minority that disrupted conventional activities while at the same time silencing and shaming more conventional and conservative citizens. Many Americans viewed this group as

a serious threat to existing society and feared that it would eventually accomplish its objectives of radically transforming the country.

Some of the groups on today's ideological left and ideological right that are identified with terrorism have roots in the social activism of this earlier period. Other groups have coalesced as activist supporters of single issues, such as the pro-lifers and pro-choice activists, gay rights activists, feminism advocates, animal rights activists, environmental preservationists, and the militant Jewish Defense League (JDL). Still other groups reflect nationalistic concerns: the Puerto Rican independence movement supporters; the anti-Castro Cubans; the Croatian separatists; and the Armenian nationalists.

It is easy to get lost in this bewildering welter of names, acronyms, and initials, many of which closely resemble one another. The specific groups and their nomenclature are less important, in our judgment, than is the underlying ideological or psychological motivation that allows them to resort to terrorist methods to achieve their objectives.

The Ideological Left

In the late 1960s and into the 1970s, according to FBI Special Agent Thomas Strentz (1988), most American terrorist groups were composed of urban, college-educated, middle-class young people. They were disciplined, well trained, and sophisticated enough to deal with last-minute alterations in plans; they could adjust to change and still complete the mission. Strentz provides a demographic profile of the 1960s and 1970s leftist groups. This profile shows a blend of highly motivated and well-educated members, with the additional involvement of a criminal element.

White Leftists

A prototypical organization of this period was the Weather Underground (WU), which originated at a May 1969 meeting of the Students for a Democratic Society (SDS) Convention in Chicago. The group called itself the Weathermen (after a line in Bob Dylan's "Subterranean Homesick Blues"). Later it changed its name to the Weather Underground because of the sexist connotations of the original name. The expressed views of the Weather Underground delineate their ideological position on the extreme left: "Our intention is to disrupt the empire . . . to incapacitate it, to put pressure on the cracks, to make it hard to carry out its bloody functioning against the people of the world, to join the world struggle, to attack from the inside" (Homer, 1983, 149). During October 1969, the Weather Underground staged demonstrations in Chicago, where they had several encounters with the police. The demonstrations were denounced by both the Students for a Democratic Society and the Black Panthers as counterproductive (Parry, 1976, 334). In December 1969, they decided to turn the WU into an elite, paramilitary organization to carry out urban guerrilla warfare; thus, according to Marsha McKnight Trick (1976, 519), it became "the grandperson of American revolutionary organizations." Activities shifted to bombing police buildings and courthouses in California, New York, and other cities. In September 1970, they arranged the escape of Timothy Leary from prison in San Luis Obispo, California, and helped him to reach Algeria. The Weather Underground continued to publish magazines and took credit for bombings through the mid-1970s. The Weather Underground had hoped to start a revolution, but, like most ideological terrorist groups, failed to reach its objectives.

Although these ideological terrorists professed a desire to transform society, they lacked a coherent concept of what they wished as its replacement. A dialogue between Herbert Marcuse and a student offers a graphic illustration of the nihilistic strain of this type of ideological terrorist.

STUDENT: But, Dr. Marcuse, what system of life will there be after the System is destroyed?

MARCUSE [WITH SOME SURPRISE]: You know, I've never given thought to this. I just want to see what the damned thing looks like when it is destroyed. (Parry, 1976, 528)

Another leftist group with techniques similar to those of the Weather Underground was the New World Liberation Front, a San Francisco–based group that published Marighella's *Minimanual of the Urban Guerrilla* in 1970. The NWLF espoused a variety of leftist causes and directed its attacks primarily against major corporations or government buildings. Trick (1976) identified it as the most active revolutionary group in the United States and noted that the NWLF was seen as an umbrella for other terrorist groups in California, such as the Chicano Liberation Front and the Red Guerrilla Family.

By the end of the 1970s, terrorist activities by such organizations as the Weather Underground had subsided to the point where law enforcement officials concluded that left-wing terrorism had all but ceased to be a problem. As things turned out, this judgment was premature; during the 1980s, white leftist terrorism once again became a factor after several years of relative inactivity.

According to Harris (1987), the most active New Left terrorist organization during the 1980s was the United Freedom Front (UFF). This group was quite small—four white males, three white females, and one black male who left the group when they began to participate in bombings—and had ties to radical movements of the 1960s and 1970s. In addition to a series of bombing incidents, UFF members were involved in the 1981 murder of a New Jersey State Police officer and the attempted murders of two Massachusetts State Police officers in 1982. The group also reportedly committed armed bank robberies from Connecticut to Virginia to sustain themselves. They lived under a variety of false identities and usually resided in rural areas, moving frequently. Prior to a criminal act—a bombing or robbery—group members conducted a lengthy and extensive surveillance of the target and surrounding areas.

Five UFF members were arrested in Cleveland, Ohio, in November 1984. The remaining two white members were arrested in Norfolk, Virginia, in April 1985. Automatic shoulder weapons, handguns, bomb components, and printed communiques were found in the group's safehouses. Group members were tried and convicted in New York and Massachusetts on a number of criminal charges, including murder, assault, and armed robbery.

Black Leftists

During the early 1970s, prisons were a source of recruitment for the black radical movement. Many inmates came to view themselves as "political prisoners," although they had not been convicted of offenses that had political motives or significance. They took the position that responsibility for their criminal behavior lay not with them, but with the society that had failed to provide them with equal educational opportunities, adequate housing, and the chance to compete effectively in American society. These inmates saw themselves not as aggressors, but as victims of a society that failed to provide all its members with the same kinds of opportunities and resources. They claimed that the public was misdirected in its attempts to rehabilitate them when it was really society that needed reforming.

But although many inmates felt themselves victims of society, most did not endorse the revolutionary ideology that called for the overthrow of society. The majority of inmates subscribed to a position that called for working within the existing socioeconomic structure to make the system share some of its power and influence. Although devoid of revolutionary intent, these inmates did employ strong rhetoric and even violence to pressure the system into meeting their demands.

A much smaller group adopted a class-oriented Marxist position that embraced a revolutionary political ideology (Berkman, 1979). This position was more attractive to blacks and other minorities because it provided an explanation for their current social and economic circumstances. This ideology maintains that racism is a phenomenon that is historically rooted in our capitalistic economic system. According to this position, racism is an economic strategy that is a means of keeping a "reserve army" of labor and preventing the rise of the working class. It is also a tool to keep the labor force divided. Therefore no meaningful change can occur as long as our economic and political system is based on capitalism.

An excerpt from the writings of George Jackson, one of the more articulate of the Marxist/Leninist black militants, shows how this position viewed the effects of capitalism on the black population:

> The new slavery, the modern variety of chattel slavery updated to disguise itself, places the victim in the factory or in the case of most blacks in subordinate roles inside and around the factory system (service trades), working for a wage. However, if work cannot be found in or around the factory complex, today's neoslavery does not allow even for a modicum of food and shelter. You are free—to starve. The sense in the meaning of slavery comes through as a result of our ties to the wage. You must have it, without it you would starve or expose yourself to the elements. (Jackson, 1970, 251)

This ideology also explains the conflicts among ethnic and racial minorities in our society. It argues that the ruling elite, by virtue of its control of the government and the work place, are able to effectively set one group of exploited people against another in the same way that the prison administration is able to turn blacks against whites as a method of maintaining control. In both instances, racial differences provide a basis for dividing these populations (Berkman, 1979).

It follows that blacks were not the only group viewed as oppressed by the capitalist system. Other minorities, including chicanos, Puerto Ricans, Indians, women, and many white workers are also exploited under this system. This sense of exploitation provides the basis for a coalition of groups that could jointly struggle against oppression. The need for this type of coalition was recognized by black leaders as well as other radical leaders.

Radical groups were not primarily interested in either helping the inmate or changing prison conditions; instead their primary focus was on changing society (Irwin, 1980). The group's ideology considered the prison simply a further illustration of the oppression and exploitation of the poor and nonwhites by a capitalist economic system. Some, like Huey

Newton of the Black Panthers, considered the prison experience of blacks similar to their experiences as slaves:

> Both systems involved exploitation: the slave received no compensation for the wealth he produced, and the prisoner is expected to produce marketable goods for what amounts to no compensation. Slavery and prison life share a complete lack of freedom of movement. The power of those in authority is total, and they expect no deference from those under domination. Just as in the days of slavery, constant surveillance and observation are part of the prison experience and if inmates develop meaningful and revolutionary friendships among themselves, these ties are broken by institutional transfers, just as the slave master broke up families. . . . It is generally recognized that a system of slavery is degrading for the master and slave alike. This applies to prison, too. The atmosphere of fear has a distorting effect on the lives of everyone there—from commissioners and superintendents to prisoners in solitary confinement. Nowhere is this more evident than among "correctional officers" as the guards are euphemistically called. (Newton, 1973, 258)

The attraction of radicals to the prison was twofold. They felt that prison provided an excellent issue that well illustrated the most negative consequences of the capitalistic system. Also, based on their early contacts with inmates, many were convinced that they could recruit inmate leaders for outside radical activities. Irwin (1980) also notes that some of the individuals involved in the movement developed an idealistic view of prisoners' sincerity and humanity.

The Black Panther party originated in Oakland, California, in 1966 in reaction to police brutality in the black community and as a means of protecting blacks against the police (Stratton, 1973). The group represented itself as a Marxist/Leninist revolutionary party that was directing its efforts toward freeing blacks from their suppression by corporate capitalism. Panther leaders saw inmates as embittered, disgruntled, and thus ripe for involvement in revolutionary political activity (Jacobs, 1976). The Panthers appealed to formerly apolitical prisoners by offering them the opportunity to adopt the more positive status of political prisoner. The Panthers took the position that both blacks and whites were oppressed by the capitalistic system and therefore did not advocate a racist position.

As of 1987, only three terrorist incidents had been ascribed to domestic black groups, all of which involved religious rivalry (Harris, 1987, 9). In addition, at least one other incident was averted by arrests in 1984. The three terrorist incidents were attributed to the group Fuqra, a black Islamic sect headquartered in Detroit, Michigan. Fuqra seeks to purify Islam by eliminating rival religious sects, such as the Ahmadiyya Movement in Islam (AMI). During August 1983, several terrorist acts were perpetrated against the AMI in Detroit: the AMI secretary was killed; firebombs were thrown at the home of the AMI treasurer; and an AMI temple was burned. Fuqra was implicated in these attacks because the bodies of the arsonists—Fuqra members—were found at the temple; they had become trapped while setting the blaze. The gun used to kill the AMI secretary was found on one of the bodies.

A possible terrorist plot involving a black street gang was prevented in August 1986, when several members of the El Rukns street gang were arrested in Chicago. Group members had in their possession numerous weapons, including an antitank weapon that had been sold to them in an undercover operation. This group, which has loose ties to Islam, is a violent criminal organization involved in drug trafficking and other illegal enterprises. Some group members allegedly met with agents of the Libyan government. The El Rukns apparently were seeking to commit a terrorist incident for hire. Thus far, nothing has happened.

Gurr (1988, 561) places black terrorism in its appropriate historical and contemporary perspective:

> Armed violence by handfuls of black militants was the last deadly derivative of a movement that won most of its victories through peaceful protest in the early 1960s. Black militancy had largely subsided by the early 1970s, in part because of the gains of the previous

decades and in part because of an increasingly conservative political climate and growing skepticism among black activists about the prospects for further progress. . . Black terrorists were concerned in however distorted a way with what we have called single-issue terrorism: they sought to defend and promote the rights of black Americans. Their occasional use of revolutionary rhetoric was at best a gesture of solidarity with political and intellectual movements in the Third World, not a serious or realistic aspiration for a U.S. minority.

The Ideological Right

Right-wing terrorism became an area of focus for law enforcement during the 1980s. Harris states that "Much of the rhetoric of the extreme right is particularly volatile and corrosive" (1987, 10) and is a motivating factor in the commission of violent acts—bombings, murders, assaults, and armed robberies—to further these views.

The third revival of the Klu Klux Klan began in the 1950s in the wake of the Supreme Court's *Brown v. Board of Education* decision and gained momentum in the states of the old Confederacy through the 1960s. At its peak, the Klan boasted about 700 Klaverns with a membership of 17,000. Murders, beatings, cross burnings, and other acts intended to intimidate and harass civil rights workers in their attempts to enroll black voters provoked a sharp federal reaction. FBI investigations led to successful prosecutions in the federal courts, and by the late 1960s and early 1970s, many white Southerners, both officials and ordinary citizens, were alienated by the Klan's terrorist activities. The KKK has endured, however, and so does the susceptibility of some Americans to racial and religious extremism.

In 1989, former KKK Imperial Wizard David Duke was elected to the Louisiana state legislature from the New Orleans suburb of Metairie. Duke was an avowed Nazi during his college days; and although he claimed to have left the Klan in 1979, his home address still served as the local Klan office at the time he entered the Louisiana statehouse. He also heads the National Association for the Advancement of White People from the same address.

Duke insisted that his extremism was a thing of the past and, in the statehouse, espoused a line of Republican conservatism. But in March 1989, at a conference in Chicago of the extreme right-wing Populist Party, he shared the podium with Art Jones, a member of the American Nazi Party. A couple of months later, he was found selling a collection of neo-Nazi books out of his state-funded district constituents' office. Among the titles were Hitler's *Mein Kampf; Did Six Million Die? The Truth at Last,* which claims that the Holocaust was a hoax inspired by the Jewish-controlled media; *Imperium,* which argues for the preservation of Western culture through Nazi racist policies; and numerous pamphlets published by a group that supports human breeding to create a master race.

Duke waved away press questions with vague assurances, claiming that the neo-Nazi books were simply "old stock" from his book business. Such materials, he claimed, were "not part of my agenda any longer." From the Louisiana House floor, he declared: "I want to make it very clear right now that I reject categorically racial or religious intolerance or hatred. Furthermore, I am diametrically opposed to the totalitarian politics and policies of both communism and Nazism." Skeptics point out that, while Duke professes to believe in "civil rights for all people," his new organization publishes an anti-Semitic newspaper with 30,000 subscribers that advocates restricting Jews to ghettoes (Cohler, 1989; Magnuson, 1989).

A number of right-wing organizations or groups share some common ideological themes. Ranging from the United Klans of America to the Aryan Nations, a basic belief is a religious fundamentalism that asserts the superiority of the white race. According to this dogma, blacks, other nonwhites, and Jews are racially, mentally, physically, and spiritually inferior. Much of this doctrine is espoused by the racist, anti-Semitic Christian Identity Movement, which teaches that the white race is God's chosen people and that whites, not Jews, are the true descendants of Israel. Jews are considered descendants of Satan.

Theories of economic conspiracy are also widely held by members of these groups; for example, that national and international forces, led by Jewish financiers, are responsible for hardship and economic depression in rural America (Gurr, 1988, 555). Politically, the groups reject the policies and authority of the federal government, which they refer to as ZOG (the Zionist Occupational Government), as being controlled by liberals, Jews, and blacks. They also emphasize "survivalism," contending that their members should prepare to fight in the racial or nuclear Armageddon that inevitably lies ahead.

Gurr notes that despite similar beliefs, the groups differ in the extent to which they are willing to engage in various actions to support their beliefs. He identifies the principal 1980s extremist groups on a continuum from conventional to violent activity. Advocacy and recruitment are within legal limits, paramilitary training is a borderline activity, tax resistance is illegal but nonviolent, and political killings and armed clashes with law enforcement officers are a major threat to public order.

One of the leaders of this movement is the Reverend Richard Butler of the Aryan Nations, Church of Jesus Christ Christian, headquartered near Hayden Lake, Idaho. His sermons, identity propaganda, and other hate and neo-Nazi literature and materials are distributed nationally from Hayden Lake by members of the group. Some popular titles: Richard Harwood's *Did Six Million Really Die?*, an item that David Duke's bookstore also carried; Butler's own *The Aryan Warrior;* and an obscure forty-year-old pamphlet called *The Hitler We Loved and Why*. Aryan Nation members maintain contacts with other right-wing groups. Members of the Aryan Nation and other neo-Nazi extreme groups often wear swastikas, double lightning bolts, and other symbols used by Hitler's Nazis.

The most violent extremist group during the 1980s, according to Harris (1987, 11) was The Order (otherwise known as the Bruders Schweigen or Silent Brotherhood), an offshoot of the Aryan Nations. This group was founded by Aryan Nations member Robert Mathews and is loosely based on a book entitled *The Turner Diaries*—an apocalyptic account of racial warfare in the United States. In the novel, an elite clandestine force, The Order, spearheads efforts to destroy the U.S. government and replace it with one based on white supremacy.

Members of the Order have been involved in numerous criminal activities since 1983, in-

cluding counterfeiting, armed robbery (with proceeds exceeding $4 million), bombings, assaults on federal officers, and the murders of a suspected informant, a Missouri state police officer, and a Denver talk-show host named Alan Berg. Between October 1984 and March 1986, thirty-eight members of the Order were arrested. On December 7, 1984, Robert Mathews was killed on Whidbey Island, Washington, while resisting arrest. Shoulder weapons, handguns, grenades and other explosives, ammunition, and potential target lists were recovered at various safehouses and other locations.

Another group that has been involved in criminal activity is the Covenant, the Sword, the Arm of the Lord (CSA). Beginning in 1980, some CSA members participated in bombings, arsons, robberies, and the murder of a black Arkansas state police officer. During April 1985, the CSA compound was raided by federal authorities, who arrested five persons, including four Order members (two of whom were fugitives) and CSA leader James Ellison. All the CSA and Order members arrested at that time or later pled guilty to charges or were convicted in federal or state courts.

Although aggressive Justice Department campaigns against white supremacist groups appeared to have significantly reduced their terrorist threat, recent events suggest that some groups may have made a comeback. Bombings that took place at the end of 1989 in Alabama, Georgia, Florida, and Maryland showed a similar pattern to earlier white supremacist incidents. The FBI is still investigating, but evidence so far suggests that a deadly campaign has begun to punish and deter members of the judiciary and civil rights advocates who have pushed school desegregation, offended the Ku Klux Klan, and respected the rights of blacks accused of assaults against whites.

Another right-wing faction that has drawn the attention of law enforcement officials includes tax protest and antigovernment groups. Organizations such as the Sheriff's Posse Comitatus (SPC) and the Arizona Patriots espouse parochial as opposed to national interests and, like the anarchists of the last century, desire as little government as possible. They advocate nonpayment of taxes and consider federal and state laws unconstitutional. The SPC, for example, regards the local sheriff as the only legitimate law enforcement authority and the justice of the peace as the highest court in the country!

Nationalistic Groups

Puerto Ricans

The independence of Puerto Rico, a former Spanish colony that the U.S. acquired at the end of the Spanish-American war in 1898, has been a burning political cause among a growing minority of Puerto Ricans for more than a century. In 1950, two nationalists attempted to assassinate President Harry S Truman at Blair House, across the street from the White House. President Truman escaped unharmed, but a District of Columbia police officer was shot and killed. On March 1, 1954, several Puerto Rican nationalists staged a shooting attack from the gallery of the U.S. House of Representatives and wounded five Congressmen. Organizations called, respectively, the *Comandos Armados de Liberacion* and the *Movimento de Independenza Revolucion en Armas* were suppressed by police action during the late 1960s and 1970s, but their surviving members formed a new organization known after 1974 as the Armed Forces of National Liberation (or FALN, after its Spanish name). This group, the most active in the continental U.S. since 1974, has been responsible for more than one hundred terrorist attacks.

Terrorist groups in Puerto Rico, in contrast, have been far more active in the commission of acts of violence. Nearly forty of the fifty-six terrorist acts committed in Puerto Rico have been attributed to two groups: the EPB-Macheteros (Machete Wielders) and the Organization of Volunteers for the Puerto Rican Revolution (OVRP). A majority of these actions consisted of bombings or attempted bombings; others included shootings, robberies, and two rocket attacks. Although Puerto Rican interests have been targeted in most of the incidents, U.S. government facilities and personnel have been attacked with greater frequency since 1983.

Police raids and arrests in 1985 temporarily shut down the *Macheteros*. But there is little reason to assume that terrorist actions in Puerto Rico will stop in the foreseeable future. The U.S. government, as Gurr points out, can scarcely force independence on a reluctant island to satisfy minority demands.

Émigré Nationalists

Transnational terrorism refers to terrorism that transcends national boundaries. Terrorists may originate in one country and carry out attacks in another country or may act in their own country in the name of an international cause or on behalf of a foreign government. In the United States, émigré groups nursing old grudges or fighting lost causes account for much transnational terrorism.

Armenian Nationalists During World War I, approximately 1.5 million Armenians, an ethnic minority living in Turkey, lost their lives. Armenians have claimed that this tragic predecessor to the Holocaust of a later time was the result of a deliberate attempt at genocide carried out by the successors to the "Unspeakable Turk," Sultan Abdul-Hamid II. According to the Turks, the loss of life occurred as part of the process of deportation and resettlement of the Armenians, who were viewed as a threat to Turkish internal security (ATA-USA *Bulletin,* 1982, 4–9).

Sixty years later, young Armenian nationalists, calling themselves the Armenian Secret Army for the Liberation of Armenia (ASALA), began a campaign of terror against primarily Turkish targets. The ASALA was international and Marxist-oriented and supported the ideology of national liberation. But an ideological split led to the formation of a rival anti-Marxist group, the Justice Commandos for Armenian Genocide (JCAG), which claimed that its terrorist actions were directed exclusively against Turkish targets (Wilkinson, 1983). North American members of the latter group carried out the assassination of the Turkish Consul-General in Los Angeles in May 1982.

Armenian violence was brought to an abrupt end by the arrest of six Armenian terrorists in 1982 and the life sentence given to Hampig Sassounian, convicted of the Los Angeles murder. Experts believe there is little likelihood of future terrorism, because the actions of the ASALA and JCAG have discredited them in Armenian communities in the U.S. and in other countries.

Croatian Nationalists In September 1976, five Americans of Croatian descent sky-jacked a TWA jet, had it flown to Europe, and demanded that leaflets on behalf of Croatian independence be dropped over Chicago, London, Montreal, New York, and Paris. A manifesto issued during this media event by the "Headquarters of Croatian National Liberation Forces" contained the following language:

> National self-determination is a basic human right, universal and fundamental, recognized by all members of the UN, a right which may not be denied or withheld any nation regardless of its territorial size or number of inhabitants. . . (*New York Times*, September 12, 1976)

Behind this incident was a long, complicated tangle of ethnic and political strife between the Serbs and the Croats, the two largest republics that make up present-day Yugoslavia. Neither the Kingdom of Serbs, Croats, and Slovenes, established under the Treaty of Versailles at the end of World War I, nor Yugoslavia under the Tito government at the close of World War II were politically viable states capable of resolving centuries of hostility and violence between the contending ethnic factions.

At any rate, the skyjackers of the TWA flight were extradited by French authorities to the U.S., where they were convicted and sentenced to lengthy prison terms. The convictions appear to have ended the activities of the Croatian National Resistance against the Yugoslav government, at least within the U.S. It is doubtful whether many Americans were ever aware of their existence or of the crusading cause they represented.

Anti-Castro Cubans Expatriate Cubans have carried on more than two decades of violence directed mainly against the Castro regime, but also against rival groups. The oldest anti-Castro group is Alpha 66, which is still led by members of the Cuban militia who participated in the ill-starred landing at the Bay of Pigs. The number 66 commemorates the year the group was formed as the beginning of an effort to wrest Cuba from the control of Fidel Castro and his Soviet-satellite Communist government.

Between 1968 and 1975, such groups as *El Poder Cubano* (Cuban Power) and the Cuban National Liberation Front were responsible for a series of bombings, assaults, and an assassination. Between 1975 and 1983, a group called Omega 7 was the main source of Cuban émigré terrorism and a serious threat to the U.S. and Latin American states that support Fidel Castro. Seven key members were arrested in 1982 and 1983, including Eduardo Arocena, the group's leader. Arocena was convicted and sentenced to life imprisonment. These law enforcement actions appear to have effectively curbed the violent activities of Omega 7.

Single-Issue Terrorists

Schmid and de Graaf (1982) designate as *single-issue terrorism* that committed by individuals or small groups attempting to exert pressure on authorities to grant some privilege to a larger group with which the terrorists sympathize.

Included in this category is a diverse collection of groups, ranging from the right-to-lifers and pro-choice activists to the Jewish Defense League. These groups display a number of common features.

Animal Rights Activists

In November 1988, in the parking lot of the U.S. Surgical Corporation in Norwalk, Connecticut, police arrested a woman who was attempting to place a pipe bomb in the bushes near the parking spot reserved for Leon Hirsch, the company's founder. Next day, New York City police found a shotgun and three more bombs in the woman's apartment amidst stacks of animal rights literature.

Fran Stephanie Trutt's arrest focused national attention on the controversial animal rights movement, estimated to comprise more than 7000 groups or organizations with membership in excess of 10 million and operating funds of more than $50 million—almost all raised by direct contributions. Taking their cue from militant British groups, some American activists have raided and ransacked labs where animals are used in tests of medical equipment. One faction, the Animal Liberation Front, claims responsibility for setting a California laboratory on fire.

In February 1989, two animal rights groups in Britain claimed responsibility for a bomb that caused severe damage to administration buildings at the University of Bristol. The activists stated that the device was intended as a protest against research on animal subjects at the university's medical and veterinary schools. Before the blast, a warning was received from a telephone caller claiming to belong to a previously unknown group, the Animal Abused Society. Although militant animal rights groups had previously used incendiary devices, the University of Bristol bombing is the first time that high explosives had been used. Predictably, the British Secretary of State for Education and Science referred to the incident as an "act of terrorism."

Many animal rights activists condemn violent protests, and most of the movement's 10 million members concentrate on lobbying and peaceful rallies. Several groups repudiated Fran Stephanie Trutt, fearing that her case would hurt their efforts; they contend that Trutt, a troubled loner obsessed with her cause, is hardly a representative of their crusade. Julie Lewin of the Fund for Animals said, "Violence toward people does not help animals." Some animal rights proponents contend that Trutt's aborted bomb attack is so damaging to their cause that it might have been instigated by an agent provocateur. Police say the bomb she planted was too sophisticated to have been made by Trutt herself, and Trutt is reputed to have told the FBI that she has no knowledge of explosives (*Time,* November 28, 1988, 24).

Pro-Life and Pro-Choice Activists

Gurr calls the series of arson and bombing attacks on abortion clinics, which began in the early 1980s and continued throughout the decade, "the most recent manifestation of vigilante terrorism in the United States" (1988, 558). Anti-abortion terrorists bombed more than forty abortion and birth control clinics between 1982 and 1986. Bombings reached a peak of twenty-five in 1984, then declined to eleven in 1985. But some of the 1985 bombings were potentially deadly, and two passersby were injured in an October 1986 bombing in New York City. (Hoffman, 1987, 238–239).

Nationwide, abortion clinics have been invaded, vandalized, burned, and bombed. Patients are harassed as they try to enter clinics, and "pregnancy clinics" have sprung up to lure unsuspecting women to anti-abortion lectures accompanied by gruesome visual details. Physicians who perform abortions receive hate mail and threats to their families; one Illinois physician and his wife were kidnapped and held for eight days (Kort, 1987, 49).

Some of those who take an active role in the pro-life movement share with right-wing groups a commitment to Christian fundamentalist doctrines, whereas some of those involved in the pro-choice movement endorse some of the basic principles identified with the ideological left. With regard to the depth and intensity of commitment displayed by people on both sides of the abortion issue, there is little room for civility and none whatever for dialogue or negotiation.

The Jewish Defense League (JDL)

The Jewish Defense League (JDL) was founded in 1968 to protest Soviet mistreatment of Jews. Its leaders were a lawyer, Bert Zweibon, and an Orthodox rabbi, Meier Kahane. Members were trained in martial arts and the use of weapons to defend themselves. They took their motto "Never Again" from the title of a book written by Kahane. During the JDL's first three years, the group carried out demonstrations and relatively harmless protest activities against Russians, Arabs, and Black Panthers.

Between 1977 and 1986, forty-three acts of terrorism have been attributed to the JDL. Although the JDL seldom claims responsibility for acts of violence, Kahane has consistently advocated the use of violence against those the League considers anti-Semitic or anti-Israel. Hoffman (1987, 5) states that more than thirty JDL members have been convicted in U.S. courts for committing, or conspiring to commit, terrorist crimes. The JDL has the somber distinction of having killed the only two victims of terrorist bombings in the U.S. in 1985.

Summary

Political terrorism of the kind that is familiar to the people of Europe and Latin America has not posed a serious danger to public order in the U.S. The number and seriousness of terrorist acts bombings, shootings, arson, and vandalism—have shown a decade-long decline, as measured by both official and unofficial sources.

For reasons that are deeply rooted in the American history and ethos, insurgent violence from the ideological left has never proven attractive to any but a very small minority of U.S. citizens: campus radicals, intellectuals, militant blacks, and small groups of social misfits, such as the Symbionese Liberation Army and the Manson "family." Despite saturation coverage of their activities by the media, their numbers were ineffectual and their network of support extremely limited. Most important, as Gurr suggests, they were unable or unwilling to "set aside the tactical liability of their humanitarianism" (1988, 573); that is, they were willing to blow up buildings but not people, thus sharply limiting their capacity to instill real terror.

On the ideological right we find an authentic homegrown form of terrorism: vigilantism. . . . the historical antecedents of vigilantism in the U.S. can be traced to the colonial period; the Ku Klux Klan that arose in the post-Civil War South can be recognized as a familiar specimen of this phenomenon. We are currently experiencing the third revival of Klan activity, which has found its traditional theme of racial purity even less appealing to people in the most conservative rural areas from which it once drew its main support.

An emergent New Right comprises a number of groups that are relatively small in numbers and organization but are united on such themes as fundamentalist Christian identity, survivalism, and the right of communities to self-defense. Given the close surveillance and prosecution of illegal acts committed by members of such groups as the Aryan Nation, Sheriff's Posse Comitatus, and the Klan, there is little likelihood that the country will experience the widespread terrorism that scourged the rural South during the 1950s and 1960s. Gurr (1988, 573) cautions, however, that resentment about social change and economic decline are the most fertile breeding grounds for future violence on the right.

For at least two decades, émigré nationalist groups have used the U.S. as an arena to promote political causes by means of terrorist actions. For brief periods, the media stage center has been occupied by Croatian nationalists, Serb nationalists, Armenian nationalists, and anti-Castro Cubans. The most enduring and dangerous of these factions are Puerto Ricans who seek independence for their island nation. Much of the rhetoric and some of their tactics show indebtedness to Third World insurgency, but it is far from clear whether a majority of their fellow Puerto Ricans share their aspirations.

Acts of domestic terrorism in the 1980s have been committed by extremist members of single-issue groups: animal rights protesters, pro-life and pro-choice activists, and members of the Jewish Defense League (JDL). Despite bombings, arsons, vandalism, and other acts of violence, few people have been killed or injured and property damage has been relatively light. In the open warfare between the pro-life and pro-choice forces, however, there is no room for complacency when contemplating the future. Crusaders have never been known for a disposition toward tolerance in pursuing a cause. As the struggle intensifies, extremists on both sides are increasingly likely to be heard.

References

ATA-USA. "Setting the record straight on Armenian propaganda against Turkey." *Bulletin of the Assembly of American Turkish Associations.* Washington, DC (Fall 1982): 4–9.

Berkman, B. *Opening the Prison Gates: The Rise of the Prisoners Movement.* Lexington, MA: Lexington Books, 1979.

Cohler, L. "Republican Racist: Dealing with the David Duke Problem." *The New Republic* 201 (1989): 11–14.

Committee on Internal Security, House of Representatives. *Staff Study on Revolutionary Activity Directed toward the Administration of Penal or Correctional Systems.* Washington, DC: U.S. Government Printing Office, 1973.

Gurr, T. R. "Political Terrorism in the United States: Historical and Contemporary Trends." In *The Politics of Terrorism,* edited by M. Stohl, pp. 549–578. New York: Marcel Dekker, 1988.

Harris, J. W. "Domestic Terrorism in the 1980s." *FBI Law Enforcement Bulletin* 56 (1987): 5–13.

Hoffman, B. "Terrorism in the United States in 1985." In *Contemporary Research on Terrorism,* edited by P. Wilkinson and A. M. Stewart, pp. 230–240. Aberdeen, U.K.: Aberdeen University Press, 1987.

Homer, F. D. "Terror in the United States: Three Perspectives." In *The Politics of Terrorism,* edited by M. Stohl, pp. 145–177. New York: Marcel Dekker, 1983.

Irwin, J. *Prisons in Turmoil.* Boston, MA: Little, Brown, 1980.

Jackson, G. *Soledad Brother: The Prison Letters of George Jackson.* New York: Coward-McCann, 1970.

Jacobs, J. "Stratification and Conflict among Prison Inmates." *Journal of Criminal Law and Criminology* 66 (1976): 476–482.

Kort, M. "Domestic Terrorism: On the Front Line at an Abortion Clinic." *Ms. Magazine* XV (May 1987): 48–53.

Magnuson, E. "An Ex-Klansman's Win Brings the G.O.P. Chickens Home to Roost." *Time* (March 6, 1989): 29.

National Advisory Commission on Criminal Justice Standards and Goals. *Task Force Report on Civil Disorders.* Washington, DC: U.S. Government Printing Office, 1973.

Newton, H. P. *Revolutionary Suicide.* New York: Harcourt Brace Jovanovich, 1973.

Parry, A. *Terrorism: From Robespierre to Arafat.* New York: Vanguard Press, 1976.

Reilly, S. "Life Uneasy for Woman at Center of Abortion Ruling." *The Oregonian* (May 9, 1989): A2.

Schmid, A. P., and De Graaf, J. *Violence as Communication: Insurgent Terrorism and the Western News Media.* Beverly Hills, CA: Sage Publications, 1982.

Silberman, C. *Criminal Justice, Criminal Violence.* New York: Vintage Books, 1980.

Stratton, J. Testimony before the Committee on Internal Security, House of Representatives. *Staff Study on Revolutionary Activity Directed against the Administration of Penal or Correctional Systems.* Washington, DC: U.S. Government Printing Office, 1973.

Strentz, T. "A Terrorist Psychosocial Profile, Past and Present." *FBI Law Enforcement Bulletin* 57 (1988): 13–19.

Trick, M. M. "Chronology of Incidents of Terroristic, Quasi-terroristic, and Political Violence in the United States: January 1965 to March 1976." National Advisory Committee on Criminal Justice Standards and Goals. *Disorders and Terrorism: Report of the Task Force on Disorders and Terrorism.* Washington, DC: Law Enforcement Assistance Administration, Department of Justice, 1976.

Wilkinson, P. "Armenian Terrorism." *The World Today* 39 (September 1983): 336–350.

31

The Social Origins of
Violence in the American Prison

Matthew Silberman

. . . In this chapter, we turn to the structural origins of violence in American society that contribute both directly and indirectly to violence in prison. We shall see how racial inequality contributes to the violent nature of American society, producing racial division in society as a whole and violent confrontations between ethnic groups in prison. The prison system reproduces the social conflicts that have their origins in society and the violence that results.

Because the prison world is a microcosm of the larger society, and because it acts as a cauldron for the tensions that society has produced, the prison system often releases individuals who are more dangerous than when they entered prison. This is not only expressed in the attitudes and behavior of the individuals who have been released after long-term incarceration, especially as juveniles or youthful offenders, but in the values and norms they bring back to the streets. The offender who has done hard time often becomes a role model in the community to which he returns, transmitting the culture of prison life and its violent nature to the streets.

Much of what is described as the violent ghetto culture today, the expressed need to carry weapons and the easy resort to violence in response to disputes, have their origins in prison. The dependence on a group of homeboys or a single person (prop) for survival in a hostile and dangerous world in prison is replicated on the street where guns are readily available and violent confrontations over the distribution of drugs are frequent.

The purpose of this chapter is to identify the social origins of violence in society at large and to describe the mechanisms by which that violence is transmitted to the prison world. Ironically, the violent adaptations that occur in today's prisons are brought to the streets by the released convict, creating a vicious cycle of violence between society and the prison system designed to stop the violence. This chapter synthesizes new material on politics and the economy with material on prison life . . . in order to make sense of the interaction that occurs between prison and society.

The Structural Origins of Violence

Recent research on the causes of violence has identified social inequality as one of the major factors contributing to high levels of violence in the United States today. Inequality based on race, class, or gender contributes to higher rates of criminal violence, including homicide, rape, and assault (see Krohn, 1976; Braithwaite, 1979; Messner, 1980; Schwendinger and Schwendinger, 1981; Blau and Blau, 1982; Baron and Straus, 1987; Gelles and Straus, 1988:86; Caputi, 1989).[1] Cross-cultural studies link economic inequality to criminal violence in general. These studies also show that gender inequality contributes to the incidence of rape. Gender inequality in the United States has been tied to sexual violence, including rape and serial murder. Economic inequality has been linked to family violence, and racial inequality has been linked to homicide.

Economic inequality contributes to a higher incidence of violent crime in a number of ways. When poverty is made worse because of who you are rather than what you have or have not accomplished, the frustrations associated with one's relative deprivation are made worse. When economic conditions create a large underclass, the need to resort to violence in a world of scarcity increases. And when the deprivations of the underclass lead to incarceration, the racial and ethnic conflicts that result from the competition for survival in society are made worse.

Given the frontier culture that legitimates violence in response to disputes over property and persons and given the decoupling of the official and informal control systems in prison, structural inequalities on the outside exacerbate the racial and ethnic tensions inside prison. It should not be surprising, then, that much of the violence in prison has racial undertones.

Social Inequality and the Production of Violence

One of the best studies of the effect of social inequality on criminal violence was conducted by Judith and Peter Blau (1982). The Blaus examined a large number of American cities and measured the discrepancies in wealth between the haves and have nots in each city. They found that it is not poverty per se that leads to crime, but poverty in the face of wealth that does so. Property crime was especially high in those areas where the wealthy were wealthiest and the poor were the poorest. Violent crime was at its greatest in those cities where wealth was determined in part by race. In other words, violent crime is a product of racial injustice.

Violence among racial minorities is an expression of rage not unlike that expressed by colonial peoples who have been subject to foreign controls for a long period of time (see Blauner, 1969). Third World peoples in colonial settings may organize politically to overthrow their oppressors, but in America, African Americans constitute a relatively small minority. Con-

sequently, racial tensions may erupt as they have during riots such as the one that occurred recently in Los Angeles. More often, however, the targets of criminal violence are the most available targets, members of one's own community. Consequently, African Americans are most frequently the targets of violence in African American communities.

When inequality is based on *ascribed status,* that is, status based on race, gender, age, or some other predetermined category, violence increases. The violence in Northern Ireland is a manifestation of the underclass position Catholics have experienced in a society dominated by a Protestant majority. To the extent that Palestinians are becoming a permanent underclass in Israeli society, violence in the state of Israel appears to be increasing. One of the most violent societies in the world can be found in Sri Lanka, formerly Ceylon, in which two ethnic groups, the Sinhalese and the Tamils, have been in a long-term struggle for power. Whether violence is of a criminal or political nature depends on the extent to which one group is able to dominate the political and economic system and the other has the resources to organize politically to resist domination.

Cross-cultural studies of gender inequality reveal two interesting facts. Rape is more frequent in societies characterized by a great deal of gender inequality (Schwendinger and Schwendinger, 1981), and domestic violence is widespread (see Baumgartner, 1993). Both these facts point to the importance of patriarchal relations, institutions based on the cultural and political domination of males, in explaining violence against women. Whether or not domestic violence is criminalized depends in large measure whether women are sufficiently organized politically to create legislation designed to restructure gender relations in their society (see Pleck, 1989).

Economic Instability and the Production of Violence

We have seen over the past ten to fifteen years an increase in homelessness, long-term unemployment, and most recently, a major recession. Once the leading nation in the world economy, the United States is now the greatest debtor nation in the world (*New York Times,* 1992). This rapid economic decline has been accompanied by enormous trade deficits and the export of both capital and labor to other countries (Sheinkman, 1992; Hershey, 1993). What this has meant to many middle-class Americans has been the loss of the American Dream. The number of jobs, especially good jobs, has declined dramatically, average wages have fallen, and benefits have declined since 1979 (Uchitelle, 1993). Many Americans have been forced to accept lower wages and part-time jobs. Permanent layoffs, retirees who lose their retirement benefits, and the closing of factories have created a sense of despair and anger among many. We have a large displaced homeless population, many of whom have dropped out of the ranks of the middle class. The sudden frustration associated with job loss has led to numerous incidents of violent outbursts.

One of the first incidents was the infamous mass murder at McDonald's in San Ysidro near San Diego, California, in 1984 (see Horvath, 1986). Huberty, a college-educated factory worker, had been laid off when the factory in his small Ohio town closed down permanently. Pursuing the American Dream, Huberty had invested in rental properties and had other investments. Nevertheless, joblessness created a sense of anger and frustration at the world that ultimately exploded in San Ysidro where he killed 21 people.

There have been a number of similar incidents involving angry postal workers and others who have experienced failure in a highly competitive system (Swickard, 1993; Koenig, 1993). These explosive acts, largely by white, middle-class failures, are the other side of the economic coin. Just as racial injustice produces violence among minority groups, economic injustice produces violence among those who assumed that they were immune from economic crisis.

Serial killing, too, appears to be a product of economic instability. The ability to kill repeatedly and escape detection is made possible by a society in which there are large numbers of displaced persons with no clear form of social identification. This anonymity makes the selection of vulnerable targets by serial killers possible. Henry Lee Lucas, who claimed at first to have killed several hundred persons, mostly female hitch-

hikers, did so while traveling the highways of America (Hickey, 1991:185–186). Convicted of only 10 homicides, Lucas has recanted his initial claims, but at least one investigator believes that 50 is a reasonable estimate (Hickey, 1991:186). Serial rapist Steven Judy was executed in 1981 for the rape and murder of a woman and the drowning of her three children, whom he had abducted from her disabled car on a highway in Indiana (*New York Times,* 1981a, 1981b). Judy was able to do so precisely because of the highly mobile and anonymous nature of our society. John Wayne Gacy, who resided in a working-class community in Chicago, was able to sexually assault dozens of young boys, murder them, and hide them in his basement without detection for several years (see Hickey, 1991:165–167). More recently, Jeffrey Dahmer, who maintained a residence in a transitional neighborhood in Milwaukee, admitted killing 17 young men and boys after drugging them during homosexual liaisons (Gelman, 1991; Mathews, 1992).

The Reproduction of Social Conflict in Prison

In America, the production of violence is intimately linked to racial and ethnic conflict. During periods of economic and political crisis, we have seen overt manifestations of ethnic hostilities in racially motivated attacks. Some politicians have effectively used "wedge" issues to divide the electorate on racial and ethnic lines in order to win elections. For example, the campaign of Republican candidate George Bush in 1988 used the image of a black rapist, Willie Horton, who had raped a white woman during a furlough from a prison in the home state of the Democratic candidate Michael Dukakis, to gain votes from the white electorate.

In the 1960s, the civil rights movement created the opportunity for African Americans to question their subordinate status in American society and to seek to change it. In prison, this gave rise to organized resistance to the subordinate status that blacks had experienced at the hands of prison administrators and white inmates alike. The Black Muslims, also known as the Nation of Islam, had its origins in Detroit as early as the 1930s (Lincoln, 1961:10–11). But they did not really become a force in American society until they began to recruit heavily among black prisoners in the 1950s and '60s (Pallas and Barber, 1973:243–248). The Muslims argued that "blacks as a group were victims of white society, that the miseries they faced were not the result of their own deficiencies" (Pallas and Barber, 1973:244). According to the original creed of the Muslims, all evil in the world was created by "blue-eyed devils," who used their power to dominate the nonwhite peoples of the world (Lincoln, 1961:75–80).

The Muslims told inmates that alcoholism, drug addiction, and criminality were a product of the evils of white society and the feelings of inadequacy that had been imposed on those of African descent who had had their true religion and true identities stripped away by the slave-masters. This message led to the conversion to Islam of large numbers of prisoners and to their rehabilitation in many cases. (Malcolm X was one of their most famous successes.) The additional appeal of the Muslims to black inmates was the evident success that this group had in reversing the hands-off doctrine of the courts. The power and effectiveness of the organization sent a clear message to African American inmates. They could overcome the historical racism of the prison system, and American society in general, by organizing to change prison conditions, and through this process gain self-respect.

Pallas and Barber (1973:246) argue that the Muslims became less militant over time and pursued a more separatist agenda, hoping to create a separate black nation in America. But it is clear that, even today, the Nation of Islam has retained a reputation for militancy among prison personnel. In addition, there has been a proliferation of Islamic groups in prison, including more conventional Shiite and Sunni sects whose beliefs are universal and nonracial.

The success of the Muslims may, in part, have created an incentive for prison reformers to ally themselves with increasingly politicized inmates in creating the prison movement of the late 1960s and early '70s. Many prisoners, especially blacks, defined themselves as "political prisoners," who were incarcerated because of the political and economic conditions of a society that produced both their criminality and their being caught and punished. The prison movement created a prisoners' union, organized work stoppages, and produced a manifesto declaring basic rights for prisoners (Irwin, 1980:110). This manifesto, or some derivative, often became a negotiating tool during prison strikes, demonstrations, or riots, as in the case of the Attica riot in 1971 (see Irwin, 1980:255–262). The ACLU (American Civil Liberties Union) founded the Prison Project in 1972, and the NAACP (National Association for the Advancement of Colored People) joined the fight for the civil rights of prisoners.

Although the successes of the Black Muslims contributed to the political consciousness of black prisoners (Pallas and Barber, 1973:246), others began to organize along less activist lines. Violent prison gangs first appeared in the California prison system in the late 1960s (Irwin, 1980:183–192). First, a group of urban Chicano prisoners organized the Mexican Mafia, which began to exploit less organized rural Chicanos and others. The other prisoners began to organize into defensive and retaliatory groups such as the Nuestra Familia (Hispanic), the Black Guerilla Family (black), and the Aryan Brotherhood (white). These four gangs have become the major prison gangs throughout America's prisons (Crouch and Marquart, 1989:204). Throughout the 1970s, most killings in the California prison system were attributable to the gangs (Crouch and Marquart, 1989:204). Some of these gangs began to exploit their control over members who were released from prison. The Nuestra Familia, for example, became active in promoting drug trafficking in northern California (see Lewis, 1980).

In Illinois, street gangs such as the Blackstone Rangers, a black group, and the Latin Kings, a Hispanic group, became active in the state's prisons (Irwin, 1980:191; Jacobs, 1977:158). Here, too, white prisoners organized defensively. In Texas, a small Hispanic group, the Texas Syndicate, had been around since the 1970s after developing among Hispanics of Texan origin in the California prison system to defend against the Chicano groups there. But, as the "authority vacuum" grew in the late 1970s and early 1980s in Texas, the Texas Syndicate grew in numbers and strength (Crouch and Marquart, 1989:206). The Aryan Brotherhood and Texas

Mafia, both white groups, and the Mexican Mafia emerged as powerful gangs at the same time.

Throughout the history of the prison system, inmates have associated with others with whom they shared a common interest. Irwin (1980:58–60) described these as "tips and cliques," in the correctional institutions of the '60s and '70s. Tips were groups that shared common experiences, such as juvenile institutions, neighborhoods (homeboys), or criminal activities. Irwin describes cliques as smaller groups who interacted with one another because of shared living arrangements and membership in a larger tip. By the 1980s, associating with homeboys became the major basis of group affiliation in American prisons. Of course, homeboys, because they come from the same neighborhoods and communities, usually share similar racial and ethnic backgrounds.

In the federal penitentiary at Leavenworth, geographical origin is a major source of gang affiliation. Earley (1992:91) describes "DC Blacks" as the "largest single ethnic group" in Leavenworth. A major disturbance at Leavenworth in July 1992 involved gangs from two major "geographical regions," one reportedly from Washington, D.C. and the other from Los Angeles. At the time of the riot, a prison spokesperson suggested that the fighting that took place during a takeover of the auditorium and prison yard may have been caused by "overcrowding, racial trouble and gang violence," but the precise cause had yet to be determined (Hanna, 1992:3). One inmate was killed in a melee that involved about 300 prisoners.

In one of the first accounts of race relations in prison, Leo Carroll (1974) describes the emergence of racial conflicts in the late 1960s and early '70s after a period of relative peace from 1956 to 1968 at ECI ("Eastern Correctional Institution"). White editors of the prison newspaper were accused of racism when they refused to publish articles about newly emerging black consciousness. Conflict over control of prison social clubs ensued, and ultimately blacks were permitted to form their own Afro-American Society (Carroll, 1974:40). Carroll describes the institution as racially polarized from that point on.

One of the manifestations of the struggle for power between whites and blacks was rape. As in the outside world, rape is as much an expression of power and anger (by men against women) as it is sexual. In the prison world, where opportunities for heterosexual relations is virtually nil, homosexual acts are not infrequent. Under normal circumstances, as on the outside, most such contacts are consensual and involve many but not all prisoners. But homosexual rape, like heterosexual rape, is an expression of power and anger as much as it is sexual. For this reason, most prison rapes were interracial, and most of these involved groups of black assailants and a single white victim. In 1971, Carroll (1974:182) estimates that at least 75 percent of the rapes at ECI were black on white. Carroll attributed these rapes to black rage directed at dominant white institutions and the ability to exert symbolic control over a white victim who represented these institutions. On the other hand, Lockwood (1980:78) argues that sexual aggression by blacks against whites reinforces racist attitudes among white prisoners (also see Irwin, 1980:183).

Several later studies of prison rape described essentially the same interracial pattern (Lockwood, 1980:77–79; Bowker, 1980:7–10; Wooden and Parker, 1982:60). Wooden and Parker point out that consensual homosexual relations are predominantly intraracial. The irony is that most of the homosexual "punks" or "kids" are "turned out" forcibly by members of a different ethnic group. According to Carroll (1974:183–184), at ECI, a white inmate would be repeatedly assaulted by a group or groups of black inmates until a white convict offered to take him under his wing and protect him as long as he agreed to be his "kid," in a more or less exclusive and subservient homosexual relationship. This suggests that the pattern of sexual assault at ECI served the interests of the convicts, both white and black, who dominated the social life of the institution.

The Production of the Underclass by the Prison System

There are two contrasting views of the nature of the American underclass. The first is that the underclass is a more or less permanent group stuck in the lowest stratum of the economic system. Produced by a "culture of poverty," the poor constitute a more or less permanent cadre of welfare-dependent, mostly minority group individuals who are ill-educated, untrained, and unsuited by temperament and lack of skills to participate in the industrial economy (Moore, 1985:1; Beverly and Stanback, 1986:24).

A second view takes the position that the culture of poverty thesis is essentially racist and classist in its assumptions (Moore, 1985:1; Beverly and Stanback, 1986:24). There is little evidence to support the idea that poverty and welfare dependency are transmitted from generation to generation (Wilson and Aponte, 1985:241–243). It is primarily the structure of the economy that determines economic opportunities and welfare dependency (Wilson and Aponte, 1985; Sanders, 1990).

This second approach views the underclass as a dynamic entity, one that includes many different kinds of nonproductive citizens whose life experiences have cast them out of the economic system. In addition to welfare families, this group includes the homeless, the seriously mentally ill, hustlers, winos, and habitual criminals. High levels of unemployment produced by economic recession create outcasts out of many individuals during hard times. But we must also understand that high rates of unemployment are endemic to our society. Thus, the underclass as a social position is a permanent fixture of our society, while the actual members of this underclass are being constantly produced and reproduced.

Very few of the members of the underclass were born into this status. Many, indeed, have experienced reasonably successful working-class or middle-class lifestyles at some point in their lives. Thus, the question becomes, *what are the mechanisms or processes by which productive or potentially productive citizens are transformed into social outcasts?* Once we understand that winos, addicts, and burns can be created by a society that degrades and humiliates its failures, leaving few options to return to conventionality, we can also begin to ask questions such as: How is it that society produces those groups who *appear* to be permanent members of the underclass? What role does the prison system play in producing the underclass?

As long as social and economic conditions do not change from generation to generation, the children of the underclass in one generation are likely to face the same conditions as their parents. If racism and the decay of the economic base remain problems in our inner cities, it is easy to see why racial minorities continue to be disproportionately represented among welfare and criminal populations.

The Role of the Jail in the Production of "Rabble": Winos, Addicts, and Bums

In his book on the American jail, John Irwin (1985) describes the process by which the jail system contributes to the production of "rabble": winos, addicts, and bums. Irwin points out that most people in city or county jails are either waiting for trial or have been convicted of minor offenses. Who is arrested and jailed and why? Irwin describes these individuals as "disreputables," individuals whose public behavior is unconventional or "offensive."

These disreputables include hustlers who sell small quantities of drugs, engage in unsophisticated swindles, or commit petty thefts such as rolling drunks, shoplifting, or burglarizing cars (Irwin, 1985:26). They also include skid-row drunks, released mental patients, junkies, and aliens. This last group is an unexpected category, yet the police treat those who speak and act differently in much the same way that they do other unconventional persons. Gay men were at one time treated as "rabble" and lived on the edge of legitimate society as they found themselves in and out of city jails. Today, with the gay rights movement and greater consciousness of the civil and political rights of homosexuals, there is effective pressure on police not to treat homosexuality as criminal, although police still find overt displays of a gay lifestyle as offensive.

Young black males may also get caught up in the criminal justice system because their behavior is viewed as offensive by police officers, although in many cases this is merely a first step toward further criminalization. This is especially true for junkies and a group that used to be called "corner boys" (see Liebow, 1967; Whyte,

1981). Hanging around and acting tough, inner-city kids are quickly labeled as troublemakers and may get pulled in by the police for minor offenses that might otherwise be ignored. Working-class whites, known in California as "low-riders," may find themselves in similar circumstances if they engage in behavior considered offensive to police officers and the community they represent, such as cruising noisily in a souped-up car. It is important to understand the way in which the jail contributes to the production of rabble because a major chunk of this group is likely to end up in prison, where they will be exposed to further violence.

The jail contributes to the creation of an underclass in four distinct stages: (1) disintegration, (2) disorientation, (3) degradation, and (4) preparation. During the *disintegration* stage, the new prisoner experiences several important losses, each anchoring his sense of who he is in the real world (Irwin, 1985:42–66). He loses his property, as his car may be towed and ultimately reclaimed by creditors, he loses his apartment, and his personal effects are temporarily removed and sometimes lost. He may also lose important social ties, not least of which is his job. Family and friends may disassociate themselves from someone who has been formerly considered "conventional."

For the inner-city youth, there is not much to lose since he owns little, pays no rent, and often is unemployed. But the jail experience further propels him, too, into the underclass because it diminishes whatever opportunity he had for employment before and reinforces the notion that he is indeed a propertyless individual in society who is likely to remain that way. It also means that ties to conventional others such as parents and preachers may become weakened, reducing the incentive to go "straight." The newly imprisoned individual also loses his capacity to "take care of business," that is, he loses control over his personal life. For the inner-city youth, ties to his family, wife or girlfriend, and children may be weakened, making it difficult to perform his expected roles as lover and father.

The experience of imprisonment leads to a sense of *disorientation* as the person's integrity and sense of self-worth is undermined (see Irwin, 1985:53–84). Subject to the indignities of close confinement in overcrowded cells, fear of sexual assault, and the powerlessness that comes from the regimentation and routines of those who run the jails, prisoners may be in a state of "shock." Of course, this is less likely to be the case as one has more experience in jail, but to some degree the loss of personal organization is inevitable for most people.

The disorientation experienced by being jailed is reinforced by the *degradation* rituals prisoners experience at every step of the way (see Irwin, 1985:67–84). Degradation means "loss of status" (i.e., *de-grade*), a consequence of the very fact of being jailed. But this is revealed, too, by the attitudes of those who treat them like "scum" and let them know it. Jailers are often the worst offenders because they must justify to themselves in some way the indignities that they subject their wards to. But even their defense lawyers do not treat them with respect, treating them as just another case number in a long series of cases handled each day. The net result of the disintegration, disorientation, and degradation process is the loss of commitment to conventional values and the society they represent.

Given the loss of commitment to conventionality, jail provides a psychological, sociological, and cultural environment that *prepares* the prisoner for participation in a variety of alternative lifestyles (see Irwin, 1985:85–100). Psychological preparation involves loss of conventional sensibilities concerning the senses, personal privacy, and appearance. One may also begin to think like a member of the "rabble" class, losing trust in others and respect for authority. Stealing and hoarding behavior in situations of scarcity are likely adaptations as well. This generalized preparation for rabble status is reinforced socially by association with others of similar background and experience. Here begins the specialization process, distinguishing bums and winos from addicts, tough guys from punks, and so on. And, finally, each grouping in jail has its own outlook on the world, a cultural perspective that lends legitimacy to what they have or are about to become.

For each category of ordinary rabble, a rationale or ideology provides an explanation for who they are and why they have become what they have become. For the mentally ill, the addict, the derelict, and the hustler, society has a set of available explanations for each of their failures. Most of these explanations tend to focus on the personal inadequacies and early traumatic experiences that may have caused these inadequacies.

What distinguishes those who are on their way to criminal status and life behind prison bars is, paradoxically, a more positive attitude. Those whom they encounter in jail reinforce their achievements, and when released on the street, they may become heroes to their peers since going to jail may become a badge of honor. In Chapter 8, we saw how those who rejected the therapeutic community in favor of returning to jail often had prior jail experience and displayed more self-confidence than those who chose to stay. In other words, although mortified by the jail experience, potential criminals are usually younger than ordinary rabble, have fewer commitments to conventional society in the first place, and less to lose. Although, like the others, their potential for reintegration in conventional society is reduced with each encounter with the criminal justice system, they experience support for their deviant conduct. This is especially true, it appears, if that conduct involves elements of aggression, a willingness to use force to pursue their ends.

A second group that is increasingly criminalized today are the petty hustlers who were caught up in the antidrug crusade of the 1980s and 1990s. With fewer opportunities to seek help in therapeutic environments, these petty drug dealers, who are usually users as well, find themselves at the victimized end of the stick once incarcerated in maximum security prisons.

The Role of the Prison in the Production of Violent Men: Convicts, Gangs, and Racial Politics

As we have seen, the production of the underclass begins in the city and county jails where prisoners lose their ties to conventional values and norms and begin to associate with those who support deviant or alternative lifestyles. As the accused felon makes his way from the local jail into the state or federal penitentiary, he is already prepared to some extent for the violent

world he is about to enter. But his adaptations up to this point have been to *criminal lifestyles,* as thief, drug dealer, gangster, hustler, and so on. What he must learn to survive in prison is what it means to be a *convict.*

In an early work on the prison world, Irwin and Cressey (1962) described the inmate culture as a reflection of both the criminal subcultures that prisoners brought to the prison with them and the particular adaptive strategies individual prisoners used to survive in prison. The thief subculture was considered dominant, focusing on trust among thieves and outwitting or conning others. These attitudes supported general inmate solidarity while encouraging inmates to do their own time and find their own niche in the inmate world as "politicians," "merchants," or "gamblers." Outside the mainstream, yet clearly evident were "rapos," convicted of sexual offenses against children, and "snitches" (Irwin, 1980:13). Prison "toughs" were the precursors of today's convicts. They were "openly hostile to the prison administration, the conventional society, and most other prisoners and . . . displayed a readiness to employ violence against others" (Irwin, 1980:12–13).

Today, the dominant type of prisoner is the "convict" whose commitment to violence is essential to his survival in an increasingly violent world. No longer do street values matter. Consequently, the new prisoner may give up his preprison identity, which in many cases is criminalistic, in favor of prison identities that are no longer defined in the mercantilistic language and values of the professional thief. Instead, ethnic conflicts and rivalries dominate the self-conceptions and available adaptive strategies. The new convict is less likely to experience the disintegration and disorientation that the initiate experiences in jail. He has already gone through this process. But the degradation continues in terms of invasions of privacy—body cavity searches, shakedowns, checking personal correspondence for contraband, and so on—violating the individual's ability to maintain his personal integrity. The lack of control over his daily routines and relationships and the loss of ties to conventional society are reinforced. Consequently, for the long-term prisoner, the loss of conventional sensibilities and the acquisition of a more or less permanent criminal status are inevitable.

Irwin's three types of preparation, (1) psychological, (2) cultural, and (3) social, help us to understand the transformation of the inmate into the convict in the prison system. Psychologically, prisoners experience a great deal of anxiety and outright fear for their personal safety. No matter how well run an institution, no matter how carefully prison administrators attend to the legal requirement that they not put in place policies that permit inmates to victimize one another, these victimizations are inevitable. But even those who appear on the surface to be tough guys demonstrate that for many, this is a veneer. After all, even the most experienced soldiers feel fear in times of combat. Here, where combat is always a possibility, fear is something you must live with on a daily basis.

Cultural adaptation occurs when inmates learn the values associated with the *convict code*. These values constitute the cultural life of the American prison in the late twentieth century. First, there is the *commitment to violence* when faced with threats to oneself or those with whom one identifies. Second, there is *hostility toward the prison administration and conventional society*. Third, there is the demand for *loyalty to fellow convicts*. Fourth, *never show weakness*.

These values will be expressed in specific norms such as (1) *snitches deserve to be killed*, (2) *fight to the death, if necessary, if you are threatened with sexual assault*, (3) *do not let anyone show you disrespect*, and (4) *never volunteer for prison programs*. These are all expressions of publicly held and legitimated norms that some convicts come to believe in and support, yet others may only give lip service to. For example, many prisoners may wish to pursue more education, but are less likely to do so today than in the past because it would appear that they were cooperating with the administration. In the past, prisoners were given incentives to participate in educational and other programs designed to improve their preparation for conventional roles in society. For example, completing a GED (high school equivalency diploma) might have earned credit toward parole. In today's climate of mandatory sentences and sentencing guidelines, these incentives are gone. The promise of early release provided a publicly acceptable excuse to participate in prison programs. But this is no longer true today.

Although there is a generalized convict identity that all prison inmates share, each is socialized today into different ethnic variants on the dominant theme. These variants constitute the third and final stage of the preparation process, the *social*. Prison life is organized largely in black, white, and Hispanic terms. Native Americans, relatively small in number in most prisons, have established their right to follow traditional religious practices and customs. Because group affiliation is important to survival in both an emotional and practical sense, many prisoners with some Native American background will become involved in the cultural and social life of traditional Native American practices

For many of African American heritage, the existence of a variety of Muslim religious groups in prison provides a basis for adjustment to prison life. Useem and Kimball (1991:127, 135, 154, 174) make it clear that these are *not* prison gangs and these groups did *not* participate in the riots that have occurred in American prisons between 1971 and 1986. Moreover, federal guidelines for the management of prison gangs list the Black Muslims (Nation of Islam) among those groups that are *not* prison gangs (U.S. Department of Justice, 1991:2). Nevertheless, the Black Muslims, who undermined the hegemony of white authority and prison administrations in the 1960s, are still feared by many prison administrators. In New York State, the prison system does not hire imams "with political agendas, like that of black separatists," from the Nation of Islam (Clines, 1992:B2).

In Pennsylvania, correctional officers attributed the 1989 riot at Camp Hill Correctional Institution to the Fruit of Islam (see Senate Judiciary Committee, 1989; House Judiciary Committee, 1990). Lincoln (1961:14, 118) describes the Fruit of Islam as the "paramilitary" arm of the Black Muslims (also see Duke, 1989; Foxman and Boland, 1992). There was no evidence in the Pennsylvania House and Senate Judiciary Committees documents, however, to link the Fruit of Islam at Camp Hill with the Nation of Islam or any other Muslim group. In their report on the riot at Camp Hill to the National Institute of Justice, Useem, Camp, and Camp (1993:183) describe the Fruit of Islam as "a powerful inmate group who apparently engaged in aggravating rather than mitigating influences." According to this report, inmate leaders who negotiated with the superintendent of the prison were all members of the Fruit of Islam (Useem, Camp, and Camp, 1993:194).

In contrast, Irwin (1980:196–197) describes the Black Muslims as a "stabilizing force" who "do not follow the aggressive and rapacious patterns of the gangs," but may "assume leadership in periods of disorder." During the Attica riot in 1971, it was Black Muslim guards who kept the hostages from being harmed by other inmates (Useem and Kimbal, 1991:34, 50).

The Aryan Brotherhood has become a notorious prison gang, largely because of the murders of two correctional officers by two members of the gang at the federal penitentiary in Marion, Illinois, which was considered the most secure prison in the country at the time (Earley, 1992:204). In both cases, the murders at Marion and the riot at Camp Hill, aggression was directed at representatives of authority and not other ethnic groups.

The ethnic basis of group affiliation in prison today is the dominant form of social organization. Whether or not these groups become active gangs, in the sense of organizing illicit activities or engaging in exploitive and violent relationships with other inmates, depends on a variety of conditions. Not all gang activity involves explicitly named gangs such as the Mexican Mafia. Some prison officials allege that religious groups may become fronts for gang activity. More precisely, any grouping in prison is likely to be used to the advantage of that group and for its self-defense. But these groups are considered gangs only when they (1) have a clear leadership structure, (2) are unified and well organized, and (3) pursue criminal activities as a group (see U.S. Department of Justice, 1991:2). These groupings, whether they constitute gangs or not, derive from racial and ethnic rivalries in the wider society and may, in turn, contribute to them. In this sense, these groups reflect the racial politics of the wider society.

The Impact of the Prison System on American Social Life

. . . we have seen a number of ways in which the violent nature of American society is reproduced in its prison system. The nature of punishment in society reflects the nature of the society of which it is part (see Rusche and Kirchheimer, 1968; Foucault, 1979:3–31). But it is also the case that prisons, as part of society, cannot be understood in isolation from their impact on that society. The vast majority of prisoners are eventually released. The values and beliefs they have learned, the identities they have acquired and the roles they play, and the reliance on coercive means to solve problems affect the communities to which these prisoners return.

The Regulation of Surplus Labor

Throughout modern history there have been periods of economic and social crisis. In their book *Regulating the Poor,* Piven and Cloward (1971) argue that the welfare system has functioned mainly as a tool for regulating the poor. Threatened with unrest, political and economic elites have wisely provided for the support of the "surplus labor" population created by economic downturns. On occasion, this would occur in response to social unrest. At other times, social welfare legislation was enacted in anticipation of unrest and thus would prevent its occurrence.

In the 1960s, the Great Society programs proposed by Lyndon Johnson were a response to increasing pressure from the poor, especially African Americans, whose expectations for equal treatment under the law were being resisted by authorities, especially in the South. These programs were also designed to overcome the effects of past and present discrimination in employment and housing in the North. The frustrations that led to the riots of the 1960s were not alleviated by these social programs and conservative politicians, such as Richard Nixon, who took the opportunity to promote a "law and order" agenda as an alternative to welfare to address the concerns of the economically and politically disenfranchised. Thus, in the context of the American polity of the last 30 years or so, welfare and crime control have become alternative strategies for dealing with the surplus labor population in the United States.

Several studies (see Brenner, 1976; Greenberg, 1977; Wallace, 1981) have demonstrated that incarceration rates increase with increasing unemployment. In his study of incarceration trends in the 1970s, Wallace (1981) does not use official government unemployment statistics since they are misleading. Once a person gives up looking for work, he or she is no longer counted as "unemployed," so it is possible for large numbers of people to give up looking for work while the official unemployment statistics go down. When the total number of people working full-time compared with the total number of able-bodied adults in society goes down, we find that the incarceration rate, or number of people put in prison in each year, goes up. In other words, as the number of jobs in society decline, the number of people who go to prison increases. Moreover, the effect of unemployment on the incarceration rate is independent of the crime rate! The trends that Wallace observed in the 1970s have continued into the 1980s. The number of prisoners in state and federal prisons doubled during the 1980s, the job base declined, and the crime rate was relatively stable.[2]

If the crime rate has not increased over the years, then how do we explain the increase in incarceration? Wallace (1981) has shown that welfare and incarceration are alternative mechanisms of social control in contemporary society. When the welfare system fails to provide a minimum of support and security for society, the state steps in with harsher measures. Furthermore, it appears that, historically, prisoners were going into prison at the same rate at which they came out. But when prisoners cannot make parole because they cannot find a suitable job on the outside, the prison population swells. As the number of job opportunities decline, the rate of release from prison slows down. In addition, there has been an increase in the number of parolees and probationers who have been sent to prison due to violations of their parole and probation conditions (Gilliard, 1993:7).

This situation has been aggravated over the past few years with mandatory sentencing, lengthening the average prison term. Almost half as many prisoners are released early on parole today than in the recent past, dropping from 72 percent in 1977 to 41 percent by 1990 (see Jankowski, 1991:5). About the same percentage, 40 percent, "maxed out" in 1990 (released at the expiration of their sentence or after completing the mandatory time required by law), compared with only 22 percent in 1977 (see Jankowski, 1991:5). But making things worse

is that mandatory sentencing has led to the increased incarceration of first offenders who might have been put on probation in the past (U.S. Bureau of Justice Statistics, 1993:13). Moreover, many of these new admissions have committed drug-related offenses. The number of adult drug arrests doubled and the rate of incarceration of drug arrestees has quadrupled since 1977 (Gilliard, 1993:7–8). From 1986 to 1990, the rate of incarceration in the 75 largest urban courts in the United States remained stable for violent crime but increased by 25 percent for those convicted of drug trafficking (see Langan, 1993:7). In 1986, offenders sentenced for drug possession or trafficking for the first time comprised *one-third* (33%) of the nonviolent offenders sentenced to state prisons (Innes, 1988:5). By 1991, the proportion of nonviolent first offenders sentenced to state prisons for drug violations had *doubled* to 63 percent (see U.S. Bureau of Justice Statistics, 1993:13).

Who are these new prisoners? It is increasingly evident that young African American males, who have been most hurt by the economic and social policies of the past two decades, are filling up our prisons. As many as 48 percent of prisoners in state prisons are non-Hispanic blacks, although blacks comprise only about 12 percent of the population (U.S. Bureau of Justice Statistics, 1992a:3).[3] A recent study conducted by Jerome Miller's National Center on Institutions and Alternatives reported that almost one out of four (23%) black men in their twenties are under the control of the criminal justice system on any given day, either in jail or prison or on probation or parole (Bencivenga, 1992). The U.S. Bureau of Justice Statistics (1993:5) reports that from 1986 through 1991 the number of black inmates serving time for drug-related offenses increased 447 percent, higher than the rate for Hispanics (324 percent) and four times greater than for whites (115 percent)! At the same time, the percentage of black and Hispanic inmates in prison for violent crimes went down.

The Antidrug Crusade

How have we managed to detect and punish more offenders than in the past? If the serious crime rate has not increased, where do these offenders come from? Why are they more likely to be young black males than in the past? What is the impact of this new pattern of enforcement on society, especially on inner-city ghetto youth? To answer these questions, we must turn to the drug wars and their impact on the prison population and its consequences for society.

The war on drugs has been one of the major vehicles of the anti-crime crusade for showing the effectiveness of tough law and order policies. Petty drug offenders are relatively easy to catch and prosecute. Without appreciably altering the flow of drug trafficking into a community, officers can produce high arrest statistics. For those who begin to build an arrest record, any future offense, although not serious by itself, may lead to harsher treatment by the courts since the past record is used as part of the sentencing decision. Since most street-level drug dealers are also users who sell drugs to feed their habits, the war on drugs criminalizes a large segment of the population, mostly poor and racial minorities, who in the past had been either ignored or placed in rehabilitation programs. Because many of these street dealers are young males, we see a greater number of minority males introduced to the criminal justice system relatively early in life.

Has the drug war reduced appreciably the flow of drugs into the United States? No. Has the overall consumption of drugs diminished? No. There is some evidence that there has been a change in the pattern of distribution and consumption of drugs, with declining usage in the middle class and an increase in the hard-core addict population among the poor. Why has the extent of drug usage worsened, if anything, in the inner cities? Recent rioting in Los Angeles demonstrates the level of frustration and anger inner-city residents feel at the lack of jobs in their communities and the hostility they experience from law enforcement.

John Hagedorn (1991) studied inner-city African American gang members who lived in Milwaukee between 1986 and 1990. Hagedorn showed that gang activity has changed dramatically over the years. In the past, inner-city gangs involved adolescents who engaged in a variety of criminal activities, including the distribution of drugs. As the gang members matured, they drifted from the "streets" into more conventional working-class lifestyles, getting a job, getting married, and raising a family. With the "dein-dustrialization" of the inner city, fewer opportunities for employment, and an educational system that is not meeting the needs of inner-city youth, these young black men delay entry into conventional society, continuing gang activity into their early twenties and beyond. And it is these gangs that have become the core of violent competition for control over drug trafficking in their communities. Just as Italian youth did during the 1920s and 1930s during the formation of the Italian American version of organized crime, which specialized in the distribution of alcohol to American consumers during Prohibition (see Whyte, 1981).

We see that difficult economic times have hit minority communities especially hard, creating greater incentives for participating in alternative, illegal economic enterprises. The demand for drugs is also great in such communities. At the same time, a crackdown on the drug trade disproportionately hits the street-level minority dealer and user. Keep in mind, too, that this population constitutes a major component of the surplus labor population. With policies that discourage welfare for the able-bodied male, incarceration has become the key mechanism for regulating this group.

Over the past twenty years or so, the prison system appears to have increasingly taken on a regulatory function in an economic system that is undergoing great difficulty. Increasing unemployment and underemployment has hit minority communities especially hard, leading to increasing involvement in organized criminal activity, especially involving drugs. The drug war has facilitated selective law enforcement directed at this surplus labor population, legitimating the incarceration of ever-increasing numbers of young black males.

Contemporary Inner-City Life: Violence and Values

One consequence of the selective enforcement of drug laws in minority communities has been to criminalize this population over time. By the late 1980s, young black males began to incorporate more and more violence in their daily lives. In fact, the homicide rate among young black males aged 14 through 24 rose dramatically from 1984 to 1991, while the homicide rate for all other groups remained stable during this period (Salholz, 1990:33; Eckholm, 1993; see note 2). According to a study by the Centers for Disease Control (see Salholz, 1990:33), from 1984 through 1988, most of this rise in the homicide rate among young black males, especially those between the ages of 15 and 19, was gun-related. While this rise in homicides can be explained by the increased availability of guns in the inner city and drug-related violence, it is also evident that violence has become generalized among young males in the inner city. The arrest rate for violent crimes in general, including assault, robbery, rape, and murder, for juveniles under the age of 18 increased 85 percent from 1987 through 1991, and the arrest rate for illegal weapons possession increased by 62 percent during the same period (Kantrowitz, 1993:43, 45).

In the early '90s, inner-city high schools are armed camps. About one-third (35%) of inner-city high school males carry firearms regularly or on occasion (Wright, Sheley, and Smith, 1992:85). Roughly 20 percent of the nation's high school youth carry weapons, often guns, to school (Morganthau, 1992:25). New York City schools periodically report shootings in school (see, for example, Kleinfield, 1992; Nordland, 1992). But this violence has been spreading even to America's smaller cities (Eckholm, 1993). What is more, the most frequent explanation for gun possession among these inner-city youth is the classic "frontier" rationale, "for protection." It should not be surprising that the group most involved in this violence is also the group that has been increasingly exposed to the criminal justice system over the past two decades. Black youth are three times more likely than whites to be arrested for weapons violations and six times more likely to be the victims of homicide (Kantrowitz, 1993:45). In many ways, what we are seeing today is the transformation of attitudes and behavior learned in the prison system back onto the streets, creating a vicious cycle of violence from the streets to the prison and back again.

One of the ways to demonstrate how prison life has influenced street life is to show how the way in which prisoners have learned to adapt to the violent world of the prison has manifested itself in the language and behavior of the streets.

In his autobiography, Malcolm X describes the use of the term "homeboy" to refer to someone from his hometown of Lansing, Michigan, whom he met on the street in Boston in the 1940s (Malcolm X, 1965:39–55). In his 1960s study of a federal institution for drug addicts, Tittle (1972:87) describes cliques of "homies" as "superficial reference points" for only about 5 percent of the inmates. Today, the term "homeboy" or "homey," which prisoners use to refer to others from their own neighborhood or community, has taken on greater significance. A homeboy is someone you can trust because you share a common experience. Homeboys will back you up if you are in trouble. The symbolic importance of the homeboy reflects the importance of common social origin as the basis of social organization in prison life today. By the late 1980s and early 1990s, the terms "homeboy" and "homey" appeared in popular culture, first in rap music, the expression of the frustrations of inner-city African American males, and later in other mediums as well.[4]

An older example of the way prison life both reflects and contributes to community life was the "prison 'dozens,' a verbal exchange exposing each other's vulnerable points, most often related to homosexuality" (Irwin, 1980:7). The "dozens" originated in rural areas of the Old South before it became part of the cultural life in the prisons of the 1930s and '40s (see Berdie, 1947). By the 1960s, the dozens had become a game of verbal insults in inner-city black ghettos, especially among the most "street-wise" youth (Foster, 1974:227).[5]

One of the most interesting and unique adaptations from prison life to the streets is what teenagers in New York City today call "props." A prop is someone you hang out with, a close buddy who will back you up if you get into trouble. In prison, two inmates who share a common background will provide mutual protection for one another.

In a recent shooting at Thomas Jefferson High School in Brooklyn, the fifteen-year-old assailant carried his gun to school along with 90 percent of the kids who "got guns or can get them" (Nordland, 1992:22). The fifteen-year-old shot and killed a sixteen-year-old who had been his crime partner in a mugging. The sixteen-year-old had done time and had called the fifteen-year-old a "rat" because he received probation. Since he had "called me a rat," the killer told the police, he thought the sixteen-year-old meant to kill him. It was "kill or be killed," the code of the prison convict! The victim was with his "inseparable buddy," his "prop," at the time of the shooting. The prop was also shot and killed (Nordland, 1992:22; Kleinfield, 1992:32).

The above example also illustrates the importance of the role of violence in defending oneself against attack by another. Just as the prison world has adopted its own version of the frontier culture and the self-defense attitudes that derive from it, the inner-city streets seem to have adopted that version from the prison world (Wright, Sheley, and Smith, 1992:88). But what has emerged in the late 1980s and 1990s is a particularly deadly version, one that seems to reflect the mores of the prison world rather than the traditional values of either African American or European American communities. Most high school students and incarcerated delinquents say that they carry weapons for "protection," but a substantial percentage of both groups, 10 percent and 14 percent respectively, say that people in their "crowd" carry guns to maintain "respect" (Wright, Sheley, and Smith, 1992:87). This reflects the world view of the hard-core convict. A white convict at Leavenworth expressed this view when he said, "As a child, I was taught not to be a stool pigeon. Don't tattletale on other kids. I was taught if someone hits you, you hit them back, and if they even think about hitting you again, you make them never want to see you again. That is what John Wayne always did and everyone in the country thought John Wayne was right" (Earley, 1992:181).

The Impact of the Contemporary Prison on Racial Politics

The prison system fosters racial division in a number of ways. First, the selective enforcement of the laws that places ever-increasing numbers of inner-city blacks into the prison system identifies blacks with criminality in the public mind, at least for the white public. The symbolism of a black Willie Horton raping a white woman used by the Republican presidential campaign in 1988 still evokes the fears of white Americans of black maleness and sexuality that produced lynchings in the Old South. Second, it contributes to the rage in the black community at both a white-dominated society in general and at the criminal justice system in particular. This rage was manifest in the racial violence that occurred during the Los Angeles riot in 1992 following the acquittal of four police officers accused of beating Rodney King (see, for example, *New York Times,* 1993).

But the racial politics within prison spills out into the public arena in more sinister ways. As we have seen above, the cauldron of hate and violence in prison reproduces and magnifies the conflicts of the wider society. We have seen the emergence of race and ethnicity as the dominant form of social organization among prison inmates. This has produced a number of different types of groups, from those that are strictly religious in orientation to those that are active prison gangs at war with one another. The degree of racial conflict varies over time and between prisons. But the very nature of the prison system provides a breeding ground for racism and the ideological beliefs that legitimate racial hatred.

Many groups that either originated in prisons or gained their strength in prison promote racial supremacist doctrines. Still others, incarcerated because of their militancy on the outside, may find themselves in a world in which kindred groups foster racial ideologies. The Black Guerilla Family and the Aryan Brotherhood both originated in California prisons in the late 1960s as "racist cliques" (Irwin, 1980:191). The Aryan Brotherhood, which originated as a self-defense organization for white prisoners who had become a minority in California prisons, eventually evolved a white supremacist doctrine (Ridgeway, 1990:91).

The basic philosophy of the Black Muslims is to use violence in self-defense rather than to initiate violence (Irwin, 1980:69). Known for their litigiousness in other states, the Black Muslims were closely monitored by Texas officials, but they were "not particularly disruptive" (Crouch and Marquart, 1989:205). But the doctrine of the Muslims is, nevertheless, based on the "theory of black supremacy" (Lincoln, 1961:76).

A variety of neo-Nazi groups recruited white prisoners in the 1970s (Irwin, 1980:185; Aho, 1990:60). By the 1980s, the Aryan Nations

Church (the Church of Jesus Christ Christian) had begun to recruit members from the Aryan Brotherhood prison gang (Aho, 1990:61; Ridgeway, 1990:91). Whereas the politics of some of the militant black prisoners in the late 1960s and early '70s was primarily left-wing in character, the politics of white prisoners today appears to be right-wing. Members of motorcycle gangs are prime targets for recruitment into these right-wing groups since they share many of their racial views and often display Nazi-like insignia (Watson, 1980:37). But the "military discipline and religious asceticism of the Aryan Nations Church" does not appeal to many who have enjoyed a more hedonistic lifestyle (Aho, 1990:61).

The promotion of racially oriented ideologies in prison provides a core of potential recruits for outside groups that share similar beliefs. To the extent that this racism is exported to the outside world, it reinforces and exacerbates divisions in the community at large. What we see today is the emergence of a coherent right-wing religious and social ideology for white prisoners just as such an ideology emerged for blacks in the 1960s. In both cases, they contribute to the production of racial hatred both inside and outside the prison system.

Conclusion

The social organization of prison life reflects and reproduces the social structure of the larger society and its cultural values. Social inequality based on race, class, or gender produces violence both in society and in prison. Racial inequality generates rage among its victims and a backlash by the white majority. Consequently, we should not be surprised to find that there is a long history of racial conflict in the American prison system.

The prison system controls the surplus population generated by a weak economy. The so-called underclass is a product of both joblessness and a criminal justice system that functions to regulate the poor when the welfare system fails to do so adequately. City and county jails are designed to control the disorganized and disruptive, whereas state and federal prisons control those who are more violent and deemed a "threat to social order" (Irwin, 1985:3). The antidrug crusade of the late 1980s has functioned to selectively enforce the law in the African American community, incarcerating young black males in ever-increasing numbers.

The prison system continues to grow, with the prison population doubling roughly every 10 years. With almost 900,000 prisoners in state and federal prisons and many more in city and county jails, the United States incarcerated a record 329 adults per 100,000 population at the end of 1992, up from 139 in 1980 (Gilliard, 1993:2). With an increase in the number of young black males under the supervision of the criminal justice system, we have seen the transmission of the violent values of the prison world to the streets. The availability of sophisticated weapons and the willingness to use deadly force to settle disputes has led to an increase in violence in inner-city communities.

There also have been increasing attempts on the part of radical right-wing groups to recruit white prisoners who share their racial beliefs. Consequently, the racial conflict that develops in prison has become a breeding ground for racial ideologies that divide Americans in the wider society.

Notes

1. In his book *Confronting Crime: An American Challenge,* Elliott Currie (1985:143–180) provides an excellent summary of the basic research on the effects of economic and racial inequality on criminal violence.
2. See Chapter 7, p. 137 and notes 2 and 3, for a discussion of long-term trends in incarceration and crime rates. During the 1980s, violent crime rates continued to remain relatively stable, although the trend was generally downward for property crimes (U.S. Bureau of Justice Statistics, 1992b:4). The only serious upward trend was the age-specific increase in the homicide rate for young black males who were increasingly at risk in drug-related crimes involving increasingly sophisticated guns. The *New York Times* (Eckholm, 1993) reported statistics provided by James A. Fox and Glenn Pierce of Northeastern University, describing stable homicide rates

from 1985 to 1991 for white males of all age groups, declining homicide rates for older black men (age 25 plus), and increasing rates for young black males aged 14 through 24. The Centers for Disease Control (Salholz, 1990:33) reported similar data for teenagers from 1984 through 1988. The risk of becoming the victim of homicide was stable for white males and for both white and black females. The risk of being murdered "almost doubled" for black males during the same period.

3. This represents an increase in the black population in prison during the antidrug crusade of the late 1980s. The U.S. Bureau of the Census (1990:187) reported Bureau of Justice Statistics data giving the black prison population as 46.9% as recently as 1986, but this included Hispanic prisoners of African descent. The more recent population data excludes Hispanic prisoners from the total. In 1990, 12% of the state prison population was of Hispanic origin.

4. Binder (1993:754) argues that between 1985 and 1990, rap music emerged as an expression of anger and defiance of authority among black youth. More recently, there has been a public outcry against so-called "gangster rap" for its more specifically violent themes. (See, for example, Staples, 1993).

5. There is some evidence that the dozens was played by rural whites as well as blacks in the Old South (Dollard, 1939; Elton, 1950). By the 1960s, few inner-city youth knew the game by this name, except the "more sophisticated and street-wise" (Foster, 1974:227).

References

Aho, James A. (1990). *The Politics of Righteousness: Idaho Christian Patriotism.* Seattle, WA: University of Washington Press.

Baron, Larry and Murray A. Straus (1987). "Four Theories of Rape: A Macrosociological Analysis," *Social Problems* 34:467–489.

Baumgartner, Mary Pat (1993). "Violent Networks: The Origins and Management of Domestic Conflict." Pp. 209–232 in *Aggression and Violence: Social Interactionist Perspectives,* edited by R. B. Felson and J. T. Tedeschi. Washington, DC: American Psychological Association.

Bencivenga, Jim (1992). "Prison Values Spill into Society," *Christian Science Monitor,* April 10:13.

Berdie, Ralph F. (1947). "Playing the Dozens," *Journal of Abnormal and Social Psychology* 42:120–121.

Beverly, Creigs C. and Howard J. Stanback (1986). "The Black Underclass: Theory and Reality," *The Black Scholar* 17:24–32.

Binder, Amy (1993). "Constructing Racial Rhetoric: Media Depictions of Harm in Heavy Metal and Rap Music," *American Sociological Review* 58:753–767.

Blau, Judith R. and Peter Blau (1982). "The Cost of Inequality: Metropolitan Structure and Violent Crime," *American Sociological Review* 47:114–129.

Blauner, Robert (1969). "Internal Colonialism and Ghetto Revolt," *Social Problems* 16:393–408.

Bowker, Lee H. (1980). *Prison Victimization.* New York: Elsevier.

Braithwaite, John (1979). *Inequality, Crime, and Public Policy.* London: Routledge and Kegan Paul.

Brenner, M. Harvey (1976). "Time Series Analysis: The Effects of the Economy on Criminal Behavior and the Administration of Criminal Justice." Pp. 25–68 in *Economic Crises and Crime.* Rome, Italy: United Nations Social Defense Research Institute.

Caputi, Jane (1989). "The Sexual Politics of Murder," *Gender and Society* 3:437–456.

Carroll, Leo (1974). *Hacks, Blacks, and Cons: Race Relations in a Maximum Security Prison.* Prospect Heights, IL: Waveland Press.

Clines, Francis X. (1992). "Prison Has the Body, but Allah Has the Spirit," *New York Times,* July 2:A1, B2.

Crouch, Ben M. and James W. Marquart (1989). *An Appeal to Justice: Litigated Reform of Texas Prisons.* Austin, TX: University of Texas Press.

Currie, Elliott (1985). *Confronting Crime: An American Challenge.* New York: Pantheon Books.

Dollard, John (1939). "The Dozens: The Dialect of Insult," *American Imago* 1:4–20.

Duke, Lynne (1989). "Big Demand for Drug Patrols Forces Muslims to Face Economics," *Washington Post,* February 12:B, 1:1.

Earley, Pete (1992). *The Hot House: Life Inside Leavenworth Penitentiary.* New York: Bantam Books.

Eckholm, Erik (1993). "Teen-Age Gangs Are Inflicting Lethal Violence on Small Cities," *New York Times,* January 31: 1, 1:2.

Elton, William (1950). "Playing the Dozens," *American Speech* 25: 230–233.

Foster, Herbert L. (1974). *Ribbin', Jivin', and Playin' the Dozens: The Unrecognized Dilemma of Inner-City Schools.* Cambridge, MA: Ballinger.

Foucault, Michel (1979). *Discipline and Punish: The Birth of the Prison.* Translated by Alan Sheridan. New York: Vintage Books.

Foxman, Abraham and Mira Boland (1992). "Fruit of Islam on U.S. Tab?" *Washington Times,* August 19:F, 3:1.

Gelles, Richard J. and Murray A. Straus (1988). *Intimate Violence.* New York: Touchstone Books.

Gelman, David (1991). "The Secrets of Apt. 213," *Newsweek,* August 5:40–42.

Gilliard, Darrell K. (1993). *Prisoners in 1992.* Washington, DC: Bureau of Justice Statistics, U.S. Department of Justice.

Greenberg, David (1977). "The Dynamics of Oscillatory Punishment Processes," *Journal of Criminal Law and Criminology* 68:643–651.

Hagedorn, John M. (1991). "Gangs, Neighborhoods, and Public Policy," *Social Problems* 38:529–542.

Hanna, John (1992). "Inmates Restricted after Riots in Kansas," *Boston Globe,* July 7:3.

Hershey, Robert D. (1993). "Trade Gap Widened in April," *New York Times,* June 16: D1.

Hickey, Eric W. (1991). *Serial Murderers and Their Victims.* Pacific Grove, CA: Brooks/Cole.

Horvath, Imre (1986). *Acts of Violence.* Stamford, CT: Lightning Video.

House Judiciary Committee (1990). *HR 226: State Correctional Institution at Camp Hill.* Transcript of public hearing, March 7, Harrisburg, PA.

Innes, Christopher A. (1988). "Profile of State Prison Inmates, 1986," *Bureau of Justice Statistics Special Report* Washington, DC: U.S. Department of Justice

Irwin, John (1980). *Prisons in Turmoil.* Boston, MA: Little, Brown.

Irwin, John (1985). *The Jail: Managing the Underclass in American Society.* Berkeley, CA: University of California Press.

Irwin, John and Donald R. Cressey (1962). "Thieves, Convicts, and the Inmate Culture," *Social Problems* 10:142–155.

Jacobs, James B. (1977). *Stateville: The Penitentiary in Mass Society.* Chicago, IL: University of Chicago Press.

Jankowski, Louis (1991). "Probation and Parole 1990," *Bureau of Justice Statistics Bulletin.* Washington, DC: U.S. Department of Justice.

Kantrowitz, Barbara (1993). "Wild in the Streets," *Newsweek,* August 2: 40–46.

Kleinfield, N. R. (1992). "The Fatal Vortex: Collision of 3 Lives in East New York," *New York Times,* March 1:1, 32.

Koenig, Robert L. (1993). "Postal Service Takes Hard Look at Policies," *St. Louis Post-Dispatch,* May 9: D6.

Krohn, Marvin D. (1976). "Inequality, Unemployment and Crime: A Cross-National Analysis," *Sociological Quarterly* 17:303–313.

Langan, Patrick A. (1993). "Felony Sentences in State Courts, 1990," *Bureau of Justice Statistics Bulletin.* Washington, DC: U.S. Department of Justice.

Lewis, George H. (1980). "Social Groupings in Organized Crime," *Deviant Behavior* 1:129–143.

Liebow, Elliot (1967). *Tally's Corner: A Study of Negro Streetcorner Men.* Boston, MA: Little, Brown.

Lincoln, C. Eric (1961). *The Black Muslims in America.* Boston: Beacon Press.

Lockwood, Daniel (1980). *Prison Sexual Violence.* New York: Elsevier.

Malcolm X (1965). *The Autobiography of Malcolm X.* New York: Ballantine Books.

Mathews, Tom (1992). "Secrets of a Serial Killer," *Newsweek,* February 3:44–49.

Messner, Steven F. (1980). "Income Inequality and Murder Rates: Some Cross-National Findings," *Comparative Social Research* 3:185–198.

Moore, Joan W. (1985). "Isolation and Stigmatization in the Development of an Underclass: The Case of Chicano Gangs in East Los Angeles," *Social Problems* 33:1–12.

Morganthau, Tom (1992). "It's Not Just New York," *Newsweek,* March 9:25–29.

New York Times (1981a). "Indiana Murderer Executed at Prison," *New York Times,* March 9:A1.

New York Times (1981b). "Murderer of Four Awaits Electric Chair in Indiana," *New York Times,* February 18:12.

New York Times (1992). "U.S. Is Bigger Debtor Nation," *New York Times,* July 4: A44.

New York Times (1993). "5 Blacks Dismissed from Jury Panel in Beating Case," *New York Times,* August 8:36.

Nordland, Rod (1992). "Deadly Lessons," *Newsweek,* March 9:22–24.

Pallas, John and Robert Barber (1973). "From Riot to Revolution." Pp. 237–261 in *The Politics of Punishment,* edited by Erik Olin Wright. New York: Harper & Row.

Piven, Frances Fox and Richard A. Cloward (1971). *Regulating the Poor.* New York: Pantheon Books.

Pleck, Elizabeth (1989). "Criminal Approaches to Family Violence." Pp. 19–58 in *Family Violence,* edited by L. Ohlin and M. Tonry. Chicago, IL: University of Chicago Press.

Ridgeway, James (1990). *Blood in the Face.* New York: Thunder's Mouth Press.

Rusche, Georg and Otto Kirchheimer (1968). *Punishment and Social Structure*. New York: Russell and Russell.

Salholz, Eloise (1990). "Short Lives, Bloody Deaths," *Newsweek*, December 17:33.

Sanders, Jimy M. (1990). "Public Transfers: Safety Net or Inducement into Poverty?" *Social Forces* 68:813–834.

Schwendinger, Julia R. and Herman Schwendinger (1981). "Rape, Sexual Inequality, and Levels of Violence," *Crime and Social Justice* 16:3–31.

Senate Judiciary Committee (1989). *Public Hearing on Recent Incidents at Pennsylvania State Correctional Institutions: Transcript of Proceedings,* November 27, Harrisburg, PA.

Sheinkman, Jack (1992). "How Washington Exports U.S. Jobs," *New York Times*, October 18:3, 3.

Staples, Brent (1993). "The Politics of Gangster Rap," *New York Times*, August 27:A, 28:1.

Swickard, Joe (1993). "A Crime for Our Time: 'Get Back at the Boss'," *Detroit News and Free Press,* May 8:A7.

Tittle, Charles R. (1972). *Society of Subordinates*. Bloomington, IN: Indiana University Press.

Uchitelle, Louis (1993). "Stanching the Loss of Good Jobs," *New York Times*, January 31:3, 1.

U.S. Bureau of the Census (1990). *Statistical Abstract of the United States, 1990* (110th ed.). Washington, DC: U.S. Government Printing Office.

U.S. Bureau of Justice Statistics (1992a). *Census of State and Federal Correctional Facilities, 1990*. Washington, DC: U.S. Government Printing Office.

U.S. Bureau of Justice Statistics (1992b). *Criminal Victimization in the United States, 1990*. Washington, DC: U.S. Department of Justice.

U.S. Bureau of Justice Statistics (1993). *Survey of State Prison Inmates, 1991*. Washington, DC: U.S. Department of Justice.

U.S. Department of Justice (1991). *Management Strategies in Disturbances and with Gangs/Disruptive Groups*. Washington, DC: U.S. Government Printing Office.

Useem, Bert, Camille Camp, and George Camp (1993). *Resolution of Prison Riots*. Report to the National Institute of Justice. Washington, DC: U.S. Department of Justice.

Useem, Bert and Peter Kimball (1991). *States of Siege: U.S. Riots 1971–1986*. New York: Oxford University Press.

Wallace, Don (1981). "The Political Economy of Incarceration Trends in Late U.S. Capitalism: 1971–1977," *Insurgent Sociologist* 10:59–66.

Watson, J. Mark (1980). "Outlaw Motorcyclists: An Outgrowth of Lower Class Cultural Concerns," *Deviant Behavior* 2:31–48.

Whyte, William Foote (1981). *Street Corner Society: The Social Structure of an Italian Slum*. Chicago, IL: University of Chicago Press.

Wilson, William J. and Robert Aponte (1985). "Urban Poverty," *Annual Review of Sociology* 11:231–258.

Wooden, Wayne S. and Jay Parker (1982). *Men Behind Bars: Sexual Exploitation in Prison*. New York: Plenum.

Wright, James D., Joseph F. Sheley, and M. Dwayne Smith (1992). "Kids, Guns, and Killing Fields," *Society* 30:84–89.